THE HISTORICAL GEOGRAPHY OF THE HOLY LAND

GEORGE ADAM SMITH (1856-1942) was a distinguished Old Testament scholar and an impassioned teacher and lecturer. The scientific knowledge that he brought to his biblical criticism was well in advance of his time, and the lucidity and liveliness of his writing gave him a wide readership.

He read first for a degree in Arts at Edinburgh University, attending courses in Political Economy at the same time, and followed this with a degree in Divinity at New College. Before his ordination he studied Arabic in Cairo, and made the first of his visits to Palestine—travelling the country on foot.

For ten years he was a Free Church Minister in Aberdeen. The lecture-sermons he gave at this time formed the basis of *The Book of Isaiah*, his first and one of his finest books, which, published in two volumes, 1888-90, at once established him as an Old Testament scholar.

In 1891 he toured Palestine again to get further material for *The Historical Geography* and the following year accepted the post of Professor of Hebrew and Old Testament Exegesis in the Free Church College, Glasgow. *The Historical Geography of the Holy Land* was published in 1894, had gone through three impressions by 1896, when it was brought out with supplementary notes, and was completely revised and brought up to date for its twenty-fifth impression in 1931. It has remained a classic study to this day.

Between 1896 and 1909 George Adam Smith made four visits to the United States, lecturing at Johns Hopkins, Chicago, Yale, Western Reserve and Berkeley Universities, and made two more visits to Palestine, in 1901 and 1904.

In 1909 he was appointed Principal of the University of Aberdeen, where he remained until his retirement in 1935. In 1916 he was knighted and became Moderator of the General Assembly of the United Free Church of Scotland, and in 1918 he again toured the United States, this time at the request of the Foreign Office.

He was the author of a number of other books: *Book of the Twelve Prophets*, *The Life of Henry Drummond*, *Modern Criticism and the Preaching of the Old Testament*, *Jerusalem*, *The Early Poetry of Israel*, and Commentaries on Deuteronomy and Jeremiah. He was a member of the Alpine Club, and received honorary doctorates in Laws, Divinity and Literature from many Universities in Great Britain and the United States. He died in 1942.

GEORGE ADAM SMITH

THE HISTORICAL GEOGRAPHY OF THE HOLY LAND

COLLINS

THE FONTANA LIBRARY
THEOLOGY AND PHILOSOPHY

First published by Hodder & Stoughton Ltd., 1894
Fourth edition with supplementary notes, 1896
Twenty-fifth edition, revised throughout, 1931
First issued in the Fontana Library of Theology and Philosophy, following the 1931 edition 1966
Second impression in the Fontana Library, March 1968
Third impression January 1973
Fourth impression October 1974

TO THE MEMORY
OF
MY FATHER
GEORGE SMITH LL.D., C.I.E.

Printed in Great Britain
Collins Clear-Type Press
London and Glasgow

INTRODUCTION

by Professor H. H. Rowley

George Adam Smith's *Historical Geography of the Holy Land* is a classic which has fascinated and instructed generations of students and which has passed through a remarkable number of editions. I remember the impression it made on me when I first read it in my youth. It illuminated for me many Biblical passages and helped me to realise, as I had not realised before, the close interrelation between geography and history, and to understand the history better.

This still valuable work has long been out of print, and many will welcome its reissue in a paperback edition. It is reissued unchanged from the latest edition the author saw because if it had been revised to take account of all the archaeological work of the last few decades and the discussions of scholars on the identification of Biblical sites it would no longer have been George Adam Smith's work, and it would also have been difficult for anyone to sew new patches on this garment without spoiling it. Something of the grace of style which gave such charm to all George Adam Smith wrote would inevitably have been lost. Readers who want the latest views will find them in the various Bible Atlases which have been published in recent years, or in a variety of other works, but a great deal of what is here offered can be found only here. The descriptions of Palestine, with all their intimate detail, and the fine scholarly setting of the history in the background of what is known from ancient and mediæval sources give this volume a character all its own, and it will continue to delight readers as well as to inform.

In one respect there has had to be change. The coloured maps found in the old editions could not be reproduced at a cost consistent with a paperback edition, and black and white maps have had to be substituted. The reader who shares my regret at this may reflect that the additional cost they would have entailed might have made it difficult for many other readers to share his pleasure in reading it.

I am conscious of the impertinence of my writing an "Introduction" to a book which was written when I was in my infancy and which had achieved a great reputation before I was heard of. All I desire to do is to introduce it to readers who do not already know it and to express the hope that this masterpiece among the vast literature on the Bible will come to mean as much to them as it has long meant to me.

H. H. Rowley

CONTENTS

Contents

CHRONOLOGICAL TABLE

			B.C.
	Entrance of Israel into Palestine	*circa*	1400
	Deborah and her Song / Gideon	,,	1200
	Saul anointed	,,	1030
	David, King	,,	1010
	Solomon, King	,,	970
	Disruption of the Kingdom and invasion by Shisha	,,	930
	Elijah	,,	870
	Israel comes into touch with Assyria: Battle of Ḳarḳar		854
	Elisha		850-800
	First Writing Prophets: Amos, Hosea	*circa*	750
Isaiah	Uzziah dies		742
Isaiah	Northern Israel falls		722
Isaiah	Deliverance of Jerusalem		701
Jeremiah	Discovery of Book of the Law		621
Jeremiah	Death of Josiah at Megiddo		608
Jeremiah	Fall of Assyria: Rise of Babylonia		606
Jeremiah; Ezekiel	First Great Captivity of Jerusalem		597
Jeremiah; Ezekiel	Second ,, ,, ,,		587
Second Isaiah	Fall of Babylonia: Rise of Persia		538
Second Isaiah	First Return of Jews from exile		536
Second Isaiah	Temple rebuilt		515
	Ezra and Nehemiah		457-430
	Erection of Temple on Gerizim		360
	Alexander the Great in Syria		332
	Beginning of the Seleucid Era		312
	Kingdom of Parthia founded		250
	Rome defeats Antiochus the Great at Magnesia		190
	The Maccabees		168-135
	John Hyrcanus		135-105
	Alexander Jannæus		104-78
	Arrival of Pompey: Roman Province of Syria		64
	Parthians invade Syria		40
	Battle of Actium		31

Chronological Table

Herod the Great		37-4
His kingdom divided among Archelaus, Herod Antipas, and Philip		4
		A.D.
Archelaus banished: Judæa under Roman Procurator		6
Caiaphas, High Priest		18-36
Pontius Pilate, Governor		26
Death of Philip		34
Banishment of Antipas		39
Agrippa I		37-44
Agrippa II		50-100
Felix Procurator		52
Festus succeeds him		60
Jewish Rebellion against Rome		66
Siege of Jerusalem		70
Formation of Roman Province of Arabia by Trajan		106
Final overthrow of the Jews under Bar Cochba by Hadrian		135
Origen in Palestine	*circa*	218
Decian Persecution	"	250
Diocletian's Persecution	*on from*	303
Eusebius, Archbishop of Cæsarea		315-318
Constantine the Great		323-336
Final overthrow of Paganism in Palestine	*circa*	400
The Hejra		622
Death of Mohammed		632
Moslem conquest of Syria		634-638
Omaiyade Khalifs make Damascus their Capital		661
Invasion of Seljuk Turks		1070-1085
First Crusade and Latin Kingdom of Jerusalem		1098-1187
Battle of Ḥaṭṭin won by Saladin		1187
Third Crusade, Richard of England		1191
Sultan Bibars, and overthrow of the Franks	*circa*	1270
Mongol Invasions, the last by Timur		1240, 1260, 1400
Napoleon in Syria		1799
The Great War		1914-1918

ABBREVIATIONS

A.V. = Authorised English Version of the Scriptures.
Baudissin, *Stud.* = *Studien zur Semitischen Religionsgeschichte*, 1876.
Beha ed-Din, *Vit. Sal., ed. Schult.* = *Vita Saladinis*, with excerpts from the geography of Abulfeda, ed. Schultens. See p. 36, n. 3.
BSAJ = British School of Archæology, Jerusalem.
Budde, *Ri. u. Sa.* or *Richt. Sam.* = *Die Bücher Richter u. Samuelis.*
Buhl = *Geographie des alten Palästina*, 1896.
CIS = *Corpus Inscriptionum Semiticarum*, cf. p. 34, n. 7.
Conder, *TW* = *Tent Work in Palestine*, 1878.
De Saulcy, *Num. de la TS* = *Numismatique de la Terre Sainte*, 1874.
Enc. Bibl. = *Encyclopædia Biblica*, 1899-1903.
Garstang, *Josh. Jud.* = *Joshua, Judges*, 1931.
Geog. Gr. Min. = *Geographi Graeci Minores*, edd. Hudson and Müller. See p. 35, n. 2.
Hastings, *DB* = *Dictionary of the Bible*, 1898-1904.
Hend. *Pal.* = *The Historical Geography of Palestine*, by Rev. A. Henderson, D.D. 2nd ed. In "Handbooks for Bible Classes".
Josephus, *Antt.* = *Antiquities.*
" *Wars* = *Wars of the Jews.*
JPOS = Journal of the Palestine Oriental Society of Jerusalem.
KAT = E. Schrader's *Keilinschriften u. das Alte Testament*; also 3rd ed. by H. Zimmern and H. Winckler, 1903.
LXX, The Septuagint, the Greek Version of the O.T.
Macc., Books of the Maccabees, 1 and 2.
Neubauer, *Géog. Tal.* = *La Géographie du Talmud*, Paris, 1868.
PEF Mem. = *Memoirs of the Palestine Exploration Fund.*
PEFQ = *Quarterly Statement of the Palestine Exploration Fund.*
PEF Red. Map = *Reduced Map of the Palestine Exploration Fund*, edd. 1890 f.
PPT = Palestine Pilgrims' Text Society's Series of Publications.
Robinson, *BR* or *Bib. Res.* = *Biblical Researches*, 1841.
" *LBR* or *LR* = *Later Researches*, 1852.
Siegfried-Stade = Siegfried's and Stade's *Handwörterbuch*, 1893.
W. R. Smith, *OTJC* = *Old Testament in the Jewish Church*, 2nd ed., 1892.
Stade, *GVI* or *Gesch.* = *Geschichte des Volkes Israel*, 1888.
Wadd. = Le Bas and Waddington, *Inscriptions Grecques et Latines recueillies en Grèce et en Asie Mineure.* See p. 34, n. 7.
Wetz. = Wetzstein.
ZATW = *Zeitschrift für die Alt-testamentliche Wissenschaft.*
ZDMG = *Zeitschrift der Deutschen Morgenländischen Gesellschaft.*
ZDPV = *Zeitschrift des Deutschen Palästina-Vereins.*
MuNDPV = *Mittheilungen und Nachrichten des Deutschen Palästina-Vereins.*

In the transliteration of Hebrew and Arabic words *'Aleph* is usually rendered by a light, *'Ayin* by a rough, breathing; but at the beginning of Arabic names the former is omitted; *Ḥeth* by *Ḥ*; *Ṭeth* by *Ṭ*; *Kaph* by *K* or sometimes as in R.S.V. by *Ch*, or *C*; *Qoph* by *Ḳ*; *Ṣade* usually by *Ṣ*. Biblical names are given as in R.S.V.

In ancient names *Gimel* is rendered by *G* (hard), in modern names by *J*. When soft after a vowel the letter *Beth* is sometimes *Bh*, sometimes just *B*; the Palestine Jews transliterate it *V*. I have left their *z* in the names of some of their colonies. In Arabic names final silent *H* is sometimes omitted as in *Lejá*, but in many cases is retained.

In this edition Biblical place-names are usually given in the forms used in the R.S.V. Greater uniformity in the spelling of modern Arabic place-names—at least in the consonants—has been secured with the help of Professor H. H. Rowley.

FROM THE PREFACE TO THE FIRST EDITION, 1894

There are many ways of writing a geography of Palestine, and of illustrating the History by the Land, but some are wearisome and some vain. They do not give a vision of the Land as a whole, nor help you to hear through it the sound of running history. What is needed by the reader or teacher of the Bible is some idea of the outlines of Palestine—its shape and disposition; its plains, passes and mountains; its rains, winds and temperatures; its colours, lights and shades. Students of the Bible desire to see a background and to feel an atmosphere; to discover from "the lie of the land" why the history took certain lines and the prophecy and gospel were expressed in certain styles; to learn what geography has to contribute to questions of Biblical criticism; above all, to discern between what physical nature contributed to the religious development of Israel, and what was the product of moral and spiritual forces. On this last point the geography of the Holy Land reaches its highest interest. It is also good to realise the historical influences by which our religion was at first nurtured or exercised, as far as we can do this from the ruins which these have left in the country. To go no further back than the New Testament, there are the Greek art, the Roman rule, and the industry and pride of Herod. But the remains of Scripture times are not so many as the remains of the centuries since. The Palestine of to-day is more a museum of Church History than of the Bible, a museum of living as well as of ancient specimens of its subject. East of Jordan, in the indestructible basalt of Hauran, are monuments of the passages from Paganism to Christianity even more numerous and remarkable than the catacombs or earliest Churches of Rome; there are also what Italy cannot give us, the melancholy wrecks of the passage from Christianity to Mohammedanism. West of Jordan are the castles and churches of the Crusaders, the impression of their brief kingdom and its ruin; the trail of the march and retreat of Napoleon. And after the long silence and crumbling of all things native, are the living Churches of to-day, and the lines of pilgrims coming up to Jerusalem from the four corners of the world.

For a historical geography compassing such a survey, the conditions are to-day three: personal acquaintance with the land; a study of the exploration, discoveries and decipherments, especially the most recent; and the employment of the results of Biblical criticism.

1. The following chapters have been written after two visits to the Holy Land. In the spring of 1880 I made a journey through Judæa, Samaria, Esdraelon, and Galilee: that was before the great changes which were produced on many of the most sacred landscapes by European colonists, and by the rivalry in building between the Greek and Latin Churches. Again, in 1891, I was able to extend my knowledge of the country to the Maritime Plain, the Shephelah, the wilderness of Judæa, including Masada and Engedi, the Jordan Valley, Hermon, the Beḳa', and especially Damascus, Hauran, Gilead and Moab. Unfortunately—in consequence of taking Druze servants, we were told—we were turned back by the authorities from Bozrah and Jebel-Druz, so that I cannot write from personal acquaintance with those interesting localities, but we spent the more time in Hauran, and at Gadara, Gerasa and Pella, where we were able to add to the number of discovered inscriptions.

2. With the exception of the results of early geographers, summarised by Reland, the renewal of Syrian travel in the beginning of the nineteenth century, and the work of Robinson—the real exploration of Palestine has been achieved during the last twenty years. It has been the work of no one nation; its effectiveness is due to its thoroughly international character. America gave the pioneers in Robinson, Eli Smith and Lynch. To Great Britain belong, through the Palestine Exploration Fund—by Wilson, Warren, Drake, Tristram, Conder, Kitchener, Mantell, Black and Armstrong—the results of a trigonometrical survey of all Western, and part of Eastern, Palestine, a geological survey, the excavations at Jerusalem and Tell el-Ḥesy, numerous discoveries and identifications, and the earliest summaries of natural history and meteorology. But we cannot forget that this work was prepared for, and has been supplemented both by French and Germans. The French have been first in the departments of art and archæology—witness Waddington, Renan, De Vogüé, De Saulcy, Clermont-Ganneau and Rey. In topography, also, through Guérin and others, the French contributions are important. To Germany we owe many travels and researches, which, like Wetzstein's, have added to the geography, especially of Eastern Palestine. The Germans have also given what has been lacking in Britain, a scientific treatment of the geography in the light of Biblical criticism; the work of Socin, Guthe, and their colleagues in the Deutsches Palästina-Verein, has been thorough and of example to ourselves. The notes in this volume will show how much I am indebted to material provided by the journals of both the British and German societies, as well as to other works issued under their auspices. Recent

American literature on Palestine is valuable, chiefly for the works of Merrill and Clay Trumbull.

But the most distinctive feature of the last twenty years has been the aid rendered by the European inhabitants of Syria. Doctors and missionaries, the children of the first German colonists and of the earlier American missionaries, have grown into a familiarity with the country, which the most expert of foreign explorers cannot rival. Through the British and German societies, Chaplin, Schumacher, Schick, Gatt, Fischer of Sarona, Klein, Hanauer, Baldensperger, Post, West and Bliss have contributed so much topographical detail, nomenclature, meteorology and information of the social life of the country, that there seems to lie rather a century than a score of years between the present conditions of Syriology [1894] and what prevailed when we were dependent on the records of travellers and pilgrims.

During recent years a great deal has been done for the geography of Palestine from Assyrian and Egyptian studies, such as by the younger Delitzsch, Maspero, Sayce, Tomkins, and W. Max Müller, whose work, *Asien u. Europa nach den altägyptischen Denkmälern*, has altered and increased the Egyptian data. I need not dwell on the information of the Tell el-Amarna tablets as to the condition of Palestine before the coming of Israel.

On the Roman and Greek periods there appeared the works of Mommsen, Mahaffy, Morrison, Neubauer, Niese's edition of Josephus, Boettger's Lexicon to Josephus, the collection of Nabatæan inscriptions in the *Corpus Inscriptionum Semiticarum*, and Schürer's *History of the Jewish People in the Time of Christ*. I have constantly referred to the latter on the Maccabæan and Herodian periods; and where I venture to differ from his conclusions this is with hesitation.

The last fifteen years have also seen the collection and re-publication of the pilgrim literature on Palestine, a more thorough research into the Arab geographies, of which Mr. Guy Le Strange's *Palestine under the Moslems* affords a valuable summary, and works on the Crusades and the Frank occupation and organisation of Palestine, of which the chief are those of Rey, Röhricht and Prutz. The French collection of the Historians of the Crusades, begun in 1843, largely falls within this generation.

From one source, hitherto unused, I derive great help: Napoleon's invasion of Syria and his conduct of modern war upon its ancient battle-fields. It is great to follow Napoleon on the routes taken by Thothmes, Sennacherib, Alexander, Vespasian and the Crusaders, amidst the same difficulties of forage and locomotion, and against much the same kind of enemies; and I am surprised that no geographer of the country has availed himself of the opportunity afforded by the full records of Napoleon's Asiatic campaign, and by the journals of British officers, attached to the Turkish army which followed up his retreat.

Of all these materials I make such use as contributes to the aim of this work. I add few original suggestions. I have felt that at present the geographer of Palestine is more usefully employed in reducing than in adding to the identifications of sites. British surveyors have been tempted to over-identification by the zeal of a portion of the religious public, which subscribes to exploration according to the number of immediate results. In Germany this temptation has been felt, though from other causes, and the Zeitschrift des Deutschen Palästina-Vereins has almost as many rash proposals as the Quarterly Statement and Maps of the Palestine Exploration Fund. I have, therefore, ignored a number of identifications and contested more. If the following pages leave many problems stated rather than solved, this has been done of purpose. The work of explorers and critics has secured an enormous number of results which cannot be doubted. But in other cases what has been achieved is simply the collection of evidence that exists above ground, which is conflicting, and can be settled only by such further excavations as Flinders Petrie and Bliss have inaugurated at Tell el-Ḥesy. The exploration of Western Palestine at least, is almost exhausted on the surface, but there is a great future for it under-ground. We have run most of the questions to earth: it only remains to dig them up.

3. An equally strong reason for the appearance of a Historical Geography of Palestine is the progress of Biblical criticism. The relation of the geographical materials at our disposal and the methods of historical reconstruction have been altered by Old Testament science, since, for instance, Dean Stanley wrote *Sinai and Palestine.* That part of criticism which consists of the distinction and appreciation of the documents, of which the Books of Scripture are composed, has contributed to the elucidation and arrangement of geographical details in the history of Israel, which without it had been left by archæology in obscurity. I heartily agree with most that is said on the duty of regulating the literary criticism of the Bible by the archæology of Syria and neighbouring countries, but there is a converse duty. We have had too many instances of the embarrassment and confusion into which archæology and geography lead us apart from the methods of Biblical criticism. To those who are distrustful of the latter, I venture to say that there is no sphere in which the helpfulness of criticism, in removing difficulties and explaining contradictions, has been more apparent than in Biblical Geography. I have felt forced by geographical evidence to contest some of the textual and historical conclusions of recent critics, but I have accepted the critical methods, and I believe this to be the first geography of the Holy Land in

which they are employed. At this time of day, it would be futile to think of writing the geography of Palestine on any other principles.

It is as a provisional attempt to collect old and new material from all these sources that I offer the following pages. I have not aimed at exhausting the details of the subject, but I have tried to lay down the best lines both for the arrangement of what has been acquired, and for fitting on to it what may still be discovered. The omissions the reader will notice. I have excluded the topography of Jerusalem, the geography of Phœnicia and Lebanon, because Phœnicia and Lebanon lie properly outside the Holy Land, and an adequate topography of Jerusalem, while not contributing to the aim of the volume, would have unduly increased the size of a work already too great. I was anxious to give as much space as possible to Eastern Palestine, of which we have had hitherto no complete geography.

28*th April*, 1894

FROM THE PREFACE TO THE TWENTY-FIFTH EDITION, 1931

This new edition has been revised throughout and as far as possible brought down to date, 1931.

The Additional Notes to previous editions have been incorporated in the body of the work, and supplemented by others. Since the last additions in 1896, and especially since the publication in 1914 of *The Historical Atlas of the Holy Land*, by the late Dr. J. G. Bartholomew and myself, numerous excavations and other discoveries have been made in Palestine, and the increase of the relevant literature—historical, philological, and archæological—has been enormous. Of all these I have made large use.

I have twice again gone through the Land, in 1901 and 1904.

The political and social conditions of Palestine and Transjordan have been transformed by the Great War, and by the passing of the government of Syria from the Turks to the British and the French under Mandate, and in Eastern Palestine and the land of Edom to Arabs in consultation with and under the advice of the British High Commissioner in Jerusalem.

In this edition I have traced the successive stages of General Allenby's campaign of 1917-18 (in conjunction with the Arab advance northwards from the Gulf of 'Aḳaba) along with their illustrations or repetitions of the ancient campaigns described in previous editions. The main administrative changes, the new lines of road and railway, the recent Jewish immigration and colonies, as well as the increase of agriculture and woodlands, have also been noted.

A wholly new chapter on the Land of Edom has been added; and this not only because of the kinship and neighbourhood of Edom and ancient Israel, but because the new Province or Emirate of Transjordan extends across Mount Edom to 'Aḳaba or Elath, as once did the government and commerce of the Kings of Judah.

I have been much encouraged by the generous tributes from Field-Marshal Viscount Allenby and many of his officers in Palestine to the real usefulness of my volume in framing the strategy and tactics of their campaign; as well as from Mr. Rowe (see p. 239) and others for the help it gave them in their recent excavations. May it be of equal service to those who have charge of the settlement of the Land and of peace and order among the inhabitants!

Finally the volume owes very much to the advice and careful supervision of my wife.

George Adam Smith

The University of Aberdeen,
19*th October*, 1931

BOOK ONE

THE LAND AS A WHOLE

I. *THE PLACE OF SYRIA IN THE WORLD'S HISTORY*[1]

Between the Arabian Desert and the eastern coast of the Levant there stretches—along almost the full extent of the latter, or for nearly 400 miles—a tract of fertile land varying from 70 to 100 miles in breadth. This is so broken up by mountain range and valley that it has never all been brought under one native government; yet its well-defined boundaries—the sea on the west, Mount Taurus on the north, and the desert to east and south—give it unity, and separate it from the rest of the world. It has rightly, therefore, been covered by one name, Syria. Like that of Palestine, the name is due to the Greeks, but by a reverse process. While "Palestina", which is really Philistina, was first the name of only a part of the coast, and thence spread inland to the desert, Syria, either a shorter form of Assyria,[2] or derived from the Babylonian *Suri* (the region from Cappadocia to Media)[3] was originally applied by the Greeks to the Assyrian Empire from the Caucasus to the Levant, then shrank to this side of the Euphrates, and finally within the limits drawn above. The Arabs call the country Esh-Sham, or "The Left", for it is the northern or north-western end of the great Arabian Peninsula, of which they call the southern side El-Yemen, or "The Right".[4]

The name Palaistiné, which Josephus uses only of Philistia, was employed by the Greeks to distinguish Southern Syria, including Judæa, from Phœnicia and Cœle-Syria. They called it Syria Palaistiné, using the word as an adjective, and then Palaistiné alone. From this the Romans got their Palestina, which in the second century was a separate province, and later on divided into Palestina Prima, Secunda, Tertia. It survives in the Arab *gund* or canton, Filistin.[5]

[1] For this chapter, see Maps 1-10 and page 56

[2] Herodotus, vii. 632.

[3] Winckler, *Der Alte Orient*, i. 23; *KAT*[3], 27 f.

[4] Syria, as a modern geographical term, is distinct from the *Syria* and *Syrians* of the A.V. The Hebrew is *Aram*, *Aramæans*, a northern Semitic people in Mesopotamia, Aram-Naharaim, and west of the Euphrates—as far as the Phœnician coast, and Damascus. Some, however, hold that Aram-Naharaim was on this side the Euphrates. The Roman Province of Syria extended from the Euphrates to Egypt. Its eastern boundary ran from the head of the Gulf of Suez past the south-eastern end of the Dead Sea, the east of Gilead, Hauran and Palmyra, to the Euphrates. East of this line was Arabia (see ch. xxv).

[5] The history of the word: Philistines, פלשתים or פלשתיים is rendered by LXX

These were foreign names: the much older and native name Canaan is of doubtful origin, perhaps racial, but more probably geographical, meaning "sunken" or "low" land. It seems to have at first belonged to the Phœnician coast as distinguished from the hills above. Thence it extended to other lowlands—Sharon, the Jordan valley—and thence over the whole country, mountain as well as plain.[1]

The historical geography of Syria, so far as her relations with the rest of the world are concerned, may be summed up in a paragraph. Syria is the northern and most fertile end of the great Semitic home, the peninsula of Arabia. But the Semitic home is distinguished by its central position, between Asia and Africa, between the Indian Ocean and the Mediterranean, which is Europe; and the *rôle* in history of the Semitic race has also been intermediary. The Semites have proved the middlemen of the world. Not second-rate in war, they have risen to the first rank in commerce and religion. They have been the carriers between East and West, they have stood between the ancient civilisations and those which go to make up the modern world; while by a higher gift, for which their conditions neither in place nor in time fully account, they have been mediary between God and man, and proved the religious leaders of the world, through whom have come its three highest faiths, its only universal religions. Syria's history is her share in this great

---

Hexateuch *φυλιστιείμ*; cf. I Macc. iii. 24, Sirach xlvi. 18. From this Josephus has *φυλιστῖνος*, i *Antt.* vi. 2. His usual form is *παλαιστῖνος*. He knows the noun *'Η Παλαιστίνη*, and uses it of Philistia, xiii *Antt.* v. 10: "Simeon traversed Judah *καὶ τὴν Παλαιστίνην* to Askalon." Cf. i *Antt.* vi. 2: "The country from Gaza to Egypt . . . the Greeks call part of that country Palestine." In *Contra Apion*, i. 22, he quotes Herodotus as using the name inclusive of Judæa. Herodotus, who describes Syria as from Cilicia to Mount Carius, distinguishes the Phœnicians from the *Σύριοι οἱ ἐν τῇ Παλαιστίνῃ*, or *οἱ Παλαιστίνοι καλεόμενοι* (ii. 104, iii. 5, 91; vii. 89), and defines it as *τῆς Συρίης τοῦτο τὸ χωρίον καὶ τὸ μέχρι Αἰγύπτου πᾶν Παλαιστίνη καλέεται.* Willrich, *Juden u. Griechen der Makk.-Erhebung*, 43, takes Herodotus' Palaistina to be Philistia. Kirchhoff (Peterm. Mitth. 1895, p. 10) finds a threefold use by Herodotus. Arrian (*Anabasis*, ii. 25) speaks of *ἡ Συρίη Παλαιστίνη*. Syria was divided into S. Palestina, S. Punica, and S. Cœla; Herod. i. 105. Cf. Appian, *Præmium*, 2, *De Rebus Syr.* 50, *De Bello Mithr.* 116, etc.; Epiphanius, *De Mens. et Pond.* xiv. Palestine was made a separate province, A.D. 67.

[1] Land of Canaan is applied in the Amarna Correspondence of the fourteenth century B.C. (Tab. Berlin, 92) to the Phœnician coast, and by Egyptians to all W. Syria. Acc. to Josh. xi. 3, Canaanites were east and west of the land; acc. to Jud. i. 9 f. all over, in the Mount, Negeb, and Shephelah and Hebron. The spread of Canaanites spread the name. Isa. xix. 18, *the lip of Canaan* is the language of which Phœnician Hebrew, Moabite, etc., were dialects. In Zech. xiv. 21, Canaanite = Phœnician = merchant.

function of inter-medium, which has endured from the earliest times to the present day.

To put it more particularly, Syria lies between two continents—Asia and Africa; between two primeval homes of men—the valleys of the Euphrates and the Nile; between two centres of empire—Western Asia and Egypt: between all these, representing the Eastern and ancient world, and the Mediterranean, the gateway to the Western and modern world. Syria has been likened to a bridge between Asia and Africa—a bridge with the desert on one side and the sea upon the other; and, in truth, all the great invasions of Syria, with two exceptions, have been delivered across her northern and southern ends. But these exceptions—the invasions of Israel and Islam—prove the insufficiency of the bridge simile, not only because they were but the highest waves of an almost constant tide of immigration which has flowed upon Syria from Arabia, but because they represent that gift of religion to her, which in its influence on her history far exceeds the influence of her central position. Syria is not only the bridge between Asia and Africa: she is the refuge of the drifting populations of Arabia. She has been not only the highroad of civilisations and the battle-field of empires, but the pasture and the school of innumerable little tribes. She has been not merely an open channel of war and commerce for nearly the whole world, but the vantage-ground and opportunity of the world's highest religions. In this strange mingling of bridge and harbour, of highroad and field, of battle-ground and sanctuary, of seclusion and opportunity—rendered possible through the division of her surface into mountain and plain—lies the secret of Syria's history, under the religion which has lifted her fame to glory. As to her western boundary, no invasion, save of hope, came over that. Even when the nations of Europe sought Palestine, their armies did not enter by her harbours till the coast was in their possession. But across this coast she felt from the first her future to lie; her expectation went over the sea to isles and mainlands far beyond her horizon; and it was into the West that her spiritual empire—almost the only empire Syria ever knew—advanced upon its most glorious course.

In all this there are four chief factors of which it will be well to have some outline before we go into details: Syria's Relations to Arabia, from which she drew her population; her position as Debatable Ground between Asia and Africa, and between both of these and Europe; her Influence Westwards; her Religion. These outlines are meant to introduce the reader to the extent and the interest of the historical geography which he is beginning, as well as to indicate our authorities.

1. *The Relation of Syria to Arabia*

We have seen that Syria is the north end of the Arabian world, that great parallelogram, bounded by the Levant with Mount Taurus, the Euphrates with the Persian Gulf, the Indian Ocean, and the Red Sea with the Isthmus of Suez. Within these limits nature is wonderfully uniform: the mass of the territory is high, barren table-land, but dotted by fertile oases and surrounded by a lower level, most of which is also fertile.[1] The population is Semitic. It is numerous for so bare a land, hardy and reproductive. But it is broken up into small tribes, with no very definite territories. These tribes have gone forth united as a nation only at one period in their history, and that was the day of Islam, when their dominion extended from India to the Atlantic. At other times they have advanced either by single tribes or by a few tribes together. Their outgoings were four—across the Straits of Bab-el-Mandeb into Ethiopia, across the Isthmus of Suez into Egypt, across the Euphrates into Mesopotamia, across the Jordan into Western Syria. Of these Syria became the most common receptacle of the Arabian drift. She lay, so to speak, broadside-on to the desert; part of her was spread east of the Jordan, rolling off undefended on to the desert steppes; she was seldom protected by a strong government, like Egypt and Mesopotamia; and so in early times she received not only the direct tides of the desert but the back-wash from those harbours as well. Of this the Hebrews were an instance, who came to her, first from Mesopotamia and then from Egypt. The loose humanity of the Semitic world has been constantly beating upon Syria, and almost as constantly breaking into her. Of the tribes who crossed her border, some flowed in from the neighbourhood only for summer, and ebbed with autumn, like the Midianites in Gideon's day, or various clans of the 'Aneezeh in our own.[2] But others came up out of the centre or from the south of Arabia—like the Beni Jafn who migrated from Yemen in the first Christian century, and, being made by the Romans wardens of the eastern marches of the Empire, founded in time a great dynasty, the Ghassanides. And others came because crowded or driven out of the Nile or the Euphrates valley, like the Syrians, the Philistines, and the Children of Israel.

Thus Syria was peopled. Whenever history lights up her borders we see

[1] The coast of the Indian Ocean open to the monsoons, some coasts of the Red Sea and Persian Gulf, Syria, the slopes of Taurus, and the Euphrates valley, are fertile. The rest of the Persian Gulf and Red Sea coasts, the Isthmus of Suez, and forty miles along the Levant, are desert.

[2] See Schumacher, *ZDPV*, xx. 72 ff. Burton and Conder spell 'Anazeh, Wetzstein 'Anezeh.

the same process at work[1]: when Israel crosses the Jordan; when the Midianites follow and oppress her; when, the Jews being in exile, the Idumæans come up on their seats; when the Decapolis is formed as a Greek league to keep the Arabs out; when the Romans, with their wonderful policy, enrol some of the immigrants to hold the others in check; especially at the Moslem invasion; but also during the Latin kingdom of Jerusalem, when various nomadic tribes roaming certain regions with their tents are assigned to the Crown or to different Orders of Chivalry[2]; and even to-day, when parts of the Survey Map of Palestine are crossed by the names of the Beni Sab, the Beni Humar, the 'Arab el-'Amarin, and so forth, just as the map of ancient Palestine is distributed among the B'ne Naphtali, the B'ne Yoseph, the B'ne Yehudah, and other clans of Israel. All these, ancient and modern, have been members of the same Semitic race. Some have carried Syria by sudden war; others have ranged for long up and down the Syrian border, or settled peacefully on neglected parts of the land, till they were weaned from nomadic habits, and drawn in among the agricultural population. To-day we do not see single tribes coming up from the centre or other end of Arabia to invade Syria; but we have seen a powerful tribe like the Ruwalla ranging every year between the Euphrates and the Jordan; or clans like the Ta'amirah of the Judæan wilderness, or the 'Adwan of Moab, after living for centuries on blackmail from the *fellahin*, gradually taking to agriculture, and submitting to the government of the country.[3]

From all this have ensued two consequences:

First. The fact, that by far the strongest immigration into Syria has been of a race composed of small independent tribes, both suits and exaggerates the tendencies of the land itself. Syria, as we shall see, is broken up into petty provinces, as separated by desert and mountain as some Swiss cantons are by the Alps. Those clans, which swarmed out of Arabia, fitted the shelves and corners of Syria, so that Syria was tribal both by her form and by the character of her population. Partly this, and partly her position between great and hostile races, have disabled her from political empire.

Second. The population of Syria has always been essentially Semitic. There are few lands into which so many divers races have come: as in ancient times Philistines and Hittites; then in large numbers, Greeks; then with the Crusades a few hundred thousands of Franks; then till the present day more

[1] On the Ḥabiri, Winckler, *Völker Vorderasiens*, 13; Garstang, *Josh. Jud.*

[2] Prutz, *ZDPV*, x. 192, mentions so many "tents" or "tribes" as assigned to the Order of St. John, and argues that the rest belonged to the king.

[3] For Hauran see *ZDPV*, xx, and generally *MuNDPV*, 1900, 69. For Turks and Transjordan, ch. xxiv. *Letters of Gertrude Bell*, i. 206.

Franks, more Greeks, Turks, Kurds, and some colonies of Circassians. But these have scarcely been grafted on the stock[1]; and the stock is Semitic. The Greek has been the one possible rival of the Semite; but Greeks have inhabited only cities, where the death-rate has exceeded the birth-rate, and were they not renewed from abroad, they would disappear in the mass of the Arab or Syrian population.[2] Immigrations of Jews, and the multiplication of their colonies, have added to the Semitic elements.

2. *Syria's Relation to the Three Continents*

When Arab tribes came up from their desert into Syria, they found themselves on the edge of a great highroad and looking across a sea. The highroad is between Asia and Africa; the sea leads from the East to Europe. From one of the most remote positions on the earth they were plunged into the midst of the world's commerce and war. While this prevented them from consolidating into an empire of their own, it proved the opportunity for the development of the gifts which they brought with them from their age-long seclusion in the desert.

Syria's position between two of the oldest homes of the human race made her a passage for the earliest intercourse and exchanges of civilisation. There is probably no older road in all the world than that which can still be used by caravans from the Euphrates to the Nile, through Damascus, Galilee, Esdraelon, the Maritime Plain, and Gaza. It is doubtful whether history has to record any great campaigns—as distinguished from tribal wars—earlier than those which Egypt and Assyria waged against each other across the extent of Syria, and continued to the sixth century before Christ. But more distant powers broke across this land from both Asia and Africa. The Hittites came south from Asia Minor over Mount Taurus, and the Ethiopians north from their conquest of the Nile.[3] Towards the end of the duel between

[1] In face of the fair hair and blue eyes you meet in Bethlehem and on the Lebanon, it is perhaps too much to say with Socin ("Syria", *Enc. Brit.*) "that *every* trace of the presence of Greeks, Romans, and Franks has disappeared". Yet see R. A. S. Macalister "Palestine", *Enc. Brit.*

[2] "In Eastern cities the death-rate exceeds the birth-rate, and the urban population is maintained only by recruital from the country, so that the blood of the peasantry ultimately determines the type of the population. Thus after the Arab conquest of Syria the Greek element in the population rapidly disappeared. Indeed, one of the most palpable proofs that the populations of all the old Semitic lands possessed a remarkable homogeneity of character is the fact that in them, and in them alone, Arabs and Arab influence took permanent root."—W. R. Smith, *Religion of the Semites*, 12, 13.

[3] 2 Chron. xiv. 9.

Assyria and Egypt, the Scythians from north of the Caucasus devastated Syria.[1] When the Babylonian Empire fell, the Persians made her a province of their empire, and marched across her to Egypt. Near the beginning of our era, she was overrun by the Parthians.[2] The Persians invaded her a second time,[3] just before the Moslem invasion of the seventh century; she fell under the Seljuk Turks in the eleventh[4]; and in the thirteenth and fourteenth the Mongols thrice swept through her.[5]

Into this stream of empires and races, which swept through Syria from the earliest ages, Europe was drawn under Alexander the Great; and now that the West began to invade the East, Syria was found to be as central between them as between Asia and Africa. She was Alexander's pathway to Egypt, 332 B.C. She was scoured by the wars of the Seleucids and Ptolemies, and her plains planted with their essentially Greek civilisation. Pompey brought her under the Roman Empire, 65 B.C., and in this and the Byzantine she remained till the Arabs took her, A.D. 634. The Crusaders held her for almost a century, 1098-1187, and parts of her for a century more: coming to her, not, like most other invaders, because she was the road to somewhere else, but because she was herself, in their eyes, the goal of all roads, the central[6] and most blessed province of the world, and yet but repeating upon her the old contest between East and West. Napoleon made her the pathway of his ambition towards that empire on the Euphrates and Indus whose fate was decided on her plains, 1799. Since then and up to 1914 Syria's history has mainly consisted in a number of attempts by the Western world to plant upon her both their civilisation and her former religion.

Thus in Syria history has very largely repeated itself; and since history never repeats, without explaining, itself, we shall see the value of these invasions from Asia, Africa, and Europe for illustrating that part of Syrian history which is especially our interest. What, then, are our authorities for them all?

Many of these invasions have left on the land no trace readable by us, but others have stamped their impression both in monuments we can decipher, and in literature. Of monuments Hittites,[7] Assyrians, and Egyptians have each left a few—upon stones north of the Lebanon, on the rocks by the old

[1] Zeph. ii; Jer. i. 14 ff. Cf. Herodotus, i. 104 ff.

[2] 40 B.C.

[3] A.D. 612-616, under Chosroes II.

[4] 1070-1085.

[5] In 1240 Syrians and Crusaders stood together to beat back the Kharesmians; a second Mongol invasion took place in 1260, and a third in 1400 under Timur, which repeated the exportations of early Assyrian days, and carried off the effective classes of Damascus and other towns to Samarcand.

[6] See Marino Sanuto's map in *Historical Atlas of the Holy Land*, Smith and Bartholomew.

[7] Wright, *Empire of the Hittites*; Conder, *Heth and Moab*; Sayce, *Races of the Old*

coast road at the mouth of the Dog River,[1] on a solitary stone near the high-road across Hauran,[2] on a stele of Sety I discovered by the present writer at Tell esh-Shihab in 1901,[3] on a clay tablet found at Lachish,[4] and on other fragments, especially those of the ruins at Beth-shan. But in the Egyptian and Assyrian annals we have itineraries through Syria, and records of conquest, profuse and informing.[5] The only records left by the Antiochi and Ptolemies, besides the names of certain towns with a few inscriptions, are coins, still picked up by the traveller.[6] On the other hand, Greece and Rome have left their monuments over the land, but especially on the plains and plateaus: in Lebanon solitary Greek temples, with inscriptions to the gods of Greece and the native gods; but across Jordan whole cities, with the usual civil architecture of theatres, amphitheatres, forums, temples, baths, and colonnaded streets. Yet you will see none earlier than the time Rome threw her shield between the Greek civilisation and the Arab drift from the desert. There are Roman pavements, bridges, and milestones; tombstones of legionaries and officials; imperial and provincial edicts; ascriptions of glory and deity to the emperors.[7] The ruins of the buildings of Herod the Great which survive at Samaria, Cæsarea, and elsewhere are of Greek character, and must be added to the signs of Western influence, which found so strenu-

Testament, etc.; Léon de Lantsheeres, *De la race et de la langue des Hittites*, 1891; V. Luschan, etc., *Ausgrabungen in Sendschirli*, 1893, 1898, 1902; Winckler, *Vorläufige Nachrichten über die Ausgrabungen in Boghaz-Keui*, 1907; and above all Garstang, *The Land of the Hittites*, 1910. Also G. A. Smith, *Jerusalem*, ii. 16 f., 1908; Cowley, Hogarth, and S. A. Cook in their Schweich Lectures for 1918, 1924, and 1925.

[1] Robinson, *Later B.R.*, 618 ff.; Layard, *Discov. in Ninevéh*, etc., 211 n.; Conder, *Syrian Stone Lore*, 56, 124.

[2] *ZDPV*, xii.

[3] G. A. Smith, *Jerusalem*, ii. 19 with plate.

[4] Conder, *Tell-el-Amarna Tablets*; *PEFQ*, 1893, Jan.

[5] Lepsius, *Denkmäler aus Aegypten*; *Records of the Past*, esp. 2nd Series with Sayce on Amarna Tablets; Tomkins on Campaigns of Thothmes III; papers in the *PEFQ* and *Trans. of the Society of Bibl. Archæology*; above all, W. Max Müller, *Asien u. Europa n. altägyp. Denkmäler*, 1893.

[6] The authorities are: Gough's *Coins of the Seleucidæ*, 1803; Gardner, *Catalogue of Coins in the British Museum*; *The Seleucid Kings of Syria*, 1878; De Saulcy in *Mélanges de Numismatique* (pp. 45-64); the relevant sections in Eckhel, *Doctrina numorum veterum*, in Mionnet, and in George Macdonald, *Greek Coins in the Hunterian Collection*, 1905.

[7] The fullest collection is in vol. iii of Le Bas and Waddington, *Inscriptions Grecque et Latines, recueillies en Grèce et en Asie Mineure*. Cf. Wetzstein, *Ausgewählte Griech. u. Lat. Inschriften gesammelt auf Reisen in den Trachonen u. um das Haurangebirge*, from *Transactions of the Royal Acad. of Sciences*, Berlin, 1863; Clermont-Ganneau, *Recueil d'Archéologie Orientale*, Paris, 1888, and papers in *PEFQ*; Mordtmann in the *ZDPV*, vii. 119-124; Allen, "On Various Inscriptions found by Merrill East of Jordan", in the *American Journal of Philology*, vi; Rendel Harris, *Some Recently Dis-*

ous an ally in that extraordinary Idumæan. Coins also abound from this period—imperial coins and those of the free Greek cities.[1]

Through all these ages the contemporary Hebrew, Greek, and Latin literatures supplement the monuments. The historical books of the Old Testament, in their extant form, were composed some centuries after the earliest events of which they treat; but, so far as their geography is concerned, they reflect with accuracy the early invasions and immigrations into Syria, which we have other means of following. In the Hebrew prophets we have contemporary evidence of the Assyrian, Egyptian, Scythian, Babylonian, and Persian invasions: to these the pages of prophecy are as sensitive as the reed-beds of Syria to the passage of the wind and the flood. Later books, like Daniel and Ecclesiasticus, and some Psalms betray by their style of thought, and by their language, that Israel has felt the first Greek influences. The books of the Maccabees and Josephus trace Greek and Roman advance, the long struggle over plain and mountain—the Hellenisation of the former, the final conquest of the latter by Rome. The Gospels are full of signs of the Roman supremacy—publicans, taxes, Cæsar's superscription on coins, centurions, the incubus of the Legion, the authority of Cæsar. The Acts tell us how west of Jordan Rome defended Christianity from Judaism, as upon the east she shielded Hellenism from the desert barbarians. In Pagan literature we have many histories and geographies with large information about the Græco-Roman influence in Syria up to the Fall of Jerusalem.[2]

For the first six centuries of our era Syria was a province of the Empire, in which, for a time, Hellenism was more at home than in Hellas itself, and Christianity was first persecuted and then established by Western edicts and arms. The story is told by Syrian and Greek historians of the Church, the

---

covered Inscriptions; my paper in the *Critical Review*, Jan. 1892, on "Some Unpublished Inscriptions from Ḥauran", twelve in all, see below chs. xxix f. For Semitic inscriptions, see *Corpus Inscriptionum Semiticarum*, Paris, 1881 ff. Also Ewing, *PEFQ*, 1895.

[1] These are still being found in considerable numbers. The authorities are: F. de Saulcy, *Numismatique de la Terre Sainte*, Paris, 1874; Madden, *Coins of the Jews*; Eckhel, Mionnet, Macdonald (see previous page).

[2] Polybius *passim*; Diodorus Siculus; Arrian's *Anabasis of Alexander*, ii; Quintus Curtius, iv; Appian and Dio Cassius; Strabo's *Geography*, especially xvi. ii, and Ptolemy's; *Geographi Græci Minores* (edd. Hudson, Oxford, 1698-1712, and Müller, Paris, 1855-61); Pliny's *Hist. Nat.* v. 13-19; Tacitus. In English, Gibbon; Mommsen's *Provinces of the Roman Empire*; Schürer's *Hist. of the Jewish People in the Time of Christ*, Eng., 1890 ff.; Morrison's *The Jews under Roman Rule*, 1890; Mahaffy, *The Greek World under Roman Sway*, 1890; Kiepert, *Formæ Orbis Antiquæ*; Hölscher, *Pal. in der Pers. u. Hellen. Zeit*, 1903; Bevan, *The House of Seleucus*; G. A. Smith, *Jerusalem*, ii, chs. xv ff.

lives of some saints, and some writings of the Fathers.[1] It is supplemented by Christian remains (especially east of Jordan), churches, tombs, and houses, with many inscriptions in Greek and Aramaic.[2] The latest Greek inscription in Eastern Palestine appears to be from a year or two after the Moslem invasion.

The next European settlement in Syria was much more brief. The Latin kingdom of Jerusalem *de facto* lasted from 1099 to 1187—not ninety years; and the coast was Western a century longer. All the more are we astonished at the impression left on the land. In their brief day, these few hundred thousands of colonists and warriors, though the sword was never out of their hand, organised the land into a feudal kingdom as fully assigned, cultivated, and administered as any part of contemporary France or England. Their chroniclers[3] do justice to their courage and exploits on the field, as well as to their treachery, greed, and lust: but to see how truly they made Syria a bit of the West, we need to go to that wonderful work, the *Assizes of Jerusalem*, to the documents of the Orders of Chivalry,[4] and to the buildings they have scattered all over the land.[5]

[1] Eusebius, *History of the Church* and *Life of Constantine*. The *History* was continued by Socrates for 306-439, by Sozomen, and Theodoret and Evagrius to 594. Stephanus Byzantinus (probably in Justinian's reign) wrote the *'Εθνικά*, of which we have only an epitome. The history of Zosimus is of the Empire from Augustus to 410. Jerome's *Letters* and *Commentaries, passim*. The lives especially of Hilarion by Jerome, and of Porphyry in the *Acta Sanctorum*. See ch. xi.

[2] See chs. xxix f.

[3] The best are William, Archbishop of Tyre (1174-1188?), *Historia rerum in partibus transmarinis gestarum a tempore successorum Mahumeth usque ad A.D.* 1184; *Itinerarium Regis Anglorum Ricardi*, attributed to Geoffrey of Vinsauf, but probably a translation by Richard, Canon of London of *L'Estoire de la Guerre Sainte*, a chronicle in verse of the Third Crusade by Ambroise, a minstrel on that Crusade, ed. by Gaston, Paris, 1897; Bongar's *Gesta Dei per Francos*; Jacques de Vitry; De Joinville's *Memoirs of Louis IX*. From the Saracen side, Beha ed-Din's *Life of Saladin*, with excerpts from the *History* of Abulfeda, etc., ed. Schultens, 1732; and Imad ed-Din El-Katib el-Isfahani, *Conquête de la Syrie et de la Palestine*, publié par le Comte Carlo de Landberg: 1, Texte Arabe. Leyden, 1888.

[4] The authorities are: E. Rey, *Les Colonies Franques de Syrie, aux xiime et xiiime Siècles*, 1883; Prutz, *Entwicklung u. Untergang des Tempel-Herren Ordens*, 1888; Prutz's and Röhricht's papers on Charters, Bulls, and other documents on the Orden der Deutsch Herren and other Orders in *ZDPV*, viii, x. Conder's papers in *PEFQ*, 1889 ff. The best edition of the *Assizes of Jerusalem*, by John d'Ibelin, is Beugnot's in *Recueil des Historiens des Croisades* (1841-1881). On the Crusades generally, cf. Gibbon; Cox in the *Epochs of History*; Sybel, *Geschichte der Kreuzzüge*; *Karten u. Pläne sur Palästina-kunde aus dem 7 bis 10 Jahrhundert*, by Röhricht, i, ii, iii, *ZDPV*, xiv, xv; Röhricht's *Regesta Regni Hierosolymitani*, 1893; W. B. Stevenson, *The Crusaders in the East*, 1907.

[5] On Crusading masonry, see Conder in *PEF Mem.*, Samaria under Cæsarea and

The pilgrim literature, which, apart from trade, represents the sole connection between the West and Syria in the centuries between the Moslem invasion and the Crusades and between the Crusades and last century, is exceedingly numerous. Most of it, too, is accessible in modern translations.[1] After the Crusades the Venetians and Genoese continued for a century or two their factories on the Phœnician coast, by which the products of the Far East came to Europe.[2]

Of Napoleon's invasion we have full information, which not only illustrates the position of Syria as debatable ground between the East and the West, but is valuable for the light it throws upon the military geography of the Holy Land. One cannot desire a more comprehensive, or lucid, outline of the relations of Syria to Egypt, to Asia, to Europe, than is given in the memoirs of his campaigns, dictated by Napoleon himself[3]; while the accounts of his routes and the reasons given for them, his sieges, losses from the plague, and swift retreat enable us to understand the movements of ancient invaders of the land. Napoleon's memoirs may be supplemented by the accounts of English officers who were with the Turkish forces.[4]

The literature on the Great War, 1914-1918, so far as it was waged in Palestine, is already extensive, both official and otherwise.[5] I will deal with it section by section through the land.

Judæa under Ashkelon. On the fortresses, see Rey, *op. cit.* ch. vii, with plans and views. On the churches, De Vogüé, *Églises de la Terre Sainte*; cf. his *Architecture civile et religieuse de la Syrie.*

[1] Bohn's *Early Travels in Palestine*; translations of the Palestine Pilgrims' Text Society; Tobler's *Itineraria Hierosolymitana*; the French *Archives de la Société d'Orient Latin*; Carmoly's *Itinéraires de la Terre Sainte des xiime-xviime Siècles*, 1847. I have found useful *Reyssbuch des heiligen Landes, das ist eine grundtliche Beschreibung aller u. jeder Meer u. Bilgerfahrten zum heyl. Lande*, etc., etc., mdlxxxiii.; the indispensable Quaresmius, *Historica, Theologica, ei Moralis Terræ Sanctæ Elucidatio*, 1639; and Pietri Della Valle's *Reisebeschreibung*, from the Italian, 1674, but few of his "Sendschreiben" refer to Syria.

[2] Besides Rey, who treats of the commerce of the Crusades (*op. cit.* ch. ix), the authorities I know are Heyd, *Geschichte des Levantenhandels im Mittelalter*, 1879, 2 vols.; in French, much enlarged, 1885-1886, 2 vols., incl. *Les Consulats Établis . . . Pour La Protection des Pélerins*; and *Discorso sopra il Commercio degli Italiani nel sec. xiv*, 1818.

[3] *Guerre de l'Orient: Campagnes d'Égypte et de Syrie.* Mémoires dictées par Napoléon lui-même et publiées par Général Bertrand, Paris, 1847.

[4] Walsh, *Diary of the Late Campaign, 1799-1801*; Wittman, M.D., *Travels in Syria, etc., 1799-1801 . . . in company with the Turkish Army.* See, too, Sir C. M. Watson, *PEFQ*, 1917, p. 17.

[5] Official—*Military Operations, Egypt and Palestine, from June 1917 to the End of the War*, Compiled by Captain Cyril Falls, Maps compiled by Major A. F. Becke,

Modern European invasion of Syria has long been impressing the land. Nothing surprised the writer more, on his return to the Holy Land in 1891 after eleven years, than the increase of red and sloping roofs in the landscape. These mean the presence of Europeans: and where they appear, and the flat roofs beloved of Orientals are not visible, then the truly Western aspect of so much of the Holy Land asserts itself, and one begins to understand how Greeks, Italians, and Franks colonised, and were at home in, this province of Asia. The Temple Christians from Württemberg did much to improve the surface of the country.[1] A Roman Catholic colony was planted on the shore of the Lake of Galilee. Large Circassian colonies, placed by the Turkish Government near Cæsarea and east of Jordan, considerably affected both the soil and the population about them.[2] Of the many changes effected since the Great War by the British and French Governments and the Jewish Colonies I hope to write later in this volume. The most important material innovations are the railways. The line between Jaffa and Jerusalem will be useful for more than pilgrims; but even greater effects may be expected from the line which follows the natural routes of commerce and war through the land from Haifa to Damascus and onward.[3] Not only does it open the most fertile parts of the country, and may bring back European civilisation to where this once was supreme, on the east of Jordan; but like the others it is of strategic value.[4]

1930. Other—*How Jerusalem was Won*, by W. T. Massey, 1919; *Crusader's Coast* Edward Thompson, 1927; *Enc. Brit.*, 14th ed., "Palestine, Military Operations", by Wavell, 1930. On the British Administration, H. C. Luke and E. Keith-Roach, *The Handbook of Palestine and Transjordan*, 2nd ed., 1930.

[1] See their journal, *Die Warte des Tempels*; papers in the *ZDPV*; and D. M. Ross, *Cradle of Christianity*, 1891. There were other sects.

[2] Their chief colonies were Cæsarea, Jerash, and Rabbath Ammon, the last two of which I visited in 1891. The Turks played them and the Bedouin off against each other. They increased the area of cultivated land, and improved agriculture. The greatest change was their introduction of wheeled vehicles, which had not been seen in Palestine since the Crusades, except within the previous twenty years, when they were confined to the Jaffa-Jerusalem and Beyrout-Damascus roads and the Temple colonies. See Appendix on "Roads and Wheeled Vehicles".

[3] Across Esdraelon, over the Jordan, round the SE of the Lake of Galilee, up the gorge of Fiḳ to Dera'a, Hauran and Damascus.

[4] When writing in 1894 I added here: "If ever European arms return to the country —as in a contest for Egypt or for the Holy Places, when may they not return?—this railway running from the coast across the central battle-field of Palestine will be of immense strategic value."

3. *Syria's Opportunity Westward*

In the previous sections of this chapter we have seen Syria only in the passive state, overrun by those Arabian tribes who have formed the stock of her population, and conquered and civilised by the great races of Asia, Africa, and Europe. But in the remaining sections we are to see Syria in the active state—the Arab tribes, who made her their home, pushing through their single opportunity, and exercising that influence in which their glory and hers has consisted. It will be best to describe first the Opportunity, and then the Influence—which was mainly that of religion.

In early times Syria had but one direction in which she could influence the rest of the world. We have seen that she had nothing to give to the empires of the Nile and Euphrates on either side of her; from them she could be only a borrower. Then Mount Taurus, though no barrier to peoples descending upon Syria from Asia Minor, seems to have barred the passage in the opposite direction. The Semitic race has never crossed Mount Taurus, except possibly once as far as the Halys.[1] Practically, therefore, early Syria's only opening lay seawards. If she had anything to pour forth of her own, or of what she had borrowed from the civilisations on either side of her, this must be the direction of outflow. So some of her tribes, whose race had hitherto been known only as land traders, voyagers of the desert, pushed out from her coasts upon the sea. They found it as studded with islands as the desert is studded with oases, and by these they gradually reached the west of Europe.

The first of these islands is within sight of Syria. Cyprus is visible from the hills of northern Syria immediately opposite, and at certain seasons may even be seen from Lebanon above Beirut.[2] From Cyprus the coast of Asia Minor is within reach, and the island of Rhodes at the beginning of the Greek Archipelago; whence the voyage was easy, even for primitive navigation, to the Greek mainland, Sicily, Malta, the African coast, Spain and the Atlantic, or north by Italy to Sardinia, Corsica and the coast of Gaul. Along those islands and coasts the line of Phœnician voyages can be traced by the deposit of Semitic names, inscriptions, and legends.[3] It is not surprising that early Greek civilisation, which they did so much to form, should have given

[1] Garstang, *The Land of the Hittites*, 79.

[2] See ch. vii, on The Coast.

[3] For Phœnician inscriptions in Cyprus, Rhodes, Sicily, Malta, Carthage, Sardinia, Spain, and Marseilles, see the *Corpus Inscriptionum Semiticarum*, vol. i, part i. For names, take these: Kition, in Cyprus, is the Hebrew Kittim (see ch. vii). Mount Atabyrus, in Rhodes, is Tabor, a Semitic term for height. Here Diodorus says Zeus

the Phœnicians the fame of inventors. But they were not much more than carriers. At this early stage of her history Syria had little to give to the West except what she had wholly or partly borrowed. Her art was Egyptian or Hittite; the letters she introduced to Europe were from Egyptian or other sources; even the commercial terms which she brought into Greek may not have been her own. But original were other droppings of her trade on Greece—names of the letters, of vegetables, metals, and some wares,[1] and most, though not all, of the religion she conveyed. The exact debt of Greek religion to Phœnicia will never be known, but the more we learn of both races the more we see how big it was. Myths, rites, morals, all spread westwards, and formed early constituents of Greek civilisation. The most of the process was probably over before history begins, for Tarshish was in existence by 1100 B.C.[2]; and perhaps the Phœnician migration and establishment of colonies was connected with the disturbances in Syria in the fourteenth century. Another important migration took place five centuries later. About 800 fugitives from Tyre founded near an old Phœnician settlement on the coast of Africa, opposite Sicily, another colony called Ḳarta Ḥadasha. That is almost good Hebrew for "the New City", corrupted by the Greeks into Carchedon, and by the Romans into Carthago. In the sixth century Carthage obtained the sovereignty over her sister colonies in the West[3]; and in the fifth century, while the Northern East under Persia assailed Greece across Asia Minor, the Semitic East twice assailed Greece across Sicily under the leadership of Carthage.[4] The second assault was led by one whose name was

---

was worshipped as a bull, a trace of the Baal-Moloch worship. On Ægean islands the worship of Kronos points to the same source. The Cyprian Aphrodite is Ashtoreth; and her feast was at the Semitic festival season in the beginning of April, her sacrifice a sheep (W. R. Smith, *Religion of the Semites*, 387). One proof of Phœnician influence is the presence of *Βετυλαί* (= Beth-el), sacred stones, conical or ovoid pillars. One was in the temple of Aphrodite at Paphos (Tacitus, *Hist.* ii, 3). In Sicily a Carthaginian coin was found with the legend "BARAT" = "the wells", the Phœnician for Syracusa. Carthage is Ḳarta Ḥadasha, "the New City"; Cadiz, or Gades, is Gadira, from "gadir", a fenced place (Bloch's *Phœnician Glossary*). Tarshish is of Semitic form, but doubtful meaning. Port Mahon, Minorca, is from the Carthaginian Mago. Among the legends are those of Perseus and Andromeda, Cadmus (from "Ḳedem", the East), Europa, etc.

[1] Phœnician loanwords: The names of the letters Alpha, Beta, etc.; commercial terms, *ἀρραβών*, interest = ערבון; *μνᾶ*, weight or coin = מנה; *κιξάλλης*, pirate, from שלל, booty. The names of one animal, גמל = the camel; of vegetables, like *ὕσσωπος* = אזוב; *βάλσαμον* = בשׂם; *κύπρος*, Lawsonia alba = כפר; *λίβανος*, frankincense tree = לבנה; *κασία* = קציעה, etc.; of other objects, *χιτών* = כתנת(?); *κλωβός*, bird-cage = כלוב, etc. *Βετυλαί* = sacred stones, is the Semitic Beit-el, Bethel.

[2] Pietschmann, 287 n.

[3] Freeman's *Sicily* (*Story of the Nations* series), p. 56.

[4] 480-473, and again 413-404.

Hannibal, and whose title, like that of all Phœnician magistrates, was Shophet. But Shophet, "Judge", is Hebrew, the title of Israel's rulers from Joshua to Samuel. And Hannibal is "the grace of Baal". Put Yah for Baal, and you have the Hebrew Hananiah; or reverse the word and you have Yohanan, the Greek Ioannes and our John.[1] The Greek colonies in Sicily held their own—held their own, but did not drive the invaders forth. It was reserved for another power to do this and keep the Semite out of Europe.

The first Punic—that is, Poinic, *φοίνικος*, Phœnician—War, in which Rome engaged, was for Sicily, and Rome won it, expelling the Syrian colonists from the island. In revenge, Hamilcar crossed the Straits of Gibraltar in 237; and by 218 his son, Hannibal the Great, conquered Spain, and crossed the Alps into Italy. But again it was proved that Europe was not to be for the Semites, and Hannibal was driven back. By 205 the Romans conquered the Iberian peninsula, passed over to Africa, and made this a Roman province.[2] How desperate was the struggle, how firmly the Syrians had planted themselves in the West, may be seen from the fact that seven hundred years after the destruction of Carthage men still talked Punic or Phœnician in North Africa; the Bible was translated into the language,[3] and this only died out before its kindred dialect of Arabic in the eighth century of our era.

During the glory of Carthage the Phœnician navies, crowded out of the Mediterranean by Greeks and Italians, pushed through the Straits of Gibraltar to the Canary Isles,[4] to a sea of weeds which may have been the same Columbus met towards America,[5] to west Gaul, the Scilly Isles,[6] and therefore surely to Britain; while an admiral of Tyre, at the motion of Pharaoh Neco, circumnavigated Africa in 600 B.C.,[7] 2000 years before Vasco da Gama.[8]

After the fall of Carthage—Tyre had fallen a hundred years before—the Phœnician genius confined itself to trading, with occasionally a little mercenary war. Under the Romans, Phœnicians were found all round the Mediterranean, with their quarters and temples in the towns. When Rome's hold on the East became firm at the beginning of our era, Syrians[9] flowed into Italy, as Juvenal puts it the Orontes into the Tiber. A few good rhetoricians, grammarians, poets and wits were among them, but the mass were slave-dealers, panders and mongers of base superstitions.

[1] Cf. Freeman, *op. cit.*, p. 21.

[2] Fifty years later they were interfering in the affairs of the real Phœnicia, and one hundred and fifty later they had reduced Syria to a province also.

[3] Augustine.

[4] Diodorus Siculus, v. 19-20.

[5] Scylax, *Periplus*, 112, in the *Geographi Græci Minores* (ed. Müller, i. 93).

[6] Cassiterides, or tin islands (Strabo, iii. v. 11).

[7] Herodotus, iv. 42.

[8] Pietschmann, 290 f.

[9] Also Nabatæans, cf. *CIS*, Pars i, tom. ii. 183 ff.

During this time—from the thirteenth century of the old era to the first of the new—there had stood upon the highlands immediately behind Phœnicia a nation speaking almost the same dialect; and this nation had heard the Phœnician tales of those western isles and coasts: of Kittim, that is Cyprus, and of Rodan, that is Rhodes; Javan, or the Ionians; Elissa, some farther coast of Sicily or Italy; and Tarshish, the limit in Spain.[1] And though this tribe had no port, nor were in touch with the sea, their imagination followed the Phœnician voyages, but with a nobler ambition than of gain, and claimed those coast-lands, on which the gross Semitic myths had caught, for ideals of justice, mercy, and the knowledge of the true God.[2] When one has learned the impressionableness of the early Greek to the religion which Syria sent him by the Phœnicians, and remembers how closely Israel stood neighbour to Phœnicia in place, in language, in political alliance, one's fancy starts the question, What if Phœnicia had also been the carrier of Israel's faith, as of Egypt's letters, Babylon's wares and the wild Semitic myths! It was impossible. When Phœnicia was still a religious influence in the West, Israel either had not arrived in Palestine, or was not so expert in the possibilities of her religion as to commend it to other peoples—though those were her neighbours and kinsmen; and when Israel knew herself as God's servant to the whole world, and conceived Phœnician voyages as means of spreading the truth, the Phœnicians were no longer the correspondents, but the enemies, of other races upon the north and west shores of the Mediterranean. Take the time of Elijah, when Israel and Phœnicia stood together perhaps more closely than at any other period. The slope of religious influence was then, not from Israel to Phœnicia, but from Phœnicia to Israel. It is the attempt to spread into foreign lands the worship of Baal, not the worship of Yahweh, that we see. Jezebel is the missionary, not Elijah; and the paradox is intelligible. The zeal of Jezebel proceeded from these two conceptions: that among the same people several gods might be worshipped side by side—Phœnician Baal in the next temple to Yahweh of Israel; and that religion was largely a matter of politics. Because she was queen in Israel, and Baal was her god, he ought to be one of Israel's gods as well. But it is better not to be a missionary-religion at all than one on such principles; and Israel's task just then was to prove that her God was the one and only God for her own life. If she first proved this on the only true ground—that He was the God of justice and purity—then the time would come when He would appear, for the same reason, the God of the whole earth, with irresistible claims upon

[1] Ramsay, *Expositor*, April, 1906, 366 f., argues that Tarshish = Tarsus and Elisha = Alasia.

[2] Isa. xlii.

the allegiance of Phœnicia and the West. So, with one exception, Elijah confined his prophetic work to Israel, and looked seaward only for rain. But by Naboth's vineyard and other matters he taught his people so well the utter difference of Yahweh from other gods—being as He was identical with righteousness, and therefore supreme—that it followed that Israel should see This was the Deity whose interests, activity, and dominion were universal. But that carries us to our next subject, the Religion of Syria—the inquiry, why Israel alone of Syrian tribes came to so pure a faith, and so sure a confidence of its victory. Let us finish this section by pointing out that when the prophets of Israel did rise to the consciousness of the universal dominion of their religion, it was to Phœnician means—those far Phœnician voyages we have been following—that they looked to carry it into effect. To the prophets Phœnicia and her influence are a great and a sacred thing. They exult in her opportunities, in her achievements. Ezekiel and another prophet bewail the destruction of Tyre and her navies as desecration. That other prophet cannot believe it to be final. He sees Phœnicia rising purified by her captivity to be the carrier of true religion to the ends of the earth.[1]

4. *The Religion of Syria*

We have seen that Syria, Esh-Sham, is but "the north" end of the Semitic world, and that from early times her population has been essentially Semitic. By this it was determined that her *rôle* in history should be predominantly the religious. The Semites are the religious leaders of humanity. The three great monotheisms have risen among them; the grandest prophets of the world have been their sons. For this destiny the race were prepared by their age-long seclusion. In the deserts of Arabia life is wonderfully tempered. Nature is monotonous, the distractions are few, the influence of things seen is as weak as it may be in this universe; the long fasts every year purge the body of grosser elements, the soul detaches itself, and hunger lends the mind a curious passion, mixed of resignation and hot anger. The only talents are those of war and of speech, the latter cultivated to a singular augustness of style by the silence of nature and the long leisure of life.[2] It is the atmosphere in which seers, martyrs, and fanatics are bred. Conceive a race subjected to

[1] Isa. xxiii; Ezek. xxvi ff.

[2] Our authorities for life in Arabia, ancient and modern, are Ludovico Varthema, who went with the Hajj to Mecca in 1503 (Hakluyt Society's publications); Burckhardt, Burton, and especially Doughty (*Arabia Deserta*, 1887), who knew the Bedawee, "the unsophisticated Semite", as never Western did. Cf. Wellhausen, *Reste des Arabischen Heidentums*; W. R. Smith, *Marriage and Kinship in Arabia* and *Religion of the Semites*.

its influences for thousands of years! To such a race give a creed, and it will be a devoted and apostolic race.

Now, it has been maintained that the desert did furnish the Arab with a creed, as well as with a religious temperament. Renan declared that the Semite, living where nature is so uniform, must be a monotheist[1]; but this thesis has been disproved by every fact discovered among the Semites since it was promulgated. The Semitic religions, with two exceptions (one of which, Islam, is largely accounted for by the other, Judaism), have not been monotheistic. Introduced to the Euphrates valley, or to Syria, where the forces of nature are as complex and suggestive of many gods as in any part of the Aryan world, the Semite has gone the way of the Aryans—nay, has preceded them in this way, not only developing a luxuriant polytheism and mythology, but becoming its missionary to the Greeks. The monotony of the desert, however, counts for something; the desert does not tempt to polytheism. Besides, all Semitic religions have been distinguished by a tendency which makes for unity. Within each tribe there was a tribal god, bound up with his people's existence, and their lord. This was favourable to monotheism. It trained men to think towards one cause, to fix their attention on a sovereign deity; and the desert, bare and monotonous, conspired with the habit.

We may, then, replace Renan's thesis, that the Semite was a born monotheist, by this: that in the Semitic religion, as in the Semitic world, monotheism had a great opportunity. There was no necessary creed in Arabia, but for the highest form of religion room and sympathy as nowhere else to the same degree.

Of this opportunity only one Semitic tribe took advantage, and the impressive fact is that the advantage was taken, not in Arabia, but in Syria herself, that is to say, on the soil whose rich and complex forces drew other Semitic tribes away from the austerity of their desert faith, and turned them into rank polytheists. The natural fertility of Syria, as we shall see, intoxicated her immigrants with nature-worship; the land was covered, not by one nation with one god, but by many tribes, each with its patron and lord; while, to make confusion worse, the influence of the idolatries of Egypt and Mesopotamia met and were combined upon her. Yet Syria, and not the Desert of Arabia, was the cradle of monotheism. The period in which this became manifest was, no doubt, one when her history for the first time counteracted to some degree the variety of her natural charms, the confusion of her many faiths. Israel's monotheism became indisputable in the centuries

[1] *Histoire des langues sémitiques*, ed. 3, 1863; "De la part des peuples sémitiques", *Asiatic Rev.*, Feb., May, 1859; and modified, *Histoire d'Israël*, i.

from the eighth to the sixth B.C., the period of the Assyrian invasions described above. Before the irresistible Assyrian advance the tribal gods of Syria—always identified with the stability of their peoples—went down one after another, and history became reduced to a uniformity analogous to that of nature in the Semitic desert. It was in meeting the problems which this excited, that the genius of Israel rose to a grasp of the world as a whole, and to faith in a sovereign Providence. This Providence was not the military Empire which had levelled the world; He was not any of the gods of Assyria. He was Israel's own Deity, who was known to the world but as the God of the few hills on which His nation hardly maintained herself. Fallen she was as low as her neighbours; taunted she was by them and by her adversaries to prove that her God could save her any more than the gods of Hamath or Damascus or the Philistines had saved them[1]: yet both on the eve of her fall, and in her deepest abasement, Israel affirmed that Yahweh reigned; that He was Lord of the hosts of heaven and earth; that Assyria was but a tool in His hand.

Why did Israel alone rise to this faith? Why did no other of the gods of the Syrian clans, Baals and Molochs, take advantage of the opportunity? Why should the people of Yahweh alone see a universal Providence in the disasters which they shared, and ascribe it to Him?

The answer to these questions is the beginning of Syria's supreme rank in the religious history of mankind. It is writ, beyond all misreading, in the prophets of the time and in the history of Israel which preceded the prophets. To use their own phrase, the prophets saw *Yahweh exalted in righteousness.* And this was not their invention: it had been implicit in Israel's conception of her God from a very early age. In what are confessedly ancient documents Yahweh is the cause of Israel's being, of the union of their tribes, of their coming to Palestine, of their instinct to keep separate from other peoples, even when they do not seem to have been conscious of a reason why. But from the first this influence upon them was ethical. It sifted the body of custom and law which was their common heritage with other Semitic tribes; it added to this both mercy and justice, mitigating the cruelty of some laws, where innocent or untried life was in danger, but enforcing others, where custom, greed, or tyranny had introduced carelessness with regard to the most sacred interests of life.[2] We may not be sure of the dates of these laws, but it is past doubt that the ethical agent at work in them was at work in Israel from the beginning, and was the character, the justice, the holiness of

[1] Isa. x. 8-11; xxxvi. 18-20; xxxvii. 12, 13.

[2] As, for instance, on homicide. The contrast of Israel's laws on this with Semitic customs, is significant of the ethical superiority of Israel.

her God. Yet at first it was not in law so much as in the events of the people's history that this character impressed them. They knew that He had found them, chosen them, brought them to the land, borne with them, forgiven them, redeemed them in His love and in His pity, so that, though it were true that no law had come to them from Him, the memory of all He had been to them, the influence of Himself in their history, would have remained their distinction among the peoples. Even in that rude time His grace had been mightier than His law.[1]

On such evidence we believe the assertion of the prophets, that what had made Israel distinct from her kinsfolk, and endowed her alone with the solution of the successive problems of history and with her high morality, was the knowledge of a real Being and intercourse with Him. This is what Revelation means. Revelation is not the promulgation of a law, nor the prediction of future events, nor "the imparting to man of truths, which he could not find out for himself". These ideas are modern, and proved false by the only true method of investigation into the nature of Revelation, a comparison of Scripture with those heathen religions out of which the religion of Israel sprang, but was so differentiated by the Spirit of God. Such a comparison shows that the subject of Revelation is the character of God Himself. God had chosen the suitable Semitic temper and circumstance to make Himself known through them in His righteousness and love for men. This alone raised Israel to her mastery of history in the Assyrian period, when her political fortunes were as low, and her extinction, humanly speaking, as probable as those of her kindred. This alone kept her loyal to her God and obedient to His law, during the following centuries, when other Syrian peoples gave way to the inrush of the Hellenic spirit, and Zeus, Athene, Apollo, Aphrodite and the goddesses of Fortune and Victory displaced, or were amalgamated with, the discredited Semitic deities.

Having solved with the prophets the problem set to her faith by the Oriental empires, Israel entered—upon the same floor of Syria—on her struggle with the stranger forces of the West, with the genius of Hellenism and the dominion of Rome. It is interesting, but vain, to speculate on what would have happened if the Maccabæan age had produced a mind like Isaiah's or Jeremiah's, or had met Greece with another spirit than that of Ecclesiastes, or of the son of Sirach. As it was, the age fell far below that of the Prophets in insight and in faith. The age of the Maccabees is a return to that of the Judges and Saul, with the Law as a new inspiration. The spiritual yields to the material, though the material is fought for with a heroism which makes

[1] See more fully the writer's essay on *The Hebrew Genius as Exhibited in the O.T.* in *The Legacy of Israel*, 1927.

the period as brilliant as any in the history of Israel. For a few years the ideal borders of Israel are regained, the law of Moses is imposed on Greek cities, the sea is reached, and the hope of Israel looks westward from a harbour of her own.[1] The conflict with Hellenism intensifies the passion for the Law, the conflict with Rome the passion for the land and political independence. In either case it is the material form which becomes the main concern of the people. Nevertheless, as Paul has taught us to see in his explanation of history,[2] this devotion to the letter of Law and Prophecy was a discipline for something higher. By keeping the commandments, and cherishing the hopes, in however mechanical a way, Israel held herself distinct and pure. And, therefore, though she felt the land slipping from under her, and consoled herself, as her hold on this world became less sure, with an extraordinary development of apocalypse—visions of another world that are too evidently the refuges of her despair in this—she still kept alive the divinest elements in her religion, the gifts of a tender conscience, and of the hope of a new redemption under the promised Messiah.

He came in Jesus of Nazareth. He came when the political estate of Israel was very low. He was born into the Empire: He grew up within twenty miles of the great port by which Rome poured her soldiers and officials upon His land. His youth saw Herod's embellishment of Palestine with Greek architecture. The Hellenic spirit breathed across all the land. Jesus felt the might and the opportunity of these forces, which now conspired to build upon Syria so rich a monument of Pagan civilisation. When He had been endowed by the Spirit with the full consciousness of what He could be, He was tempted, we are told, to employ the marvellous resources of Greece and Rome. *The Devil taketh Him up into an exceeding high mountain and showeth Him all the kingdoms of the world, and the glory of them.* In that day such a vision was nowhere so possible as in Syria. But He felt it come to Him wedded to apostasy. *All these things will I give thee, if thou wilt fall down and worship me.* And He replied from the Hebrew Scriptures with a confession of allegiance to the God of Israel: *Get thee hence, Satan, for it is written, Thou shalt worship the Lord thy God, and Him only shalt thou serve.* Also on other occasions He made an absolute distinction between Israel and the Gentiles: *Not as the Gentiles*, He said, *for after all these things do the Gentiles seek, but your heavenly Father knoweth that ye have need of these things. Ye worship ye know not what, we know what we worship, for salvation is from the Jews. I am not sent but to the lost sheep of the house of Israel.*

But within Israel and her Scriptures Jesus made great distinctions. He

[1] See p. 107. [2] Cf. W. R. Smith, *OTJC*, 315 ff.

said that much of Scripture was temporary, given at the time because of the hardness of the people's hearts, laws and customs that had passed away with the rise to a new stage in God's education of the world. The rest He confirmed, He used for feeding His own soul, and for teaching and leading others to God. Within the nation, also, He distinguished between the true and the false Israel. He insisted that, especially of late, Judaism had gone astray, laying too much emphasis on the letter of the law, nay, adding intolerably to this, and wrongly, foolishly, desiring the external kingdom. He insisted on the spiritual as against the external, on the moral as against the ceremonial, on grace as above law. So the religious authorities were moved against Him.

But their chief cause of offence—and it has ever since been the stumbling-block of many who count His ethical teaching supreme—was the claim He made for Himself. He represented Himself not only as the Messiah, but as indispensable to the race; He not only read the history of Israel as a preparation for Himself, but, looking forward, He claimed to inspire, to rule, and to judge all history of men for all time to come. A little bit of Syria was enough for His own ministry, but He sent His disciples out upon the world. Morality He identified with obedience to Himself. Men's acceptance by God He made dependent on their acceptance of His claims and gifts. He announced the forgiveness of sins absolutely, yet connected it with His own death. He has given the world its highest idea of God, yet He made Himself one with God. He predicted His death, and that He should rise again: and to His disciples not expecting this He did appear, and, in the power of their conviction that God had proved His words and given Him the victory over death, He sent them into the whole world—the whole world to which every port in Syria, on sea or desert, was at the time an open gateway.

To the story of His life and death, to the testimony of His resurrection, to His message from God, the Greek world yielded, which had refused to listen to Judaism. The little frontiers and distinctions of Syria melted before Him. For the first time, without force of arms, the religion of Israel left the highlands, to which it had been confined, and flowed upon the plains. With the Book of Acts we are on the sea-coast and among Greek cities; Peter is cured of his Judaism in Cæsarea, and the Holy Ghost descends on the Gentiles; the chief persecutor of the Church is converted on pagan soil, at Damascus; the faith spreads to Antioch, and then bursts westward along the old Phœnician lines, by Cyprus, the coasts of Asia Minor, the Greek isles and mainland, to Italy, Africa, and Spain.

But Christianity had not yet left Syria. As we shall see when we come to the Maritime Plain and Hauran, there are no fields in the world where the contest of Christianity and Paganism was more critical, or has left more traces. The histories of Eusebius and his followers, the lives of such saints as Porphyry and Hilarion, relate the missionary labours, persecutions, martyrdoms, and ambiguous political triumphs of the Church in Philistia and the Shephelah.[1] In the indestructible basalt of Hauran are monuments of the passage from Paganism to Christianity even more numerous and remarkable than the catacombs and ruins of ancient Rome. There are also what Italy cannot give us—the melancholy wrecks of the passage from Christianity to Mohammedanism. This passage was accomplished within a few years. The Mohammedan era began in 622, Damascus fell in 634, Jerusalem in 637, Antioch in 638. The last Greek inscription in Hauran is about 640, and has no emperor's name, but simply, "Christ being King".[2] The reasons of this rapid displacement of the one religion by the other are clear. When they met and fought for Syria, Christianity was corrupt, and identified with a political system sapped by luxury and rent by national strifes; Mohammedanism was simple, austere, full of faith, united, and not yet so intolerant as it afterwards became. Many Christians accepted with joy the change of ruler; few believed that, in the end, he would enforce a change of faith as well. But then the persecution settled steadily down. The Christians were driven to the heights of Lebanon, or suffered to remain only about Jerusalem, Bethlehem, Damascus, and a few other localities.

Then came what we have already glanced at in our catalogue of Western influences on Syria, the impression made by the Crusades. Seen across the shadow of their great failure, the Crusades shine but a gleam of chivalry and romance. Only when you visit Syria do you learn with what strenuous faith and purpose those ventures of a mistaken Christianity were waged. Syria was settled, organised, and built over almost as fully as any part of contemporary England. The reason that the remains of Greek civilisation are so meagre west of the Jordan is the activity of the Crusaders. Large cities famous in ancient times, like Ashkelon and Cæsarea, bear now in their upper ruins few but Crusading marks. How firmly they were built! To-day the mortar in them is harder than the stone it binds. But it is not by these coast fortresses, nor by the castles crowning the heights far inland, that the Crusades impress you, so much as by the ruins of lonely churches and cloisters, scattered over the land, far from the coast and the shelter of the Frankish citadels.[3] After this interval of Christian rule comes the long period of

[1] For the Hauran monuments, see ch. xxx; for Eusebius and other historians, p. 36, n. 1.

[2] See ch. xxx.

[3] For authorities on the Crusades, see pp. 36, 37.

silence and crumbling, till we see the churches of to-day, the missions and schools of nearly every sect in Christendom, and the long lines of pilgrims coming up to Jerusalem from the four corners of the world.[1]

In all this the Palestine of to-day is more a museum of church history than of the Bible—a museum full of living as well as ancient specimens of its subject.

The present state of Christianity in Syria is of interest, showing most of the faults, as well as the virtues, conspicuous in church history from the beginning. Greeks and Latins have warred for the possession of holy places, real and feigned. They have disfigured the neighbourhood of Jerusalem, and threatened the rest of the land, with rival sanctuaries, planted side by side as even at Gethsemane.[2] Behind the Churches move, as of old, political interests, complicating and debasing the quarrel. The native Christians, partly excusable by the long oppression they have suffered, came to feel that they held no mission to Mohammedanism, and, it would appear, hardly believed that

[1] The native churches of Syria are (1) the Orthodox Greek, with two patriarchates in Syria—Antioch and Jerusalem; the patriarchs are nominally subject to the Patriarch and Synod at Constantinople. (2) The Maronites (from John Maro, their first bishop) originally Monothelites, were, in 1182, received to communion with Rome, giving up their Monothelite doctrines, but retaining Syriac for the mass, and the marriage of their priests. They have one "Patriarch of Antioch and all the East", elected by bishops and archbishops, and confirmed by the Pope. A college for them is conducted by Jesuits, near Nahr el-Kelb. The best account is by Bliss, *PEFQ*, 1892-93. (3) In the seventeenth century Roman missions detached a large number of the Greek Church, allowing mass in the vernacular Arabic or Greek, communion in both kinds, and marriage of the clergy; but insisting on recognition of the Pope, adoption of the *Filioque*, and the Latin Easter. These are the Melchites, or Greek Catholics, who own one "Patriarch of Antioch, Jerusalem, and Alexandria", elected by bishops, confirmed by the Pope. (4) The old Syriac Church. (5) The Armenians, Armenian Uniates and Copts.

Protestant missionaries came in the beginning of last century, *via* Cyprus, where their earliest tombstones are. American Presbyterians have worked longest and most powerfully—their greatest works the College and Press at Beyrout, and translation of the Bible into Arabic. Irish Presbyterians labour in Damascus and about; Church of Scotland Chapel and Hospice, Jerusalem, Missions to Jews in Beyrout, Shweir in Lebanon, Tiberias and Safed; Anglican Missions all over, with bishop in Jerusalem; Jewish Missionary Societies in Jerusalem, Damascus, and elsewhere; Quaker and other missions. Other societies with schools at Nazareth, Jaffa, etc., especially Edinburgh Medical Mission at Damascus, and British Syrian Schools which well covered Lebanon. E of Jordan are the C.M.S. church and schools at Es-Salṭ, etc., and there was an independent mission at Kerak.

[2] The feeling between the two Churches may be seen in the title of a paper in the R.C. *Das Heilige Land*, 1890, 137-148, *Die jungsten Gewaltthaten der schismatischen Griechen in Jerusalem.*

a Mohammedan can be converted. Protestant missions did also, under the Turks, find it impossible to influence any but individual Moslems; but they introduced the Bible in the vernacular, and this has had important effects on the native Churches. It is well to say, as certain have said within the Anglican Church, that the Western Churches are in Palestine for other purposes than building rival conventicles to the Eastern; but once the Bible was introduced in the vernacular, and studied by the common people, secession was certain from the native Churches, and for this the Western missionaries were bound, whether willing or no, to provide congregations and pastors. It is by a native Church whose mother-tongue is Arabic that the Moslems will be reached, though we do not see whether this is to take place through the older bodies, that give evidence of new life, or through the new congregations of the Western missions. Meantime two things are coming home to the Moslem: opportunities of education of a high kind are within reach of all portions of the population, and even the Moslems of Damascus were roused by the heroic services of the late Dr. Mackinnon to the real meaning of Christianity, through that aspect of her which represents most vividly the Lord's own love and power—medical missions.

With the large immigration of Jews into Palestine in recent times centres of Jewish worship in the land have naturally increased, a congregation being organised in every community of thirty or more adults. Over all there is a Rabbinic Council of two chief Rabbis, one of the Sephardim, one of the Ashkenazim, with six associate Rabbis. There appear to be also Jewish congregations with arrangements of their own for ritual and other religious purposes. Hebrew, the ancient language of Israel, which had ceased to be used except in worship and some religious writings, has by the help of an enlarged vocabulary in order to meet the needs of modern science, commerce and politics (an enlargement similar to that which happened to Hebrew in Greek and Roman times) achieved a wonderful revival in the everyday talk especially of the youth of the people; and this not merely by the influence of the synagogues, but through Hebrew schools and newspapers.[1]

To contribute to this revival and generally to serve as an intellectual centre of Judaism in Palestine, are among the objects of the Hebrew University on Mount Scopus opened in 1925 by the late Earl Balfour. The University is for qualified men and women of any race or creed, and provides not only undergraduate teaching through efficient staffs in the Faculties of the Humanities and the Sciences (Mathematics, Chemistry, Biology) but also training in, and facilities for, research, literary, historical and scientific.

[1] The High Commissioner's *Interim Report* for 1920-21; W. M. Christie, *The Renaissance of Hebrew*, Victoria Institute Transactions, January 19, 1931.

II. *THE FORM OF THE LAND AND ITS HISTORICAL CONSEQUENCES*[1]

We have seen that Syria's closest relations are with the Arabian peninsula, of which it forms the north end. That Syria is not also Arabian in character—that the Arabian Desert does not sweep on to the Mediterranean except at the south-east corner—is due not only to the neighbourhood of that sea, but more to the configuration of the land itself. The Arab plateau ceases nearly ninety miles from the Mediterranean, with a threefold barrier intervening. Parallel to the coast of the Levant, and all the way from Mount Taurus to near the Red Sea, run two mountain ranges with an extraordinary valley between them. These ranges shut out the desert, and by help of the sea charge the climate with moisture—providing rains and mists, fountains and several rivers and lakes. They and their valley and their coastland are Syria; Arabia is all to the east of them. The Syrian ranges reach their summits about midway in the alpine heights of the Lebanons. The Lebanons are the focus of Syria. Besides the many streams which spring full-born from their roots, and lavish water on their neighbourhood, four rivers pass from the Lebanons across the province. The Orontes flows north, and waters most of north Syria, creating Antioch; the Abana, or Barada, flows east, and reclaims for Syria a portion of what would otherwise be desert, creating Damascus; the Liṭany, or el-Ḳasimiyah, rushes west in a bed too deep and narrow for any work save that of intersecting the land; and the Jordan flows south, forming three lakes, and otherwise intensifying the division between the two ranges. Of these rivers, only the Orontes and Liṭany reach the open sea; the Jordan comes to an end in the Dead Sea, and the Abana dies out in combat with the desert. The fate of the Abana is a proof of how desperately Syria has been rescued from Arabia, and a symbol of the influence which the invading desert has had upon her culture and civilisation.

The part of Syria with which we have to do is all to the south of the summits of the Lebanons. On their western slope the gorge of the Liṭany may be taken as the natural limit, though we shall sometimes pass a little beyond it. On the eastern slope we shall not go north of the Abana and Damascus. We have first to survey the great triple barrier against the desert,

[1] For this chapter, see Maps 1-10 and page 56.

and we commence with its most distinctive feature—the valley between the two great ranges.

South of the Lebanons, this valley, with the young Jordan in its embrace, begins to sink below the level of the sea. At the Lake of Ḥuleh it is seven feet above that level; at the Lake of Galilee, ten miles farther south, it is 680 feet below, and for sixty-five miles more it continues to descend, till at the Dead Sea it is 1290 feet below. From here it rises to about 800 feet above the sea, and then slowly sinks to the Gulf of 'Aḳaba, which forms its southern continuation. For this unique and continuous trench from the Lebanons to the Red Sea there is no single designation. By using two of its names, which overlap each other, we may call it the Jordan-Arabah Valley. From the Lake of Galilee to the south of the Dead Sea it is called by the Arabs the Ghor, or Depression.[1]

On either side of this run the two great Syrian ranges. Fundamentally of the same formation, they differ in disposition. The western is a deep wall of limestone, extending from Lebanon to a line of cliffs opposite the Gulf and Canal of Suez—the southern edge of the Desert of the Wandering. In Lebanon this limestone is disposed in lofty ranges running north and south; in Upper Galilee, it descends to a plateau walled by hills; in Lower Galilee it is a series of still less elevated ranges, running east and west. Then it sinks to the plain of Esdraelon, with signs of having once bridged this by a series of low ridges.[2] South of Esdraelon it rises again, and sends forth a branch in Carmel to the sea, but the main range continues parallel to the Jordan Valley. Scattering through Samaria into separate groups, it consolidates towards Bethel on the narrow table-land of Judæa, with an average height of 2400 feet, continues so to the south of Hebron, where by broken and sloping strata it lets itself down, widening the while, on to the plateau of the Desert of the Wandering. This Western Range we call the Central Range, for it, and not the Jordan Valley, is historically the centre of the land. The watershed lies, not down the middle of the range, but nearer the east. The west flank is long and gentle, falling to a maritime plain of varying breadth, a few hundred feet above the sea; but the east is short and precipitous, dragged down by the fissure of the Jordan Valley to far below sea-level. The effect appears in the map on page 56.

Down the east of the Jordan Valley the range is more continuous than that down the west. Sinking swiftly from Mount Hermon to 2000 feet above the sea, it preserves that average level southward across the plateau of Hauran to the cleft of the river Yarmuk; is still high, but more broken by cross valleys, through Gilead; and forms again an almost level table-land over

[1] See more fully ch. xxii.

[2] At Sheikh Abreḳ and Lejjun.

Moab. Down the west of Hauran, on the margin of the Jordan Valley, the average level is raised by a number of extinct volcanoes, which have their counterparts also to the south and east of Damascus, and these have covered the limestone of the range with a volcanic deposit as far as the Yarmuk. South of the eastern line of volcanoes runs Jebel Hauran, or Druze Mountain, as it is called from its latest colonists, and forms the border in that direction —the eastern border of Syria. Farther south the range has no definite limit, but rolls off onto the high Arabian Desert. Here we may take for a border the great Hajj Road, past the Upper Zerḳa to Ma'an.

We see, then, that Palestine is disposed, between the Sea and the Desert, in four parallel lines north and south[1]:

Sea	The Maritime Plain	The Central Range	The Jordan Valley	The Eastern Range	Desert

Now, were there no modifications of these four long bands between the Sea and the Desert, the geography of Palestine would indeed be simple, and in consequence the history of Palestine very different from what it has actually been. But the Central Range undergoes three modifications which considerably complicate the geography, and have had as powerful an influence on the history as the four long lines themselves. In the first place, the Central Range is broken in two, as we have seen, by the Plain of Esdraelon, which connects the Jordan Valley with the Maritime Plain. Again, from Judæa the Central Range does not fall immediately on the Maritime Plain, as it does farther north from Samaria. Another smaller, more open range comes between—the hills of the so-called Shephelah. These are said to be of a different kind of limestone from that of the Central Range, and they are certainly separated from Judæa by a well-defined series of valleys along their whole extent.[2] They do not continue opposite Samaria, for there the Central Range itself descends on the plain; but, as we shall see, they have a counterpart in the soft, low hills which separate the Central Range from Carmel. And thirdly, south of Judæa the Central Range droops and spreads upon a region distinct in character from the table-land to the north of Hebron—the Negeb, or South Country as translated in our version. As these three—Esdraelon, the Shephelah and the Negeb—have also proved their distinctness from the Central Range, as from the Maritime Plain, by their differing his-

[1] This is the division adopted by Robinson in his *Phys. Geog.*, p. 17, and by Henderson, *Palestine*, pp. 15-21.

[2] See ch. x.

tories, we add them to our catalogue of the ruling features of the land, which we now reckon as seven. From the west these lie:

1. The Maritime Plain.
2. The Low Hills or Shephelah.
3. The Central Range—cut in two by
4. Esdraelon, and running into
5. The Negeb.
6. The Jordan Valley.
7. The Eastern Range.

In addition are the Lebanons and Carmel. For some reasons the Lebanons ought to be at the head of the list, because the four long strips flow from and are dominated by them. But the Lebanons are too separate, and stand by themselves. Carmel, on the other hand, is not separate enough. Geographically a branch of the Central Range, though cut off from it by lower and softer hills like the Shephelah, Carmel has never had a history of its own, but has been merged in that either of the coast or of Samaria.[1] Carmel, however, was held distinct in the imagination of Hebrew writers, as, with its forward leap to the sea, it could not but be; nor will anyone, who desires to form a vivid picture of the country, leave this imposing headland out of his vision.

The whole land may then be represented as on pages 56-7.[2]

In the summary descriptions of the Promised Land in the Old Testament we find all these features mentioned, with the exception of Esdraelon, which falls under the general designation of valley-land, and with the addition sometimes of the slopes or flanks[3] of both ranges, which are distinct in character, and often in population, from the broad plateaus above them. An account of these passages, and of the general geographical terms of the Bible, will be found in an appendix. Here it is enough to give a few of the proper names. We have mentioned that for the Jordan Valley, the Arabah; that for the Low Hills, the Shephelah; and that for the South, the Negeb. The Maritime Plain between Carmel and Joppa was called in Hebrew Sharon, probably meaning the Level, but in Greek the Forest, from a great oak forest which once covered it.[4] To the south the name for it was Pelesheth, Philistia, or, poetically, *the Shoulder of the Philistines*, from its shape as it rises from the sea.[5] The Hebrew word *Darom* or *Daroma*,[6] meaning south, was applied

[1] See chs. vii, xvi.

[2] Other works: V. Schwöbel, *Die Landesnatur Palästinas*, 2 pts., 1914; R. Koepel, *Palästina die Landschaft in Karten u. Bildern*, 1930.

[3] Ashdoth = אשדות. See Appendix I. [4] See pp. 112 f. [5] Isa. xi. 14.

[6] דרום, or with the Aramaic definite article דרומא.

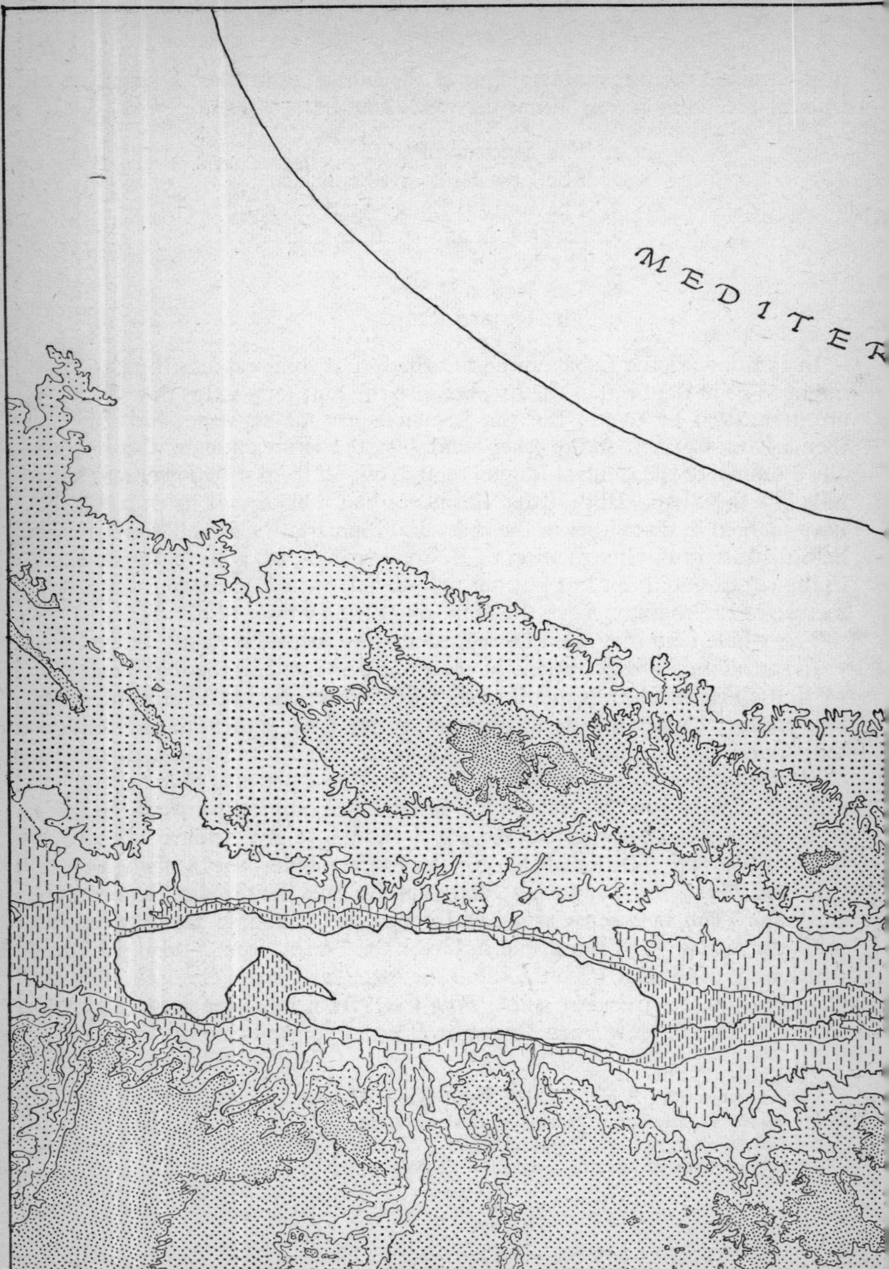
MEDITER

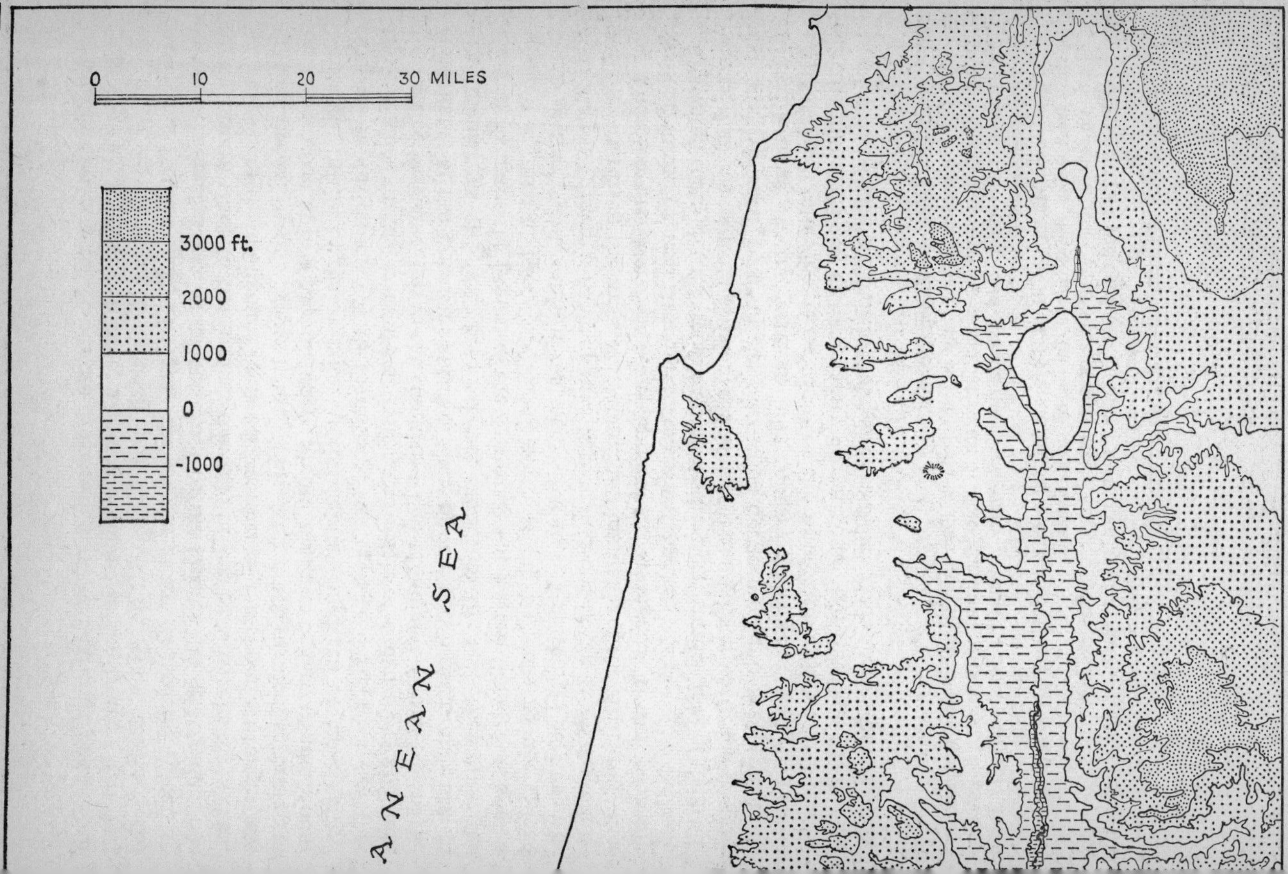
0
10
20
30 MILES
3000 ft.
2000
1000
0
-1000
ANEAN SEA

by the Jews shortly before our era to the whole of the Maritime Plain south from Lydda[1]; in Christian times Daroma extended inland to the Dead Sea, and absorbed both the Shephelah and Negeb.[2] The Arabs confined the name to a fortress south of Gaza—the Darom of the Crusaders.[3] What we know as Esdraelon was, in its western part, the Open Plain of Megiddo, but on its eastern slope to the Jordan, the Vale of Jezreel.[4] Except by Ezekiel, who speaks of the mountains of Israel,[5] neither of the two great ranges was wholly covered by one proper name. The Central was divided, according to the tribes upon it, into Mount Judah, Mount Ephraim or Israel,[6] and Mount Naphtali. In the English version Mount is often rendered by *hill-country*,[7] but this is misleading. With their usual exactness, the Hebrews saw that these regions formed part of one range, the whole of which they called not by a collective name, but in the singular—The Mountain—just as to-day the inhabitants of the Lebanons speak of their double and broken range also in the singular, as el-Jebel. Before Israel came into the land they knew the Central Range as the Mount of the Amorite.[8] The Eastern Range was known under the three divisions of Bashan north of the Yarmuk; Mount Gilead south of that[9]; and south of that across Moab, Ha-Mishor, The Level, or The Plateau. Another name applied to the north end of the Moab mountain-wall, as seen from the west, the Mount or Mountains of the Abarim[10]—that is, Those-on-the-Over-Side—was applicable, as indeed it was probably applied, to the Eastern Range in its entire extent.[11]

Viewing, then, all these modifications of the great parallel lines of the land, we see that this fourfold division, fundamental as it is, is crossed, and to some extent superseded, by a simpler distinction between mountain and plain, or, to speak more exactly, between hilly country and level country. This is obvious geographically; it has been of the utmost importance historically, for the mountain was fit for infantry warfare only, but the plain feasible for cavalry and chariots; and, as Palestine from her position was bound to be

[1] Neubauer, *Géog. du Talmud*, p. 62.

[2] In the *Onomasticon*, not only is Eshtemoa in Dan said to be in the Daroma, and Ziklag and other towns of Simeon far south of Beit-Jibrin; but Maon and Carmel on the Judæan table-land, and Gadda *imminens mari mortuo*. There was a Daroma Interior (see Art. "Iether").

[3] Now Deir el-Belaḥ. Will. of Tyre, xx. 19, derives Darom from Deir Rum, Convent of the Greeks, but the other is the probable derivation.

[4] See ch. xix. [5] vi. 2, xix. 9, etc. [6] See ch. xvi.

[7] Hill-country of Judæa, Luke i. 39, 65; Josh. xxi. 11; but always Mount Ephraim.

[8] Deut. i. 7. [9] But see ch. xxv. [10] Num. xxvii. 12.

[11] Traces of this in Ezek. xxxix. 11, where read עֲבָרִים.

crossed by the commerce and the war of the two continents on either side of her, her plains would bear the brunt of these, while her mountains would be comparatively remote from them. All the Central Range, and the centre of the Eastern Range, was mountain, fit for infantry only. The Maritime Plain, Esdraelon, and the Jordan Valley, along with the plateaus of the Eastern Range, Hauran and Moab, were plains, bearing the trunk roads and feasible for cavalry and chariots. Now, it is of the greatest importance to observe that all the mountain-land, *viz.* the Central Range and Gilead, represents Israel's proper and longest possessions, first won and last lost—while all the valley-land and table-land was, for the most part, hardly won and scarcely kept by Israel; but at first remained for long in Canaanite keeping, and towards the end was the earliest to come under the invading empires. Not only the course of Assyrian and Egyptian war but the advance of Greek culture and of Roman conquest is explained (as we shall see in detail) by this general distinction between hilly and level land, which, especially on the east of Jordan, does not correspond to the distinction of mountain range from Jordan Valley and Maritime Plain. Enisled by that circuit of lowland—the Ghor, Esdraelon, and the Maritime Plain—the Central Range in Judah and Ephraim formed Israel's most constant sanctuary, and Gilead was generally attached to it. But from the table-land of Hauran Israel were driven by the chariots of Syria; they held Moab only at intervals; the Canaanites kept them for long periods out of the Upper Jordan Valley and Esdraelon; and, except for a brief triumph in the evening of their history, the Philistines kept them from the Maritime Plain. So, when the Greeks came, the regions they covered were the coast, the Jordan Valley, Hauran, the eastern levels of Gilead, and Moab; but it is notable that in Gilead itself the Greek cities were few and late, and in the Central Range not at all. And so, when the Romans came, the tactics of their generals, as may be illustrated from Vespasian's campaign, were to secure the plains, then Samaria, and last the high, close Judæa.

But this distinction between mountain and plain, which accounts for so much of the history of the land, does not exhaust its extraordinary variety. Palestine is almost as much divided into petty provinces as Greece, and far more than those of Greece are her divisions intensified by differences of soil and climate. The two ends of the Jordan are not thirty miles away from those parts of the Maritime Plain which are opposite them, yet they are as separate from these as, in Switzerland, Canton Bern is from Canton Valais. The slopes of Lebanon are absolutely distinct from Galilee; Galilee is cut off from Hauran, and almost equally so from Samaria. From Hauran the Jebel Druz stands off by itself, and Gilead holds aloof to the south, and again Moab is distinct from Gilead. On each of the four lines, too, desert marches with fertile soil, implying the neighbourhood of different races and systems of civilisation. Upon the Central Range itself Judah is bare, austere, secluded —a land of shepherds and unchanging life; Samaria is fertile and open—a land of husbandmen, as much in love with, as they were liable to, foreign influences. These differences of soil are intensified by differences of climate. In Palestine there is every climate between the sub-tropical of one end of the Jordan Valley and the sub-alpine above the other end. There are palms in Jericho and pine forests in Lebanon. In the Ghor in summer you are under a temperature of more than 110° Fahrenheit, and yet you see glistening the snows of Hermon. All the steps between these extremes the eye can see at one sweep from Carmel: the sands and palms of the coast; the wheat-fields of Esdraelon; the oaks and sycomores of Galilee; the pines, the peaks, the snows of Anti-Lebanon. How closely these differences lie to each other! Take a section of the country across Judæa. With its palms and shadoofs the Philistine Plain might be a part of the Egyptian Delta; but on the hills of the Shephelah, which overlook it, you are in the scenery of Southern Europe; the Judæan moors which overlook them are like the barer uplands of Central Germany, the shepherds wear sheepskin cloaks and live under stone roofs—sometimes the snow lies deep; a few miles farther east and you are down on the desert among the Bedouin, with their tents of hair and cotton clothing; a few miles farther, and you drop to torrid heat on the Jordan; a few miles beyond that and you rise to the plateau of the Belḳa, where Arabs say "the cold is always at home". Yet from Philistia to the Belḳa is scarcely seventy miles.

All this means separate room and station for a far greater variety of race and government than could have been effected in so small a land by the simple distinction of Mountain and Plain. What is said of the people of Laish, in the north nook of the Jordan Valley, is characteristic of the country. *And the five men* of Dan *came to Laish, and saw the people who were in its midst, peaceful and careless, possessing riches, and far from the Phœnicians, and without any relation with the Aramæans.*[1] Laish is only twenty-five miles from the Sidonian coast, and about forty from Damascus, but mountains intervene on either side. Her unprovoked conquest by the Danites happened without the interference of either of these powerful states. From this single case we may understand how often a revolution, or the invasion or devastation of a locality, might take place without affecting other counties of this province —if one may so call them, which were but counties in size though kingdoms in difference of race and government.

[1] Judges xviii. 7: according to Budde's separation of the two narratives intertwined in this chapter (*Bücher Richter, etc.*, p. 140).

The frequent differences of race in the Palestine of to-day must strike the most careless traveller. The Christian peoples, more than half Greek and partly Frank, who were driven into the Lebanon at various times by the Arab and Turk, still preserve on their high sanctuary some racial distinctions. How much taller and whiter and nobler are the Druzes of Carmel than the fellahin of the plain at their feet![1] How distinct the Druzes of Jebel-Hauran are from the Bedouin around them! The Greeks of Beyrout are half the world away from the Arabs of Damascus. On the Central Range, in Judæa itself, the desert has preserved the Bedouin unchanged within a few miles of that medley of nations, Jerusalem. Within the Arab family are differences that approach racial degree. The tropical Ghor has engendered, or fostered, a variety of Arab, the Ghawarineh, whose frizzled hair and blackened skin contrast with the Semitic features of the Bedouin of the plateaus above him —the 'Adwan or the Beni Ṣakhr.

Therefore, while the simple distinction between mountain and plain enabled us to understand the course of the invasions of the empires which burst on Syria, these more intricate distinctions of soil, altitude, and climate explain how it was that the minor races pouring into Palestine from regions so different as Asia Minor, Mesopotamia, Arabia, Egypt, and the Greek islands, sustained their own characters in this little, crowded province through so many centuries. Palestine has never belonged to one nation, and probably never will. As her fauna and flora represent many geological ages, and are related to the animals and plants of other lands,[2] so varieties of the human race, culture and religion, the most extreme, preserve themselves side by side on those different shelves and coigns of her surface, under those different conditions of her climate. Thus when history first lights up within Palestine, what we see is a confused medley of clans—that crowd of Canaanites, Amorites, Perizzites, Kenizzites, Hivites, Girgashites, Hittites, sons of Anak and Zamzummim—which perplexes the student, but is yet in such harmony with the natural conditions of the country and with the rest of the history.[3] Again, if we remember the fitful nature of Semitic warfare—the rush, and if this be not successful, the resting content with what has been gained—we can appreciate why, in so broken a land, the invasion of the

[1] To a less extent the same contrast prevails between the peasants of the Ghuta round Damascus and the finer peasants of Hauran, but the population of Hauran is, in many cases, so very recent an immigration (see chs. xxiv, xxx), that it is difficult to estimate the causes of this difference.

[2] For the diversity see Tristram; Merrill's *East of the Jordan*; the summary in Henderson's *Palestine*; Thompson, *Crusader's Coast*.

[3] Some represent various races like Amorites, Hittites, and probably Zamzummim. Others get their name from localities or the life they lead.

Hebrew nomads was partial, and left, even in parts it covered, many Canaanite enclaves. And within Israel herself, we understand why her tribes remained distinct, why she split into two kingdoms on her narrow Highlands, and why even in Judah were clans like the Rechabites who preserved their life in tents and their austere desert habits beside the Jewish vineyards and cities.

Palestine, formed and surrounded as it is, is a land of tribes. That it can ever belong to one nation, even though this were the Jews, is contrary to Nature and Scripture.

III. *THE CLIMATE AND FERTILITY OF THE LAND, WITH THEIR EFFECTS ON ITS RELIGION*[1]

We have seen some peculiarities of the climate and soil of Palestine. We are able to appreciate the immense differences of temperature and fertility, due, *first*, to the unusual range of level—from 1300 feet below the sea with a tropical atmosphere to 9000 feet above it with an alpine; and, *second*, to the double exposure of the land—seawards, so that the bulk is subject to the influences of the Mediterranean basin, and desert-wards, so that part exhibits the characteristics of desert life. Within these conditions we have to look at the details of the climate and fertility, and to estimate their social and religious influence.

1. *Climate*

The ruling feature of the Syrian climate is the division of the year into a rainy and a dry season.[2] Towards the end of October[3] heavy rains begin to fall for a day or several days at a time. These are what the English Bible

[1] For this chapter, see Maps 1-10 and page 56.

[2] On the climate, besides meteorological statistics, see Lynch's *Narrative and Official Reports*; Barclay's *City of the Great King*; Robinson, *Phys. Geog. of the Holy Land*, ch. iii; *PEFQ*, esp. 1872; 1883, Chaplin, *Obs. on Climate of Jerus.*; 1888-1893, Glaisher, *Meteoro. Obs. at Sarona*; 1893 ff., *Ib. at Jerus.*; Anderlind, *ZDPV*, viii. 101 ff.; Der Einfluss der Gebirgswaldungen in N. Palästina auf die Vermehrung der wässerigen Niederschlage, *Id.* xiv; Ankel, *Grundzüge der Landesnatur des Westjordanlandes*, iv. Das Klima; Wittmann, *Travels*, 561-570; Chaplin and Kersten, *ZDPV*, 1891, 93 ff. —Since 1896: Zumoffen, *Bulletin de la Soc. de Géogr.*, 1899; *PEFQ*, 1897 ff. *passim*; *MuNDPV*, 1899, and onward *passim*; H. Hilderscheid, Die Niederschlagsverhältnisse Pal. in alter u. neuer Zeit., *ZDPV*, 1902 (xxv); Elsworth Huntington, *Palestine and its Transformation*, 1911, ch. xii; I. E.-Volcani, *The Fellah's Farm*, 1930.

Average annual rainfall in Jerusalem about 25 inches; in London (1881-1930), 24·47; British Isles (1881-1915), 41·4.

[3] In Lebanon often a month earlier.

calls the *early* or *former* rain, literally the *Pourer*.[1] It opens the agricultural year; the soil hard and cracked by the long summer is loosened, and the farmer begins ploughing.[2] Till the end of November the rainfall is not large, but increases from December to February, abates in March, and is practically over by the middle of April. The *latter rains* of Scripture are the heavy showers of March and April.[3] Coming before the harvest and the summer drought, they are of more importance to the country than the rains of the winter, and that is why these are passed over in Scripture, and emphasis is laid on the *early and the latter rains*. This has given most people the idea of only two intervals of rain in the Syrian year, at the vernal and the autumnal equinox; but all winter is the rainy season, as we are told in the Song of Songs:

Lo, the winter is past,
The rain is over and gone.[4]

During most winters both hail and snow fall on the hills. Hail is common, and often mingled with rain and thunder-storms, which happen at intervals through the winter, and are frequent in spring. The Old Testament mentions hail and thunder together.[5] On the Central Range snow is known to reach nearly two feet, and lie for five days or more, and pools at Jerusalem are sometimes covered with ice. But this is rare: on the Central Range the ground seldom freezes, and the snow disappears in a day.[6] On the plateaus east of Jordan snow lies for days every winter, and on Hermon fields of it last through the summer. None has been seen in the tropical Ghor. This explains the feat of Benaiah, who *went down and slew a lion in the midst of a cistern in the day of the snow*.[7] The beast had strayed up from Jordan, and been caught in a snowstorm. Where else could lions and snow come together?

In May showers are rare, and from then till October not only is no rain, but a cloud seldom passes over the sky, and a thunderstorm is a miracle.[8] Morning mists are not uncommon—in midsummer, 1891, we twice woke into one as chill and dense as a Scotch "haar"[9]—but are soon dispersed. In Bible lands vapour is the symbol of what is frail and fleeting, as it cannot be to us

[1] יורה, Deut. xi. 14, Jer. v. 24, Hos. vi. 3. מורה, Joel ii. 23, Ps. lxxxiv. 7 (*E.V.* 6). Cf. James v. 7. On rains and seasons generally see Book of Enoch.

[2] The later Jewish year began in spring with the month Nisan.

[3] מלקוש. Besides the references in the last note but one, cf. Prov. xvi. 15, Jer. iii. 3, Zech, x. 1. Rain generically = מטר. A burst of rain = גשם.

[4] ii. 11; winter, סתיו = rainy season; Ar. shita.

[5] Ps. xviii, etc.

[6] On snow in Jerusalem, *PEFQ*, 1883, 10 f.; Robinson, *Phys. Geog.*, p. 265; a snowstorm kept Trypho from Judæa, 1 Macc. xiii. 22, cf. Jos. xiv *Antt.* xv. 4.

[7] 2 Sam. xxiii. 20.

[8] 1 Sam. xii. 17, 18.

[9] At Ghabaghib in Hauran on 19th, and Irbid in Gilead on 25th, June, temp. 48°. On mists and dews, cf. Book of Enoch lx.

northerners, to whose coasts the mists cling with a pertinacity suggestive of opposite ideas. On the other hand, the dews of Syrian nights are excessive; on many mornings it looks as if there had been heavy rain, and this and mist are the sole slackening of the drought from May till October. Through summer prairie and forest fires are not uncommon. The grass and thistle of the desert will blaze for miles, driving scorpions and vipers from their holes, as the Baptist describes in one of his vivid figures;[1] sometimes, as the prophets tell us, the air is filled with the smoke of a whole wood.[2]

The winds of Syria are regular, and their place obvious in the economy of her life. *He maketh His ministers of winds.*[3] They prevail from the west, and, with the help of the sea, fulfil two functions throughout the year. In the winter the west and south-west winds, damp from the sea, as they touch the cold mountains, drop their moisture and cause the winter rains. So our Lord said: *When ye see a cloud rise out of the west, straightway ye say, There cometh a shower, and so it is.*[4] In summer the winds blow chiefly out of the drier north-west, and meeting only warmth do not cause showers, but mitigate the daily heat.[5] This latter function, even more regular than the former, is fulfilled morning by morning with almost perfect punctuality. Those who have not travelled through a Syrian summer cannot realise how welcome, how unfailing, a friend is the forenoon wind from the sea, how he is strongest just after noon, and does not leave till the need for his freshness passes with the sunset. He strikes the coast soon after sunrise; in Hauran, in June and July, he used to reach us between 10 and 12 o'clock, and blew so well that the hours previous were generally the hottest of our day. The peasants do their winnowing against this steady wind, and no happier scene is in the land than afternoon on the threshing-floors, when he rustles the thickly-strewn sheaves, and scatters the chaff before him.[6]

[1] Luke iii. 7.
[2] Isa. v. 24; ix. 18; Joel i. 19 f.; ii. 3.
[3] Ps. civ. 4; Book of Enoch lxxvi.
[4] Luke xii. 54.
[5] Ankel, *op. cit.*, pp. 84 ff., gives a number of figures for Jerusalem. From May to October dry winds blow from NW 78·8 days; from W 27·5; from N 26·5. In the rainy months W and SW winds blow for an average of 60·7 days, from NE, E, and SE, 67·4. For wind at Sarona see *PEFQ*, 1892.
[6] The explanation of this is that the limestone of Syria heats up under the sun more quickly than the sea, but after sunset cools more rapidly, so that the night breezes, after an interval of stillness following sunset, blow opposite to the day ones. On the evening breeze see Gen. iii. 8, Song ii. 17. Ankel (*op. cit.*, p. 85) emphasises the importance of those winds. Robinson, *Phys. Geog.*, p. 278, remarks on their regularity. June 3 to 16 they had the NW wind "from the time we left the Ghôr till we arrived at Nazareth. The air was fine and mostly clear, and, although the mercury ranged from 80° to 96°, the heat was not burdensome." Yet at Ekron, under the same wind, the thermometer rose to 105°, and in the sun only to 108°.

The other winds are much more infrequent and irregular. From the north wind blows chiefly in October, and brings a dry cold.[1] The name Sherkiyeh, our Sirocco, literally "the east", is used of winds blowing from the desert—E, SE, S and even SSW. Except for one in winter off the snows of the Belḳa,[2] they are hot winds: *when ye see the south-wind blow, ye say, There will be heat, and it cometh to pass.*[3] They come with a mist of fine sand, veiling the sun, scorching vegetation, and bringing languor and fever to men. They are painful airs, and, if the divine economy were only for our physical benefit, inexplicable, for they neither carry rain nor help at harvest. *A dry wind off the bare heights in the wilderness towards the daughter of My people, neither to fan nor to cleanse.*[4] They blow chiefly in spring, and for a day at a time. The following extracts, from our diary in 1891, give some impression of what these hot sandy winds make of the atmosphere. It will be noticed how readily they pass into rain, by a slight change from SSW to full SW:

Edh-Dhaheriyah, Saturday, April 25 (in the Negeb, four hours south of Hebron), 8 P.M.—Night dark and clear, with moon in first quarter. Temp. 58° Fahr.; 11 P.M. 62°, moon hazy.

Sunday.—8 A.M. 78°. Hot wind from south, yet called Sherkeh or Sherkiyeh, *i.e.* east wind, by our men. Temperature rises to 88° at 10, and 90° at 12. Sky drumly all forenoon, but the sun casts shadows. Atmosphere thickening. At 1.45 wind rises, 93°; 2.30, gale blowing, air filled with fine sand, horizon shortened to a mile, sun not visible, grey sky, but a slight shadow cast by the tents. View from tent-door of light grey limestone land under dark grey sky, misty range of hills a mile off, and one camel visible; 3.40, wind moderate, temp. 93°; 4.40, strong wind, half-gale, 83°; 5 P.M., wind SSW, temp. 78°. Wind veers a little farther W in the evening; 6 P.M., temp. 72°; sunset, 68°; 10.30 P.M., 63°. A slight shower, stormy-looking night, clouds gathering from many quarters. The grey town's eastern face lit by the moon, and weird against the clouds, heaped together on the western sky, reflecting the moonlight.

Monday, April 27.—Rain at intervals through the night, with high SW wind endangering the tents; 5.45 A.M., temp. 58°. Distant hills under mist, with the sun breaking through. Scudding showers, grey clouds, no blue sky. Landscape as in Scottish uplands with little agriculture. Left camp 6.30. Most of the day dull and windy. Cleared up towards evening, with sunshine.

[1] Job xxxvii. 9. Cf. Ankel, *op. cit.*, p. 86. [2] *PEFQ*, 1899, 309. [3] Luke xii. 55.
[4] Jer. iv. 11. Cf. Ezek. xvii. 10; xix. 12; Hos. xiii. 15; Jon. iv. 8.

Here is another Sherkiyeh (called also Khamsin) a fortnight later, in Samaria, between Sebastiyeh and Jenin:

May 11.—At Sebastiyeh at sunrise only 48° with slight west wind. Towards noon, under the same wind, 80°. Then the wind changed. A Sherkiyeh blew from SSE, and at 2 P.M., at our resting-place, Ḳubaṭiyeh, high and open, 92°. Sun veiled, afternoon dull. At 5, at Jenin, En-gannim, 88°, with more sunshine. At 10, still 84°. A few hours later we were wakened by cold. The wind had changed to W, the temperature was 72°, at sunrise, 68°.

These two instances—and we experienced two others at Jerusalem, one lasting for two days—will give the reader some idea of the east wind, or sirocco. It will be seen that in Palestine this does not inflict on men more than great discomfort, with a possibility of fever. In the desert, where the sand is loose, it is different: caravans have been overwhelmed by the sirocco between Egypt and Palestine; but on the fertile hills there is no danger to life from the sand-clouds, and the farther north they travel, the less disagreeable does their haze become.[1]

Yet sometimes the east wind breaks with violence even on the coast. Tents may be carried off by wicked gusts.[2] To an east wind Jeremiah likened the scattering of Israel, by an east wind Ezekiel saw ships of Tyre broken, and the Psalmist ships of Tarshish.[3]

We have seen how broken the surface of Palestine is; how opposite its various aspects, seaward and towards the desert; how suddenly changing and contrary its winds. This will have prepared us for the fact that its differences of temperature are also great—great between one part of the country and another, great between summer and winter, but relatively greater between day and night and between one part of the day and another. Here are instances: Robinson experienced in May, in the mountains of Judæa, a pleasant temperature of from 80° to 96° under a fresh west wind; but at Ekron in the plain, though the wind was the same, the heat had risen to 105°, and the sultry air had the characteristics of a sirocco. Coming down from Moab to the Jordan, on 7th July, we found the temperature at Heshbon at 9 A.M., when the sun was near his full strength, only 76°; but on the edge of the Ghor at noon it was 103°; on Jordan, at 2.30 P.M., 101°; and at Jericho throughout the night not less than 89°. On the heights of Gadara, from afternoon of the 23rd to forenoon of the 27th June, the mid-day temperature had ranged under the west wind from 82° to 90°, between 6 and 10 P.M. from 70° to 76°,

[1] Cf. Robinson, *Phys. Geog.*, pp. 279, 280.
[2] Lynch, *Official Report*, p. 74.
[3] Jer. xviii. 17; Ezek. xxvii. 26; cf. xix. 12; Ps. xlviii. 7; Jos. xiv *Antt.* ii. 2.

while the lowest morning temperature just before sunrise was 65°. But at the sulphur baths of Hammath below Gadara the mid-day temperature on 24th June was 100°, and at 3 P.M. still 96°; while at Pella, in the Jordan Valley, on 28th and 29th June, we had a mid-day temperature from 98° to 101°, at sunrise 74°, and at 10 A.M. 78°. Yet after we rose to the Wady Yabis in Gilead, at 10 P.M., it was only 69°, next mid-day at Ajlun 86°, at 10 P.M. 64°, and at sunrise next morning 58°. These are changes between different localities, but even at the same spot the range is great. We have seen that caused by the sirocco—once from 48° at sunrise to 92° by 2 P.M. But take an instance with no sirocco. On the 23rd April, at Beit-Jibrin at sunrise, the thermometer stood at 42°; from 11 to 3 it ranged over 85°. At Laish it sank, in a storm of wind and rain, from 88° to 72° in little over a quarter of an hour; but changes as sudden and even more extreme are not uncommon down the Jordan Valley.[1]

But these extremes of heat which surround the Central Range, and these ample changes of temperature must not be allowed to confuse our minds with regard to the climate which this part of the land, Israel's proper territory, enjoys through the year. In the world there are few healthier homes. The mean annual temperature varies from 62° to 68°. Except under the sirocco the warmest days of summer seldom exceed 90°, and the cold of winter still more seldom falls to freezing-point; February is the coldest month, with a mean temperature of about 46°. Through March and April this rises from 54° to 61°; in May and June from 65° to 74°; July and August, 76°; September and October, 75° to 68°. After the rains there is a fall in November to about 60°, and in December to 52°. The snows, the less sunshine, and the cold north-east winds, are sufficient to account for the further fall in January to 49°.[2]

We have carefully surveyed the rains, winds, and temperatures of Palestine. For the mass of the land lifted from 1000 to 2000 feet above the sea, the result is a temperate climate, with the annual seasons perhaps more regular, but the daily variations of heat much greater, than throughout the most of the temperate zone. On her hills and table-lands Israel enjoyed the advantages of a healthy and bracing climate, with the addition of such stimulus and strain as come from a considerable range of the daily temperature, as well as from

[1] Lynch's *Narrative*; cf. Daily Range, Sarona, *PEFQ*, 1891; Jerus., *id.*, 1893. On Tiberias, *PEFQ*, 1896, p. 92; cf. below, ch. xxi.

[2] These figures are arrived at after a comparison of Barclay's for the years 1851 to 1855 (*City of the Great King*, p. 428), and those given by Chaplin, *PEFQ*, 1883, and Glaisher, *id.*, 1893-1894. Cf. Wittmann, 561-570.

the neighbourhood of extreme heat, in the Jordan Valley and on the Western Plain, to which the business of their life obliged most of the nation often to descend. Some tribes felt these changes more regularly than others. Most subject to them were the highlanders of Mount Ephraim, who had fields in the Jordan Valley, and the Galileans, whose province included both the heights of Naphtali and the sub-tropical basin in which the Lake of Galilee lies. In their journeys from the Jordan to Cana, from Nazareth to Capernaum, from Capernaum to the highlands of Cæsarea Philippi our Lord and His disciples, often with no roof to cover their heads at night, must have felt the full range of the Syrian temperature. But these are conditions which breed a hardy and elastic frame of body. The national type formed in them was certain to prove at once tough and adaptable. To the singular variety of the climate in which the Jewish nation grew up we may trace some of the physical persistence and versatility which has made Jews at home in every quarter of the globe. This is different from the purely Semitic frame of body, which has been tempered only by the monotonous conditions of the desert. The Arab has not proved himself so successful a colonist as the Jew. And in our own times we have had another instance of the tempering influences of the climate of Palestine. The emigration of Syrians from the Turkish Empire was for a time considerable and the Syrians have been good colonists in America and Australia.

One other effect of the climate of the Holy Land is as important. It lends itself to the service of moral ideas.

In the first place, it is not mechanically regular. Unlike that of Egypt, the climate of Syria does not depend upon a few simple and unfailing phenomena—upon one great instrument like the Nile to whose operations man has but to link his own and the fruits of the year are inevitable. In the Palestine year there is no inevitableness. Fertility does not spring from a source which is within control of man's spade, and by which he can defy a brazen and illiberal heaven. It comes down from heaven, and if heaven sometimes withholds it, nothing else in man's reach is a substitute for it. The climate of Palestine is regular enough to provoke men to methodical labour for its fruits, but the regularity is often interrupted. The early or the latter rains fail, drought comes occasionally for two years in succession, and that means famine and pestilence. There are the visitations of the locust, said to be bad every fifth or sixth year, and earthquakes, also periodical in Syria. Thus a purely mechanical conception of nature as something inevitable, whose processes are more or less under man's control, is impossible; and the imagination is roused to feel the presence of a Will behind nature, in face of whose interruptions of the fruitfulness or stability of the land man is helpless. To such a climate is partly due Israel's doctrine of Providence. The Book of Deuteronomy, to which we owe so much insight into the religious influences of the Promised Land, emphasises this by contrasting it with Egypt. *For the land, whither thou goest in to possess it, is not like the land of Egypt, whence ye came out, where thou sowedst thy seed, and wateredst it with thy foot, as a garden of herbs*—that is, where everything is so much under man's control, where man has nature at his foot like a little garden, and has but to link himself to the mechanical processes of nature, and the fruits of the year are inevitable. *But the land, whither ye are passing over to possess it, is a land of hills and valleys, of the rain of heaven it drinketh water: a land which The Lord thy God Himself looketh after; continually are the eyes of The Lord thy God upon it, from the beginning even to the end of the year.* That is, the climate of Egypt does not suggest a personal Providence, but the climate of Palestine does so. *And it shall be, if ye indeed hearken to My commandments, which I am commanding you to-day, to love The Lord your God, to worship Him with all your heart, and with all your soul, that then I will give the rain of the land in its season—early rain and latter rain,—and thou shalt gather thy corn and thine oil. And I will give grass in thy fields for thy cattle, and thou shalt eat and be full. Take heed to yourselves, lest your heart be beguiled, and ye turn aside and worship other gods and bow down to them; and the wrath of The Lord grow hot against you, and He shut up the heaven, that there be no rain, and the ground yield not her increase; and ye perish off the good land which The Lord is giving you* (Deut. xi.).

Two passages in the prophets give instances of this principle. Through Amos God reminds His people of recent drought, famine, mildew and blasting, pestilence and earthquake, and reproaches them that after each of these they did not turn to Him[1]: *yet have ye not returned unto Me, saith The Lord.* Isaiah, alluding to the same series of disturbances, speaks in a different order of earthquake, drought with forest fires and famine, and complains that the people are still impenitent: *for all this His anger is not turned away, but His hand is stretched out still.*[2]

It was a moral Providence, then, which the prophets read in the climate of their land. But Israel could not have read this high moral Providence with a God of another character than her own. Look at her neighbours. They experienced the same droughts, thunderstorms, and earthquakes; but these

[1] Amos iv. 6-11.

[2] Isa. v. 25, ix. 18-21, v. 26-30. These passages are connected by the same refrain, they belong to the same series, and must originally have stood together. We need not suppose that either prophet was bound to follow the real sequence. Amos puts famine before drought.

do not appear to have suggested to them other ideas than the wrath of the Deity, who had therefore to be propitiated by the horrible sacrifices of manhood, feminine purity, and child life, which have made their religions so revolting. Israel also felt God was angry, but because He was such a God, and had revealed Himself as in the past, they knew that He punished them through their climate, not to destroy, but to warn and turn, His rebel folk. The Syrian year and its interruptions play an equal part in the Phœnician religions and in the Hebrew prophets' doctrine of Providence. But while in the former they lead to mutilation and cruel sacrifices, in the latter they are the reminder that man does not live by the bread of the year alone: they are calls to conscience, to repentance, to purity. And what makes the difference on that same soil, and under those same heavens, is the character of Israel's God. All the Syrian religions reflect the Syrian climate; Israel alone interprets it for moral ends, because Israel alone has a God who is absolute righteousness.

Here, then, is another of those many points at which the Geography of Syria exhausts the influence of the material and the seen, and indicates the presence on the land of the unseen and the spiritual.

2. *The Fertility of the Land*

The long rainy season in Palestine means a considerable rainfall,[1] and while it lasts the land gets a thorough soaking. Every highland gorge and lowland valley-bed—nearly every one of those wadies which are dry in summer, and to the traveller at that season seem the channels of some ancient flood—is filled annually with a roaring torrent, while many of the high meadows are lakes, and plains like Esdraelon become in part quagmires. But the land is limestone and porous. The rains are quickly drained away, the wadies are left dry, the lakes become marshes, or dwindle to dirty ponds,[2] and on the west of Jordan there remain only a few perennial streams, of which but one or two, and these mere rills, are found in the hill-country. At the foot of the hills,[3] however, there burst forth through the summer not only such springs as we have in our own land, but copious fountains, from three to twenty feet in breadth, and one to three feet in depth—some with broad pools full of

[1] Annual rainfall at Nazareth is about 61 centimetres; at Jerusalem, 57; while at Athens it is 40; Constantinople, 70; Vienna, 44; London, 58; Paris, 50; Rome, 80. —So Anderlind, *ZDPV*, viii. 101 ff. Cf. *PEFQ*, 1894.

[2] Occasionally winter lakes will be large through summer. Merj el-Ghuruk, in May, 1891, was a large lake. So Buṭṭauf in Galilee.

[3] *i.e.* where the hard dolomitic limestone comes to the surface (as at the Virgin's Well on Kidron), but in the porous cretaceous limestone springs are wanting.

fish, and some sending forth streams strong enough to work mills a few yards away. These fountain-heads, as they are called,[1] are characteristic features of the Syrian summer; in the dust and rust of the rest of the land they surprise you with their wealth of water and rank vegetation. They are chiefly found at the foot of Hermon, where three give birth to the Jordan, along both bases of the Central Range, in the Jordan Valley and the Western Plain, and on Esdraelon at the foot of Gilboa and of the Samarian hills. There are smaller editions among the hills of Galilee and Samaria, but on the table-land of Judæa springs are few and mostly meagre, and the inhabitants store the winter rain in pits, partly natural, partly built. On the plains water may be got in most places by boring and pumping.[2]

[1] Ras el-'Ain.

[2] 'Ain, *well* or *spring*, in place-names is common, but we must not infer that living water is present. It is not at 'Ain Shems; at 'Ain Sinia there is only a cistern (Robinson, *Phys. Geog.*, 219, 220), but to the NE a spring (Conder, *Crit. Review*, iv. 293). At the foot of the hills the chief large fountains are: On the W Plain, between Tyre and 'Akka at Ras el-'Ain, 'Ain el-Musheirifeh, el-Kabireh, Birweh, and Tell Kurdany, source of the Belus. Along the N base of Carmel the Kishon is fed by springs. S of Carmel are the sources of the Zerḳa, Subbarin and Umm esh-Shukaf, whence aqueducts led to Cæsarea; and other spots at the roots of the Samarian hills, like Ras el-'Ain, whence the 'Aujeh flows. In the Shephelah several wells; water can be got by boring on the Philistine plain; Ashkelon and Gaza are noted for wells, and the wadies near the sea have water for much of the year. The streams in the Negeb are winter streams (Psalm cxxvi); wells are few. Along the W base of the Judæan range are fountains, chiefly at faults in the strata of gorges leading to the plateau, *e.g.* 'Ain el-Ḳuf, in the W el-Ḳuf. In a cave in a gorge off W en-Najil I found abundant water in May. The Judæan plateau has cisterns and pools, but few springs, almost no large ones. Two springs between Edh-Dhaheriyah and Hebron are perhaps *the upper and nether springs* of Caleb (Josh. xv. 19); twelve small about Hebron, and over thirty have been counted within 10 miles from Jerusalem, but only those at Solomon's Pools yield considerable water. Samaria is more favoured, esp. at Khan Lubban, W Ḳanah, Salim, Nablus (where the vale between Gerizim and Ebal has water the year round), Fendaḳumieh, Jeba', Tell Dothan, Lejjun, and Jenin. On the N base of Gilboa are 'Ain Jalud and three other fountains, yielding a stream. In Galilee are springs at Shunem, Khan el-Tajjar (two, one large), Ḥaṭṭin (large), Nazareth, Ṣeffuriyeh (large), Gischala, Tibnin, Ḳedesh (two, large), and other places. Along the E base of the Central Range are many copious fountains—most more or less brackish and warm—opposite Merom, 'Amudiyeh, Belateh, Mellaḥah, the smaller Mughar and Kuba'a. On the E shore of the Lake eṭ-Ṭabighah, with stream, 'Ain et-Tineh and Mudawarah, with pools; 'Ain el-Baridah, with small pools; hot springs at Baths of Tiberias; about Beisan many springs and thence down Jordan, esp. at Saḳut, W Maliḥ (salt and warm), Ḳarawa, Fusail, 'Aujeh, 'Ain Duḳ, 'Ain es-Sulṭan (near Jericho), 'Ain Ḥajla on the plain. Along the coast of the Dead Sea Jehayir, Feshkhah (brackish and warm), Ghuweir (small), Terabeh, 'Ain Jidy, and 'Areijeh, whose streams produce thickets and fields, but are lost before the sea is reached. Of longer streams from the W Jordan receives

East of Jordan water is more plentiful. Several long perennial rivers drain the eastern desert, and water the plateaus between it and the Jordan Valley, the eastern half of which might be irrigated in its entire extent. Springs are more frequent, and, although streams are fewer north of the Yarmuk than on the south, the soil on the north is deep volcanic mould on a basalt basis, and holds its winter moisture longer than the limestone.

The distribution of water, then, unequal as it is, is another factor in heightening the complexity of this land of contrasts. Take it with the differences of level and temperature, and of aspect, seaward and to the desert, and you understand what a mixture of soils Palestine is, and how her fauna and flora range between the alpine and the tropical, between the forms of the Mediterranean basin and those of desert life, while she still cherishes, in that trench down her middle, animals and plants related to those of distant lands, with which in previous geological periods she had closer relations.

As to soils, the reader of the Bible feels how near in Palestine the barren lies to the fruitful. Apart from the desert proper, which comes up almost to the gates of Judæan cities, how much land is described as only pasture, and this so dry that there is constant strife for the wells upon it! How often we hear of *the field*, the rough, uncultivated, but not wholly barren, bulk of the hill-country, where the *beasts of the field*, wild beasts, found room to breed and become a serious hindrance to Israel's conquest of the land.[1] This *field* is a great element in the Old Testament landscape, as we recognise it in the tracts of moorland, hillside and summit, jungle and bare rock, which make up much of the hill-country, and can never have been cultivated even for vines. How much of this *field* was forest is debatable. On the one hand, where are now only fragments of wood, writers,[2] even down to the Crusades, describe forests like that of North Sharon; the word for wood occurs in place-names, where are now few trees, as in Judæa and Jaulan; you see enormous roots here and there even in Judæa; palm groves have disappeared from the Jordan Valley, and elsewhere you may take it that the Turk did not leave the land so wooded as he found it. On the other hand, copse and wood cover old clearings as on Carmel; on the Central Range, the Old Testament speaks only of isolated large trees, of copses and small woods, but looks for

---

the Jalud at Beth shan, the Fari'ah, and the Ḳelt—the first two perennial, the last almost.

[1] Field, שׂדה, is used not only for this wild moorland and hillside, but also for cultivated soil, and for the territory belonging to a town.

[2] Arculphus, A.D. 670, describes a pine forest S of Bethlehem; remains still exist —Conder, "Palestine" in Hastings, *D.B.*

forests to Gilead, Bashan, and Lebanon; and there is little mention of the manufacture of large native wood.[1]

The truth is, that the conditions for the growth of such forests as we have in Europe and America are not present in Palestine: the Hebrew word we translate *forest* ought to be *woodland*, perhaps only *copse* or *jungle*,[2] and we may conclude that the land was never much more wooded than it is to-day. The distribution of woodland may have been different, but the woods were what we find the Palestine wood still to be—open and scattered, trees distinguished rather for thickness than height, and little undergrowth when compared with a northern or a tropical forest.[3] Here and there groves of larger trees, or solitary giants of their kind, may have stood conspicuous on the bare landscape. The chief trees are varieties of oak, including the ilex, of terebinth,[4] and carob, and box that grows to a height of 20 feet, with few pines and cypresses, and (by water) planes. These were *trees of God*, planted by Him and not by man. The only others of size were the walnut, mentioned by Josephus, above the Lake of Galilee, and the sycomore, used for both fruit and timber.[5] But these were cultivated. The acacia or shittimwood is common towards the desert.[6] In Sharon the eucalyptus has been introduced against malaria.

Next to the woods of Palestine, a thick bush forms one of her sylvan features. It consists of dwarf oak, terebinth and pine, dwarf wild olive, wild vine, arbutus and myrtle, juniper and thorn. This mixture of degraded forest and fruit-trees represents the remains of former woods and the sites of abandoned cultivation. In the bush *forest* and *garden* meet half way. Sometimes old oil and wine presses are found beneath it, sometimes great trees, survivors of old woods, tower above it. A few wadies in Western Palestine, and many in Eastern, are filled with oleanders, ribbons of pink across the landscape. Willows are common, and cane-brakes where there is water. The

[1] Isa. ix. 10. For the temple cedar was imported from Lebanon. The Israelites do not appear to have used coffins, 2 Kings xiii. 21; cf. Ankel, *op. cit.*, p. 104; Post "Forest" in Hastings, *D.B.*

[2] יַעַר. The corresponding Arabic *wa'ar* is rocky ground.

[3] Richard found undergrowth difficult in Sharon. *Itin. Ricardi*, iv. 12.

[4] It is often impossible to tell whether oak or terebinth is meant in the O.T. There are four words, אֵלָה and אַלָּה; אֵלוֹן and אַלּוֹן.

[5] Amos vii. 14; Isa. ix. 9 (*E.V.* 10); 1 Kings x. 27; 1 Chron. xxvii. (xxviii.), 28; 2 Chron. i. 15; Luke xix. 4.

[6] Blanckenhorn, *ZDPV*, xv. 62, and Buhl, *Geogr.*, 54 f., take the decrease of cultivation to be due to less cold and damp from prehistoric times (proved by geology) to historic; cf. Fraas, *Aus dem Orient.*, i. 198 ff. But Benzinger, *Archäologie*, 32, agrees with me that this "cannot be proved either from the O.T. or present conditions".

rank jungle of the Jordan and stunted flora of the desert fall to be separately described.

If Palestine be not a land of forests, it is a land of orchards. Except chestnuts, which are not found, the fruit-trees of the temperate zone flourish in Syria. The most common are the apricot, "to Syria what the fig is to Smyrna and Ephesus", figs themselves, orange, citron, pomegranate, mulberry, pistachio, almond, and walnut.[1] The sycomore, which is easily grown, is cultivated for its timber and rough tasteless figs, which, as well as the carob, are eaten by the poor.[2] The date-palm used to be cultivated both on the Maritime Plain and in the Jordan Valley, where it might still be.[3] Near Jericho, balsam groves were farmed down to Roman times.[4] But the two chief fruit-trees of Palestine are the olive and the vine, the olive certainly, and the vine probably, native to Syria. The cultivation of the olive has been sustained to this day, and was probably never much greater than now. That of the vine is being revived. The disappearance of vineyards and not of forests is the difference with which we have to reckon in the landscape of Palestine. Innumerable hillsides, not capable of other cultivation, which were terraced with vineyards to their summits, now in their ruin only exaggerate the stoniness of the land.[5] But some Germans on Carmel and Judæa, some French firms, the Jesuits in the Beḳa' and the Jewish Colonies are changing this. At Salṭ there has always been a cultivation of grapes for manufacture into raisins.[6]

The cultivation of grain was confined to the lower plateaus, broader valleys, and plains. The best wheat-fields are Philistia, Esdraelon, the Mukhneh east of Nablus, and Hauran. The wheat of Hauran springing from volcanic soil, is famed through the East.[7] Barley, given to horses and other beasts of burden, was the despised food of the poorer peasants, or of the whole nation when the Arabs drove them from the plains to the hills. It was in the shape of a barley cake that the Midianite dreamt he saw Israel

[1] Tristam, *Natural History of the Bible*. Cf. Anderlind, *Die Fruchtbäume in Syrien insbesondere Palästina*, *ZDPV*, xi. 69. Plums, pears, and apples seldom in Palestine. Cherries and bananas lately introduced.

[2] Amos was a gatherer of sycomore figs, vii. 14; the carob fruit was the food of the Prodigal, Luke xv. 16. Pictures, Volcani, *op. cit.* 124.

[3] See pp. 60, 80, 113 and chs. xxi, xxii.

[4] *Balsamodendron Gileadense*, still in S Syria. Cf. Jer. viii. 22.

[5] See the chapter on Judæa, xv.

[6] Honey in *milk and honey*, Gen. xliii. 11, etc., seems not to be that of bees but grape-syrup, Benzinger, *Archäol.*, 91, Buhl, *Geogr.*, 57. Yet this does not suit Isa. vii. 22 f. On orchards, I. E.-Volcani, *op. cit.* 120.

[7] See the chapter on Hauran.

rolling down from the hills and overturning his camp on Esdraelon.[1] Oats were not grown, but millet was common in ancient times, and maize is now. Beans, pulse, and lentils were largely grown. Garden vegetables thrive richly where there is summer irrigation—tomatoes, onions, cucumbers, pumpkins, and melons chiefly in the plains; but we received all these from the peasants of Gilead and the Bedouin of Moab.[2] It is doubtful whether the sugar-cane was known.[3]

There is no turf in Palestine, and little grass that lasts through summer. After rain, *the field* springs thick with grasses and wild grains of many kinds,[4] some clover, lupins, many succulent plants, aromatic herbs, lilies, anemones, and hosts of other wild-flowers, but early summer sees much withered away. Lupins, clover and other plants are cultivated for fodder; but cattle and sheep must trust to the wild pasture, over whose meagre vegetation their range has to be large. Only by fountains and pools can they find grass through the year.[5] The Jewish colonies are changing this.

Such, then, is the fertility of the Holy Land in forest, orchard, and field. To a western eye it must, at certain seasons, seem meagre and uninfluential —incapable of stirring the imagination, or enriching the life of a people. Yet come in with the year at the flood, the springing of the grain, the rush of colour across the field, the flush of green on the desert, and in imagination clothe the stony terraces with the vines which once trailed from foot to summit of many of the hills—then, even though your eye be western, you will feel the charm of the land. It is not, however, the western eye we have to consider. It is the effect of this fertility on the desert nomads from whom the population of Syria was chiefly drawn. If even at the season of its annual ebb the fertility of the whole land affords a contrast to the desert—how much more must its eastern forests, its wheat-fields, its streams, the oases round its perennial fountains, the "pride of Jordan", impress the immigrant nomad. If he settles among them, how wholly must they alter his mode of life!

This fertility affected immigrants from the desert, among whom were

[1] Judges vii. 13. [2] The potato, I think, has recently been introduced to Syria.

[3] Isa. xliii. 24; Jer. vi. 20. Eng. *Sweet Cane*; but, according to most authorities, identical with the Calamus (Exod. xxx. 23; Ezek. xxvii. 19), a kind of spice, probably imported.

[4] Three Hebrew words are translated grass: ירק, *yereḳ*, which means any green herb; דשא, *deshe'*, which is our grass; חציר, *ḥāsîr*, which is our grass or hay. Hay has been infrequent, Buhl, *Geogr.*, p. 56, n. 33.

[5] On the grains and flora of Palestine, see the works of Tristram and Post, articles in *PEFQ*, *Enc. Bib.*, and Hastings, *D.B.*; and other works reviewed in *ZDPV*, xxiii (1900); also Thompson's *Crusader's Coast*, *passim*.

Israel, in two ways. It meant to them at once an ascent in civilisation and a fall in religion.

1. It meant a rise in civilisation. To pass from the desert into Syria is to leave the habits of the nomadic life for those of the agricultural. The change may be gradual, and generally has been, but the end is inevitable. Immigrant tribes, with herds and tents, have roamed the Syrian fields for generations, but at last settled in villages and townships. The process can be illustrated all down the history of Syria: it can be seen to-day. Israel also passed through it, and the passage made them a nation. From a series of loosely-connected pastoral clans, they became a united people, with a definite territory, and its culture as the means of their life. The story is told in two passages of such beauty that I translate the whole of them. The first is from the Song of Moses, the other from the Blessing of the Tribes—in chapters xxxii and xxxiii of Deuteronomy. It is to be noticed that neither carries the origin of Israel further back than the desert. Neither even hints at the sojourn of the people in Egypt. Israel are a purely desert tribe, who by the inspiration of their God are stirred up to leave their desert home, and settle as agriculturists in Palestine:

Remember the days of old,
Scan the years age upon age;
Ask of thy sire that he show thee,
Thine elders and they will tell thee.
When the Highest gave nations their heritage,
When He sundered the children of men,
He set the bounds of the peoples,
By the tale of Israel's sons (?).
For Yahweh's lot, it is Jacob,
Israel the scale of His heritage.
He found him in a land of the desert,
In a waste, in a howling wilderness.
He swept around him, He scanned him,
As the apple of His eye He watched him.
As an eagle stirreth his nest,
Fluttereth over his young,
Spreadeth his wings, doth take them,
Beareth them up on his pinions,
Yahweh alone was his leader.
And no strange god was with him.
He made him to ride on the highlands,

And to eat of the growth of the field.
Suckled him with honey from the crag,
And oil from the flinty rock.
Cream of kine and milk of sheep,
With the fat of lambs and rams,
Bulls of Bashan and he-goats,
With fat of the kidneys of wheat;
And the blood of the grape thou drankest in foam!

How could the passage from the nomadic life to the agricultural be more vividly expressed than by this figure of a brood of desert birds stirred to leave their nest by the father bird![1] The next poem is full of the same ideas—that it was in the wilderness their God met the people, that their tribes first became a nation by settlement in Canaan, and by the new habits which its fertility imposed:

Yahweh from Sinai is come,
And risen from Seir upon us;
He shone from the hills of Paran,
And sped from Meribah of Kadesh.[2]
From the South[3] *fire . . . to them.*
Also He loved His people,
Their saints were all in Thy hand (?),
They pressed to Thy feet (?),
They took of His words.[4]

Law did Moses command us,
A Domain had the assembly of Jacob,—
So He became king in Jeshurun,
When the heads of the people were gathered,
When the tribes of Israel were one.

There is none like the God of Jeshurun,
Riding the heavens to thy help,
And the clouds in His highness!
The Eternal God is thy refuge,
And beneath are the arms everlasting.

[1] Cf. Ibn Khaldun on the effects of civilisation on the Arabs, in *Literary History of the Arabs*, by R. A. Nicholson, 439 ff.
[2] Text altered (partly after LXX) gives this parallel to the other lines.
[3] Reading very corrupt. I suggest *the south* as a parallel to the other lines.
[4] LXX, these lines are very uncertain.

And He drove from before thee the foe,
And He said—Destroy!
So Israel dwelt in safety,
Secluded was Jacob's fount
In a land of corn and wine,
Also His heavens dropped dew.
Happy thou, Israel! Who is like unto thee!
A people saved by Yahweh,
He is the shield of thy help,
Yea, the sword of thy highness;
And thy foes shall fawn upon thee,[1]
And thou—on their heights shalt thou march!

2. But this rise from the nomadic level to the agricultural, which the passage from the desert into Syria implied, this ascent in social life, meant at the same time almost inevitably a descent in religion.

It is intelligible. The creed of the desert nomad is simple and austere—for nature about him is monotonous, silent, illiberal. But Syria is a land of lavish gifts and oracles—where woods are full of mysterious speech, and rivers burst suddenly from the ground, where the freedom of nature excites, and seems to sanction, the passions of the human body, where food is rich and men drink wine. The spirit and the senses are equally captured. No one can tell how many voices a tree has who has not come up to it from the silence of the great desert. No one may feel how "possessed" a landscape can be—as if singled out and endowed by some divinity for its own domain and residence—who has not, across the forsaken plateaus of Moab or Anti-Lebanon, fallen upon one of the sudden Syrian rivers, with its wealth of water and of verdure.

But with the awe comes the sense of indulgence, and the starved instincts of the body break riotously forth. It is said that Mohammed, upon one of his journeys out of Arabia, was taken to look upon Damascus. He gazed, but turned away. "Man", he said, "can have but one Paradise, and mine is above." This may be a legend, but it is a symbol of the effect which Syria exercises on the imagination of every nomad who crosses her border.

All this is said to have happened to Israel from almost their first encampment in Canaan. *Israel settled in Shittim, and the people began to commit whoredom with the daughters of Moab . . . Israel joined himself to Baal-peor.* And still more, when they settled west of Jordan among the Canaanites, and had adopted the life of the land, did they lapse into polytheism, and the

[1] To adopt the happy translation of Mr. Addis.

sensuous Canaanite ritual. In every favoured spot their predecessors had left a Baal, a Lord or Possessor, to whom the place was Beulah, subject or married, and to these innumerable Baalim they turned aside. *They went astray on every high hill, and under every green tree,*[1] *they did according to all the abominations of the nations which the Lord cast out before the children of Israel.*[2] The poem we have quoted directly connects this lapse into idolatry with the change from the nomadic to the agricultural life. These next lines follow immediately those on pages 76, 77:

And Jeshurun waxed fat, and struck out
—Thou art fat, thou art thick, thou art sleek!—
And cast off the God that had made him,
And despised the Rock of his salvation.
With strange gods they moved Him to jealousy,
With abominations provoked Him to anger.
They sacrificed to monsters undivine,
Gods they never had known,
New things, lately come in,
Their fathers ne'er had them in awe.
Of the Rock that bare thee thou wast unmindful,
And forgattest the God who gave thee birth.

All this makes two things clear. The conception of Israel's early history which prevails in Deuteronomy, *viz.* that the nation suffered a declension from a pure and simple estate of life and religion to one which was gross and sensuous, from the worship of their own deity to the worship of many local gods, is justified in the main—I do not say in details, but in the main—by the geographical data, and by what we know to have been the influence of these at all periods in history. And, secondly, this survey of the fertility of Syria, and of its social and religious influences, has surely made clear to us how unlikely a soil this was for monotheism to spring from. We must feel that it has brought into relief the presence and the power of those spiritual forces, which, in spite of the opposition of nature, did create upon Syria the monotheistic creed of Israel.[3]

[1] The worship of the host of heaven did not become general in Israel till the ninth and eighth centuries.

[2] 1 Kings xiv. 23, 24. Cf. 2 Kings xvii. 9-12; Hos. ix. 10.

[3] On soils, cereals, and fodder crops see Reports by Sir E. J. Russell, F.R.S., and Dr. J. B. Orr, D.S.O., in *The New Judæa*, July 29, 1927.

IV. *THE SCENERY OF THE LAND AND ITS REFLECTION IN THE BIBLE*

It once was the fashion to despise the scenery of Palestine. The tourist, easily saddle-sore and missing the comforts of European travel, found the landscape deteriorate almost from the moment he left the orange-groves of Jaffa behind him, and arrived in the north with a disappointment which Lebanon itself could not appease. The Plain was commonplace, the glens of Samaria only "pretty", but the Judæan table-land revolting in its stony dryness, and the surroundings of the Lake of Galilee feverish and glaring. Now it is true that the greater part of Palestine, like other countries not unknown for beauty, requires all the ornament which cultivation can give it, and it has been deprived of this. The land has been stripped and starved, its bones protrude, in parts it is very bald—a carcase of a land, if you like, from some points of view, and especially when the clouds lower, or the sirocco throws dust across the sun. Yet, even as it lies to-day, there are in the Holy Land some prospects as bold and rich as any you will see in countries famed for their picturesqueness. There is the coast-line from the headland of Carmel—northwards the Gulf of Ḥaifa, with its yellow sands and palms, across them brown, crumbling Acre, and in the haze the white Ladder of Tyre: southwards Sharon with her scattered forest, her coast of sand and grass, and the haggard ruins of 'Athlit, last foothold of the Crusaders: westwards the green sea and the shadow of the clouds upon it, grey when you look at them with your face to the sun, but, with the sun behind you, purple, and more like Homer's "wine-coloured" water than anything I have seen on the Mediterranean. There is the *excellency of Carmel* itself: wheat-fields from Esdraelon to the first bare rocks, then thick bush and scrub, young ilex, wild olives and pines, with undergrowth of purple thistles, mallows with blossoms like pelargoniums, stocks of hollyhock, golden broom, honeysuckle and convolvulus[1]; then, between the shoulders of the mountain, olive-groves, their dull green mass banked by the lighter forest trees, and on the flanks broad lawns, where in the shadow of oaks you look far out to sea. There is the Lake of Galilee seen from Gadara, with the hills of Naphtali above, and Hermon

[1] For the flower scenery, see Thompson's *Crusader's Coast*, for the whole R. Koeppel, *Palästina*, as above.

filling the north. There is the perspective of the Jordan Valley as you look up from over Jericho, between the bare ranges of Gilead and Ephraim, with the winding ribbon of the river's jungle, and the top of Hermon, a white cloud in the infinite distance. There is Gilead, where you ride, 2000 feet high, under the boughs of trees creaking and rustling in the wind, with Western Palestine before you. There is the moonlight view out of the bush on the north flank of Tabor, the leap of the sun over the edge of Bashan, summer morning in the Shephelah and sunset over the Mediterranean, when you see it from the gate of the ruins on Samaria down the glistening Vale of Barley. Even in the barest provinces you get many a little picture that lives with you—a chocolate-coloured bank with red poppies against the green of the prickly-pear hedge above it, and a yellow lizard darting across; a river-bed of pink oleanders flush with the plain; a gorge in Judæa, where you look up between limestone walls picked out with tufts of grass and black-and-tan goats cropping at them, the blue sky over all, on the edge of the only shadow, a well, a trough, and a solitary herdsman.

And then there are those prospects in which no other country can match Palestine, for no other has a valley like the Ghor, or a desert like that which falls from Judæa to the Dead Sea.[1] There is the view from the Mount of Olives, down 20 miles of hill-tops to the deep blue waters, with the wall of Moab glowing on the further side like burnished copper, and staining the blue sea red with its light. There is the view of the Dead Sea through hazy afternoons, when across the yellow foreground of Jeshimon the white Lisan rises like a pack of ice from the blue waters, and beyond it the Moab range, misty, silent, and weird. There are the precipices of Masada and En-gedi sheer from the salt coast. And, above all, there is the view from En-gedi under the full moon, when the sea is bridged with gold, and the eastern mountains are black with a border of opal.

But, whether there be beauty or not, there is on all the heights that sense of space and distance which comes from Palestine's high position between the great desert and the great sea.

Of all this such use was made by Israel as served the expression of her high ideals, or was necessary in the description of her warfare. Israel was a nation of prophets and warriors. But prophets, like lovers, offer you no more reflection of nature than as she sympathises with their passion; nor warriors, except as they wait impatiently for her omens, or are excited by her freshness and motion, or lay down their tactics by her contours. *Let it be when thou hearest the sound of a going in the tops of the mulberry trees, that then thou*

[1] De Saulcy calls the Dead Sea, "le lac le plus imposant et le plus beau qui existe sur la terre".—*Voyage autour de la Mer Morte*, i. 154.

bestir thyself, for then shall The Lord have gone out before thee to smite the host of the Philistines.[1]

The torrent of Kishon swept them away,
That torrent of spates, torrent Kishon.[2]

My God, make them like a whirl of dust,
Like stubble before the wind;
As a fire burns up a wood,
And as flame sets the mountains afire.[3]

Oh that I had wings like a dove,
I would fly away and be at rest!
I would hasten my escape
From the storm and tempest.[4]

The God of my rock; in Him will I trust:
My shield, and the horn of my salvation,
My high tower and my refuge.
He matches my feet to hinds' feet;
He sets me upon my high places.
Thou hast enlarged my steps beneath me;
So that my ankles swerve not.[5]

Of the brook shall he drink by the way:
Therefore shall he lift up the head.[6]

The gazelle, Israel, is slain on thy heights,
How fallen are the heroes![7]

When the Almighty scattered kings upon her,
It was as when it snoweth on Zalmon.[8]

How vividly these cries from Israel's mountain-war bring before us all that thirsty, broken land of crags and shelves, moors and gullies, with its mire and its rock, its few summer brooks, its winter spates and heavy snows; the rustling of its woods, its gusts of wind, and its bush fires; its startled birds,

[1] 1 Chron. xiv. 15. [2] Judges v. 21. [3] Ps. lxxxiii. 13, 14. [4] Ps. lv. 6-8.
[5] 2 Sam. xxii. 3, 34, 37. [6] Ps. cx. 7. [7] 2 Sam. i. 19. [8] Ps. lxviii. 14.

when the sudden storms from the sea sweep up the gorges, and its glimpses of deer, poised for a moment on the high sky-line of the hills. The battle-fields, too, are accurately described. The features of the Vale of Elah, of Michmash, of Jezreel, and of Jeshimon can be recognised to-day from the stories of David and Goliath, of Jonathan and the Philistine host, of Saul's defeat and Gideon's victory, and Saul's pursuit of David.[1]

The little details, which thus catch a soldier's ear and eye, are of course not so frequent with the prophets as the long lines of the land, and its greater natural phenomena.

He that sits on the circle of earth,
And the dwellers thereon are as grasshoppers;
That stretches the heavens as a curtain,
And spreads them out as a tent to dwell in.[2]

Men who looked at life under that lofty imagination did not always notice the details of their country's scenery. What filled them was the sense of space and distance, the stupendous contrasts of desert and fertility, the hard, straight coast with the sea breaking into foam, the swift sunrise, the thunder-storms sweeping the length of the land, and the earthquakes. For these were symbols of the great prophetic themes: the abiding justice and mercy of God, the steadfastness of His providence, the nearness of His judgements to life, which lies between His judgements as the land between the Desert and the *Great Deep*; His power to bring up life upon His people as spring rushes up on the wilderness; His awful last judgement, like *morning scattered on the mountains*, when the dawn is crushed upon the land between the hills and the heavy clouds, and the lurid light is spilt like the wine-press of the wrath of God. And if those great outlines are touched here and there with flowers, or a mist, or a bird's nest, or a passing thistledown, or a bit of meadow, or a quiet pool, or an olive-tree in the sunshine, it is to illustrate human beauty, which comes upon the earth as fair as her wild-flowers, and as quickly passes away, which is like a vapour that appears for a moment on the hillside and then is gone; or it is to symbolise God's provision of peace to His people in corners and nooks of this fiercely-swept life of ours:

[1] The most careful study of these battle-fields is given by Principal Miller in *The Least of all Lands*, with plans. See also Conder's identification of the scene of David and Goliath, and description of Mount Hachilah (*Tent Work*, 277 and 244).

[2] Isa. xl. 22.

He makes me to lie down in green pastures:
He leads me beside the still waters.[1]

They looked unto Him, and were lightened[2]*;*

where the effect is of liquid light, when the sun breaks through the clouds, rippling across a wood or a troubled piece of water.

But I am like a green olive in the house of God.[3]

I will be as the dew unto Israel:
He shall blossom as the lily,
And strike forth his roots like Lebanon:
His branches shall spread,
His beauty shall be as the olive,
And his scent as Lebanon.[4]

Bring up man and the animals, and you see those landscapes described by Old Testament writers as you see them to-day—valleys covered with corn, pastures above clothed with flocks, shepherds and husbandmen calling to each other through the morning air, narrow high-banked hill-roads brimming with sheep, long and stately camel trains, herds of wild cattle—*bulls of Bashan have compassed me about.* You see the villages by day, with the children coming to meet the traveller[5]; the villages by night, without a light, when you stumble on them in the darkness, and the dogs begin barking—*at evening they return and make a noise like a dog, and go round about the city.* You see night,

Wherein all the beasts of the forest creep forth,
The sun arises, they shrink together,
And lay them down in their dens.
Man goes forth unto his work,
And to his labour till evening.[6]

You see those details which are characteristic of every Eastern landscape: the chaff and rolling thorns blown before the wind, the dirt cast on the streets; the broken vessel by the well; the forsaken house; the dusty grave.

Let us pay attention to all these, and we shall surely feel ourselves in the

[1] Ps. xxiii. 2.
[2] Ps. xxxiv. 5, Massoretic text.
[3] Ps. lii. 8.
[4] Hos. xiv. 5, 6.
[5] 2 Kings ii. 23; Mark x. 13.
[6] Ps. civ. 20, 22, 23.

atmosphere and scenery in which David fought and Elisha went to and fro, and Malachi saw the Sun of Righteousness arise with healing in His wings.

There are three poems in the Old Testament which give a more or less comprehensive picture of the scenery of Palestine: the Twenty-Ninth Psalm, the Song of Solomon, and the Hundred and Fourth Psalm.

The Twenty-Ninth Psalm describes a thunderstorm travelling the far length of the land, rattling and stripping it: so that you see its chief features sweeping before you on the storm. Enough to give the translation of verses 3-9, which contain the description. It begins among the thunder-clouds:

The voice of The Lord is upon the waters,
The God of Glory is thundering;
The Lord is upon great waters.
The voice of The Lord with power,
The voice of The Lord with majesty,
The voice of The Lord breaks the cedars;
Yea, The Lord breaks the cedars of Lebanon.
He makes them skip like a calf;
Lebanon and Sirion like a wild ox in his youth.
The voice of The Lord hews out flames of fire.
The voice of The Lord makes the wilderness whirl;
The Lord makes the wilderness of Kadesh to whirl.
The voice of The Lord makes the hinds to travail,
And strips bare the forests;
In His palace every one saying, Glory.[1]

Here all the scenery appears to us, as in flashes of lightning, from the storm-clouds that break on the peaks of Lebanon, down Lebanon's flanks to the lower forests where the deer lie, and so out upon the desert. In the last verse there is a wonderful contrast between the agitation of earth at one end of the storm, and the glory of the heavenly temple at the other.[2]

In the Song of Songs we have a different aspect of the country: springtime among the vineyards and villages of North Israel, where the poem was composed. The date does not matter:

For, see, the winter has passed,
The rain is over and gone;

[1] Ps. xxix. 3-9.

[2] I feel no reason to depart in this from the Massoretic. But see Cheyne *in loco*, who reads *oaks* for *hinds*.

The flowers appear on the land;
The time of singing is come,
And the turtle dove's murmur is heard in our land.
The fig-tree is reddening her figs,
And blossoming vines give forth their fragrance.

Come, my beloved, let us forth to the field,
Let us lodge in the villages,
Let us early up to the vineyards,
Let us see if the vine flourish,
If its blossom have opened,
The pomegranates bud.
There will I give thee my loves,
The mandrakes are fragrant,
And round our gates are all rare fruits,—
I have stored them for thee, my beloved.

Lebanon is in sight and Hermon:

Come with me from Lebanon,
My bride with me from Lebanon,
Look from the top of Amana,
From the top of Senir and of Hermon.[1]

And the bracing air from snow-fields and pine-forests wafts down

The scent of Lebanon.

There are the shepherds' black tents, the flocks of goats that swarm from Mount Gilead, the sheep that come up from the shearing and washing, and the pomp which now and then passes by the high road across North Israel from Egypt to Damascus—royal litters, chariots, and regiments with banners, heralded by clouds of dust.

I have likened thee, O my love,
To a horse in the chariots of Pharaoh.[2]

What is this up from the wilderness
Like pillars of smoke?

[1] Song ii. 11-13; vii. 11-13; iv. 8. [2] Song i. 9.

Behold! it is the palanquin of Solomon;
Threescore mighty are round it,
Of the mighty of Israel;
Each of them grasping a sword,
Experts in war.
Each with his sword on his thigh,
Against the alarms of the night.[1]

Who is she looking forth like the dawn,
Fair as the moon, pure as the sun,
Glorious as bannered hosts?[2]
I went down to the garden of nuts,
To see the fruits of the valley;
To see if the vine had flourished,
The pomegranates budded.
Or ever I knew,
My soul brought me on the chariots of my willing people.[3]

The text of the last verse is corrupt, but the sense is clear. The country girl has gone into the valley, where she thinks herself alone with the nut-trees and pomegranates, when suddenly a military troop, marching by the valley road, surprise her. We shall see, when we come to Galilee, that the character of the province is that of a garden, crossed by many of the world's high roads. Nothing could better illustrate this character than the procession and pomp, the chariots and banners, which break through the rural scenery of the Song of Songs.

We have no space here for the Hundred and Fourth Psalm, and must refer the reader to the Revised Version. He will find a more comprehensive view of the Holy Land than in any other Scripture, for it embraces both atmosphere and scenery—wind, water and light, summer and winter, mountain, valley, and sea, man and the wild beasts.

Before we pass from the scenery, it may be well to draw the reader's attention to one feature of its description in the Old Testament. By numerous little tokens, we feel that this is scenery described by Highlanders: by men who, for the most part, looked down upon their prospects and painted their scenes from above. Their usual word for valley is *depth*[4]—something below them; for terror and destruction some of their commonest names mean originally *abyss*.[5] God's unfathomable judgements are *depths*, for the narrow

[1] Song iii. 6-8. [2] Imposing. [3] Song vi. 10-12. [4] עמק.
[5] בלע, פחת, etc.

platform of their life fell eastward to an invisible depth; their figure for salvation and freedom is a *wide* or a *large place*.[1] Their stage slopes away from them, every apparition on it is described as *coming up*.[2] And there is that singular sense, which I do not think appears in any other literature, but which pervades the Old Testament, of seeing mountain-tops from above. Israel *treadeth upon his high places*, as if mountain-tops were a common road; and The Lord *marcheth upon His high places*, as if it were a usual thing to see clouds below, and yet on the tops of hills. Joel looks from his high station eastward over the tops of the mountains that sink to the Dead Sea, and speaks of *morn above the mountains* broken and *scattered upon them* by the heavy thunder-clouds. And, finally, we owe to the high station of Israel, those long approaches and very distant prospects both of war and peace: the trails of armies across the plains in fire and smoke, the land spreading very far forth, and, though Israel was no maritime people, the wonderful visions of the coast and the sea.

V. *THE LAND AND QUESTIONS OF FAITH*

These questions have, no doubt, already suggested themselves to the reader, and will do so again and again as he passes through the land—How far does the geography of Palestine bear witness to the truth and authenticity of the different books of the Bible? How far does a knowledge of the land assist our faith in the Word of God and Jesus Christ His Son? It is well for us, before we go through the land, to have at least the possibilities of its contribution in these directions defined, were it for no other reason than that it is natural to expect too much, and that part of the religious public, and some writers for them, exaggerate the evidential value of the geography and archæology of Palestine, and by emphasising what is irrelevant, especially in details, miss the essential contents of the Land's testimony to the divine origin of our religion.

We have seen how freshly the poetry and narrative of the Bible reflect the natural features of Palestine both in outline and in detail. Every visitor to the land has felt this. Napoleon himself may be quoted: "When camping on the ruins of those ancient towns, they read aloud Scripture every evening in

[1] מרחב.

[2] So high the land also appeared from Egypt (Erman, *Life in Ancient Egypt*, trans. by Tirard, 538), and from Mesopotamia (where Ezekiel talks of the Mountains of Israel).

the tent of the General-in-Chief. The analogy and the truth of the descriptions were striking: they still fit this country after so many centuries and changes."[1] This is not more than the truth, yet it does not carry us far. That a story accurately reflects geography does not necessarily mean that it is a real transcript of history, else were the Book of Judith the truest man ever wrote, instead of being what it is, a pretty piece of fiction. Many legends are wonderful photographs of scenery. And, therefore, let us admit that, while we may have other reasons for the historical truth of the patriarchal narratives, we cannot prove this on the ground that their directions and place-names are correct. Or, again, that the Book of Joshua, in marking tribal boundaries, gives us a detailed list of towns, the most of which we can identify, does not prove the date or authorship of these lists, nor the fact of the partition of the land in Joshua's time. Again, that Israel's conquests under Moses east of Jordan went so far north as described, is not proved by the discovery in these days of the towns mentioned. In each of those cases all that is proved is that the narrative was written in the land by some one who knew the land, and this has never been called in question. The date, the accuracy of the narrative, will have to be discussed on other grounds. All that geography can do is to show whether or not the situations were possible at the time to which they are assigned, and even this is a task often beyond her resources.

At the same time, there are in the Old Testament pictures of landscape, and descriptions of the geographical relations of Israel, which we cannot but feel as testimonies to the truth of the narratives in which they occur. If you can to-day follow the description of a battle by the contours, features, and place-names of the landscape to which it is assigned, that is a strong, though not a final, proof that the description is true. One thinks of the battles of the Vale of Elah, Michmash, and Jezreel. And surely it is striking that in none of the narratives of these is any geographical impossibility. Again, nothing that the Pentateuch tells us about the early movements of the Philistines and Hittites disagrees with the evidence we possess from geography and archæology[2]; while Israel's relations to the Philistines in the record of the Judges and early Kings, contrasted with her relations to the same people in the prophetic period, is in accordance with the data of the historical geography of Syria.[3]

[1] "En campant sur les ruines de ces anciennes villes, on lisait tous les soirs l'Écriture Sainte à haute voix sous la tente du général en chef. L'analogie et la vérité des descriptions étaient frappantes; elles conviennent encore à ce pays après tant de siècles et de vicissitudes."—*Campagnes d'Égypte et de Syrie, dictées par Napoléon lui-même*, vol. ii. For similar experiences in the last war, Thompson, *Crusader's Coast*, ii.

[2] See chapter ix on the Philistines.

[3] *Ibid.*, p. 130 f.

As to questions of authorship, the evidence of geography mainly comes in support of a decision already settled by other proofs. One thinks especially of the accurate pictures of the surroundings of Jerusalem given in the prophecies of Isaiah and Jeremiah, both of them her citizens, contrasted with the very different geographical reflection in the earlier prophecies of Ezekiel, or in the second half of the Book of Isaiah. Geography, too, assists us in the analysis of the composite books of the Old Testament into their various documents, for in the Pentateuch, for instance, each document has often its own name for the same locality, and, as has just been said, the geographical reflection in the first half of the Book of Isaiah is different from that in the second half.[1] But in the Old Testament geography has little contribution to make to any question of authenticity, for, with the exceptions stated, the whole of the Old Testament is admitted to have been written by natives of Palestine familiar with their land.

It is different with the New Testament, where authorship outside Palestine is sometimes a serious possibility. Here questions of authenticity are bound up with those of geographical accuracy. Take the case of the Gospel of St. John. It has been held that the writer could not have been a native of Palestine, because of alleged errors in his description of places. I show, in a chapter on the Question of Sychar, that this opinion finds no support in the passage most loudly quoted in its defence.[2] And, again, the silence of the synoptic Gospels concerning cities on the Lake of Galilee like Tiberias and Taricheæ, which became known over the Roman world in the next generation, and their mention of places not so known, has weight in the argument for the early date of the Gospels, and for the authorship of these by contemporaries of Christ's ministry.[3]

But if on all such questions of date, authorship, and accuracy of historical detail, we must be content to admit that geography has not much more to contribute than a proof of the possibility of certain solutions, it is very different when we rise to the higher matters of the religion of Israel, to the story of its origin and development, to the appearance of monotheism, and to the question of the supernatural. On these the testimony of the historical geography of the Holy Land is high and clear.

For instance, to whatever date we assign the Book of Deuteronomy, no one who knows the physical constitution of Palestine, and her relation to the desert, can fail to feel the essential truthfulness of the conception, which rules in that book, of Israel's entrance into the land as at once a rise in

[1] Duhm thinks he can make out that part of Isa. xl-lxvi was composed in Lebanon.
[2] Ch. xviii.
[3] See chapter on the Lake of Galilee, ch. xxi.

civilisation from the nomadic to the agricultural stage, and a fall in religion from a faith which the desert kept simple to the rank polytheism that was provoked by the natural variety of the Paradise west of Jordan.[1] Or take another critical stage of Israel's education: no one can appreciate the prophets' mastery of the historical forces of their time, or the wisdom of their advice to their people, who has not studied the relations of Syria to Egypt and Mesopotamia or the lines across her of the campaigns of these powers.

But these are only details in larger phenomena. In the economy of human progress every race has had its office to fulfil, and the Bible has claimed for Israel the specialism of religion. It represents Israel as brought by God to the Holy Land—as He also carried other peoples to their lands—for the threefold purpose of being preserved through the changes of ancient history, of being educated in true religion, and sent forth to the world as apostles and examples. But how could such a people be better framed than by selection out of that race of mankind which has been most distinguished for its religious temperament, and by settlement on a land both near to, and aloof from, the main streams of human life, where they could be at once spectators of history and yet not its victims, where they could enjoy personal communion with God and yet have some idea also of His providence of the whole world; where they could gather up the experience of the ancient world, and break with this into the modern? There is no land which is at once so much a sanctuary and an observatory as Palestine: no land which, till its office was fulfilled, was so swept by the great forces of history, and was yet so capable of preserving one tribe in national continuity and growth: one tribe learning and suffering and rising superior to the successive problems these forces presented to her, till upon the opportunity afforded by the last of them she launched with her results upon the world. It is the privilege of the student of the historical geography of Palestine to follow this process of development in detail. If a man can believe that there is no directing hand behind our universe and the history of our race, he will say that all this is the result of chance. But for most of us only another conclusion is possible. It may best be expressed in the words of one who was no theologian but a geographer—perhaps the most scientific observer Palestine has ever had. Karl Ritter says of Palestine: "Nature and the course of history show us that here, from the beginning onwards, there cannot be talk of any chance."[2]

But while the geography of the Holy Land has this positive evidence to

[1] See ch. iii, especially pp. 76 ff.

[2] "Die Natur und der Hergang der Geschichte zeigt uns dass hier von Anfang an von keiner Zufälligkeit die Rede sein kann."—K. Ritter, *Ein Blick auf Palästina u. seine christliche Bevölkerung*.

offer, it has also negative evidence to the same end. The physical and political conditions of Israel's history do not explain all the results. Over and over again we shall see the geography of the land forming barriers to Israel's growth, by surmounting which the moral force that was in her becomes conspicuous. We shall often be tempted to imagine that Israel's geography, physical and political, is the cause of her religion; but as often we shall discover that it is only the stage on which a spirit—that, to use the words of the prophets, is neither in her mountains nor in her men—rises superior alike to the aids and to the obstacles which these contribute. This is conspicuous in the case of Israel's monotheism. Monotheism was born not, as Renan says, in Arabia, but in Syria. And the more we know of Syria and of the other tribes that inhabited her, the more we shall be convinced that neither she nor they had anything to do with the origin of Israel's faith. For myself, I can only say that all I have seen of the land, and read of its history, drives me back to the belief that the monotheism which appeared upon it was ultimately due to the revelation of a character and a power which carried the evidence of their uniqueness and divine sovereignty.

But the truth and love of God have come to us in their highest power not as a book, even though that be the Bible, nor as a doctrine, even though that be the monotheism of the Bible, with its intellectual and moral consequences, but as a Man, a native and a citizen of this land: whose education was its history, whose temptation was some of its strongest political forces, who overcame by loyalty to its distinctive gospel,[1] who gathered the significance of its history into Himself, and whose ministry never left its narrow limits. He drew His parables from the fields its sunshine lights, and from the bustle of its daily life; He prayed and agonised for us through its quiet night scenes; He vindicated His mission to mankind in conflict with its authorities, and He died for the world on one of its common places of execution. For our faith in the Incarnation, therefore, a study of the historical geography of Palestine is a necessary discipline. Besides helping us to realise the long preparation of history, Jewish and Gentile, for the coming of the Son of God, a vision of the soil and climate in which He grew and laboured is the only means of enforcing the reality of His Manhood. It delivers us, on the one hand, from those abstract views of His humanity which have been the error and curse of Christianity; and, on the other hand, from what is to-day a more present danger—the interpretation of Christ (prevalent with many preachers to the times) as if He were a son of our own generation.

The course of Divine Providence in Syria has not been one of mere development and cultivation, of building and planting. It has been full also of

[1] See pp. 35, 47 f.

rebuke and frustration, of rooting up and tearing down. Judgement has all along mingled with mercy. Christ Himself did not look forward to the history of the kingdom which He founded as an unchecked advance to universal dominion. He took anything but an optimist's view of the future of His Church. He pictured Himself not only as her King and Leader to successive victories, but as her Judge: revisiting her, and finding her asleep; separating within her the wise from the foolish, the true from the false, the pure from the corrupt, and punishing her with sore and awful calamities. Ought we to look for these visitations only at the end of the world? Have we not seen them fulfilled in the centuries? Has not the new Israel been punished for her sin, as Israel of old was, by the historical powers of war, defeat, and captivity?

It is in the light of these principles of Christ's teaching that we are to estimate the portentous victory of Mohammedanism over Christianity on the very theatre of our Lord's revelation. The Christianity of Syria fell before Islam, because it was corrupt and deserved to fall. And again, in attempting by purely human means to regain her birthplace, the Church was beaten back by Islam, because she was divided, selfish, and worldly. In neither case was it a true Christianity which was overthrown, though the true Christianity bears to this day the reproach and the burden of the results. The irony of the Divine Judgement is clearly seen in this, that it was on the very land where a spiritual monotheism first appeared that the Church was first punished for her idolatry and materialism; that it was in sight of scenes where Christ taught and healed and went about doing good with His band of poor, devoted disciples, that the envious, treacherous, truculent hosts of the Cross were put to sword and fire. They who in His name sought a kingdom of this world by worldly means, could not hope to succeed on the fields where He had put such a temptation from Him. The victory of Islam over Christendom is no more an obstacle to faith than the victory of Babylonia over Israel upon the same stage. *My threshing-floor* said God of these mountains, and so they proved a second time. The same ethical principles by which the prophets explain the overthrow of Israel account for the defeat of Christianity. If the latter teach us, as the former taught them, the folly of making a political kingdom the ambition of our faith, the fatality of seeking to build the Church of God by intrigue and the sword, if it drive us inward to the spiritual essence of religion and outward to the Master's own work of teaching and healing, the Mohammedan victory will not have been in vain any more than the Babylonian. Let us believe that what Christ promised to judge by the visitations of history is not the World, but His Church, and let us put our own house in order. Then the reproach that rests on Palestine will be rolled away.

VI. *THE VIEW FROM MOUNT EBAL*[1]

It may assist the reader to grasp the various features of the Holy Land, which we have been surveying in the last four chapters, if he be helped to see it with his own eyes as it lies to-day. The smallness of Palestine enables us to make this view nearly complete from two points.

First let us stand off the land altogether, and take its appearance from the sea. As we sail north from Jaffa, what we see is a straight line of coast in alternate stretches of cliff and sand, beyond this a Plain varying from eight to thirty miles in width, and then the Central Range itself, a persistent mountain-wall of nearly uniform level, rising clear and blue from the slopes which buttress it to the west. How the heart throbs as the eye sweeps that long and steadfast sky-line! For just behind, upon a line nearly coincident with the water-parting between Jordan and the sea, lie Shechem, Shiloh, Bethel, Jerusalem, Bethlehem, and Hebron. Of only one of these does any sign appear. Towards the north end of the range two bold round hills break the sky-line, with evidence of a deep valley between them. The hills are Ebal and Gerizim, and in the valley, the only real pass across the range, lies Nablus, anciently Shechem.

That the eye is thus drawn from the first upon the position of Shechem—and we shall see that what is thus true of the approach from the west is also true of that from the east—while all the other chief sites of Israel's life lie hidden, and are scarcely to be seen till you come upon them, is a remarkable fact which we emphasise in passing. It is a witness to the natural, an explanation of the historical, precedence enjoyed by this northern capital over her more famous sister, Jerusalem.

But now let us come on to the land itself, and take our second point of view at this, its obvious centre. Of the two hills beside Shechem, Gerizim is the more famous historically, but Ebal is higher and has the further prospect. The view from Ebal virtually covers the whole land, with the exception of the Negeb. All the four long zones, two of the four frontiers, specimens of all the physical features, and most of the famous scenes of the history, are in sight. No geography of Palestine can afford to dispense with the view from the top of Ebal. In detail it is this:

Looking south, you have at your feet the pass through the range, with

[1] For this chapter, see Map 5 and page 56.

Nablus, which has replaced in name and partly in site the ancient Shechem[1]; then over it the mass of Gerizim, with a ruin or two; and then twenty-four miles of hill-tops, at the back of which you dimly discern a tower. That is Nebi Samwil. Jerusalem is only five miles beyond, and to the west the tower overlooks the Shephelah. Turning westwards, you see—you almost feel—the range letting itself down by irregular terraces to the plain; the plain itself flattened by the height from which you look, but really undulating to mounds of one and two hundred feet; beyond the plain the gleaming sandhills of the coast and the infinite blue of the sea. Joppa lies south-west thirty-three miles; Cæsarea north-west twenty-nine. Turning northwards, we have the long ridge of Carmel running down from its summit, perhaps thirty-five miles distant, to the low hills that separate it from our range; over the rest of this the hollow that represents Esdraelon; over that the hills of Galilee in a haze, and above the haze the glistening shoulders of Hermon, at seventy-five miles of distance. Sweeping south from Hermon, the eastern horizon is the edge of Hauran above the Lake of Galilee, continued by the edge of Mount Gilead exactly east of us, and by the edge of Moab away to the south-east. This line of the Eastern Range is maintained at a pretty equal level, nearly that on which we stand,[2] and seems unbroken, save by the incoming valleys of the Yarmuk, and the Jabbok. It is only twenty-five miles away, and on the near side of it lies the Jordan Valley—a wide gulf, of which the bottom is out of sight. On this side Jordan the foreground is the hilly bulwark of Mount Ephraim, penetrated by a valley coming up from Jordan on to the plain of the Mukhneh to meet the pass that splits the range at our feet.

The view is barer than a European eye desires, but softened by the haze the great heat sheds over all. White clouds hang stagnant in the sky, and their shadows crouch below them among the hills, as dogs that wait for their masters to move. But I have also seen the mists, as low as the land, sweep up from the Mediterranean, and so deluge the range that, in a few hours, the valleys which lie quiet through the summer are loud with the rush of water and the rattle of stones; and though the long trails of cloud wrap the summits, and cling about the hillsides, the land looks barer and more raw than in the sunshine. The hills are brown, with here and there lighter shades, here and there darker. Look through the glass, and you see that the lighter are wheat-fields ripening, the darker olive groves, sometimes two miles in

[1] Stanley, *Sinai and Palestine*, 234, calls it "the most beautiful, perhaps, it might be said, the only very beautiful spot in central Palestine", and traces this to its damp atmosphere, quoting Van de Velde.

[2] Ebal is 3077 feet.

extent, not thickly planted like woods in our land, but with the trees wide of each other, and the ground broken up beneath. Had we looked west even so recently as the Crusades, we should have seen Sharon an oak forest from coast to mountain. Carmel is green with its carobs and oak saplings. But near us the only great trees are the walnuts and sycomores of Nablus, immediately below. In valley-beds, or on the brow of a steep slope, but mostly occupying the tops of island-knolls, are the villages. When I looked from here in 1891 there were no farmsteads, villas, nor lonely castles, for the land was still what it had been from Gideon's and Deborah's time—a disordered land, where homes could not safely lie apart. In all the prospect the one town, the most verdant valley, lie at our feet, and the valley flows out on the east to a sea of yellow corn that fills the plain below Gerizim. Anciently more villages would have been visible, and more corn, with vineyards where now ruined terraces add to the stoniness of the hills. In Herod's day the battlement of Cæsarea and its white temple above the harbour would have flashed to us in the forenoon sun; behind Ebal the city of Samaria would have been still splendid and populous; a castle would have crowned Gerizim; there would have been more coming and going on the roads, and the sound of trumpets would have risen oftener from the garrison below. In Christian times we should have seen the flat architecture of the villages, which you can scarce distinguish from the shelves of the mountains, break into churches, with gables, cupolas, and spires. For the century of the feudal kingdom at Jerusalem castles were built here and there, and under their shelter cloisters and farmsteads dared to be where they never could be before or since. That must have been one of the greatest changes the look of the land has undergone.

But during all these ages the long lines of the land would be spread out in the same way as now—the straight coast, and its broad plain; the range that rolls from our feet north and south, with its eastern buttresses falling to the unseen bottom of the Jordan Valley, and across this the level edge of the tablelands of the East.

It is on Ebal, too, that we feel the size of the Holy Land—Hermon and the heights of Judah both within sight, while Jordan is not twenty, nor the coast thirty miles away—and that the old wonder comes strongly upon us of the influence of so small a province on the history of the whole world. But the explanation is also within sight. Down below us, at the mouth of the glen, lies a little heap of brown stones.[1] The road comes up to it by which the

[1] Or did, when the writer was there in 1891; but the Greek Church have built over it. Thompson, *Crusader's Coast*, 120 f. says: "Here was a well, thirty years ago

Patriarchs first entered the land, and the shadow of a telegraph post falls upon it. It is Jacob's well: *Neither in this mountain nor in Jerusalem shall ye worship the Father; but the hour cometh, and now is, when the true worshippers shall worship the Father in spirit and in truth.*

---

left in ruin amid its fig-trees, now with one more church desecrating it. . . . The well is buried in a building."

BOOK TWO

WESTERN PALESTINE

VII. *THE COAST*[1]

"Ante importuosas Asceloni ripas."

Every one remembers, from the map, the shape of the east end of the Levant. An almost straight line runs from north to south, with an inclination westward. There is no large island off it, and upon it no deep estuary or fully sheltered gulf. North of the headland of Carmel nature has so far assisted man by prompting here a cape, and dropping there an islet, that some harbours have been formed which have been, and may again become, historical. When we remember that the ships of antiquity were small, propelled by oars and easily beached, we understand how those few advantages were sufficient to bring forth the greatest maritime nation of ancient times—especially with the help of the mountains behind, which, pressing closely on the coast, compelled the population to push seaward for the means of livelihood.

South of Carmel the Syrian coast has been more strictly drawn. The mountains no longer come so near as to cut up the water with their roots. But sandhills and cliffs, from thirty to a hundred feet high, run straight on to the flat Egyptian delta, without either promontory or recess. A forward rock at 'Athlit, two curves of the beach at Ṭanṭurah, twice low reefs—at Abu Zaburah and Jaffa—the faint promise of a dock in the inland basin of Ashkelon, with the barred mouths of five or six small streams[2]—such are all the possibilities of harbourage on this coast. The rest is merely a shelf for the casting of wreckage and the roosting of sea-birds. The currents are parallel to the coast, and come north laden with sand and Nile-mud, that helps to choke the few faint estuaries and creeks.[3] It is almost always a lee-shore; the prevailing winds are from the south-west.

Of this inhospitality two consequences followed in the history of the land. In the first place, no invader disembarked an army south of Carmel, till the

[1] For this chapter, see Maps 1, 3, 4, 7.

[2] The mouth of the Rubin is seventy yards across, and six feet deep, yet by the bar, *amoncellement du sable*, it can be forded: Guérin, *Judée*, ii. 53. For the other streams, see pp. 104, 112 f., etc.

[3] Admiralty Charts, 2633, 2634. Cf. Otto Ankel, *Grundzüge der Landesnatur des Westjordanlandes*, 32, 33. Thus the Nile has not only created Egypt, but helped to form the Syrian coast. The currents seem to be the reason why Alexander built his harbour at the W end of the Delta and not at Pelusium, which is choked by Nile-mud.

country behind the coast was already in his power. Even invaders from Europe—the Philistines themselves (if indeed they came from Crete),[1] Alexander, Pompey, the first Crusaders, Napoleon, and the British in the Great War, found their way into Palestine by land, either from Egypt or from Asia Minor. Other Crusaders disembarked farther north, at Acre or Tyre, and in the Third Crusade Richard, though assisted by a fleet, won the coast fortresses south of Carmel from the land.[2] But again, this part of the coast has never produced a maritime people. It is true that the name Phœnicia once extended as far south as Egypt[3]; Phœnician masonry has been uncovered at Ṭanṭurah, the name of Arsuf is probably from the Phœnician god Resheph,[4] and we have records of Sidonian supremacy at times over Dora and Joppa, as of Tyrian over Joppa and Ashkelon.[5] But the Phœnicians cannot be said to have been at home south of Carmel. Phœnicia proper lay north of that headland; from Carmel to Egypt the tribes were agricultural, or interested in the land trade alone. It was not till a seafaring people like the Greeks planted their colonies in Sharon and Philistia that harbours were seriously attempted. Of this a striking illustration is given by the generic name of the landing-places from Gaza to Cæsarea. This is not Semitic but Greek: El-mineh, by a usual transposition of the vowel and consonant of the first

[1] See pp. 125 ff.

[2] Richard came to Acre by Cyprus. Philip and Konrad landed there. Frederick II, in 1228, came by Cyprus to Baṭrun, S of Tripoli. Galleys from Venice or Genoa touched at Corfu, Crete, Rhodes, and Cyprus, from which they made for Jaffa as the nearest point to Jerusalem. See Felix Fabri (in *PPT* series), vol. i.

[3] So Strabo; Josephus, xv *Antt.* ix. 6; Pliny, *Hist. Nat.* v. 14, speaks of Joppa of the Phœnicians.

[4] See *Survey Memoirs*, ii. 137 ff. Clermont-Ganneau, *Recueil d'Archéologie Orientale.* M. Ganneau proposed the identification of Horus, Resheph, Perseus, and St. George. The myths of Perseus and St. George were both born on this coast, see p. 161. A stone hawk, which he takes as the symbol of Horus, was found at Arsuf. He adds that Resheph was probably equivalent to Apollo, and in Egypt Apollo and Horus were equal. But the classical name of Arsuf, Apollonia, cannot be used for this identification, and was probably conferred by Apollonius, son of Thraseas, who governed Cœle-Syria for Seleucus Antipater, 1 Macc. x. 69 ff. Rebuilt by Gabinius in 57 B.C., in the Crusades it was besieged by Godfrey, taken by Baldwin, again by Richard; Louis restored the fortifications, and it was destroyed by Bibars in 1265. Cf. Clermont-Ganneau, *PEFQ*, 1896. On Resheph, see S. A. Cook, *Rel. of Ancient Palestine*, etc., 112 ff.

[5] Inscription of Eshmunazar, ll. 18, 19, in the *CIS* i. 19, 20, which records the grant of Dora and Joppa to Sidon. Scylax (*Geographi Græci Minores*, ed. Müller i. 79) assigns Dora to Sidonians and Ashkelon to Tyrians in the Persian period. For Phœnician trade with Joppa, cf. Jonah i. 3, 2 Chron. ii. 16. But the name of Joppa is not in the parallel 1 Kings v. Early notices of Joppa in Amarna Letters, Brit. Mus. 57, 71, Egyptian Travels, Josh. xix. 46, Heb. Yapho.

yllable, is the Greek *Limen*[1]; Leminah is in the Talmud the name for the ort of Cæsarea.[2] The other name for harbour on this coast, Mayumas, has ot been explained.[3]

But the failure even of these attempts to establish permanent ports for eep-sea vessels is a yet stronger proof of the inhospitable character of the oast. Let us take them in series from the north. ‘Athlit has twice been held gainst the rest of Palestine. In A.D. 130 it was the last stronghold of Jewish ndependence: in the thirteenth century the last fortress of the Cross.[4] Yet eaward ‘Athlit is unsheltered. The blunt foreland suggests the only kind of arbour possible on the Syrian shore—a double port facing north and south, vhose opposite basins might compensate for each other's exposure; yet no uch harbour seems to have been attempted. The Crusading ruins at ‘Athlit re numerous and solid: a castle, a church, and remains of a mighty sea-wall. ′et the men who built these built out to sea nothing but a jetty now covered y the waves. Farther south at Ṭanṭurah, the ancient Dora, Merla or La Ierle of the Crusaders,[5] there are also great buildings and the suggestion of double harbour. If this was ever achieved, it has disappeared, and but a ew coasting vessels now put in to the unprotected rock. Cæsarea had a great ort; yet nothing but part of its mole remains. Within the reefs at Minet bu Zaburah the inhabitants of Nablus used to keep a few boats, but little nasonry is visible.[6] At Arsuf[7] there is a tiny harbour, yawning thirty feet etween a jetty and a reef; it is used by fishermen. Every one knows the open

[1] Like Arsuf from Resheph.

[2] למינה, Talmud Jerus., Gittin, i. 1. Cf. Conder, *Tent Work*, p. 283.

[3] Conder makes it equivalent to watering-place.

[4] Then known as Castellum Peregrinorum.

[5] Dor or Dora till recently was identified by all (as in previous edd. of this work f. S. A. Cook, *Enc. Bibl.*) with Dor of the O.T., but against this see below, ch. xix. 'ull details of the history and antiquities of the site in G. Dahl, *Materials for the Hist. f Dor* (1915), and *Bulletin* 4, with Plates of *BSAJ* (1924); *Bulletin* 6, p. 67, reports eposits of fish-scales and shells (there was a purple-fishery off the place) by what 'as probably a temple of a sea-god. About 1050 B.C. (according to Pap. Golenischeff) alled Dora, occupied by Zakkara, a sea-folk "from the isles of Greece or beyond"; "Zakkara vase" and Cypriote ware have been found on it. *Periplus of Scylax* about 50 B.C. assigns it to Sidon. In 219-218 B.C., and 137-138 its holders held it against eleucid forces. Under Zoilus in 104 it may have been destroyed, but was restored y Pompey in 63; its coins dated from then and it was (save possibly for a time under leopatra) in the Rom. Province of Syria. Described as Phœnician in the first cenry A.D. from 64 to 222 it issued its own coins and after decay had in the fifth century bishop till its destruction by the Saracens. For La Merle see *Itin. Ricardi*, iv. 14. onder on doubtful grounds identifies it with el-Mezr‘a between Dor and Cæsarea. n Dor see Garstang, *Josh. Jud.*, 89, 232 n.

[6] The famous water-melons of Mukhalid are exported hence.

[7] See p. 102.

roadstead at Jaffa, with the reefs that are more dangerous in foul weather than they are useful in fair.[1] In olden days Jamnia had a Limen at the mouth of the Nahr Rubin, but the Minet Rubin, as it is now called, is a little way off this, and by a few rocks with some masonry provides only a landing-place for small boats.[2] At the mouth of the Nahr Sukreir the Navy landed supplies for the British Forces in 1917 before they occupied Jaffa. The Limen of Ashdod is now the Minet el-Kulah, with a landing-place between reefs "at which ships occasionally touch".[3] At Ashkelon are visible at low water two shallows of crescent shape, perhaps remains of ancient moles, and at the bottom of the rocky basin, in which the mediæval city was confined explorers have traced the lines of a little dock; but the sand, which drifts up the coast, has choked the dock, and in the sea only a jetty is left.[4] The Limen of Gaza was once a considerable town, if we may judge from the ruins that break from the sand, but the beach is now straight and low, and the roadstead as unsheltered as at Jaffa.

Thus, while the cruelty of many another wild coast is known by the wrecks of ships, the Syrian shore south of Carmel is strewn with the fiercer wreckage of harbours.

I have thrice sailed along this coast on a summer afternoon with the western sun illuminating it, and I remember no break in the long line of foam where land and sea met, no single spot where the land gave way and welcomed the sea to itself. On each occasion the air was quiet, yet all along the line was disturbance. It seemed as if the land were everywhere saying to the sea: I do not wish you, I do not need you. And this echoes through most of the Old Testament. The sea spreads before us for spectacle, for symbol, for music, for promise, but never for use—save when a prophet sought it as an escape from his God.[5] In the Psalms the straight coast serves to illustrate the immovable limits set by the Almighty between sea and land. In the Prophets its roar and foam symbolise the futile rage of the heathen beating on God's steadfast purpose for His people: *Ah! the booming of the peoples the multitudes—like the booming of seas they boom; and the rushing of nations like the rushing of mighty waters they rush; nations—like the rushing of many waters they rush. But He checks it, and it flees far away, and is chased like*

[1] Pliny's description (*H.N.* v. 14) suits the Jaffa of to-day: "Insidet collem præjacente saxo."

[2] Guérin, ii. 54.

[3] *PEF Mem.* ii. 426, all signs of a harbour are covered with drifting sands. Pomponius Mela (first century) gives the *portus* of Azotus as the port for Arabia.

[4] *ZDPV*, ii. 164, with a plan. Guérin, *Judée*, ii. 155.

[5] Though elsewhere, *that go down to the sea in ships, that do business in great waters* are Hebrews, Ps. cvii. 23, 24.

chaff on the mountains before wind, and like swirling dust before whirlwind.[1]

As in the Psalms and the Prophets, so in the History the sea was a barrier and not a highway. From the first it was said: *Ye shall have the Great Sea for a border.*[2] Throughout the language the sea is a horizon: the Hebrew for West is *The Sea.* There were three tribes, who seem to have reached the maritime frontier appointed for them: Dan, who in Deborah's time was *remaining in ships*,[3] but he left them and his bit of coast for the inland sources of Jordan; and Asher and Zebulun, whose territory was not south but north of Carmel. Even in their case no ports are mentioned, the word translated *haven*, in the blessing of Zebulun and in the blame of Asher,[4] being but *beach*, land *washed* by the sea, and the word translated *creeks* meaning no more than *cracks* or *breaks.* Again, when the builders of the second temple hire Phœnicians to bring timber from Lebanon to Joppa, it is not written "to the harbour or creek of Joppa", but to the *sea of Joppa.*[5] So that the only mention of a real harbour in the Old Testament is in the general picture of the storm in Psalm cvii, where the word means *refuge.* Of the name or idea of a *port*, gateway in or out, there is no trace; and, as we have seen, in the name for the port of Cæsarea in the Talmud, Leminah, and in the term still given to some landing-places on the coast, El-Mineh, it is no Semitic root, but the Greek *Limen* which appears. In this inability of their coast-line to furnish the language of Israel with even the suggestion of a port, we have the crowning proof of the peculiar security and seclusion of their land so far as the sea is concerned.

We can now appreciate how much truth there is in the contrast commonly made between Palestine and Greece. In respect of security the two lands do not much differ; the physical geography of Greece is even more adapted than that of Palestine for defence. But in respect of seclusion from the sea, and the world reached by the sea, they differed entirely. Upon almost every league of his broken and embayed coast-line, the Greek had an invitation to voyage. The sea came inland to woo him: by island after island she tempted him to other continents. She was the ready means of commerce, of colonising, and of that change and advantage with other men, which breed openness, originality and subtlety of mind. But the coast of the Hebrew was very different, and from his high inland station he saw it only far off—a stiff, stormy line, down the length of which as there was nothing to tempt men in, so there was nothing to tempt them out.[6]

The effect of a nation's physical environment upon their temper and ideals

[1] Isa. xvii. 12, 13. [2] Num. xxxiv. 6. [3] Judges v. 17. See p. 128.

[4] Gen. xlix. 13; Judges v. 17. [5] Ezra iii. 7.

[6] Hull (*PEF Mem. on Geology of Palestine, etc.*) proves that, at no remote date, the

is always interesting, but can never be more than vaguely described. Whereas of greater interest, and capable of exact definition, because abrupt, imperious and supreme, is the manner in which a nation's genius, by sheer moral force and Divine inspiration, dares to look beyond its natural limits, feels at last too great for the conditions in which it was developed, and appropriates regions and peoples, towards which nature has provided it with no avenue. Such a process is nowhere more evident than in the history of Israel; we find the history not only as in other lands, moulded by the geography, but also breaking the moulds, and seeking new spheres. The first instance of this meets us now. In the development of the religious consciousness of this once desert tribe, there came a time when her eyes were lifted beyond that iron coast, and *her face*, in the words of her prophet, *became radiant and her heart large with the sparkle of the sea: for there is turned upon thee the sea's flood-tide, and the wealth of the nations is coming unto thee. Who are these like a cloud that fly, and like doves to their windows? Surely towards Me the isles are stretching, and ships of Tarshish in the van, to bring thy sons from afar, their silver and their gold with them, to the name of* THE LORD *of Hosts and to the Holy of Israel, for He hath glorified thee. Isles* here are any lands washed by the sea, but what the prophets had chiefly in view were those islands and coasts of the Mediterranean which, within physical sight of the Greek, to the Hebrew could be the object only of spiritual ambition. Six at least are named in the Old Testament. The nearest is Cyprus, whose people are called Kittim, from the town of Ktî or Kition.[1] Cyprus is not in sight of any of the territories of Israel, but its hills can be seen at most times from the hills of northern Syria immediately opposite, and even from southern Lebanon above Beyrout, during a few weeks about midsummer, when the sun sets behind Mount Tröodos, and the peak of that mountain comes out black against the afterglow.[2] It was these glimpses of land in the setting sun, which first drew the Phœnicians westward, and from the Phœnicians the Israelites had their knowledge of them. Beyond Cyprus is Rhodes, and that was called Rodan among the Hebrews and its people Rodanim.[3] Crete was

---

sea washed the foot of the hills. Had this lasted to historical times the story of Judæa and Samaria would be utterly different.

[1] *CIS.* i. 137; cf. Gen. x. 4; Num. xxiv. 24; Isa. xxiii. 1, 12.

[2] So Dr. Carslaw and I saw it, July 1891, from a hill in front of Shuweir, six hours from Beyrout, 5000 feet above the sea. For the converse Felix Fabri, *PPT*, i. 198.

[3] In Ezek. xxvii. 20, for דדן Dedan read רדן Rodan, and in Gen. x. 4, for דדנים Dodanim read רדנים Rodanim, where the LXX have Ῥόδιοι.

known to them under the name Caphtor.[1] These, the only three islands of the Mediterranean mentioned in the Old Testament, were evidently the line of Phœnician progress westward: they are also the three that occur in nearly every mediæval voyage from Syria to Europe.[2] Beyond them loomed to the Hebrews farther and more uncertain coasts. The name Javan came from the Ionians or Iafones, on the Asian shores of the Ægean,[3] but is used of all Greeks down to Alexander the Great.[4] Tubal and Meshech, often mentioned with Javan,[5] were tribes in the interior of Asia Minor. Beyond Javan were the coasts of Elisha,[6] perhaps Sicily, and Tarshish, the Phœnician colony in Spain. To all these ships traded from Tyre and Sidon, Acco and Joppa. Their outward cargoes were wheat, oil, and balm, with Oriental wares, and they brought back cloth, purple and scarlet, silver, iron, tin, lead, and brass.[7] Sometimes they carried west Hebrew slaves[8] and outlaws,[9] forerunners of the Dispersion.

The isles shall wait for His law; let them give glory to Yahweh, and publish His praise in the isles: unto Me the isles shall hope. When, at last, the Jews got their first and only harbour,[10] it was such a prophecy as this which woke up within them. Of Simon Maccabæus it was said: "With all his glory he took Joppa for an haven, and made an entrance to the isles of the sea."[11] The exultation of this—the glad "At last!" audible in it—was natural; and we sympathise with it the more when we learn that this was no mere military operation by Simon, but, according to his light, a religious measure. In those days, when Jews took a town within the promised boundaries, they purged it of the heathen and their idols, and settled in it "such men as would keep the Law".[12] *The Law*, then, was at last established on the sea, with an

[1] This is more probable than that Caphtor should be Kaft-ur, an Egyptian name for the Delta. See notes on p. 126.

[2] Cf. p. 102, n. 2.

[3] Isa. lxvi. 19; Ezek. xxvii. 13, 19. In the last verse, for *Dan also* read *Vedan*, which is unknown.

[4] Dan. viii. 21; x. 20; xi. 2.

[5] Gen. x. 2; Ezek. xxvii. 13. Tubal was the Tibarenians; Meshech the Moscho of Herodotus. Schrader, *KAT*, 82-84.

[6] Gen. x. 4, Elisha, son of Javan; 1 Chron. i. 7; Ezek. xxvii. 7.

[7] Ezek. xxvii. 6, 12, 13, 17. [8] Amos ii. 9. [9] Jonah i. 3.

[10] Ezion-geber was probably held for them, and we speak now of the W.

[11] 1 Macc. xiv. 5: *Καὶ μετὰ πάσης τῆς δόξης αὐτοῦ ἔλαβε τὴν Ἰόππην εἰς λιμένα καὶ ἐποίησεν εἴσοδον ταῖς νήσοις τῆς θαλάσσης*; about 144 B.C. Jonathan had captured Joppa in 148 (1 Macc. x. 76), and in 145 made Simon lord of the coast from the Ladder of Tyre to the Border of Egypt. But this was only nominal, till next year, when the Greek natives of Joppa being about to revolt, Simon occupied it and later (about 141), fortified it.—S. Tolkowsky, *The Gateway of Palestine*, 1924.

[12] So Simon did at Gazara, 1 Macc. xiii. 47, and, we can understand, in Joppa also,

open gate to the isles,[1] and the people of Yahweh had more reason to be rapturous than at any time since the prophecies of their western progress were first uttered. Their hopes, however, were defeated by the rigour of the measures they took to fulfil them. In every town the Hellenised population[2] rose against this fanatic priest from the highlands with no right to the sea, and intrigued for the return of Antiochi or Ptolemies, who allowed them to worship their own gods. It was the old opposition between Philistia and Israel, on the old ground. Twice the Syrians retook Joppa, twice Hyrcanus (Simon's successor) won it back. Then, after twenty years of Jewish possession, Pompey came in 63 B.C., and decreed that, with the other coast towns, it should be free.[3] But in 47 Cæsar excepted Joppa, "which the Jews had originally", and decreed "it shall belong to them, as it formerly did"[4]; and later Augustus added it, with other cities, to Herod the Great's kingdom.[5] Joppa was therefore Jewish as no other town on the Coast or Maritime Plain became, and so continued till the campaign of Vespasian in A.D. 68. It was violently Jewish. Though Joppa was tributary to Herod he never resided there, nor tried to rebuild it, nor to plant heathen features upon it. Alone of the cities of the region, it had no Greek or Latin name attached to it. In close commerce with Jerusalem, Joppa was infected with the fanatic patriotism of the capital; as were rebels and assassins there, so were rebels and pirates here. The spirit of disaffection towards Rome passed through the same crises in the coast-town as in Jerusalem. In the outbreak of 66, when every other town of the Maritime Plain was divided into two camps,[6] and Jews and Hellenised Syrians massacred each other, Joppa remained Jewish, and it was Joppa that Cestius Gallus first attacked on his march to Jerusalem.[7] In the years before the Jews thus took to arms Joppa had doubtless been distinguished by the more peaceful exercises of the same Judaistic spirit. On ground free from heathen buildings and rites the Pharisees must have imitated as far as possible the rigorous measures of the Maccabees, and cherishe- the ancient hopes which the sea inspired in their race, along with petty pred

---

though in a sea-town full of foreigners the task would be more difficult, and not so perfectly accomplished.

[1] For a coin of Alex. Jannæus with an anchor, see *Palestine in General History*, 74 f. with plate.

[2] In the coast-towns at this time, though the bulk of the people were from the old stocks and spoke Aramaic, the upper classes were Greek, and Greek was official; the native deities were amalgamated with Greek counterparts.

[3] Josephus, xiv *Antt.* iv. 4; i *Wars*, vii. 7: "He restored to their own citizens."

[4] Josphus, xiv *Antt.* x. 6; Strabo xvi. ii. 28.

[5] Josephus, xv *Antt.* vii. 3; ii *Wars*, vi. 3.

[6] ii *Wars*, xviii. 2.

[7] *Ib.* 10.

cautions against the foreigners whom it drifted to their feet. This was the state of affairs when Peter came from Jerusalem to Joppa, and dreamt of things clean and unclean on the housetop overlooking the harbour.[1]

If we turn to the neighbouring Cæsarea, we see as great a contrast as possible on the same coast. Was Joppa Jewish, national, patriotic? Cæsarea was Herodian, Roman in obedience, Greek in culture. At first the Herodian strongholds had lain on the east of Palestine, and for the most part in wild places, like Machærus and Masada, as became a family not sure of its station, and sometimes chased from power by its enemies. But when Herod won the favour of Augustus, and time made clear that the power of Augustus was to be permanent, Herod came over the Central Range of Palestine, and on sites granted by his patron built himself cities looking westward. He embellished and fortified both Jerusalem and Samaria. Then he sought a seaport. Augustus had given him Gaza, with Anthedon, Joppa and Straton's Tower.[2] He chose the last, Josephus says because it was more fit to be a port than Joppa. But this was not so. His reasons were political. It was more important for Herod to have a harbour suited to Sebasté than to Jerusalem, for Sebasté was nearer the sea and more in his hands than the Holy City. Besides, Joppa, as we saw, was national rather than Herodian, in spirit. Straton's Tower was a fresh site. Here Herod laid the lines of "a magnificent city", and spent twelve years in building it.[3] He erected sumptuous palaces and edifices for "containing the people", a temple on raised ground, a theatre, and an amphitheatre with prospect to the sea. There were also a number of arches, cellars, and vaults for draining the city, "which had no less of architecture bestowed on them than had the buildings above ground". But the greatest work was the haven. A breakwater 200 feet wide was formed in 20 fathoms by dropping in the waves enormous stones. The half was opposed to the waves, so as to keep off those which were to break upon it, and so was called Procymatia, or "first breaker of waves", while the other half had a wall with towers. There were also arches, where sailors lodged, and before them a quay round the whole haven, "a most pleasant walk for such as had a mind to that exercise". The entrance of the port was on "the north, on which side was the gentlest of all the winds in this place". On the left of the entrance was a round turret, made strong in order to meet the waves, while on the right stood two enormous stones upright and joined together, each larger than the turret opposite.[4] To-day the mole is 160 yards from shore; the mouth of the harbour is 180.[5] This haven had a name to itself—Sebastos

[1] Acts x.
[2] i *Wars*, xx. 3.
[3] Josephus, xv *Antt.* ix. 6; but in xvi *Antt*, v. 1, "ten years".
[4] Josephus, xv *Antt.* ix. 6, abridged.
[5] *PEF Mem.* ii.

Limen—which even dwarfed the name of the city, Cæsarea.[1] In later times the latter is called The Cæsarea beside the August Harbour,[2] and Jews, as we have seen, spoke of the Leminah by itself; for it was *the* harbour, the first real port upon that coast. Cæsarea speedily became, and long continued to be, the virtual capital of Palestine—the one instance of a coast town which ever did so. "Cæsarea Judææ caput est", says Tacitus[3]; he means the Roman province. Judæan in truth Cæsarea never was. The gateway to Rome, the place was a piece of Latin soil.[4] The Procurator had his seat in it, there was an Italian garrison, and on the white temple that shone over the harbour to the sea, stood two statues of Augustus and of Rome.[5] It was heathendom in its glory at the door of the true religion! Yes, but the contrast might be reversed. It was justice and freedom in the most fanatic and turbulent province of the world. In seeking separation from his people, and an open door to the West, Herod had secured these benefits for a nobler cause than his own, to which we now turn.

Peter came to the Joppa described, and it is interesting that he came by Lydda, in those days another centre of Jewish feeling. Joppa, Lydda, and Jerusalem Cestius Gallus marked out as centres of the national revolt.[6] To Jewish Joppa Jewish Peter came; and we understand that as he moved about its narrow lanes, leading to the sea, where his scrupulous countrymen were jostled by foreign sailors and foreign wares, he grew more concerned than ever about the ceremonial law. While food was prepared—observe the legal moment—*he saw*, above this jealous bit of earth, *heaven opened, and a certain vessel descending as it had been a great sheet*—perhaps the sail of one of the large Western ships in the offing—*let down by the four corners to the earth, wherein were all the four-footed beasts of the earth, and wild beasts, and creeping things, and fowls of the air. And there came a voice to him, Rise, Peter, kill and eat! But Peter said, Not so, Lord, for I have never eaten anything common or unclean.* To his conscience the contents had been a temptation. *And the voice said unto him a second time, What God hath cleansed call not thou common!*

[1] *Καισαρεία Σεβαστή*: *Καισαρεία Παραλιός, Καισαρεία ἡ ἐπὶ θαλάττῃ*. Cæsarea Stratonis, Cæsarea Palestinæ, and, after Vespasian Colonia Prima Flavia Augusta Cæsarea. Pliny, *Nat. Hist.* v. 69, and a Latin inscription in the neighbourhood.

[2] On a coin of Nero: *ΚΑΙΣΑΡΕΙΑ Η ΠΡΟΣ ΣΕΒΑΣΤΩ ΛΙΜΕΝΙ*. The coin is given in De Saulcy's *Numismatique de la Terre Sainte*, p. 116.

[3] *Hist.* ii. 78; Josephus, iii *Wars*, iii. 5, extends Judæa to Ptolemais. But in Acts xii. 21 (cf. xxi. 10) Cæsarea is distinct from Judæa. In the Talmud Antipatris is the border-town.

[4] The Jews called Cæsarea the daughter of Edom—their symbolic name for Rome. *Talmud Babyl. Megillah*, 6a.

[5] Josephus as above.

[6] ii *Wars*, xviii. 10.

This was done thrice, and the vessel was received up again into heaven. The vision took place in Joppa, but was fulfilled in Cæsarea. Here, on virtually Gentile soil, amid surroundings not very different from those of Paul's sermon on Areopagus,[1] Peter made his similar declaration, *Of a truth I perceive that God is no respecter of persons; but in every nation he that feareth Him and worketh righteousness is accepted with Him.* In a Roman soldier's house, in face of the only port broken westward through Israel's stormy coast, the Gentile Pentecost took place, and *on the Gentiles also was poured out the gift of the Holy Ghost.*[2]

Again, in the narrative of Paul's missions, Cæsarea is the harbour by which he reaches Syria from Ephesus, and from which he sails on his last voyage for Italy.[3] More significant were his removal to Cæsarea from Jerusalem, and the anxiety of the Jewish authorities to get him back to Jerusalem.[4] In the Holy City they would not give him a hearing; they lay in wait to kill him. In Cæsarea he was heard to the end of his plea; but for his appeal to Cæsar he would have been acquitted, and during two years in which he lived there, receiving friends, and enjoying a certain liberty—though the place had many Jewish inhabitants[5]—no one ventured to waylay him. There were only 60 miles between Cæsarea and Jerusalem, but in A.D. 60 Cæsarea was virtually Rome.

The subsequent history of Herod's harbour repeats what we have learned of it. As long as the land was held by men with interests in the West, the town triumphed over the unsuitableness of its site; but when Palestine passed into the hands of an Eastern people, with no maritime ambitions, it dwindled, and was finally destroyed by them. Cæsarea was Vespasian's headquarters, equally opportune for Galilee, Samaria, and Judæa, and there he was proclaimed Emperor in 69. He also established close by a colony, Prima Flavia Augusta Cæsarea. Very early there was a Christian bishop of Cæsarea, who became Metropolitan of Syria. Origen fled there, and Eusebius was Archbishop from 315-318. When the Moslems came, Cæsarea was the headquarters of Sergius, the Byzantine general: in 638 it was occupied by Abu 'Obeida. Under the Arabs its importance sank. The town continued opulent, but famous only for agricultural products,[6] and Herod's harbour must have fallen into decay. The town was left alone by the first Crusaders, but King Baldwin took it in 1102, and thus passing once more into the hands

[1] Josephus says that the Limen of Cæsarea was like the Piræus; and the great temple and court of justice stood hard by.

[2] Acts x. f. [3] Acts xviii. 22; xxvii. 1. [4] Acts xxv. 3.

[5] ii *Wars*, xiv. 4.

[6] Mukaddasi in the tenth, and Nasir-i-Khusrau in the eleventh, century, quoted by Le Strange, *Pal. under Moslems*, 474.

of seafarers it was re-built, so that the ruins of to-day are mostly of Crusading masonry.[1] Saladin won it in 1187, and reduced it.[2] Richard took it back in 1191, and built it again. Louis of France added fortifications. And then Sultan Bibars, consummating the policy of his race by his destructive march in 1265, on which every coast fortress was battered down, laid Cæsarea low, and scattered its inhabitants. It is said that he himself, pick in hand, assisted at its demolition.[3]

When we come to deal with the strongholds of Samaria, we shall see how Sebasté, only some twenty-five miles inland from Cæsarea, with the same western exposure, suffered similar changes of fortune according as an Eastern or a Western race dominated the country.

VIII. *THE MARITIME PLAIN*[4]

Beyond the forbidding coast there stretches, as you look east, a prospect of plain, the Maritime Plain, on the north cut swiftly down upon by Carmel, whose headland comes within 200 yards of the sea, but at Carmel's other end 6 miles broad, and thence gradually widening southwards, till at Joppa there are 12 miles, and farther south 30 miles between the blue mountains of Judæa and the sea. The Maritime Plain divides into three parts. The corner between Carmel and the sea is bounded on the south by the Crocodile River,[5] the Nahr ez-Zerḳa, and is nearly 20 miles long. From this River the Plain of Sharon, widening from 8 miles to 12, rolls southwards 44 miles to the mouth of the Nahr Rubin and a line of low hills south of Ramleh. The country is undulating, with groups of hills from 250 to 300 feet high. On the north it is largely wild moor and marsh, with long tongues of sand running in from the coast. The marshes on the Zerḳa are intricate, and formed the refuge of Arabs who kept themselves free from the requisitions of the Turkish Government. There is one oak-wood in the very north, and groves of the same scatter southward. These are the remains of a forest so extensive, that it sometimes gave its name to the plain. The Septuagint translates Sharon by *Drumos*.[6] Josephus describes it as the "place called the Forest",[7] or "The Forests",[8] and Strabo as "a great Forest".[9] The Crusaders named

[1] *PEF Mem.* ii. [2] Beha ed-Din, *Life of Saladin*, ch. 35. [3] Makrisi.

[4] For this chapter, see Maps 1, 3, 4, 7.

[5] Pliny, *N.H.* v. 17; Robinson, *Phys. Geog.* 189; *PEF Mem.* ii. 3; *MuNDPV*, 1902, 64; Gray, *PEFQ*, 1920, 167; Masterman, *id.* 1921, 19; 1923, 102.

[6] Isa. xxxv. 2, xxxvii. 24, lxv. 10. [7] i *Wars*, xiii. 2. [8] xiv *Antt.* xiii. 3.

[9] xvi: δρυμὸς μέγας τις.

it the Forest of Assur,[1] Tasso Enchanted Forest,[2] Napoleon Forest of Meski.[3] Now scattered and ragged, it must originally have swept from the heights of Carmel to Aijalon. Besides the streams mentioned, north Sharon is crossed by these perennial waters: the Mefjir or Dead River of the Crusaders,[4] the Iskanderuneh or their Salt River, and the Falik or their Rochetaille.[5] In the other half of Sharon, south of the ʻAujeh in front of the broad vale of Aijalon, there is far more cultivation—fields of corn and melons, gardens, orange-groves, and groves of palms, with strips of coarse grass and sand, frequent villages on mounds, the once considerable towns of Jaffa, Lydda and Ramleh, and the high road and railway to Jerusalem. South of the low hills bounding Sharon, the Plain of Philistia rolls on to the River of Egypt, about 40 miles, rising now and again into gentle ranges 250 feet high, and cut here and there by a deep gully, with running water. But Philistia is mostly level, nearly all capable of cultivation, with few trees, and presenting the view of a vast series of corn-fields. Wells may be dug almost anywhere. The only difficulty to agriculture is the drifting sand, which in places has come 2½ miles inland.

The Maritime Plain possesses a quiet but rich beauty.[6] If the contours are gentle the colours are strong and varied. Along almost the whole seaboard runs a strip of links and downs, sometimes of drifting sand, sometimes of grass and sand together. Outside this border of broken gold is the blue sea, with its fringe of foam. Landward the soil is a chocolate brown, with breaks and gullies, now bare to their dirty shingle and puddles, and now full of green reeds and rushes telling of ample water beneath. Over field and moorland millions of flowers are scattered—poppies, pimpernels, anemones, the convolvulus and the mallow, narcissus and blue iris—*roses of Sharon and lilies of the valley*. Lizards haunt the sunny banks. The shimmering air is filled with bees and butterflies, and the twittering of small birds, hushed now and then as the shadow of a hawk blots the haze. Nor when darkness comes is all a blank. The soft night is sprinkled with glittering fireflies.

Such a plain, rising through the heat by dim slopes to the persistent range of blue hills beyond, presents a prospect of nothing but fruitfulness and peace. Yet it has ever been one of the most famous war-paths of the world.

[1] *Itiner. Ricardi*, iv. 16. One near feudal manor was Casale de la Forest, Röhricht, *Stud. z. mittelalt. Geog. u. Topogr. Syrien's ZDPV*, x. 200.

[2] *Gerusalemme Liberata*, ii, xiii. [3] From the village Miskieh.

[4] But see Röhricht, 251. Nahr el-Ḳaṣab, River of Reeds, of Beha ed-Din, is either the Mefjir or the Falik (Guérin, *Samaria*, ii. 384 ff.).

[5] *Itiner. Ricardi*, iv. 17.

[6] Geologically, raised beaches and sea-beds from the Pliocene downwards to Upper Eocene Sandstone.

It is not only level, it is open. If its coast-line is destitute of harbours, both its ends form wide and easy entrances. The southern rolls off upon the great passage from Syria to Egypt, those illustrious, as well as horrible, ten sandy marches from Gaza—past Rafia, Rhinocolura, "the Serbonian Bog", and the sands where Pompey was stabbed to death—to Pelusium and the Nile. Of this highway between Asia and Africa, along which Thothmes, Ramses, Sennacherib, Cambyses, Alexander, Pompey, Titus, Saladin, Napoleon, Allenby, and other generals have led their armies—of this highway the Maritime Plain is but the continuation.

Nor is the north end of the plain shut in by Carmel, as the view from the sea clearly shows. From the sea the sky-line of Carmel, running south-east, does not sustain its level up to the Central Range. It is bow-shaped, rising from the sea to its centre, and drooping again inland. At the sea end, under the headland, a beach of 200 yards is left, and southwards there is always from a mile to 2 miles between the hill-foot and the shore. But this passage, though often used, by Richard for instance, and by Napoleon on his retreat, is not the historical passage round Carmel, and could not be. Broken by rocks, and difficult to force if defended, the Crusaders called part of it the House of the Narrow Ways, Les Destroits, and Petra Incisa.[1] It is at the other, the inland, end of Carmel that the historical passage lies. Here a number of low hills, with wide passes, and a valley—the Vale of Dothan—intervene between Carmel and the Central Range, and offer alternative routes from the Maritime Plain to Esdraelon. Napoleon, who followed one of these routes on his northern march, has stated his reasons for doing so in words which emphasise the points we consider: "Carmel se lie aux montagnes de Nablouse, mais elle en est séparée par un grand vallon"—that is, the hills of softer formation, whose subdued elevation seems as a valley between the harder heights of Carmel and Samaria. "On a l'avantage de tourner Mont Carmel par la route qui suit la lisière de la plaine d'Esdrelon"—that is, after it reaches the watershed—"au lieu que celle qui longe le mer arrive au détroit de Haifa"—that is, the sea-pass which the Crusaders called Les Destroits—"passage difficile à forcer s'il était défendu".[2] The route Napoleon chose east of Carmel, was of the three which are usually followed the most westerly, for his goal was Acre. From the end of Sharon it strikes due north, past Subbarin, and, descending to the east of the Maḥrakah, reaches Esdraelon at Tell Ḳeimun. The shortest road from Sharon and Egypt to the Phœnician cities, it is now followed by the telegraph wire. Another route leaves Sharon at Khurbet es-Sumrah, strikes north-east up Wady 'Arah to the watershed

[1] *Itiner. Ricardi*, iv. 12, 14. Les Destroits survives in Khurbet Dustrey.
[2] *Campagnes d'Égypte et de Syrie. Mémoires . . . dictées par lui-même*, ii. 55.

at 'Ain Ibrahim, and thence descends to Lejjun, from which roads branch to Nazareth, Tiberias, and by Jezreel to Jordan. A third and more frequented route leaves Sharon still farther south, and, travelling almost due east by a long wady,[1] emerges upon the Plain of Dothan, and thence descends north-east to Jenin in Esdraelon. This road is about 17 miles long, but for Beisan and the Jordan Valley it is shorter than the route by Lejjun, and is, no doubt, the historical route from Egypt to the east of the Jordan and Damascus. On this road, near Dothan, Joseph's brethren, having cast him into a pit, *lifted up their eyes, and behold, a travelling company of Ishmaelites came from Gilead, with their camels, bearing spicery and balm and myrrh, going to carry it down to Egypt.*[2]

To this issue of Sharon into Esdraelon, which is hardly noticed in manuals of sacred geography, too much attention cannot be paid. Its presence is felt by all the history of the land. No pass had more effect upon the direction of campaigns, the sites of battles, or the limitation of Israel's possessions. We shall fully see the effects of it when we come to the Plain of Esdraelon. Here it is enough to mention such facts as illustrate the continuity of Esdraelon and Sharon. In ancient Egyptian records of travel and invasion,[3] names on Esdraelon and the Jordan are almost as frequent as those on the Maritime Plain, and a journey is recounted in a chariot from the Lake of Galilee to Egypt. On this Bethshan and Megiddo, which is Tell el-Mutesellim by Lejjun, and Joppa were stations. In the Bible the Philistines and Egyptians are frequently represented in Esdraelon. It surprises the reader, that Saul and Jonathan came so far north as Gilboa to fight with Philistines, whose border was to the south of them, and that King Josiah should meet the Egyptians at Megiddo. The explanation is found in the easy passage from Sharon to Esdraelon. The Philistines had come by it, either to use the more open entrance into Israel from the north, or to hold the trade route to Gilead;

[1] W. Abu-Nar, afterwards Nahr el-Mefjir.

[2] Gen. xxxvii. 25. The levels on these routes are: The headland of Carmel is some 500 feet above the sea; thence the ridge rises, in over 11 miles, to 1810 feet; thence suddenly sinks to 800 or 1000, the height of the pass by Subbarin to Tell Ḳeimun. Then come, almost at right angles to Carmel, the series of lower ranges—for 8 miles the Belad er-Ruhah, "bare chalk downs, with an average elevation of 800 feet" (*PEF Mem.* ii), fertile but treeless, except on the west slope; then 8 or 10 miles of higher hills, some reaching 1600 feet; then Dothan, then the hills of Samaria. The watershed at 'Ain Ibrahim, where the Lejjun road crosses, is 1100 feet. Dothan is 700. Sharon, at its margin, is 200, and this may be taken as the level of Esdraelon, though Lejjun is over 400 and Jenin over 500.

[3] *Travels of an Egyptian*, I, *R.P.* ii. 107 ff.; *Annals of Thothmes III*, *ib.* 39 ff. Cf. W. Max Müller, *Asien und Europa*, 195 ff., and Schumacher, *Die Ägyptische Hauptstrasse, etc.*, *MuNDPV*, 1903, 4 ff.

the Egyptians had come by it, because making for Damascus and the Euphrates.

Between these, its open ends, the Maritime Plain was traversed by highways, following through all ages much the same direction. Coming up from Egypt, the trunk road crossed the Wady Ghuzzah near Tell el-'Ajjul—Calf's Hill—the pre-historic site of Gaza,[1] a favourite Saracen camp, and in 1917 a Turkish outpost captured by Allenby, and continued through Gaza and past Mejdel to Ashdod, avoiding the coast, for the sand on the Philistine coast drifts far, and is loose.[2] After Ashdod it forked. One branch struck through Jamnia to Joppa, and thence up the coast by Arsuf and Cæsarea to Ḥaifa,[3] with Roman bridges over the streams. The other branch, used in the most ancient times, as well as by the Romans and Saracens, and still the main caravan road between Egypt and Damascus, strikes from Ashdod farther inland, by Ekron to Ramleh,[4] and thence by Lydda, Antipatris and Gilgal to the passes leading to Esdraelon. This road was joined by roads from the hills at Gaza, Ashdod, Ramleh—where the Beth-horon road from Jerusalem, and another from Beit-Jibrin through the Shephelah came in,—at Antipatris, —where the road from Jerusalem to Cæsarea, by which Paul was brought down, crossed it[5]—and near Gilgal and Kakon, where passes descended from Shechem and Sebasté. The inland high-road was also joined by a cross-road from Joppa near Antipatris. All these roads were fairly supplied with water.

The natural obstacles were few and easily turned. The inland road avoided streams and marshes which the coast road had to traverse, and which seem not to have been bridged till the Romans came. Some fortresses, as in the south the Philistine cities, and in the north Arsuf and Cæsarea, might form bases or flanks for lines of defence, but they stood by themselves, and could be turned, as Godfrey turned Cæsarea in the First Crusade. Strong lines were drawn across the Plain at two places that we know of. The deep, muddy bed of the 'Aujeh[6] tempted Alexander Jannæus to build a wall from Kapharsaba to the sea at Joppa, with wooden towers and intermediate redoubts; but "Antiochus soon burnt them, and passed his army that way to Arabia".[7] And Saladin's army, with its left on the fortress of Arsuf, and its right on the Samarian hills, strove to keep Richard back, but was dispersed after two battles.[8] Napoleon's march we know in more detail. He was under

[1] See p. 133, n. 3. [2] *PEF Mem. Jerus.* 427. [3] Royal Egyp. road (Brugsch).

[4] Through Burkah and Beshshit.

[5] The part through the hill-country was traced by Eli Smith in 1840.

[6] "The Crooked" also "River of the Father of Peter" by Moslem chroniclers (Le Strange, pp. 54 f.), scene of battles between rival Moslems A.D. 750, 884, 975. Crusaders called it La Grande Rivière.

[7] Josephus, xiii *Antt.* xv. 1. Cf. i *Wars*, iv. 1. [8] *Itiner. Ricardi*, iv. 14-24.

the necessity of taking two fortresses, Gaza and Joppa, and was attacked by a body of Samarians from Nablus as he passed Kakon. His experiences may be taken as those likely to have happened to most invaders from north and south, except that when it was the Jews who opposed the invader, they came down Aijalon, and flung themselves across his path from Lydda, Gezer, and Joppa.

We now see why the Maritime Plain was so famous a war-path. It is really not the whole of Palestine which deserves that name of The Bridge between Asia and Africa, but this level and open coastland along which the embassies and armies of the two continents passed to and fro, not troubling themselves, unless provoked, with the barren, awkward highlands to the east. So Amenhotep II and Thothmes III passed north to the Hittite frontier and the Euphrates. So came Sety and the Ramses. So, from 740 to 710, Tiglath-Pileser, Shalmaneser, and Sargon swept south across Jordan and Esdraelon to the cities of the Philistines, entering Samaria, whose gateways they found at Jenin and Kakon,[1] but leaving Judah alone. So, in 701, Sennacherib marched his army to the borders of Egypt, and detached a brigade for the operations on Jerusalem, which Isaiah had described. So Necho went up to the border of Assyria, and Nebuchadrezzar came down to the border of Egypt. So Cambyses passed and left Judah alone. So Alexander the Great passed between his sieges of Tyre and of Gaza, and passed back from Egypt to Tyre, entering Samaria by the way to punish the inhabitants of Shechem.[2] So the Antiochi from Syria and the Ptolemies from Egypt surged up and down in alternate tides, carrying fire and rapine to each other's borders. From their hills the Jews could watch the spectacle of war between them and the sea—the burning villages, the swift, busy lines of chariots and cavalry—years before Jerusalem herself was threatened.[3] When Judas Maccabæus burnt the harbour and ships at Jamnia, "the light of the fire was seen at Jerusalem, two hundred and forty stadia off".[4] Roman legions marched and counter-marched too often to mention, and made roads and bridges, some lasting to this day.

In the first Moslem assaults the Maritime Plain bore less of the brunt than the east of the land, but in the European invasions of the eleventh to the thirteenth centuries the Plain was, as in Greek and Roman times, scoured by war. While Godfrey and the First Crusade passed unhindered from Ḥaifa to Ramleh,[5] Richard and the Third Crusade had to skirmish every league of

[1] Jenin on Esdraelon, Kakon on Sharon.
[2] The account of his march into Jerusalem is fictitious.
[3] Isa. v. 26 ff.
[4] 2 Macc. xii. 9. The real distance is about 300 stadia.
[5] William of Tyre, vii. 22.

the way with an enemy that harassed them from the Samarian valleys, and to fight one battle under Arsuf, and another east of Joppa.[1] On the Philistine Plain innumerable conflicts, sieges, and forays took place, for while the Latin kingdom of Jerusalem lasted, it met here the assaults of the Egyptian Moslems, and when Richard came he had here at once to repel the sallies of the Moslem from Jerusalem, and intercept the aid coming to them from Egypt. In 1265 Bibars came north and so demolished the fortresses that some, like Ashkelon and Cæsarea, famous for centuries before have been desolate ever since. But this garden of the Lord was never more violated than when Napoleon, in the spring of 1799, brought up his army from Egypt, or when, in the heat of summer, he retreated, burning the towns and harvests of Philistia and massacring his prisoners.[2]

A different story is that of General Allenby's advance in November 1917, after taking Beersheba and Gaza, with help from air and from sea. Suffering want of water but hardened by vigorous training during the previous months, and assisted with supplies by railroad, steamer, and camels, the three Corps of the British Army, two diagonally from Beersheba over the Judæan hills and the Shephelah and one directly north from Gaza, mastered by severe fighting successive lines and positions of the German-Turkish defence, often behind broad barriers of prickly pear or on rocky ridges, all from November 1 to noon on November 16, when they occupied Jaffa. Never were invaders more welcome to the natives to whom their victories meant at last peace and security from exactions.[3]

Not only war swept the Maritime Plain. The Plague came up this way from Egypt. Throughout antiquity the north-east corner of the Delta was regarded with reason as its home. The natural conditions of disease were prevalent. The eastern branch of the Nile, then entering the sea at Pelusium, supplied a stretch of mingled salt and fresh water under a high temperature.[4] To the west there is the swampy Delta; and on the Asian side sand-hills, with brackish wells. Along the coast there appear to have been a number of lagoons, separated from the sea by bars of sand, and used as salt-pans.[5] In Greek and Roman times the largest was known as the Serbonian Bog or Marsh.[6] It had an evil repute. The dry sand blowing across it gave the

[1] *Itiner. Ricardi*, as above.

[2] *Op. cit.* ii. 109. Wittmann, *Travels*, pp. 128, 136.

[3] Massey, *How Jerusalem Was Won*, chs. x-xii; see further below, pp. 196 ff.

[4] Always accompanied by fevers, as round the Gulf of Mexico.

[5] Cf. Martin Baumgarten's *Travels* (1507) in Churchill's Collection, i. 410.

[6] λίμνη Σερβωνίς, Strabo, i. iii. 4, and Diod. Sic.; *Serbonis Lacus*, Pliny, *Nat. Hist.* v. 13; Ptol. iv. 5, § 12, 20. Cf. *Fragmenta Hist. Graec*, ii. 391, Reinach's *Textes*, 14 f. It lay parallel to the sea, and was about 200 stadia by 50. See Stark's *Gaza*, 270 ff.

appearance of solid ground, which was sufficient to bear those who ventured only till they were beyond flight or rescue, and it swallowed part of more than one unfortunate army.[1] In Justinian's time, the "Bog" was surrounded by salt-makers and fishcurers; filthy villages of underfed and imbecile people, who always had disease among them.[2] The extremes of temperature are excessive. It was a state similar to that observed in an outbreak of plague in Astrakhan.[3] Armies from the north reached these unhealthy conditions exhausted by their march across the desert. Those from the south picked up the infection, with the possibility of its breaking out, when the desert was passed, in the damper climate of Syria. Their camps, their waste and offal, with an occasional collapse of their animals in a sandstorm, were frequent aggravations.[4]

Relevant instances are not few. Here Sennacherib's victorious army was infected by pestilence, and melted north like a cloud; here in Justinian's time the Plague started more than once a course across the world; here a Crusading expedition showed symptoms of the Plague; here, in 1799, Napoleon's army was infected and carried the disease into Syria: while the Turkish force marching south in 1801 found the Plague about Jaffa and in the Delta.[5]

These facts provide us with a probable explanation of two records of disease in the Old Testament. The Philistines, who occupied the open door by which the infection entered Syria,[6] were struck when in camp against

[1] Diod. Sic. i. 5 gives a graphic account of this. Artaxerxes Mnemon lost part of his army here in 350. Cf. *Paradise Lost*, ii; Felix Fabri, *PPT*, ii. 470.

[2] Gibbon.

[3] *On the Outbreak of Plague in Astrakhan*, 1878-79, by Dr. Giovanni Cabriadus, *Transactions of the Epidemiological Society*, vol. iv, pt. iv, 449. Cf. *Reports of the German and English Commissions*, *ib.* vol. iv, 362, 276; also W. J. Simpson, *Report on the Causes of the Plague in Hong-kong*, 1903.

[4] Baumgarten in 1507 saw such a collapse: "10,000 sheep and asses and other creatures lying on the ground rotten and half consumed, the noisome smell of which was so insufferable that we were obliged to make all haste"; these were herds which the Sultan of Egypt had seized in Syria in default of tribute. Cf. the tribute Isaiah describes going down to Egypt, xxx. 6: *Oracle of the Beasts of the Negeb*. In the year 189 of the Hegira was the plague of 'Amwas, Clermont-Ganneau, *Arch. Res.* i. 489. See Wittmann, *Travels*, 122 f.

[5] On Sennacherib, see my *Isaiah*, i. On the Plague in Justinian's time, Evagrius, xxix; Gibbon, xliii; on Napoleon, *Memoirs of Campaigns*; Walsh, *Journal of the late Campaign in Egypt*, 1803, p. 136; Wittmann, *Travels*, chs. viii, x, xi on Plague and Ophthalmia in Maritime Plain. Volney, who says (*Travels*, i, 253) that the Plague always on the coast is brought from Greece and Syria, ignores the fact that its home was in the NE corner of the Delta.

[6] All the Commissioners of Inquiry on the Plague of Astrakhan were not convinced that the infection can be carried by clothes, but the Germans had no doubt that it was

Israel by two symptoms of the Plague—tumours in the groin and sudden, numerous deaths.[1] Among the Israelites, again, the only country which gave its name to a disease was Egypt. *All the sore sicknesses of Egypt of which thou art afraid* is a curse in Deuteronomy, eloquent of the sense of frequent infection from that notorious quarter. One of these sicknesses is specified as the *Boil* or *Tumour of Egypt*.[2] That it occurs in the singular number may be due to its being a continuous eruption on the body, but it seems rather to mean a solitary tumour, and it is interesting that in modern instances the tumours have generally been one on each person, while in India a local name for the Plague is The Boil.[3]

However this may be, it seems certain that Israel was sometimes attacked by epidemics, which, starting from the north-east corner of Egypt, travelled by the desert route to Syria, and passed up the avenues of trade from the Maritime Plain. The Philistines, as traders, would stand in special danger of infection.

These, then, were the contributions of the Maritime Plain to the history of Israel. It was a channel always busy with Commerce, and often scoured by War and the Plague.

The positions of the cities of the Maritime Plain are of interest. We have surveyed those on the coast. Those inland are in two groups. Coming from the north, we find no inland town of consequence till the ʻAujeh is passed,

---

caused by the carriage of spoil of war.—*Trans. of Epidem. Soc.* iv. 376 ff., *Report of German Commission*; cf. *The Account of the Endemic Plague in India*, *ib*. p. 391, where it is said that it is traders who are mostly attacked. Cf. *Brit. Med. Journ.*, Nov. 7, 1896.

[1] The name of that with which they were smitten, עפלים, ʻŏphālîm, is *swellings* or *boils*, 1 Sam. v. 6, 9, 12; and the offerings to avert the calamity were not only golden boils but golden mice, the symbol of the Plague, *ib*. vi. 5. In Ustinow's Jaffa collection are images of mice, *PEFQ*, 1893, 294, 306; 1894, 189. Cf. Herodotus' account of the disaster to Sennacherib, in which mice play a part, ii. 1. The disease which beset Napoleon's army in Philistia was the same—a *fièvre à bubons*.

[2] Deut. vii. 15, xxviii. 60; *pestilence in the way*, or *after the manner*, *of Egypt*, Amos iv. 10. The Boil (=שחין shĕḥîn) is both a single tumour like a carbuncle, as in 2 Kings xx. 7, and an extensive eruption, as in Job ii. 7, where it is supposed to be elephantiasis. In Deut. xxviii. 27, 35 it is a disease of the skin, *from the sole to the crown*.

[3] *Trans. of the Epidem. Soc.* iv, pt. i, 129 ff., *On Plague and Typhus Fever in India*, Surgeon-General Murray. On solitary tumours, *id. Report of German Commission on the Astrakhan Plague*, 376, and cases by Dr. Cabriadus, *id.* iv, pt. iv, 449, and Colville's *Notes on Plague in Province of Baghdad*, *id.* iv, pt. i, 9, where the sign of Plague was an enlargement of glands in groin or armpit. Rev. T. G. Selby tells me that in 1894 in Hong-kong the plague, with swellings in the armpits and on the loins, was preceded by great mortality among rats, and similarly in Central China.

and then the first group appear at the mouth of the Vale of Aijalon. The second group are separated from these by low hills on the Nahr Rubin, and are the towns of Philistia.

The incoming Vale of Aijalon explains the first group—Ramleh, Lydda and her sisters, with, perhaps, Antipatris. Lydda, or Lod, with Ono a little farther out on the plain, and Hadid, on the edge of the hills behind, formed the most westerly Jewish settlements after the Exile. The returned Jews pushed down the only broad valley from Jerusalem till they touched the edge of the thoroughfare which sweeps past it. The site of their settlements was named the Ge-haḥarashim—*Valley of the Smiths* or *Craftsmen*, a recollection of the days when there was no *ḥarash* in Israel, but Hebrews came down to the Philistine border to get their plough-shares and mattocks sharpened.[1] The frontier position of Lydda—according to Josephus, "a village not less than a city"—made it the frequent subject of battle and treaty between the Jews and their successive enemies.[2] Like other inland towns of Sharon, it appears not to have been fortified. It was one of the centres of Jewish feeling throughout Roman times, and on the destruction of Jerusalem formed a refuge for the leaders of Judaism. After one or other of those revolts of despair, into which the Jews burst during the second and third centuries, Lydda emptied of everything Jewish was made pagan under the name of Diospolis.[3] Judaism disappeared, but Christianity survived, and finally got the upper hand. There was a Bishop of Diospolis in the fourth century, and a Synod of Diospolis, at which Pelagius was tried, early in the fifth.[4] The Christian interest of Lydda, however, centres round her St.

[1] I Sam. xiii. 19. Lod, Ono, and Hadid are not given in Joshua (only in I Chron. viii. 12); but Ezra ii. 33 implies they were Jewish towns before the exile, cf. Neh. vii. 37. Neh. xi. 35 relates their rebuilding, and gives the name of the district, גֵּי הַחֲרָשִׁים—LXX, γῆ Ἀρασείμ. Conder suggests Ḥarashim "in the present Hirshah", *PEFQ*, 1878, 18.

[2] Especially between Syrians and Jews, and Romans and Jews. It was confirmed by Ptolemy to Jonathan, I Macc. xi. 34, and by Cæsar, with the right to make it Jewish, xiv *Antt.* x. 6; capital of a toparchy, iii *Wars*, iii. 5. For its adherence to the national side, and occupation by Cestius Gallus, see p. 139, as by Vespasian, iv *Wars*, vi. That he met no opposition was due to the town's want of fortification.

[3] This is supposed to have happened as early as Hadrian, when Jerusalem was desecrated. But Schlatter, *Zur Topographie u. Geschichte Palästinas*, No. 2, sets the change under Septimius Severus about A.D. 202, when Beit-Jibrin was put under a Greek name. The earliest coins found of Diospolis bear "L. Septimia Severa Diospolis". Eusebius and Jerome know that name, though neither Diospolis nor Lydda is the subject of an article in the *Onomasticon*, but Diospolis occurs in fixing towns like Arimathæa, Addara, Adithaim, etc.

[4] 415. He got off, to the wrath of Jerome: *Dialogi adv. Pel.*

George. There is no hero whom we more frequently meet in Palestine, and especially east of Jordan. Indeed, among the saints, there was none with a history like his, who from obscure origins became not only virtual patron of Syrian Christendom, and an object of Moslem reverence, but patron as well of the most western of Christian peoples. St. George of Lydda is St. George of England; he is also venerated in Moslem legend. This triple fame is due to his martyrdom on the eve of the triumph of Christianity (to the early Church George is Megalo-martyr and Tropaiophoros), the neighbourhood of his shrine to the scene of a Greek legend, the removal of his relics to Zorava in Hauran, where his name rapidly spread, and the effect of all this Syrian reputation, first upon the Moslems before they grew impervious to Christian influences, and then on the Crusaders at a crisis in their first invasion. The original George was a soldier of good birth, and served as a tribune under Diocletian. In 303 he was martyred. According to some, Lydda was the scene of his martyrdom; others place there the property of his family, but say that he suffered in Nicomedia.[1] In either case Lydda received his relics; through the following centuries pilgrims visited his tomb in the town,[2] and there was a monastery dedicated to him. A church had stood in Lydda from the earliest times, but was destroyed on the approach of the First Crusade. A new cathedral was built by the Crusaders over the tomb, and partly because of this, but also in gratitude for the intervention of the saint in their favour at Antioch, they dedicated it to him. It was a great pile, capable of use as a fortress. So, on the approach of Richard, Saladin destroyed it. Richard, who did more than any to identify St. George with England,[3] is said to have rebuilt the church; there is no record of this, and it is more likely that the great bays which the traveller to-day admires are the ruins that Saladin made.[4] By Crusading times the name of the saint had displaced both Diospolis and Lydda, and the town might have been called St. George till now but for the break in Christian pilgrimage from the sixteenth

[1] Eusebius, *Eccl. Hist.* viii. 5, tells of "a certain man of no mean origin, but highly esteemed for his temporal dignities", who, in Nicomedia, tore down Diocletian's edicts against Christianity, and then heroically met death.

[2] Antonini Placentini, *Itinerarium* (*cir.* 570), c. 25: "Diospolis . . . in qua requiescit Georgius martyr." The same sentence confounds Diospolis with Ashdod and Cæsarea. Arculf, before 683, Willibald, 728, and Bernard, 865, also mention the tomb. The church does not appear to have been dedicated to St. George; travellers quote only the monastery and the tomb.

[3] It was under Edward III that St. George became patron of England.

[4] Robinson's reasons against Richard's building seem conclusive, *Bib. Res.* iii. 54 f.; De Vogüé, *Les Églises de la Terre Sainte*, 363 ff. with plans. Cf. Phocas, 39; Beha ed-Din, ch. 121.

to the eighteenth centuries.[1] The Arabs have perpetuated the Hebrew Lod in their Ludd.

The connection of St. George with a dragon can be traced to the sixth century. It was probably due to two sources—the coincidence of the rise of the martyr's fame with the triumph of Christianity, and, as M. Clermont-Ganneau has argued, the conveyance to St. George of the legend of Perseus and Andromeda. Near Lydda—at Arsuf or Joppa—Perseus slew the sea-monster which threatened the virgin; and we know how Christian saints have been served heir to the fame of heathen worthies who preceded them in the reverence of their respective provinces. But the legend has an even more interesting connection. Mohammedans, who usually identify St. George with the prophet Elijah—El-Khaḍr,[2] the forerunner of Messiah—at Lydda confound his legend with another about Christ Himself. Their name for Antichrist is Dajjal, and they have a tradition that Jesus will slay Antichrist by the gate of Lydda. This notion sprang from a bas-relief of St. George and the Dragon on the Lydda church. But Dajjal may be derived, by a common confusion between *n* and *l*, from Dagon, whose name two neighbouring villages, Dajun and Bet Dajon, bear to this day, while one of the gates of Lydda used to be called the Gate of Dagon.[3] If the derivation be correct, it is indeed a curious process by which the monster symbolic of heathenism conquered by Christianity has been evolved out of the first great rival of the God of Israel. And could there be a fitter scene for such a legend than the town where Hebrew touched Philistine, Jew struggled with Greek, and Christendom contested with Islam? To-day the population is mostly Mohammedan,[4] and part of the cathedral a mosque; but there is still a Christian congregation in Lydda, who worship in the nave and an aisle; and once a year, on the anniversary of their saint, whom even Moslems reverence, they are permitted to celebrate Mass at the high altar over his tomb.[5] Lydda has long been noted for the grey olive groves which surround it.

About 700 Lydda suffered one of her many overthrows. The Arab general[6] who was the cause saw the necessity of building another town in the neigh-

[1] So in Crusading documents (*ZDPV*, x. 215), but as late as 1506, in *Die Jerusalemfahrt des Caspar von Mulinen*: "Und reit der Herre fon Ramen und der Herre fon Sant Joergen uncz gon Jaffen" (*ZDPV*, xi. 195).

[2] Or El-Khiḍr, "the ever-green" or "ever-youthful", a mythical figure originally heathen, personifying the animating power of nature.

[3] Clermont-Ganneau, *PEF Mem.* ii. Cf. *PEFQ*, 1895, 114.

[4] Some 5000 out of about 7000; the rest are of the Orthodox Greek Church.

[5] Details of the above not in Clermont-Ganneau's papers are in Guérin's *Judée*, i. On Elijah, St. George, El-Khaḍr, *ZDPV*, 1894.

[6] Suleiman, son of the Khalif 'Abd-el-Melek, according to Abulfeda.

bourhood to command the junction of the roads from the coast to the interior with the caravan route from Egypt to Damascus. He chose a site nearly 3 miles from Lydda, and called it Ramleh, "the sandy"; no other feature characterises it; though owing to its position and the fertility of the surrounding fields it enjoyed for a long time considerable prosperity. Like the cathedrals of the plains of Europe the mosque has a lofty tower, from which the convergent roads may be surveyed for miles. Ramleh was once fortified. It suffered the varying fortunes of the wars of the Crusades, and after it became again Mohammedan, in 1266, its Christian convent provided shelter for pilgrims to Jerusalem.[1]

In 1917 Allenby's Army, having captured the Abu Shusheh ridge and driven the enemy northwards on the Maritime Plain, detachments of Australian and New Zealand Cavalry, along with the Inverness Battery of Artillery, entered Ramleh on the forenoon of November 15, and advancing by the Lydda road, on which they dispersed a Turkish column in retreat and too weak to offer resistance, peacefully occupied Lydda itself. Of all these operations the result was to split in two the German-Turkish host.[2]

From Ramleh it is a long way back in time to Antipatris. Antipatris was a creation of Herod, and appears to have been built not as a fortress, but as a peasant residence. Its site was probably not where Robinson placed it, at Kefr Saba, but southward at Ras el-'Ain near El-Mir. Here is the wealth of water which Josephus describes, as well as ruins sufficient to demonstrate that the site was once of importance.[3]

[1] Pilgrims used to wait here till the frequently delayed permission was granted them to go on to Jerusalem. Felix Fabri, i, etc., etc.

[2] *Military Operations, Egypt and Palestine*, 181.

[3] Robinson, *Bib. Res.* ii. 45-47. The credit of the other site is due to the *PEF* Survey under Conder (see *Mem.* ii. 258 ff.). Though Josephus says Antipatris was on the site of Kefr Saba (xvi *Antt.* v. 2), he describes it more generally as in the Plain of Kefr Saba (ii *Wars*, xxi. 9). Šanda, *Untersuchungen zur Kunde des Alten Orients* chooses Mejdel Yaba. See my art. in *Enc. Bibl.*

IX. *THE PHILISTINES AND THEIR CITIES*[1]

The singularity and importance of the Philistine towns demand their separation from the rest of the Maritime Plain, and treatment by themselves.

The cities of the Philistine League were five—Gaza, Ashkelon, Ashdod Ekron,and Gath; but Jamneh, or Jamniel, was associated with them. Only, one, Ashkelon, is on the sea; the others dominate the trunk-road which through Philistia keeps inland. None lie north of the low hills by the Nahr Rubin. These facts, with the well-known distinction of the Philistines from the Canaanites or Phœnicians, point to an immigration from the south and an interest in the land trade.

This is confirmed by all we know of the history of this people. In the LXX the name Philistines is generally translated by Allophuloi (Vulg. *aliegenæ*) "aliens"; and it has suggested a derivation from *falash*, a Semitic root, "to migrate".[2] In the Old Testament there is a distinct memory of such a migration: *O children of Israel, saith Yahweh, have I not brought up Israel out of the land of Egypt, and the Philistines from Caphtor, and the Syrians from Kir? The Caphtorim, which came forth from Caphtor, destroyed the Avvim, which dwelt in open villages as far as Gaza, and dwelt in their stead.*[3] Where the Philistines came from, and what they originally were, is not clear. That they moved up the coast from Egypt is certain[4]; also that they came from Caphtor.

[1] For this chapter see Maps 4 and 7.

[2] The name was not given by the Semites, Hebrews or Canaanites. That it was the Philistines' name for themselves appears from its use by other peoples in connection with them. In Egyptian inscriptions it is Purasati; in Assyrian Pulistav and Pilista; Schrader, *KAT*, 102, 103, argues that by Pilista Assyrians meant Judah as well as the Philistine cities—a remarkable precedent for the Greek Philistia extended across the whole country behind. Pelesheth has a Semitic appearance which Pelishtim, showing the root to be quadriliteral, has not. The name is supposed to survive in localities in the Shephelah—Ḳeratiyeh el-Fenish by Beit-Jibrin, 'Araḳ el-Fenish, Bestan el-Fenish—also at Laṭrun, Ṣoba, 'Amwas, and Khurbet Ikbala. All these are on the border of Philistia, and the name does not occur elsewhere. Conder in *PEF Mem.* iii. 294, Cl.-Ganneau, *Arch. Res.* I. 497, Pietschmann *Gesch. der Phön.* 253 f., Macalister, *The Philistines*, etc. (1911).

[3] Amos ix. 7; Deut. ii. 23.

[4] From the unlikelihood of their landing on the coast, traces in O.T. of their settlement S of Gaza before they occupied it (the stories of the patriarchs and Bk. of Joshua), and Gen. x. 14, whether you read the clause in brackets as it stands, or at the end of the verse. Pathrusim and Casluhim are practically Egypt; *out of whom* should be *whence*. But some take this as a gloss.

But it by no means follows that Caphtor and Egypt are the same region.[1] On the contrary, Caphtor seems to be outside Egypt[2]; and as the Philistines are also called Kerethîm,[3] the connection between Egypt and Crete was always close, and traditions trace the inhabitants of Palestine to Crete, it appears more safe to identify Caphtor with that island.[4] But to have traced the Philistines to Crete is not to have cleared up their origin, for early Crete was full of tribes from both east and west.[5] The attempt has been made to derive the name Philistine from the Pelasgians, or a Pelasgic clan called Peneste, and to prove that Philistine names and institutions are Aryan.[6] But Crete shows signs of having been once partly colonised by Semites, and it is possible that some of these, after contact with Greek tribes, returned eastward.[7] In that case their natural goal, as with the east-faring Greeks, would be, not the harbourless coast of South Syria, but the mouths of the Nile. Now, the little

[1] Ebers (*Ægypten u. die Bücher Mosis*) and Sayce (*Races of the O.T.* 53-54, 127) asserted that Caphtor is Kaft-ur, "the greater Phœnicia", applied to the Delta by the Egyptians. Later (*Academy*, 1894) Sayce withdrew his acceptance of Ebers' etymology; "it cannot be a compound of Kaft and the Eg. *ụr*, great. But the spelling equally shows that W. Max Müller is incorrect in making Kaft a part of Asia Minor. The Decree of Canopus states that Kaft was Phœnicia." Reland (p. 74) placed Caphtor "in ora Maritima Ægypti contra Pelusium", and "suspected" a connection between Pelusium and Pelesheth. Plutarch's *De Isi et Osiri*, xvii, speaks of a youth, Pelusius or Palæstinus, after whom Isis names Pelusium. *PEFQ*, 1931, 203 ff., "Caphtor, Keftiu and Cappadocia", by G. A. Wainwright, B.Litt.

[2] I cannot think that, if Caphtor had been part of the Delta, it would have been given as distinct from Egypt, Amos ix. 8. On the other hand, the reason given by Dillmann (on Gen. x. 14), that אִי is applied to Caphtor in Jer. xlvii. 4, is not conclusive, for אִי is also applicable to the Delta coast.

[3] Zeph. ii. 5; Ezek. xxiv. Cf. 1 Sam. xx. 14.

[4] That Caphtor is not mentioned in Gen. x. 4, with other Mediterranean islands, as a son of Javan, is due to this that Crete was regarded as connected, not with the N but with the S coast of the Mediterranean. The arrangement in Gen. x is not ethnological, but mainly geographical. The traditions referred to above are the connection which the inhabitants of Gaza alleged between their god Marna and the Cretan Jove, and Tacitus, *Hist.* v. 2: "Judæos Creta insula profugos, novissima Libyæ insedisse, memorant, qua tempestate Saturnus vi Jovis expulsus cesserit regnis." He explains this tradition by the analogy between Idæi, from Mount Ida, and Judæi. But these late traditions may have risen from a connection between Crete and the Philistine coast in Hellenic times. Gaza had then great trade with the west.

[5] Cf. *Odyssey*, xix. 170 ff. Achæans, Kydonians, Dorians, Pelasgians, and aboriginal Cretans—ἐτεόκρητοι.

[6] Hitzig, *Urgeschichte u. Mythologie der Philistäer*, where extraordinary Sanscrit analogies are suggested. The argument is still more overdone in Schenkel's *Bibel-Lexicon*. Phil. *seren* may be τύραννος, but also =*axle*.

[7] Knobel's opinion (*Völkertafel Gen.* x) was that the Philistines were Egyptians who had sojourned in Crete.

we know of the Philistines, while not proving such a theory, does not contradict it. Take them as a whole, and the Philistines appear a Semitic people, with some non-Semitic habits, institutions, and words. Putting aside the names of their towns, as probably due to their Canaanite predecessors,[1] we find a number of their personal names also Semitic.[2] Their religion seems to have consisted of the Semitic fashion of reverencing a pair of deities, male and female. Dagon had a fish-goddess by his side, and the names Dagon and Beelzebub are Semitic. Nor is this evidence counterbalanced by the fact that the Philistines did not practise circumcision, for they may have abandoned the custom during their western sojourn, as later Phœnicians did in contact with the Greeks. But even when we have admitted the Semitic features, it is possible to argue that the Philistines received these from the civilisation which they succeeded and absorbed. This is certain in the case of their towns, and of the giants among them, who belonged to remains of the Canaanite population.[3] Indeed, with the exception, perhaps, of Abimelech, there is no Philistine name of a Semitic cast of which this may not be true. It is possible that neither Delilah nor Obed-edom the Gittite was a pure Philistine.[4] As for language, there is little argument either way; but if, as there is reason to suppose, incoming Israel acquired theirs from the Canaanites, it is not impossible for the Philistines to have done the same.[5] As for religion, if in antiquity the religion of a province was usually adopted by its invaders, and if even Israel fell under the power of Canaanite worship, so as only with difficulty to escape from succumbing to it, how much more likely were the Philistines, who had not the spirit of Israel, to yield to the *manner of the gods of the land*.[6] The case, therefore, is complex. As to the non-Semitic elements in Philistinism, some maintain that they are Greek, or at least Aryan.[7] Now,

[1] This disposes of part of Stade's argument, *Gesch. des V. Israel*, i. 142.

[2] Abimelech, Delilah, Obed-edom. But see below. Perhaps also Ishbi, Saph, Goliath, Raphah. Achish, אכיש, son of Maoch, מעוך, king of Gath, 1 Sam. xxvii. 2. Achish, son of Maachah, מעכה, king of Gath, 1 Kings ii. 39. W. Max Müller (*Asien, u. Eur.* 389) gives a name Bi-d-ira.

[3] Josh. xi. 21, 22. Cf. xv. 13, 14.

[4] Gath was so near the Israel border, and so often under Israel, that Obed-edom may have been a Hebrew, though this is not likely from his name.

[5] Nothing can be argued from this, that in Aramæan times they seem from two coins of Ashdod to have spoken a dialect of Hebrew.

[6] 2 Kings xvii. 26.

[7] Riehm (*Handwörterbuch*) says of the Philistines, "sie sind mit Griechischen, bestimmter Karischen, Elementen stark versetzten Semiten aus Kreta". Isa. ix. 11; LXX has Ἕλληνες for Philistines. W. Max. Müller, *As. u. Eur.*, etc., 361, 387 ff., says of the "Purasati from the midst of the sea" of Ramses III (Danoma, Takkara, perhaps Δαναοί, Τεῦκροι) they may have been Ancient-Lysians, not impossibly pre-

it would be interesting if we were sure that in the early Philistines Israel already encountered that Hellenism with which she waged war on the same fields under the Maccabees. But we cannot affirm more than that this was possible; and the above ambiguous results are all that are afforded by our knowledge of this perplexing people. The excavations of this century add practically little to it.

The Philistines appear to have come into the Maritime Plain of Syria either shortly before or shortly after Israel left Egypt. In the Tell el-Amarna Letters from South Palestine, in the beginning of the fourteenth century B.C., they are not mentioned; and in the latter half of that century the monuments of Ramses II represent the citizens of Ashkelon with faces that are not Philistine. This agrees with the traditions in Genesis, one of which places the Philistine centre still south of Gaza, at Gerar identified by the excavations of Sir Flinders Petrie as Tell el-Jemmeh on the south side of Wady Ghuzzeh about a mile above the point at which Wady esh-Sheriah enters it[1]; while another states that the Canaanites once held the coast from Gaza northwards[2]; as well as that of Deuteronomy,[2] that *the Caphtorim* had to *expel the Avvim, who dwelt in open villages, as far as Gaza.* This northern advance of the Philistines may have been going on when the Israelites were invading the Canaanites from the east. But if so, it cannot have been either powerful or ambitious, for of the various accounts in Joshua and Judges of the first Hebrew conquests none bring the Hebrews even into conflict with the Philistines.[3] By Deborah's time, the tribe of Dan had touched the sea, and when afterwards they were driven back to the hills, the pressure came not from Philistines, but from Amorites.[5] Afterwards, however, the Philistines,

---

Hellenic people of the Greek Isles, perhaps the 'Ετεόκρητες of *Odyssey*, xix. 176, thrown into movement by the Greek advance westward. See R. N. Salaman, *PEFQ*, 1925; Garstang, *Josh. Jud.* 313, "by their arms and organisation akin to the Iron Age peoples of the Achæan world, particularly those of the Homeric age".

[1] Gerar, Gen. xx, xxvi, taken by Rowlands, *Holy City*, i. 464 (cf. Van de Velde, *Memoir*, 1858, 115), as Umm el-Jerar, 6 m. SSE of Gaza after *Onomasticon's*, 25 Rom. m. S of Eleutheropolis, and generally accepted, *PEF Mem. Jerus.* 438 ff.; suggested by Phythian-Adams, *PEFQ*, 1923, 140 ff., as Tell el-Jemmeh, 2 m. farther up (Map 4, *Military Operations Egypt and Palestine*, etc.); and this is proved by Flinders Petrie, *Gerar*, Brit. Sch. of Archæol. in Egypt, 1928; remains from Thothmes III onward.

[2] Gen. x. 19. [3] ii. 3.

[4] Josh. xi, xiii, Jud. i, especially 18, where with LXX insert *not*. Josh. xiii. 2: *the land that remains, all the Gĕlîlôth, circuits, of the Philistines.*

[5] Judges v. 17, *Dan abides in ships*, i. 34, *Amorites forced Danites into the hills, they would not suffer them to come down into the Vale* of Aijalon, where the Amorites settled till subdued by Ephraim. How, then, can it be said that Dan *abode in ships*? It is one of the many difficulties we meet in the accounts of Israel's occupation. As against

adding to their effective force the tall Canaanites[1] whom they had subdued, and strengthened, perhaps, by clans from their earlier seats—for, like Israel, they had several tribes among them[2]—moved north and east. Overflowing from what was especially known as their districts, the Gĕlîlôth Pelesheth,[3] they seized the coast to beyond Carmel, and spread over Esdraelon. It was during this time that they also invaded the highlands to the east of them, and began that conflict with Israel which alone has given them fame and a history.

We cannot have followed this history without being struck by the strange parallel which it affords to the history of Israel—the strange parallel and the stranger divergence. Both Philistines and Hebrews were immigrants into the land for whose possession they fought through centuries. Both came up to it from Egypt. Both absorbed the populations they found upon it. Both succeeded to the Canaanite civilisation, and came under the fascination of the Canaanite religion. Each people had a distinctive character, and both were at different periods so victorious that either, humanly speaking, might have absorbed the other. Indeed, so fully was the Philistine identified with the Land that his name has for ever become its name—a distinction which Israel never reached. Yet Israel survived and the Philistine disappeared. Israel attained to a destiny, equalled in history only by Greece and Rome, whereas the fame of the Philistines lies in having served as a foil to the genius of the Hebrews, and to-day his name against theirs is the symbol of impenetrableness and obscurantism.

What caused this difference between peoples whose earlier fortunes were so similar? *First*, we may answer, their geographical position, and *Second*, the spirit in one of them. The same Hand[4] which brought in Israel from the east brought up the Philistine from the south. It planted Israel on a rocky range of mountain, aloof from the paths of the great empires, and beyond their envy. It planted the Philistines on an open doorway and a great thoroughfare, amidst the traffic and the war of two continents. They were bent now towards Egypt, now towards Assyria, at a time when youthful Israel was growing straight and free as one of her own forest trees. They were harassed

---

Stade, Budde and Kittel, I venture to believe Dan did reach the sea, for Judges v. 17 is one of the best assured parts of Deborah's Song, and not to be put aside because in conflict with another statement.

[1] Sons of Anak. [2] Caphtorim, Philistines, Thekels (Zakkara) Kerethim.

[3] One instance of the use of Gĕlîl, or Gĕlîlah, apart from Galilee (ch. xx). It was applied by the foreign Hebrews, and one might see a trace of it in the Galilea of the Crusaders, E of Cæsarea, and Jelil, NE of Jaffa. See the opening of ch. xx.

[4] See Amos viii. 9.

by intrigue and battle, when her choicest spirits had freedom for the observation of the workings of an omnipotent and righteous Providence; and when, at last, they were overwhelmed by the streams of Greek culture which flowed along their coast in the wake of Alexander the Great, she upon her heights still stubbornly kept the law of her Lord. Yet, to ascribe this difference of destiny to difference of geographical position were to dignify the mere opportunity with the virtue of the original cause; for it was not Israel's geographical position which prevented her from yielding to the Canaanite religion, or moved her, being still young and rude, to banish from her midst the soothsayers and necromancers, to whom the Philistines were given over.[1] But from the first Israel had within her a spirit, and before her an ideal, of which the Philistines knew nothing, and always her prophets identified the purpose—which they clearly recognised—of her establishment on so isolated and secure a position with the highest ends of righteousness, wisdom, and service to all mankind.

It is outside the purpose of this work to follow in detail the history of the relation of the two peoples, but it may be useful to define the main periods into which that history falls, with their relevant portions of geography.

There was *first* a period of military encounters, and alternate subjugation of the one people by the other. This passed through its heroic stage in the times of Samson, Saul, and David, entered a more peaceful epoch under Solomon, and for the next three centuries of the Hebrew monarchy was distinguished by occasional raids from both sides into the heart of the enemy's country. The chief theatres of the events of this period are the Shephelah hills and the valleys leading up through them upon Judah and Benjamin.[2] At one time the Philistines are at Michmash, on the very citadel of Israel's hill-country, and at another near Jezreel, by its northern entrances.[3] In both cases their purpose may have been to extend their supremacy over the trade routes which came up from Egypt and crossed the Jordan; but it seems as probable that, by occupying Michmash and the Plain of Esdraelon, they sought to separate the tribes of Israel from one another.[4] Occasionally Philistines penetrated to the neighbourhood of Jerusalem,[5] or the Israelite

[1] Cf. 1 Sam. xxviii. 3 with Isa. ii. 6.

[2] See next chapter.

[3] 1 Sam. xiii, xxix, and xxxi.

[4] This seems the more likely at Michmash, for although there was a trade route from Jordan by Jericho and Michmash to the coast, much used by the Crusaders, a garrison at Michmash could not have kept it open while Saul had his camp at Gilgal, and commanded Jordan.

[5] 2 Sam. v. 22 ff.

raids swept to the gates of Gaza[1]; but neither people ever mastered the other's chief towns.

The *second* period is that of the centuries from the eighth to the fourth before Christ, when the contests of the two nations are stilled before the advance of the world-powers—Egypt, Assyria, Babylon, and Persia. Now, instead of a picture of forays and routs up and down the intervening passes, Philistine and Hebrew face to face in fight, we have the gaze of the Hebrew prophets looking down on Philistia, and marking her cities for destruction by the invader. It is, indeed, one of the many signs of the sobriety of the prophets, and of their fidelity to fact, that they do not seek to revive in Israel her earlier ambitions for victory over her ancient foe. The threats of prophecy against Philistia are, with one exception, threats of destruction from Egypt and Mesopotamia. Isaiah, Jeremiah, Zephaniah, Zechariah speak of the Philistine cities, not hotly, as of enemies shortly to be met in battle, but pitifully, as victims of the Divine judgement, which lowers over Philistia and Israel alike.[2]

A change of attitude and temper came with the *third* period, from the third century before Christ to the close of the Jewish revolts against Rome, in the third century after Christ. With Alexander's invasion the Philistine coast and cities were opened to Greek influence. There was traffic with Greece through the harbours, such as they were; there were settlements of Greek men in the cities; Greek institutions arose; the old deities were identified with Greek gods; and, though the Philistine stubbornness persisted, it was exercised in the defence of civic independence, according to Greek ideas and of Greek manners and morals. But it was just against this Hellenism, whether of Syria or of the half-free Philistine cities, that the wars of the Maccabees broke out. The aloofness of the prophetic period was over, and Israel returned to close quarters with her ancient foes. Their battles raged on the same fields; their routs and pursuits up and down the same passes. Did Samson arise in the Vale of Sorek, and David slay Goliath in the Vale of Elah, both leading down into Philistia?—then the birthplace of the Maccabees was in the parallel Valley of Aijalon at Modein, and their exploits within sight of the haunts of their predecessors a thousand years before. So through the literature of this time, and of the times leading up to it, we miss the wide prophetic view, and in Psalms that exult in the subjugation of the Philistines

[1] 2 Kings xviii. 8.

[2] Isa. xiv. 29-32; Jer. xlvii; Zeph. ii; Zech. ix. The one exception is Isa. xi. 14, where it is said Judah and Ephraim shall swoop upon the shoulder of the Philistine towards the sea. Some maintain this is not Isaiah's. But there was occasion for it in Isaiah's days, in the expeditions of Uzziah and Hezekiah up to the gates of Gaza.

to Israel, and *triumph over Philistia,*[1] we seem to breathe again the ruder, military spirit of the times of Samson and of Saul. This active warfare persisted till the last Jewish revolts under the Roman emperors. Then the Jews gave way, withdrawing into Galilee, and Christianity succeeded to the heritage of the war against Hellenism.

The slow conquest of heathenism by the Church forms the *fourth* period of the history of Philistia, from the first, to the beginning of the fifth, century after Christ. It is typical of the whole early progress of Christianity, and as full of pathos and romance as this was in any other part of the world. In Philistia Christianity rose against a Hellenism proud of its recent victories over the Jews. Flourishing schools and notable philosophers were in every city. The gods, identified with the deities of Greece and Rome, were favoured equally by the common people and by the governing classes. The Marneion, or Temple of Marna, at Gaza was regarded as a stronghold of heathendom only second to the Serapeum at Alexandria.[2] Beside so elaborate a paganism the early Christians of Philistia, though organised under many bishops, were a small and feeble folk. Like the Church of Pergamos, they *dwelt by Satan's throne*, and like her, in consequence, they had their martyrs.[3] Neighbours to the Church of Egypt, they imitated the asceticism of Antony, and avowed the orthodoxy of Athanasius. The deserts of Egypt sent them monks, who, scattered over the Plain and the Shephelah, gradually converted the country people, with a power which the Hellenism of the cities had no means to counteract.[4] It is their caves and the ruins of their cloisters which we come across to-day in the glens of the Shephelah, especially near Beit-Jibrin.[5] For a little Constantine's favour gave them a freer course in the cities, but this was closed by the hostility of Julian; and it was not till 402, under the influence of Theodosius and at the hands of the vigorous Bishop Porphyry of Gaza,[6] that the Cross triumphed and idolatry was abolished. Then the Marneion was destroyed, almost on the site on which Samson drew down the Temple of Dagon fifteen hundred years before. But this was only the climax of a process of which the country monks deserve the credit. In the

[1] Psalm lx (cviii), lxxxiii, etc. Of course, it is possible that such Psalms are earlier, for Hezekiah carried fire and sword into Philistia—a reminder of how impossible it is to be dogmatic on the date of any Psalm, simply because it reflects the feeling of the literature of the time to which we assign it.

[2] Jerome *ad Lætam*, ep. vii, and *Commentary to Isaiah*, c. xvii.

[3] Rev. ii. 13. For martyrs see Eusebius, *H.E.* viii. 13, Sozomen *passim.*

[4] Jerome, *Life of Hilarion*, Sozomen's *History*, vi. 31.

[5] See ch. xi. The labours of these monks were especially numerous in the νόμος of Eleutheropolis (Eusebius).

[6] *Life of Porphyry*, by Marcus the Deacon, in the *Acta Sanctorum.*

same glens where the early peasants of Israel had beaten back the Philistine armies with ox-goads,[1] and David with his shepherd's sling had slain the giant, simple monks with means as primitive gained the first victories for Christ over as strenuous a paganism.

After this life in Philistia is almost silent till the Crusades, and after the Crusades till the Great War.

This sketch of the four periods of Philistine history will prepare us for our review of the Philistine cities in this chapter, and of the Shephelah in the next. The Philistine cities we take from the south northwards.

Gaza may best be described as in most respects the southern counterpart of Damascus. It is a site of abundant fertility on the edge of a great desert[2] —a harbour for the wilderness and a market for the nomads; once, as Damascus is, the rendezvous of a pilgrimage; and as Damascus was the first Syrian station across the desert from Assyria, so Gaza is the outpost across the desert from Egypt. This is to summarise her position and history.

Gaza lies to-day where she lay in ancient times,[3] on and around a hill, which rises 100 feet above the plain, at 3 miles from the sea. Fifteen wells of fresh water burst from the sandy soil, and render possible the broad gardens and large population.[4] The Bedouin from a hundred miles away come to the bazaars for cloth, weapons, and pottery. When the pilgrimage to Sinai was made rather from Syria than from Egypt, the caravans were organised in Gaza for the desert march.[5] The inhabitants were characterised as "lovers

[1] Shamgar and his slaughter of 600 Philistines with an ox-goad (Judges iii. 31) are typical of the fact above stated.

[2] ἐπὶ τῇ ἀρχῇ τῆς ἐρήμου Arrian, *Anabasis*, ii. 26. For Damascus see ch. xxxi.

[3] But not in prehistoric. Flinders Petrie, after excavating Tell el-'Ajjul, says that site "was occupied from the Neolithic to the Bronze Age and appears to have been the old Gaza. As there are no remains of an age later than that of the Shepherd Kings, it would seem that the place was abandoned" probably because of its malarial conditions during summer (*The Times*, Feb. 9, 1930). On Tell el-'Ajjul, see p. 116.

[4] Arrian, *Anab. Alex.* ii. 26, reckons Gaza at twenty stadia from the sea. The hill is not extensive. The gardens spread 4 miles north and south by 2½ east and west. The population was 18,000 in 1894, and, except when ruined, the town was described by writers of all ages as large, splendid, opulent. For descriptions see *PEF Mem.* iii; *ZDPV*, viii, but especially xi, with plan by Gatt, p. 149; on the walls J. Garstang, *PEFQ*, 1920, 156. In 1483 twice as big as Jerusalem: Felix Fabri (*PPT*, ii. 450).

[5] Rather than at Hebron, even when the pilgrimage was to or from Jerusalem, for Bedouin avoided Hebron, but came to Gaza: Robinson, *BR*, i. Cf. Anton. Placen., *Itiner.* (A.D. 570), which describes (ch. xxxiii) Gazans as "homines honestissimi, omni liberalitate decori, amatores peregrinorum". Antoninus took 18 or 19 days to Sinai. Antonius de Cremona: "De monte Synay usque ad Gazam fuimus xv diebus

of pilgrims", whom, no doubt, like the Damascenes they found profitable. As from Damascus, so from Gaza trade-routes travelled in all directions—to Egypt, to South Arabia, and in the times of the Nabatæan kingdom to Petra and Palmyra.[1] Amos curses Gaza for trafficking in slaves with Edom.[2] When Strabo and Pliny reach Gaza, almost the only fact they find relevant is her distance from Elath, on the Gulf of 'Akaba.[3] From those eastern depots on sea and desert Gaza, by her harbour,[4] in Greek times forwarded the riches of Arabia and India across the Mediterranean, as Acco did by the Palmyra-Damascus route. The Crusaders do not appear to have used Gaza for commerce, because this part of Palestine was never so securely in their hands as to permit them to dominate the roads south and east for any distance, and they tapped the eastern trade by the route Moab, Jericho, Jerusalem, Joppa.[5] But through Moslem times the stream has partly followed its old channel. Caravans setting out from Gaza would meet the Damascus Hajj at Ma'an with pilgrims and supplies.[6] Their common interest in those routes has generally kept the people of Gaza and the Bedouin on good terms. Bates, the Persian who defended Gaza against Alexander, employed Arab mercenaries[7]; in the military history of Judah, Arabs are twice joined with Philistines[8]; the excursions of the Maccabees against the Philistine towns were usually directed against the "nomads" as well[9]; and, on the eve of her desolation by Alexander Jannæus, Gaza was looking across the desert for King Aretas, the Arabian, to come to her help.[10] In the Moslem invasion Gaza was one of the first points which Abu Bekr's soldiers struck,[11] and the Byzantine army was defeated in the suburbs. After that the Mohammedans called Gaza Dehliz el-Moulk, "the Threshold of the Kingdom".

But Gaza has even closer relations with Egypt. The eight days' march

---

in deserto." Cf. Bertrand de la Brocquière (1432), Felix Fabri (1483), ii. 93, who spells Gaza Gazara.

[1] Pliny, *Hist. Nat.* v. 12. Cf. ch. xxix. [2] Amos i. 6.

[3] Strabo, xvi. ii. 30; Pliny, *Hist. Nat.* v. 12, cf. 14. Marciani Her. *Periplus*, etc. (Müller, G. C. Min. i. 522), "Gaza distant from head of Aelanitic Gulf 1260 stadia".

[4] D. Mackenzie, "The Port of Gaza", *PEFQ*, 1918, 73.

[5] Rey's *Les Colonies Franques aux xii et xiii siècles*, ch. ix.

[6] Burckhardt's *Travels in Syria*, 436, 658; Doughty's *Arabia Deserta*, I, 133, where it is said that caravans also come from Hebron to Ma'an.

[7] Arrian, *Anab.* ii. 26, 27; Quintus Curtius, iv. 6.

[8] In bringing tribute to Jehoshaphat, 2 Chron. xvii. 11, and invading Jehoram, 2 Chron. xxi. 16.

[9] 1 Maccabees. [10] Josephus, xiii *Antt.* xiii. 3.

[11] By the most southerly of the three brigades—that of Amr-Ibn-el-Assi—Gaza seems to have been taken in 634.

across the sands from the Delta required that, if an army came up that way into Syria, Gaza, being their first relief from the desert, should be in friendly hands. Hence the continual efforts of Egypt to hold the town. Alike under the Pharaohs of the sixteenth to the fourteenth centuries, and the Ptolemies of the third and second, we find Gaza occupied, or fought for, by Egyptian troops.[1] Alexander invading Egypt and Napoleon invading Syria had both to capture her. Napoleon has emphasised the indispensableness of Gaza, whether in the invasion or in the defence of the Nile Valley.[2] Gaza is the outpost of Africa, the door of Asia.

Gaza never lay within the territories of early Israel,[3] though Israel's authority, as in Solomon's time,[4] and temporary conquests, as in Hezekiah's,[5] might extend to her gates; and this is to be explained by the prestige which Egypt, standing immediately behind, cast upon her. Under the Maccabees Jewish armies carried fire and sword across Philistia. Ekron and Ashdod were taken, Ashkelon came to terms, and, after Jonathan had burnt her suburbs, Gaza was forced to buy him off.[6] It was not till 96 B.C. that Jews crossed her walls, but then the pent-up hatred of centuries burst in devastation upon her. Alexander Jannæus, taking advantage of the withdrawal of the Egyptian troops, invested Gaza. After a year's siege, in which the whole oasis was laid waste, the town was captured by treachery, her buildings burned, and her people put to the sword.[7] Gaza, to use the word echoed of her by one writer after another for the next century, lay desert.[8] In 62,

[1] *Annals of Thothmes III*; *Tell el-Amarna Letters* of the 15th cent.; records of Ramses' conquests in the 14th. Sayce supposed the Philistines were planted by the Egyptians in Gaza and her sister cites as outposts of Egypt (*Races of the O.T.* 54), yet Egypt is always represented as hostile to them, Müller, *Asien u. Europa*, 388 ff.; and in a review of the 1st ed. of this work, Sayce acknowledged that I was "fully justified in rejecting" his view of the Philistines as "a sort of Egyptian outpost". Cf. Jer. xlvii. But see Garstang, *Josh. Jud.* 375, on traces of brick ramparts of Egyptian style. From 323, when Ptolemy Lagi took it (Diod. Sic. xix. 59), Gaza frequently passed from the Ptolemies to the Antiochi, and back again, till 198 B.C. (Polybius, v), when it fell to Antiochus the Great, and was part of the Syrian kingdom for a century.

[2] *Op. cit.* II, ch. vii. For the British capture of it in 1917, see p. 196 f.

[3] Addition to Josh. xv, viz. vv. 45-47, sets Gaza within the ideal borders of Judah; this has no confirmation, and is contradicted by the LXX of Judges i. 18, where *not* is inserted. G. B. Gray rejects this *not*. The Gaza of 1 Chron. vii. 28 is another near Shechem.

[4] 1 Kings iv. 24 'Azzah, or rather Ghazzah, is the more correct spelling of Gaza.

[5] 2 Kings xviii. 8.

[6] Josephus, xiii *Antt.* v. 5; 1 Macc. xi. 61 ff. In xiii. 43 read Gazara for Gaza.

[7] Josephus, xiii *Antt.* xiii. 3.

[8] πολὺν χρόνον ἐρήμους, xiv *Antt.* v. 3; μένουσα ἔρημος, Strabo, xvi. 2, 30; and ἡ ἔρημος Γάζα, the anon. Greek in Hudson's *Geographi Græci Minores*, iv, 39.

Pompey took Gaza—now called a maritime city like Joppa—from the Jews, and made it a free city.[1] In 57 Gabinius rebuilt it,[2] on a new site, possibly close to its harbour, which through the Greek period had been growing in importance. In 30, Gaza, still called "a maritime city", was granted by Cæsar to Herod,[3] but at the latter's death, being Greek, as Josephus says, it was again taken from the Jews, and added to the Province of Syria.[4] "New" Gaza flourished at this time, but Old or Desert Gaza was not forgotten, probably not even abandoned, for the trunk-road to Egypt still travelled past it. In the Book of Acts, in the directions given to Philip to meet the Ethiopian eunuch, this is accurately noted: *Arise, and go toward the south, unto the way that goeth down from Jerusalem to Gaza; this is desert.*[5] Most connect the adjective, not with Gaza, but with *the way*; yet no possible route from Jerusalem to Gaza could be called desert, and this being so, and several writers of the period preceding having used the phrase of the town itself, it seems we are shut up to the same reference here. If New Gaza, as is probable, lay at this time upon the coast, then we know that the road the Ethiopian travelled did not take that direction, and in describing the road it was natural to mention the old site—Desert not necessarily in reality but still in name—which was a station upon it. That Philip was found immediately after at Ashdod suggests that the meeting and the baptism took place on the Philistine Plain, and not on the hills of Judæa, where tradition has placed them. But that would mean the neighbourhood of Gaza, and an additional reason for mentioning the town.[6]

[1] Josephus, xiv *Antt.* iv. 4.

[2] Josephus, xiv *Antt.* v. 3; i *Wars*, vii. 7. In both Gaza is separated from the inland towns and called Maritime.

[3] Josephus, xv *Antt.* vii. 3.

[4] Josephus, xvii *Antt.* xi. 4; ii *Wars*, vi. 3; the earliest imperial coins of Gaza date from a year or two after this (De Saulcy, *Numismatique de la Terre Sainte*, p. 213).

[5] Acts viii. 26.

[6] My only difficulty in coming to this conclusion is that many are against it; but it seems so impossible to describe any route from Jerusalem to Gaza as desert—whether tha: by Beit-Jibrin, which Robinson (*BR*, ii; *Phys. Geog.* 108, 109) selects, or the longer by Hebron, which Räumer and Guérin prefer (*Judée*, ii. 204), Guérin supporting his choice by the unfounded remark that fewer people took this route, and so it might be distinguished as ἔρημος from the other—that I feel shut up to taking ἔρημος as referring to Gaza. Had Acts viii been a document of the first century B.C., there could have been no doubt about the reference, for Gaza was then left "desert", as stated by Josephus, xiv *Antt.* v. 3, and remained desert, as witnessed by Strabo, xvi. 2. 30, and by the Fragment in *Geogr. Græc. Minores*, ed. Hudson, iv. 39. This gives a list of towns from S to N, and says that after Rinocoloura, ἡ νεά Γάζα κεῖται, πόλις οὖσα καὶ αὐτή, εἶθ' ἡ ἔρημος Γάζα εἶτα ἡ Ἀσκάλον πόλις. Diodorus Siculus (xix 80) had spoken of an Old Gaza where Ptolemy Lagi, in 312, defeated Demetrius Polior-

The subsequent history of Gaza is identified, as we have seen, with the struggle of Christianity against heathendom. In the second and third centuries Gaza became a prosperous centre of Greek commerce and culture. Her schools were good, but her temples were famous, circling round the Marneion, or House of the city's god, Marna. Marna, Lord or our Lord,[1] was the Baal of Gaza, Lord of Heaven and sun and rain, whom it was easy to identify with Zeus. A statue, discovered a long time since at Tell el-'Ajjul, is supposed to be the image of Marna, and bears resemblance to the Greek face of the Father of gods and men.[2] Around him were Zeus Nicephorus, Apollo, Aphrodite, Tyche, Proserpina, Hecate—nearly the whole Syrian pantheon. Truly the Church of Gaza dwelt, like the Church of Pergamos, where Satan's throne was: and like her she had her martyrs.[3] Constantine, finding the inland Gaza's authorities obdurately pagan, gave a separate constitution to the sea-town, or Mayumas, which he entitled Constantia, and there was a bishop of this besides the Bishop of Gaza. But Julian took away these privileges. For generations the rival cries "Marna", "Jesus", rent the

---

cetes, as if to distinguish it from New Gaza of Diodorus' own time. Schürer, *Hist.* Div. II, vol. i. 71, holds that New Gaza was not the port, but another town inland, and, according to the Fragment, S of Old Gaza; there is no evidence of this. New Gaza of the Fragment might as well be a coast-town as Ashkelon; and Josephus' statement that the Gaza Pompey enfranchised in 62 was not inland, like Ashdod and Jamnia, but maritime, like Joppa and Dora (Josephus, xiv *Antt.* iv. 4; cf. xv *Antt.* vii. 3, where again it is "maritime", like Joppa) seems to make it probable that the Gaza which Gabinius rebuilt (*id.* v. 3) was on the coast. If this be so, it lay off the road to Egypt, which still passed by the Desert Gaza. It is not necessary to suppose that this was absolutely deserted even in Philip's time. The fertile site and neighbouring great road would attract people; but, even though it were like its old self, the name *Ἔρημος* might stick to it. Gaza is said to have been demolished by the Jewish revolt of A.D. 66 (ii *Wars*, xviii. 1), and if this had been true, we might have had a new reason why Acts viii added the gloss "this is desert" to a description of Gaza; but, as Schürer remarks, we have coins of the years following, which testify to the city's continued prosperity (cf. De Saulcy, *Num. de la T.S.* p. 214). However this may be, the return of the city to its old site, which may have begun before Philip's time, was completed in the following centuries, and the reason is clear. The land trade was always likely to prevail over the sea trade on such a coast, and the old site had, besides the road, its fertility and 15 wells. In A.D. 363 the Gazans believed themselves to be on the same site as Old Gaza; and the temples destroyed in 402, and churches built in their stead, occupied the site of the city to-day, which agrees with the description of the Gaza taken by Alexander (Arrian, *Anab.* ii. 26). Jerome, in the *Onomasticon*, is too vague to be taken into account. Bertrand de la Brocquière says that between Hebron and Gaza he crossed "a desert country". Against my view, see Phythian-Adams, *PEFQ*, 1923, 30, "The Problem of 'Deserted' Gaza".

[1] Cf. *Μαρὰν ἀθά* of 1 Cor. xvi. 22. [2] *PEFQ*, 1882.

[3] Euseb. *HE* and Sozomen *passim*.

streets and circuses. How the Church in 402 finally won the political victory under Theodosius and her Bishop Porphyry we have seen.[1] After this the schools of Gaza in philosophy and rhetoric grew more and more distinguished. Students, it is said, left Athens to learn the Attic style in Philistia, and even Persia borrowed her teachers.[2] We get a glimpse of the citizens in the close of the sixth century, "very honest, beautiful with all liberality, lovers of pilgrims".[3] But in 635 Gaza became Moslem, and, for obvious reasons, gradually declined to the rank of a respectable station of traffic. Even with the Crusaders her military importance did not revive. They found her almost deserted and took no trouble to fortify her. Their chief fortress in Philistia was Ashkelon, and their southern outpost Daroma, now Deir el-Belaḥ, on the Wady three hours south of Gaza.

Near Gaza was a town, Anthedon,[4] which occurs in Josephus, and is mentioned by Pliny, Ptolemy, and Sozomen. Alexander Jannæus took it when he took Gaza: it was rebuilt and enfranchised under the Romans, and in Christian times had a bishop.[5] Near this town, then called Tadun, the Moslems defeated the Byzantines in 635. The site was lost till Herr Gatt heard the name Teda given by a native to some ruins twenty-five minutes north of Gaza harbour, and near the sea.[6] Anthedon must have been virtually a suburb of Gaza.

We take next Ashkelon, or as the Greeks called it, Askalon. The site, which to-day bears the name,[7] has been described: a rocky amphitheatre on the low bank of the coast, filled by Crusading ruins.[8] Since the fortifications, as at Cæsarea, are bound together by pillars of Herod's time, it is certain that the Ashkelon which Herod embellished[9] stood here also, though extending inland: and there is no hint in Josephus that Herod's Ashkelon occupied any other site than that of the Philistine city, where traces of the Philistines

[1] P. 132. [2] For details see Stark, pp. 631-645. [3] See p. 134, n. 5.

[4] Josephus, xiii *Antt.* xiii. 3; xv. 4; i *Wars*, iv. 2; Pliny, *Hist. Nat.* v. 14; Ptol., *Geogr.* v. 16.

[5] *Acta Conciliorum.*

[6] This proves that Pliny was wrong in putting Anthedon inland and Ptolemy right in calling it a coast-town. For Gatt's discovery see *ZDPV*, vii. 5 ff.; cf. 140, 141. It contains this beautiful summary of tradition. After asking the name and hearing it was Teda, Gatt said to his informant: "Whence knowest thou that?" "From those who have lived before me have I heard it. Is it not with you as with us—some are born and others die, and the old tell the young what they know?"

[7] In Arabic 'Asḳalan, with initial 'Ayin instead of Aleph.

[8] Description by Guthe, plan by Schick, *ZDPV*, ii. 164 ff.; on excavations, etc., *PEFQ*, 1921, 12, 73, 76, 162; 1922, 112; 1923, 60; J. Garstang, *id.* 1924, 24 ff.; *Josh. Jud.* 357 f. with plan.

[9] i *Wars*, xxi. 11.

are still clear. If this be so, then of all the Philistine Pentapolis Ashkelon was the only one immediately on the sea.[1] This fact, combined with distance from the trunk-road on which Gaza, Ashdod, and Ekron stand, perhaps explains a singularity in Ashkelon's history, when compared with that of her sisters. The town has no natural strength, but is well watered.

Take her in her period of greatest fame. During the Crusades Ashkelon combined the significance of all the fortresses of Philistia, and proved the key to south-west Palestine. To the Arabs she was the "Bride of Syria", "Syria's Summit".[2] The Egyptians held her long after the Crusaders settled in Jerusalem. She faced the Christian outposts at Ramleh, resisted assaults, and sent two expeditions up to the walls of Jerusalem, before she was captured by Baldwin III in 1154. The scene of two more battles, Ashkelon was retaken by Saladin in 1187, and dismantled five years later when he retired upon Jerusalem. The Christians tried to rebuild the fortress, but the truce came, one of the articles of which was that the town should be fortified by neither party, and it was finally demolished by Bibars in 1270. This fierce contest and jealousy between powers occupying respectively Syria and Egypt, the plains and the hills, certify the strategical importance of the old Philistine site. That through the Crusades Ashkelon should have enjoyed the chief importance, while Gaza had hardly any, is due to the situation on the coast. Both Moslems and Christians had fleets which from time to time supplied Ashkelon from the sea.

It may have been this touch with the sea which proved Ashkelon's value to

[1] Doubt on this has risen solely from the facts, that in the Acts of the Council of Constantinople, 536, are mentioned both a Bishop of Ashkelon and a Bishop of the Port or Mayumas of Ashkelon, and that Antoninus Placentinus (c. 33), A.D. 570, and Benjamin of Tudela mention two Ashkelons from which Pusey concluded that the Philistine city lay inland (*PEFQ*, 1874). These data cannot counterbalance the assertions of Josephus that Herod's Ashkelon, which was the Crusader's Ashkelon on the coast, was an ancient city (iii *Wars*, ii. 1), 520 stadia from Jerusalem, too great a distance for any but a coast-town. Josephus nowhere describes Ashkelon as maritime (as just quoted he says it was walled about), unless i *Wars*, xxi. 11, which describes the Laodiceans as dwelling on the sea-shore, covers Ashkelon in the next clause. Possibly ancient Ashkelon spread inland: the hollow by the sea is small, the Crusading town was little more than a fortress, and ancient ruins, of what must have been large edifices, lie inland (cf. Guérin, *Judée*, ii. 134). The harbour town may have been separated from the town behind. Conder's suggestion, that Khurbet 'Asḳalan in the Shephelah may be the Askalon of the Acts of the Council of Constantinople, has nothing to support it but the name (*PEF Mem.*). Guérin's idea that the inhabitants tried to create a better port than that at their feet, either north or south, may solve the difficulty. He found no traces of such; but note that the next stream to the south bears the name among others of the Nahr 'Asḳalan.

[2] Le Strange, *Palestine under the Moslems.*

its ancient masters, especially if it be here that the Philistines were reinforced by direct immigration from Crete.[1] Jeremiah connects it with the sea-shore.[2] In David's lamentation over Saul, it is not Gath and Gaza, but Gath and Ashkelon which are taken as two typical Philistine cities. *Publish it not in the streets of Ashkelon*: it may be that these were bazaars[3]; and there is a sound of trade, a clinking of shekels, about the city's name.[4] Ashkelon was always opulent and spacious.[5] The Assyrian flood covered all things, and Ashkelon suffered from it as much as her neighbours.[6] But in the times of the Maccabees she recovered her distinction. She was not so bitter to Judaism as other Hellenic towns, and escaped their misfortunes at the hands of Jonathan.[7] When Alexander Jannæus devastated Gaza, Ashkelon kept her peace with that excitable savage. She was the first in Philistia to secure the protection of Rome, and enjoyed her freedom earlier and more continuously than the rest. Through Roman and Byzantine times she was a centre of Hellenic culture, producing even more grammarians and philosophers than her neighbours.[8]

If Ashkelon takes her name from trade, Ashdod, like Gaza, takes hers from her military strength.[9] Her citadel was probably the low hill, beside the present village Esdud, well watered, and commanding the mouth of the most broad and fertile wady in Philistia. It served, also, as the half-way station on the great road between Gaza and Joppa, and, as we have seen, the inland branch broke off here for Ekron and Ramleh. The ruins of a khan have outlived those of the fortresses from which the city took her name. Ashdod also, like her sisters, had her varying fortunes in the war with Israel, and like them suffered for her position on the way between Assyria and Egypt. Sargon besieged and took her[10]: Sennacherib besieged and took her,[11] but her most wonderful siege, which Herodotus calls the longest in history, was that for twenty-two years by Psammetichus.[12] Judas Maccabæus cleared Ashdod of idols in 163, and in 148 Jonathan and Simon burnt her temple of

[1] Hence the Cherethim, but see pp. 125 f. Ashkelon was a fortress in Ramses II's time, before the Philistines came: taken by Ramses II from the Hittites, cf. Brugsch, *Geogr. Inschr. altägyptischer Denkmäler*, ii.

[2] xlvii. 7. [3] 2 Sam. i. 20.

[4] Ashkelon, from *shākal*, to weigh, or to pay. Hence sheḳel or shekel.

[5] For Herod's time cf. Josephus, iii *Wars*, ii. 1, etc.; under the Moslems, Le Strange, *op. cit.*

[6] Cf. *Conquests of Sargon and Sennacherib*; *Records of the Past.*

[7] 1 Macc. x. 86; xi. 60.

[8] *PEFQ*, 1888, 22-23, describes two statues found at Ashkelon. Reinach (*Revue des Études Juives*, 1888) ascribes them to the first century B.C. They are Victories.

[9] 1 Sam. v; 2 Chron. xxvi. 6. [10] Isa. xx. 1. [11] 1 *Rec. of Past*, v.

[12] Herod. ii. 157.

Dagon.[1] But, like Ashkelon, Ashdod was now thoroughly Greek, and was enfranchised by Pompey.

Ekron, the modern 'Aḳir, as Robinson discovered, won its place in the league by possession of an oracle of Baalzebub, or Baal of the Flies,[2] and by a site on the northern frontier of Philistia, in the Vale of Sorek, where a pass breaks through the low hills to Ramleh. That is, like so many more ancient cities Ekron had the double fortune of a sanctuary and a market on a trade route. Ekron was nearer the territory of Israel than the other Philistine towns, and from this consequences flowed. It was from Ekron that the ark was returned to Israel, by the level road up the Sorek valley to Beth-shemesh, not twelve miles away. Amos uses a phrase of Ekron as if she were more within reach than her sister towns[3]: she was ceded to the Maccabees by the Syrians[4]; and, after the destruction of Jerusalem, the Jews readily came to her, for like Lydda she was in a valley that led down from Jerusalem. To-day the Joppa-Jerusalem railway travels past her. With Ekron we may take a town that stood near in rank to the first Philistine five—Jabneh, or Jabneel,[5] but in Greek times Jamnia, with a harbour at the mouth of the Rubin, famous in the history of the Jews for their failure to capture it,[6] and for the settlement there of the Jewish Sanhedrin and a Rabbinic school after the destruction of Jerusalem.[7] Yebna, as the town is now called, lies in a fertility of field and grove that helps us to understand the repute of the district for populousness.[8] The ruins are of churches built by the Crusaders, who called the place by a corruption of its full name, reversing *l* and *n* as usual, Ibelin for Jabneel.

Now, where is Gath? Gath the city of giants died out with the giants. That we have to-day no certain knowledge of her site is due to the city's early disappearance. Amos, about 750 B.C., points to her recent destruction by Assyria as a warning that Samaria must follow. Before this, Gath has invariably been mentioned in the list of Philistine cities, and frequently in the account of the wars between them and Israel. But, after this time, the names of the other four cities are given without Gath—by Amos himself, by Jeremiah, by Zephaniah, and in the Book of Zechariah[9]—and Gath does not again appear in either the Old Testament,[10] or the Books of the Maccabees, or those parts of Josephus which treat of centuries subsequent to the eighth. This can only mean that Gath, both place and name, was destroyed about

[1] 1 Macc. v. 68; x. 83, 84. [2] 2 Kings i. 2. [3] Amos i. 8. [4] 1 Macc. x. 89.
[5] That is, God buildeth, Josh. xv. 11. [6] 1 Macc. v. 58 ff.
[7] Dowling, *PEFQ*, 1914, 84.
[8] Strabo, xvi. ii. 28. Philo in his account of his embassy to Caligula.
[9] Amos i. 6-8; Jer. xlvii; Zeph. ii. 4-7; Zech. ix. 5-7.
[10] Micah i. 10: *Tell it not in Gath* is hardly an exception, for the expression is proverbial.

750 B.C.; and renders valueless statements as to the city's site based on evidence subsequent to that date—as that of the *Onomasticon*, on which stress has been laid by recent writers,[1] or that of the Crusaders, who identified Gath with the site of Jabneh.[2]

When we turn to the appearances of Gath in history before the time of Amos, what they tell is this: Gath lay inland, on the borders of Hebrew territory, and probably in the north of Philistia. When the ark was taken from Ashdod, it was *brought about*, that is *inland*, again to Gath.[3] Gath was the Philistine city most frequently taken by Israel, and, indeed, was considered along with Ekron as having belonged to Israel[4]: after taking Gath, Hazael *set his face to go up to Jerusalem*.[5] This implies an inland position, and hence nearly all have sought Gath among the hills of the Shephelah or at their junction with the plain—at the south-east angle of the plain,[6] at Kefr Dikkerin,[7] at Deir Dubban,[8] and at Beit-Jibrin, or "home of big men".[9] The only argument for so southerly a position is Gath's connection with Ziklag in the story of David and Achish,[10] and this is scarcely conclusive. On the other hand, Gath is mentioned between Ashkelon and Ekron,[11] several times with Ekron, and especially in the pursuit of the Philistines from the Vale of Elah.[12] In a raid of Uzziah, Gath is coupled with Jamnia and Ashdod.[13] None of this prevents us from fixing on a site favoured by modern writers, Tell eṣ-Ṣafiyeh, commanding the entrance to the Vale of Elah and looking across Philistia to the sea. Steep limestone scarps rise from the plain to a broad plateau, still known by the natives as the Castle. During the Crusades King Fulke fortified it, it was destroyed by Saladin, and is said to have been restored by Richard. They called it Blanchegarde, from its white frontlet.

[1] *Onomasticon*, art *Γέθ*, "even now a village as you go from Eleutheropolis (Beit-Jibrin) to Diospolis (Lydda), about the fifth milestone from Eleutheropolis". Robinson, Conder, Guérin make much of this tradition.

[2] Will. of Tyre, xv. 24; Fel. Fab. ii. 425.

[3] 1 Sam. v. 8.

[4] Gath was taken under Samuel (1 Sam. vii. 14), and is then described as originally Israelite. Taken also by David, 1 Chron. xviii. 1; but this may be due to reading the parallel text, 1 Sam. vii. 14: Metheg Ha-Ammah, *bridle of the mother-city*, as if it were Gath Ha-Ammah, *Gath the metropolis*. Taken also by Uzziah (2 Chron. xxvi. 6), early in his reign. But 2 Chron. xi. 5-8, that Gath was among the cities rebuilt by Rehoboam may, if Gath be the true reading (Josephus, viii *Antt*. x. 1 gives Ipa or Ipan), mean, from other towns mentioned, another Gath, near Beit-Jibrin.

[5] 2 Kings xii. 17.

[6] Trel. Saunders, *Introd. to Survey*, etc.

[7] Guérin, *Judée*.

[8] Robinson.

[9] Albright suggests 'Araḳ el-Menshiyeh; no pottery being found here of Persian or Greek times.

[10] 1 Sam. xxvii. 2-6.

[11] *Ibid*. v. 8.

[12] *Ibid*. xvii. 52.

[13] 2 Chron. xxvi. 6.

It is too important a site to have been neglected by either Israel or the Philistines, and this lends the argument in its favour some weight, but not enough for proof. Tell eṣ-Ṣafiyeh may have been Libnah, the White,[1] or the Mizpeh of the Shephelah.[2] Gath has also been placed at Beit-Jibrin, the "home of big men", both because this might have served as a by-name for the city of giants,[3] and is in the neighbourhood of Mareshah,[4] and because Beit-Jibrin is not identified with any other town of antiquity. But Beit-Jibrin is too far south, and does not lie on the line of the rout of the Philistines after the battle of Socoh.[5] We must look farther north towards Ekron. First Chronicles mentions a Gath convenient to Aijalon and the hills of Ephraim,[6] but this may be Gath-rimmon, which lay towards Joppa. The case is made more difficult by the fact that Gath is a generic name, meaning "winepress", and was applied to several villages, usually with another name attached.[7] Remarkably enough, like their namesake they have disappeared, and in that land of the vine almost no site called after the winepress has held its name.

This then,—that Gath lay inland, on the borders of Israel, probably near Ekron, and perhaps in the mouth of a pass leading to Jerusalem,—is all we know of the town which was once famous, and which vanished 2500 years ago.[8] Gath perished with its giant race.[9]

X. *THE SHEPHELAH*[10]

Over the Plain, as you come up from the coast, you see a sloping moorland break into scalps and ridges of rock, and over these a loose gathering of chalk and limestone hills, round and featureless, with an occasional bastion flung out in front of them. This is the Shephelah—a famous theatre of the history of Palestine—debatable ground between Israel and the Philistines, the Maccabees and the Syrians, Saladin and the Crusaders.

[1] Josh. x. 29, 31 f.; 2 Kings viii. 22, etc. [2] Josh. xv. 38. [3] 2 Sam. xxi. 22.
[4] Cf. Moresheth-gath, Mic. i. 14. [5] 1 Sam. xvii. 52. [6] 1 Chron. vii. 21; viii. 13.
[7] Cf. Gath-ha-hepher, the birthplace of Jonah, in Galilee, Gath-rimmon near Joppa: Gath-rimmon in Eastern Manasseh, Josh. xxi. 25.
[8] For Gath in the Egyptian records see 2 *RP*, v. 48, Nos. 63 and 70; ii. 64, 65. Assyrian lists mention a Gûnti or Guntu near Ashdod, which some identify as Gath. Guntu may be the Egyptian Ka-na-ti in Thothmes' list (Müller, *Asien u. Europa*, etc., 161). Müller (*ib.* p. 159 and p. 393) suggests Kn-tu of Shishak's list as one of the many Gaths. In the Amarna Letters Gimti.
[9] On Tell eṣ-Ṣafiyeh and excavations there, Garstang, *Josh, Jud.* 392 f. with plan and picture.
[10] For this chapter, see Maps 4, 7 and 8.

Shephelah means *low* or *lowland*.[1] The Septuagint mostly renders it by *plain*,[2] and even in recent works[3] it has been applied to the Plain of Philistia. But the towns assigned by the Old Testament to the Shephelah are all situated in the low hills and not on the plain.[4] The Philistines are said to have made a raid on the cities of the Shephelah, which, therefore, must have stood outside their territory, and indeed did so[5]; and in another passage[6] the time is recalled when Jews *inhabited the Shephelah*, yet it is well known they never then inhabited the Maritime Plain. In First Maccabees I notice that the town of Adida is described in one passage as "in the Shephelah", and in another as "over against the Plain"[7]; while in the Talmud the Shephelah is expressly distinguished from the Plain, Lydda, at the base of the Low Hills, being marked as the point of division.[8] We conclude, therefore, that though

[1] A feminine form from the verb in the passage, *every mountain shall be made low*. It occurs with a like meaning in Arabic, and has been suggested as the root of *Seville* (Gesenius, *Thesaurus*).

[2] τὸ πεδίον or ἡ πεδινή.

[3] Stanley, *Sin. Pal.*, Kittel, *Gesch.* i. 14, Sieg. Stade, *Wörterbuch*, Shephelah = Küstenebene. Stade, *Gesch.* i. 157, has the opposite error of calling the Shephelah the "westliche Abdachung", as the Negeb is the "südliche Abdachung" of the Judæan range. This is to recognise the distinction of the Shephelah from the Maritime Plain; but it overlooks the valley between it and the Judæan range, which prevents it from being the mere "glacis" of the latter. Knobel and Dillmann, on Josh. xv. 33, are more correct, but fail to appreciate the break between the Judæan range and the Shephelah. On this see pp. 146 ff.

[4] Josh. xv. 33, 2 Chron. xxviii. 18. Aijalon in its vale, Gimzo to W of it; Zorah, to Eshtaol, Beth-shemesh in Sorek; Gederah to the north, and En-gannim, Zanoah, and Jarmuth within 3 miles S of Sorek: Adullam and Socoh up the Vale of Elah (W es-Sunṭ): Tappuah in the W el-Afranj; Mareshah, Lachish, Eglon SW of Beit-Jibrin. Others have not been identified. Vv. 45-47 of Josh. xv, which give Philistine towns in the Plain, are a later addition. 2 Chron. xxvi. 10 distinguishes Shephelah from Mishor, probably the Philistine plain. Eusebius describes the Shephelah as the low country (πεδινή) about Eleutheropolis (Beit-Jibrin) to the N and W. About Beit-Jibrin Clermont-Ganneau and Conder claim to have re-discovered the name in Arabic, Sifla (*Tent Work*, 277). See also my answer to Buhl (*Geog.* 104) in *Expositor*, Dec. 1896.

[5] 2 Chron. xxviii. 18; cf. Obad. 19. [6] Zech. vii. 7.

[7] 1 Macc. xii. 38, xiii. 13. ἐν τῇ Σεφηλᾷ, κατὰ πρόσωπον τοῦ πεδίου: Hadid, a town of Benjamin, Ezra ii. 33, Neh. xi. 34; in lists of Thothmes III, Hadita ii *RP*, 48; now el-Ḥaditheh.

[8] Talmud, *Jer. Shebiith*, ix. 2: ההר שפלה והעמק ביהודה. "In Judah mountain, Shephelah, and valley land", or "plain". A note to the Mishna on the country from Beth-horon to the sea: אמר ר׳ יהונן עוד היא יש בה הר ושפלה ועמק מבית חורזן ועד אמאוס הר מאמאוס ועד לוד שפלה מלוד ועד הים עמק "In that region are Mountain, Shephelah, and Plain. From Beth-horon to Emmaus Mountain, from Emmaus to Lydda Shephelah, from Lydda to the sea Plain."

the name may occasionally have been used to include the Maritime Plain,[1] and this wider use may have been occasionally revived, yet the Shephelah proper was the region of low hills between that Plain and the Central Range.[2] Shephelah would thus be equivalent to our "downs", low hills as distinguished from high, did it not include the flat valley land, which is as characteristic of this broken region as the subdued elevation of its hills. The name has been more fitly compared to the Scottish "Lowlands", which are not entirely plain, but have groups and ranges of hills.

How far north did the Shephelah run? From the sea, and across the Plain, low hills are seen buttressing the Central Range all along. Now the name Shephelah might be applied to the whole length of these low hills; but with one exception—in which it is probably used for the low hills that separate Carmel from Samaria[3]—it does not appear to have extended north of the Vale of Aijalon. The towns mentioned in the Old Testament as in the Shephelah are south of this; and if the identification be correct of "Adida in the Shephelah"[4] with Ḥaditheh, 4 miles ENE of Lydda, then this is the most northerly instance of the name. Roughly speaking, the Shephelah meant the low hills south, and not those north, of Aijalon. This distinction corresponds with a physical difference in the relations of these two parts of the low hills to the Central Range. North of Aijalon the low hills which run out on Sharon are connected with the mountains behind them. You ascend to the latter from Sharon either by sloping ridges, such as that which carries the high road from Jaffa to Nablus; or you climb up terraces, such as the succession of ranges closely built upon one another, by which the country rises from Lydda to Bethel. That is, the low hills west of Samaria are (to use the Hebrew) *'ăshēdôth*, Slopes, of the Central Range, and not a separate group. But south of Aijalon the low hills do not hang upon the Central Range, but are separated from the mountains of Judæa by valleys, both wide and narrow, which run from Aijalon to near Beersheba; and it is only where the low hills are thus flung off the Central Range into an independent group, separating

[1] No proof of this in O.T., but perhaps in Eusebius.

[2] It is easy to see why, if it had once extended to the coast, it shrank to the low hills, for the Plain had a name of its own, Philistia, while the Jews required to distinguish the low hills from the Central Range.

[3] In Josh. xi. 16, after the Mount, Negeb, Arabah are mentioned, comes *the Mount of Israel and its Shephelah*. As I elsewhere point out, this can only be that part of the Central Range which fell within the kingdom of N Israel, and the low hills between it and Carmel, Josh. xi. 2. Jer. Talmud gives an application of the name Shephelah across Jordan (Reland, ch. xlvii, p. 308), שפלתו חשבון.

[4] 1 Macc. xii. 38: *Σίμων ᾠκοδόμησε τὴν Ἀδιδὰ ἐν τῇ Σεφηλᾷ*—as a cover to the road from Joppa which he had won for the Jews (Conder).

Judæa from Philistia, that the name Shephelah seems to have been applied to them.[1]

This difference in the relation of the low hills to the Central Range, north and south of Aijalon, illustrates two historical phenomena. It explains some of the difference between the histories of Samaria and Judah. While the low hills opposite Samaria are really only approaches, slopes, and terraces of access to Samaria's centre, the southern low hills opposite Judah offer no furtherance towards this more isolated province: to have conquered them is not to have got footing upon it. And this division between the Shephelah and Judah explains why the Shephelah has so much more importance in history than the northern low hills, which are not so divided from Samaria. It is debatable as they cannot be. They are merged in Samaria. The Shephelah has a history of its own, for while they cannot be held by themselves, it can be, and was, so held at frequent famous periods of war and invasion.

This division between the Shephelah and Judæa is of such importance in the history of the land that it will be useful for us to follow it in detail.

As we ride across the Maritime Plain from Jaffa towards the Vale of Aijalon by the main road to Jerusalem, we become aware, as the road bends south, of getting behind low hills, which gradually shut out the view of the coast. These are spurs of the Shephelah: we are at the back of it, and in front of us are the high hills of the Central Range, with the wide gulf in them of the Vale of Aijalon. Near the so-called half-way house, the road to Jerusalem enters a steep and narrow defile, the Wady 'Ali, which is the real entrance to the Central Range, for at its upper end we come out among peaks over 2000 feet high. But if, instead of entering this steep defile, we turn to the south, crossing a broad low watershed, we find ourselves in the Wady el-Ghurab, a valley running south-west, with hills to the east of us touching 2000 feet, and hills to the west seldom above 800. The Wady el-Ghurab brings us out upon the broad Wady eṣ-Ṣurar, the Vale of Sorek, crossing which we find the mouth of the Wady en-Najil,[2] and ride still south along its straight narrow bed. Here again the mountains to the east of us are over 2000 feet, cleft by narrow and tortuous defiles, difficult ascents to the Judæan plateau, while to the west the hills of the Shephelah seldom reach 1000 feet, and the valleys among them are broad and easy. They might stand—especially if we remember that they have respectively Jerusalem and Philistia behind them

[1] True of the only other application of the name W of Jordan, as in n. 3 on the previous page. The low hills between Carmel and Dothan are flung off the Central Range as the Shephelah proper is.

[2] All g's are soft in the modern Arabic of Palestine; gh is like the French gr in *grasseyé*.

—for the narrow and broad ways of our Lord's parable. From the end of Wady en-Najil the passage is immediate to the Vale of Elah, the Wady es-Sunṭ, at the spot where David slew Goliath, and from there the broad Wady eṣ-Ṣur runs south, separating by 2 or 3 miles the lofty and compact range of Judæa on the east from the lower, looser hills of the Shephelah on the west. The Wady eṣ-Ṣur terminates opposite Hebron[1]: and here the dividing hollow turns south-west, and runs between peaks of nearly 3000 feet high to the east, and almost nothing above 1500 to the west, into the Wady esh-Sheri'a, which finds the sea south of Gaza, and may be regarded as the southern boundary of the Shephelah. I have ridden nearly every mile of this great fosse, that has been planted along the ramparts of Judæa, and describe from my own observations the striking difference of its two sides. All down the east, let me repeat, runs that close and lofty barrier of the Central Range, penetrated only by difficult defiles,[2] its edge turreted here and there by a town, giving proof of a table-land behind; but all down the west the low scattered ranges and clusters of the Shephelah, with their shallow dales and softer brows, much open ground and wide passes to the sea. Riding along the fosse between, I understood why the Shephelah was always debatable land, open equally to Israelite and Philistine, and why the Philistine, who so easily overran the Shephelah, seldom got farther than its eastern border, on which many of his encounters with Israel took place.[3]

From this definition of its boundaries—necessary to our appreciation of its independence alike of plain and of mountain—let us turn to survey the Shephelah itself.

The mountains look on the Shephelah, and the Shephelah looks on the sea—across the Philistine Plain. It curves round this plain from Gaza to Jaffa like an amphitheatre.[4] But the amphitheatre is cut by three or four great gaps, wide valleys that come right through from the foot of the Judæan hills to the sea. Between these gaps the low hills gather in clumps and in short ranges from 500 to 800 feet high, with one or two summits up to 1500.

[1] Near Terḳumieh. [2] See ch. xii, sec. 3.

[3] The geology of this district has not yet been completely studied; but the distinction between the Central Range and the Shephelah seems coincident with the border between the Nummulite limestone on the west and the cretaceous on the east. Cf. Hull, p. 63, of the *Geological Memoir of the PEF*: "The calcareous sandstone of Philistia", is "the key to the physical features of this part of Palestine, and accounts for the abrupt fall of the table-land of Central Palestine along the borders of Philistia, and along a line extending to the base of Mount Carmel; as the harder limestones dip under and pass below the comparatively softer formation which has been more deeply denuded than the former." See also p. 63.

[4] Trelawney Saunders, *Introduction*, p. 249.

The formation is of limestone or chalk, and very soft—therefore irregular and almost featureless, with a few prominent outposts upon the Plain. In the cross valleys there are perennial, or almost perennial, streams, with broad pebbly beds; the soil is alluvial and red, with corn-fields. But on the slopes and glens of each hilly maze between the cross valleys the soil is a grey white; there are no perennial streams, and few springs, but many reservoirs of rain-water. The corn-fields straggle for want of level space, yet the olive-groves are finer than on either the plain below or the range above. Inhabited villages are frequent; the ruins of abandoned ones more so. But the prevailing scenery of the region is of short, steep hillsides and narrow glens, with few great trees, and thickly covered by brushwood and oak-scrub—crags and scalps of limestone breaking through, and a grey torrent-bed at the bottom of each glen. In the more open passes of the south, the straight line of a Roman road dominates the brushwood, or you see the levelled walls of an early Christian convent, and perhaps the solitary gable of a Crusaders' church. In the rocks are older monuments—large wine and oil presses cut on platforms above ridges that may have been vineyards; and once or twice on a braeside a huge boulder has well-worn steps up it, and on its top little cuplike hollows, evidently an ancient altar. Caves abound—near the villages gaping black dens for men and cattle, but up the unfrequented glens hidden by hanging bush, behind which you disturb only the wild pigeon. Bees murmur everywhere, larks are singing; and, although in the maze of hills you may wander for hours without meeting a man or seeing a house, you are seldom out of sound of the human voice, shepherds and ploughmen calling to their cattle and to each other across the glens. Higher up you rise to moorland, with rich grass if there is a spring, but otherwise heath, thorns, and rough herbs that scent the wind. Bees abound here too, and dragon-flies, kites, and crows; sometimes an eagle floats over from the cliffs of Judæa. The sun beats strong, but you see and feel the sea; the high mountains are behind, at night they breathe upon these lower ridges gentle breezes, and the dews are heavy.

Altogether it is a rough, happy land, with its glens and moors, its mingled brushwood and barley-fields; frequently under cultivation, but for the most part broken and thirsty, with few wells and many hiding-places; just the home for strong border-men like Samson, and just the theatre for that guerilla warfare, varied occasionally by pitched battles, which Israel and Philistia, the Maccabees and the Syrians, Saladin and Richard waged with each other.

The chief encounters between those foes naturally took place in the wide valleys, which cut through the Shephelah maze. The strategic importance of these valleys can hardly be overrated, for they do not belong to the Shephelah alone. Each of them is continued by a defile into the heart of Judæa, not far from an important city, and each has at its other end one of the five cities of the Philistines. To realise these valleys is to understand the wars that have been fought on the western watershed of Palestine from Joshua's time to Saladin's.

1. Take the most northerly of these valleys. The narrow plain, across which the road to Jerusalem runs, brings you up from Lydda, to opposite the high Valley of Aijalon. The Valley of Aijalon, really part of the Shephelah,[1] is a fertile plain gently sloping up to the foot of the Central Range, the steep wall of which seems to forbid further passage. But three gorges break through, and, with sloping ridges between them run up past the two Beth-horons on to the plateau at Gibeon, a few flat miles north of Jerusalem.[2] This has always been the easiest passage from the coast to the capital of Judæa—the most natural channel for the overflow of Israel westwards. In the first settlement of the land, it was down Aijalon that Dan pushed and touched the sea[3]; after the exile, it was down Aijalon that the returned Jews cautiously felt their way, and fixed their westmost colonies at its mouth on the edge of the Plain.[4] Throughout history we see hosts swarming up this avenue, or swept down it in flight. At the head of it invading Israel emerged from the Jordan Valley, and looked over the Shephelah towards the sea. Joshua drove the Canaanites down to Makkedah in the Shephelah on that day when such long work had to be done that he bade the sun stand still for its accomplishment[5]; down Aijalon the early men of Ephraim and Benjamin

[1] Thus Aijalon and Gimzo were in the Shephelah (2 Chron. xxviii. 18), and the Talmud says the Shephelah extended from Emmaus to Lydda.

[2] The five roads from the Vale of Aijalon to Jerusalem are: (1) On one of the sloping ridges between the gorges, you rise rapidly from W Selman 818 feet, by Beit-Liḳia 1600, Beit-'Anan 2070, el-Ḳubeibeh 2570, and along the ridge by Biddu and Beit-Iksa 2525, across W Beit-Ḥanina to Kh. el-Bedr 2519, thence to Jerusalem. (2) Or you follow W Selman from 818 feet to 1157, 1610, 1840, till it brings you out at its head on the plateau of el-Jib 2400 feet, about 5 m. N of Jerusalem. (3) Or you take the more famous Beth-horon road, which rises from Beit-sira 840 feet on a spur to the lower Beth-horon 1240 feet, and thence traverses a ridge with the gorges of W Selman to the S, and W es-Sunṭ and W el-Imeish to the N, to the upper Beth-horon (2022), and still on the ridge, comes out on the plateau of el-Jib, a little to the north of No. 2. (4) From Beit-Nuba in mid Aijalon a road (Derb es-Sulṭain as I heard it before I took it) strikes E over Aijalon, entering the hills by W el-Burj (?), and so to Kh el-Buruj (1440), after which it turns S below the ridge of Beit-'Anan with ruins of a khan, and joins the road from the latter a little NW of el-Ḳubeibeh. See (1). (5) From Yalo to Ḳuryat el-'Enab.

[3] Chapter iii.

[4] Lydda, Ono, Hadid on the Ge-Haḥarashim, pp. 121 f.

[5] Josh. x. 10. Makkedah is identified by Warren as el-Mughar to the south of Ekron, but this is doubtful.

raided the Philistines[1]; up Aijalon the Philistines swarmed to the heart of Israel's territory at Michmash, disarmed the Israelites, and forced them to come down the Vale to get their tools sharpened, so that the mouth of the Vale was called the Valley of the Smiths even till after the exile[2]; down Aijalon Saul and Jonathan beat the Philistines from Michmash,[3] and by the same way, soon after his accession, King David *smote the Philistines*—who had come up about Jerusalem either by this route or the gorges leading from the Vale of Sorek—*from Gibeon until thou come to Gezer*,[4] that looks right up Aijalon. Ages later this rout found a singular counterpart. In A.D. 66 a Roman army under Cestius Gallus came up from Antipatris on the 'Aujeh by way of Aijalon. When they entered the gorges of the Central Range, they suffered from the sudden attacks of the Jews; and, although they set Jerusalem on fire and occupied part of it, they suddenly retreated by the way they had come. The Jews pursued, and, as far as Antipatris, smote them in thousands, as David had smitten the Philistines.[5] It may have been because of this that Titus, when he came to punish the Jews two years later, avoided Aijalon and the gorges at its head, and took the higher and less covered road by Gophna to Gibeah.[6]

The Vale of Aijalon was also overrun by the Egyptian invasions. Egypt long held Gezer at the mouth of it, and Shishak's campaign included the capture of Beth-horon, Aijalon, Makkedah and Jehudah near Joppa.[7]

But it was in the time of the Maccabæan wars and in the time of the Crusades that this part of the Shephelah was most famously contested.

We have already seen that the Plain of Aijalon, with its mouth turned slightly northwards, lay open to the roads down the Maritime Plain from Carmel. It was, therefore, the natural entrance into Judæa for the Syrian armies who came south by the coast; and Modein, the home of the Maccabees, and the origin of the revolt against Syria, lies on the edge of Aijalon by the path the invaders took.[8] Just as at Lydda, in this same district, the revolt afterwards broke out against the Romans in A.D. 66, so now in 166 B.C. it

[1] 1 Chron. vii. 21; viii. 13.

[2] 1 Sam. xiii. 19. See p. 121 for the origin of the name, Ge-Haḥarashim.

[3] 1 Sam. xiii, xiv; *ap.* xiv. 31. Aijalon survives in Yalo.

[4] 2 Sam. v. 25; 1 Chron. xiv. 16. [5] Josephus, ii *Wars*, xix. [6] v *Wars*, ii.

[7] On Gezer, 1 Kings ix. 15-17. On "Shishak's Campaign": Maspero in *Transactions of Victoria Institute*; W. Max Müller, *Asien u. Eur. nach. altägypt. Denkm.*, 166 f. The town of Aijalon is mentioned, in the Tell el-Amarna Tablets, as one of the first to be taken from the Egyptian vassals.

[8] 1 Macc. ii. 1, 15, 23, 70; xiii. 25, 30; xvi. 4; 2 Macc. xiii. 4, *Μωδείν* or *Μωδεείν*. Variants, *Μωδεείμ*, 1 Macc. ii. 23; ix. 19; xiii. 25, 30; *Μωδαείμ*, xvi. 4; *Μωδιείμ*, 2 Macc. xiii. 14. In Josephus, *Μωδεεῖμ* or *Μωδεεί*, xii *Antt.* vi. 1, xi. 2; xiii *Antt.*

broke out against the Hellenising Syrians.[1] The first camps, both Jewish and Syrian, were pitched about Emmaus, not far off the present high road to Jerusalem.[2] The battles rolled—for the battles in the Shephelah were always rolling battles—between Beth-horon and Gezer, and twice the pursuit of the Syrians extended across the last ridges of the Shephelah to Jamnia and Ashdod.[3] Jonathan swept right down to Joppa and won it.[4] But the tide sometimes turned, and the Syrians mastering the Shephelah fortresses, swept up Aijalon to the walls of Jerusalem[5]; though they preferred on occasions to turn the flank of the Jews by coming through Samaria,[6] or gaining the Judæan table-land at Bethsura by one of the southern defiles.[7]

Now, up and down this great channel thirteen centuries later the fortune of war ebbed and flowed in an almost precisely similar fashion. Like the Syrians, and, indeed, from the same centre of Antioch, the Crusaders took their way to Jerusalem by Tyre, Acre, and Joppa, and there turned up through the Shephelah and the Vale of Aijalon. The First Crusaders found no opposition; two days sufficed for their march from Ramleh by Beth-horon to the Holy City. Through the Third Crusade, however, Saladin firmly held the Central Range, and though parties of Christians swept up within sight of Jerusalem their camps never advanced beyond Aijalon. But all the Shephelah rang with the exploits of Richard. Fighting his way, as we have seen, from Carmel along the foot of the low hills, with an enemy perpetually assailing his flank, Richard established himself at Joppa, opposite the mouth of Aijalon. Thence he pushed gradually inland, planting forts or castles—on the plain, Plans and Maen; on the edge of the Shephelah, Mirabel and Mont-

---

vi. 6; *Μωδεείν*, i *Wars*, i. 3. *Onomast.* Euseb. *Μηδεείμ*, Jerome, Modeim. Evidently a plural, now in the Hebrew form, now in the Aramaic. So Talmud, Môdî'îm מודיעים: but also Môdî'îth מודיעית (Neubauer, *Geog. Talm.* § 99). Either would give the present Medieh or Midieh, 7 m. ESE of Lydda (Neubauer), which suits Eusebius' statement that Medieh was near Lydda, and 1 Macc. xiii. 29, that the monument of the Maccabees could be seen from the sea. Forner had also proposed Medieh, *Le Monde*, 1866 (Guérin). Robinson takes Laṭrun, and in *Judée*, i. 311, Guérin inclines to this. In *Rev. Bibl.* Le Camus contests the interpretation of 1 Macc. xiii. 29 f. that Modeeim was visible from the sea, but Buhl (p. 198) says he gives no good reasons for a more southerly position. Maundrell says Modon "a village on a high hill in sight of the convent of St. John".

[1] 1 Macc. ii. [2] *Ibid.* iii. [3] *Ibid.* iii, iv, vii, ix. [4] *Ibid.* x. 75, 76.

[5] In Judas' lifetime, but when he was absent the Jews were pursued "to the borders of Judæa", *ibid.* v. 56-61. And again in the campaign in which Judas was slain, *ibid.* ix; and the battle between Jonathan and Bacchides, when the latter took Emmaus and Gezer, *ibid.* ix. 50, 52.

[6] Probably the line of Bacchides' advance, *ibid.* ix. 1-4.

[7] *Ibid.* iv. 29, vi. 31, 49, 50, ix. 52, etc.

gisard; and up the Vale of Aijalon, the Château d'Arnauld, perhaps the present El-Burj; Turon (now Laṭrun) on one side and Emmaus (now 'Amwas)[1] on the other side of the present road to Jerusalem—till he reached Betenoble, far up the vale, and near the foot of the Central Range.[2] But Richard did not confine his tactics to the Vale of Aijalon. Like the Syrians, when he found this blocked, he turned south and made a diversion upon the Judæan tableland, up one of the parallel valleys of the Shephelah, and then, when that failed, returned suddenly to Betenoble.[3] All this cost him from August 1191 to June 1192. He was then within 12 miles of Jerusalem as the crow flies, and on a raid he saw the secluded city, but he retired. His funds were exhausted, and his followers quarrelsome. He feared, too, the summer drought of Jerusalem, which had compelled Cestius Gallus to withdraw in the moment of victory. But, above all, Richard's retreat from the foot of the Central Range illustrates what I have emphasised, that to have taken the Shephelah was to be no nearer Judæa. The baffled Crusaders fell back through their castles in the Shephelah to the coast. Saladin moved after them, occupying Mont Gisart, and taking Joppa; and though Richard relieved the latter, and the coast remained with the Crusaders for the next seventy years, the Shephelah, with its European castles and cloisters, passed from Christian possession.

[1] See Clermont-Ganneau, *Arch. Res.* i, ch. xix.

[2] The sites of most of these are uncertain. Plans and Maen lay east of Joppa, but not east of Ramleh (*Itiner. Ricardi*, iv. 29). So Maen cannot be el-Burj or Deir Ma'in (Guérin, *Jud.* i. 337), and of Conder's two suggestions (*Syr. Stone Lore*, 398) the second is correct. Plans has not been found.—The difficulty in accepting Conder's identification of Mirabel with el-Mirr, near Ras el-'Ain, NE of Joppa, is that the latter is on the plain, where the *Itiner.* says the Turks whom Richard scattered fled to Mirabel, that is, if el-Mirr be Mirabel, NW and *towards* the plains which the Christians held.—On Montgisard (Rey) or Mont Gisart (C.-Ganneau), see next pages.—Château d'Arnauld is described by William of Tyre as "in descensu montium, in primis auspiciis campestrium, via qui itur Liddam". The site is uncertain—el-Burj (De Saulcy), Kharubeh (Guérin).—Laṭrun derived by mediævals from Latro, and supposed to be the den Boni Latronis of the Good Thief, Dismas (Quaresm. *Eluc. Terr. Sanct.* ii. 12), is really el-Aṭrun. This may be from either (1) old French *touron* or *turon*, an isolated hill, for in 1244 Laṭrun was called Turo Militum (Rey, *Colon. Franques*, 300, 413), and Turon might become, according to a law in the Arab adoption of foreign words, Atron, like *itfa* from *tafa*; or (2) Arabic Naṭrun, post of observation, with article en-Naṭrun, that might become el-Laṭrun, or the present el-Aṭrun. Cf. Nöldeke, *ZDPV*, vii. 141.—Betenoble: "Near the foot of the mountains", *Itiner.* iv. 34. Betenoble is philologically liker Beit-Nabala, on the edge of the Maritime Plain, 4 m. NE of Lydda, than Beit-Nuba, which is at the other end of Aijalon, near Yalo. But other references in the *Itiner.*, though not conclusive (v. 49, vi. 9), imply it was well inland from Ramleh.

[3] *Itiner. Ricardi*, v. 46-48.

We have won a more vivid imagination of the campaigns of Joshua and David by following the marches of Judas Maccabæus, the rout of the Roman legions, and the advance and retreat of Richard Lionheart—the last described with so much detail. The natural lines, which those armies had to follow, remained through the centuries the same: the same were the difficulties of climate, forage, and locomotion; so that the best commentaries on many chapters of the Old Testament are the Books of the Maccabees, the Annals of Josephus, and the Chronicles of the Crusades. History never repeats, without explaining itself.[1]

One point in the Northern Shephelah, round which these tides of war have swept, deserves special notice—Gezer, or Gazar. It is one of the few remarkable bastions which the Shephelah flings out to the west—on a ridge running towards Ramleh, the most prominent object in view of the traveller from Jaffa towards Jerusalem. It is high and isolated, but fertile and well watered, a very strong post and striking landmark. The name occurs in the Egyptian correspondence of the fourteenth century, where it is described as being taken from the Egyptian vassals by the tribes whose invasion agitates that correspondence.[2] A city of the Canaanites, under a king of its own—Horam—Gezer is not given as one of Joshua's conquests, though the king is[3]; but the Israelites *drave not out the Canaanites who dwelt at Gezer*,[4] and in the hands of these it remained till its conquest by Egypt whose Pharaoh gave it, with his daughter, to Solomon, and Solomon rebuilt it.[5] Judas Maccabæus was strategist enough to gird himself early to the capture of Gezer, and Simon fortified it to cover the way to the harbour of Joppa, and caused John, his son, the captain of the host, to dwell there.[6] It was virtually the key of Judæa at a time when Judæa's foes came down the coast from the north; and, with Joppa, it formed part of the Syrian demands upon the Jews.[7] But this is by no means the last of it. M. Clermont-Ganneau, who discovered the site,[8] identified Gezer with the Mont Gisart of the

[1] For the British campaign of 1917, see below, pp. 154, 196 f.

[2] See 2 *RP*. 74, 78; Conder's *Tell-el-Amarna Tablets*, 122, 134-138, 147. On the Amarna tablets Gezer is Gazri; in Egyptian Kadiru.

[3] Josh. x. 33.

[4] *Ibid*. xvi. 3, 10; Judges i. 19.

[5] 1 Kings ix. 15-17. See W. Max Müller, *op. cit*. 160, 390.

[6] 1 Macc. xiii. 43 (where Gaza should read Gazara, cf. Josephus, xiii *Antt*. vi. 7; i *Wars*, ii. 2) and 53.

[7] 1 Macc. xv. 28.

[8] By finding upon it two stones, dated from the time of the Maccabees, *PEFQ*, 1875. On the extensive and fruitful excavations by R. A. S. Macalister, 1902-8, through 40 feet of accumulations from the Neolithic Age to the time of the Maccabees, see the *PEF Mem. The Excavation of Gezer*, 3 vols. (1912); *inter alia*, two walls, each 16

Crusades.[1] Mont Gisart was a castle and fief in the county of Joppa, with an abbey of St. Katherine of Mont Gisart, "whose prior was one of the five suffragans of the Bishop of Lydda". It was the scene, on 24th November 1174, seventeen years before the Third Crusade, of a victory won by a small army from Jerusalem under the boy-king, the leper Baldwin IV, against a much larger host under Saladin, and, in 1192, Saladin encamped upon it during negotiations for a truce with Richard.[2]

On the morning of 14th November 1917, Gezer, now Tell Jezer, was rushed and taken by a Brigade of English Yeomanry with a battery of machine-guns.[3]

Shade of King Horam, what hosts of men have fallen round that citadel of yours! On what camps and columns has it looked down through the centuries, since first you saw the strange Hebrews burst with the sunrise across the hills, and chase your countrymen down Aijalon—that day when the victors felt the very sun conspire with them to achieve the unexampled length of battle. Within sight of every Egyptian and Assyrian invasion of the land, Gezer has also seen Alexander pass by, the legions of Rome in unusual flight, the armies of the Cross struggle, waver and give way, Napoleon come and go, and British yeomen come and stay. If all could rise who have fallen around its base—Ethiopians, Hebrews, Assyrians, Arabs, Turcomans, Greeks, Romans, Celts, Saxons, Mongols, and English—what a rehearsal of the Judgement Day it would be! Few travellers who rush across the plain realise that the first conspicuous hill they pass in Palestine is also one of the most thickly haunted, even in that narrow land into which history has so crowded itself. But upon the ridge of Gezer no sign of all this now remains, except in the name Tell Jezer, the traces of the modern excavations, and in a hollow to the north, beside a fountain, the scattered Christian stones of Deir Warda, the Convent of the Rose.

Up none of the other valleys of the Shephelah has history surged as up and down Aijalon and past Gezer, for none are so open to the north, nor present so easy a passage to Jerusalem.

2. But the next valley, Wady eṣ-Ṣurar, or Vale of Sorek,[4] has an importance of its own, and remarkably enough, is now the main road to Jerusalem. The railway from Jaffa, instead of being carried up Aijalon, turns south at Ramleh

---

feet thick, ruins of a citadel, a great water-tunnel, group of seven monoliths, traces of infant sacrifices, Egyptian hieroglyphs, two cuneiform tablets.

[1] *Recueil d'Archéol. Orient.*, Paris, 1888, pp. 351-92.

[2] *Ibid.* p. 359.

[3] Massey, *op. cit.* 120 ff.

[4] Albright, *Bull. American Sch. of Oriental Research,* thinks Sorek = W Suriḳ.

by the pass through sandhills to Ekron, and thence runs up the Wady eṣ-Ṣurar and its continuing defile through the Judæan range to that plain south-west of Jerusalem, which is probably the Vale of Rephaim. It is the way the Philistines came in the days of the Judges and David; there is no shorter road into Judæa from Ekron, Jamnia, and perhaps Ashdod.[1] Ashkelon would be better reached—as it was by the Crusaders when they held Jerusalem—by the Wady es-Sunṭ and Tell eṣ-Ṣafiyeh.

Just before the Wady eṣ-Ṣurar approaches the Judæan range, its width is increased by the entrance of Wady Ghurab from the north-west, and by Wady en-Najil from the south. A great basin is formed with the low hill of 'Artuf, and its village in the centre. Ṣur'a the ancient Zorah, and Eshua',[2] perhaps Eshtaol, lie on the slopes to the north; 'Ain Shems, certainly Beth-shemesh, lies on the southern slope opposite Zorah. When you see this basin, you perceive its importance. Fertile and well-watered—a broad brook runs through it, with tributary streamlets—it lies immediately under the Judæan range, and at the head of a valley passing to Philistia, while at right angles to this it is crossed by the great hollow which separates the Shephelah from Judæa. Roads diverge in all directions. Two ascend the Judæan plateau by defiles from the Wady en-Najil; another and greater defile, still under the name Wady eṣ-Ṣurar, runs up east to the plateau next Jerusalem, and others north-east into the rough hills known to the Old Testament as Mount Jearim, while the road from Beit-Jibrin comes down the Wady en-Najil, and continues by an easy pass to 'Amwas and the Vale of Aijalon. As a centre, then, between the southern and northern valleys of the Shephelah, and Judæa and Philistia, this basin was sure to become important. Immediately under the central range it was generally held by Israel, who could pour down upon it by five or six different defiles.[3] It was also open to Philistia, and had

[1] By W eṣ-Ṣurar Jerusalem is some 28 miles from Ekron, 32 from Jamnia, 38 from Ashdod, 45 from Ashkelon.

[2] Ṣur'a صرعا is Hebrew צרעה, 1100 feet above the sea, say 800 above the valley. Eshua' اشوع is far in sound from Eshtaol אשתאול, but the shrinkage is possible, and the village lies near Ṣur'a. Guérin heard at Beit-'Aṭab "an old tradition" that Eshua' was originally Eshu'al or Eshthu'al. This deserves confirmation—if possible. Kh. Suriḳ seems an echo of the ancient Sorek. On 'Ain Shems and its excavation, S. A. Cook, *PEFQ*, 1910, 220; D. Mackenzie, *id.* 1911, 69, 139, 143, 169; 1912, 171; Mackenzie and Newton, *PEF Annual*, 1911, pp. 41 ff., 1912-13; E. Grant, *PEFQ*, 1928, p. 179; 1929, p. 201.

[3] Of the two roads to the S of the main defile the more southerly leaves 'Ain Shems, crosses the Wady en-Najil, enters a defile S of Deir Aban, and reaches the plateau at Beit 'Aṭab, 2052 feet: thence over stony moorland to el-Khuḍr, on the Jerusalem-Hebron road: a bare road, with no obstacles after the defile, it may be shortened by

easy passage to the Vale of Aijalon, whose towns are often classed with its own.[1]

On the northern bank of this basin the tribe of Dan found a temporary settlement. The territory, which Joshua assigns to Dan,[2] lies down the parallel valleys that lead through the Shephelah to the sea, Aijalon and Sorek, and the Song of Deborah seems to imply that they reached the coast,—*why did Dan abide in ships?*[3] But either Deborah speaks in scorn of futile ambitions westward, which were stirred in Dan by the sight of the sea from the Shephelah, and Dan never reached the sea at all; or else the tribe had been driven back from the coast, for now they lay poised on the broad pass between their designated valleys, retaining only two of their proper towns, Zorah and Eshtaol. This was under the eaves of Israel's mountain home, yet open to attacks from the plain. They found it so intolerable that they moved north to the sources of Jordan; but not without stamping their name on the place they left, in a form which showed how temporary their hold of it had been —the Camp of Dan. Here, in Zorah, either before or after the migration, their hero, Samson, was born.[4]

---

cutting across to Bittir. The other is almost parallel to this; it rises to the plateau at Deir el-Ḥawa, crosses to Er-Ras, and so by Milḥah to Jerusalem. The road up the main defile follows it to Khurbet el-Loz, then crosses to the Jerusalem-Jaffa road. Another road crosses from Zorah to the foot of Mount Jearim, and traverses this to Ṣoba, and another follows W Ghurab to the Jerusalem high-road.

[1] Zorah and Aijalon are also coupled in one of the Tell el-Amarna Letters, 137, Berlin collection; Conder, *Tell-el-Amarna Tablets*, 156. Josh. xix. 40-48: towns assigned to Dan. 2 Chron. xi. 10, *Zorah and Aijalon*, fortified by Rehoboam.

[2] Josh. xix. 40-48, J and P.

[3] Judges v. 17. But see Budde's reading of this, *Richt. Sam.* p. 16, n. 2.

[4] In Judges the Camp of Dan is twice mentioned: in the life of Samson, part of the body of the Book, where it is *between Zorah and Eshtaol*, xiii. 25; and in the account of the Danite migration, one of some appendages to the Book, where it is the muster-place of the soldiers of Dan when they *came up from Zorah and Eshtaol*, and said to be *in Kiriath-jearim in Judah*, xviii. 12, 13; a clause adds, *lo, it is behind*, i.e. *west of Kiriath-jearim*. The same place could not have lain between Zorah and Eshtaol, and away from both in Kiriath-jearim. We have evidently two narratives, distinguished by critics on other, textual grounds. (Budde, *Richt. Sam.*, assigns the former to the Yahvist, the latter to the Elohist, 138 ff.) In this case the clause on xviii. 12, *it is west of Kiriath-jearim*, is a gloss to modify what precedes it, and bring it into harmony with xiii. 25, for the locality between Zorah and Eshtaol may be described as lying W of Kiriath-jearim, and that, whether the latter be Ḳuryat 'Enab or Khurbet 'Erma. Again, since xviii. 11-13 is part of the appendix to the Book, and therefore not in chronological sequence from the earlier chapters, it is difficult to say whether Dan's migration came before or after the events of Samson's life. If before, then some Danite families had stayed behind in Zorah and Eshtaol, which is likely, and the theory

It is as fair a nursery for boyhood as you will find in the land—a hillside facing south against the sunshine, with corn, grass, and olives, scattered boulders and winter brooks, the broad valley below with the pebbly stream and screens of oleanders, the south-west wind from the sea blowing over all. There *the child Samson grew up; and the Lord blessed him, and the Spirit of the Lord began to move him in the camp of Dan between Zorah and Eshtaol.* Across the Valley of Sorek, in full view, is Beth-shemesh, now 'Ain Shems, House and Well of the Sun, with which name it is natural to connect his own—Shimshon, "Sun-like".[1] Over the low hills beyond is Timnah, where he found his first love and killed the young lion. Beyond is the Philistine Plain, with its miles upon miles of corn, which, if as closely sown then as now, would require scarce three, let alone three hundred foxes, with torches on their tails, to set it all afire. The Philistine cities are but a day's march away, by easy roads. And so from these country braes to yonder plains and the highways of the great world—from the pure home and the mother who talked with angels, to the heathen cities, their harlots and their prisons—we see at one sweep of the eye the course in which this uncurbed strength, at first tumbling, and sporting with laughter like one of its native brooks, like them also ran to the flats and the mud, and, being darkened and befouled, was used by men to turn their mills.[2]

---

becomes possible, though not probable, that the name Camp of Dan, given, as in xviii. 13, to a particular spot in Kiriath-jearim, had extended to the whole district, which the settlement of Dan had covered. The one thing certain is, we have two documents. See also Cook, *Camb. Ancient Hist.* ii. 314 n.

[1] Mackenzie (*PEF Annual*, 1912-13, p. 83) found a head "representing some divinity, and if we were to ask what Canaanite male divinity were most likely to be adored at Beth-shemesh the answer would be Shemesh himself".

[2] The other scenes of Samson's life are not satisfactorily identified. For the rock Etam and its cleft Conder proposes (also Henderson, *Pal.* p. 109) a cave at Beit-'Aṭab (*b* and *m* interchangeable) on the Judæan plateau. But the cave at Beit-'Aṭab (I have visited it) is too large to be described as a cleft, and if Etam had been so high up the narrative would not have said (Judges xv. 8) that Samson *went down* to it. Coming up from Zorah to Beit-'Aṭab on a summer day, one feels that strongly. Schick, *ZDPV*, x. 143, proposes plausibly (Guthe thinks correctly) the 'Araḳ Isma'in a cave in a rock N of Wady Isma'in. Lehi he finds, in Khurbet eṣ-Ṣiyyagh (الصياغ in the Name Lists, *PEF Mem.*), ruins at mouth of W en-Najil. Aquila and Symmachus, and Jos. (v *Antt.* ix. 8, 9) translate Lehi *Σιαγών*, and Schick reports E of Ṣiyyagh an 'Ain Nakura. But Ṣiyyagh could have come from Siagon only through Greeks and Christians, and is a late valueless tradition. Conder suggests for Ramath-lehi and En-hakkore, the 'Ayun Abu-Meḥarib, "founts of the place of battles", sometimes called 'Ayun Ḳara, "founts of a crier", near Kesla, where is a chapel to Sheikh Nedhir, "the Nazarite chief", and a ruin Ism-Allah, which he suggests is a corruption of Esm'a Allah, "God heard". Interesting, but inconclusive. Henderson, *Pal.* 110, suggests the serrated

The theory that the story of Samson is a mere sun-myth, edited for the sacred record by an orthodox Jew, has never received acceptance from leading critics, who have been convinced that, though containing elements of popular legend, its hero was an actual personage. Those who study the story of Samson with its geography must feel that the story has a basis of reality. Unlike the exploits of the personifications of the Solar Fire in Aryan and Semitic mythologies, those of Samson are confined to a limited region. The attempts to interpret them as phases or influences of the sun, or to force them into a cycle like the labours of Hercules, have broken down.[1] To me it seems just as easy and just as futile to read the story of this turbulent strength as the myth of a mountain-stream, at first exuberant and sporting with its powers, but when it has left its native hills, mastered and darkened by men, and yet afterwards bursting its confinement and taking its revenge upon them. For it is rivers, and not sunbeams, that work mills and overthrow temples. But the idea of finding any nature-myth in such a story is far-fetched. As Hitzig emphasises, it is not a nature-force but a character with whom we have to deal here, and, above all, the religious element in the story, so far from being a later flavour imparted to the original material, is the life of the whole.[2]

The head of the Vale of Sorek has usually been regarded as the scene of the battle in which the Philistines took the ark.[3] The place, as we have seen, was convenient both to Israel and Philistia, and it has been argued that in afterwards bringing back the ark to Beth-shemesh,[4] the Philistines were seeking to make their atonement exact by restoring their booty at the spot where they had captured it; and that the stone on which they rested the ark may have been the Eben-ezer, Stone of Help, near which they had defeated the Israelites, and the Israelites are said (in another document)[5] afterwards to

---

appearance of W Isma'in as originating the name Lehi: Hashen, the tooth, occurs up it. Guérin heard the Weli Sh. Gharib called Ḳabr Shamshun, but this may be a recent legend. He puts these scenes at 'Ain el-Lekhi, NW of Bethlehem (*Jud.* ii. 317 ff., 396 ff.). Buhl (p. 91) counts Schick's identifications uncertain. Timnah perhaps Kh. Tibneh.

[1] Goldziher, *Hebrew Mythology*. E. Wietzke, *Der Biblische Simson der Ægyptische Horus Ra*: 1888. The etymologies of this work illustrate the length that men will go when hunting for myths.

[2] This point is well put by Orelli, Herzog's *Real-Encycl.* Cf. Hitzig, Ewald, Stade, Kittel, in their histories of Israel. All deny the myth, admit legend, and allow that the hero was historical. Budde, *Richt. Sam.* 133, holds to Kuenen's position that the narrator knew nothing of a myth, but says "the legendary nature of the narratives is *selbst verständlich*".

[3] 1 Sam. iv. [4] 1 Sam. vi. [5] 1 Sam. vii.

have defeated them. But these reasons are not more than probable. The name neither of Eben-ezer nor of Aphek has been identified in the neighbourhood, and on the data of the narratives Eben-ezer may just as probably have lain farther north—say at the head of Aijalon.[1]

The course of the ark's return, however, is certain. It was up the broad Vale of Sorek that the untended kine of Beth-shemesh dragged the cart behind them with the ark upon it, *lowing as they went, and turned not aside to the right or to the left, and the lords of the Philistines went after them unto the borders of Beth-shemesh. And Beth-shemesh*—that is to say, all the villagers, as is the custom at harvest-time—were *in the valley* (the village itself lay high up on the valley's southern bank) *reaping the wheat harvest, and they lifted up their eyes and saw the ark, and came rejoicing to meet it.*[2] *And the cart came into the field of Joshua the Bethshemite and stood there, and a great stone was there, and they clave the wood of the cart, and the kine they offered as a burnt-offering to Yahweh*—certainly upon the stone.[3] *And the five lords of the Philistines saw, and returned to Ekron the same day. . . . And the great stone whereon they set down the ark of Yahweh is a witness thereof in the field of Joshua the Bethshemite.*

In the Shephelah, however, the ark was not to remain. The story continues that some of the careless harvesters, who had run to meet the ark, treated it too familiarly—*gazed at it and Yahweh smote of them threescore and ten men.*[4] The plague which the ark had brought upon Philistia clung about it still. As stricken Ashdod had passed it on to Gath, Gath to Ekron, and Ekron to Beth-shemesh, so Beth-shemesh now made haste to deposit it upon Yahweh's own territory of the hills: *To whom shall He go up from us?* The nearest hill-town was Kiriath-jearim, *the Town of the Woods.*[5] This must have lain

[1] The argument stated above for the identity of the great stone by Beth-shemesh (1 Sam. vi. 14, 18) with Eben-ezer (iv. 1, v. 1, and vii. 12) is M. Clermont-Ganneau's (*PEFZ*, 1874, 279; 1877, 154 ff.). Wilson thinks Deir Aban too remote from Shiloh and Mizpah. It does not suit the topography of 1 Sam. vii. 11, 12, which is from another document than chs. iv-vi. According to the Hebrew of vii. 11, 12, Eben-ezer is under Beth-car, perhaps but not certainly 'Ain Karim, and between Mizpah and Hashen, *the tooth*; but according to the LXX under Beth-jashan, between Mizpah and Jashan or Jeshanah, that is, 'Ain Sinia north of Bethel (as M. Clermont-Ganneau suggests), and therefore on a possible line of Philistine advance. Chaplin (*PEFQ*, 1888, 263 ff.) suggests Beit-Iksa for Eben-ezer; Conder, Deir el-'Azar, near Ḳuryet el-'Enab, and finds the name Aphek in Merj Fiḳieh, near Bab el-Wad. See Milner, *PEFQ*, 1887, iii.

[2] So the LXX of 1 Sam. vi. 13.

[3] Mackenzie (*PEF Annual*, 1911, pp. 48 ff.) says of a rock terrace on which a shrine or wely now stands at 'Ain-Shems, "we can imagine no more likely halting-place for the Ark on its arrival from Ekron".

[4] Most authorities omit the added *fifty thousand*.

[5] Jer. xxvi. 20.

somewhere about Mount Jearim, the rugged, wooded highlands, which look down on the basin of Sorek from the north of the great defile. But the exact site is not known. Some think it was the present Ḳuryet-'Enab to the north of Mount Jearim, and others Khurbet-'Erma to the south, near the mouth of the great defile. Each of these, it is claimed, echoes the ancient name; each suits the descriptions of Kiriath-jearim in the Old Testament. For the story of the ark Khurbet-'Erma has the advantage, lying close to Beth-shemesh, and yet in the hill-country. Leaving open the question of the exact site we must be satisfied with knowing that Kiriath-jearim lay on the west border of Benjamin; once the ark was there, it was off the debatable ground of the Shephelah and within Israel's proper territory. Here, in *the field of the woods,*[1] it rested till David brought it up to Jerusalem, and that was probably why Kiriath-jearim was also called Kiriath-baal, or Baal of Judah, for in those times Baal was not a name of reproach, but the title even of Yahweh as Lord and Preserver of His people's land.[2]

3. The third valley which cuts the Shephelah is the Wady es-Sunṭ, which, when it gets to the back of the low hills, turns south into the Wady eṣ-Ṣur, the great trench between the Shephelah and Judah. Near the turning the narrow Wady el-Jindy curves off north-east to the neighbourhood of Bethlehem. The Wady es-Sunṭ is probably the Vale of Elah.[3] Its entrance from the Philistine Plain is commanded by the famous Tell eṣ-Ṣafiyeh,[4] the Blanchegarde of the Crusaders, whose high white front looks west across the plain 12 miles to Ashdod. Blanchegarde must always have been a formidable position, and it is simply inability to assign to the site any other Biblical town—for Libnah has no satisfactory claims—that makes the case so strong

[1] Psalm cxxxii. 6.

[2] Robinson suggested K. 'Enab, and this suits the data of the *Onomasticon,* which places Kiriath-jearim at the ninth milestone from Jerusalem towards Lydda. It lies also convenient to the other towns of the Gibeonite League to which it belonged, Gibeon, Chephirah, and Beeroth (Josh. ix. 17; cf. Ezra ii. 25); it suits the place of Kiriath-jearim on the borders of Judah and Benjamin (Jos. xv. 9, xviii. 14), and it can be reached by an easy road from Beth-shemesh. Khurbet-'Erma was suggested by Henderson, and examined and accepted by Conder (Henderson's *Palestine,* 85, 112, 210). The name has the consonants of Je'arim (exactly those in Ezra ii. 25, where the name is 'arim), but it also means "heaps of corn", and may not be derived from the ancient name. The site is ancient, with a platform of rock that has the appearance of a high-place or shrine (Conder, *PEFQ,* 1881, 265). But it is far from the other members of the league. On Baal-Jehudah, see 2 Sam. vi. 2. Garstang, Deir el-'Azar above el-'Enab.

[3] Sunṭ is mimosa. Elah, any large evergreen tree, ilex or terebinth (Baudissin, *Stud.* ii. 185, n. 1). Vale of Elah, 1 Sam. xvii. 2, 19; xxi. 9.

[4] For Bliss' and Macalister's excavations see *PEFQ,* 1899.

for its having been the site of Gath. Blanchegarde is 23 miles from Jerusalem, but the way up is most difficult after Wady es-Sunṭ. It is remarkable that, when Richard decided to besiege Jerusalem, and had marched from Ashkelon to Blanchegarde, instead of pursuing the Wady es-Sunṭ and its narrow continuation to Bethlehem, he preferred to turn north two days' march across the Shephelah hills with his flank to the enemy, and attack his goal up the Valley of Aijalon.[1]

An hour's ride from Tell eṣ-Ṣafi up the winding Vale of Elah brings us through the Shephelah, to where Wady eṣ-Ṣur turns south towards Hebron,[2] and the narrow Wady el-Jindy strikes up towards Bethlehem. At the junction of the three there is a level quarter of a mile, cut by two brooks, which form the stream down Wady es-Sunṭ. This plain is probably the scene of David's encounter with Goliath; for to the south on the low hills that bound the Wady es-Sunṭ is the name Shuweikeh, probably the Socoh,[3] on which the Philistines rested their rear and faced Israel across the valley.

The "Gai", or ravine, which separated them has been recognised in the trench which the combined streams have cut through the level land, and on the other side is the Wady el-Jindy, a natural road for the Hebrews to have come down from their hills. Near by is Beit-Fased, probably an echo of Ephes-dammim, and on the spot where we should seek for the latter. It is the very battle-field for those ancient foes: Israel in one of the gateways to her mountain-land; the Philistines on the low hills they often overran; and between them the valley that divides Judah from the Shephelah. Major Conder and Principal Miller have given detailed descriptions of the battle and its field.[4] Only the following needs to be added: Socoh is a strong position isolated from the rest of the ridge, and keeps open the line of retreat down the valley. Saul's army was probably not exactly opposite, but a little way up on the slopes of the incoming Wady el-Jindy, and so placed that the Philistines, in attacking it, must cross not only the level land and the main stream, but one of the two other streams as well, and must also climb the slopes for some distance. Both positions were thus strong, and this perhaps explains the long hesitation of the armies in face of each other, even though the Philistines had the advantage of Goliath. The Hebrew position certainly looks the stronger. It is interesting, too, that from its rear the narrow pass

[1] *Itin. Ric.* v. 48. *L'Estoire de la Guerre Sainte*, 797 ff.

[2] The Wady eṣ-Ṣur and the Wady es-Sunṭ are parts of the same Wady.

[3] Shuweikeh is a late site. For Socoh, Bliss (*Development of Pal. Exploration*, 292) suggests Tell Zakariyah, which is either that or Azekah.

[4] Conder, *PEFQ*, 1876, 40; *TW*, 279. Miller, *Least of all Lands*, ch. v, with a plan of the field. Cf. Cheyne, *Hallowing of Criticism*.

goes right up to the interior of the land near Bethlehem; so that the shepherd-boy, whom the story represents as being sent by his father for news of the battle, would have not more than 12 miles to cover between his father's house and the camp.

If you ride south from the battle-field up Wady eṣ-Ṣur, you come in about two hours to a wide valley running into the Shephelah on the right. On the south side of this is a steep hill, with a well at its foot and at the top the shrine of a Moslem saint. They call the hill by a name 'Aid-el-ma, in which it is possible to hear Adullam,[1] and its position suits what we are told about David's stronghold. It stands well off the Central Range, and is very defensible. There is water in the valley, and near the top large low caves, partly artificial. If we can dismiss the idea that all David's 400 men got into the cave of Adullam—a pure fancy for which the false tradition, that the enormous cave of Khareitun near Bethlehem is Adullam, is responsible—we shall admit that this hill was such a *stronghold* as David is said to have chosen. It looks over to Judah, and down the Wady es-Sunṭ; it covers two high-roads into the former, and Bethlehem, from which David's three mighty men carried the water he sighed for, is, as the crow flies, not 12 miles away. The site is, therefore, entirely suitable; and yet we cannot say that enough resemblance is in the modern name to place it beyond doubt as Adullam.[2]

[1] Cf. Nestle, *MuNDPV*, 1895, 43; Seybold, *id.* 1896, 25.

[2] The tradition that Adullam is the cave of Khareitun (*i.e.* Saint Chariton, p. 410), SE of Bethlehem, cannot be traced behind the Crusaders. It is probably due to them. The Adullam of the O.T. lay off the Central Range, for men from the latter *went down* to it (Gen. xxxviii. 1; 1 Sam. xxii. 1; 2 Sam. xxiii. 13). The prophet Gad bids David leave it and go *into the land of Judah* (1 Sam. xxii. 5); and it is reckoned with Socoh, Azekah (supposed to be Tell Zakariyeh, for excavations on which see *PEFQ*, 1899, cf. April 1901; *MuNDPV*, 1896, 25), Gath, Mareshah, and other towns in the Shephelah W of Hebron (Josh. xv. 35, in the towns *in the Shephelah*, v. 33; Neh. xi. 30; Micah i. 15; 2 Chron. xi. 7; cf. 2 Macc. xii. 38). So great a mass of evidence is conclusive for a position somewhere in the Shephelah. It is not contradicted in the two passages (2 Sam. xxiii. 13; 1 Chron. xi. 15) describing how water was brought to David in Adullam from the well at Bethlehem, 12 miles from the nearest site on the Shephelah. Stade (*GVI*, i, 244) reads 1 Sam. xxiii. 3 as placing Adullam in Judah, but he manages this only by reading xxii. 5 as a gloss, for which there are no grounds. Retain xxii. 5, which tells how David went back from Adullam to Judah, and xxiii. 3, though probably from another document than xxii, follows on correctly. Finally, there is no reason for separating the cave from the city Adullam (so Birch, *PEFQ*, 1884, p. 61; 1886, p. 31). Adullam being proved to be on the Shephelah, the next question is the exact site. It is safest to say that, while many sites are possible, 'Aid-el-ma is the preferable. It is the only one that has an echo of the old name, and, lying on the E of the Shephelah, it suits Adullam's association in the O.T. with Socoh and Azekah, while it is only some 7 miles from Mareshah, with which Micah joins it. Deir Dubban, suggested by V. de Velde (*Reise*, etc., ii. 155 ff.), is on the

The only other famous site up the Wady eṣ-Ṣur is that of Keilah, or Ḳegilah. It is probably the present Ḳila, a hill covered with ruins on the Judæan side of the valley. When David returned from Adullam to Judah, he heard that the Philistines were besieging Keilah, a fenced town *with bolts and bars.*[1] In obedience to an oracle he attacked the Philistines, and relieved it. But Saul heard he was there, and hoped, with the help of the inhabitants, to catch him in a trap. David hurriedly left Keilah, and for a time the whole Shephelah, for the wilderness on the other side of Judah.[2]

4. The fourth of the valleys that cut the Shephelah is that now named the Wady el-Afranj, which runs from opposite Hebron north-west to Ashdod and the coast. It is important as containing the real capital of the Shephelah, the present Beit-Jibrin.[3] This site has not been identified with any Old Testament name,[4] but, like many other places in Palestine, its permanent importance is illustrated by its use during Roman times, and especially during the Crusades. It is not a place of natural strength, and this is perhaps why we hear nothing of it, so far as we know, during the older history; but it is the converging point of many roads,[5] and the soft chalk of the district lends itself admirably to the hewing of intricate caves—two facts which account for its later importance. Indeed, these caves have been claimed as proof that the Horites, or cave-dwellers, of the early history of Israel, had their centre here,[6] but none of them bear any mark older than the Christian era. The first possible mention of Beit-Jibrin is an emended passage of Josephus, where he describes it as a village of the Idumæans, who overran

W slope of the Shephelah, and has no point in its favour but its caves. Clermont-Ganneau is the discoverer of ‘Aiḍ-el-ma. The *Onomasticon* need not be taken into account. It confounds Adullam and Eglon.

[1] 1 Sam. xxiii.

[2] Khurbet Ḳila was proposed by Guérin, *Jud.* iii. 341. In Josh. xv. 43, 44, it is mentioned with Nesib, and this is probably the neighbouring Beit-Naṣib. It is mentioned in *Tell-el-Amarna Tablets*, Conder, pp. 143, 144, 151-155, and Nasib 157 in revolt from Egypt. It is practically on the Shephelah (this against Dillmann). The *Onomasticon* puts *Κεειλά* on Hebron and Beit-Jibrin road 7 or 17 m. from Hebron. This is evidently Beit-Kahil, not in the Shephelah, but on Judah.

[3] Ptolemy, xv "Betogabra"; Tab. Peut. "Betogubri". Nestle, *ZDPV*, i. 222-225, takes it to be the Aramaic בית גברא—"House of the Men", or "Strong Men"—and shows its identity with Eleutheropolis from a Syrian MS. of the third century. Robinson, *BR*, ii. 61, had put this past doubt. Nestle, on good grounds, places Elkosh, the birthplace of Nahum, close by.

[4] Thomson, *L. and B.*, proposes it as the site of Gath, but see p. 143.

[5] Perhaps the ancient city lay on a neighbouring height Tell Sandaḥannah or at Kh. Mer‘ash, Mareshah or Marissa. For this and the converging roads, see Peters and Thiersch, *Painted Tombs of Marissa*, 6 f.

[6] *Talm. Bereshith Rabba*, xlii, describes Eleutheropolis as inhabited by Horites, and

the Shephelah in the last centuries before Christ, and as taken by Vespasian when he was blockading the approaches to Jerusalem.[1] The Romans built roads from it in all directions, the high straight lines of which still dominate the brushwood and corn-fields of the neighbouring valleys. About A.D. 200 Septimius Severus refounded it, and its name was changed to Eleutheropolis.[2] It was the centre of the district, the half-way house between Jerusalem and Gaza, Hebron and Lydda, and the *Onomasticon* measures from it all distances in the Shephelah.

Many times, as our horses' hoofs strike pavement on the Roman roads of Palestine, and we lift our eyes to the unmistakable line across the landscape, we pilgrims from the far north are reminded that these same straight lines cross our own island, that by our own doors milestones have been dug up similar to those which lie here, and we are thrilled with some imagination of what the Roman Empire was, and how it grasped the world. But by Beit-Jibrin this feeling grows still more intense, for the Roman buildings there are mostly the work of the same emperor who built the wall on the Tyne, and hewed his way through Scotland to the shores of the Pentland Firth.

There are early Christian remains at Beit-Jibrin, both caves and churches, but we shall take them up afterwards in speaking of the rise of Christianity throughout the Shephelah. The Crusaders came to Beit-Jibrin, or Gibelin as they called it, and thought it Beersheba.[3] They made it their base against Ashkelon and Fulke of Anjou built the citadel. It was in charge of the Knights of St. John, and they attempted to colonise the neighbourhood in 1168.[4] Their monuments are ruins of a Gothic church, some fortifications, and their name in the Wady el-Afranj, "Valley of the Franks".

Not two miles from Beit-Jibrin lies Mer'ash, the Mareshah or Moresheth-gath of the Old Testament,[5] and birth-place of the prophets Eliezer and

---

derives the name Free-town from the fact that the Horim chose these caves to dwell there in liberty! So Jerome, *Comm. in Obadiam.*

[1] iv *Wars*, viii. 1, by reading βήγαβρις for βήταβρις.

[2] The date is fixed by the earliest coins of the city, with its new name and that of Severus, of A.D. 202, 203. Cf. Robinson, *LBR*, 194.

[3] Gibelin, Begibelinum, Bersabe Judæa. Röhricht, *ZDPV*, x. 240.

[4] Will. of Tyre, xiv. 22. On the colony see Prutz, *ZDPV*, iv. 113; on discovered graves, Thiersch and Peters, *MuNDPV*, 1902, 40.

[5] Josh. xv. 44; 2 Chron. xi. 8; xiv. 9, 10; xx. 37; Micah i. 1, 15; Jer. xxvi. 18; 2 Macc. xii. 35. Mareshah and Moresheth Gath were distinct (see my *Twelve Prophets*, i. 402). Mer'ash, 1 mile S of Beit-Jibrin, is spelt the same as מָרֵאשָׁה, Josh. xv. 44. Micah i. 14 f. and Jerome (*Onom.* and *Epitaph. S. Paulæ*) both distinguish the two, the latter placing Morasthi E of Eleutheropolis and Maresa as at the second milestone

Micah. In the reign of Asa an army of Kushim under Zerah, came up this avenue through the Shephelah, but by Mareshah Asa defeated them, and pursued them to Gerar.[1] In 163 B.C. Judas Maccabæus laid Mareshah waste in his campaign against the Idumæans.[2] John Hyrcanus took it again from their hands in 110, and Pompey gave it back to them.[3] Mareshah was one of the towns Gabinius rebuilt, but the Parthians in 40 B.C. swept down on it,[4] and thereafter we hear no more till Eusebius tells us it is desert.[5] Thus it was an important and "a powerful town"[6] as long as Beit-Jibrin was unheard of; when Beit-Jibrin comes into history, it disappears. Can we doubt that we have here one of those frequent instances of the transference of a community to a new and neighbouring site? If this be so, we have full explanation of the silence of the Old Testament about Beit-Jibrin; it was really represented by Mareshah.

5. The last of the valleys through the Shephelah is Wady el-Ḥesy, or Wady el-Jizair, running from a point about 6 miles south-west of Hebron to the sea, between Gaza and Ashkelon. This valley also has its important sites; for Lachish, which used to be placed at Umm Lakis, on the slopes to the south, is since the English survey, and excavations claimed to have been Tell el-Ḥesy, a mound in the bed of the valley, and Eglon—the present 'Ajlan—is not far off.[7] These two were ancient Amorite fortresses. Eglon disappeared at an early period, but Lachish endured, always fulfilling the same function, time after time suffering the same fate. Her valley is the first in the Shephelah which the roads from Egypt strike, and Gaza stands at its lower end. Lachish has therefore through history played second to Gaza, now an outpost of Egypt and now a frontier fortress of Syria. In the Tell el-Amarna Letters we read of her in Egyptian hands. She is the farthest city Egyptwards which Rehoboam fortifies.[8] Sennacherib must take her before he invades Egypt.[9] During the Latin kingdom of Jerusalem, her successor

---

from the same. Benjamin of Tudela equates Mareshah and B. Jibrin (Bohn, *Early Travels*, 87). See also Bliss, *Excavations in Pal.* 1898-1900. Peters and Thiersch, *PEFQ*, 1902, 303 ff. Their *Painted Tombs*, etc., give an inscription with *Μαρισῃ*, which records a Sidonian colony there after 198 B.C.

[1] 2 Chron. xiv. 9 ff. The Massoretic Text places the battle in the Valley of Zephathah (גי צפתה) at Mareshah, LXX gives north of Mareshah. Robinson, *Bib. Res.* ii. 31, compares Zephathah with Tell eṣ-Ṣafiyeh. Cf. *PEFQ*, 1886, 50 ff., 148 ff.

[2] 163 B.C., as he went from Hebron to Ashdod, Josephus, xii *Antt.* viii. 6. In 1 Macc. v. 66, read *Μάρισσα* for *Σαμαρεία*.

[3] Josephus, xiii *Antt.* ix. 1; xiv *Antt.* iv. 4. [4] *Ibid.* xiii. 9. [5] *Onom.* *Μάρησα*.

[6] So Josephus.

[7] Albright takes T. el-Ḥesy for Eglon and T. ed-Duweir for Lachish.

[8] 2 Chron. xi. 9.

[9] 2 Kings xviii. 14, 17; xix. 8; Isa. xxxvi. 2; xxxvii. 8; 2 Chron. xxxii. 9.

at Umm Lakis is held by the Order of the Hospitallers,[1] for the same strategical reasons.[2] Again, some 5 miles above Lachish, at the Wells of Ḳaṣṣaba, or "the Reeds", there is usually wealth of water, and all the year round a stream. Latin chronicles of the Crusades know the place as Cannetum Esturnellorum, or "the Cane-brake of the Starlings": and Richard twice made it his base, once on coming up the Wady el-Ḥesy from the coast, when he advanced on Beit-Jibrin, and once when he came south to intercept, in the Wady esh-Sheri'a, a caravan on its way from Egypt.[3] Through these ages, then, Lachish was an outpost, and, as we should now say, a customs-station, between Judæa and Egypt. War and commerce both swept past her. But this enables us to understand her neighbour Micah's word about her. In his day Judah's *sin* was to lean on Egypt, to accept Egyptian subsidies of horses and chariots. So Micah mocks Lachish, playing on the assonance of her name to that for a horse: *Yoke the wagon to the steed, O inhabitress of Lachish; beginning of sin is she to the daughter of Zion for in thee are found the transgressions of Israel.*[4]

I have now explained the strategic importance of the Shephelah, and especially of the five valleys which are the only possibilities of passage through it for great armies. How much of the history of all these centuries can be placed along one or other of them; and, when we have placed it, how much more vivid that history becomes!

There is one campaign in the Shephelah which we have not discussed in connection with any of the main routes, because the details are obscure—Sennacherib's invasion of Syria in 701 B.C. But the general course of this, as told in Assyrian annals and the Bible, becomes plain in the light of the geography we have been studying. Sennacherib, coming down the coast like the Syrians and Crusaders, like them also conquered first the towns about Joppa. Then he defeated an Egyptian army before Alteku, somewhere near Ekron, on the Philistine Plain,[5] and took Ekron and Timnah. With

[1] Their name for Lachish, Malagues or Malaques (cf. Röhricht, *ZDPV*, x. 239)—that is Umm Lakis—is a good instance of what the unfortunate names of this country have suffered at the mouths of its conquerors.

[2] On Lachish excavated see Petrie, *Tell el-Hesy*, 1891; Bliss, *PEFQ*, 1892 f., and *A Mound of Many Cities* (1894).

[3] *Itin. Ricardi*, v. 41; vi. 4. On the identification of Ḳaṣṣaba with the Cannetum Esturnellorum, see Clermont-Ganneau, *Recueil*, etc., 378.

[4] Micah i. 13.

[5] Alteku, the Eltekeh of Josh. xix. 44, cannot be where the *PEF Red. Map* (1891) makes it, at Beit-Liḳea, far up Aijalon—for how could an Egyptian and Assyrian army have met there?—but was near Ekron, on the road to Egypt. I now think of it in Sorek not far E from Ekron. See my art. in *Enc. Bibl.*

Egypt beaten back, and the Northern Shephelah mastered, his way was open into Judah, the invasion of which and the investment of Jerusalem appear next in the list of his triumphs. These must have been effected by a detachment, for Sennacherib himself is next heard of in Southern Shephelah, besieging Lachish and Libnah, no doubt with the view of securing his way to Egypt. At Lachish he received the tribute of Hezekiah, who hoped to purchase the relief of the still inviolate Jerusalem; but, in spite of the tribute, he sent to Hezekiah from Lachish and Libnah two peremptory demands for her surrender. Then suddenly in Zion's despair, the Assyrian army was smitten, not, as we usually imagine, round Jerusalem, for the Bible nowhere implies that, but under Sennacherib in the main camp and headquarters. Either these were still in Southern Shephelah—for Sennacherib's annals do not carry him south of Lachish, and Egypt often sent her plagues up this way to Palestine[1]—or, if we believe Herodotus, they had crossed the desert to Pelusium, and were overtaken in that pestiferous region, which has destroyed so many armies.[2]

XI. *EARLY CHRISTIANITY IN THE SHEPHELAH*
ITS CAVES AND CHURCHES[3]

Our study of the Shephelah has covered only the campaigns and battles which have ranged over its very debatable ground. But the region had its victories of peace as well as of war, and throughout it we find to-day ruins of cloisters and of churches, and caves with Christian symbols. Many of the former are, no doubt, ruins of Crusaders' buildings; but some go back to the Byzantine period, and the caves with the crosses marked on their walls are probably early Christian. Christianity conquered the Shephelah almost before any other part of Palestine, and the story of the conquest is a heroic one.[4]

Among the crowds who followed our Lord at the beginning of His ministry were many from Idumæa,[5] then virtually the southern Shephelah with the Negeb. The Edomites had come up on it during the Jewish exile, and after the return of the Jews they continued to hold the greater part of it. Judas

[1] 1 *RP*, I; Schrader, *KAT*, I, p. 218 ff.; Stade, *Gesch.* i. 620 ff.; my *Isaiah*, i, chs. xix to xxiii. Schrader wrongly makes the crisis at the battle of Eltekeh.

[2] See pp. 118 ff. [3] For this chapter, see Map. 7.

[4] It is told in the histories of Eusebius, Socrates, and Sozomen, in Jerome's Letters, and in his *Life of Hilarion.* Stark's *Gaza*, etc., § 16, takes it up at points.

[5] Mark iii. 8.

Maccabæus conquered their territory,[1] but John Hyrcanus brought them under the law and circumcised them.[2] By the Law the third generation of Edomites were admitted to the full privileges of Israel,[3] so that in our Lord's time Idumæa was practically a part of Judæa, with a Jewish population.[4] Many out of Idumæa heard Him, and it is probable that Idumæans were present on the day of Pentecost. Apostles and evangelists went down into the Shephelah. Peter we have seen at Lydda, and from the Christians at Lydda influences might easily pass across the whole region by the high-road to Beit-Jibrin. Philip met the Ethiopian somewhere in the southern Shephelah, and was afterwards found at Ashdod.[5] Very early, then, little communities of Christians must have been formed among these beautiful glens and moors. Tradition assigns one of the Twelve, Simon Judas, to Beit-Jibrin.[6] When persecution came, we can understand how readily this land of caves, where David and his men had hid themselves from Saul, would be used by Christian fugitives from the Greek cities of the coast. The habits of the ascetic life also spread here from Egypt. Monks and hermits settled first to the south of Gaza,[7] then came up the Wady el-Ḥesy to the district round Beit-Jibrin, and found among the villages of the Shephelah a nobler work than their brother-monks of the Libyan and Arabian deserts. With a persistence and success, the proof of which appeared in the aid rendered by the rural districts to the Christians of the cities in the struggles of the fourth century, they converted the peasants and built them up in the faith. Here the contrast which was seen over the rest of the world was reversed, and "urban" might have been taken as the synonym of idolater, but "heathen" and "pagan" as by-names for Christians. Even so early as the Decian persecutions, and still more in those under Diocletian and Maximin, many confessors were brought in "from the country" to martyrdom at Cæsarea, or sent back to their glens mutilated and branded.[8] Some have been named for us. Romulus, a sub-deacon of the Church at Lydda, was one of six young men, who, first binding their hands, went to the amphitheatre of Cæsarea, where some of their brethren were being thrown to the beasts, and boldly declared themselves to the governor as Christians.[9] They were beheaded. Zebina of Beit-Jibrin was one of three who defied the Governor of Cæsarea, when he was sacrificing

[1] See p. 165.

[2] About 125 B.C. Josephus, xiii *Antt.* ix. 1; i *Wars*, ii. 6.

[3] Deut. xxiii. 8, 9 (Heb., but Eng. Version 7, 8).

[4] How violently Jewish may be seen from the part they took in the Jewish revolt of A.D. 66—Jos. iv *Wars*, iv. 4 f.

[5] Acts viii. 39 f.

[6] Stark's *Gaza*, etc., p. 613—after the *De LXX Domini discipulis*.

[7] Jerome's *Life of Hilarion*.

[8] Euseb. *HE*, viii. *passim*.

[9] *Ibid.* 3.

to idols. They were executed.[1] Petrus Asketes, a youth from Anea in the borders of Beit-Jibrin, was burned to death in the same city.[2] The Shephelah lay at the doors of that slaughter-house, into which the fury of Maximin converted the Syrian coast from Egypt to Cilicia; and during the eight[3] years of the persecution its Christian communities must have been thrilled by the stories of heroism, martyrdom, and miracle which came up to them from the sea-board. Lying in caves, the mouths of many of which look over the plain upon Gaza and Ashkelon, they were told how the gates of these cities were beset by spies, and Christians were caught as they came in from the country or were travelling between Cilicia and Egypt; how some were found in the towns reading the Scriptures, and dragged before the prefect; how some were burned, and all tortured; how some were thrown to the wild beasts, and some trained for pugilistic combats to make a Roman holiday; how human heads and limbs were sometimes scattered about the gates to terrify the peasants; and how a strange dew once broke out on the buildings of Cæsarea, and people said that the stones must weep at cruelties so terrible. Men wanting a foot, or hand, or eye, or seared across the face, or with their sides torn by hooks, would come to these caves to die; and some country youths, emulous of martyrdom, would rush to Cæsarea and defy the governor in the great theatre. These things are told by Eusebius, who lived through them, and is a sober writer.[4]

The most intricate caves of the Shephelah are those about Beit-Jibrin—the district of whose Christianity we hear most. The yellow chalk of the ridges there is easy to carve, and hardens on exposure. Some of the old caves, which had probably been used from time immemorial[5] must have lately been enlarged as quarries for the building of Eleutheropolis; others had been used by the Jews as tombs. But by the Christians they were greatly increased. There is in them, as they now lie, no such wealth of inscriptions as in the Roman catacombs, but that their form is due to the early Christians seems proved by these facts: that the chambers have in many cases been run through Jewish tombs[6]; that almost the only ornament is the Cross, and that the only Moslem inscriptions yet discovered are early ones in the Cufic character.[7] A few notes, taken on the spot, will perhaps give a vivid idea of the caves about Beit-Jibrin:

[1] *Ibid.* 9.

[2] *Ibid.* 10.

[3] So *ibid.* 13; but "ten years", *ibid.* 15.

[4] *History*, Bk. viii.; cf. Theodoret, iii. 7; Evagrius, i. 21, etc.

[5] See p. 163.

[6] *PEF Mem.* Judæa, 268.

[7] Robinson (and Eli Smith), *BR*, ii. Guérin, *Jud.* ii. Conder doubts whether these are older than Cent. xii (*Critical Rev.* iv. 295).

"... Down a steep grass gully to some rough steps—evidently not the original entrance, but one broken by the fall of the rock—and so, lighting our candles, into a large chamber. Thence we crept, by a passage as high as my walking-stick, to a larger room, of elegant shape, with a pillar in the centre, 2 ft. thick each way. Climbing to the top of some rubbish, we found a hole in the wall, and passed through into a great bell-shaped chamber, round which there descended a spiral staircase with a balustrade. We went down to the bottom, 50 steps. Returning, half-way up we found a door into another series of chambers, which we penetrated for about 200 feet; they went on further. We came back to the staircase, and passed by it out of the solid rock into a narrow vaulted passage choked with rubbish, at what seemed to be the proper entrance to the labyrinth."

This describes but a part of one series of caves in one district. Elsewhere round Beit-Jibrin there are other series, in which you may wander for hours through cells, rooms, and pillared halls with staircases and long corridors, all cut out of the soft yellow chalk. There is almost no ornament, nor trace of ornament having been removed. Where the walls are preserved, they have no breaks save niches for holding little lamps. The low passages, along which you have to creep, suggest their origin in times of terror; and the natural mouths of many, hidden by bush, and overlooking the plain to the sea, are splendid posts of observation for sentinels of hunted men. But the vaulted masonry of other entrances speaks of more peaceful days; and all the chambers are dry, and in summer delightfully cool. While then, some caves about Beit-Jibrin may have been inhabited, or even formed, during the persecutions, the bulk are probably due to monks and hermits who came up from Egypt. The caves at Deir Dubban north of Beit-Jibrin, have also a few crosses, and what look like Cufic inscriptions high up on the walls. They, too, are to be assigned to the Byzantine period.[1]

When the Christianity of the Shephelah came above ground, it built some noble churches. Close by the caves described stands the ruin Sandaḥannah, Church of Sancta Anna, mother of the Virgin. It is the east end of a basilica, and with the foundations, which can still be traced for the rest of the building, implies a church as great and beautiful as the Basilica of Justinian in Bethlehem. Probably it dates from the same age, when the famous Marcian, who built the churches of Gaza, was bishop there, and his brother Bishop of Eleutheropolis.[2] Byzantine remains have been recognised in other parts of the Shephelah, as at Deir el-Bedawiyeh, Deir el-Botum, and Deir el-Mokhalliṣ

[1] Guérin, *Jud.* ii. 105, 106. [2] Stark, *Gaza, etc.*, p. 625.

or Convent of the Saviour.[1] Some of the untraceable ruins, which are strewn across these hills, must belong to the same period; but other remains, such as the chapel within the citadel at Beit-Jibrin, are French architecture of the thirteenth century, and the scattered stones to the north of Tell Jezer may also be the work of the Crusaders.[2]

XII. *JUDÆA AND SAMARIA—THE HISTORY OF THEIR FRONTIER*[3]

Over the Shephelah we advance upon the Central Range. Our nearest goal is that part of the range which is called the *Hill-country*, or *Mount*, *of Judah*. But it is necessary to look at the range as a whole, and see how, and why, its short extent was divided first into the two kingdoms of Northern Israel and Judah, and then into the provinces of Samaria and Judæa.

We have seen[4] that a long, deep formation of limestone extends all the way from Lebanon in the north to a line of cliffs opposite the Gulf and Canal of Suez in the south. Of this backbone of Syria the part between Esdraelon and the Negeb is historically the most famous. Those 90 miles of narrow highland from Jezreel to Beersheba were the chief theatre of the history of Israel. As you look from the sea they form a persistent mountain wall of nearly uniform level, rising clear and blue above the low hills which buttress it to the west. The one sign of a pass across it is the cleft we noticed,[5] between Ebal and Gerizim, in which Shechem, the natural capital of these highlands, lies.

But uniform as that persistent range appears from the coast, almost the first thing you remember as you look at it is the prolonged political and religious division of which it was capable—first into the kingdoms of Northern Israel and Judah, and then into the provinces of Samaria and Judæa. Those ninety narrow miles sustained the arch-schism of history. Where did the line of this schism run? Did it correspond to any natural division in the range itself?

A closer observation shows that there was a natural boundary between northern and southern Israel. But its ambiguity is a curious symbol of the uncertain frontier of their religious differences.

We have seen, *first*, that the bulk of Samaria consists of scattered mountain

[1] Guérin, *Jud.* ii. 27, 97, 98. [2] See p. 154. [3] For this chapter, see Maps 3, 4, 5 and 6.
[4] P. 53. [5] P. 94.

groups, while Judæa is a table-land; and, *secondly*, that while the Samarian mountains descend continuously through the low hills upon the Maritime Plain, the hill-country of Judæa stands aloof from the Shephelah Range, with a well-defined valley between.[1] Now, these two physical differences do not coincide: the table-land of Judæa runs farther north than its isolation from the low hills. Consequently, we have an alternative of frontiers. If we take the difference between the relations of the two provinces to the Maritime Plain, the natural boundary will be the Vale of Aijalon, which penetrates the Central Range, and a line from it across the water-parting to the Wady es-Suweiniṭ, the deep gorge of Michmash, which will continue the boundary to the Jordan at Jericho. If we take the distinction between the scattered hills and the table-land, then the natural boundary from the coast eastwards to the Jordan will be the river 'Aujeh, the Wady Deir Balluṭ, the Wady Nimr, a line across the water-parting to the Wady Samieh, and so down this and the other Wady 'Aujeh to the Jordan, 8 miles above Jericho.[2] For it is just where this line crosses the water-parting, about the Robber's Well on the road from Jerusalem to Nablus, that travellers coming north find the country change. They have descended from the plateau, and their road onward lies through valleys and plains, with ridges between. This second natural border is easily remembered by the fact that it begins and ends with streams of the same name—'Aujeh, "the crooked"—and that, while the western stream reaches the sea a little above Joppa, the eastern falls into the Jordan a little above Jericho. Somewhat farther north than this second line is a third and even more evident border, which leaves Wady Deir Balluṭ by Wady Ishar, and runs north-east deep and straight to 'Aḳrabbeh. Still farther north is a fourth line, which leaves the western 'Aujeh by Wadies Ishar and Ḳanah—the latter probably the Brook Kanah,[3] the frontier between Ephraim and Manasseh—but this line we need not take into our reckoning.

Thus we have not one, but three possible frontiers across the range: south of Bethel, the line from the head of Aijalon to the gorge of Michmash; north of Bethel, the change from table-land to valley, with deep wadies both to Jordan and to the coast; and, more northerly still, Wady Ishar. None of these is a "scientific frontier", and their ambiguity is reflected in the fortunes of the political border, which oscillated among them.

Take the most southerly—the line up Wady es-Suweiniṭ, across the plateau south of Bethel, and down Aijalon. This was a real pass across the range. Not only did Israel by it first come up from the Jordan on to the table-

[1] See pp. 146 ff. [2] Trel. Saunders, *Introd. to Survey of W. Palestine*, p. 229.
[3] Josh. xvi. 8, xvii. 9.

land, and by it sweep down towards the sea, but it was in all ages a regular route for trade.[1] Its use, and the close connection into which it brought the Maritime Plain with the Jordan Valley, could not be more clearly proved than by the name Dagon at its eastern as well as its western end. A little way north of Jericho there was, down to the time of the Maccabees, a fortress called by the name of the Philistine god.[2] In Saul's days the Philistines were naturally anxious to hold this route and, invading Israel by Ephraim, they planted their garrisons upon its northern side at Ramallah[3] and Michmash, while Saul's forces faced them from its southern side.[4] This is the earliest appearance of this natural border across the Central Range as a political frontier. The next is a few years later: while David was king only of Judah, his soldiers sat down opposite those of Abner at Gibeon,[5] on a line between Aijalon and Michmash. After the disruption the same line seems to have been the usual frontier between the kingdoms of Northern Israel and Judah; for Bethel,[6] to the north, was a sanctuary of Israel, and Geba, to the south, was considered as the limit of Judah.[7] But though the Vale of Aijalon and the gorge of Michmash form such a division down both flanks of the plateau, the plateau itself offers no real frontier, but stretches level from Jerusalem to the north of Bethel. Consequently we find Judah and Israel pushing each other up and down on it, Israel trying to get footing south, Judah trying to get footing north, of Michmash. For instance, Baasha, king of Israel, *went up against Judah, and built*, or *fortified*, *Ramah*, the present er-Ram, 4 miles north of Jerusalem, *that he might not suffer any to go out or come in to Asa, king of Judah*[8]; but, Asa having paid the Syrians to invade Israel from the north, *he left off building Ramah*, and Asa made a levy throughout Judah, *and they took away the stones and timber of Ramah wherewith Baasha had builded, and King Asa built*, or *fortified*, *with them Geba of Benjamin and Mizpah.*[9] And conversely to Baasha's attempt on Ramah we find the kings of Judah making attempts on Bethel. Soon after the disruption, Abijah won it for

[1] The Crusaders used it. See p. 134.

[2] Josephus, xiii *Antt.* viii. Probably the same as Dok (1 Macc. xvi. 15), now 'Ain Duḳ, N of Jericho, a holy place of Jews, Vincent, *Rev. Bib.* 1919, 532 ff.; S. A. Cook, *PEFQ*, 1920, 82, 139.

[3] 1 Sam. x. 5. *The hill of God*, perhaps Ramallah, SW of Bethel.

[4] 1 Sam. xiii, xiv. Seneh, so called from the *thorns* upon it, lay on the south side of the Michmash gorge. Bozez, *the shining*, for it lay facing the south, was opposite to Seneh on the north.

[5] 2 Sam. ii. 13.

[6] 1 Kings xii. 29; 2 Kings x. 29; Amos iii. 14, iv. 4, vii. 10, 13; Hosea x. 15.

[7] The formula, *from Dan to Beersheba*, meaning all Israel, was replaced *from Geba to Beersheba* (2 Kings xxiii. 8; cf. 1 Kings xv. 22).

[8] 1 Kings xv. 17.

[9] *Ibid.* 21, 22.

Judah,[1] but it must have quickly reverted to the north. Similarly to the Bethel plateau, the Jordan valley offered no real frontier between Judah and Northern Israel, and we find Jericho, though a Judæan city, in possession of the northerners.[2] On the west, Northern Israel did not come south of the Vale of Aijalon, for in that direction the Philistines were still strong.[3]

When the kingdom of Northern Israel fell, Jericho and Bethel reverted to Judah; but Bethel was a tainted place, and Josiah destroyed it,[4] and still in his time Geba was the formal limit of Judah.[5] Only formal, however, for Bethel and other villages to the north must have been rebuilt and occupied by Jews. Men of Bethel returned in Zerubbabel's company from exile along with men of Ai, Michmash, Gibeon, Anathoth, Azmaveth, Beeroth, Ramah, and Geba,[6] on the plateau; Lydda, Hadid, and Ono in Aijalon; and Jericho and Senaah[7] in the Jordan Valley. All these are either upon or south of the line from Michmash to Aijalon, except Bethel, which is a little to the north. Beth-horon, which was also on the line, but belonged to Ephraim,[8] is not mentioned among them. This proves that, after the northern kingdom fell, Judah had only slightly pushed her frontier northwards. She got Jericho back, and a little place to the north of it, and Bethel, but she did not get Beth-horon.

Except, then, for the northward bulge at Bethel, the frontier between Judah and Israel was till the Exile the most southerly of the three natural borders.

During the Exile the Samaritans must have flowed south into the vacant or weakened Jewish cities, but the only evidence we have of this concerns Lod, or Lydda, and its neighbourhood. Long after Lod's reoccupation by the Jews, the district was still nominally a Samaritan toparchy.[9] When the Jews returned they found the frontier obliterated; their countrymen who had not gone into exile were fallen into idolatrous practices, and the Samaritans came up to Jerusalem and offered to join them in building the Temple. The offer was rejected; but after the Temple was finished in 516 the Jewish exclusiveness gave way, and such intercourse was held with the Samaritans,

[1] 2 Chron. xiii. 19. [2] 1 Kings xvi. 34; 2 Kings ii. 4 ff.

[3] 1 Kings xvi. 15 ff., where we find Gibbethon, on the borders of Ephraim, to the north of Aijalon, in Philistine possession.

[4] 2 Kings xxiii. 4, 15. [5] *Ibid.* 8. [6] Ezra ii. 23 ff.; Neh. vii. 25 ff.

[7] Probably 5 miles north of Jericho; cf. *Onom.* Megdalsenna.

[8] Josh. xvi. 3, 5, xxi. 22.

[9] Lydda was a Samaritan νομός up to the time of Jonathan Maccabæus (about 145 B.C.), 1 Macc. xi. 34, Josephus, xiii *Antt.* iv. 9. Another proof that the neighbourhood of Lydda is Samaritan is found in the fact that Sanballat asks Nehemiah to meet him there (Neh. vi. 2).

by marriage and other relations, as must have scattered many Jews northwards across the old frontier.[1] Then under Ezra and Nehemiah (460-432), when the Samaritans were again excluded, they seem to have overthrown the walls of Jerusalem, and at the rebuilding of these they appeared in force.[2] All this time it is evident there was no real frontier north of Jerusalem. Soon after, as Nehemiah intimates, the Jews were again settled in the frontier towns of Geba, Michmash, 'Aija, Beth-el, Ramah, and down Aijalon in Hadid, Lydda, and Ono, and even at Neballat north-west of Lydda.[3] As before the Exile, Beth-horon is not mentioned among the Jewish towns; and Sanballat, the Samaritan, is called the Horonite.[4] For 160 years we hear no more of the frontier, except that in a time of the Jews' distress the Samaritans cut off their lands[5]; and then under Judas Maccabæus, Beth-horon is mentioned as a village of Judæa.[6] Proofs multiply that since Nehemiah's time the Jews were pushing steadily northwards. In 161 B.C. Beth-horon, Bethel, and even Timnath-pharathon, in the interior of the old Samarian territory,[7] are described as towns of Judæa.[8] By 145 the Jews demand from the Syrian king the transference of the Samaritan toparchies, Aphærema, Lydda, and Ramathaim, to Judæa.[9] Lydda we know, Aphærema is the city of Ephraim, 5 miles north-east of Bethel; the site of Ramathaim is doubtful, but it also

[1] Ezra ix. 2; Neh. xiii. 23 ff., especially 28.

[2] Neh. iv. 2, in the Massoretic or the LXX reading, which latter, to my mind, makes better sense: *Is this the power of Samaria, that these Jews can build their city?* But Ryle (*Camb. Bible for Schools*) thinks LXX fails to throw light.

[3] Neh. xi. 31-36. The other towns north of Jerusalem which are mentioned are Anathoth, Nob, Ananiah (Beit-Ḥanina), Hazor (Ḥazzur), all near Jerusalem; Gittaim and Zeboim, unknown. Schlatter (*Zur Topog. u. Gesch. Palästinas*, 53) has tried to prove that this list refers to pre-exilic times, and is out of date in Nehemiah. He holds Neh. xi is taken from 1 Chron. ix which belongs to the Books of the Kings of Judah. But, with his usual method of special pleading, he omits to say that the verses he is dealing with in Neh. xi, *viz.* 25 ff., do *not* appear in the document, 1 Chron. ix, which invalidates his argument. There is no reason to believe that Neh. xi. 25 ff. is not authentic; while the Jewish occupation of Lod and Ono is put past doubt by their later history. None who helped Nehemiah in building the walls came from the north of Gibeon, Meronoth (?), Mizpah, (Neh. iii.).

[4] Schlatter (*op. cit.* 4, *War Beth-horon der Wohnort Sanballat's?*) seeks to prove, without success, that Sanballat was neither a Samaritan nor of Beth-horon. But Buhl points out that the LXX of Josh. x. 10 (cf. that of 2 Sam. xii. 34) confirms Sanballat's title *Horoni*, Neh. ii. 10, 19, xiii. 28 (*Geog.* 169).

[5] Josephus, xii *Antt.* iv. 1.

[6] *Id.* vii. 1. That this is no anachronism is seen from xiii *Antt.* i. 3.

[7] On any theory of its site; see ch. xvii.

[8] 1 Macc. ix. 50; Josephus, xiii *Antt.* i. 3.

[9] 1 Macc. xi. 28, 34; Josephus, xiii *Antt.* iv. 9.

lay within Mount Ephraim.[1] Taken along with the capture of Joppa, which happened about the same time, this addition of Samarian territory shifted the frontier of Judæa to the line of the 'Aujeh and Wady Deir Balluṭ, or the second of the three natural borders.[2] John Hyrcanus (135-105) overran Samaria; in 64 Pompey separated it again[3]; in 30 it fell to Herod the Great; in A.D. 6 it was taken with Judæa from Archelaus, and put under a Roman procurator.[4] In 41 Claudius gave it, with Judæa, to Agrippa. During that time, therefore, there was no political frontier between Judæa and Samaria. The religious difference, however, kept them apart as much as ever, and the necessity felt by the scrupulous Judaism of the time to distinguish heathen from holy soil ensured a strict drawing of their frontier. Josephus[5] puts the boundary at the Acrabbene toparchy, and again at the "village Anuath, also named Borcæus", which the English Survey has identified with Burḳit and 'Aḳrabbeh.[6] This gives the frontier along the northmost of the natural borders, Wady Ishar. On the Maritime Plain Jewish Judæa ceased at the 'Aujeh,[7] though the Roman province of Judæa covered the plain to the north of that, as it covered Samaria, and indeed had its chief town in Cæsarea. On the eastern side the border between Samaria and Judæa probably ran down Wady Far'ah to the Jordan, just north of Ḳurn Ṣurṭabeh.[8] The northern boundary of Samaria was the edge of Esdraelon.

These were practically the limits of Samaria during our Lord's ministry. Samaria extended from the edge of Esdraelon to Wady Ishar and Wady Far'ah, and from the Jordan to the edge of the Maritime Plain, where it touched heathen territory. To go through Samaria, therefore, our Lord and His disciples had only some 23 miles to cover[9]; while if they wished to avoid

[1] On the city of Ephraim see ch. xvii. Ramathaim, Ῥαμαθέμ, is Ramathaim or Ramah, Samuel's city in Mount Ephraim (1 Sam. i. 1; other passages in 1 Sam. throw no light). It has been identified with Beit-Rima, 13 miles NE of Lydda, which agrees with the *Onomasticon*, art. Ἀρμαθέμ Σειφά, where it is identified with the Arimathæa of Joseph. On the mosaic map of Madaba Armathem or Arimathe see Schulten's note, *Mos. Karte v. Madaba*, 15.

[2] Unless Timnath-pharathon was Judæan, and lay at the head of Wady Far'ah; in that case the frontier was the northmost of the three borders.

[3] Josephus, xiv *Antt.* iii. 4, speaks of Pompey's arrival at Koreæ, "which is the first entrance to Judæa when one passes over the midland countries"; but it is uncertain whether Josephus speaks of his own or Pompey's time, nor are we sure where Koreæ was. See ch. xvii.

[4] Samarians enrolled in Roman forces, and probably formed part of the garrison in Jerusalem, Schürer, *Jewish People in Time of Christ*, i. ii. 51.

[5] iii *Wars*, iii. 4, 5. [6] *PEFQ*, 1881, 48; *ZDPV*, xxxiv. 110. [7] Talmud.

[8] Conder, *Handbook*, 310 f. Talmud (Bab. Gittin, 76*a*) counts all heathen between Kefr Outheni on Esdraelon and Antipatris.

[9] That is, by the present high-road from the Wady Ishar, past Sychar to Jenin or

Samaria and all other unclean soil in passing from Galilee to Judæa, they had to cross the Jordan north of Bethshan, come down through the hot Jordan valley, and recross by one of the fords at Wady Far'ah, or between this and Jericho.[1] *The city of Ephraim*, to which our Lord retired, was, and had been since the times of Jonathan Maccabæus, a city of Judæa.[2]

XIII. *THE BORDERS AND BULWARKS OF JUDÆA*[3]

We now reach the stronghold and sanctuary of the land, Judæa, physically the most barren and awkward, morally the most potential and famous of the provinces of Syria. Like her annual harvests, the historical forces of Judæa have always ripened later than those of Samaria. She had no part in Israel's earliest struggles for unity and freedom—indeed, in these she is named only as a traitor[4]—nor did the beginnings either of the kinghood or of prophecy spring from her. Yet the gifts, which her older sister's more open hands were the first to catch—and lose, were by her redeemed, nourished, consummated. For this more slow and stubborn function Judæa was prepared by her isolated and unattractive position, which kept her for longer than her sister out of the world's regard, and, when the world came, enabled her to offer a more hardy defence. Hence, too, sprang the defects of her virtues, her selfishness, provincialism and bigotry. With a few exceptions, due to the genius of some of her sons, who were inspired beyond other Israelites, Judæa's character and history may be summed up in a sentence. At all times, in which the powers of spiritual initiative or expansion were needed, she was lacking, and so in the end came her shame. But when the times required concentration, indifference to the world, loyalty to the past, and passionate patriotism, Judæa took the lead, or stood alone, in Israel, and these virtues rendered brilliant even the hopeless, insane struggles of her end. Judæa was the seat of the one enduring dynasty of Israel, the site of their temple, the platform of their chief prophets. After the Exile Israel rallied round her capital, and centuries later expended upon her fortresses the last efforts of their freedom. From the day when the land was taken in pledge by the dust of the patriarchs, till the remnant of the garrison of Jerusalem slaughtered

---

Engannim; cf. Luke ix, John iv. See also Josephus, xx *Antt.* vi. 1, for a quarrel between Galilean pilgrims and Samaritans.

[1] Cf. Mark x. [2] John xi. 54.

[3] For this chapter, see Maps 4, 6, 7, 8, 9, 10.

[4] Deborah's Song names not Judah. Men of Judah betrayed Samson.

themselves out at Masada, rather than fall into Roman hands, or till at Bether the last revolt was crushed by Hadrian, Judæa was the birthplace, the stronghold, the sepulchre of God's people. It is not wonderful that they should have won from it the name which is now more frequent than either their ancestral designation of Hebrews or their sacred title of Israel.

For us Christians it is enough to remember, besides, that Judæa contains the places of our Lord's Birth and Death, with the scenes of His Temptation, His more painful Ministry, and His Agony.

Judæa is very small. Even when you extend the surface to the promised border at the sea, and include all of it that is desert, it does not amount to more than 2000 square miles, or the size of one of our average counties.[1] But Judæa, in the days of its independence, never covered the Maritime Plain; and even the Shephelah, as we have seen, was frequently beyond it. Apart from Shephelah and Plain Judæa was 55 miles long, from Bethel to Beersheba, and 25 to 30 broad, or about 1350 square miles, of which nearly half was desert.[2]

It ought not to be difficult to convey an adequate impression of so small and separate a province. The centre is high and broken table-land from 2000 to 3000 feet above the sea, perhaps 35 miles long by 12 to 17 broad.[3] You will almost cover it by one sweep of the eye. But surrounding this are borders and bulwarks of extraordinary variety and intricacy; and as it is they which have largely made the history of the land and the culture of the inhabitants, it will be better for us to survey them, before we come to the little featureless plateau, which they lift and isolate from the rest of the world. We begin with the Eastern.

I. *East: the Great Gulf with Jericho and En-gedi. The Entrance of Israel*

You cannot live in Judæa without being daily aware of the awful deep which bounds it on the east—the lower Jordan Valley and Dead Sea. From Bethel,

[1] Aberdeenshire is 1955 square miles; Perth, 2528; Cumberland, 1516; Northumberland, 2015; Norfolk, 2017; Essex, 1413; Kent, 1515; Somerset, 1659; and Devon, 2015.

[2] Jer. xxxii. 44, xxxiii. 13 divide it into *places about Jerusalem*, *cities of Judah*, *cities of the hill-country*, *cities of the Shephelah*, *cities of the Negeb*. For *The Administrative Divisions of Judah*, W. F. Albright, *JPOS*, v. 17 ff.

[3] From the centre of Wady 'Ali to the E base of the Mount of Olives (1520 feet), 14 miles. From Wady en-Najil on the Shephelah border to the descent from the plateau E of Mar Saba, 17 miles; a line across Hebron from edge to edge of the plateau gives 14 miles.

from Jerusalem, from Bethlehem, from Tekoa, from the heights above Hebron, and from fifty points between, you look down into that deep, and feel Judæa rising from it almost as a sailor feels his narrow deck or a sentinel the sharp-edged platform of his high fortress. From the hard limestone of the range on which you stand, the land sinks swiftly, and, as it seems, shuddering through softer formations, desert and chaotic, to a depth of which you cannot see the bottom; but you know that it falls far below the level of the ocean to the coasts of a bitter sea. Across this emptiness rise the hills of Moab, high and precipitous, and it is their bare edge, almost unbroken, and with nothing visible beyond save a castle or a crag, which forms the eastern horizon of Judæa. The simple name by which that horizon was known to the Jews—The Mountains of the Over-side, or of Those-Across[1]—is more expressive than anything else could be of the great vacancy between. The depth, the haggard desert through which the land sinks into it, the singularity of that gulf and its prisoned sea, and the high barrier beyond conspire to produce on the inhabitants of Judæa a moral effect such as, I suppose, is created by no other frontier in the world.

It was only, however, when we had crossed into Moab that we fully appreciated the significance of that frontier in the history of God's separated people. The table-land east of the Dead Sea is about the same height as the table-land of Judæa to the west, and of almost exactly the same physical formation. On both are landscapes from which it would be impossible to gather whether you were in Judæa or in Moab—impossible but for one thing, the feeling of what you have to the east of you. To the east of Judæa there is that great gulf fixed. But Moab to the east rolls off imperceptibly to Arabia: a few low hills, and no river or valley, are all that lie between her pastures and the deserts, out of which, in every age, wild and hungry tribes have been ready to swarm. Moab is open to the east; Judah, or Judæa, with the same formation, and imposing the same habits of life on a kindred stock of men, has a great gulf between herself and the east. In this fact lies a large part of the reason why she was chosen as the home of God's peculiar people.

The Wilderness of Judæa, which is piled up from the beach of the Dead Sea to the edge of the Central Plateau, may be reserved for later treatment. Here it is only needful to ask what passes break up through it to the centre of the province? The answer is, that passes, strictly so called, do not exist. There are gorges torn by winter torrents—between Jericho and Jebel Usdum at the south end of the Dead Sea there cannot be fewer than twenty—but all are too narrow and crooked to carry roads. Real gateways and roads into Judæa on this border are only five: and these are determined not by lines of

[1] הרי עברים or הר.

valley, but by another feature which in this region is more indispensable to roads. That is the presence of an oasis. The roads from the east into Judæa have to cross, for five to eight hours, a waterless desert; it is necessary that they start from the few well-watered spots on its eastern edge. There are practically only three of these: Jericho, 'Ain Feshkhah, some 10 miles south, and 'Ain Jidi, or En-gedi, 18 miles farther. From Jericho there start into Judæa three roads, from 'Ain Feshkhah one, and from En-gedi one.

The roads from Jericho—north-west to Ai and Bethel, south-west to Jerusalem, and south-south-west to the Lower Kidron and Bethlehem—do not keep to any line of valley; for, as has been said, this flank of Judæa is cut only by deep gorges, but for the most part they follow the ridges between the latter. The most northerly of these three routes into Judæa[1] ascends behind Jericho to the ridge north of the Ḳelt, follows it to Michmash, and so by Ai to Bethel. This is an ancient road, and was probably the trade route between the Lower Jordan and the coast, both in ancient and mediæval times.[2] It is the line of Israel's first invasion, described in the seventh and eighth chapters of Joshua; and its fitness for that is obvious, for it is open, and leads on to a broad plateau in the centre of the country. The middle route of the three is now the ordinary road from Jerusalem to Jericho. It is impossible to think that an invading army fearing opposition ever attempted its higher end.[3] But it is the shortest road from Jericho to Jerusalem, and therefore the usual pilgrim route in both directions. Peræans and Galileans came up to the Temple by it: it was the path of our Lord and His disciples, when He set *His face steadfastly towards Jerusalem*; and from then till now it has been trodden in the opposite direction by pilgrims from all lands to the scene of His baptism. When taken upwards a more hot and heavy way it is impossible to conceive—between blistered limestone rocks, and in front the bare hills piled high, without shadow or verdure. There is no water from Jericho till you reach the roots of the Mount of Olives.[4] Curious red streaks appear from time to time on the stone, and perhaps account for the sanguinary names which attach to the road—the present Red Khan, the Chastel Rouge of the Crusaders and the Tala'at ed-Dumm or Ascent of Blood[5]—but the crimes committed

[1] More northerly still a road goes up from Jericho by the first pass into the more open Mount Ephraim. Its course is marked by Roman pavement past 'Ain Duḳ, round Umm Sirah, and up the Wady Ṭaiyibeh to eṭ-Ṭaiyibeh, the Biblical city of Ephraim. See ch. xvii.

[2] See pp. 129 f.

[3] Pompey may have come this way, but more probably approached Jerusalem from the north; Josephus, xiv *Antt.* iv. 1.

[4] 'Ain Ḥauḍ or 'Ain Shems, the En-shemesh of Josh. xv. 7.

[5] Khan el-Aḥmar, one of the sites for the Inn of the Good Samaritan (St. Luke

here make these doubly deserved. The surrounding Arabs have always found the pilgrims a profitable prey. The third road[1] from Jericho leaves the Arabah about 5 miles south of Jericho, and, coming up by el-Munṭar, crosses the Kidron near Mar Saba. Thence one branch strikes north-west to Jerusalem, and another south-west to Bethlehem; before they separate they are joined by a road from 'Ain Feshkhah, the large oasis 10 miles south of Jericho, on the Dead Sea coast. We are not certain of an invasion of Judæa by these avenues, unless Judah and Simeon went up by one of them at the first occupation of the land.[2] But one or other was undoubtedly the road up which Naomi brought Ruth, and down which David took his family to the King of Moab.[3] This double connection of Bethlehem with Moab comes back to you as you ride along these roads with the cliffs of Moab in sight. Moab is visible from Bethlehem: when Ruth lifted her eyes from gleaning in the fields of Boaz, she saw her native land over against her.

These roads then debouch from the Judæan hills, and join a little above the end of the Dead Sea. Opposite their junction at least two fords cross the Jordan,[4] by no means so easy as the numerous fords opposite Mount Ephraim, yet passable for most of the year, and meeting highways from Gilead and Moab. A road also comes down the Arabah west of Jordan, and another from Mount Ephraim by 'Ain Duḳ.

Follow these roads, passes, and fords to where they meet at the foot of the Judæan hills; observe the streams breaking from the hill-foot at their junction, and rendering possible an elaborate irrigation. Then, where lately but a few hovels and a tower on the edge of a swamp mocked the imagination, you will see a city rise in the midst of a wonderful fertility of grove and garden. Jericho was the gateway of a province, the emporium of a large trade, the mistress of a palm forest, woods of balsam, and rich gardens. To earliest Israel she was the City of Palms[5]; to the latest Jewish historian "a divine

---

x. 34). Tala'at ed-Dumm is applied to a hill and fortress north-east of the Khan, and to the wady which the road pursues thence towards Jericho. It is doubtless the ancient Ma'aleh Adummim (Josh. xv. 7, xviii. 17) on the border between Judah and Benjamin. The fortress was the Crusaders' Chastel Rouge (not Tour Rouge, which stood near Cæsarea), or Citerne Rouge, built by the Templars for the succour of pilgrims, and also called la Tour Maledoin. Rey, *Colonies Franques*, 387.

[1] There is really a fourth between our second and third, which passes the Mohammedan place of pilgrimage, Nebi Musa.

[2] Judges i. 3 ff.

[3] 1 Sam. xxii. 3, 4.

[4] Makhaḍet el-Ḥajlah (near el-Ḥajlah, ancient Beth-hoglah, Josh. xv. 6, xviii. 19, 21) and the Makh. el-Henu. *PEF Mem.* iii. 170 and Sheet xviii counts three more.

[5] Deut. xxxiv. 3; Judges i. 16, iii. 13; 2 Chron. xxviii. 15.

region", "fattest of Judæa".[1] Greeks and Romans spread her fame, with her dates and balsam, over the world, and great revenue was derived from her.[2] Her year is one long summer; she can soak herself in water, and the chemicals with which her soil is charged seem to favour her peculiar products. Like Bethshan, she can make a swamp about her; five miles in front is a river, which, if she oppose, cannot be crossed; and immediately behind are her own hills, with half a dozen possible citadels. Jericho is thus a city surrounded by resources. Yet in war she has always been easily taken. That her walls fell at the sound of Joshua's trumpets is a summary of her history. Judæa could never keep her. She fell to Northern Israel till Northern Israel perished.[3] She fell to Bacchides and the Syrians.[4] She fell to Aristobulus when he advanced on his brother Hyrcanus and Judæa.[5] She fell without a blow to Pompey,[6] and at the approach of Herod and of Vespasian

[1] Josephus, iv *Wars*, viii. 3; i *Wars*, vi. 6. Cf. iv *Antt.* vi. 1; xiv *Antt.* iv. 1; xv *Antt* iv. 2; i *Wars*, xviii. 5.

[2] Strabo, xvi. ii. 41, the palms covered 100 stadia. Diod. Siculus, ii. 48. 9; cf. xix. 98. 4. Pliny, *Hist. Nat.* xiii. 4: the finest dates are those of Jericho, grown in salt soil; cf. Horace, *Epistles*, ii. 2. 184: "Herodis palmetis pinguibus." Mark Antony gave the region to Cleopatra; Herod farmed it of her (xv *Antt.* iv. 2; i *Wars*, xviii. 5); but in 30 B.C., from Augustus he got it to himself (xv *Antt.* vii. 3; i *Wars*, xx. 3). He built a palace, which Archelaus rebuilt, baths and theatres; and fortified a citadel on the hill behind, calling it Kypros after his mother (xvi *Antt.* v. 2; i *Wars*, xxi. 4, 9; ii *Wars*, xviii. 6), probably the ruin Beit-Gubr or Ḳubr. Herod lived much and died in Jericho. In our Lord's time, Jericho was under the Romans, who farmed its revenues; Pressel's *Priscilla an Sabina*, letters from a Roman lady on the imperial farms, to her friend at home, gives a vivid picture. Zacchæus was connected with the imperial farms, or sat in this border town at receipt of custom—probably the former, since he proposed to restore the money he had exacted, impossible to a toll-keeper with a passenger constituency. In Josephus' time the region still flourished. In the 4th cent. were many palms ("Descriptio Orbis Totius", Müller, *Geogr. Græci Minores*, ii. 513). The Christian population was mainly monks and anchorites, with keepers of inns for pilgrims; and cultivation seems to have declined. In the 7th cent. Adamnan, and in the 8th another, still saw palm groves; but at the Moslem invasion the town was deserted. The Saracens revived the culture, and introduced sugar, which the Crusaders found growing (Rey, *Col. Franques*, etc., 248). There are ruins called Ṭawaḥin es-Sukker, "sugar-mills", not far from the fount of Elisha. The revenues were great (Will. of Tyre, xv. 27) under the Latin kingdom. There were still palms. After the Crusades, the place was more neglected, till reduced to its late pitiful condition. The last palm was seen by Robinson in 1838; it is gone. The present village occupies the site neither of the O.T. nor of the N.T. Jericho. The former lay round 'Ain es-Sulṭan; the latter to the S on Wady Ḳelt. Robinson, *Bib. Res.* i; Zschokke, *Topographie der westlichen Jordans'Au*, Jerusalem, 1866; on the mounds, *PEF Mem. Jerus.* 507; on W el-Ḳelt, *MuNDPV*, 1897, 21, on Gilgal, *id.* 1899, 30, 97.

[3] See last chapter.

[4] 1 Macc. ix. 50-53; xiii *Antt.* i. 3.

[5] xiv *Antt.* i. 2; cf. xiii *Antt.* xvi. 3.

[6] xiv *Antt.* iv. 1.

her people deserted her.[1] It is interesting that three invaders of Judæa—Bacchides, Pompey, and Vespasian—took Jericho before attempting Jerusalem, although she did not lie on their way to the latter, and fortified her, not, it is to be supposed, as a base of operations, but as a source of supplies. This weakness of Jericho was due to two causes. An open pass came down on her from Northern Israel, and from this both part of her water supply could be cut off, and the hills behind her occupied. But besides her people seem never to have been distinguished for bravery; and indeed in that climate how could they? Enervated by the heat, which degrades the inhabitants of the Ghor, and unable to endure on their bodies aught but linen,[2] they could not be warriors, or anything but irrigators, paddlers in water and soft earth. We forget how near neighbours they had been to Sodom and Gomorrah. No great man was born in Jericho; no heroic deed was done in her. She has been called "the key" and "the guardhouse" of Judæa; she was only the pantry.[3] She never stood a siege, and her inhabitants were always running away.

Recent excavations, German and British,[4] have made important discoveries, especially of the earlier history of Jericho: City walls round the great mound of to-day, Kom es-Sulṭan, with remains of the Stone, Middle and Late Bronze Ages, 3000?-1200 B.C., and proofs of the destruction of the City by a general conflagration about 1400, to which it has been found apposite to quote the words in Joshua, *they burned the city with fire*, for they had *devoted all that was in the city*[5]; and of another destruction in the Early Iron Age, 1400-900 B.C.

The next road from the East into Judah leads up through the wilderness from En-gedi.[6] The oasis of En-gedi is the cause of this road, for other gorges breaking upwards from the Dead Sea are not so difficult as the rocky stair that climbs from it. Here again we see what we saw at Jericho, and to a less degree at 'Ain Feshkhah—that on this side of Judæa the presence of water and gardens is more necessary to a road than an open pass.

He who has been to En-gedi fears lest he exaggerate its fertility to those who have not. The oasis bursts upon him from one of the driest and most poisoned

[1] xiv *Antt.* xv. 3; iv *Wars*, viii. 2, ix. 1. [2] Jos. iv *Wars*, viii. 3.

[3] Jos. xiv *Antt.* xv. 3, 10.

[4] German, 1907-8, see *MuNDPV*, v, 1907, 65; *Mitteil d. deutsch. Orient. Gesellschaft*, Dec. 1908; S. A. Cook, *PEFQ*, 1910, 54. British, by Garstang on Sir Charles Marston's Expedition, the approximate dates for the strata tested by Dr. Fisher and Père Vincent, see *PEFQ*, July 1930, 123 ff., with plates and plans, 1931; *Scotsman*, 10th March 1931; *PEFQ*, April 1931, 104 ff.; Garstang, *Josh. Jud.* 1931, *passim*; *PEFQ*, 1931, 186 ff., "The Walls of Jericho", by Prof. J. Garstang, M.A., D.Sc., LL.D.

[5] Josh. vi. 24, 21. [6] "The well of the wild goat"; modern name, 'Ain Jidi.

regions of our planet. Either he has ridden across Jeshimon, seven hours without a spring, three with hardly a bush, when suddenly, over the edge of a precipice, 400 feet below him he sees a river of verdure burst from the rock, and scatter, reeds, bush, trees, and grass, down other 300 feet to a mile of gardens by the beach of the blue sea; or he has come along the coast, through sulphur smells,[1] with the bitter sea on one side, the desert cliffs on the other, and a fiery sun overhead, when round a corner of the cliffs he sees the broad fan of verdure open and slope before him. He passes up it, through gardens of cucumber and melon, small fields of wheat, and a scattered orchard, to a brake of reeds and bushes, with a few trees. He hears what perhaps he has not heard for days—the rush of water; and then through the bush he sees the foam of a waterspout, 6 feet high and almost 2 feet broad, which is but one branch of a fresh stream that breaks from boulders above on the shelf at the foot of the precipices. The verdure and water, strange and sudden, with the exhilaration of the view across the sea, produce most generous impressions of this oasis, and tempt to exaggerate its fertility. The most enthusiastic, however, could not too highly rate its usefulness as a refuge, for it lies at the back of a broad desert, and is large enough to sustain an army. Its own caves are insignificant, but in the neighbourhood there is one "vast grotto".[2] More obvious are the sites of ancient "strongholds", such as David held; and over the neighbourhood of the stream are scattered the ruins of masonry—remains of the town which Solomon perhaps fortified,[3] which was the centre of a toparchy under the Romans,[4] still a large village in the fourth century,[5] and during the Crusades gathered round a convent,

[1] S of Engedi we failed to find Tristram's hot sulphur springs where marked on the Survey Map, but the smell was apparent, and the gravel badly stained. Heat 94° in shade of thorn-bush, in spite of a strong breeze.

[2] Guided by a negro slave of the Rushaideh Arabs, who own the oasis, I searched for caves. A tiny one is on the terrace, where the water springs, and three lower down, almost on the plain. My guide said these were all. None was large enough to have been the scene of 1 Sam. xxiv. *The strongholds* (xxiii. 29, xxiv. 22) must have lain by the water, and the cave below them (xxiv. 3, 22). Tristram (*Land of Israel*, p. 286): "a fairy grotto of vast size".

[3] In 1 Kings ix. 18, Hebrew text Tamar, while Hebrew margin and 2 Chron. viii. 4 Tadmor. The latter is not correct, for the town was *in the wilderness in the land.* Tamar must be sought for in the wilderness of Judæa, and where more suitably than in this frontier village of Hazazon-tamar? Perhaps Tamar of Ezek. xlvii. 19, xlviii. 28 (?) is the same. See next page, n. 3; and n. 10, p. 185.

[4] Josephus, iii *Wars*, iii. 5, omitted by Pliny in the toparchies, *H.N.* v. 14, 70.

[5] Eusebius, *Onomast.* art. Ἐγγαδδὶ: καὶ νῦν ἐστὶ κώμη μεγίστη Ἰουδαίων. Both Eusebius and Jerome place it vaguely in the wilderness, in the Aulôn, or Plain of Jericho, and on the Dead Sea. Cf. Ptolemy, v. 16. 8.

with vineyards celebrated through Syria.[1] Ancient Engedi was also famous, like Jericho, for palms and balsam.[2] From the former it derived one of its names, Hazazon-tamar[3]—"Hazazon of the Palm"—but this tree has disappeared as wholly as the vine. If we thus feel the fitness of Engedi for a refuge, we can also appreciate why it should rank only second to Jericho as a gateway into Judæa and a source of supplies for the march through the wilderness behind. The way up from it is steep, not a pass so much as a staircase, which has had partly to be hewn and partly built over the rocks.[4] When you climb it, you stand on a rolling plateau. The road breaks into two branches, both in parts with ancient pavement. One turns north-west by Wady Ḥuṣaṣeh—in which Ḥaṣaṣon perhaps survives—to Herod's Herodeion, Bethlehem and Jerusalem. It is a wild, extremely difficult road, and almost never used by caravans.[5] The other branch turns south-west to Juttah and Hebron,[6] the proper route from En-gedi into Judæa. As the roads from Jericho make for Bethel or Jerusalem, so this from En-gedi makes for Hebron. Hebron and En-gedi have always been connected. David came to En-gedi from the Hebron neighbourhood, and the Crusading convent of En-gedi was under the Bishop of Saint Abraham.[7]

In the reign of Jehoshaphat, Moab and Ammon with allies invaded Judæa by En-gedi[8]—a route which they chose, not because they had come round the south of the Dead Sea, but because Jericho then belonged not to Judæa but to Israel. From En-gedi they followed neither of the roads just described, but struck up between them, through the *wilderness*, probably north-west towards Tekoa, not a difficult route for an army, less steep than any other approach to the Central Plateau from the desert.[9] They came by *the ascent of Ziz*.[10] Jehoshaphat went out through *the wilderness of Tekoa* to meet them in the *wilderness of Jeruel*, but found them slaughtered and dispersed in a

[1] Rey, *Colonies Franques*, 384, under Hebron, "J'y ai retrouvé en 1858 des restes de constructions médiévales". Scott places here an episode of the *Talisman.*

[2] Josephus, ix *Antt.* i. 2.

[3] 2 Chron. xx. 2, *the same is Engedi.* But see Holzinger on Gen. xiv. 7; Winckler, *Gesch.* ii. 34 ff.; Cheyne, *Enc. Bibl.*

[4] This staircase is only some 500 feet, but, owing to its steepness and narrowness, which allow beasts to carry only a fraction of their usual burdens, our mules took two hours to bring our baggage up.

[5] Salt-carriers from Jebel Usdum to Jerusalem seem, from answers they made to us, to prefer to go farther north, before turning to Jerusalem.

[6] For a full description, see Robinson, *BR*, ii. pp. 209 ff.

[7] Crusaders' name for Hebron, Rey, *loc. cit.*

[8] 2 Chron. xx. 1 ff.; 16 Ziz.

[9] We followed it, for the sake of our mules, in preference to the rough road towards Bethlehem.

[10] *Flowers*, unless it was a proper name; cf. LXX Ἀσσεῖς, L. Ἀσισά; cf. חצצון,

valley, which was called by the relieved Judæans Berachah, or "Blessing". These places are as unknown as the agents of the mysterious slaughter. This is said to have been by *ambushments*, and in that tangle of hills and water-courses, enough men might hide to surprise and overcome an army. The Bedawee camps are unseen till you are upon them, and the bare banks of a gulley, up the torrent-bed of which a caravan is painfully making its way, may be dotted in two minutes with armed men.[1] It was probably some desert tribes which thus overcame Jehoshaphat's enemies before he arrived. The narrative is obscure, but through it we can see the characteristics of this region—the tangled hills, ambushes, sudden surprise, the bare valley strewn with slain and their spoil.

South of En-gedi, on the desert as it falls to the precipices of the Dead Sea, the traveller comes across traces of a military road. We found these on a line making for the edge of the precipice above Masada, but how they continued down the cliff we could not discover. It had been a road suitable for wheeled vehicles, but now mules can scarcely descend to Masada. This road has for our present task no importance. It was not an entrance to the land, but an inland way between the Herodian fortresses of Masada and Herodium.

I have refrained from touching upon Israel's entrance into Western Palestine, which took place across this border. But, after what we have seen, we can judge how far the geography of the latter corresponds to the narratives in Joshua and Judges. These narratives are from several sources, which differ in their testimony.[2] But they agree that Israel's invasion of Western Palestine was by the nation as a whole and under Joshua; that it was through

---

2 Chron. xx. 2, LXX Ἀσασάν, Gen. xiv. 7 Ἀσασάν. With Berachah, cf. the ruins Berekut. Another place in this wilderness is "the water of the pool Asphar" or "Asphal", 1 Macc. ix. 33. This is probably the Bir-Selhub, a large cistern 6 m. WSW of Engedi near the junction of several roads (Robinson, *BR*, ii. 202), the hills here still bear the name Sufra. Others (Buhl, *Geog.* 158) identify Asphar with the ruin and cistern ez-Zaʻferane S of Tekoa.

[1] We had experience between En-gedi and Tekoa. We were coming up a winding gully, with no creature in sight save a shepherd on a distant height. He gave a cry, which was answered from a farther hill, and, in a short time, we were surrounded by armed and yelling Arabs, on foot and horseback. They were of the Rushaîdeh tribe, and their anger was that we had taken as guides through their land some Jâhalin. We invited the chiefs to dinner, paid two dollars toll, and were not further troubled.

[2] For instance, as to the name Gilgal. On the other hand, it is a question whether we find such a difference, amounting to contradiction, between Josh. vi. 24-27, in the document of the Hexateuch, J, E, relating how Israel burnt Jericho and all that was therein, and Joshua cursed the rebuilder (1 Kings xvi. 34 narrates the fulfilment),

siege and battle, that the crossing of Jordan was near Jericho, that Jericho was the first town taken, that Joshua set the camp at Gilgal, and that thence Israel divided, Judah and Simeon with the Kenites attacking Central and Southern Judæa, but the House of Joseph under Joshua, going up to Ai, Bethel, and Mount Ephraim.

The truth of this narrative has been denied in almost every particular by Stade, who maintains that all Israel did not invade Western Palestine at one time, that Joshua did not lead them, that they did not wage war on the Canaanites, and did not cross in the region of Jericho. In an Appendix I try to show the baselessness of Stade's presuppositions, singularly opposed to the traditions we possess.[1] Here I may point out how the evidence of the geography we have been surveying is—as far as it can go—against Stade's theory, and agrees with the main lines of the biblical narrative. Let us bear in mind the limits of geographical evidence. It cannot prove a narrative correct, but if its data agree with the line the narrative takes, especially if the narrative like this has come down several lines of tradition, that must create a presumption in favour of the narrative. Again, it may prove other and rival versions of the events, which the narrative describes, to be improbable or absurd, and so it lends the narrative additional support. Geography does this in the issue between Stade's theory and the account of Israel's invasion. Stade's theory fits the conditions neither on the east nor on the west bank of Jordan.

Stade declares that Israel cannot have crossed at Jericho, because the Plain of Shittim opposite Jericho then belonged to Moab; but it is generally admitted, even by critics in sympathy with Stade,[2] that Moab was then south of Arnon, and that Israel occupied all to the north. It is true that later Moab did hold the country opposite Jericho, but this proves that the tradition of Israel's crossing there could not have arisen at the late date to which Stade assigns it. Again, when he maintains that Israel could not have beaten the Canaanites on the Plain of Jordan, we point to the fact that Jericho never did stand a siege. But the strongest argument against Stade's theory lies in

---

and Judges iii. 13, from a different document, which tells how Eglon of Moab smote Israel and took the City of Palmtrees. One might try to solve this contradiction by emphasising that Jericho has changed its site more than once; and that Judges iii. 13 speaks of a Jericho which had risen on another from that cursed by Joshua. But there is no sign of this, and, on the data before us, it seems more probable that the writer of Judges iii. 13 was unacquainted with the facts in Josh. vi. 24-27.

[1] Appendix II. Joshua's reality is supported by the fact that he is mentioned not only in Document E, as Stade avers, but in J also.

[2] *E.g.* Wellhausen, *Hist.* p. 5.

the double direction which the invasion is said to have taken from Jericho. All agree that Israel won a footing on two parts of the Central Range—Mount Ephraim and opposite the Dead Sea—between which there lay for a time a belt of Canaanite country. But from what centre except Jericho could these separate positions be equally reached? Certainly not from the Jabbok; it is hard to see how, if Judah crossed at the Jabbok, as Stade thinks the rest of the tribes did,[1] she fought her wars so far south as the Negeb of Judæa.

On the other hand, the main lines of the biblical narrative agree with the geographical data. The crossing of Jordan is possible and likely.[2] The quick conquest of Jericho is in harmony with all we have learned of that city's characteristics and her failure through history to stand a siege[3]; the double direction of the subsequent invasion, north-west and south-west, agrees with the standing camp of Israel near Jericho at Gilgal, and with the lines of road we have followed from Jericho to the interior; while the return of Joshua to Gilgal after the first conquests on the Central Range,[4] and the authority which, it is to be presumed, Israel continued to exercise from Gilgal upon the Central Range, have an analogy in the description (from the same source)[5] of the district of Gilgal, as a centre of Canaanite authority over the Central Range before Israel's time; while both facts are possible in face of the passes from this part of the Jordan Valley into Mount Ephraim.

The route by which Judah and Simeon went up to *their lots*[6] cannot be definitely traced. But we may notice that two of the most ancient settlements of Judah—Bethlehem and Hebron[7]—correspond to the two great routes from the Jordan Valley into Central Judæa, by 'Ain Feshkhah and En-gedi. With them went up the nomadic tribe which at Sinai had attached itself to the fortunes of Israel. *The sons of Hobab, the Kenite, brother-in-law of Moses, went up out of the Town of Palms with the sons of Judah into the wilderness of*

[1] Some think Judah with the Kenites came from Kadesh through the Negeb. Stade allows not more than a *perhaps* to this (*Gesch.* 132; nothing of it in his account of Judah, 157-160). Oort adopts it in his Atlas. But indications show that Judah entered her territory from the N, her first seats Bethlehem and Baale-Judah (Kiriath-jearim); only later did she come S to Hebron.

[2] Meyer, whose analysis of the Documents (*ZATW*, I) is unsparing, firmly believes in this part of the narrative.

[3] The bulk of Josh. iv, on the fall of Jericho, belongs to the oldest documents J, E.

[4] Josh. x. 43. On Gilgal, *MuNDPV*, 1899, 30 f., 97 f.

[5] Deut. xi. 30, from the same hand as Josh. x. 43. If it means that Ebal and Gerizim are over against Gilgal, this was the present Juleijil (Schlatter, *Zur Topogr.* 246 ff., 274; Buhl, *Geog.* 202).

[6] Judges i. Meyer and Budde have shown the true course and connection of this chapter (mainly from J). See Budde, *Ri. u. Sam.* 1-24, 84-89.

[7] Judges i. 3-11.

Judah at the going down of Arad, and they *went and dwelt with the Amalekite.*[1] While the main Judæan stock settled on arable ground, and in cities, and inter-married with Canaanites, the Kenites, true to their nomadic origin, turned into the wilderness of Judah, and dwelt with the Amalekites. The *going down of Arad* is the south-eastern buttress of the Judæan plateau, at the head of the gorge which runs up from Masada, the Wady Seyyal. The name Arad exists 17 miles south-east of Hebron. The rocky dwelling of the Kenite, visible from Nebo,[2] cannot be identified. It is probably not the heights of Yekin, to which it has been assigned,[3] for those are not sufficiently in the desert. En-gedi is possible. The stronghold and oasis must have been possessed by somebody: to-day they are cultivated by the Rushaîdeh, a Bedawee tribe like the Kenites.

2. *The Southern Border: the Negeb*

The survey of the southern border of Judæa leads us upon a region of immense extent and historical interest—the Negeb, translated *The South* in our version,[4] literally Dry or Parched Land. The character and story of the

[1] Judges i. 16. The corrupt text must be emended in such way as above. Meyer and Hollenberg (*ZATW*, 1), Budde, *Ri. u. Sam.* 9-11 and 86, Kittel, *Gesch.* 242, 243. There is no reason to omit *sons of* with Budde; it is justified by different LXX sources, and the passage from a plural verb to the singular verbs need give no trouble. That a proper name has fallen out of the text is obvious. *Brother-in-law* needs it, and LXX MSS. give us a choice of two, of which Hobab is to be preferred in this J Document. Kittel is right in rejecting Meyer's *and Cain*. The *going down of Arad*, LXX Vat. is to be preferred to the Massoretic *Negeb* or *south of Arad*, for, as Budde says, if *Arad* is in the wilderness of Judah, it cannot be connected with the Negeb. In v. 17, Budde and Kittel rightly retain Arad. All agree with Hollenberg that העם, people, must read העמלק, 'Amalek, or Budde more correctly העמלקי, the Amalekite. LXX has Amalek, in conformity with 1 Sam. xv. 5 ff.

[2] Num. xxiv. 21 ff.

[3] *PEF Red. Map*, Henderson, 71. The name has no similarity.

[4] *E.g.*, Gen. xiii. 1; 1 Sam. xxx. 1; Ps. cxxvi. 4. The Negeb extended from the Arabah to the coast, and was variously named according to the people on the north of it. There was the נ׳ הכרתי, to the south of Philistia; נ׳ הירחמאלי, S of the Shephelah; נ׳ כלב, S of Hebron (there is a W el-Kulâb about 10 miles SW of Hebron); the נ׳ יהודה or אשר ליהודה, which covered the same central portion, and the נ׳ הקיני which was the eastmost part S of the seats of the Kenites (1 Sam. xxvii. 10, xxx. 14; 2 Sam. xxiv. 7). Used for Judah, Ezek. xxi. 2 f. (Heb.); in Daniel it stands for Egypt, viii. 9, xi. 5 ff. As ים Sea is used in Palestine for West, so Negeb came to be used for South; the S border, Josh. xv. 2, 4, xviii. 19; of Gennesareth, Josh. xi. 2, cf. Zech. xiv. 10. The name occurs on the Egyptian monuments: W. Max Müller,

Negeb require a separate study: here we deal with it as the southern border of Judæa.

From Hebron the Central Range lets itself down by broad undulations, through which the Wady Khalil[1] winds as far as Beersheba, and then, as Wady es-Seba', turns sharply west, finding the sea near Gaza. It is a country visited by annual rains, with a few perennial springs, and in early summer abundance of flowers and corn. We descended from Hebron to Dhaheriyah, possibly Kiriath-sepher, over moors and through wheat-fields, arranged in the narrower wadies in terraces, but lavishly spread over many of the broader valleys. A thick scrub covered most of the slopes. There were olive groves about the villages, but elsewhere few trees. We passed a stream and four springs,[2] two with tracts of marsh, and, though it was the end of April, heavy showers fell. South of Dhaheriyah—which may be regarded as the frontier town between the hill-country and the Negeb[3]—the soil is barer, but

---

Asien u. Europa nach altägypt. Denkm. 148. See Blanckenhorn, *MuNDPV*, 1895, 35; W. F. Albright, *JPOS*, iv. 131, "Egypt and the Early History of the Negeb"; *JPOS*, xi. 1931, 204 ff., "Beiträge zur historischen Geographie des Negeb", by A. Alt.

[1] El-Khalil, "the friend", that is, of God, a title of Abraham, is also the modern name of his city, Hebron, near which the Wady starts.

[2] N of Seil ed-Dilbeh is 'Ain Hejireh, with a shadoof for irrigation, and on the S Ain Dilbeh, a square pool covered with weeds, supposed to be the upper and nether springs granted by Caleb to his daughter, to compensate for the dryness of her domain n the Negeb (Jud. i. 14 f.). The valley is fertile and the hills feed flocks. But springs are farther S.

[3] Edh-Dhaheriyah is possibly Debir, known also as Kiriath-sepher (Josh. xv. 15), LXX *πόλις γραμμάτων*, city of letters. Moore קרית סְפָר, Border-town. Why not Pay, or Toll-town? (סְפָר payment, 2 Chron. ii. 16, Heb.; 17, Eng.) It lies on a high-road. Another name is קרית סנה (Josh. xv. 49), thorn-town (?), perhaps a misreading of K-Sepher. דביר or Debir, means part behind; Dhaheriyah may mean that also. It lay near Hebron on the hills (Josh. xi. 21, xv. 48), a chief town of the Canaanites (xii. 13), and was set apart for priests (xxi. 1, 15), but might also be said to be on the Negeb, xv, cf. v. 15 with v. 19 (though not necessarily). Dhaheriyah suits this double designation, on the hills, but at the *back*, just over the edge of the fertile country. I have let the above stand, but reviewing this work in *The Academy*, Sayce (cf. *PEFQ*, Jan. 1893) says, "O.T. information on this site seems to exclude its identification with Dhaheriyah", where Petrie found no early remains. Debir more naturally signifies *Sanctuary* (1 Kings vi. 5) than *Back*. Now it is claimed that excavations at Tell Beit-Mirsim, 15 m. SW of Hebron, prove it as Debir, Garstang, *Josh. Jud.* 210, 370; *PEFQ*, 1931, 175. W. Max Müller suggested Beth-Thupar of *The Travels of a Mohar* as = Heb. Beth Sopher, *Scribe's House* and supposing that the writer transposed Kiriath and Beth identifies Beth-Thupar with Kiriath-sepher, which he accordingly points K. Sopher as against both Massoretic and LXX. This is precarious. See Muss-Arnolt, *Christ. Intelligencer*, Feb. 17, 1892.

travellers from the desert delight in the verdure which meets them as soon as they pass Beersheba and Wady es-Seba‘.[1] The disposition of the land—the gentle descent cut by the broad Wady—and its fertility render it as open a frontier, and easy an approach to Judæa, as it is possible to conceive. But it does not roll out upon the level desert. South of Beersheba, before this is reached and the region of roads from Arabia to Egypt and Philistia, lie 60 miles of mountainous country, mostly disposed in "steep ridges running east and west",[2] whose inaccessibleness is further certified by the character of the tribes that roam upon it. Wilder sons of Ishmael are not found on the desert.[3] The vegetation, even after rain, is meagre, and in summer disappears. "No great route now leads, or ever has led, through this district"[4]; but the highways which gather upon the south of it from Egypt, Sinai, the Gulf of ‘Aḳaba, and Arabia, are thrust by it either to the east up the Wady ‘Arabah to the Dead Sea, or to the west towards Gaza and Philistia. Paths indeed skirt this region, and even cross its corners, but are not war-paths. When Judah's frontier extended to Elath, Solomon's cargoes from Ophir[5] and the tribute of Arab kings to Jehoshaphat[6] were doubtless carried through it. When any one power held the whole land, merchants traversed it from Petra to Hebron or Gaza,[7] or skirted it by the Roman road up the west of it from ‘Aḳaba to Jerusalem[8]; and even whole tribes might drift across it in days when Judah had no inhabitants to resist them. When the Jews came back from exile, they found Edomites settled as far north at least as Hebron. But armies of invasion, knowing that opposition awaited them upon the Judæan frontier, would hardly venture across those steep and haggard ridges, especially when the Dead Sea and Gaza routes lay convenient on either hand, and led to regions much more fertile than the Judæan plateau.

Hence until the Great War in 1917 Judæa was almost never invaded from the south. Chedorlaomer's expedition, on its return from Paran, swept north by the Arabah to the Cities of the Plain, sacking En-gedi, but leaving Hebron untouched.[9] Israel themselves were repulsed seeking to enter the Promised Land by this frontier[10]; and, perhaps most significant, the invasion by Islam, though its chief goal may have been the Holy City of Jerusalem,

[1] Robinson, *BR*, i. 305, 306.
[2] Robinson, *BR*, i. 275.
[3] Azazimeh; cf. Trumbull's *Kadesh Barnea*.
[4] Robinson, *BR*, i. 275.
[5] 1 Kings ix. 26-28.
[6] 2 Chron. xvii. 11.
[7] As they do to this day. See p. 134.
[8] As shown in the *Tabula Peutingeriana*.
[9] Gen. xiv.
[10] The theory that Judah and Simeon, or the Kenites, did not cross Jordan like the rest of Israel, but came up through the Negeb, has no evidence beyond the fact that for a time Judah was separated from the other tribes by a Canaanite belt crossing the range near Jerusalem; and this is explained by the double and far-parting entrance into the land at Jericho. See pp. 187 ff.

and its nearest road to this lay past Hebron, swerved to east and west, and entered, some of it by Gaza, and some, like Israel, across Jordan. The most likely foes to swarm upon Judah by the slopes of Hebron were the natives of this wild desert, *Arabs*, or, as they were called from Egypt[1] to Philistia,[2] *Amalekites*; but it is to be remarked that though they sometimes invaded the Negeb,[3] they must have been oftener attracted, as they still are, to the fertile and more easily over-run fields of the Philistines. *Nine furlongs from Jamnia* Judas Maccabæus defeated in a great battle *the nomads of Arabia*[4]; and the proper harbour of the desert and emporium of Arabian trade was, as we have seen, not Hebron but Gaza.[5] The best defences of a road or a frontier against these impetuous swarms were strong towers such as protect the Hajj road between Syria and Mecca from the Bedouin,[6] and of these Uzziah built a number in the desert south and east of Judah.[7] The symbolic use of towers in the Bible is well known.

The most notable road across this border of Judah was the continuation of the highway from Bethel, which kept the watershed to Hebron, and thence came down to Beersheba. From here it struck south across the western ridges of the savage highland district and divided into several branches. One, the Roman road already noticed, curved round the south of the highland district to 'Aḳaba and Arabia; another, the way perhaps of Elijah when he fled from Jezebel,[8] and used by mediæval and modern pilgrims, crossed to Sinai; while a third struck direct upon Egypt, the *way to Shur*. By this Abraham passed and repassed through the Negeb[9]; Hagar, the Egyptian slave-woman, fled from her mistress, perhaps with some wild hope of reaching her own country[10]; and Jacob went down into Egypt with his wagons.[11] In times of alliance between Egypt and Judah, this was the way of communication between them. So that fatal embassy must have gone from Jerusalem, which Isaiah describes struggling *through the land of trouble and anguish, whence are the young lion and the old lion, the viper and fiery flying serpent*[12]; and so, in the time of the Crusades, those caravans passed from Cairo for

[1] Exod. xvii. 8. [2] 1 Sam. xxx. 1. [3] 1 Chron. iv. 43. [4] 2 Macc. xii. 11.
[5] See p. 134. [6] Cf. Doughty, *Arabia Deserta*, i. 13. [7] 2 Chron. xxvi. 10.
[8] 1 Kings xix. [9] Gen. xiii. 1.
[10] Gen. xvi. 7, 14. The *well was called Beer-Lahai-Roi = The Well of the Living One who seeth me*, but it may be *The Well* called "*He that seeth me liveth*" (Wel.), *behold*, it is *between Kadesh and Bered* (for the latter the Targum Ps. Jonathan gives Ḥaluṣa, *i.e.* the present Khalaṣah, ruins 13 m. S of Beersheba). Twelve miles NW of 'Ain Ḳadis is 'Ain el-Muweileh, which Rowlands says is pronounced Moilahhi by the Arabs, and so may be Ma-leḥayi-rai, or "water of the living one seeing" (*PEFQ*, 1884, 177).
[11] Gen. xlvi. 1, 5 f. [12] Isa. xxx. 6.

Saladin at Jerusalem, one of which Richard intercepted near Beersheba.[1] It is an open road, but wild, and never, it would seem until the Great War, used for the invasion of Judæa from Egypt.[2] The clearer way to most of Syria from Egypt lay along the coast, and, passing up the Maritime Plain, left the hill-country of Judæa to the east.

This, then, was the southern frontier of Judah, in itself an easy access, with one trunk-road, but barred by the desert ridges to the south, and enjoying even greater security from its more lofty and barren position between two regions of such attractiveness to invaders as the Valley of the Jordan and the Plain of Philistia. Before we leave this, it is well to notice that the barrier of highlands south of Beersheba represents the difference between the ideal and the practical borders of the Holy Land. Practically the land extended from Dan to Beersheba, where, during the greater part of history, the means of settled cultivation came to an end; but the ideal border was the River of Egypt, Wady el-'Arish, whose chief tributary comes up to the foot of the highlands south of Beersheba, and passes between them and the level desert beyond.

Of names in Palestine hardly any are better known than Beersheba. Nothing could more aptly illustrate the defencelessness of these southern slopes of Judah than that this site which marked the frontier of the land was neither fortress nor gateway, but a cluster of wells on the open desert. Yet, like Dan at the other end of the land, Beersheba was a sanctuary. These two facts—its use for their flocks, its holiness to themselves—are intermingled in the stories of the Patriarchs, whose herdsmen strove for its waters; who themselves *plant a tamarisk, and call on the name of Yahweh, the everlasting God*. Two narratives of the Pentateuch differ in describing the origin of Beersheba. One imputes it to Abraham, the other, in similar circumstances, to Isaac.[3] The meaning of the name as it stands might either be the Well of Seven or the Well of (the) Oath, and in one passage both etymologies seem to struggle for decision,[4] though the latter prevails. Seven wells are there

[1] See p. 166.

[2] Unless Shishak came up this way. In his lists of conquests occur some names in the Negeb, but not far enough south to prove that he took this road. See Maspero in *Trans. Vict. Inst.* W. Max Müller, *Asien u. Europa*, 148.

[3] Gen. xxi. 22-32, to Abraham, E; Gen. xxvi. 26-33, v. 33, to Isaac, J.

[4] Gen. xxi. 22-31*a* implies Well of Seven, but 31*b*-32, Well of the Oath. It almost seems as if two accounts were mingled; though there is no linguistic proof of this, al from 22 to 32 belonging to E, one is inclined to extend J back from 33, 34 to 31*b*. Stade thinks Seven Wells was the Canaanite name (the form in that sense being un-Hebraic), and that Well of the Oath was what the Hebrews changed it to in conformity with their syntax, *Gesch.* i. 127, LXX, Gen. xxi. 31, φρέαρ ὁρκισμοῦ, xlvi. 1, τὸ φρέαρ τοῦ ὅρκου.

now, and to the north, on the hills round the valley, are scattered ruins nearly three miles in circumference. Beersheba was of importance under Samuel; his sons judged there.[1] Elijah fled to Beersheba.[2] It was a sanctuary in the eighth century, and frequented even by Northern Israel.[3] During the separation of the kingdoms the formula, *from Dan to Beersheba*, became *from Geba to Beersheba*,[4] or *from Beersheba to Mount Ephraim*.[5] On the return from exile, Beersheba was again peopled by Jews, and the formula ran *from Beersheba to the valley of Hinnom*.[6] In Roman times Beersheba was "a very large village" with a garrison.[7] It was the seat of a Christian bishopric.[8] The Crusaders did not come so far south, and confused Beersheba with Beit-Jibrin.[9]

South of Beersheba, for thirty miles, the country, although mostly barren, is sprinkled with ruins of villages, gathered round wells. They date mostly from Christian times, and are eloquent in their testimony to the security which Rome imposed on the most lawless deserts. Old Testament sites of importance are the city of Salt[10] and Moladah,[11] Zephath or Hormah and Ziklag, all unknown; Rehoboth is probably Ruḥeibeh. The ascent of Akrabbim was on the south-east corner of Judæa, going up from the Arabah, near the end of the Dead Sea.[12]

One other thing we must note. As on her east border Judah was in touch with the Arab Kenites, so on the Negeb she touched, and absorbed, the Amalekite or Edomite clan of Jerahmeelites.[13]

[1] 1 Sam. viii. 2. [2] 1 Kings xix. 3. [3] Amos v. 5, viii. 14. [4] 2 Kings xxiii. 8. [5] 2 Chron. xix. 4. [6] Neh. xi. 27, 30.

[7] Euseb. and Jerome, *Onom.* Βηρσαβεέ, Bersabee.

[8] Socrates, *Hist. Eccl.*—Christian Inscriptions, *PEFQ*, 1920, 15.

[9] For its condition before the War, *MuNDPV*, 1899, 62 (cf. *Biblical World*, April, July 1901), 1903, 176. Massey, *op. cit.*; in 1917 "no signs of elaborate ruins to indicate anything larger than a native settlement", till the Germans came and built barracks, hospital station, mosque, etc., a base for attacking the Suez Canal.

[10] Josh. xv. 62; Conder, Tell el-Milḥ, Mound of Salt.

[11] Josh, xv. 26, xix. 2; 1 Chron. iv. 28; Neh. xi. 26. Robinson, Tell el-Milḥ, *MuNDPV*, 1901, 9 ff.

[12] For the geography of this region, cf. Rob. *BR*, i, Trumbull's *Kadesh Barnea*, Palmer's *Desert of the Exodus*, Drake's and Kitchener's reports, *PEFQ*; A. Musil, *Arabia Petraea*, vol. ii (1908), C. L. Woolley and T. E. Lawrence, *The Wilderness of Zin*, *PEF Annual*, 1914-15.

[13] 1 Sam. xxvii. 10, xxx. 29; 1 Chron. ii. 9. Stade, *Gesch*, i. 159.

3. *The Western Border: the Defiles*

The ideal boundary of Judæa on the west was the Mediterranean, but, as we have seen, the Maritime Plain was never in Jewish possession (except for intervals under the Maccabees), and even the Shephelah was debatable, as often out of as within Judah. The most frequent border of Judah to the west was the edge of the Central Range. In the chapter on the Shephelah it was pointed out how real a frontier this was. A long series of valleys running south from Aijalon to Beersheba separate the low loose hills of the Shephelah from the lofty compact range to the east—*the hill-country of Judæa.* This barrier, which repelled the Philistines, even when they had conquered the Shephelah, is penetrated by defiles, none more broad than those of Beth-horon, of Wady 'Ali along which the high-road to Jerusalem travels and of Wady eṣ-Ṣurar up which the railway runs. Few are straight, most sharply curve. The sides are steep, and often precipitous, frequently with no path between save the torrent bed, in rapids of loose shingle or level steps of the strata, which at the mouth of the defile are often tilted almost perpendicularly into easily defended obstacles of passage. The sun beats down upon the limestone; springs are few, though sometimes generous; a thick bush fringes the brows, and caves abound and tumbled rocks.[1]

Everything conspires to give the few inhabitants means of defence against large armies. It is a country of ambushes, entanglements, surprises, where armies have no room to fight, and the defenders can remain hidden; where the essentials for war are nimbleness and the sure foot, power of scramble and of rush. We see it in the Eighteenth Psalm: *By thee do I run through a troop, and by my God I leap a wall; God Who girds me with strength and makes my way perfect. He makes my feet like hinds' feet, and sets me on my high places. Thou hast enlarged my steps under me, and my feet have not slipped.*

Yet with negligent defenders the western border of Judæa is quickly penetrated. Six hours will bring an army up any of the defiles, and they stand on the central plateau, within a few miles of Jerusalem or of Hebron. So it happened in the days of the Maccabees. The Syrians, repelled at Beth-horon and at Wady 'Ali, penetrated twice the unwatched defiles to the south, the second time with a number of elephants, of which we are told

[1] I describe from observation of Wady el-Ḳuf from Beit-Jibrin to Hebron, and of three defiles that run up from W en-Najil to the plateau of Beit 'Aṭab. So too Schick, *ZDPV*, x. 131, 132, on W Ismain: "dass das Thal viele und grosse Krummungen hat tief eingeschnitten und stets von steilen Böschungen eingeschlossen ist, und keine Ortschaften trägt."

that they had to come up the gorges in single file.[1] What a sight the strange huge animals must have been, pushing up the narrow path, and emerging for the first and almost only time on the plateau above. On both occasions the Syrians laid siege to Beth-zur, the stronghold on the edge of the plateau, which Judas had fortified for the western defence of the country. The first time, they were beaten back down the gorges; but the second time, with the elephants, Beth-zur fell, and the Syrians advanced on Jerusalem. After that attacks from the west failed, and the only other successful Syrian invasion was from the north.[2]

Beth-zur, the one fortress on the western flank of Judæa south of Aijalon, is due to the one open valley on that flank, the Vale of Elah, above the higher end of which it stands. The need of it could not be more eloquently signified than by the fact that it was up the Vale of Elah that the Philistines, the Syrians in the second century B.C., and Richard with the Third Crusade, all attempted to reach the central plateau—the Syrians and the Crusaders both choosing this entrance after their attack by Aijalon had failed.

But if invaders came up these defiles to the plateau, the settlers on the latter more easily passed down them to the Shephelah. Over the Shephelah Judah claimed, if she did not always exercise, dominion; and the claim did not rest so much on conquest as on kinship. In the earliest times the tribe had intermarried with the Canaanites of the Shephelah, especially with those round Adullam. This is the meaning of the adventures in Genesis xxxviii: *Judah went down from his brethren, and turned in to a certain Adullamite whose name was Hirah.* To lovers of the Bible this result of criticism must come as a relief, that the following verses relate, not the intercourse of individuals, but the intermarriage of families.[3] As Judah, then, had Arab allies and kinsfolk on her eastern and southern borders, so on her western she mixed with Canaanites.

How did the British in 1917 overcome this hard border and the armies of Turks and Germans established along it?[4]

The British had the experience of the defence of the Suez Canal under General Maxwell, of their advance over the desert under General Murray, and of two unsuccessful battles before Gaza; with an invaluable review of the whole situation by Sir Philip Chetwode. Their resources were such as

[1] Josephus, xii *Antt.* ix. 4. [2] By Bacchides in 160 B.C.

[3] Lagarde explains Tamar, or Palm, by Phœnicia, Zerah (זרח=אזרח indigenous) by the aboriginal inhabitants of the land, the Canaanites, and Pharez or Perez by the Hebrews (*Orientalia*, ii. 1880).

[4] W. T. Massey, *op. cit.*; Cyril Falls, *Military Operations, Egypt and Palestine, from June 1917*, 1-140; Wavell, *Enc. Brit.* 14th ed.

no invader of Palestine had enjoyed—a double railway-track from Ḳanṭara on the Canal to within eight miles of Gaza, some supplies by steamers from Port Said to the coast at Deir el-Belaḥ, and a pipe-line of Nile water, flowing and pumped from 200 miles away. The Army itself was the largest that ever entered Palestine, over 200,000 men (besides 60,000 labourers and followers) in three Corps, XXth, XXIst, and Desert Mounted, and it was led by a strong and able general, personally inspiring to all ranks—Sir Edmund Allenby.

After three months of preparation, Corps XXI remaining before the strengthened defences of Gaza, the other two moved along the face of the enemy's long line to the left of this at Beersheba and the neighbourhood, and after assaults from the west, south, and east occupied Beersheba by the night of 31st October, with as much land to the north as kept the place and its wells safe from Turkish guns.

Meantime, 27th to 31st October, Gaza was bombarded from sea and land, and, 1st and 2nd November, its outer redoubts captured, not without heavy casualties to our forces, till after further bombing and assault, they entered the city on 7th November to find it a shell of ruin, deserted by the enemy. Next day a part of Corps XXI, taking the Turkish redoubts at Atawineh east of Gaza, linked up with a Division of Corps XX, of which other Divisions, along with the Desert Mounted Corps, had, by 4th November, driven the left of the Turkish line north to Khuweilfeh and two days later taken, by the 74th Division, the strong positions at Sheri'a. Part of the force swept back by Karm to Gaza, while another part, fighting over the Shephelah, occupied by the 8th en-Najileh on the Wady el-Ḥesy. Huj to the west also fell to them, with Bureir (on the 9th). After a halt at Kaukaba they crossed the Maritime Plain towards the main Ramleh road at Es-Suafir-el-Gharbiyeh and reached el-Mejdal within a few miles of the coast—in time not to intercept the Turks now on retreat from a second line of defence on the Wady el-Ḥesy, but to share in the British pursuit of these up the Plain. Some squadrons had already occupied Ashkelon. Through constant fighting and in spite of several costly repulses the British advance went steadily on from Ashdod (Esdud). One by one strong positions, Ḳaṭra, Mughar and others on the plain, Gezer and Abu Shusheh on the Shephelah, fell to it till Ramleh and Ludd were occupied on 15th November and the next day Jaffa itself.

Thus were two borders of Judah disposed of: the southern and part of the immediate western with all the coast beyond this, and the British Army looked up Aijalon towards Jerusalem. The enemy was split in two.

4. *The Northern Border: the Fortresses of Benjamin*

The narrow table-land of Judæa continues ten miles to the north of Jerusalem, before it breaks into the valleys and mountains of Samaria. These last ten miles of the plateau—with steep gorges on the one side to the Jordan and on the other to Aijalon—were the debatable land across which, as we have seen, the most accessible frontier of Judæa fluctuated; and therefore became the site of more fortresses, sieges, forays, battles, and massacres than perhaps any other part of the country. Their appearance matches their violent history. A desolate and fatiguing extent of rocky platforms and ridges, of moorland strewn with boulders, and fields of shallow soil thickly mixed with stone, they are a true border—more fit for the building of barriers than for the cultivation of food. They were the territory of Benjamin, in whose blood, at the time of the massacre of the tribe of Judah,[1] they received the baptism of their awful history. As you cross them their aspect recalls the temper of their inhabitants. *Benjamin shall ravin as a wolf*, father of sons who, noble or ignoble, were passionate and unsparing—Saul, Shimei, Jeremiah, and he that *breathed out threatenings and slaughter against the disciples of the Lord*, and *was exceeding mad against them.*[2] In such a region of blood and tears Jeremiah beheld the figure of the nation's woe: *A voice is heard in Ramah, lamentation and bitter weeping, Rachel weeping for her children: she refuseth to be comforted for her children, because they are not.*[3]

But it is as a frontier that we have now to do with those ten northmost miles of the Judæan plateau. Upon the last of them three roads concentrate —an open highway from the west by Gophna, the north road from Shechem, and a road from the Jordan Valley through the passes of Mount Ephraim. Where these draw together,[4] about three miles from the end of the plateau, stood Bethel, a sanctuary before the Exile, thereafter a strong city of Judah.[5] But Bethel, where she stood, could not by herself keep the northern gate of Judæa. For behind her to the south emerge the roads we have followed—that from the Jordan by Ai and those from Aijalon up the gorges and ridge of Beth-horon. The Ai route is covered by Michmash, where the Philistines encamped against Saul and Jonathan,[6] and where the other hero called

[1] Judges xx. 35. [2] Acts ix. 1, xxvi. 11. [3] Jer. xxxi. 15. [4] *ZDPV*, xxxiv. 99.

[5] 1 Macc. ix. 50; see *MuNDPV*, 1900, 1 ff.

[6] 1 Sam. xiii. In vv. 17, 18 the three directions which the three foraging bands of Philistines took are plain; N to Ophrah, and the City of Ephraim, Eṭ-Ṭaiyibeh, W to Beth-horon, SE *over the ravine of Zeboim*, *i.e.* Wady Abu Duba, running NE into W Far'ah, afterwards W Ḳelt (cf. Neh. xi. 35), down which there is the name Shukh ed-Duba. But see Buhl, 98 f.

Jonathan—Maccabæus—held for a time his headquarters.[1] The Beth-horon roads were covered by Gibeon,[2] the frontier post between David and Saul's house.[3] Between Michmash and Gibeon are six miles, and on these lie others of the strong points that stand forth in the invasion and defence of this frontier: Geba, long the limit of Judah to the north[4]; Ramah, which Baasha of Israel built for a blockade against Judah[5]; Adasa, where Judas Maccabæus pitched against Nicanor, coming up from Beth-horon.[6] These, with Michmash and Gibeon, formed a line of defence valid against the Aijalon and Ai ascents, as well as against the level approach from the north. There have also been discovered at Tell en-Naṣbeh, seven miles north of Jerusalem, remains of a walled town with "exceeding strong" walls, which some think the ancient Mizpah.[7]

The earlier invasions delivered upon this frontier of Judah are difficult to follow. Before it was a frontier in the days of Saul, the Philistines overran it either from Aijalon, or from Mount Ephraim; Saul's centre was in Michmash. Whether, in their attacks upon Jerusalem,[8] Joash or Rezin and Pekah crossed it we cannot say; probably the latter at least came up from the Arabah. Isaiah pictures a possible march this way by the Assyrians after the fall of Samaria. *He is come upon Ai; marches through Migron, at Michmash musters his baggage; they have passed the Pass; "Let Geba be our bivouac." Terror-struck is Ramah; Gibeah of Saul has fled. Make shrill thy voice, O daughter of Gallim. Listen Laishah, answer her Anathoth; in mad flight is Madmenah; dwellers in Gebim gather their stuff to flee. This very day he halts at Nob; he waves his hand at the mount of the daughter of Zion, the hill of Jerusalem.*[9] This is not actual fact—for the Assyrian did not then march upon Zion, and when he came twenty years later it was probably by the Beth-horon or another of the western passes—but this was what might have happened any day after Samaria fell. The prophet is describing how easily the Assyrian

[1] Josephus, xiii *Antt.* i. 6. [2] Josh. x. 1-12. [3] 2 Sam. ii. 12, 13. [4] 2 Kings xxiii. 8.

[5] 1 Kings xv. 17.

[6] Josephus, xii *Antt.* x. 5; 1 Macc. vii. 40-45. Probably the present Khurbet Adasa on the road N from Jerusalem. Schürer (*Hist.* i. 1, 129) prefers a site nearer Gophna; Eusebius (*Onom.* Ἀδασά) says near Gophna. But that describes Khurbet Adasa, on the same road as Gophna.

[7] W. F. Badè, *PEFQ*, 1927, 7 ff., condensed from the *Bulletin* (vol. v. 3) of the Pacific School of Religion; E. Grant, *id.* 159 ff.; Phythian-Adams, *JPOS*, iii. 13; Albright, *JPOS*, iii. 3, refutes this, vii. 3, identifies it with Beeroth, and supports the identification of Mizpah with Nebi Samwil.

[8] 2 Kings xiv. 11, xvi. 5.

[9] Isa. x. 28-32: for Laishah van Kasteren (*ZDPV*, xiii. 101) suggests 'Isawiye. Geba is Jeba', Gibeah probably Tell el-Ful.

could advance by this open route upon Zion; and yet, if he did, God would cut him down in sight of his goal.[1] All the places mentioned are not known; of those that are some are off the high-road. How Nebuchadrezzar came up against Jerusalem is not stated[2]; but we can follow the course of subsequent invasions. In the Syrian war in 160 B.C. Nicanor and Bacchides both attempted the plateau—the former unsuccessfully by Beth-horon, the latter with success from the north. In 64 Pompey marched from Beth-shan through Samaria, but could not have reached Judæa had the Jews persevered in their defence of the passes of Mount Ephraim.[3] These being left open, Pompey advanced easily by Koreæ and Jericho upon Bethel, and thence unopposed to the walls of Zion.[4] In 37 B.C. Herod marched from the north and took Jerusalem.[5] In A.D. 66 Cestius Gallus came up by Beth-horon and Gibeon to invest Jerusalem, but speedily retreated by the same way.[6] In 70, after Vespasian had spent two years in reducing the strong places round Judæa, Titus led his legions to the siege past Gophna and Bethel. It seems to have been by Pompey's route that the forces of Islam came upon Jerusalem; they met with no resistance in either Ephraim or Judah, and the city was delivered into their hands by agreement, A.D. 637.

In 1099, the first Crusaders advanced to their successful siege by Aijalon; in 1187, Saladin, having conquered the rest of the land, drew in on the Holy City from Hebron, from Ashkelon and from the north. The Third Crusade, after reaching Jaffa and even Ashkelon, occupying Ramleh and Lydda and penetrating the Shephelah as far at least as Tell eṣ-Ṣafi, their Blanchegarde, were prevented by Saladin from advancing from Aijalon, except on an occasional raid, and all they enjoyed of Jerusalem was a distant view.[7]

In November, 1917, after evacuating Lydda, Ramleh, and Jaffa[8] the German-Turkish armies divided, the 8th lining the River 'Aujeh north of Jaffa, the 7th occupying the upper end of the Vale of Aijalon, and the hills and passes between that and Jerusalem. Setting a force to "contain" the 8th Army, General Allenby on 17th November sent others of his Divisions up the ancient routes, some of these with stretches of Roman roads, towards Jerusalem and in particular towards the road thence to Nablus. I can give but a summary of their advance, on which were equally conspicuous the ability of their commander, controlled by the desire above all to avoid every risk to the Holy City, and the devotion and heroism of his troops, bivouacking under heavy rain, marching on "abominable roads", up narrow defiles and

[1] Isa. x. 32, 33. [2] 2 Kings xxiv. 10.
[3] But see p. 232, n. 8, on another possible route for Pompey. [4] xiv *Antt.* iii. 3.
[5] xiv *Antt.* xvi. [6] See p. 150. [7] *L'Estoire de la Guerre Sainte, Itiner. Ricardi*, etc.
[8] See p. 197.

steep slopes, in almost constant encounter with a numerous foe often strongly entrenched. For details the reader is referred to works already cited.[1]

The 75th Division, with a brigade of the Australian Mounted Division covering its right, marched by the main, metalled road to Jerusalem; on their left the 52nd Division followed the Lydda-Jerusalem road, a route nearly parallel to but converging on that of the 75th; and on the left again of the 52nd the Yeomanry Mounted Division took the Beth-horon route. Having occupied Laṭrun, the 75th fighting for two days more[2] took Ḳuryat el-'Enab in a mist, then Ḳusṭul, and turning north by Biddu in face of heavy firing won Nebi Samwil by midnight on 21st November, and then Beit-Izza, but failed to take el-Jib, Gibeon. Meanwhile the 52nd Division by Beit-Liḳia reached Beit-'Anan, Beit-Dukku and Beit-Izza, thus covering the flank of the 75th at Nebi Samwil. The other Division by the classic Beth-horon route actually reached Betunia, only some five miles from the Jerusalem-Nablus road, which Allenby had planned as the objective of all three Divisions; but under the bad weather and in face of fierce opposition from superior numbers they had to fall back almost to Lower Beth-horon, Beit-'Ur et-Taḥta.[3] The troops were exhausted, the roads, bad enough for the infantry, were on many stretches impassable for our artillery; and the advance of all three Divisions was delayed for days during which, while enemy attacks had to be repelled, better roads were made, and reliefs and reinforcements brought up.

The enemy's line, partly entrenched, now ran from Bethlehem northwards and west of Jerusalem by 'Ain Karim to near Lifta, thence west to Beit-Iksa and again northwards east of Nebi Samwil (which they continued fiercely to bombard) but west of el-Jib to Upper Beth-horon, Beit-'Ur el-Foḳa, and beyond. Along this they still sprang counter-attacks upon the British between 27th November and 3rd December; for the most part these were repelled, but not without heavy British casualties. Another British force, however, was to appear from the south summoned by telegraph and aeroplane. The 53rd Division with a Cavalry Corps and batteries of guns, having come up from Beersheba by Dhaheriyah, advanced between the 5th and 7th December from Hebron to Solomon's Pools in face of little resistance,

[1] See p. 37, n. 5.

[2] Small parties of the enemy had to be dislodged, but our Indian troops, "highly skilled in operations of this type, completely out-manœuvred the Turks" (Falls, *Military Operations*, etc., 191).

[3] "The difficulties of this abortive but doggedly-conducted operation can scarcely be exaggerated. The ground, rocky, boulder-strewn, often precipitous, slippery from the rain, would have been hard enough to advance across had there been no enemy, and there was actually an enemy superior in numbers and infinitely superior in artillery" (Falls, *Milit. Operations*, 200).

and on the 8th found that the enemy had quitted Bethlehem. A general attack on this day from the west brought the British somewhat nearer the City, till in parts they were held up by heavy Turkish fire. The attack was to be resumed on the 9th, but when that day dawned the British found no enemy to oppose them and entered the City. Jerusalem was won. General Allenby made his official entry on the 11th. This capture of the Holy City was the thirty-fourth or thirty-fifth in her history.

Through the rest of December the enemy made several attempts to regain Jerusalem, especially on the 26th, but failed, and counter-attacks carried the British front five or six miles on, thus safeguarding the City on the north. By the end of the year the British line ran from the Mount of Olives northwards, some three miles east of the Nablus road, to three miles north of Bireh, thence south-west to upper Beth-horon and thence north-west all the way to Arsuf on the Maritime Plain, to which the 52nd British Division had driven back the enemy's 8th Army from the line it had taken up on the 'Aujeh after evacuating Jaffa.

During January 1918, and the first half of February the British front to the east of Jerusalem advanced as far as Michmash, and plans were made for a descent upon Jericho. On 19th February the 60th Division, with the Wellington Mounted Rifles and Anzac Mounted Division, aided by the Royal Flying Corps, advanced in three columns, through some fighting and over country "the most difficult yet encountered" to a line from Ras eṭ-Ṭawil east of Michmash to 'Iraḳ Ibrahim some five miles north-east, and el-Munṭar some six miles south-east, of the Mount of Olives. On the 20th, fighting still, they got to Tala'at ed-Dumm (or Dam) on the Jericho road and Jebel Ekteif. On the 21st they followed the retreating foe to the edge of the cliffs from Nebi Musa to Jebel Ḳurunṭul, which overlook the Jordan Valley, establishing on that edge the security of Jerusalem against invasion from the east; and the same day they entered Jericho and cleared the enemy out of the Jordan Valley as far north as the Wady 'Aujeh.[1]

We have now compassed the Four Borders of Judæa—east, south, west, and north—and have followed all the approaches and invasions across and through them, on to the Great War itself.

[1] See above, p. 172.

XIV. *AN ESTIMATE OF THE REAL STRENGTH OF JUDÆA*[1]

Having gone round about Judæa, and marked well her bulwarks, we may draw some conclusions as to the measure of her strength—physical and moral. Judæa has been called impregnable, but, as we must have seen, the adjective exaggerates. To the north she has no frontier; her southern border offers few obstacles after the desert is passed; with all their difficulties, her eastern and western walls have been carried again and again; and even the dry and intricate wilderness, to which her defenders have more than once retired, has been rifled to its recesses. Judæa, in fact, has been overrun as often as England.

And yet, like England, Judæa, though not impregnable, has the advantages of insularity. It is singular how much of an island is this inland province. With the gulf of the Arabah to the east, with the desert to the south, and lifted high and unattractive above the line of traffic that sweeps past her on the west, Judæa is separated as much as by water from the two great continents, to both of which she otherwise belongs. So open at many points, the land was yet sufficiently unpromising and remote to keep unprovoked foreigners away. When they were provoked and did come upon her, they found the waterlessness of her central plateau an almost insuperable obstacle to the prolonged sieges, which the stubbornness of her people forced them to make against her capital and other fortresses. There was this further difficulty. Judæa's borders may be more or less open, but they are such as to compensate for each other's weakness. For an invader might come over one frontier and make it his own; but the defeated nation could retreat upon any of the others. In the intricacy of these or of the great desert, they had room to rally and sweep back upon the foe when he was sufficiently disheartened by the barrenness of the plateau he had invaded. Hence we never find, so far as I know, any successful invasion but one of Judæa, which was not delivered across at least two of her borders. The exception was the First Crusade; and there is enough to account for it in the laxity of the defence it encountered. It is significant that neither of the two greatest invaders of Judæa, who feared a real defence of her central plateau, ventured upon this till they had mastered the rest of Palestine, and occupied the strongholds

[1] For this chapter, see Maps 4, 6, 7, 9.

round the Judæan borders. At the interval of more than a millennium, the tactics of Vespasian and of Saladin were practically identical. Vespasian not only overran Galilee and Samaria, but spent nearly another year in taking and refortifying Jamnia, Ashdod, and Hadid in the west, Bethel and Gophna to the north, Jericho to the east, and Hebron with other "Idumæan strongholds" to the south, before he let slip his impatient legions upon Jerusalem. His own officers, as well as deserters from the city, urged him at once to march upon it, but Josephus says that Vespasian "was obliged at first to overthrow what remained elsewhere, and to leave behind him nothing outside Jerusalem, which might interrupt him in that siege"[1]; and he closes the list of the Roman conquests around Judæa with the remark, "now all the places were taken, except Herodium, Masada, and Machærus, so Jerusalem was now what the Romans aimed at". Similarly, in 1187, Saladin, even after his victory at Ḥaṭṭin, did not venture to attack Jerusalem till the Jordan Valley, most of the Maritime Plain, with Ashkelon and even Beit-Jibrin, had fallen into his hands.[2] Nothing could more clearly prove that Judæa, though not impregnable, was extremely difficult to take, and that a rush across one of her borders, like that of Cestius Gallus in A.D. 66, was sure to end in disaster. To succeed, an invader must master at least two of her frontiers, both to prevent the nation from rallying and to secure sources of supplies.

To have followed these campaigns, the details of which are known to us, is to understand more clearly what, indeed, this province herself tells you by mute eloquence of rock, mountain, and desert—her value to the people for whom she was shaped by the Creator's hands. Judæa was designed to produce in her inhabitants the sense of seclusion and security, though not to such a degree as to relieve them from the attractions of the great world, which throbbed closely past, or to relax in them those habits of discipline, vigilance, and valour, which are the necessary elements of a nation's character. In the position of Judæa there was not enough to tempt her people to put their confidence in herself; but there was enough to encourage them to defend their freedom and a strenuous life.[3] And while the isolation of their land was sufficient to confirm their calling to a discipline and destiny separate from other peoples, it was not so complete as to keep them in ignorance of

[1] iv *Wars*, vii. 3; on the capture of Jamnia and Ashdod, vi *Wars*, iii. 2; strongholds of Idumæa, viii. 1; Jericho, 2 ff.; Jericho and Hadid, ix. 1; Hebron with the unknown Kaphethra and Kepharabis, 9.

[2] Cf. *Itiner. Ricardi*, vi. 1, 7, *L'Estoire de la Guerre Sainte*, 10, 137 ff., 10, 593 ff. Both emphasise the waterlessness round Jerusalem.

[3] In the *Least of all Lands*, Principal Miller has valuable remarks on the influence of the physical geography on the character of the people.

the world, or to release them from those temptations to mix with the world, in combating which their discipline and destiny could alone be realised.

All this receives exact illustration from both Psalmists and Prophets. They may rejoice in the fertility of their land, but they never boast of its strength. On the contrary, of the measure of the latter they show a sagacious appreciation. Thus Isaiah's faith in Zion's inviolableness does not blind him to the openness of Judah's northern entrance: it is in one of his passages of exultation about Zion that he describes the easy advance of the Assyrian to her walls.[1] Both he and other prophets recognise how swiftly the great military powers will overrun Judah; and when they except Jerusalem from the consequences, it is not because of her natural strength, but by their faith in the intervention of God Himself. So at last it happened. In the crisis of her history, the invasion by Sennacherib, Judah was saved, as England was saved from the Armada, neither by the strength of her bulwarks, for they had been burst, nor by the valour of her men, for the heart had gone out of them, but because, apart from human help, God Himself crushed her insolent foes in the moment of their triumph.[2]

Of this feeling, perhaps the most concise expression is found in the Forty-Eighth Psalm, where, though *beautiful for situation is Mount Zion on the sides of the north,*[3] and *established for ever*, it is *God* Himself who *is known in her palaces for a refuge*; and when the writer has *walked about Zion and gone round her*, and *told the towers thereof*, *marked well her bulwarks* and *considered her palaces*, it is not in these that he triumphs, but this is the result of his survey: *this God is our God for ever and ever, He will be our Guide even unto death.* Judah was not impregnable, but better—in charge of an invincible Providence.

With their admission of the weakness of Judah's position, there runs through the prophets an appreciation of her unattractiveness, and this leads them, especially Isaiah, to insist that under God her security lies in that and in her people's contentment with it. Though they recognise how vulnerable the land is, the prophets maintain that she will be left alone if her people are quiet upon her, and if her statesmen avoid intrigue with the powers of the world. To the kings of Israel, to Ahaz, to Hezekiah's counsellors, to Josiah, the same warnings are given[4]: *Asshur shall not save us: we will not ride upon*

[1] Isa. x. 32. See p. 199 above.

[2] See p. 166f; 2 Kings xviii, xix; Isa. xxxvii, and probably xxxiii.

[3] Perhaps a phrase for the sacred inviolableness of the site; but it is remarkable that, owing to the strong sun (perhaps also to the geological formation), the northern aspect of hills in W Palestine is more fruitful and beautiful than the S aspect; *e.g.* Ebal and Gerizim.

[4] Ahaz, cf. 2 Kings xvi with Isa. vii.

horses.[1] *Woe to them that go down to Egypt for help, and stay on horses and trust in chariots. In returning and rest shall ye be saved: in quietness and in confidence shall be your strength.*[2]

Thus we see how the physical geography of Palestine not only makes clear such things as the campaigns and migrations of the Old Testament, but signalises the providence of God, the doctrine of His prophets, and the character He demanded from His people. It was a great lesson the Spirit taught Israel, that no people dwells secure apart from God, from character, from common-sense. But the land was the illustration and enforcement of this lesson. Judæa proved, yet did not exhaust, nor tempt men to feel that she exhausted, the will and power of God for their salvation. As the writer of the Hundred and Twenty-First Psalm feels, her hills were not the answer to, but the provocation of, the question, *Whence cometh my help?* and The Lord Himself was the answer. As for her prophets, much of their sagacity is but the true appreciation of her position. And as for the character of her people, while she gave them room to be free and to worship God, and offered no inducement to them to put herself in His place, she did not wholly shut them off from danger or temptation, for without danger and temptation a nation's character cannot be strong.

XV. *THE CHARACTER OF JUDÆA*[3]

We have seen how much of Judæa is borderland, and how strongly this fact has determined her history. But after all it is the plateau, which her bulwarks lift and isolate from the rest of Palestine, that remains the characteristic part of Judæa. Here lay her chief towns, and her people were most themselves. This plateau is little more than thirty-five miles long, from Bethel to the cities south-east of Hebron. The breadth varies from fourteen to seventeen, when reckoned from the western edge, above the valley that cuts off the Shephelah, to where on the east the level drops below 1700 feet and into desert.

The greater part of the Judæan plateau consists of stony moorland, on which rough scrub and thorns, reinforced by a few dwarf oaks, contend with multitudes of boulders, and the limestone, as if impatient of the pretence of soil, breaks out in bare scalps and prominences. There are patches of cultivation, but though the grain springs bravely from them, they seem more

[1] Hos. xiv. 3, cf. xii. 1. [2] Isa. xxxi. 1, xxx. 15.
[3] For this chapter, see Maps 6, 9, 10.

beds of shingle than of soil. The only other signs of life, besides the wild bee and a few birds, are flocks of sheep and goats, or a few cattle, cropping apart in melancholy proof of the scantiness of the herbage. Where the plateau rolls, the shadeless slopes are for the most part divided between brown scrub and grey rock; the hollows are stony fields traversed by dry torrent-beds of boulders and gashed clay. Where the plateau breaks, low ridge and shallow glen are formed, and the ridge is often crowned by a village, of which the grey stone walls and mud roofs look from the distance like a mere outcrop of the rock; yet round them, or below in the glen, there will be olive-groves, figs, and perhaps terraces of vines. Some of these breaks in the table-land are rich in vegetation, as at Bethany, the Valley of Hinnom, the Gardens of Solomon and other spots round Bethlehem and in the neighbourhood of Hebron, the famous Vale of Eshcol or Vine-Cluster. Again between Hebron and the wilderness are nine miles by three of plateau, where the soil is almost free from stones, and the fair, red and green fields, broken by a few heathy mounds, might be a scene of upland agriculture in our own country.[1] This is where Maon, Ziph, and the Judæan Carmel lay with the farms of Nabal, on which David and his men, like the Bedouin of to-day, levied blackmail from Horesh in the wilderness below.[2]

But the prevailing impression of Judæa is of stone—the torrent beds, the paths that are no better, the heaps and heaps of stones gathered from the fields, the fields as stony still, the moors strewn with boulders, the scalps and ribs of the hills. In the more desolate parts, which otherwise were covered

[1] "At 2.30 we left Hebron. Rough limestone country. Paths execrable, slippery rock and rolling stones. In an hour we came on the Ziph-Maon-Carmel plateau, like a bit of higher, less fertile Kincardineshire—rolling red ground, mostly bare, partly wheat and barley, broken by limestone scalps partly covered by scrub, and honeycombed by caves. We came on this at Tell Zif (Ziph), cantered across it one and a half hours to Kurmul, with ruins of Crusaders' Castle, large blue pool below, black Bedawee tents near. Thence 20 minutes to Ma'in through barley-fields. The view from Maon is extensive. The plateau spreads due N, hills sweep round two sides from SW to NE; due N at the mouth of an opening through them is Hebron with white buildings, the mosque clear through a glass. WNW Yuṭṭah on a peak, NE Beni Na'ûn. E a decisive fall of about 400 feet from cultivated land to desert, thence Yeshimon, rolling hills and irregular ridges backed by the range of Moab."—*Extract from my Diary*.

[2] בחרשה: A.V. *in the wood*, 1 Sam. xxiii. 15. But this implies both an unusual grammatical form, and *a wood*, or *thicket*, if it existed in these desert regions, would be too prominent to be used as a hiding-place. The LXX understood a proper name, though they spelt it differently (Josephus follows LXX). Conder discovered SE of Ziph, in the desert, the Ruin Khoreisa and Wady Abu Hirsh, in both of which he sees Horeshah (R.S.V Horesh), *TW*, 243 f. On Nabal, Maon and Carmel see 1 Sam. xxv. 2 ff.

with scrub, this impression is increased by ruins of cultivation—cairns, terrace walls, and vineyard towers.

Now if you aggravate this stony appearance by two other deficiencies, you will feel to the full that dreariness which most bring away with them as their whole memory of Judæa. First, there is no water. No tarns break into streams and quicken the landscape, as they quicken even the most desolate moors of our north, but at noon the cattle go down by dusty paths to some shadowless gorge, where the glare is broken only by the black mouth of a cistern with troughs around. On the plateau the only gleams of water are the pools at Gibeon, Jerusalem, Bethlehem, Hebron, and I do not suppose that from Bethel to Beersheba there are, even in spring, more than six or seven tiny rills. No water to soothe the eye, there are no great hills to lift it. The horizon has no character or edge. Of course from the western boundary of the plateau you see the blue ocean with its border of broken gold, and from the eastern boundary the Moab Hills, that change colour all day long above the changeless blue of the Dead Sea. But, in the centre of the hill-country there is nothing to look to past the featureless roll of the moorland, and the low blunt hills with flat-roofed villages.

Was the land always like this? For answer, we have three portraits of ancient Judah. The first is perhaps the most voluptuous picture in the Old Testament[1]:

Binding to the vine his foal
And to the choice vine his ass's colt,
He hath washed in wine his raiment,
And in the blood of the grape his vesture:
—Heavy in the eyes from wine,
And white of teeth from milk.

This might be the portrait of a Bacchus in the vineyards of Sicily; but of Judah we can scarcely believe it, as we stand in his land to-day. And yet on those long, dry slopes with their ruined terraces—no barer than the banks of Rhine in early spring—and even more in the rich glens around Hebron and Bethlehem, where the vine has been preserved,[2] we perceive the possibilities of such a portrait. *Heavy in the eyes from wine, he hath washed in wine his raiment*—but Judah has lost his eyes, and his raiment is in rags. The Judæan landscape of to-day is liker the second portrait which Isaiah drew in prospect

[1] Gen. xlix. 11 f.

[2] Until the revival of vineyards by foreigners, Hebron and Bethlehem were almost the only places in the Holy Land where wine was made. The grapes of Es-Salṭ have always been turned into raisins.

of the Assyrian invasion. *In that day shall the Lord shave, with a razor that is hired, the head and the hair of the feet and the beard. And it shall be in that day, a man shall nourish a young cow and a couple of sheep; and it shall be, because of the abundance of the making of milk, he shall eat butter,—for butter and honey shall everything eat which is left in the midst of the land. And it shall be in that day, that every place in which there were a thousand vines at a thousand silverlings—for briars and for thorns shall it be.... And all the hills that were digged with the mattock, thou shalt not come hither for fear of briars and thorns; but it shall be for the sending forth of oxen and for the treading of sheep.*[1] With the exceptions named above, this is the Judah of to-day. But we have a third portrait, by Jeremiah,[2] of what Judah should be after the Restoration from Exile, and in this it is remarkable that no reversion is promised to a high state of cultivation, with olives and vines as the luxuriant features of the country, but that her permanent wealth and blessing are conceived as pastoral.... *For I will bring again the captivity of the land as in the beginning, saith Yahweh. Thus saith Yahweh of Hosts: Again shall there be in this place—the Desolate, without men or even beast—and in all its cities, the habitation of shepherds couching their flocks. In the cities of the Mountain,* or *Hill-country, of Judah, in the cities of the Shephelah, and in the cities of the Negeb, and in the land of Benjamin, and in the suburbs of Jerusalem, and in the cities of Judah, again shall the flocks pass upon the hands of him that telleth* them. Now, though other prospects of the restoration of Judah include husbandry and vine culture,[3] and though Jews after the Exile speak of their property as vineyards, olive-yards and cornland, with sheep,[4] the prevailing aspect of Judah is pastoral, and the fulfilment of Jacob's luscious blessing must be sought for in the few fruitful corners of the land, especially at Hebron. As Judah's first political centre, Hebron would in the time of her supremacy be the obvious model for the nation's ideal figure.[5]

But this has brought us to the first of those three features of Judæa's

[1] Isa. vii. 20 ff.   [2] Jer. xxxiii. 12, 13. The passage begins with ver. 10.

[3] Micah iv. 4, 1 Kings iv. 25 give the ideal, *every man under his own vine and fig-tree.* Jer. (xxxi. 24) places husbandmen before *them that go forth with flocks.* Habakkuk puts vines, figs, olives before flocks, iii. 17. Isa. lxv. 10 says, *Sharon shall be a fold of flocks, and the valley of Achor a place for herds to couch, for My people that have sought Me*; but 21, *they shall plant vineyards*, cf. Isa. lxi. 5, *strangers shall stand and feed your flocks, and sons of the alien shall be your plowmen and vine-dressers.*

[4] Nehemiah v. Haggai speaks only of husbandry, Malachi of flocks and vines, Joel of corn, wine, oil, figs, pomegranates, palms, apples (chap. i), cattle and herds in the background. New wine and milk are of the future, iii. 18.

[5] One is tempted to ask whether any inference as to the date of Gen. xlix can be drawn from its representation of Judah as chiefly a wine-growing country; I do not think so; cf. passages cited in the above notes.

geography which are significant in her history—her pastoral character, her neighbourhood to the desert, her unsuitableness for the growth of a great city. With these the rest of this chapter will be occupied.

1. If the prevailing character of Judæa be pastoral, with husbandry only incidental to her life, it is not surprising that the forms which have impressed her history and her religion upon the world should be those of the pastoral habit. Her origin; more than once her freedom and power of political recuperation; more than once her prophecy; her images of God and her poetry of the spiritual life have been derived from this source. It is the stateliest shepherds of all time whom the dawn of history reveals upon her fields—men sprung from her own remote conditions, nor confined to them, but moving across the world in converse with empires, and bringing down from heaven truths sublime and universal to wed with the simple habits of her life. These were the patriarchs of the nation. The founder of its one dynasty, and the first of its literary prophets, were *taken from following the flocks.*[1] The king and every leader of men was called a shepherd. God was the Shepherd of His people, and they the sheep of His pasture. In Judæa Christ called Himself the Good Shepherd, and in Judæa, taking another feature of her life, He said He was the True Vine.[2]

Judæa offers as good ground as there is in the East for observing the grandeur of the shepherd's character. On the boundless Eastern pasture, so different from the narrow meadows and dyked hillsides with which we are familiar, the shepherd is indispensable. With us sheep are often left to themselves; I do not remember to have seen in the East a flock without a shepherd. In such a landscape as Judæa, where a day's pasture is thinly scattered over an unfenced tract, covered with delusive paths, still frequented by wild beasts, and rolling into the desert, the man and his character are indispensable. On some high moor, across which at night hyenas howl, when you meet him, sleepless, far-sighted, weather-beaten, armed, leaning on his staff, and looking out over his scattered sheep, every one on his heart, you understand why the shepherd of Judæa sprang to the front in his people's history; why they gave his name to their king, and made him the symbol of Providence; why Christ took him as the type of self-sacrifice.

Sometimes we enjoyed our noonday rest beside one of those Judæan wells, to which three or four shepherds come down with their flocks. The flocks mixed with each other, and we wondered how each shepherd would get his own again. But after the watering and the playing were over, the shepherds one by one went up different sides of the valley, and each called out his peculiar call; and the sheep of each drew out of the crowd to their own

[1] 2 Sam. vii. 8; Amos vii. 15.

[2] Stanley, *Sinai and Palestine*, xiii.

shepherd, and the flocks passed as orderly as they came. *The shepherd of the sheep, when he puts forth his own sheep, he goes before them, and the sheep follow him, for they know his voice, and a stranger will they not follow. I am the Good Shepherd, and know Mine own, and am known of Mine.* These words our Lord spake in Judæa.

2. With the pastoral character of the hill-country of Judæa we may take its neighbourhood to the desert—the wilderness of Judæa. In the Old Testament this land is called the Jeshimon, a word meaning *devastation*,[1] and no term could better suit its haggard and crumbling appearance. It covers some thirty-five miles by fifteen. We came upon it from Maon. The cultivated land east of Hebron sinks quickly to rolling hills and waterless vales, covered by broom and grass, across which it took us all forenoon to ride. The wells are few, and almost all cisterns of rain-water, jealously guarded through summer by their Arab owners.[2] For an hour or two more we rode up and down steep ridges, each barer than the preceding, and descended rocky slopes to a wide plain, where we left behind the last brown grass and thistle; the last flock of goats we had passed two hours before. Short bushes, thorns, and succulent creepers were all that relieved the brown and yellow bareness of the sand, crumbling limestone, and scattered shingle. The strata were contorted; ridges ran in all directions; distant hills to north and south looked like gigantic dust heaps; those near we could see to be torn as by waterspouts. When we were not stepping on detritus, the limestone was blistered and peeling. Often the ground sounded hollow; sometimes rock and sand slipped in large quantity from the tread of the horses; sometimes the living rock was bare and jagged, especially in the frequent gullies, that glowed and beat with heat like furnaces. Far to the east ran the Moab hills, and in front of them we got glimpses of the Dead Sea, the deep blue of which was a refreshing sight across the desert foreground. So we rode for two hours, till the sea burst upon us in all its length, and this chaos, which we had traversed, tumbled and broke, down 1200 feet of limestone, flint, and marl—crags, corries, and precipices—to the broad beach of the water. Such is Jeshimon, the wilderness of Judæa. It carries the violence and desolation of the Dead Sea Valley right up to the heart of the country, to the roots of the Mount of Olives, to within two hours of the gates of Hebron, Bethlehem, and Jerusalem.

When you realise that this howling waste came within reach of nearly

[1] In Deut. xxxii. 10, applied to the Arabian Desert, from which God brought Israel, the waste and howling wilderness, תהו וילל ישימן.

[2] The *PEF Survey* map shows that almost the only names in this part of Judæa are compounded with Bîr, "cistern".

every Jewish child; when you climb the Mount of Olives, or any hill about Bethlehem, or the hill of Tekoa, and, looking east, see those fifteen miles of chaos, sinking to a stretch of the Dead Sea, you begin to understand the influence of the desert on Jewish imagination and literature. It gave the ancient natives of Judæa, as it gives the visitor of to-day, the sense of living next door to doom; the sense of how narrow is the border between life and death; the awe of the power of God, who can make contiguous regions so opposite in character. *He turneth rivers into a wilderness, and watersprings into a thirsty ground.* The desert is always in face of the prophets, and its howling of beasts and dry sand blow mournfully across their pages the foreboding of doom.

But this is not the only influence of the desert. Meteoric effects are nowhere in Palestine so simple or so brilliant. And there is the annual miracle, when, after the winter rains, even these wastes take on a glorious green. Hence the sudden rushes of light and life across the prophet's vision; it is from the desert that he mostly borrows his imagery of the creative, instantaneous Divine grace. *The wilderness and the solitary place shall be glad for them: the desert shall rejoice, and blossom as the rose.*

Two, at least, of the prophets were born in face of the wilderness of Judæa—Amos and Jeremiah—and on both it has left its fascination. Amos lived to the south of Jerusalem, at Tekoa. No one can read his book without feeling that he haunted heights, and lived in the face of wide horizons. But from Tekoa you see the exact scenery of his visions. The slopes on which Amos herded his cattle show the mass of desert hills with their tops *below* the spectator, and therefore displaying every meteoric effect in a way they could not have done had he been obliged to look *up* to them. The cold wind that blows off them after sunset; through a gap the Dead Sea, with heavy mists; beyond the gulf the range of Moab, cold and grey, till the sun leaps from behind his barrier, and the world of hill-tops below Tekoa is flooded with light—that was the landscape of Amos. *Lo, He that formeth the mountains, and createth the wind, and declareth unto man what is His thought; that maketh the morning darkness, and treadeth on the high places of the earth, Yahweh, God of Hosts, is His name; that maketh the Seven Stars and Orion, and turneth the shadow of death into morning, and maketh the day dark with night; that calleth for the waters of the sea, and poureth them out on the face of the earth—Yahweh His name.*

Jeremiah grew up at Anathoth, a little to the north-east of Jerusalem, across Scopus, and over a deep valley. It is the last village eastward, and from its site the land falls in broken, barren hills to the north end of the Dead Sea. The vision of that desert maze was burnt into the prophet's mind, and he contrasted it with the clear, ordered Word of God. *O generation, see ye the word of the Lord: Have I been a wilderness unto Israel, a land of darkness?*[1] He had lived in face of the scorching desert air—*A dry wind off the bare heights in the wilderness toward the daughter of My people, not to fan nor cleanse.* And in face of the chaotic prospect, he described doom in these terms: *I beheld the earth, and lo, it was without form and void, I beheld, and lo, the fruitful place was a wilderness at the presence of Yahweh, by His fierce anger.*[2]

But the wilderness affected Judæa by more than its neighbourhood. There can be little doubt but that the more austere and fanatic temper of the Jew was begotten in him by the absorption of such desert tribes as the Kenites. Israel was everywhere a mixed race, but while in Samaria and Galilee the foreign constituents were mostly Canaanite, in Judæa they were mostly Arabian.[3]

The wilderness of Judæa played also a great part as the refuge of political fugitives and religious solitaries—a part it still continues. The story of Saul's hunt after David, and of David's narrow escapes, becomes vivid among those tossed and broken hills, where the valleys are all alike, and bodies of men may camp near each other without knowing it. Ambushes are everywhere possible, and alarms pass rapidly across the bare and silent hills. You may travel for hours, and feel as solitary as at sea without a sail in sight; but if you are in search of any one, your guide's signal will make men leap from slopes that did not seem to shelter a rabbit, and if you are suspected, your passage may be stopped by a dozen men, as if they had sprung from the earth.[4]

We cannot pass from the wilderness of Judæa without remembering two more holy events of which it was the scene. Here John was prepared for his austere mission, and found his figures of judgement. Here you understand his description of his preaching—like a desert fire when the brown grass and thorns on the fertile portions will blaze for miles, and the unclean reptiles creep out of their holes before its heat: *O generation of vipers, who hath taught you to flee from the wrath to come?* And here our Lord suffered temptation. *Straightway the Spirit driveth Him into the wilderness.* For hours, as you travel across these hills, you may feel no sign of life, except the scorpions and vipers which your passage startles, in the distance a few wild goats or gazelles, and at night the wailing of the jackal and the hyena's howl. *He was alone with the wild beasts.*

3. But the most impressive fact about Judæa—at least in face of her history—is her natural unfitness for the growth of a great city.

[1] Jer. ii. 31. [2] Jer. iv. 11, 23, 26. [3] Wellhausen, *De Gentibus*, etc. [4] See p. 186.

All the townships of Judæa were either fortresses, shrines, or villages. The fortresses we have already seen on the borders, chiefly on the west and north. And on the western border we have seen one of the shrines—Kiriath-jearim, or Baale-judah. The rural townships lay chiefly on the east,—Tekoa and the group on the fertile plateau south-east of Hebron[1]. But up the centre of the plateau ran a road, and all the places of greatest importance lay upon it—Beersheba, Kiriath-sepher (?), Hebron, Bethlehem, Jerusalem, and Bethel. Of these, Beersheba (as we have seen), Hebron, and Bethel were sanctuaries before Israel entered the land; and Jerusalem, from the earliest times, had been a fortress and probably also a shrine. Hebron and Bethlehem, the two earliest seats of Judah, have the greatest natural possibilities. Ancient Hebron lay on a hill to the north-west of the present site; it commands an entrance to the higher plateau, and is within hail of the desert, which means trade with Arabs. The valleys around are fruitful. Like so many ancient towns, Hebron combined the attractions of a market and a shrine.[2]

Beth-lehem-ephratah was no shrine, but, as its double name implies, it lies in the midst of great fertility, with water not far away.[3] The position is

[1] Eshtemoa, Maon, Carmel, Juttah, Ziph, Janum, etc.

[2] The origin of Hebron is obscure, in the Hexateuch mentioned by all documents. J calls its earlier name Kiriath-arba, and Caleb drave from it sons of Anak, Sheshai, Ahiman, Tolmai (Judges i. 10, 20; Num. xiii. 22; cf. Josh. xv. 4. According to Josh. xi. 21, Joshua cut off the Anakim from Hebron). J also says that *Hebron was built seven years before Zoan* (Num. xiii. 22), but which building of Zoan? J mentions *the terebinths of Mamre*, but does not identify them with Hebron (Gen. xiii. 18, xviii. 1). E confirms J: Hebron earlier called *Kiriath* (*city of*)*-arba*: *he was the mightiest among the Anakim* (Josh. xiv. 15). A verse by the Redactor calls Arba *the father of Anak* (Josh. xv. 13; cf. xxi. 11). E puts Vale of Eshcol near Hebron (Num. xiii. 23). P identifies Kiriath-arba and Hebron (Gen. xxiii. 2, Josh. xx. 7, a city of refuge; cf. xxi. 13), and Mamre (the sacred terebinths of which it does not mention) with Hebron (Gen. xxiii. 19, etc., xxxv. 27. According to xxv. 9, xlix. 30, l. 13, Machpelah lies in front of Mamre). In Gen. xxxv. 27, Arba bears the article, *City of the Arba*, or *of the Four*, and so in Neh. xi. 25. In Gen. xiv. 13, 24, a chapter not assignable to any document, Mamre is called Amorite and brother to Eshcol and Aner. In Samuel, Kings, Chronicles, Hebron is the only name given to the city: 1 Sam. xxx. 31; 2 Sam. ii. 1, etc.; iii. 2, 32; iv. 1-12; v. 1-13; xv. 7, 10, Absalom's vow in Hebron, and his revolt there; 1 Chron. ii. 42, Mareshah, father of Hebron, 43, Korah, Tappuah, Rekem, Shema, sons of Hebron; vi. 55, 57, Hebron given to sons of Aaron; 2 Chron. xi. 10, fortified by Rehoboam; 1 Macc. v. 65, destroyed by Judas in campaign against Edomites.

[3] Tomkins (*PEFQ*, 1885, 112) suggests Beth-lehem as originally the sacred place of Lakhmu, a Chaldæan god of fertility (Smith, *Chald. Genesis*, 58, 60), and compares Lahmi (1 Chron. xx. 5); Lahmam, the present el-Laḥm, was near Beit-Jibrin. Had Beth-lehem, however, been originally a shrine, some trace must have survived in the

one of considerable strength, and not far from that citadel which Herod the Great made famous under his own name. Beth-lehem, indeed, though *too little to be placed among the families of Judah*, is the finest site in the whole province.

Yet neither Beth-lehem nor Hebron, nor any other part of that plateau, bears tokens of civic promise. Throughout Judæa these are lacking. She has no harbours, no river, no trunk-road, no convenient market for the nations on either side. In their commerce with each other these pass by Judæa, finding their emporiums in the cities of Philistia, or, as of old, at Petra and Bozrah on the east of the Jordan. Gaza has outdone Hebron as the port of the desert. Jerusalem is no match for Shechem in fertility or convenience of site. The whole plateau stands aloof, waterless, on the road to nowhere. There are none of the natural conditions of a great city.

And yet it was here that She arose who, more than Athens and more than Rome, taught the nations civic justice, and gave her name to the ideal city men are ever striving to build on earth, to the City of God that shall one day descend from heaven—the New Jerusalem. For her builder was not Nature nor the wisdom of men, but on that secluded and barren site the Word of God, by her prophets, laid her eternal foundations in righteousness, and reared her walls in her people's faith in God.

Old Testament. "House of Bread" is a natural name for so fertile a site, and has continued into Arabic, in which, however, the same letters mean "house of meat". In J E it is *Ephrath, that is B.* (Gen. xxxv. 16, 19; cf. xlviii. 7 R). Ibzan, a judge, sprang from it (Judges xii. 8-10). In Judges xvii. 7, xix. 1, 2, etc., it is *B. in Judah*; in Ruth i. 1, etc., *B. Judah,* or *B.* alone. So in 1 and 2 Sam., *passim,* 1 Chron. xi. 16, Jer. xli. 17, they came to *the inn of Chimham, which is by B., to go and enter into Egypt.* Micah v. 2, *B. Ephratah,* though thou be too *small to be among the families of Judah.* The natives were called Ephrathites (Ruth i. 2; 1 Sam. xvii. 12). But in Judges xii. 5, 1 Sam. i. 1, 1 Kings xi. 26, Ephrathite = Ephraimite. Herod's citadel near Beth-lehem was the Herodium, now Jebel Fureidis, or Frank Mountain, from its use by the Crusaders after the capture of Jerusalem (Felix Fabri, *PPT,* ii. 403 f.). Conder suggests Fureidis = a corruption of Herodium (cf. Furbia = Herbia). Herod is buried here. On the reasons for supposing that the Church of the Nativity occupies the site of the inn, see Conder, *TW,* ch. x, Henderson's *Palestine,* p. 149.

XVI. *SAMARIA*[1]

From Judæa we pass to Samaria. Halves of the same range, how opposite in disposition and in history! The northern is as fair and open as the southern is secluded and austere, and their fortunes correspond. To the prophets Samaria is the older sister,[2] standing nearer the world, taking precedence in good and evil. The more forward to attract, the more quick to develop, Samaria was the less able to retain. The patriarchs came first to Shechem, but chose their homes about Hebron; the earliest seats of Israel's worship, the earliest rallies of her patriotism, were upon Mount Ephraim,[3] but both Church and State ultimately centred in Jerusalem; after the disruption of the kingdom the first prophets and heroes sprang up in the richer life of Northern Israel, but the splendour and endurance both of prophecy and of kingship remained with Judæa. And so, though we owe Samaria some of the finest of Israel's national lyrics, she produced no literature of patriotism, but the literature about her is full of scorn for her traffic with foreigners, for her luxury and her tolerance of idols. "Pride, fulness of bread and prosperous ease", then rottenness and swift ruin, are the chief notes of prophecy concerning her. And so while pilgrims throng on either hand to Judæa and to Galilee, none seek Samaria save for one spot of her surface—neither a birthplace nor tomb nor battle-field nor city, but the scene of a wayside saying by Him who used this land only as a passenger.

But if hardly Holy Land—if hardly ever national land—no region of Syria is more interesting and romantic. The traveller, entering from Judæa, is refreshed by a far fairer landscape. When he reaches the Vale of Shechem he finds himself at the physical centre of Palestine, from which the features of the country radiate and group themselves most clearly. Historical memories, too, burst about the paths of Samaria more lavishly than even those fountains, which render her a contrast to Judæa—the altars at Shechem[4] and Shiloh, the fields round Dothan, the palm-tree of Deborah, the wine-press of Ophrah, Carmel and Gilboa, the columns in Samaria, the vineyard of Naboth, the gates of Jezreel and Beth-shan, the fords of Jordan; the ap-

[1] For this chapter, see Maps 1, 2, 3, 4, 5, 6.

[2] Jer. iii; Ezek. xvi. 46, and especially xxiii.

[3] *He blew a trumpet in Mount Ephraim*, Judges iii. 27. *Palm-tree of Deborah between Ramah and Bethel in Mount Ephraim*, iv. 5; cf. vi. 11.

[4] See pp. 222 f.

proach of the patriarchs, Elijah's apparitions, Elisha passing to and fro, John baptising at Ænon near to Salim; Ahab and Herod; Gideon's campaign; Jehu's furious driving, Judith and Holofernes, battles of the Maccabees, the strategy of Pompey and of Vespasian.

It has been shown how the southern frontier of Samaria gradually receded from the Vale of Aijalon to the Wady Ishar and 'Aḳrabbeh.[1] The northern was more fixed, and lay from the Mediterranean to Jordan, along the south edge of Esdraelon, by the foot of Carmel and Gilboa. If we shut off Carmel, the edge of Sharon may be taken as the western boundary; the eastern was Jordan. These limits enclose a territory nearly square, or some forty miles north and south by thirty-five east and west—the size of an average English shire.[2]

The earliest name given to this section of the Central Range (we exclude Carmel) was *Mount Ephraim*[3]: just as the whole table-land of Judah was called *Mount Judah*.[4] When you stand off the country you see, as you do not when within it, the propriety of the singular name *mount*. Broken up as Samaria is into more or less separate groups of hills, yet when you view her from Gilead, or from the Mediterranean, she presents the aspect of a single mountain *massif*, with entrances indeed, but apparently as compact as the table-land of Judæa.

Take first the western flank. Here from summits of 3000 feet, and an average watershed of 2000, Mount Ephraim descends upon Sharon by uninterrupted ridges. The general aspect of the slope is "rocky and sterile"; with infrequent breaks of olive-woods,[5] fields, and a few villages. This

[1] See pp. 173-176.

[2] See p. 178. The distances are: from Bethel to Jezreel, 42 miles; from the edge of Sharon to Jordan between 33 and 36; but from the point of Carmel to Beth-shan 40; and to the SE corner of the province (east of Bethel) about 67 miles. Without Carmel Samaria is about 1400 square miles; Carmel 180 or 200 more. Judæa was estimated at 2000 square miles, of which only about 1400 were habitable. On *The Administrative Divisions of Israel*, W. F. Albright, *JPOS*, v. 17 ff.

[3] הַר אֶפְרַיִם, Josh. xvii. 15, xix. 50, etc. Judges iii. 27, iv. 5, etc.; 1 Sam. i. 1, ix. 4, etc. (also הַר יִשְׂרָאֵל Josh. xi. 16, 21). That the whole known as Samaria is covered by the name is proved by the facts that between Ramah and Bethel is styled as in Mt. Ephraim (Judges iv. 5); also Shechem (1 Kings xii. 25; Josh. xx. 7, etc.); and that in Jer. xxxi. 6, Mt. Ephraim is parallel to Mountains of Samaria (v. 5). The name spread originally from the hill-country north of Benjamin's territory, which fell to the tribe of Ephraim, and in which we must seek for the *city called Ephraim* (2 Chron. xiii. 19, 2 Sam. xiii. 23, John xi. 45)—perhaps eṭ-Ṭaiyibeh.

[4] Josh. xxi. 11, where it is translated *hill-country of Judah*.

[5] Robinson, *LBR*, 135.

bareness is not because of steepness; the descent, which is unbroken, is gradual—only some 1800 feet in eighteen miles. The whole flank lies in contrast to the precipices and defiles which run down the west of Judæa; and, whether you ascend by its valleys or by its broad ridges, the way is easy and open. That little history was enacted upon this flank of Mount Ephraim seems to be due to—besides the comparative sterility of the soil—the impossibility of anywhere making a stand, the uselessness of building a fortress.

On the water-parting the one pass conspicuous from the sea is that in which Shechem lies between Ebal and Gerizim. It crosses to the east of the range, and is continued by a valley with a southerly trend, the Wady el-Ifjim, which runs out upon the Jordan below the Horn or Promontory of Ṣurṭabeh, and divides the east flank of Mount Ephraim into two sections. South of the Wady el-Ifjim, Mount Ephraim presents to Eastern Palestine a bulwark of mountain closely piled, with corries running up it—the most difficult corner of the frontier. Seen from Nebo it looks inaccessible. The descent is over 2800 feet in nine miles, or three times the gradient of the western flank. But north of Wady el-Ifjim and Ṣurṭabeh this flank of Mount Ephraim opens, and a series of valleys descend from the interior. From the water-parting the level drops 2500 feet in ten miles. Opposite the centre of the province the hills fall close on Jordan, but farther north they recede to five miles, and at Bethshan turn west in the range of Gilboa, leaving the valley of Jezreel to run up on the north of them towards the sea.

Within those bulwarks Mount Ephraim surprises us with the number of its plains, meadows, and vales. These begin from the north with the gap between Carmel and Gilboa, through which a gulf of Esdraelon gapes for seven miles to Jenin. Thence a succession of spaces, more or less connected, spreads south through the centre of the province to within a few miles of its border. First from Jenin is the Plain of Dothan,[1] reached by a pass through low hills; thence another pass leads to spacious meadows lying across the country from the south end of Mount Gilboa to the range of hills which bulwark the city of Samaria on the north[2]; and thence another pass leads to a third series of plains running south into the great Sahel Mukhneh opposite Gerizim. Now upon this succession of level lands running south from

[1] Sahel 'Arrabeh. Robinson (*Phys. Geogr.* 122) a bay of Esdraelon; but they are separated by low hills. Wellhausen (*Hist.* 39) as merging into Sharon, but a long pass connects them; see p. 115.

[2] Cf. *PEF Mem.* ii. Samaria, 38. Trel. Saunders, *Introd. to Survey*, 136. The Plains of 'Arrabeh, Selhab and Zebabdeh drain to the Mediterranean; Merj el-Ghuruḳ has no outlet. In May 1891, it held a shallow lake; cf. Robinson, *BR*, iii. 153. The Mukhneh drains to Jordan.

Esdraelon, there emerge valleys,—those that come up from Sharon and those that come up from Jordan. Of the former the chief is the broad Barley-Vale, Wady esh-Sha'ir, which sweeps up past Samaria upon Shechem. In this direction, too, the gentle ridges offer almost everywhere easy access from the coast. On the other side running down to Jordan, are the Wady el-Far'ah, that winds from a little south of Shechem to opposite the Jabbok, the trunk road to the east, farther north the Buḳei'a, or Little-Dale; then Salt-Vale, or Wady el-Maliḥ, issuing at Abel-Meholah, and Wady el-Khashneh, with the road from Shechem to Beth-shan, up which came perhaps Pompey and certainly Vespasian. These are *the outgoings of Mount Ephraim*,[1] broad, fertile, of easy gradients. But besides these, and even where the mountains crowd together in the south-east corner are frequent meadows and corn lands. Travellers from Judæa will remember the open vales which they crossed before they reached the Mukhneh; of the less visited country to the east, Robinson says: "It was a surprise to find in this *break-down* of the mountains so much good land; so many fine and arable, though not large, plains."[2]

I. Therefore the openness of Samaria is her most prominent feature, and tells most in her history. Few invaders were successfully resisted. It is singular that we have no account of the invasion by Israel. Bethel falls, and after that the tribe of Joseph, to whom the region is allotted, express no fear, record no struggle, till they come to Esdraelon and the Canaanite cities, Beth-shan and Jezreel.[3] Under the invasion of the Canaanites, Israel's law could be administered only in the south-east, between Ramah and Bethel, where stood the palm-tree of Deborah.[4] In Gideon's day Midianites swept south from Esdraelon, so that the use of the open threshing-floors was impossible even at Ophrah.[5] In Elisha's time, the Syrians, by apparently annual invasions, swept west as far as the citadel of Samaria, behind the watershed. The Assyrians overwhelmed the land, and carried off the greater part of the population. In the Book of Judith Holofernes is represented as easily bringing in his army from Esdraelon by the plains described above.[6] Vespasian, seeking to blockade Judæa, marched from Antipatris by Shechem to Koreæ, and thence to Jericho and back again, then to Gophna, Ephraim and back again, within a week.[7] And Titus came easily upon Jerusalem from Cæsarea past Gophna and Bethel.[8] How differently all this reads from the history of the invasion of Judæa through her narrow defiles—the sallies from

[1] Josh. xvii. 18. [2] *LBR*, 296. [3] Josh. xvii. 14. [4] Judges iv. 5.
[5] Perhaps Ferata, south-west from Shechem (Conder). Judges vi. 11.
[6] Bethulia must be sought for somewhere about the Merj el-Ghuruḳ. See p. 234.
[7] Josephus, iv *Wars*, viii, ix, x. [8] *Id.* v *Wars*. ii. 1.

the hills, the ambushes of the Wady ʻAli, the routs down by the two Beth-horons and Aijalon!

One effect of the openness of Samaria is the frequency with which the chariot appears in her history. In the annals of Judah chariots are seldom mentioned.[1] The long drives of the Old Testament are in Samaria—the race of Ahab against the storm from Mount Carmel to Jezreel[2]; his funeral in his battle-chariot stained with his blood from Ramoth-gilead to Samaria, *and they washed his chariot by the pool of Samaria, and the dogs licked up his blood*[3]; the drive of Jehu from Ramoth-gilead past Bethshan and up the Vale of Jezreel, and *the watchman in Jezreel told, saying, . . . the driving is like the driving of Jehu the son of Nimshi, for he drives furiously; and Joram said, Yoke, and they yoked his chariot, and Joram king of Israel and Ahaziah king of Judah went out each in his chariot to meet Jehu, and found him in the portion of Naboth the Jezreelite*; the chariot-race from there between Jehu and poor Ahaziah *by way of the garden house, the ascent of Gur, which is by Ibleam*, where Ahaziah was smitten, and Megiddo, where he died, *and his servants carried him in a chariot to Jerusalem*[4]; Jehu's drive again from Jezreel to Samaria, *and he lighted on Jehonadab son of Rechab coming to meet him, and he gave him his hand, and took him up into the chariot, and said, Come with me and see my zeal for the Lord*[5]; and the drive of Naaman from Damascus, across Hauran, over Jordan and up Jezreel, *with his horses and his chariots*, to the house of Elisha, presumably at Samaria, and the drive back, and the pursuit by Gehazi, and when *Naaman saw one running after him, he lighted down from his chariot to meet him.*[6] Contrast this with the two meagre references to chariot-driving in Judæa—in the one case the chariot carried a corpse, in the other a dying man[7]—and you have illustrated the difference between the level stretches of Samaria, and the steep, tortuous roads of her sister province. The prophet emphasises this contrast: *I will cut off the chariot from Ephraim, and the horse from Jerusalem.*[8]

More important than chariots, and even than easy invasion by enemies, is that effect of Samaria's openness, to which I alluded in the beginning of this chapter. Judæa, earning from outsiders little but contempt, inspired the people, whom she nursed in seclusion from the world, with a patriotism that has survived two thousand years of separation, and still draws her exiles from all countries of the world to pour their tears upon her dust, though it be the most barren the world contains. Samaria, fair and facile, lavished her favours on foreigners, and was oftener the temptation than the discipline,

[1] See Appendix, on Roads and Wheeled Vehicles in Syria. [2] 1 Kings xviii. 44 ff.
[3] 1 Kings xxii. 29 ff. [4] 2 Kings ix. 16 ff. [5] 2 Kings x. 12, 15 ff. [6] 2 Kings v. 9 ff.
[7] 2 Kings ix. 28; 2 Chron. xxxv. 24. [8] Zech. ix. 10.

the betrayer than the guardian, of her own. The surrounding paganism poured into her ample life; and although to her were granted the first victories against it—Gideon's and Elijah's—she suffered the luxury that came after to take away her crown. From Amos to Isaiah the sins she is charged with are those of a civilisation once ripe, now rotten—drunkenness, clumsy art, servile imitation of foreigners, thoughtlessness and cruelty. For these she falls, and her summer beauty is covered by the mud of a deluge. *The crown of the pride of the drunkards of Ephraim is trodden under foot, and the fading flower of his glorious beauty, which is on the head of the fat valley, shall be as the first ripe fig before the summer, which when he that has caught sight of it sees it, while it is yet in his hand he eats it up.*[1] Poor province, she grew ripe and was ravished before the summer of her people!

II. The second characteristic of Samaria is her central position. Jerusalem has acquired such historical importance that we are apt to imagine her as the natural head and centre of the land. But nothing comes with greater surprise upon the visitor to Palestine than to discover that, with her advantages of defence, Jerusalem lies on a barren, awkward site, and that natural and historical precedence have to be given, not to Mount Zion and the City of David, but to Mounts Ebal and Gerizim, with Shechem between.

We have noticed how this suggests itself before we touch the land. In the Central Range as seen from the sea, the only sign of a pass is that between Ebal and Gerizim, whose summits conspicuously rise above the general level of the sky-line. It is the same on the other side of the land. Seen from Moab, the Central Range runs unbroken, save by narrow corries. But stand farther north, on the hills of Gilead opposite Ephraim—on Jebel Osha', above es-Salṭ, or on the castle of er-Rubad, above 'Ajlun—and there open to you across Jordan the mouths of valleys which run up to the plains in front of Shechem. There is thus a pass right across Samaria, from the coast to Jordan, and where it pierces the watershed, with Ebal on one side and Gerizim on the other, Shechem lies at the parting of the waters, some of its fountains flowing seawards, the rest to Jordan. Joppa, down an open incline, stands three or four miles nearer than to Jerusalem. Cæsarea is but thirty away; Jenin, the gateway to Esdraelon, eighteen; Beth-shan twenty-five; while none of the roads which fall directly east take more than eighteen to reach the fords of Jordan. We have also seen that from Mount Ebal all the chief

[1] One proof of how Samaria was permeable from the west is Beit-Dejan, *i.e.* the House of Dagon, a village 6½ m. SE of Shechem. Cf. the name Amalek (Judges v. 14, xii. 15). This, however, is perhaps due to some Arab element which, like the Kenites in S, entered with Israel.

features and most of the borders of the land are visible.[1] To this may be added, that under the Turks Nablus or Shechem was the seat of the government of the province and the link of the telegraphic systems of the east and west of Jordan, and under British administration has a District Court.

Excavations of this century, before and after the War, have discovered the site of the ancient Shechem (or as some think that of the *Tower of Shechem*) at Balaṭa about a mile east of Nablus, and exposed four stages of its history: Canaanite 2000-1400 B.C. with bronze weapons, and proofs of Babylonian and Egyptian influence, as well as of Hittite, similar to what we shall see at Beth-shan, and also small figures of the mother goddess Ashtoreth; Early Israelite 1400-900, broken (it is claimed) about 1100 by Abimelech's destruction of Shechem, but the walls[2] were rebuilt; Late Israelite, with among other details domestic altars assigned through the pottery to the eighth and seventh centuries; and Samaritan-Hellenistic, the pottery inscribed with Aramaic letters perhaps of the fifth and sixth centuries.[3]

It is therefore in harmony with the geographical and archæological data that the story of the patriarchs brings Abraham and Jacob, on their entrance into the Promised Land, at once to Shechem,[4] and that Deuteronomy selects Ebal and Gerizim as the scene of an inaugural service by Israel on taking possession of the country, a service which the Book of Joshua duly records. Both passages, in Deuteronomy and in Joshua, are from the Deuteronomist, whose principle is the centralisation of Israel's worship in one sanctuary, and that ostensibly Jerusalem. His mention of Ebal, therefore—it is the only sacred site which he names—stands out in the greater relief, as proof of the attractiveness and central position of Shechem.[5] After the disruption of Israel, these qualities were not found to atone for her weakness as a fortress, and she soon ceased to be the capital of the Northern Kingdom. To the Samaritans the district owed the revival of its claims to be the religious centre

[1] The View from Mt. Ebal, ch. vi.   [2] Judges ix. 30 ff.

[3] These excavations begun by Sellin before 1914 were continued by him and others in 1926; summaries in *PEFQ*, 1926, 206 f.; 1927, 54 f.; cf. 1929, 59 (Phythian-Adams). Further, that Balaṭa is Shechem is probable from the statement of Eusebius and Jerome that Neapolis, Nablus, was a little way from Shechem.

[4] Abraham, Gen. xii. 6 (J); Jacob, Gen. xxxiii. 18 (P and E, cf. xxxiv).

[5] Deut. xxvii; Josh. viii. 30 ff. The former is difficult, breaking the connection between xxvi and xxviii, and compiled from several narratives (Dillmann *in loco*, Driver, *Introd.* 88). But all agree that a national service was to take place at Shechem soon after the crossing of Jordan, which Josh. viii. 30 ff. (Deut.) records. That the only sanctuary mentioned by Deuteronomy should be the capital of Samaria, is an element to be considered on the question whether that book rose out of an agitation for a central sanctuary at Jerusalem. If so, it is strange that Ebal is honoured, while Jerusalem is not mentioned.

of the land. But this was in the interest of as narrow a sectarianism as ever sought to monopolise the liberal intentions of nature. The abuse was gloriously atoned for. It was by this natural capital of the Holy Land, from which the outgoings to the world are many and open, that the religion of Israel rose above every geographical limit, and the charter of a universal worship was given. *Neither in this mountain, nor yet at Jerusalem, shall ye worship the Father; but the hour cometh, and now is, when the true worshippers shall worship the Father in spirit and in truth.*[1]

III. The third feature of Samaria is her connection with Eastern Palestine. This has existed from the earliest times, save for the interruption of the Samaritan schism, down to the present day. Both Abraham and Jacob came from the East to Shechem. Israel, leaving to Ammon and Moab the regions of Eastern Palestine opposite Judah, occupied those which march with Samaria. In this latitude, one tribe, Manasseh, settled on both sides of the river[2]; another, Ephraim, gave its name not only to the western mountains, but to a *wood* or *jungle* on the eastern side[3]; in the days of the Judges, Midian-

[1] Among other assumptions, the Samaritans fixed on Gerizim as the site of the offering of Isaac, and this is supported by Stanley (*Sinai and Palestine*, n. to ch. v) on the ground that Gerizim is visible from a distance, as Mt. Moriah in Jerusalem is not. *Abraham lifted up his eyes, and saw the place afar off* (ver. 4). But the vagueness of *the land of Moriah* and *one of the mountains* (ver. 2) prevents us from fixing on a definite hill; while there is reason to believe that *Moriah* is not the original reading, but a late gloss inserted to give the Temple at Jerusalem the credit of the narrative. Cf. Baudissin, *Stud. zur Semit. Religions-gesch.* ii. 252, Dillmann on Gen. xxvii, Henderson's *Palestine*, §48.

[2] See chs. xxv and xxvi for the Eastern Conquests of Israel.

[3] *Forest* or *Jungle of Ephraim*, in which the battle was between David and Absalom (2 Sam. xviii. 6). Reuss (*in loco*) insists that a forest named Ephraim must have lain W of Jordan. He claims that this agrees with the narrative which represents the bearer of the news to David at Mahanaim, taking the direction of the Jordan, which he would have done had he started from W of the river, and explains the absence of mention of David's force recrossing the river to meet Absalom by supposing gaps in the narrative. Putting aside this, by which one might prove anything, I may point out that *both* messengers had to run from the scene of Absalom's defeat to David, and ask, if that was W of Jordan, how could it be said that only *one* of the messengers ran from it by the plain (ver. 23)? This disposes of Reuss, and proves the *forest* E of the river. Lucian's LXX gives *Μααινάν* (for מחנים) instead of Ephraim as the forest. But this is the kind of correction Lucian would make to relieve a difficulty. And why should it be unlikely that the name Ephraim crossed the river, and fastened on the E bank? In the history of that tribe, especially under the Judges, many adventures may have occurred to cause Ephraimites, who frequently passed over, to leave their name when they went back. Or a colony may have settled there. Ephraimites settled in Gilead in such numbers that the western Ephraimites call the Gileadites fugitives from Ephraim (Judges xii. 4).

ites, *sons of the East*, swept annually across Jordan, and up to the recesses of Mount Ephraim; Gideon drove them back, and the rout extended from Esdraelon to Heshbon; it was from a tryst in Ephraim that Saul, though a Benjamite, marched to relieve Jabesh Gilead.[1] As before the disruption the Trans-Jordan provinces were connected with the tribe of Joseph, so after it they fell to that tribe's successor, Northern Israel; as formerly the Midianites made yearly incursions across the river, so now the Syrians. Jeroboam, the first king, fortified Penuel after Shechem,[2] and Ramoth Gilead was an outpost under Ahab, from which chariots drove to Jezreel and Samaria.[3] Elijah, the prophet of Samaria, came from Tishbeh in Gilead; Elisha crossed Jordan to anoint Jehu. After the exile, the impotence of the Samaritans broke the connection of their territory with the land over Jordan, and Peræa, as the latter was now called, formed the link between Galilee and Judæa.[4]

The reason of this immemorial connection is clear. We have seen that a number of valleys lead down through Mount Ephraim upon Jordan, while Esdraelon, with offsets into Northern Samaria, presents a still easier highway in the same direction. Now, to Esdraelon and those passes the Jordan, dangerous river as it is, offers many fords; while farther south, where the passes into the Western Range are few and more difficult, there are in Jordan hardly any fords.[5] The passage, therefore, from Samaria to Gilead was comparatively easy; hence their frequent invasions of each other, and their long political union. With this contrast the separation of Judæa from the east by the gulf of the Dead Sea.

In connection with the chariots, Ahab's, Jehu's, and Naaman's, the question rises, How did they cross Jordan? Till the Romans came no bridges were in Palestine. Like the name for *port*, that for *bridge* does not occur in the Old Testament, probably because the thing itself was unknown. It is unlikely that chariots were driven through the river, for the shallowest ford is three feet deep, and the bottom muddy. Either the body of the chariot was floated over, as baggage is still, by inflated skins, or else such ferry-boats existed as Cæsar found on the rivers of Gaul.[6]

[1] From Bezek, Khurbet Ibziḳ, 13 m. NE from Shechem.

[2] 1 Kings xii. 25.

[3] 1 Kings xxii; 2 Kings ix.

[4] Though Beth-shan went with Decapolis.

[5] On the Survey map not more than *five* fords are marked south of the Horn of Ṣurṭabeh, but at least *twenty-two* north of this.

[6] *Bell. Gall.* iii. 29. The depth of the fords is variable. Burckhardt tells of one 2 hrs. SE from Beisan 3 ft. deep (*Syria*, 344, 345); Lynch, of one that a donkey crossed with difficulty (*Narrative*, 224). Of three Hebrew forms from the root, *to cross*—מַעֲבָר, מַעְבָּרָה and עֲבָרָה, the first two mean both a ford (Gen. xxxii. 23, מַעֲבַר;

IV. The fourth feature of Samaria is her connection with Carmel. To Samaria Carmel holds much the same place on the west as Bashan or Gilead on the east. Seen from Ebal or Jezreel, they stand on either hand of Mount Ephraim, carrying the eye along the only high and sustained sky-lines in sight, and forming with Hermon the three dominant features of the view. Both have always been better wooded than Mount Ephraim. And so, because they stand in similar relation and contrast to Samaria, we find them, though at opposite sides of the Holy Land, frequently mentioned together. *Bashan and Carmel shake off their fruits. Israel shall feed in Bashan and Carmel. Feed thy people in the forest in the midst of Carmel: let them feed in Bashan and Gilead.* Sometimes Lebanon is added: *Bashan languishes, and Carmel and the flower of Lebanon languish.*

Though of the same rock as the Central Range, Carmel is separated from the latter by a softer formation, in which the more denuded hills offer easy passages from Sharon to Esdraelon. These hills are the *Shephelah of Israel*,[1] as debatable ground as the Shephelah of Judah, but lying, more openly than the latter, on the line of foreign traffic and war. Carmel was, therefore, no integral part of the body politic of Samaria. The kings of Northern Israel held it as they held Gilead. But in later history Carmel lay outside the province of Samaria—sometimes reckoned to Galilee, sometimes taken by Tyre.[2] Nor was Carmel a threshold to the land: his isolated range could not be used by Israel, as Gilead was, for the basis of foreign campaigns. Indeed we have seen how the campaigns of Syrian history treated Carmel as a thing to avoid, sweeping past on either side of him. The ridge was so cultivated that the villages must have been many, but there was neither site nor occasion for a town. Carmel had no political or military history. His influences were of another kind.

Throughout the Old Testament Carmel appears as a symbol or as a sanctuary. His bulk, visible from many quarters, makes him the picture of what is fact and not dream: while his head-long sweep seawards is the token of what will surely come and not fail. *Pharaoh is but a rumour*, do they say? *As I live, saith the Lord, surely like Tabor among the mountains, and like Carmel by the sea, shall he come!* The two hills stand at opposite ends of

---

Josh. ii. 7, etc., מעברה) and a pass (1 Sam. xiii. 23, xiv. 4; Isa. x. 29). The third is only in 2 Sam. xix. 18, and may be either a ford or more probably as in A.V., a ferry, as it is nominative to the active verb *caused to pass over*. In 2 Sam. xv. 28, xvii. 16, the plural עברות must mean fords; but Hebrew margin and LXX read ערבות, plains. In Rabbinic מעברא and מעברה both mean a ferry. In Jer. li. 32, Hitz. transl. מעברה by "bridge".

[1] Josh. xi. 16. See p. 145.

[2] Josephus, iii *Wars*, iii. 1.

Esdraelon, each separate from other hills and imposing its bulk upon the plain. But Carmel's long sweep north-westward gives him the appearance of having *come* there. Some hills suggest immovableness, and others, with their "long greyhound backs", are full of motion. Carmel combines these effects, and impresses those who look upon him with the sense of one long stride over the plain and firm foothold upon the sea. Not only his shape is symbolic. Sweeping seawards, Carmel is the first of Israel's hills to meet the rains, and they give him of their best. He is clothed in verdure. To-day it is mostly wild—fresh open jungle, coppices of oak and carob, with here and there a grove of great trees. But in ancient times most of the hill was cultivated. The name means Garden, and in the rock, beneath the wild bush, grooved floors and troughs have been traced, numerous enough to be proof of large harvests of grape and olive. The *excellency of Carmel* was now the figure of human beauty,[1] and now the mirror of the lavish goodness of God[2]; that Carmel should languish—Carmel in the gateway of the rains—is the prophets' most desperate figure of desolation.

But it is as a sanctuary that the long hill is best remembered. In its separation from other hills, position on the sea, visibleness from all quarters of the country,[3] uselessness for war or traffic, profusion of flowers, high platforms and groves with glorious prospects of land and sea, Carmel must have been a place of retreat and of worship from the earliest times.[4] It was claimed for Baal; but, even before Elijah's day, an altar had stood upon it for Yahweh. About this, as on a spot whose sanctity they equally felt, the rival faiths met in that contest, in which for most of us the history of Carmel consists. The story in the Book of Kings is too vivid to be told again; but it is not without interest to know that the debate, whether Yahweh or Baal was lord of the elements, was fought out for a day in face of the most sublime prospect of earth and sea and heaven. Before him, who stands on Carmel, nature rises in great stages from Sea to Alp: the Mediterranean, the long coast north and south, with its hot sands and palms; Esdraelon covered with wheat, Tabor and the lower hills of Galilee with their oaks—then, over the barer peaks of Upper Galilee and the haze about them, the clear snow of Hermon, hanging like an only cloud in the sky. It was in face of that miniature universe that the Deity who was Character was vindicated as Lord against the deity who was not. It was over all that realm that the rain swept up at the

[1] Song vii. 5. [2] Isa. xxxv. 2.

[3] Carmel is visible not only from the hills of Samaria, from Jaffa, from Tyre, from Hermon, from the hills of Naphtali, but also from the hills behind Gadara, east of Jordan, and from other points in Gilead.

[4] For Elijah 1 Kings xviii. 19 ff., Elisha 2 Kings ii. 25, iv. 25, for fugitives Amos ix. 3.

call of the God who exposed the injustice of the tyrant and avenged the wrongs of Naboth.

V. The last great feature of Samaria was the fortresses, which were necessitated by the peculiar formation of the province, and which lay all around and across her. But the number of them was so great, and the part they played in her history so important—repeating on several sites the function usually discharged in a country by one capital city—that the description of them must be left for another chapter.

XVII. *THE STRONG PLACES OF SAMARIA*[1]

Last chapter closed with the designation of her many fortresses as the fifth great feature of Samaria. It is these which this chapter is to describe. The large number of them was due to the openness of the land, and to the fact that, unlike Judæa, Samaria had no central position upon which her defence might be consolidated. Her fortresses lay around and across her, but chiefly, as was natural, upon the passes which draw up to her centre. They were mostly built on the high isolated knolls, which are a frequent feature of her scenery.

Of those strong places, the chief was that which was so long the capital and gave its name to the whole kingdom. *The head of Ephraim is Samaria.*[2]

This is to dethrone Shechem, the earliest capital of the land, the place to which the government has gravitated again and again. But Shechem is no fortress. The natural centre of the land, as we have seen, well furnished with water, and attracted also by its sacred associations, the site is incapable of defence. This was discovered by Jeroboam himself, for even in his reign we find the court at Tirzah,[3] by the head of one of the eastern passes. Tirzah, was retained by the following dynasty, but when the next usurper, Omri, shaped his policy, he turned westward, and chose a virgin site in that valley which leads down from Shechem to the coast, Wady esh-Sha'ir or Barley-Vale. Here, in a wide basin, formed by a bend of the vale and an incoming glen, rises a round, isolated hill over three hundred feet. It was not already a city, but probably, as in recent times, covered with soil and arable to the top. Omri fortified it and called it Shomeron, Wartburg, Watch Tower.[4] The name is appropriate. Although the mountains surround and overlook

[1] For this chapter, see Maps 1, 2, 3, 5. [2] Isa. vii. 9. [3] 1Kings xiv. 17, xv. 33, etc.

[4] שֹׁמְרוֹן from שָׁמַר to watch, with the termination frequent in place-names. Aramaic is שָׁמְרַיִן and from this the Greek *Σαμάρεια* and Latin Samaria are formed.

it on three sides, Samaria commands a view to the west. The broad vale is visible for eight miles, then a low range of hills, and over them the sea. It is a position out of the way of most of the kingdom, of which the centre of gravity lay upon the eastern slope; but it was chosen by a dynasty whose strength was alliance with Phœnicia. The coast is but twenty-three miles away. In her palace in Samaria Jezebel can have felt far neither from her home nor from the symbols of her ancestral faith. There flashed the path of her father's galleys, and there her people's god sank to his rest in the same glory betwixt sky and sea, which they were worshipping from Tyre.

But the position has other advantages than its western exposure. "Though it would now be commanded from the northern range, it must before the invention of gun-powder have been almost impregnable."[1] The sieges of Samaria were always prolonged. In Elisha's day there was the blockade by the Syrians; when, *behold, an ass's head was sold for fourscore shekels, and the fourth part of a kab of dove's dung*(?) *for five*.[2] Even the Assyrians did not capture the town till after an investment of three years, 723-721. In 331, it yielded to Alexander the Great, who visited it on his way back from Egypt, in order to punish the Samaritan murderers of the Governor he had appointed over Cœle-Syria.[3] Ptolemy Lagi deemed it dangerous enough to have it dismantled before he gave over Cœle-Syria to Antigonus[4]: and being rebuilt it was again destroyed fifteen years later.[5] Fortified once more, it was able in 120 to resist for a year the flood-tide of Jewish conquest under John Hyrcanus.[6] He demolished the city, but, like so many other places devastated by the Jews, it was rebuilt by Gabinius, the successor of Pompey.[7] And then as the site had suited the Phœnician alliance of Ahab, so it fell in

---

LXX gives also *Σεμερών* and *Σομορών*, and Josephus *Σωμαρεών* (viii *Antt.* xii. 5): Stade, *ZATW*, 1885, 165 ff., *Der Name der Stadt Samarien*, disputes 1 Kings xvi. 24, that Omri gave the place its name, and takes the original to have been שַׁמְרִין.

[1] Major Conder, *Tent Work*. [2] 2 Kings vi. 25.

[3] Andromachus, whom they burnt alive. Q. Curtius, iv. 5, 9, iv. 8, 9. Others add that Alexander settled Macedonians in the town, Euseb. *Chron.* ii. 114, Syncell. i. 496, quoted by Schürer, *Hist*, Div. ii, vol. i. 123. Eusebius speaks of Perdiccas as refounding the town.

[4] Diodorus Siculus, xix. 93.

[5] Demetrius Poliorcetes against Ptolemy. Stark, *Gaza*, 361.

[6] Josephus, xiii *Antt.* x. 2, 3; i *Wars*, ii. 7. How Hyrcanus demolished Samaria is interesting: "He destroyed it utterly, and brought streams to drown it, for he made such excavations as might let the waters run under it; nay, he demolished the very signs that there had ever been so great a city there." This can only mean that there was a good part of the city below the hill.

[7] Josephus, xiv *Antt.* v. 3; i *Wars*, viii. 4. Germer Durand, in *Rev. Bibl. Trimestrielle*, tells of an inscription in Sebasṭiyeh from the 15th year after the rebuilding.

with the Roman policy of Herod, and especially with his plan of building a port at Cæsarea, and holding the roads from the coast to the interior. Augustus gave Samaria to Herod, who fortified and embellished it in honour of his patron, and, as upon other high places, a temple to Cæsar arose where there had been a temple to Baal.[1] Herod called it Sebaste, the Greek for Augusta, and this name has survived till now with the remains of his colonnades and gateways. The Herodian town probably covered and overflowed the large hill; it is said to have been not less than two miles and a half in circumference.[2] Herod settled in it a number of veterans, and used it as a recruiting-ground for mercenary troops. The character of its population—half Greek, half Samaritan—agreed with his policy of building fortresses for himself on what was virtually pagan soil; while the Gentile character of the soldiers whom he recruited is proved by their desertion to the Romans, in the great Jewish revolts.[3] In spite of its re-creation as a *colonia* under Septimius Severus,[4] Sebaste dwindled to a small town,[5] though the seat of a bishop, and the centre of a large civil district. The Crusaders restored the Episcopal See, with a Gothic cathedral, whose ruins stand by the columns of Herod. Then the town shrank to a miserable village. For as long as there ruled in the land a power with no interests towards the coast and sea, Samaria was forced to yield again to the central Shechem the supremacy which Ahab and Herod, with their western obligations, had taken from Shechem to give her.[6]

Amid the peaceful beauty of the scene—the secluded vale covered with corn-fields, through which winding streams flash and glisten into the hazy distance, and the gentle hill rises without a scarp to the olives waving over its summit—it is possible to appreciate Isaiah's name for Samaria, *the crown of pride of Ephraim, the flower of his glorious beauty which is on the head of the fat valley*.[7] Only the more hard is it to realise how often such a landscape became

[1] Cf. 1 Kings xvi. 32, i *Wars*, xxi. 2. Reisner excavated foundations of Ahab's palace, Herod's Senate, Forum, portions of masoned ramparts, W gate. Further *PEFQ*, July 1931, "nothing older than Omri".

[2] Josephus, xv *Antt.* viii. 5; i *Wars*, xxi. 2.

[3] In Josephus, xvii *Antt.* x. 3, Herod's soldiers, and in 9, the city of Samaria, are said to have gone over to the Romans. In ii *Wars*, iii. 4, and iv. 3, these soldiers are called Sebastenes. *Σεβαστηνοί*, cf. ii *Wars*, xii. 5, *μίαν ἴλην καλουμένην Σεβαστηνῶν*. These prove the opinion wrong which takes the *σπειρὴ Σεβαστή* of Acts xxvii. 1 for a cohort enlisted at Sebaste. Had it been so, its name would have run *σπειρὴ καλουμένη Σεβαστηνῶν*. It is the Augustan or Imperial cohort.

[4] De Saulcy, *Numis. de la Terre Sainte*, 274, quotes Ulpian (lib. i. tit. 15), and 280, gives a coin of Caracalla, COL. L. SEP. SEBASTE.

[5] The *Onomasticon, sub Σομερών*, calls it a *πολίχνη*, in the fourth century.

[6] For Sebasṭiyeh in the Great War see next chapter.

[7] Isa. xxviii. 1.

the theatre of war and of the worst passions of tyranny and religious strife.

Sinister fate to have belonged both to Ahab and to Herod! There by the entrance of the gate Ahab drew his sentence of death from the prophet of God; and there they washed his blood from his chariot, when they brought him back to his burial.[1] There Jezebel slew the prophets of Yahweh and Jehu the priests of Baal.[2] There Herod married Mariamne, and when in his jealousy he had slain her for nothing, there she haunted him, till his remorse "would frequently call for her and lament in a most indecent manner, and he was so far overcome of his passion that he would command his servants to call for Mariamne, as if she were still alive and could hear them".[3] There, too, he strangled his two sons.[4] Like most of Herod's palaces, Sebaste was a family shambles. It is not without fitness that a tradition, otherwise unjustified, should have assigned to this place of blood the execution of John the Baptist. The church was dedicated to him, and his tomb is pointed out in the rock beneath.

On this western flank of Samaria there was no other town of the first rank. But the passes as they emerged upon Sharon must have been guarded by forts. Some hold that Fer'on due west of Sebaste was Pirathon,[5] birthplace of one of the Judges. A more likely site of importance, both in the attack and defence of the east border of Mount Ephraim, is Kakon, a little way out upon the plain. Kakon commands the entrances to the roads up to Sebaste, and through by Dothan to Esdraelon. Kakon was always a frontier position. In the Crusades it was the limit of the territory of Nablus[6]; and in March 1799 it was at Kakon that a force from Nablus, coming down the Wady esh-Sha'ir and over the low hills by Bela' and Shuweikeh, met Turkish cavalry from Acre, and attempted to check Napoleon's march northward.[7] If it be in Northern Sharon that we must seek for the Aphek, at which the Philistines twice assembled their forces—once before invading Israel, and once before crossing to Esdraelon[8]—there is no more suitable spot than Kakon.

On the road from Shechem to Joppa—part of which runs along one of the natural frontiers between Samaria and the south[9]—there is no town of commanding strength, except el-Jit, and none of the names either upon the road or near it has been satisfactorily identified with any famous name of

[1] 1 Kings xx. 42, xxii.

[2] 1 Kings xviii. 13; 2 Kings x. 17 ff.

[3] Josephus, xv *Antt.* vii. 7.

[4] *Id.* xvi *Antt.* xi. 7.

[5] Judges xii. 15. But see pp. 231, 233.

[6] Röhricht, *ZDPV*, x. 246, at Kakon or Cacho, as it was then called, the Knights of St. John had a Casale.

[7] *Guerre de l'Orient*: *Campagnes d'Egypte et de Syrie*, ii.

[8] 1 Sam. iv. 1; xxix. 1. But, on the various Apheks, see pp. 219 f., 400.

[9] The Wady Ḳanah, see p. 172.

ancient history.[1] The other road from Sharon up the south frontier of Samaria to Bethel, passes nothing important,[2] till at the junction with the Shechem-Bethel road, in the extreme south-west corner of Mount Ephraim, lies Jufna. Though not mentioned in the Old Testament,[3] it must have played an important part in the defence or invasion of Samaria. Jufna is the Gophna of Josephus, the head of a toparchy in Judæa.[4] Judas Maccabæus fell back on Gophna after his defeat by Antiochus Epiphanes[5]; and it was occupied by Vespasian in his blockade of Judæa and by Titus in his advance upon Jerusalem. Whether Paul was taken to Cæsarea by this or by Beth-horon is uncertain.[6]

The south frontier of Samaria was defended, when it lay so far south,[7] by Bethel, and by the city of Ephraim or Ephron,[8] if the conjecture be correct that the latter is the strong village eṭ-Ṭaiyibeh, on the road up from Jericho. Behind these outposts, the avenues northward are covered by a series of strongholds, chiefly on the tops of high knolls, like Jiljilia, probably the Gilgal of Elijah's last journey[9]; Sinjil, a Saint Giles of Crusading times[10]; Seilun a

[1] On the road and its neighbourhood cf. Robinson, *LBR*, 133-141. El-Jit is probably *Γίττων* or *Γιτθῶν* of early Christian writers, who give it as the birthplace of the Samaritan, Simon Magus, Acts viii. 9; Just. Mart. *Apolog.* 11; Euseb. *H.E.* ii. 1, 13, etc. El-Funduḳ is the Pundeḳa of the Talmud, doubtless an ancient inn, πανδοκεῖον (Neubauer, *Géog. Talm.* 172). Fer'ata, east of Funduḳ, has been suggested both for Pirathon and Gideon's Ophrah. "Ophra, nicht zu weit von Sichem u. Tebes, wohl im sudösten des westmanassitischen Gebietes zu suchen" (Budde, *Ri. u. Sa.* 107). Kefr Thilth, on W Ḳanah, is claimed as Baal-shalishah (2 Kings iv. 42), cf. Baith-Sarisa of Eus. 13 m. W of Lydda (1 Sam. ix. 4); the last spur of hill which the road descends has a village (Hableh), a good site, unidentified; and little more than a mile out on the plain is Jiljuliyeh, an ancient Gilgal, but not (as Robinson) the place in Joshua xii. 23, where with LXX we ought to read Galilee.

[2] Ḳibbiah, to the S among the hills NE from Lydda, is probably Gibbethon, which Northern Israel sought to take from the Philistines (1 Kings xv. 27). Timnath-heres (Judges ii. 9), Timnath-serah (Josh. xix. 50; xxiv. 30), the city of Joshua has been placed at Kefr Haris, 9 m. S of Shechem. Buhl (p. 170) identifies the former with Timnath (1 Macc. ix. 50) and modern Tibne.

[3] Unless it be the Ophni of Benjamin (Josh. xviii. 24). [4] Josephus, iii *Wars*, iii. 5.

[5] *Id.* i *Wars*, i. 5. [6] Robinson, *Bib. Res.* iii. 77 ff.; *LR*, 138. [7] See pp. 172 f.

[8] 2 Sam. xiii. 23; 2 Chron. xiii. 19, Hebrew text Ephron, margin Ephraim, John xi. 54 (the city to which our Lord retired before the passover)—the Aphairema of 1 Macc. xi. 34; xiii *Antt.* iv. 9, one of three toparchies taken from Samaria and added to Judæa (see p. 250), about 145 B.C. Cf. Schürer, *Hist.* Div. i, vol. i, 246. Schlatter, *Z. Topog. u. Gesch. Pal.* 243-246, quotes Hecatæus for the opinion that Alexander ceded these districts to the Jews (?).

[9] 2 Kings ii. 1.

[10] Sinjil, a Casale or manor of the Order of St. John, was presented to them by a Robert of St. Giles, Prutz, *ZDPV*, iv. 166. Hence its name: one of the few which the Crusaders stamped on the land.

tell, probably identical with Shiloh, the sanctuary of the Ark, destroyed by the Philistines after the battle of Ebenezer, and desolate till about 300 B.C., in Christian times with two large churches[1]; and Ḳuriyat, one of the sites proposed for Koreæ,[2] which Pompey occupied on his march from Scythopolis to Jericho. Somewhere near Koreæ lay the Hasmonæan fortress of Alexandrium—"a stronghold fortified with the utmost magnificence on a high mountain".[3] Alexandrium played a frequent part in the civil wars of the Jews, in the Roman invasions, and in Herod's life. Pompey occupied it. Gabinius besieged it, during which siege Mark Antony distinguished himself.[4] Herod confined Mariamne within it,[5] and buried his strangled sons there, "where their uncle by their mother's side, and the greatest part of their ancestors had been deposited".[6] Neither Koreæ nor Alexandrium has been identified past doubt. If Ḳuriyat be Koreæ, Alexandrium, no resemblance of which name survives, may be the Mejdel Beni-Fadl, from which a Roman road went down to Phaselis or Khurbet Faṣ-ail farther south.[7] But some recognise Koreæ in Ḳurawa, at the mouth of the Wady Far'ah on the Jordan Valley, and place Alexandrium above it on the prominent Horn of Ṣurṭabeh. Till traces of the name Alexandrium be discovered, the matter remains uncertain.[8]

We are now round upon the eastern flank of Samaria. At no time do the passes penetrating this appear to have been protected by fortresses on the Jordan. The kings of Israel held both sides of the Jordan, and built their

[1] All which has been suggested by the excavations in 1929 of Hans Kjaer and a Danish Society, *JPOS*, x. 1920, 87-174; *PEFQ*, 1927, 202 ff.; *id.* 85, A. T. Richardson prefers Beit-Sila in Benjamin; *id.* 157 f., W. F. Albright: "the first stratum [at Seilun] represents the transition from Late Bronze to Early Iron—from the 13th to the 11th cents." B.C. Later excavations in *PEFQ*, April 1931, 71 ff., illustrate the ruin of Shiloh by the Philistines, 1 Sam. iv; and reveal remains of Byzantine churches.

[2] Robinson, *Bib. Res.* iii. 83. [3] Josephus, i *Wars*, vi. 5. [4] *Id.* xiv *Antt.* v. 2-4.

[5] Josephus, xv *Antt.* vii. 1.

[6] *Id.* xvi *Antt.* xi. 7.

[7] Mejdel B. Fadl is 2146, Kh. Bkt. el-Ḳusr 2906 feet above the sea.

[8] Not Gildemeister, *ZDPV*, 1881, 245, as Schürer says (*Hist.* Div. i., vol. i, 320 n.), proposed Ḳurawa and Ṣurṭabeh; but Zschokke, in 1866 in *Beiträge z. Topogr. der westl. Jordan's Au* (Jerusalem, 1866). The case between the two Koreæs is: (1) Josephus says "Pompey passed by Pella and Scythopolis, he came to Koreæ, the first entrance into Judæa, when one comes through the inlands" (xiv *Antt.* 3, 4). This suits both Ḳurawa and Ḳuriyat, for both are on what was then the frontier between Samaria and Judæa. (2) Pompey took Koreæ and Alexandrium on the way from Scythopolis to Jericho. His straightest line would be down the Ghor, and past Ḳurawa. But this road down the Ghor was dangerous and very warm: it was not longer to come up into Mt. Ephraim as far as Koreæ, and then go down to Jericho. (3) No city, village, or ruin is called Ḳurawa; but a village is at Ḳuriyat. (4) On Ṣurṭabeh are ruins, but

fortresses to the east, like Jeroboam's Penuel and Ahab's Ramoth; while the towns which the Herods built in the Valley were not intended for military, but for agricultural purposes. Herod the Great founded Phaselis, near the mouth of Wady Faṣ-ail; and the "village" which his son Archelaus built and called after himself Archelais, probably lay close by to the south. The district is fertile, but had not been cultivated before it was thus colonised. It became one of the famous gardens of Syria, and its palm-groves stretched to those of Jericho.[1]

But if the eastern passes of Mount Ephraim had no fortresses by their mouths in the Jordan Valley, several guarded their upper ends. There were Bezek on the road from Shechem to Beth-shan, Tirzah (if Tirzah be Teiaṣir, and not, as is more probable, Ṭulluzah) at the junction of the Beth-shan and Abel-Meholah roads, and Thebez at the top of the road down the Buḳei'a. Some fortress surely covered the top of the Wady Far'ah—Pirathon, I suggest, the name of which contains the same radicals as Far'ah, and is probably the Pharathon that is combined in First Maccabees with Timnath, another name of which are echoes in the district.[2] At the top of Wady el-Ifjim stood Taanath-shiloh.[3]

---

not corresponding to Josephus' account of the size of Alexandrium. No other passage in which the latter is mentioned throws light. The question is by no means so clear as Schürer feels, who decides for Ḳurawa and Ṣurṭabeh.—Further on Alexandrium, see Strabo, xvi, ii. 40. Cf. Clermont-Ganneau, *PEFQ*, 1896, p. 79.

[1] Josephus (xvi *Antt.* v. 2; i *Wars*, xxi. 9), Pliny (*H.N.* v. 15), and others speak of the palms of Jericho, Phaselis, Archelais, and Livias; cf. Ptolemy, v. 16, (7.) Herod left Phaselis to Salome (xvii *Antt.* viii. 1, ii *Wars*, vi. 3). She bequeathed Phaselis and Archelais, "where is a great plantation of palm-trees" (xviii *Antt.* ii. 2), "her plantation of palm-trees that was in Phaselis" (ii *Wars*, ix. 1), to Julia, wife of Augustus. Brocardus (12th cent.) mentions the village Phasellum in the Ghor, and Eli Smith discovered the name Fuṣail attached to ruins, a great spring and the wady. Phaselis, therefore, is beyond doubt. But the name Archelais has not been found. Josephus calls it a "village" (xvii *Antt.* xiii. 1), and puts it near Neara—probably *Νοοράθ* of the *Onom.*, 5 miles from Jericho; The *Tabul. Peuting.* fixes it on the Roman road, 12 m. N of Jericho. If this figure is right (another, stating Archelais is only 24 miles from Scythopolis, is wrong, since the whole distance from Jericho to Scythopolis is 48, not 15, Schürer, Div. i, vol. ii. 41), that would bring us to a heap of ruins, nearly 2 miles south of Phaselis, at the mouth of W Unkur edh-Dhib. The *PEF* map places Archelais at the mouth of W Far'ah, and Boettger (*Topogr. Hist. Lexicon zu den Schriften des Fl. Josephus*) at Buseiliyeh, in the same valley.

[2] For Pirathon, פרעתון, Judges xii. 13-15. *Τὴν θαμναθὰ φαραθων* (1 Macc. ix. 50) is one place; and *θαμναθὰ*, Timnah, perhaps, may be recognised in the name Tammun, common at the head of W Far'ah.

[3] Josh. xvi. 6: identified by Van de Velde with Ta'ana, Thena.

On the north frontier the fortresses were of greater importance. We have seen that from the Plain of Esdraelon there leads south into the heart of the province a succession of plains, connected by easy passes. It is the widest avenue into both Samaria and Judæa,[1] and has an issue to Sharon as well as to Esdraelon. It was, therefore, sought not only by invaders of Israel from the north, but by those from east and west[2] as well. The writer of the Book of Judith, whether his book be history or not, testifies to the strategical importance of this line of entrance into Samaria. He calls its various steps the "Anabases of the hill-country, for by them was the entry into Judæa", and says, "it was easy to stop the invaders as they advanced (the pass being narrow) in double file at most".[3]

Commanding the passes and plains are a series of promontories and isolated knolls; some of these were Samaria's northern fortresses. The Book of Judith mentions three, of which the farthest south was Geba, another Dothan, both still so called, and a third Bethulia, whose name cannot be recovered with certainty—it may lurk in Meselieh or Meithalun, or have been succeeded by Sanur.[4]

At the mouth of the pass which leads from Esdraelon lay En-gannim, the present Jenin. This was never a fortress, for it is strong only in water,

[1] Even Judæa, as the Book of Judith emphasises.

[2] So the Midianites penetrated Mount Ephraim so far as to make the Israelites hide themselves even at Ophrah (Judges vi. 11); and the Philistines appear to have come by this way (1 Sam. iv).

[3] . . . *τὰς ἀναβάσεις τῆς ὀρεινῆς ὅτι δι' αὐτῶν ἦν ἡ εἴσοδος εἰς τὴν 'Ιουδαίαν καὶ ἦν εὐχερῶς διακωλῦσαι αὐτοὺς προσβαίνοντας, στενῆς τῆς προσβάσεως οὔσης, ἐπ' ἄνδρας τοὺς πάντας δύο* (Judith iv. 7). The extract is from the letter of the high priest charging the inhabitants to hold the passes. The last remark is exaggerated. On "La Véracité du Livre Judith" see Raboisson, *Revue Illustrée de la Terre Sainte*, 1894.

[4] Geba, Judith iii. 10, now Jeba', 4 m. N of Sebasṭiyeh, Geba' of the Talmud (Neubauer, *Géogr. du T.* 264). Dothan, a strong place in Elisha's time, 2 Kings vi. 13; in Judith it is Dothaim, iv. 6, vii. 3, 18, viii. 3. Bethulia, the stronghold of Israel against Holofernes, iv. 6, vi. 10, 11, 14, vii. 1-20, etc., is placed at Meselieh by Conder, *Handbook*, 289; Sanur, which in 1830 stood a long siege, has also been suggested, the chief fortress on the line. Marta (quoted in *ZDPV*, xii. 117) says Bethulia was near el-Barid, NW of Jenin, and believes to have found in Kh. Ḥaraiḳ el-Mellaḥ an Arabic repetition of the name Beit-Falo, which stands for Bethulia in the Syriac version. But C. C. Torrey (*Journ. Amer. Oriental Soc.*) points out it was a large city, and argues for its being a pseudonym for Shechem with the topography of which it agrees. Also in the *Florilegium Melchior de Vogué*, 1909, he takes Betomesthaim (Judith iv. 6, xv. 4) as a pseudonym for Samaria, reading Betomesphai, = בית מצפה = שמרון Heb. for Samaria. A. Condamin, agreeing, suggests through Gk. and Syriac Betomesthaim = בית משטמה, *place of enmity* (*Recherches de Science Religieuse*, Nov. Dec. 1910, 570 f.).

but was known as the frontier town between the later Samaria and Galilee.[1] Seven miles north of Jenin, across the plain, on a cape of Gilboa, with a view that sweeps Esdraelon east and west, stood Jezreel. Built by the same dynasty which built Samaria, like Samaria it lay convenient to their alliance with Phœnicia. Jezreel also covered the highways from the coast to Jordan and from Egypt to Damascus.[2]

As you look from Jezreel eastward, there is visible in the distance down Esdraelon another fortress, Beth-shan, the position of which, with its relation to the province of Samaria and all Western Palestine, demands description.

The broad Vale of Jezreel comes gently down between Gilboa and the hills of Galilee. Three miles after it has opened round Gilboa to the south, but is still guarded by the northern hills, it suddenly drops over a basalt[3] bank some three hundred feet into the valley of Jordan. This bank, or brow, which runs north and south for nearly five miles, is cut by the Jalud and three other streams falling east in narrow ravines, in which the black basalt lies bare, and the water breaks noisily over it. Near the edge of the brow, between two of the ravines, and on the south bank of the Jalud (where this is joined by another of the streams) rises a commanding mound, Tell el-Ḥoṣn, Mound of the Fortress, once the citadel of Beth-shan, the other quarters of which lay southward. The position, which may be further fortified by scattering the abundant water till marshes are formed,[4] is one of strength and immense prospect. The eye sweeps from four to ten miles of plain all round, and follows the road west to Jezreel, covers the thickets of Jordan where the fords lie, and ranges the edge of the eastern hills from Gadara to the Jabbok. It is almost the farthest-seeing, farthest-seen fortress in the land, and lies in the main passage between Eastern and Western Palestine. You perceive the meaning of its history. Beth-shan ought to have been to Samaria what Jericho was to Judæa—a cover to the fords of Jordan three miles off, a key to the passes westward. But there is this difference: while Jericho lies well up to the Judæan hills, and has no strength apart from them, Beth-shan is isolated, strong and fertile enough to stand alone. Alone it has stood—less often an

[1] In O.T. only Josh. xix. 21, xxi. 29. Josephus calls it *Γημά*, ii *Wars*, xii. 3, *Γιναία*, xx *Antt.* vi. i, iii *Wars*, iii. 4. The two former passages describe a quarrel at Ginæa between Galilean pilgrims to Jerusalem and Samaritans, which illustrates Luke ix. 52 ff.

[2] Jezreel is now Zer'in. The first clear references date from Ahab's time (1 Kings xviii. 45, 46; xxi. 1, 23, etc.). Previous instances of the name (1 Sam. xxix. 1, 11; 2 Sam. ii. 9; iii. 2; iv. 4; 1 Kings iv. 12) may as well be referred to the plain. See on the name, pp. 249 f. Macalister found no old pottery.

[3] The whole formation here is volcanic.

[4] As the Byzantine army did against the Mohammedans in A.D. 634.

outpost of Western Palestine than a point of vantage against it. The one event by which it becomes vivid in the Old Testament—the hanging of the bodies of Saul and Jonathan upon its walls—is but a symbol of the standing menace and insult it proved to Israel from its proud position across the plain. In the earlier history Beth-shan sustained an enclave of Canaanites in the midst of Israel's territory; later it was Philistine, and later, belonging neither to Samaria nor to Galilee, it was a free city, chief of the Decapolis, with an alien and provoking population.[1] In its long history, it was Jewish for only thirty years,[2] and gladly welcomed Pompey, who made it free again.[3] Other successful invaders, to whom it had opened its gates, used it as a base against the land which it ought to have defended—for example, Antiochus the Great[4] and Vespasian.[5] On the first occasion on which Beth-shan was seriously employed for the defence of Western Palestine, the stupidity of her garrison rendered her strength of no avail. In A.D. 634 the Byzantine army having suffered defeat upon the Yarmuk,[6] fell back across Jordan, fortified the bank on which Beth-shan stands, and scattered the water into marshes. The Moslem found these impassable, and sat down in blockade for some months, hoping that summer would exhaust the streams. But before summer came the Byzantines rashly attacked them on their own ground, and suffered a second and decisive defeat. Beisan surrendered. The battle was called the battle of Faḥl, Arab for Pella, which lies on the opposite side of Jordan; but in the history of Islam the day is the Day of Beisan. It settled the fate of Western Palestine.[7]

The only other serious defence of Beth-shan was also against Moslem attack, and was likewise rendered futile by the stupidity of the defenders. The Crusaders seem never to have paid the town that attention which its position invited and the presence across Jordan of the Moslem power ought to have extorted from them. Their attempts at fortification on this vulnerable portion of their frontier they concentrated on the castle of Belvoir, high above Beth-shan and the channel through which the Moslems were certain to sweep. The result proved their error. Beth-shan, unwalled and weakly

[1] Josephus, ii *Wars*, xviii. 3.

[2] Judas Maccabæus found it friendly in 164, but probably from fear or policy (2 Macc. xii. 29-31) it yielded to John Hyrcanus in 107 (?) (Jos. xiii *Antt.* x. 3), and was under Jewish rule till Pompey's arrival in 64.

[3] Jos. xiv *Antt.* iii. 4. For coins under the Empire, De Saulcy, *Numis. de la Terre Sainte*, 287-290, plate xiv. 8-13. Rebuilt by Gabinius.

[4] 198 B.C. Polybius, v. 70: its cession to Antiochus was *καθ' ὁμολογίαν*.

[5] iii *Wars*, ix. 7. Vespasian found it a good base against Galilee and Judæa.

[6] Others hold that this battle was fought at Jarmuth (Josh. x. 23).

[7] Muir, *Annals of the Early Caliphate. The Caliphate*, 104 f.

garrisoned, gallantly repulsed the first onset of Saladin, but within a year he returned and destroyed her, with Jezreel and another fortress in the neighbourhood, 'Afarbala or Fourbelet.[1] Belvoir held out for eighteen months more—as any well-manned fortress on that height could not help doing—but to what purpose? The Christian banner at Belvoir waved a mere signal, remote, ineffectual above the Arab flood that speedily covered the land. The mistake was to neglect Beth-shan. When the Crusaders left Bethshan to its fate, they sealed their own.

These few campaigns will have shown us the strategical importance of this remarkable town. But, from its position on the high-road between Damascus and Egypt, Beth-shan must have seen many other sights and persons of great name in history. It could not fail to fall in the way of Thothmes III,[2] but the earliest note of it in Egyptian literature occurs in the fourteenth century B.C., in the travels of the Mohar, who passed through it in his chariot: "Represent to me Baita-sha-al as well as Keriathaal: the fords of the Jordan —how does one cross them?—let me know the passage to enter Mageddo."[3] The name does not seem to occur in the lists of Assyrian and Babylonian conquests, but Holofernes rested here, and if he as well as Pompey and Saladin—all three advancing from Damascus to invade Western Palestine—occupied Beth-shan, then Tiglath-pileser and Sargon, with the same line of march, probably did so too. An older Cleopatra visited Bethshan when she made her treaty with Alexander Jannæus[4]; and Vespasian caused his legions to winter in its warmth.[5] Josephus says that in his time Beth-shan—then called Scythopolis—was the largest city of the Decapolis.[6] Its territory was wide and rich.[7] The ruins attest a high degree of wealth and culture. Many temples have been traced, and there is a large amphitheatre, of which so much is preserved that it requires little effort to summon back, as you stand in the arena, the throng and passion of the city in its Greek days. Twelve basalt rows of benches for the citizens—semicircles nearly two hundred feet in diameter—rise eastward just so high as to let the actors upon the arena

[1] Beha ed-Din, *Life of Saladin*, c. 24 (ed. Schultens, pp. 53, 54; William of Tyre, xxii. 26). 'Afarbala, عفربالا, is the Crusaders' Fourbelet, or Forbelet, a castle of the Hospitallers, not far from Jordan, and S of Beisan. Rey suggests Ḳula'at Maleh (*op. cit.* 427).

[2] In the list of places conquered by him in Palestine is a Bathshal; but neither Mr. Tomkins nor Professor Sayce identifies this with Beth-shan. II. *Rec. of Past*, v. 52. Müller (*op. cit.* p. 193) denies that Bet-sa-el = Beth-shan.

[3] I. *Rec. of Past*, ii. 112; cf. II. *id.* v. 52.

[4] Josephus, xiii *Antt.* xiii. 2.

[5] iv *Wars*, ii. 1. Beth-shan is 320 ft. below the sea.

[6] iii *Wars*, ix. 7.

[7] Polybius, v. 70; Josephus, *Life*, 9. It bordered with Gadara.

see, over the mass of faces, the line of the Gilead hills over Jordan.[1] No Christian can stand among these ruins—the best preserved west of the Jordan—without remembering that in the persecutions of Decius and Diocletian Syrian amphitheatres were used for the slaughter of the confessors of Christ. The citadel frowned over all from the north.

In Christian times Beth-shan was still a noble city,[2] an episcopal see,[3] full of monks, and the birthplace of some Christian literature.[4] The fertile country was well cultivated in ancient times; like Jericho, the town was surrounded by palm-groves. The linen of Scythopolis was famed over the world.[5] Moslem war and waste swept all this away. The Crusaders, as we have seen, did little to revive the town, and, since Saladin dismantled it, Beisan has been little more than the squalid village which gathers to the south of the unoccupied citadel.

In the first edition of this work, 1894, I wrote that "few sites promise richer spoil to the first happy explorer with permission to excavate". Operations were begun in 1926 by an expedition of the University of Pennsylvania, whose Field-Director, Mr. Alan Rowe, wrote me in 1926: "The wonderful truth of your forecast about the richness of the antiquities in Beisan has been amply proved by the excavations of the site."[6] Now nine strata have been uncovered, of which the lowest five, dating from the time of Thothmes III, 1501-1447 B.C., up to that of Ramses II, 1292-1225, disclose six Canaanite Temples, two on the lowest stratum for "Mekal god of Beth-shan" and his female counterpart, while of two of the time of Ramses II and in use till 1000 B.C., one to Resheph is identified as that *house of Dagon* on which Saul's head was fixed by the Philistines,[7] the other for the goddess Antit with small figures of her and a dish with the gazelles sacred to Ashtoreth, doubtless *the house of the Ashtoreth*,[8] in which they put Saul's armour, while *they fastened his body to the wall of Beth-shan* with the bodies of his sons. Other remains reveal a great serpent cult, and a *maṣṣebah*, the Canaanite image of godhead,

[1] There are fourteen entrances—for spectators, for actors, for wild beasts—and behind, beneath the seats, passages and exits. Half-way up the benches are recesses, said to have contained brass sounding-tubes (Irby and Mangles' *Travels*, 301, 302; Robinson, *LBR*, 318).

[2] Euseb. *Onom.* Bethshan, ἐπίσημος.

[3] For a list of its bishops (the bishop of the time was present at Nice) see Reland, *Palæst.*, under Scythopolis.

[4] Basilides and Cyril.

[5] On the palms, Sozomen, *H.E.* viii. 13 (in 1891 one 30 feet high); on the linen, *Totius Orbis Descriptio* (anon. 4th cent.), in *Geogr. Græci min.*, ed. Müller, ii; cf. Marquardt, *Das Privatleben der Römer*, ii. 466.

[6] I urged the Pal. Expl. Fund to excavate but in vain.

[7] 1 Chron. x. 10.

[8] 1 Sam. xxxi. 10.

was found besides Egyptian images in human and animal forms, "the whole a combination of an old Canaanite high-place and a temple with altars". In these strata and the one above them, which represents the city under Philistine, Israelite, Assyrian, Babylonian, and Persian domination, the remains reveal the influence of and relations with Egypt, Mesopotamia, Asia Minor (Hittite), and Crete. The idolatry revealed is as rank and mixed as possible, and the strictures of the prophets, *Ephraim is joined to his idols* and the like shown to be just. The three upper strata are from the Hellenistic (Jewish and Roman), Byzantine, and Arab periods to the present day.[1]

Thus, under shadow of the high mound, where the streams rattle down in the beds they have worn deep for thousands of years, and Jordan lies in front, and Gilead rises over Jordan, it is possible to dream vivid dreams of a past in which Thothmes, Ramses, Saul and Judas Maccabæus, Pompey, Cleopatra and Vespasian, the Byzantines and first Moslem invaders, the Crusaders and Saladin, have all played a part. How these memories revived when in September 1918 Beth-shan became the goal and the pivot of Allenby's cavalry![2]

With regard to the names of this town, it is well known that it had two, and less known that, for a period, it had a third. In the Old Testament it is Beth-shean or Beth-shan.[3] In the Septuagint, 2 Maccabees, Josephus, and Greek and Latin literature it is Scythopolis.[4] But it claimed also, as other towns did, to have been Nysa, where the infant Bacchus was nursed by the nymphs; and this name appears both on its coins and in classical writers.[5] Beth-shan and Scythopolis were extant till the Crusades,[6] since which an Arabic contraction, Beisan, has prevailed. Beth-shean, in the longer of the two Hebrew forms, means House of Security, or Tranquillity, or, in a bad sense, Self-confidence; any of which would be appropriate to the natural strength and fertility of so self-contained a site, while the last might well be

[1] Reports by Alan Rowe, *PEFQ*, 1928, 73 ff., 110; 1929, 78 ff.; with plans and plates; by G. M. Fitzgerald, 1931, 59 ff.

[2] For this see ch. xix.

[3] בית שאן, Josh. xvii. 11, 16; Judges i. 27; 1 Kings iv. 12; 1 Chron. vii. 29—from which verse we see that Beth-shean was a district as well as a town. But בית שן, 1 Sam. xxxi. 10, 12; 2 Sam. xxi. 12.

[4] *Σκυθῶν πόλις*, LXX, Judges i. 27; Judith iii. 10; 2 Macc. xii. 29; Polybius, v. 70. But *Σκυθόπολις*, Jos. xii *Antt.* viii. 5; xiii *id.* vi. 1; Pliny, *H.N.* v. 16 (18), etc.; Scytopolis, *Totius Orbis Descriptio. Geogr. Græ. min.* ii.

[5] Pliny, *H.N.* v. 16 (18): *Scythopolim antea Nysam.* So Stephen Byzantinus. For coins, De Saulcy, Plate xiv. 8-13, No. 10, *ΝΥΣΑ·ΙΕΡΑ*; No. 11, *ΝΥΣ·ΣΚΥΘΟ·ΙΕΡΑ*. Others have a figure supposed to be the nymph suckling Bacchus. The coins date from Nero to Gordian.

[6] Fetellus (*circa* 1130) gives both.

given by the Hebrews to a city which so long defied them. This is uncertain; and it is possible that we have here simply the name of a deity, as in Beth-dagon and Beth-peor. To Mr. Rowe the serpent-cult in Beth-shan, *house* or *temple* of *Shan*, suggests a connection between Shan and the Mesopotamian serpent-deity Shakhan or Shahan. The origin of the name Scythopolis, or Scytopolis, is as obscure. The obvious derivation is that made in one or two occurrences of the name as *Σκυθῶν πόλις* or City of the Scythians, who Herodotus says invaded Palestine in the reign of Psammetichus.[1] Bethshan is on the line of such an invasion. It is also suggested that Scythopolis is Succothopolis[2]—the name Succoth occurring in the neighbourhood—but Robinson rightly objects to such a hybrid, the like of which does not elsewhere occur. It may, however, have happened that the Greek colonists, hearing some Semitic name in the district, should have wrongly supposed it to be the same as "Scythian". This may have been Succoth; or possibly that word of similar radicals to Succoth, which is used in the Old Testament as a synonym for the second syllable of Beth-shean, if Beth-shean be really the *House of Security*.[3]

XVIII. *THE QUESTION OF SYCHAR*[4]

The identification of Sychar would be a small matter, if it were not that its difficulty, as well as that of the whole topography of the Fourth Chapter of John, has been made the ground, by some for doubting, by others for denying, that the author of the Gospel was personally acquainted with the geography of Palestine. A well-known writer has said bluntly that there was no such place as Sychar, and that the Gospel commits a blunder.[5] And another writer[6] has stated a number of difficulties in the way of accepting the Fourth of John as the account of an eye-witness. I hope, by pointing out some material things hitherto overlooked, to meet the difficulties, and if not to place the identification of Sychar beyond doubt, at least to adduce enough

[1] Herod. i. 103, 105. Pliny, *H.N.* v. 16 (18), says Bacchus settled Scythians there! It is useless to quote Syncellus, a historian of the 8th cent.

[2] By Reland, with whom Gesenius agrees: *Thesaurus*, sub voce בית שאן.

[3] סכת, to be *still* or *silent*, is related to שקט, sh-ḳ-ṭ, synonymous with שאן, used like שאן of land as well as men, Jud. iii. 11 and parallel passages. The two occur in Jer. xxx. 10, xlvi. 27: ושקט ושאן.

[4] For this chapter, see Map 5.

[5] *Supernatural Religion*, ii. 427.

[6] Cross, *Critical Review*, July 1892.

evidence in its support to prove the charge of mistake unfounded and even absurd.

The objections to the topography of Fourth John are three:—1. Sychar is not known as a *city of Samaria*. 2. Even if Sychar be proved to be Shechem or el-'Askar, no woman seeking water would have come from either to Jacob's Well. 3. Expositions based on the accuracy of the narrative involve an error concerning the direction of the main road through Samaria to Galilee.

1. *Supernatural Religion* holds that there was no such place as Sychar, and that "a very significant mistake" has been committed by the author of John's Gospel—significant of his ignorance of Palestine.

To begin with, the writer of the Fourth Gospel is admitted to have been acquainted with the Old Testament, and in this the position of the locality in question, *the parcel of ground that Jacob gave to his son Joseph*, is more than once carefully fixed. In Genesis xxxiii. 18 it is described as *in face of*, or *to the east of*, *the city of Shechem*[1]; and in Joshua xxiv. 32 as *in Shechem*. It is inconceivable that, with these passages before him, any student of the Old Testament would, in mere error, have substituted Sychar for Sychem—*Συχάρ* for *Συχέμ*. But the point goes further. Had the writer of the Gospel possessed only that knowledge of the locality which the Old Testament gave him, it is most probable that like Stephen[2] he would have used the name *Συχέμ*. That he introduces another is a sign that he employed another source of information. All now agree that Sychar is not a copyist's error.[3] If, then, the author himself wrote it, he did so in spite of two well-known passages in the Old Testament—with which his familiarity is evident—and, therefore, it may be presumed, because of his acquaintance with Sychar as a name in the topography of Samaria.

In that topography Sychar can have stood—as a second name for Shechem, or as the name of a place near Shechem.

For the first of these alternatives a good deal has been said, but all by hypothesis. It is possible that, by their habit of playing upon names, the Jews may have called Shechem Sheḳer, *false*, or Shikkor, *drunken*.[4] But we have no proof of their having done so, and it is to be noted that the passage in Isaiah xxviii, which is quoted in support of the second, and etymologically the only possible, derivation for Sychar, does not describe Shechem, but Samaria, or Sebaste, six miles away. Trench's idea, that John, in his habit

[1] That is, if we adopt the rendering which takes *Shalem* adverbially, *in peace*.

[2] Acts vii. 16.

[3] This was Jerome's way out of the difficulty.

[4] שֶׁקֶר, *falsehood*, was applied to idols (Hab. ii. 18). In Isaiah xxviii reference is made to drunkenness, שִׁכּוֹר, as the notorious sin of Samaria.

of symbolising, was the author of the nickname, is too far-fetched.[1]

We turn to the second possibility, that Sychar was the name of a place other than Shechem, but, like Shechem, in the neighbourhood of *the parcel of ground which Jacob bought*. For this the first evidence we get is in the beginning of the fourth century, when two visitors to the land, Eusebius and the Bordeaux Pilgrim (the latter A.D. 333), mention a Sychar distinct from Shechem,—lying, says the former, before Neapolis, the present Nablus,[2] and the latter adds "a Roman mile from Shechem". Jerome asserts that Shechem and Sychar are the same; but he says so without evidence except such as all now agree to be unfounded,[3] and his negative assertion cannot stand against the other two, who say that they saw this Sychar distinct from Shechem—the less so, that in translating Eusebius Jerome adopts his Sychar without question. The next traces of a separate Sychar are found in mediæval writers. Abbot Daniel (1106-1107) speaks of "the hamlet of Jacob called Sichar. Jacob's well is there. Near this place, half a verst away, is the town of Samaria, at present called Neapolis." Fetellus (1130) says: "A mile from Sichem is the town of Sychar, in it is the fountain of Jacob, which however is a well." John of Würzburg (1160-1170) says: "Sichem is to-day called Neapolis. Sichar is east of Sichem, near the field which Jacob gave his son, wherein is the well of Jacob, at which a church is now being built."[4] Again in the Samaritan Chronicle, the latest possible date of which is the fourteenth century, there occurs the name of a town "apparently near Shechem, spelt Ischar", with initial Aleph, merely a vulgar pronunciation of Sychar.[5] Quaresmius, who wrote about 1630,[6] reports that Brocardus (1283) saw "a certain large city deserted and in ruins, believed to have been that ancient Sichem, to the left" or north "of Jacob's well": "the natives told me the place is now called Istar by them." Then the traveller Berggren found the name 'Askar or 'Asgar, with initial 'Ain, given both to a spring 'Ain el-'Askar, which he identifies with Jacob's well, and—more important for our question—to the whole plain below, the Sahel el-'Askar.[7] Finally,

[1] *Studies in the Gospels*, 86.

[2] From which Eusebius distinguishes Shechem, describing this as in the suburbs of Neapolis, holding Joseph's tomb. (Euseb., *Onomasticon.*)

[3] *Viz.* the confusion by some copyist of Sychar with Sychem.

[4] I quote Daniel (who very curiously confounds Neapolis with Sebaste), Fetellus and John of Würzburg, from the translations of the Palestine Pilgrims' Text Society.

[5] Conder, *Tent Work*, 41.

[6] "*Elucidatio Terræ Sanctæ*", Lib. vii, Peregr. i, Cap. ix. That Quaresmius gives not his own but the report of Brocardus is clear, for he says: "Fateor me non vidisse nisi Neapolem, nec vetus Sychar," etc.

[7] *Reise*, ii. 267.

the name still attaches to a few ruins and hovels at the foot of Mount Ebal, one mile and three-quarters east north-east from Nablus and little over half a mile north from Jacob's well.[1] The question is, Can 'Askar be derived from Sychar through Ischar? Robinson says no: "the fact that 'Askar begins with the letter 'Ain excludes all idea of affinity with the name Sychar."[2] Robinson is wrong. Though the tendency is the other way, there are cases in which 'Ain has displaced Aleph. Conder says that the Samaritans in translating their chronicle into Arabic call Ischar 'Askar.[3] And it has been overlooked that we have an analogous case. Ashkelon in Hebrew begins with Aleph, but in Arabic this has changed to 'Ain. The case, therefore, for 'Askar, so far from being barred by the rules of the language, comes through this test in all its strength. And its strength, in short, is this. That in the fourth century two authorities independently describe a Sychar distinct from Shechem; that in the twelfth century at least three travellers, and in the thirteenth at least one, do the same, the latter quoting a corrupt but still possible variation of the name; that in the fourteenth the Samaritan Chronicle mentions another form; and that modern travellers find a third possible variation not only applied to a village suiting the site described by authorities in the fourth century, but important enough to cover the plain about the village. This may not be conclusive, but is at least strong, proof for the identification of 'Askar with Sychar. Certainly there is enough of it to expose the dictum of *Supernatural Religion*, that it is "evident" there was no such place as Sychar, and that the writer of the Gospel made "a mistake". The "evidence" is all the other way.

It may be said that the name Sychar was fastened on the district by Christian pilgrims and sacred-site jobbers of the fourth century forced to find a place for it since it occurred in the Gospel. But the answer is obvious. For centuries after the fourth it was taken for granted that Jerome was right, and that Shechem and Sychar were the same place.[4] That all this time, in spite of ecclesiastical tradition, the name Sychar should have continued in the

[1] Described by Canon Williams and with greatest detail by Conder, *Tent Work*, 40-42.

[2] *Later Researches*, 133.

[3] *Tent Work*, 41.

[4] By Arculf, 700; Saewulf, apparently 1102; Theoderich, 1172; Sir J. Maundeville, 1322; Tuchem of Nurnberg, 1480. A curious opinion is offered by the Graf zu Solms (1483) that "on the right hand of this well" of Jacob, that is, to the south, "ist ein alter grosser Fleck aber öde, dass ich meyne die alte Statt Sichem seyn gewesen, dann gross alt Gebäw da ist. Und liget von dem abgenanten Brunnen Jacob zwen steinwürff weit, gar an einer lustigen Stell, allein dass es Wasser mangelt." But from Neapolis the well was two bow-shots off, so that "some say Napolis is Thebes".

neighbourhood, and solely among the natives, is strong proof of its originality—of its having been from the first a native and not an artificial name.

2. This leaves us with the second difficulty. Granted that Sychar is either Shechem, the present Nablus, or 'Askar, is it likely that a woman from either, seeking water, should have come past streams in their immediate neighbourhood to the distant, deep and scanty well of Jacob? There is a fountain in 'Askar: and a stream, turning a mill, flows down the valley "a few rods"[1] from Jacob's well. This the woman, if from 'Askar, must have crossed, while, if from Shechem, she must have passed near it and other sources of water. Jacob's well is over one hundred feet deep,[2] and often dry.

In answer to this, it may be said that the difficulty is not why the woman should have come to the well, but why the well should be there at all. That anyone should have dug so deep a well in the neighbourhood of many streams is perplexing, unless in those far away summers the streams ran dry, and the well was dug so deep that it might catch their fainting waters below the surface.[3] Be that as it may, the well is there, testifying past all doubt the possibility of the woman's use of it. Dug for man's use by man, how impressively among the natural streams around it explains the intensity of the woman's words: *Our father Jacob gave us the well.* It was *given*, not found. The signs of labour and expense stand upon it the more pathetically for the freedom of the waters that rattle down the vale; and must have had their share in increasing the fondness of that tradition which possibly was the attraction of Jacob's fanatic children to its scantier supplies.[4]

It is impossible to say whether the well is now dry, for many feet of it are choked with stones. Robinson says there is a spring in it,[5] Conder that it fills by infiltration. If either is correct, we can understand the double titles given to it, both of which our version renders by *well.* It is *Jacob's fountain*, *πήγη* (iv. 6); *but the pit*, *τὸ φρέαρ is deep* (iv. 11); and *Jacob gave us the pit* (iv. 12). By little touches like these, and by the agreement of the rest of the topography—Mount Gerizim, and the road from Judæa to Galilee—(as well as by the unbroken traditions of three religions), we feel sure that this is the Jacob's well intended by the writer, and that he had seen the place.

[1] Robinson.

[2] "Thirty-five yards", Maundrell; "one hundred and five feet", Holmes.

[3] Robinson suggests that an earthquake may have changed the disposition of the waters in the Vale since the time of the narrative. Possible, for little could tilt the watershed west, but we dare not count on it.

[4] Porter mentions a favourite well outside Damascus which drew the inhabitants a mile away from their own abundant waters.

[5] *LBR*, 108.

Thus, then, the present topography, so far from contradicting, justifies the narrative. The author knew the place about which he was writing.

3. By Jacob's well the great north road through Samaria forks, and the well lies in the fork. One branch turns west up the vale past Shechem, and round the west of Ebal to Sebaste, and Jenin. The other holds north across the mouth of the vale and past 'Askar. Now exception has been taken[1] to Lightfoot's and Stanley's speaking of this second road as the main road to Galilee. It is said that the latter has always gone by Shechem and Sebaste, and that the road which holds across the mouth of the vale turns north-east into the Jordan Valley at Beth-shan, and leads not to Upper Galilee, where our Lord was going, but to Tiberias and the Lake. It is correct to say that the Shechem road is the ordinary road, but wrong to say there is not a road across the mouth of the vale and on to Jenin. Robinson was told of such a road; and I have to report that in 1891, being anxious to avoid the road by Sebaste, which I had traversed, I was told by my muleteers that I could reach Jenin by following the Beth-shan road, and, when it struck east, keeping due north. Moreover, this is a more natural direction for the trunk road to the north to follow than round by Shechem and Sebaste. For if one takes the Survey Map, he sees this direction to be on the line of that series of plains which come right down from Esdraelon to opposite the Vale of Shechem[2]; while the road round by Sebaste has to climb a barrier of hills. Besides, such a road would be preferred by our Lord, avoiding as it did both Shechem and Sebaste, two large towns, one Samaritan the other Greek, close to which, if He turned up the valley, He must needs have passed.

So that Lightfoot and Stanley are probably correct; but the point is a small one, and does not affect the narrative in John. Upon the data given there, our Lord and His disciples, after their rest at Jacob's well, may have intended to take any one of the three roads; and that whether the city to which the disciples went to buy bread was Shechem or was 'Askar.

In support of the above argument I have the following valuable testimony to the superior quality of the water of Jacob's Well from Dr. H. J. Bailey, a medical missionary in Nablus for two years: "Apart from the sacred character of the Well, its waters have a great reputation for purity and flavour among the natives of El-'Askar and Nablus. The respective qualities of various supplies of water are a favourite topic with Easterns, and in a hot climate, where other beverages are almost unknown, the natives are great connoisseurs. From the nature of the soil the springs at Nablus are mostly of very hard water, 'heavy' as the natives say. Not unjustly they attribute many of their

[1] By Mr. Cross, *Critical Review*, July 1892. [2] See pp. 218 f.

complaints to this, and long for the 'light' waters of Gaza and other places. Now Jacob's Well has among them the repute of containing cool, palatable, refreshing water, free from the deleterious qualities of their other supplies. Frequently I have been told that after a hearty meal (which with them is appalling) a draught of this water will disperse the feeling of abnormal fulness in a short time. The fountain at El-'Askar gushes from the limestone of Mount Ebal, and is of particularly hard or 'heavy' water. The woman would, therefore, gladly take her jar to the celebrated Well of Jacob for a supply of drinking water."

"The source of supply to the Well has not been accurately ascertained, but is doubtless greatly due to the percolation of the rainfall, which may account for some of its special quality of 'lightness' (softness). It is not uncommon in the East to send a great distance for drinking water, especially among those who can afford to do so. The Woman of Samaria may, if poor, have been hired to carry for a richer person. At Nablus I used to send to a spring some miles from my house for drinking water and soon a regular little cavalcade repaired to this spring every morning and evening to supply the richer families with water which the English doctor recommended. Bishop Blyth of Jerusalem sends three miles to 'Ain Karim for his water supply."[1]

XIX. *ESDRAELON*[2]

In our survey of Samaria we have been drawn out upon the Plain of Esdraelon. The Plain has come up to meet us among the Samarian hills. Carmel and Gilboa encompass it; half a dozen Samarian strongholds face each other across its southern bays. Nature has manifestly set Esdraelon in the arms of Samaria. Accordingly in Old Testament times they shared, for the most part, the same history: in tribal days, though Esdraelon was assigned to Zebulun and Issachar, Manasseh, the keeper of the hills to the south, claimed towns upon it[3]; in the days of the kingdom, the chariots of Samarian kings,[4] the feet of Samarian prophets, traversed Esdraelon from Carmel to Jordan.[5] But after the Exile the Samaritan Schism, confounder of many natural arrangements, divorced the plain from the hills which embrace it, and Esdraelon was counted not to Samaria, but to Galilee, the southern frontier

[1] See on this Clay Trumbull and Masterman, *PEFQ*, 1897, 149 ff.
[2] For this chapter, see Maps 1, 2. [3] Josh. xvii. 11 ff.; xix. 10-23. [4] See p. 220.
[5] 1 Kings xviii. 44-46; 2 Kings iv. 8 f.

of which became coincident with its own southern edge.[1] More important, however, than the connection of either north or south with Esdraelon, is the separation which this Plain effects between them, the break it causes in the Central Range of Palestine, the clear passage it affords from the coast to the Jordan. This has given Esdraelon a history of its own.

Esdraelon is usually regarded as one plain under one name from sea to Jordan. In reality it is several plains, more or less divided by the remains of ridges, which once sustained across it the continuity of "the backbone of Palestine". Thus, nine miles from the sea, near Tell el-Ḳassis,[2] the traditional site of the slaughter of the priests of Baal, a promontory of the Galilean hills shoots south to within a hundred yards of Carmel, leaving only that space for the Kishon to break through. Eight or nine miles farther east, at Lejjun and Tell el-Mutesellim, the ancient Megiddo, low ridges run out from both north and south, as if they had once met. And between Jezreel and a spot west of Shunem, about twenty-four miles from the coast, there is a sudden fall of level eastwards, which visibly separates Esdraelon proper from the narrower valley sloping towards Jordan and is the sign of a former connection between Gilboa and Moreh. To north and south of the Plain the geological formation is the same.

If we overlook, as we may for the moment, the slight rising ground beyond Lejjun we get upon this great opening across Palestine three divisions—to the west the Maritime Plain of Acre, bounded by the low hills near Tell el-Ḳassis; in the centre a large inland plain; and upon the east, running down to Jordan, the valley between Gilboa and Moreh. Of these the Central Plain lies as much athwart, as on a line with, the other two, spreading north and south with a breadth equal to its length. In shape it is a triangle. The southern side is twenty miles from Tell el-Ḳassis by the foot of Carmel and the lower Samarian hills south to Jenin. The other sides are equal, fifteen miles each; the northern being the base of the Nazareth hills from Tell el-Ḳassis to the angle between them and Tabor, the eastern a line from Tabor to Jenin. This side is not so bounded by hills as the other two, but has three breaks across it eastward—one between Tabor and Moreh, a mere bay of the plain, with a narrow wady down to the Jordan; one between Moreh and Gilboa, the long valley aforesaid running to the Jordan by Beth-shan; and one between Gilboa and the hills about Jenin, also a bay of the plain, but without issue to Jordan. The general level of the Central Plain is 200 feet above the sea-line, but from this the valley Jordanwards sinks gently in twelve miles to 400 feet below the sea, at Beth-shan, where it drops over a high bank on to the Jordan Plain.

[1] Josephus, ii *Wars*, iii. 4.

[2] *i.e.* the Mound of the Priest.

This disposition of the land, with all that it has meant in history, is best seen from Jezreel.

As you stand upon that last headland of Gilboa,[1] 200 feet above the plain, your eye sweeps from the foot of Tabor to Jenin, from Tell el-Ḳassis to Beth-shan. The great triangle spreads before you. Along the north of it the steep brown wall of the Galilean hills, about 1000 feet high, runs almost due west, till it breaks out and down to the feet of Carmel, in forest slopes just high enough to hide the Plain of Acre and the sea. But over and past these slopes Carmel's steady ridge, deepening in blue the while, carries the eye out to its dark promontory above the Mediterranean. From the near end of Carmel the lower Samarian hills,[2] green with bush and dotted by white villages, run south-east to the main Samarian range, and on their edge, due south, seven miles across the bay, Jenin stands out with minarets and palms, and the glen breaking up behind it to Dothan. The corresponding bay on the north between Moreh and Tabor, and Tabor itself, are hidden. But the rest of the plain is before you, a great expanse of loam, red and black,[3] which in a more peaceful land would be one sea of waving wheat with island villages; but has mostly been what its modern name implies,[4] a free, wild prairie, upon which one or two hamlets ventured forth from the cover of the hills; though now Jewish colonies seek to overtake the waste of coarse grass and thistly herbs that camels love. No water is visible. The Kishon flows in a muddy trench, unseen five yards away. But in 1891 here and there a clump of trees marked a deep well, worked to keep a little orchard green through summer; dark patches of reeds betrayed the beds of winter swamps; and the roads had no limit to their breadth, but sprawled, as if at most seasons one caravan could not follow for mud on the exact path of another. Yet such details sink in a sense of space, and of a level made almost absolute by the rise of hills on every side of it. It is a vast inland basin, and from it breaks just at your feet, between Jezreel and Shunem, the valley Jordan-wards—breaks as visibly as river from lake, with a slope and almost the look of a current upon it. Away down this, between Gilboa and Moreh, Beth-shan shines like a white island in the mouth of an estuary, and, across the unseen depth of Jordan, rises the steep flat range of Gilead—a counter-part at this end of the view to the ridge of Carmel at the other.[5]

[1] Modern name Fuḳu'a, but the old endures in Jelbon on the hill.

[2] Which we have identified as *the Shephelah of Israel*. See p. 225.

[3] "Loose soil, mostly volcanic, which is tiring to horses, unfitted for cavalry, and in winter boggy."—*PEF Mem.* ii. 36.

[4] Merj ibn 'Amir, "meadow of 'Amir's son", wild and rough.

[5] This "antiphon" of Gilead and Carmel in the view from Jezreel illustrates the remark made on p. 225.

From Jezreel you can appreciate everything in the literature and in the history of Esdraelon.

I. To begin with, you can enjoy that happiest sketch of a landscape and its history which was ever drawn in half a dozen lines, *Issachar*[1]—to whom the most of Esdraelon fell—

Issachar is a large-limbed ass,
Stretching himself between the sheepfolds:
For he saw a resting-place that it was good,
And the land that it was pleasant.[2]

Such is Esdraelon—a land relaxed and sprawling among the hills to north, south, and east, as you will see a loosened ass roll and stretch his limbs in the sun in a village yard. To the highlander looking down, Esdraelon is room to stretch in and lie happy. Yet the figure of the ass goes further, the room must be paid for,

So he bowed his shoulder to bear
And became a slave under task-work.

The inheritors of this plain never enjoyed the highland independence of Manasseh or Naphtali. Open to east and west, pleasantest stage on the highway from the Nile to the Euphrates, Esdraelon was at intervals the war-path or battle-field of empires, but more regularly the prey and pasture of Arabs, who with each spring came upon it over Jordan. Even when there was no invasion to fear, Esdraelon still suffered: when not the camp of the foreigner she served as the estate of her neighbours. About 1884 the peasants got rid of the Arabs of the desert, only to be bought up by Greek capitalists from Beyrout.

II. Another thing clear from Jezreel is the reason of the names given to the Great Plain and its offshoots. These are two: Vale, or Deepening, and Plain, or Opening; the former connected with Jezreel, the latter with Megiddo.

(1) The Vale of Jezreel. The word for Vale, 'Emeḳ, literally *deepening*, is a highlander's word for a valley as he looks *down* into it, and is never applied to an extensive plain away from hills, but always to wide avenues running up into a mountainous country like the Vales of Elah, Hebron, and Aijalon.[2] We should expect the word, when joined to Jezreel, to apply not to the Central Plain west of Jezreel, but to the deep vale east of Jezreel, which descends to Jordan between Moreh and Gilboa. And it is so applied in the story of Gideon's campaign. The Midianites when they passed over Jordan

[1] Gen. xlix. 14. [2] See Appendix I.

pitched in the Vale of Jezreel,[1] and Gideon *beside the well of Harod*; and again *the camp of Midian was by the hill of Moreh in the valley north of* Gideon,[2] who presumably occupied, like Saul, the heights of Gilboa above the wells. The same identification suits other passages where the *Vale of Jezreel* is mentioned,[3] and we conclude that in the Old Testament it is the valley down which Jezreel looks to Jordan, and not the plain across which Jezreel looks to Carmel.[4] But in later times it is this latter which is called after Jezreel—not indeed now the *Vale* of Jezreel, but *the Great Plain Esdrelom*, or *Esdrēlon.*[5] This name has survived not in the local dialect, but in various Greek and Latin forms, as Stradēla,[6] or Istradēla,[7] Esdraelon.

(2) The Plain of Megiddo. While 'Emeḳ means *deepening*, the word used here, Biḳ'ah, means *opening*. From its origin—a verb *to split*—one would naturally take it to be a valley narrower than 'Emeḳ, a cleft or gorge. But it is applied to broad vales like that of Jordan under Hermon or at Jericho, though never to table-lands or maritime plains like Sharon. The Arabic equivalent is the name of the vale between the Lebanons, as well as of other level tracts in Syria surrounded by hills. A surrounding of hills seems necessary to the name Biḳ'ah, as if land *laid open*, or *lying open*, in the midst of hills. Such is the Central Plain of Esdraelon, girt by hills, laid open or gaping in the midst of the main range of Palestine.[8]

The name Megiddo has not survived, like that of Jezreel, and much controversy has risen about its site. On the base of the Central Plain just opposite Jezreel is a place called Lejjun—the Roman Legio, Legion,[9] and about a mile to the north of it on the same low ridge a mound, Tell el-Mutesellim. As Jezreel commands the mouth of the valley towards the Jordan, so Legio guards the mouth of the chief pass towards Sharon. It was, therefore, as important a site as Jezreel, and as likely to give its name to the plain. In Roman times it did so. Jerome calls the Great Plain both the Plains of Megiddo and Campus Legionis.[10] Moreover, the town named in the immediate neighbourhood of Megiddo—*Taanach upon the waters of*

[1] Judges vi. 33. [2] Judges vii. 1; cf. 12. [3] Josh. xvii. 16; Hosea i. 5.

[4] So correctly the *PEF* map, ed. 1890.

[5] Book of Judith i. 8, *τὸ μέγα πεδίον 'Εσδρηλώμ*; cf. iii. 9, iv. 6, *'Εσδρηλών*, but again with *μ* in vii. 3.

[6] The *Jerusalem Itinerary*.

[7] *Bordeaux Pilgrim*, A.D. 333; another MS., Stradela, ed. *PPT*, 17. In Fetellus (1130) Jezrahel.

[8] See Appendix I. [9] *MuNDPV*, 1900, 1, 5.

[10] Plains of Megiddo, in his *Pilgrimage of St. Paula*, iv; Campus Legionis in the *Onomasticon*, where Eusebius has *τῷ μεγάλῳ πεδίῳ τῆς Λεγεῶνος*, etc., artt. *Ἀρβηλά*, *Βαιθακάθ*, *Γαβαθών*, etc.

Megiddo[1]—is undoubtedly the present Ta'annak, four miles from Lejjun,[2] and there even seems a trace of the name in the name the Arabs give the Kishon, Mukuṭṭa'. Even without this item there was good evidence for Robinson's identification of Lejjun with Megiddo, and it was generally accepted against the rival site which Conder proposed in Mujedda', a place with ruins at the foot of Gilboa above the Jordan and near Beisan.[3]

But this century excavations upon Tell el-Mutesellim have modified Robinson's theory by discovering ruins from remote times and down to 350 B.C., which are evidence that the Tell was Megiddo, and deserted about that date when presumably the inhabitants moved a mile south to the position which the Romans, when they came, fortified and called Legio, now Lejjun. Of the details of these arguments and discoveries, I give a summary in a note at the end of this chapter[4]; and now only emphasise what is evident as you stand at Jezreel, the equal right with Jezreel which Megiddo and Legio had to bestow their names on that great triangle of plain among hills.

III. Now when we have made out Lejjun and Megiddo as places of equal importance with Jezreel—each giving its name to the plain, as well as holding a gateway into it—we are ready to mark the next fact about Esdraelon which the view from Jezreel towards Megiddo renders clear. This is, that the passage which Esdraelon afforded across Palestine was not so much that which seems the more natural, viz., from the Plain of Acre by the glen through which Kishon breaks at Tell el-Ḳassis, but that which comes over from Sharon by the pass at Megiddo. Look from Jezreel, and you see this to be possible. The Plain of Acre is not more visible to you than the Plain of Sharon; the Galilean hills intervene, and rise almost as high and broad between Esdraelon and Acre as the Samarian hills do between Esdraelon and Cæsarea. Look at the way Carmel lies. You understand how most armies coming north over Sharon, whether making for the south of the Lake of Galilee by Beth-shan, or for the north of the Lake by the plateau above Tiberias, would prefer not to compass the prolonged ridge of Carmel by the coast and so enter Esdraelon from the Plain of Acre, for that would be a roundabout road; but they would cut across the Samarian hills south of Carmel by the easy passes which issue on Esdraelon at Megiddo and else-

[1] Jud. v. 19.

[2] How names change! Legio is the Crusading Legio, Ligio, Lyon. In a Bull of Alexander IV (30th Jan. 1255), with an inventory of the properties of the Abbey of St. Mary in the Vale of Jehoshaphat, is "the Church of Ligio with parish and tithes", as well as "the Manor of Thanis", *i.e.* Taanach.

[3] Mujedda', town and wady, Burckhardt, *Travels*, July 2, 1843.

[4] Pages 268 f.

where. And so armies from the south generally came: Thothmes and other early Pharaohs; the Philistines when they shirked attacking Israel on the steep flanks of Benjamin and camped by the most open gateway of the hill-country opposite Esdraelon[1]; Pharaoh Neco, when Josiah met him at Megiddo, and was slain *when he met him*, and *the mourning of Hadadrimmon in the Plain of Megiddo* became a proverb in Israel[2]; the Romans, who set a great garrison near Megiddo, and called it Legion; Napoleon, in 1799, who, although he was making for Acre, did not take the sea-path round Carmel, but also crossed into Esdraelon by Subbarin and Tell Ḳeimun; and the British forces in 1918. If other proof be needed that in ancient times Esdraelon's connection with the coast was south, and not north, of Carmel, we find it in that list of towns frequent in the Old Testament—Beth-shan, Taanach, Megiddo, Dor.[3] These formed a strategical line of fortresses along the south of the one great avenue across country,[4] at the mouths of passes over into Sharon. Nothing could be clearer. The chief break across Palestine which Esdraelon affords is the break into Sharon, not that into the Plain of Acre. And, indeed, the roads from Acre to the interior, whether making for Jordan above or below the Lake, travelled then as now through the long parallel valleys of Lower Galilee. If caravans entered Esdraelon from Acre, it was to seek a gateway to Samaria at Jenin, or to cross to Sharon by the pass of Megiddo.[5] Few armies going north or south kept to the beach below Carmel; if those of the Ptolemies and Antiochi did so, it was because the Jews held the hills up to Carmel; if Richard in the Third Crusade did so,[6] it was because those hills were all occupied by the Saracen.

IV. We have followed the natural avenues to Esdraelon from the rest of the land. Let us now review the points at which they enter the Great Plain; for it is from these, of course, that its various campaigns were directed. The

[1] *αἱ ἀναβάσεις τῆς ὀρεινῆς, ἡ εἴσοδος εἰς τὴν Ἰουδαίαν*; Jud. iv. 6, above, p. 234.

[2] 2 Chron. xxxv. 22; Zech. xii. 11. Hadadrimmon (LXX *ῥοῶν*, pomegranate plantation) is perhaps Rummaneh, close beside Lejjun.

[3] Not, as in previous edd. of this work, Dor (Ṭanṭurah) on the coast, but a Dor or Naphath (or Naphoth)-Dor = Height or Heights of Dor, in line with the other three along the south of Esdraelon, as pointed out in *Bulletin* 4 of *BSAJ*, 1924. Site still uncertain. See above, p. 103.

[4] Josh. xvii. 11; Judges i. 27; 1 Kings iv. 11 f.; 1 Chron. vii. 29.

[5] An incidental proof that travellers preferred this road; in 382, St. Paula, going from Ptolemais to Cæsarea, did not keep to the sea, but crossed the plain of Megiddo by the death-place of Josiah. Jerome, *Life of St. P.*, iv.

[6] *Itiner. Ricard.* iv. 12-14. Cestius took the sea road, Josephus, ii *Wars*, xviii and Napoleon on his retreat, *Campagnes d'Egypte et de Syrie*, ii. 104. The railway from the coast to Jordan keeps north of Carmel.

entrances are five in number, and all visible from Jezreel. Three are at the corners of the triangle—the pass of the Kishon at Tell el-Ḳassis, the glen between Tabor and the Nazareth hills, and the valley southward behind Jenin. The first of these is the way of advance from the Plain of Acre[1]; Harosheth of the Gentiles, from which Sisera advanced, lies upon it. The second is the road down from the plateau above Tiberias, and Northern Galilee generally; it is commanded by Tabor, on which was always a fortress. The third is the passage towards that series of meadows which lead up from Esdraelon into the heart of Samaria—the Anabases of the Hill-country.[2] The other two gateways to the Great Plain were, of course, Megiddo and Jezreel. Megiddo, and the three towns in line with it, guarded against the approach of Philistines, Egyptians, and other enemies from the south; Jezreel that of Arabs, Midianites, Syrians of Damascus, and enemies from all the east.

V. With our eyes on these five entrances, and remembering that they are not merely glens into neighbouring provinces, but passes to the sea and to the desert—gates on the great road between the empires of Euphrates and Nile, between the continents of Asia and Africa—we are ready for the arrival of those armies of all nations whose almost ceaseless contests have rendered this plain the classic battle-ground of Scripture. Was ever arena so simple, so regulated for the spectacle of war? Esdraelon is a vast theatre, with its clearly-defined stage, with its proper exits and entrances. We will still watch it from Jezreel.

(1) The earliest historical battle of Megiddo was fought in 1479 B.C. between an army of Thothmes III of Egypt, that had come over from Sharon by the middle of the three passes into Esdraelon, and the forces of certain Syrian states allied against Egypt. The geographical details of the Egyptian preparation for this campaign and advance north from Gaza are of the utmost interest[3] in their close correspondence to all subsequent advances of armies from Sharon to battle in Esdraelon including even that of the British forces under General Allenby in 1918.

(2) Significantly Israel's first battle in Esdraelon was one in which they overcame not only a foreign tyrant but the use that tyrant made of the plain

[1] From Acre itself a more usual road lay further north across the slopes of the Galilean hills.

[2] See above, pp. 234 f.

[3] See especially H. H. Nelson, *The Battle of Megiddo* (Univ. of Chicago, 1913), with the text of the relevant annals of Thothmes and a reconstruction of the battle by the physical features of the region and full use of modern authorities on the history. Cf. p. 269 below.

for the purpose of preventing Israel's unity. On the eve of Deborah's appearance in Israel, Esdraelon, which had been assigned to Issachar, was still in possession of the Canaanites, and scoured by their chariots.[1] This meant not only that the entrances to the hill-country of Israel were in Canaanite hands, but that the northern tribes, Zebulun and Naphtali, were cut off from the southern, Manasseh, Ephraim, Benjamin, and the still ineffective Judah.[2] The Canaanite camp was at Harosheth, perhaps the present Ḥarithiyeh, on the Kishon pass, where it must have paralysed the maritime tribes of Asher and Dan.[3] The evil, therefore, was far greater than the oppression of Issachar; it affected the national existence of Israel, and its removal was the concern of all her tribes. This is emphasised by both accounts of the revolt. The Song of Deborah, a contemporary document, mentions every tribe, according as it took part or did not, except the tribe of Judah.[4] The prose account, preceding the song,[5] names only northern tribes, but describes the leaders as belonging to both ends of Israel—Deborah to Mount Ephraim near Bethel, and Barak to Kedesh-naphtali.[6] With regard to the battle itself, the two accounts agree as to the chief actors, the Divine help given to Israel,[7] the battle-field upon Kishon, the total defeat of the Canaanites, and the murder of Sisera by Jael. In addition, the prose introduces Jabin, king of Canaan, at Hazor,[8] names Harosheth as Sisera's camp, and Tabor as the tryst of the Israelites, and gives a different account of how Jael struck her

[1] Oort (*Atlas*, iv) and Guthe (Droysen's *Hist. Hand Atlas*) mark a band of Israelite territory across Esdraelon, including Jezreel. This is improbable, for it shuts up the Canaanites, who were powerful on the plain, in a little enclosure about Beth-shan —a blockade which could not have been maintained by oppressed and weakened Israel. Budde, *Ri. u. Sa.* 46.

[2] Judah is not mentioned in Deborah's Song, nor, of course, Levi.

[3] See p. 128. Others take el-Harbaj for Harosheth.

[4] Machir stands for Manasseh, Gilead for Gad.

[5] Judges iv.

[6] When we grasp the national significance of the crisis, we may discount the objections to the distance which ch. iv puts between Deborah's and Barak's homes (Budde, *Ri. u. Sa.* p. 105; Cooke, *The Song and Hist. of Deborah*, p. 11; Wellhausen, *Proleg.*, Eng. ed. 241). There was no reason for inventing it, and it is natural in the circumstances. Ch. v implies that *all* the tribes on the Central Range were roused, and does not indicate, as some allege of ver. 15, that both Deborah and Barak belonged to Issachar. On ch. iv see A. B. Davidson, *Expositor*, January 1889.

[7] Wellhausen's contrast between the two chapters on this point is manifestly overdrawn, *Proleg.*, Eng. ed. 241 f.

[8] The song has *kings of Canaan* (v. 19). Some attribute the insertion of Jabin to an editor (Bertheau, *Richter*, 2nd ed.; Dillmann on Josh. xi. 1); others, after Kuenen (Wellhausen, Budde, Cooke, Driver), hold the chapter is woven from two narratives —one of Sisera's defeat by Deborah and Barak on Kishon, as in ch. v; the other of a battle by Zebulun and Naphtali against Jabin on the north Jordan. This is far from

fell blow.[1] With the first and the last of these we have nothing to do here. The addition of Harosheth[2] and Tabor is in harmony with the geographical data, and it was natural to introduce them in a prose narrative, where more attention would be paid than in the song to tactical details. Accepting, then, the geographical contributions of chapter iv in supplement to the rapid sketch of the fighting in chapter v, we may take the following as a full account of the battle.[3]

The hands of the prophetess of Mount Ephraim were required to loosen the spring of the revolt, but the spring itself was found among the northern tribes; to them belonged the military leader, Barak, and this determined the place of muster not on Gilboa where Gideon and Saul, southern chiefs, afterwards assembled their forces, but in the strong corner at Tabor, where the main road enters the plain from Northern Galilee. To this, in the loose disposition of Oriental warfare—compare Gideon's and Saul's traverse of the plain by night in presence of the enemy[4]—it would be easy for the southern tribesmen to cross, unless indeed we are to imagine, and this is not unlikely, that the Canaanites were attacked by Israel from both sides of the plain. It is not necessary to suppose that Barak arranged his men high up Tabor; though Tabor, an immemorial fortress, was there to fall back upon in case of defeat. The headquarters of the muster were probably in the glen, at Tabor's foot, in the village Deburieh—perhaps a reminiscence of Deborah herself—which also in Roman times was occupied by the natives of Galilee in their revolt against the foreigner who held the Plain.[5] Here in the northern

---

probable, for (1) there is no reason why two such stories should have got mixed (as Budde owns, p. 62). The appearance of a Barak in both has been suggested as a reason, but a double Barak would be as difficult as a double Jabin (here and Josh. xi). (2) The attempt to distinguish the two narratives (Bruston, "Les deux Jéhovistes", *Rev. de Théol. et de Phil.* 1886) has failed. (3) Ch. iv is a consistent account. On the alleged discrepancy between vv. 16 and 22, see below, p. 257. Even if the Jabin portion were detachable, this would not affect the other divergences of ch. iv from ch. v, especially the mention of Ḥarithiyeh and Tabor.

[1] See Cooke, *op. cit.*; W. R. Smith, *OTJC*.

[2] Amenhotep II (1449-23) on a Syrian campaign crossed the waters of Arseth, which LXX of Jud. iv. 2 reads (Fl. Petrie, *Hist. of Egypt*, ii. 155).

[3] The date of the battle was probably during the reign of Ramses III. Some put it to his Syrian campaign and take the foes as Egyptian, pointing to the name Sisera as of Eg. origin, and to בפרע פרעות (v. 2) as if = when Pharaohs broke loose (Knight, *Nile and Jordan*, 257); others hold that *nations* in *H. of the Nations* (iv. 2) is northern nations, a Hittite confederacy, and point to the Beni-Sisera among the Cilician foes of Ramses III (Prof. Garstang in a letter to me).

[4] Judges vii and 1 Sam. xxix.

[5] Josephus (ii *Wars*, xxi. 3) speaks of a garrison at Dabaritta, as it was called in his day, to "keep guard on the Great Plain".

angle of Esdraelon Barak watched till the lengthening line of his enemy's chariots drew out from the western angle at Tell el-Ḳassis and stretched opposite to him with Taanach and Megiddo behind them. They may even have turned north towards the Hebrew position. Then Barak gave them battle in a fierce highland charge: *into the valley* his thousands *rushed at his feet.* It has been supposed that with the charge a storm broke from the north, for *there was fighting from heaven*, according to the poem, and Kishon was in full flood:

Torrent Kishon swept them away,
Torrent of spates,[1] *torrent Kishon!*

This means that the plain must already have been in a state in which it was impossible for chariots to manœuvre. As another feature of the battle the poem remembers the plunging of horses, probably because of the swamps:

Then did the horse-hoofs stamp,
By reason of the plungings, the plungings of their strong ones.[2]

The highland footmen had it all their own way. Their charge came with such impetuosity upon a labouring and divided foe, that the latter—and this, too, shows how far Canaan had advanced across the plain—were scattered both east and west. The main flight turned back towards Harosheth, and the slaughter and the drowning must have been great in the narrow pass. But Sisera himself, who doubtless was in the van of his army as he led it east, seems to have fled eastward still, for according to the prose narrative the tent of Heber the Kenite, where he sought rest and found death, lay *by the terebinth of Bezaanannim by Kedesh* on the plateau above the Lake of Galilee.[3] It is the same direction as the French military maps show the flight of the Turks to have taken in 1799, when Kleber's small squares, reinforced by Napoleon, broke up vastly superior numbers on the same field of Sisera's discomfiture.[4]

[1] Obscure plural word, LXX *of ancient times* or *deeds*—inappropriate in a song celebrating the first of these. Others take it of *onsets, i.e. battles*, from an Arab application of the root. But, from this it is possible to deduce *onrushings of water, sudden floods* or *spates*, and this is the most natural. See Cooke, *op. cit.* 48.

[2] For an interesting parallel to this in the morass or quicksands of Kishon which happened to the British in 1918, see below, p. 268.

[3] Ewing (Hastings, *D.B.* "Meroz") takes Sisera's flight as down the Vale of Jezreel, and identifies Meroz (cursed because it assisted him!) with el-Murussus, 5 m. NW of Beisan.

[4] The above identification of Kedesh is Conder's (*TW*). Cooke, *op. cit.* 12 f., suggests Kedesh of Issachar (1 Chron. vi. 72, cf. 76; Josh. xii. 22) between Taanach and Megiddo, with which he identifies the Kedesh of Barak, counting it an error to call this Kedesh-naphtali. But Kedesh of Issachar was too near the battle and too much under the hills of Manasseh for Sisera to flee there; still less would he have

Barak's was a strange victory, in which highlanders had for once been helped, not hindered, by level ground. But the victory won that day by the Plain over the Canaanites was not so great as the victory won by Israel over the Plain. Esdraelon is broad and open enough to separate two nations; but the unselfish tribes had overcome this difference between them. What in a century or two might have yawned to an impassable gulf, they had bridged once for all by their loyalty to the Ideal of a united people and a united fatherland. And the power of that Ideal was faith in a common God. Well might Deborah open her song with the Hallelujah:

For that the leaders took the lead in Israel,
For that the people offered themselves willingly,
Bless ye the Lord.

(3) The next invaders, whom Israel met upon Esdraelon, were Arabs from over Jordan, eastern Midianites. This time therefore they drew to battle not upon Kishon and the western watershed, but at the head of the long vale running down to Beth-shan; and as Manasseh was now the heart of the defence, the muster of Israel was not at Tabor, but at Gilboa. *Gideon and all the people that were with him pitched above the well of Harod, and the camp of Midian was to the north of him from Moreh into the Vale.* The Midianites took up practically the same position about Shunem as we shall see the Philistines occupy before their defeat of Saul.[1] Due south across the head

---

gone to it, if it had been Barak's seat. The *plain of Zaanaim*, A.V., is in Hebrew *oak* or terebinth of Beṣa'ănaim (אֵלוֹן בְּצַעֲנַנִּים, Q'ri בצעננים evidently one word as LXX take it, and because אלון is in the genitive to ״ב), also in Josh. xix. 33 as Beṣa'-ănannîm, LXX *βεσεμιίν*, on the border of Naphtali—another reason against identifying Kedesh with K. of Issachar. LXX *βεσεμιὶν* suggests Kh. Bessum on the plateau west of the Lake, the name Kedesh lies E below, and Damieh, perhaps the Adami of Josh. xix. 33, close by NW. Conder's choice is well supported. Another point is the alleged discrepancy between iv. 16, where Barak pursues the Canaanites *west* to Harosheth, and 22 where he pursued Sisera to Kedesh, *i.e. east*, if the above identification be correct. Now the double flight of the Canaanites, west and east, was probable, for in both directions lay Canaanite towns. If so, Barak might despatch the main pursuit west, while he turned east after Sisera. To read the narrative as if it stated that Barak undertook *in person* both pursuits, is to treat it with a rigour which would force inconsistencies upon any succinct historical narrative.—Flinders Petrie, *Hist. of Egypt*, ii. 323, says Kedesh of Issachar was not the Qedshu of Thothmes III's list.

[1] It is doubtful how far the name Moreh extended E, but if Beth-shittah, Jud. vii. 22, be Shuṭṭa, Moreh must be to its west, and is probably the hill above Shunem, now Jebel Duḥy. On the Midianites' advance, Schumacher, *ZDPV*, xx. 72 ff.; Burney "The Rout of the Midianites", Beiheft 27 of *ZATW*, 87 ff.

of the Vale is the rugged end of Gilboa—Jezreel standing off it—and on this Gideon, like Saul, drew up his men. The only wells are three, all in the Vale: one by Jezreel, one out upon the plain, and one close under the steep banks of Gilboa. The first and second of these lie open to the position of the Midianites, and tradition has rightly fixed on the third and largest, now the 'Ain Jalud, as the well of Harod.[1] It bursts some fifteen feet broad and two deep from the foot of Gilboa, and mainly out of it, but fed also by the other two springs, it flows strongly enough to work six or seven mills. The deep bed and soft banks of this stream constitute a formidable ditch in front of the position on Gilboa, and render it possible for defenders of the latter to hold the spring at their feet in face of an enemy on the plain: and the spring is indispensable to them, for neither to the left, right, nor rear is other living water. Thus the conditions of the narrative in Judges vii are all present, though it must be left to experts to say whether ten thousand men could be deployed in the course of an evening from the hill behind to the spring and the stream flowing from it. Anybody, however, who has looked across the scene can appreciate the suitability of the test Gideon imposed on his men. The stream, which makes it possible for the occupiers of the hill to hold also the well against the enemy on the plain, forbids them to be careless in using the water; for they drink in face of that enemy, and the reeds and shrubs which mark its course afford cover for hostile ambushes. Those Israelites, therefore, who *bowed themselves down on their knees*, drinking headlong, did not appreciate their position or the foe; whereas those who merely crouched, lapping up the water with one hand, while they held their weapons in the other and kept face to the enemy, were aware of their danger, and ready against surprise. The test was a test of attitude, which, both in physical and moral warfare, has proved of greater value than strength or skill—attitude towards the foe and appreciation of his presence. In this case

[1] See *PEF Survey* large map. 'Ain el-Meiyiteh is under Jezreel. 'Ain Ṭuba'un, where Saladin camped in 1187 ("Fons Tubania"; Will. of Tyre, xxii. 26), is on the plain. The name 'Ain Jalud is interesting. Beha ed-Din (*Vit. Salad.* ch. xxiv) calls it 'Ain el-Jalut, well of Goliath, with whose slaughter by David the *Jerusalem Itinerary* connects Jezreel (ed. *PPT*, see Stradela). But Jalut and the association with Goliath may be due to a mishearing of Jalud. Jalud resembles the Gilead of v. 3 of the story. It does not contain the 'ain of the latter, but we have many cases of 'ain replaced by a long vowel. Conder suggested 'Ain el-Jem'ain, or Well of the Two Troops, at the foot of Gilboa, near Bethshan, as the well of Harod. But, in a pass which has seen countless bivouacs and forays, it is futile to suppose that this name may refer to Gideon's two troops; while if Shuṭṭa represents Beth-shittah, we must suppose the Arab position and Gideon's camp to the south of it to lie west of Shuṭṭa, up the vale. Gilead may be a misreading for Gilboa: Le Clerc's idea (1708) preferred by Driver and others.

it was particularly suitable. What Gideon had in view was a night march and the sudden surprise of a host—tactics that might be spoiled by a few careless men. Soldiers who behaved at the water as did the three hundred, showed the common-sense and vigilance to render such tactics successful.[1] First, however, Gideon explored the ground, two miles in breadth between his men and the Arab tents; and heard, holding his breath, the talk of two sentries, which revealed to him what stuff for panic Midian was. The rest is easily told. It was the middle watch, that dead of the night against which our Lord warned His disciples.[2] The wary men, behind a leader who had made himself familiar with the ground, touched without alarm the Arab lines. They carried lights, as Syrian peasants do on windy nights,[3] in earthen pitchers, and had horns hung upon them.[4] They blew the horns, brake the pitchers, flashed the lights—that to the startled Arabs must have seemed the torchbearers and pointsmen of an immense host—and shouted, *The sword! for Yahweh and Gideon!* But no sword was needed. Cumbered by their tents and cattle, the Midianites, as in other instances of Arab war, fell into a panic, drew upon each other, and *fled* down the Vale *to Beth-shittah, to Zererah* near Bethshan,[5] *unto the lip of Abelmeholah*, the deep bank over which the Vale of Jezreel falls into the valley of the Jordan, *above* the unknown *Tabbath*.[6]

(4) The next campaign on Esdraelon—the Philistines against Saul[7]—is more difficult. It is uncertain whether the narrative (1 Sam. xxviii-xxxi) runs in our Bibles in proper order, and where Aphek lay.

As the narrative runs, the Philistines gather to war against Israel (xxviii. 1), and camp at Shunem, whereupon Saul gathers Israel, and camps on Gilboa (v. 4); the Philistines assemble at Aphek, and Israel pitches by a fountain in Jezreel (xxix. 1); the battle is joined, and Israel flee, and are slain on mount

[1] V. L. Trumper, *JPOS*, vi. 10, suggests danger from leeches; see, too, S. Tolkowsky *id.* v. 69.

[2] Jud. vii. 19 f., Luke xii. 38.

[3] Thomson, *The Land and The Book*, 450.

[4] If each had a torch in a pitcher, how held he his horn (as implied in ver. 16)?

[5] Rather Zeredah, 2 Chron. iv. 17, in the Plain of Jordan. It is the same as Zarethan, 1 Kings vii. 46; cf. Josh. iii. 16; 1 Kings iv. 12.

[6] I have followed the plain course of the text, for it suits the geographical conditions. But parts are difficult. Why should the Ephraimites complain of being called too late, and Gideon represent that the work had been done by Abiezer alone (viii. 1, 2) if vi. 35 assures that Gideon had already summoned the four tribes? No doubt most were sent back after the test, but there is no sign that those who passed it were only Abiezrites. Because of this some (cf. Budde, *Ri. u. Sa.* 111 ff.) strike out vi. 35, and the story of the test vii. 2-8, and leave the narrative as if Gideon never had more than 300 men, all from Abiezer, till after the defeat of Midian.

[7] See Ovenden, *PEFQ*, 1924, 193.

Gilboa (xxxi. 1). This order implies that Aphek was close to Shunem, on the line of the Philistine advance on Gilboa; and it has been sought both at Fuleh on the Plain, where the Crusaders had a castle and Kleber's squares in 1799 beat back the Turks; and at Fuḳu'a on Gilboa itself, on the road from Jenin to Beth-shan across the hill, as if the Philistines moved from Shunem to south-east of Saul's position, and attacked him from the rear, upon his own level. But neither of these sites has been proved to be Aphek.[1]

In the order of the Philistine advance, however, ought not Shunem to be placed *after* Aphek? Probably we should rearrange the chapters, so as to put xxix-xxx between verses 2 and 3 of xxviii. Then the order would run: the Philistine muster (xxviii. 1); their gathering to Aphek and the encampment of Israel by the fountain in Jezreel (xxix. 1); the Philistines advance towards Jezreel (*id.* 11); they camp on Shunem and Israel on Gilboa (xxviii. 4) the battle on Gilboa (xxxi. 1).[2] On this order, the uncertainties are the positions of Aphek and the fountain in Jezreel. Some place Aphek in Sharon, at the mouth of a pass into Samaria, identifying it with the Aphek of the previous Philistine invasion, when the ark was taken.[3] But this is not proved

[1] Unlikely for the Philistines to move from Shunem to the present Fuleh, for this is farther off than Shunem from Gilboa. Conder suggests Fuḳu'a. We passed over the road from Jenin to Beth-shan. From the plain up to Fuḳu'a it is easy for chariots and about Fuḳu'a is open ground, but between that and part of Gilboa above 'Ain Jalud is broken by glens.

[2] So Reuss, Budde, etc.

[3] 2 Sam. iv. 1. See chs. x and xvii. On the two Apheks at which the Philistines pitched, Wellh. *Hist.* Eng. ed. p. 39, and W. R. Smith, *OTJC*, 435. They absorb in this Aphek that from which the Syrians attacked Samaria (1 Kings xx. 26). This is out of the question. For Aphek in Sharon we have this evidence (published by me in *Expositor*, Dec. 1896). In the lists of Thothmes III, No. 66, is Apuku, after Joppa, Lydda, Ono and before Suḳa and Yḥm, where he had to decide which of three roads he would take over Carmel. So it lay S of W Abu Nar and may be Yemma. Suḳa is Shuweiḳeh, 2 m. farther S and Apuku or Apuki (Max Müller, *As. u. Eur.* 161) lay between it and Ono at the mouth of Aijalon. A fragment of Esarhaddon (681-668 B.C.) gives Apḳu as 30 Kasbu-Ḳaḳḳar (double leagues) from Raphia, from which it is natural to measure a place on Sharon (though Schrader, *KAT*², 204, takes Apḳu as Fiḳ on the Lake of Galilee). Jos. ii *Wars*, xix. 1 gives "a tower of Aphek", to drive the Jews from which Cestius Gallus on reaching Antipatris from Cæsarea "sent before" a party and taking it, marched to Lydda. This agrees with Thothmes' data and implies an Aphek between the 'Aujeh and Lydda. No name can be found with an echo of this, but two may be noted: Feggeh, 9 m. NE of Joppa, is not near enough to the Plain's limit to suit Lucian's text of 2 Kings xiii. 22, *Hazael took the Philistine from his hand from the west sea to Aphek.* In Arab names about Cæsarea cited by Röhricht, *ZDPV*, 1896, are Sair Fuḳa and Faḳin. A. Šanda (in No. 2 of *Mittheilung. der Vorderasiat. Gesellschaft*, 1902) reads LXX of Josh. xii. 18 as *Αφεκ τῆς Σαρών*, and deduces from Josephus, ii *Wars*, xviii, that it lay on the low hills between Nahr

and with the passage before us, it is hard to believe that Saul's advance to Esdraelon, which is given as simultaneous with the Palestine gathering at Aphek, should have taken place while the Philistines were still in Sharon, for this would have been to leave Benjamin and Ephraim undefended. Saul must have *followed* the Philistines to Esdraelon; and it is almost impossible to think of him leaving Jenin, the entrance to the hill-country of Israel,[1] and advancing to Gilboa till he saw the Philistines move across the plain to Shunem. In this case, while Aphek remains unknown, we might take *the fountain which is in Jezreel* to be that at Jenin, En-gannim, *Jezreel* being intended for the whole district. This would give a consistent story of the earlier stages of the campaign.[2]

However that may be, the rest is clear. The Philistines entered Esdraelon, doubtless by Megiddo. Had their aim been the invasion of the hill-country, they would have turned south-east to Jenin, and Saul would have met them there. That we find them striking north-east to Shunem, at the head of the Vale of Jezreel, proves that at least their first intention had to do with the Valley of the Jordan. Either they had come to subjugate all the low country, and confine Israel, as the Canaanites did, to the hills, or they sought to secure their caravan route to Damascus and the East from Israel's descents upon it by roads from Bezek to Beth-shan and across Gilboa.[3] In either case Saul must not be permitted to remain where he was, for from Gilboa he could descend with equal ease upon Esdraelon and the Valley of the Jordan. They attacked him, therefore, on his superior position. Both the story of the battle and the Elegy in which the defeat was mourned imply that the fighting was on the heights of Gilboa, and yet upon ground over which cavalry and chariots might operate.[4] The Philistines could not carry Saul's position directly from Shunem, for that way the plain dips, the deep bed of the

---

el-'Aujeh, W Balluṭ and W esh-Shellal, without excluding the possibility of its being E of Kefr-Saba on the slope of the range. S. Tolkowsky, *JPOS*, ii. 145, argues for but one Aphek, Fuḳu'a on Mt. Gilboa; but W. F. Albright, *id.* 184, for four or five.

[1] See p. 234 f.

[2] The other alternative, of supposing two narratives, one assigning the Philistine muster to Aphek, the other to Shunem, is not so probable.

[3] This would afford a parallel to their occupation of Michmash (1 Sam. xiii. 5) on the trade-route Aijalon to Jericho, and to the trace of Philistine occupation in Beth-dagon near Shechem, on the only other pass east to west across the Range. On the Philistines as traders, ch. ix.

[4] 1 Sam. xxxi. 1, *fell down wounded on Mt. Gilboa*; 2 Sam. i. 6, *upon Mt. Gilboa, behold, Saul leaned on his spear; and the chariots and horsemen followed hard after him*; cf. vv. 19, *high places*; 21, *Ye hills of Gilboa . . . for there the shield of the mighty is vilely cast away, Saul's shield*; 25, *Jonathan, slain on thy high places.*

stream intervenes, and the rocks of Gilboa are steep.[1] But they went round Jezreel, and attacked the promontory of the hill by the easier slopes and wadies to the south, which lead up to open ground about the village of Nuris, and above the 'Ain Jalud. Somewhere on these slopes they encountered that desperate resistance which cost Israel the life of three of the king's sons; and higher up the king himself, wounded and pressed hard by the chariots and horsemen, yet imperious to the last, commanded his own death.[2]

And David sang this dirge over Saul and Jonathan his son[3]: Behold it is written in the Book of the Brave.[4]

Israel, the Beauty is slain on thy heights,
How fallen are the mighty!

Tell it not in Gath,
Publish it not in the streets of Ashkelon!
Lest they rejoice, the daughters of the Philistines;
Lest they make triumph, the uncircumcised's daughters.

Hills of Gilboa,
Let not dew, let not rain be upon you,
Ye fields of disaster![5]

See pp. 257 f.

[2] This view was formed on the ground, and in the main is the same as that of Principal Miller, who surveyed the ground in detail, and gives a description of the course of the fight and plans, that include not only the contours, but what he believes were successive positions of the Israelites. He exposes the errors of Dean Stanley who describes the battle as on the plain, and only the flight on the hills. But he is not justified in declaring from xxix. 11 that the Philistines occupied the town Jezreel before the battle. He conceives Saul's position on Gilboa to be due to his rash design of adding to his kingdom the whole of N Palestine—rash, for so he left Benjamin and Ephraim undefended. This is not certain. *Least of all Lands*, ch. vi, plans on 151 and 171. Lord Bryce wrote me in 1914: "Is it not probable that the battle was on the gentle slopes rising to Gilboa behind Jezreel? On that hypothesis Saul's journey to Endor from his camp on the hills would be easier than if the Philistines got as far SE as Bethshan."

[3] Gloss: *He bade them teach the children of Judah dirges* or *lamentations*, reading קנות for קשת.

[4] ישר, the Upright, Valiant.

[5] The text is ושדיתרומות, which is unintelligible as the Massoretes divide it, but by little alteration reads ושדי מהומות or ושדות, *fields of discomfitures, frustrations.* Other readings are Lucian's הרי מָוֶת *hills of death*, which Renan follows, taking ושדי as a later variant wrongly brought from the margin; Stade's ושדי ערמות, *nor field of sheaves*; Klostermann's שדות רמיה. Another might be שדות ראמות, cf.

For there thrown to rust is the shield of the mighty,
Shield of Saul unanointed with oil.[1]

From the blood of the slain,
From the fat of the mighty,
Bow of Jonathan never swerved
Nor sword of Saul came empty home.

Saul and Jonathan, the lovely, the pleasant,
In their lives and in their death they were not divided;
Than eagles they were swifter,
Than lions more strong.

Daughters of Israel, weep for Saul,
Who clothed you in scarlet with jewels;
Who brought up adorning of gold on your raiment.

How fallen are the mighty
In the midst of the battle!

Jonathan slain on thy heights,
Anguish is mine for thee,
O my brother Jonathan,
Dearest wert thou to me.
Thy love to me was wonderful,
Passing the love of women.

How fallen are the mighty,
And perished the weapons of war!

(5) Esdraelon was the scene of another lamentation for a king in Israel. By Jeremiah's time it had been prophesied that Egypt would come upon the land, but the people did not heed, saying, *Pharaoh is but a rumour, the time appointed is past*. Jeremiah replied he should come, *as surely as Tabor among*

Prov. xxiv. 7: Justi, *Nationalgesänge der Hebr*. i. 72, *Hohes Schlachtfeld*. It is possible that דמים, *blood*, lurks in the last letters. This would be natural, for a common Semitic idea is that no rain or dew will bless the spot stained by the blood of a slain man.

[1] The parallel shows that *oil* refers to the practice of rubbing shields with oil to preserve them, and not to Saul, as if *not Anointed*.

the mountains, and Carmel by the sea.[1] So he did by Megiddo, till his host filled the plain between these hills as solid and present a fact as either of them.[2] Josiah rashly and needlessly put himself in Pharaoh's way. His army was routed, and himself mortally wounded as they met.[3] *And Jeremiah made a dirge upon Josiah, and all the singing-men and the singing-women speak of Josiah in their dirges to this day. So they made them a custom in Israel; and, lo, they are written among The Dirges.*[4] *The mourning of Hadadrimmon in the Vale of Megiddo* became a proverb in Israel.[5] The dirges of Jeremiah have perished, and, indeed, he deprecated the extremes to which such lamentation was carried. Israel was near a greater calamity which required all her tears:

> "*Weep not for the dead, nor bemoan him,*
> *But weeping weep for him that goeth away,*
> *For he shall never come back,*
> *Nor see the land of his birth.*"[6]

(6) The rest of the historical scenes of Esdraelon down to the British advance in 1918 there is space only to enumerate. But perhaps the mere succession of them will impress us, more than details could do, with the pageant of commerce, war, and judgement, which through the centuries has traversed this arena. From Jezreel you see the slaughter-place of the priests of Baal; Jehu's ride from Beth-shan to the vineyard of Naboth at your feet; the camp of Holofernes spreading from the hills above Jenin out to Cyamon in the plain[7]; the marches and counter-marches of Syrians, Egyptians and Jews in the Hasmonæan days[8]—the elephants and engines of Anti-

[1] Jer. xlvi. 18.

[2] It is doubtful whether Neco came to Syria by the land route, or (as Vespasian sent his troops) by sea, and Cheyne suggests Dor as his landing (*Life and Time of Jerem.*, 96). But the only ground for the latter is the conjunction in Herod. ii of Neco's ship-building with his campaign; and, if he had come by sea, he would have landed not at Dor, but at Acco, in which case he would not have marched so far S again as Megiddo. The battle at Megiddo suits the land route. The *Μάγδαλος* of Herodotus is a corruption of Megiddo. *Μενδή*, in Jos. x *Antt.* v. 1, is an error, מנדי for מגדן, and proof of the risks to which names in Palestine have been subject in seven or eight languages.

[3] 2 Kings xxiii. 29, *as soon as he had seen him.* See my *Jeremiah*, 4th ed. 393.

[4] 2 Chron. xxxv. 24, 25. [5] Zech. xii. 11. [6] Jer. xxii. 10.

[7] Judith vii. 3. *Κύαμων* = bean-field, has been identified with Tell Ḳeimun below Carmel; some find it at Fuleh, which means bean. The description of *Κύαμων* opposite Esdraelon (name of plain or of city?) suits both Ḳeimun and Fuleh.

[8] 1 Macc. xii. 41-52, Trypho's treacherous capture of Jonathan Maccabæus, another of the woes of this tragic Plain. Jos. xiii *Antt.* ix. 3: Demetrius II, defeated by Alexander Zabinas, falls back on Ptolemais (Acre); x. 2, Hyrcanus moves between Sebaste

ochus, the litters of Cleopatra and her ladies. The Romans plant their camps and stamp their names on the soil, Legio and Kastra; Pompey, Mark Antony, Vespasian, and Titus pass at the head of their legions,[1] and men of Galilee sally upon them from the same nooks in the hills of Naphtali from which their forefathers broke with Barak upon the chariots of Canaan.[2] After the Roman war the Roman peace, and for an interval of centuries Esdraelon is no more blotted by the tents of the Bedouin; but a broad civilisation grows between her and Arabia, Jordan is bridged, and from the Greek cities of the Decapolis chariots, soldiers, officials, and provincial wits on their way to Rome pass to the ports of Cæsarea and Ptolemais.[3] In the fourth century Christian pilgrims arrive, and cloisters are built from Beth-shan to Carmel.[4] Three centuries of this, and then through their old channel the Desert swarms sweep back, now united by a common faith, and the vigour of a new civilisation; you see before them the rout of the Greek army up the Vale of Jezreel.[5] The Arabs stay for nearly five hundred years, obliterating the past, distorting familiar and famous names. Then the ensigns of Christendom return. Crusading castles rise—on the Plain Ṣapham and Faba[6] under the black and white banner of the Templars, and high up on the ridge north of Bethshan, so high and far that it is called by the Arabs Star-of-the-Wind, Belvoir under the Red Cross of the Hospitallers.[7] Cloisters are rebuilt, and thriving villages, for justice and shelter given, bring tribute to the Abbey of Mount Tabor; pilgrims throng, and the holy memories are replanted, not always on their proper sites.[8] Once more by Beth-shan the Arabs break the

---

and Scythopolis; xii, Jannæus takes Ptolemais, and fights with Egyptian forces between that and Jordan, 103 B.C.; xiii, Cleopatra, mother of Ptolemy Lathyrus, besieges Ptolemais, and meets Jannæus in Bethshan; xiv. 1, so Demetrius Euchærus went up to Shechem at the call of the Pharisees; xv. 2, so Aretas must have come from Damascus to Adida.

[1] Pompey, 64 B.C., xiv *Antt.* iii. 4, iv. 5, Mark Antony under Gabinius, 57-55, *Ibid.* v. Cæsar, in 47, visited Syria by sea, *Ibid.* viii. 3 and 6, by sea to Cilicia, ix. 1: we know not where he touched (cf. Sueton. *Julius*, 35). Antony again in Syria in 40, *Ibid.* xiii. 1 and from 36-33 partly, with Cleopatra in xv *Antt.* iv, i *Wars*, xviii, Plutarch, *Anton.* 36-51. Vespasian reached Ptolemais in 67 A.D. iii *Wars*, ii. ff. Titus joined him, *Ibid.* iv. For these operations in Esdraelon and Lower Galilee, *Ibid.* vi ff., cf. Sueton. *Vespasian*, 5, Tacitus, *Hist.* iv. 51.

[2] Jos. ii *Wars*, xxi. 3. [3] Mommsen, *Provinces of the Roman Empire*, Engl. ii, ch. x.

[4] For authorities see pp. 35, 36. [5] See pp. 236 f.

[6] "The Bean": also called La Fève and La Fène, Rey, *Col. Fr.* 439; Röhricht, *ZDPV*, x. 231, 232. Known to Saracens as el-Fulah = "The Bean." Beha ed-Din *Saladin*, ch. 24, Abulfeda, ed. Schultens, 41.

[7] Kaukab el-Hawa; by Franks Delehawa: Prutz, *ZDPV*, p. 168.

[8] Röhricht, *op. cit.* on pp. 17, 18.

line of the Christian defence, and Saladin spreads his camp where Israel saw those of Midian and the Philistines[1]; through a long hot summer the castles of the Cross yield one by one, till Belvoir holds out alone, flying the Red Cross for eighteen months over a Saracen country. Finally, after two forlorn hopes—one of Andrew of Hungary, who carried the Cross to the top of Tabor, and was beaten down again,[2] and one of Saint Louis of France, who marched to Jordan and back—Esdraelon is closed to the arms of the West, till in 1799 Napoleon, with his ambition of an Empire on the Euphrates, breaks into it by Megiddo, and in three months from the same fatal stage falls back upon the first great Retreat of his career.

What a Plain! Upon which not only the greatest empires, races, and faiths, east and west, have contended, but each has come to judgement—on which with all its splendour of human battle, men felt *there was fighting from heaven, the stars in their courses were fighting*—on which panic has descended upon the best equipped and most successful armies, but the humble were exalted to victory in their weakness—on which false faiths, equally with false defenders of the true faith, have been exposed and scattered—on which since Saul wilfulness and superstition, though aided by every human excellence, have come to nought, and since Josiah piety has not atoned for rash and mistaken zeal. The Crusaders repeat the folly of the kings of Israel; and, alike under the old and the new covenant, a degenerate church suffers judgement at the hands of the infidel.

They go forth unto the kings of the earth and of the whole world to gather them to the battle of the great Day of God Almighty . . . and He gathered them together unto a place called in the Hebrew tongue Har Mageddon.

The Campaign of 1918

The British advance upon Esdraelon in September 1918 was not only magnificent in numbers, in plan and execution, but also of historic interest and importance through the similarity of some of its tactics and even of its incidents to those of the campaigns we have been following from the Pharaohs to Napoleon.

For this advance General Allenby prepared by massing his troops from

[1] At the fountain of Tubania, a little out on the plain N of Jezreel, cf. p. 258, n. 1; in 1186 when Saladin had to retire, but returned, won the battle of Ḥaṭṭin, 14th June 1187, and occupied Acre 9th July, took Jerusalem 1188, but Belvoir did not fall till Jan. 1189.

[2] Andrew in 1217, the Sixth Crusade; Louis in 1270, the Eighth Crusade.

the Jordan westward to the sea, while leading the enemy to believe that the main British attack would be delivered east of the Jordan and up the Jordan Valley, in which only a skeleton British force was retained. "The enemy was thoroughly deceived, wholly unaware of the devastating blow that was about to be dealt him."[1]

By the 19th of September the British line from the Jerusalem-Nablus road wound mainly WNW by Sinjil,[2] Jiljiliyah, Rafat and Mejdel-Yba to a point on the coast one mile and a half north of Arsuf. Before dawn on the 19th, after "a terrific bombardment" by their Artillery, and aided by the Air Force, the Infantry—English, Scottish, Welsh, Irish and various Indian regiments—along with a French detachment, began their advance, and their left wing fought a successful battle where in A.D. 1191 Richard Lionheart defeated the Saracens on Sharon, between Arsuf and the Faliḳ River; thus leaving the way open for the advance of the cavalry to the passes leading over from Sharon to Esdraelon. Ṭul Karm, the junction of roads and railways to Lydda and Nablus, was taken by midnight on the 19th and Nablus (Shechem) itself by the 21st, with the outposts of the British centre now on a line north of Sebasṭiyeh (the town Samaria) and Shuweikeh and with the enemy retreating north upon Jenin and Beth-shan and east down Wady el-Far'ah[3] to the Jordan.

Meanwhile the Cavalry in three Divisions had advanced from Sharon with sweeping success. The 5th Division starting from Arsuf reached Liktera by 11 A.M. on the 19th, and, taking the most westerly of the historic passes into Esdraelon by Subbarin, up the head of Wady el-Fuwar and past Abu-Shusheh near Tell Ḳeimun,[4] crossed the Plain riding down a Turkish battalion, that had come too late to defend the pass; and one Brigade of the Division was actually attacking Nazareth before noon on the 20th and just failed to capture the German Commander-in-Chief. The 4th Division and the Australian Mounted Division crossed from Sharon by the still more famous pass up Wady 'Ara and by Musmus to Lejjun and Megiddo, the route of Thothmes and other invaders from the south. Here they divided very early on the 20th. Part turning south by Taanach reached Jenin by 5 P.M., while the main body having captured el-'Affuleh on the plain and its railway station by 8 A.M. and having sent a detachment to make for the railway bridge over Jordan, marched down the Vale of Jezreel to Beth-shan which they reached at 4.35 P.M.—having covered seventy miles in thirty-four hours—and thence despatched a Brigade south along the Jordan Valley. These last movements, combined with the steady advance of the British artillery and

[1] Falls, *op. cit.* p. 467. [2] See above, p. 202. [3] See above, p. 219.
[4] See above, p. 115.

infantry from Nablus, enveloped and "destroyed" the two German-Turkish armies in retreat, captured many thousands of prisoners, secured a number of fords and bridges across the Jordan, and on the 25th after "a fierce fight" took Semakh on the extreme south of the Lake of Galilee, and immediately thereafter Tiberias in face of little resistance. Corresponding to these victories at the east end of the Great Plain, Haifa at the other end, after one failure on the 22nd, was captured on the 23rd by squadrons of the 5th Division fighting their hard way both on the ridge of Carmel and through the narrow defile of Kishon, not without some of the fatal experiences of its swamps and quicksands which Sisera's host had encountered.[1] On the same day the 13th Brigade, advancing from Ṣeffuriyeh north of Nazareth, occupied Acre.

Allenby's conquest of Esdraelon and the approaches to it from south, east and north was complete.

NOTE TO PAGE 251—WHERE WAS MEGIDDO?

1. Conder's argument for Mujedda' was threefold: (1) Megiddo is as often mentioned, save once, with Beth-shan as with Taanach; (2) Muḳuṭṭa' is not a possible transformation of Megiddo; (3) the site on the Jordan Valley suits the flight of Ahaziah (2 Kings ix) better than Lejjun does. Each of these points fails, for (1) *Taanach by the waters of Megiddo* puts the Mujedda' site out of the question; also Josh. xii. 21 sets Taanach and Megiddo next Carmel; no definition of locality can be taken from the order of towns in Josh. xvii. 11 where the text is corrupt nor from Jud. i. 27, which, starting from Beth-shan, leaps over Gilboa to Taanach, then to Dor, then back to Ibleam (possibly Bir Bela'meh near Jenin, and to Megiddo); in 1 Kings iv. 12 is also confusion, Taanach, Megiddo, Beth-shan, Abel-Meholah then back to Jokneam on Carmel; in 1 Chron. vii. 29 the order is right from E to W. (2) Palatal *t* in Muḳuṭṭa' and Heb. *d* are interchangeable (Wright's *Comp. Gram.* 53), so are deep *ḳ* and *g*. The final ' not in Megiddo but in Muḳuṭṭa' and Mujedda' may (as Conder says) equal Heb. *n* in the form Megiddon; Muḳuṭṭa' is "ford", Arabs may have substituted it for a resembling name of which they knew not the meaning, as happens elsewhere. (3) Lejjun suits the flight of Ahaziah better than Mujedda' does; Jehu was driving up the Vale of Jezreel from Beth-shan, and Ahaziah's flight would be in the opposite direction; we do not know *the ascent of Gur*, Ibleam may be beside Jenin. Overtaken and wounded here on a path south, which Jehu afterwards took to Samaria, it was natural for Ahaziah's escort to seek another route for chariots from the plain south: that from Megiddo to Sharon. Thus the case goes against Mujedda' and for the ridge Lejjun—Tell el-Mutesellim. After the foregoing appeared in the *Expositor* I read Trelawney Saunders against Conder's theory, *PEFQ*, 1880, 223 f.; he, too, suggests that Muḳuṭṭa' may be derived from Megiddo; and with Saunders is Socin, *ZDPV*,

[1] Falls, *op. cit.* p. 536; "no more remarkable cavalry action of its scale was fought in the whole course of the campaign," *id.* p. 538.

iv. 150 f. Under the former's note Henderson cites for Mujedda', that in *Travels of the Mohar* Megiddo is presumably close to Jordan, but this cannot stand against evidence which puts it near Taanach, and W. Max Müller, *As. u. Eur.* 195 f., suggests that the writer confused Kishon with Jordan, also that in Egyptian Megiddo is spelt with a *t*; on the Amarna Tablets both Magidda and Makida. Raumer, *Pal.* 3, 402, identifies Lejjun with Maximianopolis, Buhl, 209 f. accepts Lejjun.

2. The excavations which have proved Robinson's theory of the site of Megiddo as only approximately true were those on Tell el-Mutesellim by Schumacher in 1903-5, and recently renewed at Professor Breasted's suggestion by the Oriental Institute of Chicago University. They have shown so far that not Lejjun, but the Tell or Mound about a mile farther north is the ancient Megiddo. A wall has been traced almost all round the Tell with a city gate of well-dressed ashlar, presumed to be the work of Phœnician masons employed by Solomon but bearing some Hittite features. Some debris and ashes above this stratum suggest a destruction of the city. Above all this are two strata with walls mostly of unhewn stone assigned to the period of N Israel monarchy; and here was found a cartouche of the Pharaoh Shoshenk, Heb. Shishak or Shoshak, whose record at Karnak of the cities subjected by him includes both Megiddo (Makidu) and Taanach. Above those two strata there is nothing that can be dated later than 350 B.C. about which date therefore the inhabitants of Megiddo appear to have removed to a site a mile farther south on the same ridge which the Romans when they came fortified and called Legio. See Schumacher, *Tell el-Mutesellem*, vol. i, 1908, edited by Steuernagel, with vol. of plates; vol. ii, "bearbeitet von C. Watzinger", 1929; H. H. Nelson, *The Battle of Megiddo*, 1913; Père Mallon, *Biblica*, July 1926; J. W. Crowfoot, *PEFQ*, 1930, 176; Flinders Petrie, *Hist. of Egypt*, ii. 325, on the lists of Thothmes III, says "the site el-Lejjun or Tell el-Mutesellim and not el-Mujedda' is proved, by this campaign and their relation to Taanakh", to be Megiddo; Max Müller, *Jewish Quart. Rev.* 1914, 651.

XX. *GALILEE*[1]

This name, which binds together so many of the most holy memories of our race, means in itself no more than The Ring. Galîl, as the easily slipping letters testify, is anything that rolls, or is round.[2] Like our circle, or circuit, it was applied to any well-defined region, as, for example, that east of Jerusalem, which Ezekiel calls *the Eastern Galilee*, or to *the Galilees of the Jordan*, or to *the Galilees of the Philistines*.[3] How it came to be the peculiar title of one district, and take rank among the significant names of the world, was as

[1] For this chapter, see Maps 1 and 2.

[2] גָּלִיל (cf. Greek κύλ-ινδρον), is used of balls, cylinders, rings (Esther 1. 6; Cant. v. 14), or the leaf of a door turning on its hinge (1 Kings vi. 34).

[3] But in these cases it was the feminine. הַגְּלִילָה הַקַּדְמֹנָה, the region east of Jerusalem (Ezek. xlvii. 8). Plural גְּלִילוֹת הַיַּרְדֵּן, the circles of Jordan (Josh. xxii. 10, 11); cf. "links of Forth". גְּלִילוֹת פְּלֶשֶׁת (Joel iv. 4), circles of the Philistines (cf. Josh. xiii. 2). This name may survive in the Crusaders' *Galilaea*, a casale, and "tota

follows. Gĕlîl ha-Gôîm—*Ring* or *Region of the Gentiles*, a phrase analogous to the German *Heidenmark*—was applied to the north border of Israel, pressed and permeated from three sides by foreign tribes. Thence the name spread, till in Isaiah's time it was as far south as the Lake of Gennesaret. By the time of the Maccabees it had reached the south of Esdraelon, and covered the whole of the northmost of the three provinces into which, after the Exile, the land west of Jordan was divided.[2]

The population grew even more Gentile than before. The Jews who settled in Galilee after the Return from Babylon were few, and about 164 B.C. Simon Maccabæus had to bring them all back to Judæa.[3] But the extension of the Jewish state under John Hyrcanus, 135-105, must have enabled many Jews to return to the attractive province without fear of persecution, and either that monarch or his successor added Galilee to his domains, and sought to enforce the law upon its inhabitants.[4] Soon afterwards, by 104, Galilee had developed a loyalty to the Jewish state sufficient to throw off a strong invader.[5] From this time onwards it was natural to drop out of her name the words *of the Gentiles*, which even before this were not always used; but the article was retained, and throughout the New Testament she is known as The Galilee. It would be pleasing to the patriotism of her inhabitants to call their famous and beautiful province, *The* Region.[6]

Galilea", a district near Cæsarea. Prutz, *Besitzungen des Johanniterordens in Pal. u. Syr.*, *ZDPV*, iv. 157 ff. with map. Prutz refers it to Kalkilye, but it is more probably the present Jelil, in the same neighbourhood.

[1] Isa. ix. 1 (Heb. viii. 23).

[2] In 1 Macc. the boundaries are indefinite. Galilee was still, in a sense, distinct from the Great Plain, xii. 47, 49; but it covered the neighbourhood of Ptolemais (Acre), v. 55.

[3] 1 Macc. v. 23. Schürer (*Hist.* i. 1, 192) corrects Keil on this verse.

[4] Schürer (*Hist.* i, 1, 294) and Buhl, 73, think that the Jewish conquest of Galilee was not till Aristobulus I, 105-104 B.C. But the conquest of Ituræan territory NE of Galilee (Josephus, xiii *Antt.* xi. 3), the only triumph of the brief reign of Aristobulus, could hardly have been undertaken without the previous conquest of Galilee by his predecessor; with this agrees the ambiguous statement that Hyrcanus had his son Alexander brought up in Galilee (*ib.* xii. 1). In the opening of next reign, Alexander Jannæus (104-78), we find Galilee so thoroughly Jewish that Ptolemy Lathyrus has difficulty in his siege of Asochis, and is unable to take Sepphoris (*ib.* 4, 5). This seems to require, for the Judaising of Galilee, an earlier date in the reign of John Hyrcanus. But, as xiii *Antt.* xv. 4 mentions nothing under Alexander as Jewish save Tabor and Sepphoris, the Jews probably possessed only South Galilee.

[5] See previous note.

[6] הגליל (Josh. xx. 7, xxi. 32; 1 Chron. vi. 76). ארץ הגליל (1 Kings ix. 11). גליל הגוים (Isa. viii. 23). In 2 Kings xv. 29, את־הגלילה, not the feminine form, but the masculine, with ה paragog., is used. The feminine גלילה is not applied in

The natural boundaries of Galilee are obvious. South, the Plain of Esdraelon (and we have seen why this frontier should be the southern and not the northern edge of the plain[1]); north, the great gorge of the Liṭany or Ḳasimiyah,[2] cutting off Lebanon; east, the valley of the Jordan and the Lake of Gennesaret; west, the narrow Phœnician coast. This region coincides closely with the territories of four tribes, Issachar, Zebulun, Asher, Naphtali. But the sea-coast, claimed for Zebulun and Asher, never belonged to them or to the province of Galilee: it was always Gentile. On the other hand, owing to the weakness of the Samaritans, Carmel was reckoned to Galilee when not in the hands of the men of Tyre[3]; and the eastern shores of Lake Gennesaret also fell within the province.[4] Exclusive of these two additions, Galilee measured about fifty miles north to south, and from twenty-five to thirty-five east and west. The area was only about 1600 square miles, or that of an average English shire.

From the intricacy of its highlands, the map of Galilee seems at first impossible to arrange to the eye. But, with care, the ruling features are distinguished, and the province falls into four divisions. There is the Jordan Valley with its two lakes, that singular chasm, which runs along the east to Galilee, sinking from Hermon's base to more than 700 feet below the level of the ocean.[5] From this valley, and corresponding roughly to its three divisions —below the Lake of Tiberias, the Lake itself, and above the Lake—three belts or strips run westward: *first*, the Plain of Esdraelon; *second*, the so-called Lower Galilee, a series of long parallel ranges, all below 1850 feet, which, with broad valleys between them, cross from the plateau above

---

Hebrew to Galilee (for its uses see p. 269, n. 2). But LXX render הגליל *ἡ Γαλιλαία*. In Isa. viii. 23 (LXX and Eng. ix. 1) *Γαλιλαία τῶν ἐθνῶν*. In the Apocrypha *Γαλιλαία Ἀλλόφυλων* (cf. 1 Macc. v. 15, etc.). The article is omitted only in 1 Macc. x. 30. And so in the N.T. *ἡ Γαλιλαία*, the article omitted only twice.

[1] See p. 246 f.

[2] Too readily assumed to be the Lion River, Leontes (*Λέοντος ποτάμοι ἐκβολάι*) of Ptolemy, v. 15, which he places between Sidon and Beyrout, and which, if he was right, may be the Bostrenus, the present Nahr el-Awali. There is no connection between the names Liṭany and Leontes.

[3] Josephus, iii *Wars*, iii. 1. See p. 225.

[4] Thus Judas who led the revolt against them in A.D. 6 is called the Galilean, *ἀνὴρ Γαλιλαῖος* (Josephus, ii *Wars*, viii. 1), although he was of Gamala in Gaulanitis (xviii *Antt.* i. 1). In the same way under the Turks "the whole coast district was under the administration of the Kada Tubaríya" (Schumacher, *The Jaulân*, p. 103). It is the most convenient arrangement. To-day "Palestine territory along the E bank of the Lake varies from a minimum of 10 metres parallel with high-water mark to a maximum of about 2000" (Luke and Keith-Roach, *Handbook*, 4).

[5] Opposite Beth-shan.

Tiberias to the maritime plains of Ḥaifa and Acre; and *third*, Upper Galilee a series of plateaus, with a double water-parting, and surrounded by hills from 2000 to 4000 feet.[1] As you gaze north from the Samarian border, these three zones rise in steps to the beginnings of Lebanon; and from the north-east, over the gulf of the Jordan, the snowy head of Hermon looks down athwart them.

The controlling feature of Galilee is her relation to those mountains. A native of the region has aptly described it in his picture of God's grace. *I will be as the dew unto Israel; he shall blossom as the lily, and cast forth his roots like Lebanon.*[2] Galilee seems as the *casting forth of the roots of Lebanon.* As the supports of a great oak run up above ground, so the gradual hills of Galilee rise from Esdraelon and Jordan and the Phœnician coast, upon that northern mountain. Not Lebanon, however, but the opposite range of Hermon dominates the view. Among his roots Lebanon is out of sight; whereas that long, glistening ridge, standing aloof, always brings the eye back to itself.[3] In summer hot harvesters from every field lift their hearts to Hermon's snow; and the heavy dews of night they call his gift. How closely Hermon was identified with Galilee is seen from his association with the most characteristic of the Galilean hills: *Tabor and Hermon rejoice in Thy name.*[4]

To her dependence on the Lebanons Galilee owes her water and her superiority in fruitfulness to both Judæa and Samaria. This is not because Galilee has a greater rainfall; her excess in that respect is slight,[5] and during the dry season showers are almost as unknown as in the rest of Palestine. But the moisture, seen and unseen, which the west winds lavish on the

[1] The division between Upper and Lower Galilee is evident on the map. It runs roughly, from the N end of the Lake of Galilee (to the south of Ṣafed), by Wady Maktul leading up from the Plain of Gennesaret, thence by level ground between Kefr 'Anan and er-Ramah W towards Acre. S of this there is no height over 1850 feet, the peaks run from 1000 to 1850, with Jebel es-Siḥ 1600, and Tabor 1843. But N of this line the steep constant wall of the northern plateau rises almost immediately, and figures from 2000 to 3000 are frequent. The Talmud marks this division thus: "Upper Galilee above Kefar Hananyah, a country where sycomores are not found; Lower Galilee below Kefar Hananyah, which produces sycomores." Kefar Hananyah is Kefr 'Anan. Josephus gives the breadth of Lower Galilee as from Xaloth, at the roots of Tabor, to Berseba, not identified, but possibly Kh. Abu es-Seba' very near Kefr. 'Anan.

[2] Hosea xiv. 5. Some emend *Lebanon* to *libnah, poplar.*

[3] So LXX of Deut. i. 7 for Lebanon gives *Αντιλίβανος.*

[4] Psalm lxxxix. 12. How far they believed its influence to travel may be seen from that other psalm: *The dew of Hermon that cometh down on the mountains of Zion* (Psalm cxxxiii).

[5] The figures are few for Nazareth (we owe them to Dr. Vartan). Comparing them

Lebanons, is stored by them for Galilee's sake, and dispensed to her with unfailing regularity round the year. It breaks out in the full-born rivers of the Upper Jordan Valley, and in the wealth of wells among her hills. When Judæa is dry it feeds the streams of Gennesaret and Esdraelon. In winter the springs of Kishon burst so richly that the Great Plain about Tabor is a quagmire; even in summer there are fountains on Esdraelon, round which the thickets keep green; and in the glens running up to Lower Galilee the paths cross rivulets and sometimes wind round a marsh. In the cross valleys, winter lakes last till July,[1] and farther north autumn streams descend both watersheds with a music unheard in South Palestine. The difference in this respect between Galilee and Judæa is just the difference between their names—one liquid and musical like her running waters, the other dry and dull like the fall of your horse's hoof on her blistered and muffled rock.

So much water means an exuberant fertility. We have seen what Esdraelon is, and we may leave for separate treatment the almost tropic regions of the Jordan Valley. But take Lower and Upper Galilee, with their more temperate climate. They are almost as well wooded as our own land. Tabor is covered with bush, and on its northern side with large, loose groves of forest trees. The road which goes up from the Bay of Carmel to Nazareth winds as among English glades, with open woods of oak and abundance of flowers and grass. Often, as about Nazareth, the limestone breaks out not less bare than in Judæa, but over the most of Lower Galilee there is a profusion of bush, with scattered forest trees—holly-oak, maple, sycomore, bay-tree, myrtle, arbutus, sumac, and others—and in the valleys olive orchards and stretches of corn-land. Except for some trees like the sycomore, Upper Galilee is as rich, "an undulating table-land, arable and everywhere tilled, with swelling hills in view all round, covered with shrubs and trees".[2] Above Tyre is a great plateau, sloping westwards, "all cultivated, and thronged with villages". South of Wady el-Ma the country is more rugged, and cultivation only in patches[3]; yet even here are vines and olives. Round Jotapata Josephus speaks of timber cut down for Vespasian's siege.[4] Gischala was Gush-ḥalab, "fat soil",[5] and noted for its oil. Throughout the province olives were so abundant that a proverb ran, "It is easier to raise a legion of

---

with those for Jerusalem by Dr. Chaplin, Anderlind makes out a difference of 4·16 centimetres in the annual rainfall; Jerusalem, 57·01; Nazareth, 61·17. Jerusalem is 2300 feet above the sea, Nazareth about 1000.

[1] The Plain of Buṭṭauf, Zebulun or Asochis, was then partly a lake (Conder's *Tent Work*).

[2] Robinson, *LBR*, *PEF Mem.* iii. [3] *Ibid.* [4] iii *Wars*, vii. 8; cf. vi. 2.

[5] Neubauer, *Géog. du Talmud.*

olives in Galilee than bring up a child in Palestine."[1] Even on the high watershed between Ḥuleh and the Mediterranean, the fields are fertile, the ridges covered with small oaks. To the inhabitants of such a land, the more luxuriant vegetation of the hot plains on either side spreads its temptations in vain.

Asher, his bread is fat,
And he yields the dainties of a king.
Blessed be Asher above children,
And let him dip his foot in oil!
O Naphtali, satisfied with favour,
And full of the blessing of the Lord.[2]

But it is luxury where luxury cannot soften. On these broad heights, open to the sunshine and the breeze, life is free and exhilarating.

Naphtali is a hind let loose.[3]

This figure expresses the feelings bred by the health, spaciousness, high freedom and glorious outlook of Upper Galilee.

To so generous a land the inhabitants, during that part of her history which concerns us, responded with energy. "Their soil", says Josephus, "is universally rich and fruitful, and full of the plantations of trees of all sorts, insomuch that it invites, by its fruitfulness, the most slothful to take pains in its cultivation. Accordingly it is all cultivated by its inhabitants, and no part lies idle."[4] The villages were frequent, the fortified towns not few and the population very numerous. We may not accept all that Josephus reports —he reckons a population of nearly three millions—but there are reasons for the possibility of his high figures.[5] In any case the province was thickly peopled. Save in the recorded hours of our Lord's praying, the history of Galilee has no intervals of silence and loneliness; the noise of a close and busy life is audible; and to every crisis in the Gospels and Josephus we see crowds immediately swarm.

[1] *Talmud*, quoted by Neubauer, p. 180. The abundance of oil in Galilee is well illustrated in the use made of boiling oil by the defenders of Jotapata, who poured great quantities of it on the Roman soldiers (iii *Wars*, vii. 28).

[2] Gen. xlix. 20; Deut. xxxiii. 23, 24.

[3] Gen. xlix. 21. Another reading, partly suggested by LXX, is taken by Ewald, Dillmann, etc., *Naphtali is a slender terebinth giving forth goodly boughs*. Other versions support the Massoretic text; and while the figure of a tree is not inapplicable to the mountains of Naphtali, that of a slender tree is absurd. The ordinary reading is suited to a people in the position of Naphtali.

[4] iii *Wars*, iii. 2.

[5] See those given by Dr. Selah Merrill in his valuable monograph on *Galilee in the Time of Christ*. "Bypaths of Bible Knowledge" Series, 1891.

One other feature of Galilee must not be passed over. The massive limestone of her range is broken here and there by volcanic extrusions—an extinct crater near Gischala,[1] dykes of basalt, and scatterings of lava on the plateau above the lake. Hot sulphur springs flow by Tiberias, and the province has been shaken by terrible earthquakes.[2] The nature of the people was also volcanic. Josephus describes them as "ever fond of innovations, and by nature disposed to changes, and delighting in seditions".[3] They had an ill name for quarrelling. From among them came the chief zealots and wildest fanatics of the Roman wars.[4] We remember two Galileans who wished to call down fire from heaven on those who were only discourteous to them.[5] Yet this inner fire is an essential of manhood. It burns the meanness out of men, and can flash forth in passion for righteousness. First to last, the Galileans were chivalrous and gallant.

Zebulun was a people jeoparding their lives to the death,
And Naphtali on the high places of the field.[6]

With the same desperate zeal, their sons attempted the forlorn hope of breaking the Roman power. "The country", says Josephus proudly, "hath never been destitute of men of courage."[7] Their fidelity, often unreasoning and ill-tempered, was always sincere. "The Galileans", according to the Talmud, "were more anxious for honour than for money; the contrary was true of Judæa."[8] Our Lord chose His friends from the people; and it was *not* a Galilean who betrayed Him.

When we turn from the physical characteristics of this province of subterranean fires and waters to her political geography, we find influences as bold and inspiring as those we have noted. We may select three as chief—the neighbourhood of scenes of Hebrew history; the world-roads which crossed Galilee; the surrounding heathen civilisations.

[1] Sahel el-Jish.

[2] For example that in 1837, which overthrew the walls of Tiberias, and killed so large a number of the population of Ṣafed and other towns.

[3] *Life*, xvii; xvii *Antt.* x. 5; xx *id.* vi. 1; i *Wars*, xvi. 5; ii *id.* xvii. 8; Tacitus, *Ann.* xii. 54.

[4] Judas the Galilean from Gamala in Jaulan, A.D. 6 (xviii *Antt.* i. 1; ii *Wars*, viii. 1). His sons, James and Simon, were executed by Tiberius Alexander (xx *Antt.* v. 2); his grandson, Menahem, was prominent in the revolt of 66 (ii *Wars*, xvii. 8, 9), and a descendant, Eleazar, was captain of the Sicarii, and led the defence of Masada in 73 (ii *Wars*, xvii. 9; vii *ib.* viii. 1). Cf. Schürer, *Hist.* Div. 1. vol. 1, p. 81, n. 129. John of Gischala, a passionate patriot (Jos. *Life*, x. xiii, etc.; ii *Wars*, xxi. 1, 2, etc.). Cf. the *Galileans, whose blood Pilate mingled with their sacrifices* (Luke xiii. 1).

[5] Luke ix. 54. Cf. Jos. xx *Antt.* vi. 1.

[6] Judges v. 18.

[7] iii *Wars*, iii. 2.

[8] Quoted by Neubauer, *Géog. du Talmud*, 181.

I. It is often taken for granted that the Galilee of our Lord's day was a new land with an illegitimate people, without history, traditions, or prophetic succession. The notion is inspired by such proverbs as, *Search and see, for out of Galilee cometh no prophet. Can any good come out of Nazareth?* But these were due to the spitfire pride of Judæa, that had contempt for the coarse dialect of the Galileans,[1] and for their intercourse with the heathen. The province, it is true, had been under the Law for little more than a century.[2] Her customs and laws, even on such matters as marriage and intercourse with the heathen, her coins and weights, her dialect, were sufficiently different from those of Judæa to excite popular sentiment in the latter, and provide the scribes with quotable reasons for their hostility. Do we desire a modern analogy for the difference between Judæa and Galilee in the time of our Lord, we find one in the differences between England and Scotland soon after the Union. But Galilee had as much reason to resent the scorn of Judæa as Scotland the haughty tolerance of England. Behind the Exile Galilee had traditions, a prophetic succession, and a history almost as splendid as Judah's own. She was not out of the way of the scenes of famous days. Carmel, Kishon, Megiddo, Jezreel, Gilboa, Shunem, Tabor, Gilead, Bashan, the waters of Merom, Hazor and Kedesh, were within touch or sight. She shared with Judæa the exploits of the Maccabees. By Gennesaret was Jonathan's march, by Merom the scene of his heroic rally when his forces were in flight, and of his victory; on the other side, at Ptolemais, was his treacherous capture, the beginning of his martyrdom.[3] Galilee, therefore, lived as openly as Judæa in face of the glories of their people. Her latent fires had visible provocation. The foot of the invader could tread no league of her without starting the voices of fathers who had laboured and fought for her, without rewaking promises which the prophets had lavished upon her future. *As in the former time He brought into contempt the land of Zebulun, and the land of Naphtali, so in the latter time hath He made them glorious, the way of the Sea, across Jordan, Galilee of the Gentiles. The people which walked in darkness have seen a great light; dwellers in the land of deep darkness, on them hath the light shined.*

The preparation which all this must have effected for the ministry of our Lord is clear. The Messianic tempers were stronger in Galilean than in other Jewish hearts.[4] While Judæa's religion had for its characteristic zeal

[1] The Galileans confounded the gutturals. For to-day see W. Christie, *ZDPV*, xxiv. 69, *Der Dialect der Landesbevölkerung des mittleren Galiläa*, with map, 108.
[2] See p. 270.
[3] 1 Macc. ix, xi, xii.
[4] See p. 275, on the number of Galileans in the revolt against Rome.

for the law, Galilee's was distinguished by the nobler, more potential passion of hope. Therefore to Galilee Jesus came preaching that *the Kingdom of Heaven is at hand*; it was the Galilean patriotism which He chose to refine to diviner issues.

But we usually overlook that Galilee was vindicated also in the affections of the Jews themselves. It is one of the most singular revolutions, even in Jewish history, that the province, which through so many centuries Judæa had condemned as profane and heretical, should succeed Judæa as the sanctuary of the race and the home of their theological schools—that to-day Galilee should have as many holy places as Judæa, and Ṣafed and Tiberias be reverenced with Hebron and Jerusalem. The transference can be traced by the movements of the Sanhedrim. After the defeat of the last Jewish revolt at Bittir (A.D. 134), the Sanhedrim migrated north from Jabneh on the Philistine plain to Hosah just north of Carmel, and gradually eastward across Lower Galilee to Shaphram, to Beth-shearim, to Sepphoris, to the unclean and cursed Tiberias itself. Here the last Sanhedrim sat, and the Mishna was edited. The tomb of Maimonides is in Tiberias, and most of the towns of Lower, and some of Upper, Galilee have fame from the residence or the martyrdom of famous Rabbis. It is curious to observe in the Talmuds the reflection of a state of society in Galilee of the third century more strict in some respects than that of Judæa. But, in the history of Israel, the last is ever becoming the first.[1]

II. The next great features of Galilee are her Roads. This garden of the Lord is crossed by many of the world's famous highways. We saw that Judæa was on the road to nowhere; Galilee is covered with roads to everywhere: from the harbours of the Phœnician coast to Samaria, Gilead, Hauran and Damascus; from Sharon to the valley of the Jordan; from the sea to the desert; from Egypt to Assyria. They were not confined to Esdraelon and the Jordan Valley. They ran over Lower Galilee by its parallel valleys, and even crossed the plateau of Upper Galilee on the shortest way from Tyre and Sidon to Damascus. A review of these highways will enhance our appreciation of Galilee's history. They can be traced by current lines of traffic, by the great khans or caravanserais still in use or in ruin, and by remains of Roman pavements.

From the earliest times a great thoroughfare has connected Damascus

[1] For the above, see Neubauer, *Géog. du Talmud*, 177-233, a valuable picture, but it draws too much on the Talmud's picture of Galilee to illustrate the different state in our Lord's time. The towns mentioned above are on the map of the *PEF*. Hosah is Khurbet Ḥusheh, Shaphram, Shefa 'Amr, 2 m. off; for Beth-shearim Conder proposed She'arah on the Tabor plateau.

with the sea. Its direction has varied from age to age according to political circumstances. The port of Damascus was sometimes Tripoli, sometimes Beyrout, sometimes Sidon or Tyre, sometimes ʻAkka with Ḥaifa. But between Damascus and the three first of these rises the double range of Lebanon; the roads have twice to climb thousands of feet.[1] To Tyre again the road must first compass Hermon to Banias or Ḥaṣbeya, and then cross the heights of Naphtali.[2] ʻAkka is the natural port for Damascus, and the nearest ways to ʻAkka run through Lower Galilee. Leaving Damascus, the highway kept to the south of Hermon upon the level region now called Jedur,[3] and crossed the Jordan midway between the Lakes of Merom and Gennesaret at the present Bridge of the Daughters of Jacob. Thence it climbed to the Khan, now called "of the Pit of Joseph", and divided. One branch held west past Ṣafed, by the line of valley between Lower and Upper Galilee, and came down by Wady Waziyeh upon ʻAkka.[4] Another branch went south to the Lake of Gennesaret at Khan Minyeh—one of the possible sites for Capernaum—and there forked again. One prong bent up the Plain of Gennesaret and Wady Rubadiyeh to rejoin the direct western branch at Ramah. Another left the Plain of Gennesaret up the famous Wady el-Ḥamam by Arbela[5] to the plateau above Tiberias, and thence passing the great Khan or market, now called eṭ-Ṭujjar, "of the merchants", defiled between Tabor and the Nazareth hills upon Esdraelon, which it crossed to Megiddo, on the way to Sharon, Philistia, Egypt. A third branch from Khan Minyeh continued due south by the Lake and Tiberias to Beth-shan, from which the traveller might either ascend Esdraelon and rejoin the straight route to Egypt, or go up through Samaria to Jerusalem, or down Jordan to Jericho. But at Beth-shan, or a little north of it, there came across Jordan another road from Damascus. It had traversed the level Hauran, and come down into the valley of the Jordan by Aphek[6] or by Gamala, and it went over to the Mediterranean either by Beth-shan and Esdraelon or up Wady Fejjas to the plateau above the Lake, and thence by the cross valley past

[1] The road from Damascus to Tripoli went *via* Baʻalbek and B'sherreh; that to Beyrout by the modern diligence route; that to Sidon went from Rama, past the present Ḳulaʻat esh-Shuḳif, the Crusading castle of Belfort.

[2] After Banias the road traverses the Jordan Valley by Tell el-Ḳaḍy, passes the Ḥaṣbany branch by an old bridge; thence over the first watershed N of Rubb Thelathin, through the valley near Abrikha, where are remains of pavement, and over the second watershed by Burj Alawei to Tyre. It is commanded by two Crusading castles—Hunin, at a distance of two miles, Tibnin at more.

[3] By Sʻasa and el-Ḳuneiṭra.

[4] Schumacher, *PEFQ*, 1889, 79, 80.

[5] Modern Irbid, 1 Macc. ix; Hosea x. 14.

[6] Probably Fiḳ, opposite Tiberias.

Cana and Sepphoris to 'Akka. This was also the way over Galilee from Gilead and the Decapolis.[1]

The Great West Road from Damascus to the Mediterranean, in one or other of its branches, was the famous *Way of the Sea*. It may have been so called by Isaiah when he heard along it the grievous march of the Assyrian armies, *by way of the sea, over Jordan, Galilee of the nations*. But we cannot be certain, for the phrase is ambiguous in both its terms; we do not know whether *the sea* is Gennesaret or the Mediterranean, and whether *the way* be really a road or only a direction. If the two latter alternatives be taken, the phrase means no more than westward—a rendering suitable to the context.[2] However this be, later generations applied Isaiah's words to the great caravan route between Damascus and the sea, and throughout the Middle Ages it was known as the "Via Maris". The Romans paved it, and took taxes from its traffic; at one of its tolls, in Capernaum, Matthew *sat at the receipt of custom*.[3] It was then the great route of trade with the Far East, and continued to be so. From the eleventh to the fourteenth centuries

[1] In Roman times were two bridges, one just below the Lake, the other the present Jisr el-Mujami'a. The route—Damascus, Nawa, Beth-shan, and Esdraelon—is the line of the Damascus-Ḥaifa railway. It crosses the Jordan just below the Lake.

[2] Isa. viii. 22 (Eng. ix. 1) דֶּרֶךְ הַיָּם *The Way of the Sea*. (1) The usual interpretation is Gennesaret (יָם־כִּנֶּרֶת, Num. xxxiv. 11), and *the way of the sea*, with the following words עֵבֶר הַיַּרְדֵּן, *over Jordan*, taken as a district E of the Lake. But the tribes mentioned, Zebulun and Naphtali, had their territories W of Jordan; and עֵבֶר הַיַּרְדֵּן is applicable to either side of the river. The march of the Assyrian here described swept west. But (2) does *way* mean a *highway*? I incline to think it means no more than direction, and we ought to take הַיָּם, or sea, in its sense of the West, so that the phrase in analogy to דֶּרֶךְ צָפוֹנָה (Ezek. viii. 5, xxi. 2, xl. 6) means *westward*. In that case it would be equivalent to בְּעֵבֶר הַיַּרְדֵּן יָמָּה (Josh. v. 1, etc.) *across the Jordan westwards*. It is true, however, that in these cases the particle of *direction towards* is used; whereas in our verse *sea* is in the genitive case with the article, a construction pointing to its being the title of a road rather than description of a direction. Yet not necessarily so, for הַיָּם (with the article) in the sense of west also occurs, Josh. xix. 11; Ezek. xlii. 19. But if a definite sea be meant, it is more probable that the Mediterranean, the goal of the road, would give its name to the latter, than the Lake of Gennesaret, along which only one of the road's branches passed.

[3] Mark ii. 14.

the products of India coming from the Persian Gulf by Baghdad and Damascus were carried along it to the factories of Venice, Genoa, and Marseilles in ʻAkka and Tyre, and thence distributed through Europe.[1] The commerce of Damascus gained an easier way to Beyrout by the Alpine road which the French engineers built across the Lebanons and the railway; but the Via Maris was still used for the considerable exports on camel-back of grain from Hauran.[2]

The Great South Road, the road for Egypt, which diverged from the Via Maris at the Lake of Galilee, was used equally for traffic and for war from the days of the patriarchs down to our own. One afternoon in 1891, while we were resting in the dale at the foot of Tabor, there passed three droves of unladen camels. We asked the drivers, "Where from?" "Damascus." "And whither?" "Jaffa and Gaza; but, if we do not get the camels sold there, we shall drive them down to Egypt." How ancient a succession they were following! From Abraham's time, every year that war was not afoot, camels have passed by this road to Egypt. Armies sometimes marched along it, as, for instance, the Syrians when Jonathan Maccabæus went out against them in the defiles by Arbela above Gennesaret.[3] But the open road over Hauran and across the Jordan below the Lake seems to have been the more usual line of invasion. So the Syrians came in Ahab's time,[4] and probably also the Assyrians when they advanced by Damascus.

The Great Road of the East (as we may call it) from ʻAkka across Lower Galilee to Beth-shan, and over the Jordan into Gilead, was the road for Arabia. Up it have come through all ages the Midianites, the children of the East. In the Roman period it connected the Asian frontier of the Empire with the capital. Chariots, military troops, companies of officials and merchants, passed by this road, between the Greek cities east of Jordan and Ptolemais, the port for Rome.

Of all things in Galilee it was the sight of these immemorial roads which taught and moved me most—not because they were trodden by the patriarchs, and some of them must shake to the railway train, not because the chariots of Assyria and Rome have both rolled along them, but because it was up and down these roads that the immortal figures of the Parables

[1] Rey, *Les Colonies Franques de Syrie aux xiième et xiiième siècles*, ch. iii, *Les Communes Commerciales*, and ch. ix, *La Commerce.* Heyd, *Die Italienischen Handelscolonien in Palästina.* See above, p. 18.

[2] In harvest 1891 their passage across the Jisr-Benat-Jaʻḳob never ceased.

[3] 1 Macc. ix. 2. So also came some of Saladin's army, in 1187, to the battle of Ḥaṭṭin.

[4] 1 Kings xx, xxii.

passed. By them came the merchantman seeking goodly pearls, the king departing to receive his kingdom, the friend on a journey, the householder arriving suddenly upon his servants, the prodigal son coming back from the far-off country. The far-off country! What a meaning has this frequent phrase of Christ's when you stand in Galilee by one of her great roads—roads which so easily carried willing feet from the pious homes of Asher and Naphtali to the harlot cities of Phœnicia—roads which were in touch with Rome and with Babylon.

III. Her roads carry us out upon the surroundings of Galilee. In the neighbourhood of Judæa we have seen great deserts, some of which come up almost to the gates of the cities, and have impressed their austerity and foreboding of judgement upon the feelings and the literature of the people. The different temperament of the Galilean was explained in part by his different environment. The desert is nowhere even visible from Galilee. Instead of it the Galilee of our Lord's time had for neighbours the half Greek land of Phœnicia, with its mines and manufactures, its open ports, its traffic from the West; the fertile Hauran,[1] with its frequent cities where Greek was spoken, and the pagan people worshipped their old divinities under the names of Greek gods; and Gilead, with the Decapolis, ten cities (more or less) of stately forums, amphitheatres, and temples.[2] We shall feel the full influence of all this upon Galilee when we go down to the Lake. Meantime let us remember that Galilee was not surrounded by *desert places* haunted by demoniacs, which is what a few traces in the Gospels suggest; but that the background and environment of this stage of our Lord's ministry was thronged and gay—that it was Greek in all the name can bring up to us of busy life, imposing art, and sensuous religion. The effect upon the Galilean temperament is obvious.

These then are the influences which geography reveals bearing upon Galilee. Before we go down to the Lake, let us focus them upon the one town away from the Lake, which is of supreme interest—Nazareth.[3]

Nazareth is usually represented as a secluded and obscure village. Many writers on the life of our Lord have emphasised this, holding it proved by

[1] Greek Auranitis. See ch. xxx. [2] See ch. xxix.

[3] On Nazareth see Guérin's *Galilee*; Merrill, *op. cit.*; Conder's *Tent Work*, ch. v; Schumacher, *Das jetzige Nazareth*, *ZDPV*, xiii. 234. In 1894 the population was 7500. Some have found them turbulent. Schumacher calls them pleasant and hospitable. They form a "Sprachinsel in gewissem Sinne"; for while surrounding towns pronounce *q* (*ḳ*) fully or miss it, Nazareth people pronounce it as *k*: *u* they pronounce *ü*, as in Turkish. There is want of water, "the well of Mary" being the only well. There is a market for the neighbourhood. See too F. J. Scrimgeour, *Nazareth of To-day*.

the silence of the Gospels concerning His childhood and youth. But the value of a vision of the Holy Land is that it fills the silences of the Holy Book, and from it we receive a very different idea of the early life of our Lord from the one current among us.[1]

The position of Nazareth is familiar. The village lies on the most southern of the ranges of Lower Galilee, and on the edge of this just above the Plain of Esdraelon. You cannot see the surrounding country, for Nazareth rests in a basin; but the moment you climb to the edge of this, which is everywhere within the limit of the village boys' playground, what a view you have! Esdraelon lies before you, with its twenty battle-fields—the scenes of Barak's and of Gideon's victories, of Saul's and Josiah's defeats, of the struggles for freedom in the days of the Maccabees. There is Naboth's vineyard and the place of Jehu's revenge upon Jezebel; there Shunem and the house of Elisha; there Carmel and the place of Elijah's sacrifice. To the east of the Valley of Jordan, with the range of Gilead; to the west the radiance of the Great Sea, with the ships of Tarshish and the promise of the Isles. You see thirty miles in three directions. It is a map of Old Testament history.

But equally full was the present life on which the boy Jesus looked out. Across Esdraelon, opposite Nazareth, there emerged from the Samarian hills the road from Jerusalem, thronged annually with pilgrims, and the road from Egypt with its merchants going up and down. The Midianite caravans could be watched for miles coming up from the fords of Jordan; and the caravans from Damascus wound round the foot of the hill on which Nazareth stands. Or if the boys climbed the northern edge of their hollow home, there was another road in sight, where the companies were still more brilliant—the highway between Acco and the Decapolis, along which legions marched, princes swept with their retinues, and all sorts of travellers from all countries went to and fro. The Roman ranks, the Roman eagles, the wealth of noblemen's litters and equipages cannot have been strange to the boys of Nazareth, especially after their twelfth year, when they went up to Jerusalem, or visited with their fathers famous Rabbis, who came down from Jerusalem, peripatetic among the provinces. Nor can it have been the eye only which was stirred. For the rumour of the Empire entered Palestine close to Nazareth—the news

[1] It is a merit of Merrill's monograph on Galilee, that it disproved this error in detail. See too a passage by Walter Besant in *The City and the Land*, 114 f.: "Palestine was not an obscure country. He who wandered among the hills and valley of Galilee was never far from some great and populous city. It was not as a rustic preaching to rustics that our Lord went about. He went forth in a part full of Roman civilisation, busy and populous, where, at every turn, He would meet with something to mark the empire to which He belonged."

from Rome, about the Emperor's health,[1] the changing influence of the statesmen, the prospects at court of Herod or of the Jews; Cæsar's last order on the tribute, or whether the policy of the Procurator would be sustained. Some Galilean families must have had relatives in Rome; Jews would come back to this countryside to tell of the life of the world's capital. The scandals of the Herods buzzed up and down these roads; pedlars carried them, and the peripatetic Rabbis would moralise upon them. The customs, too, of the neighbouring Gentiles—their loose living, sensuous worship, absorption in business,[2] the hopelessness of the inscriptions on their tombs, multitudes of which were readable (as some still) on the roads round Galilee—all this would furnish endless talk in Nazareth, both among men and boys.

Here He grew up and suffered temptation, Who was tempted in all points like as we are. The perfection of His purity and patience was achieved not easily as behind a wide fence which shut the world out, but amid rumour and scandal with every provocation to unlawful curiosity and premature ambition. The pressure and problems of the world outside must have been felt by the youth of Nazareth as by few others; yet the scenes of prophetic missions to it, Elijah's and Elisha's, were also within sight.[3] A vision of the kingdoms of the world was as possible from this village as from the mount of temptation. But the chief lesson which Nazareth teaches is the possibility of a pure home and a spotless youth in face of the evil world.

This comes still more home to the eye and to the heart as we visit in the town its only well, "The Well of Mary", at which she and her Son must have daily drawn water, and the ancient "Synagogue" which may have been that in which Jesus preached. Other "sacred" sites are not so authenticated.

With its many religious establishments, its industries and the surrounding agriculture, the modern town, en-Naṣira, is fairly prosperous, and of recent years its population has rapidly increased.

[1] As in the days when Vespasian was encamped in Galilee. See both Josephus and Tacitus on this.

[2] Matt. vi. 32. [3] Luke iv. 25 ff.

XXI. *THE LAKE OF GALILEE*[1]

In last chapter the dominant features of Galilee were shown to be seven. First, a close dependence on Lebanon. Second, an abundance of water, which Lebanon lavishes on her by rain, mists, wells, and full-born streams. Third, a great fertility: profusion of flowers, corn, oil, and wood. Fourth, volcanic elements: extinct craters, dykes of basalt, hot springs, liability to earthquakes. Fifth, great roads: highways of the world cross Galilee in all directions, from the Levant to Damascus and the East, from Jerusalem to Antioch, from the Nile to the Euphrates. Sixth, in result of the fertility and of the roads, busy industries and commerce with a large population. And seventh, no neighbouring desert, such as infects Judæa with austerity, but in its place a number of heathen provinces, pouring upon Galilee the full influence of their Greek life.

These seven features of Galilee in general were concentrated upon her Lake and its coasts. The Lake of Galilee was the focus of the whole province. Imagine that wealth of water, that fertility, those nerves and veins of the volcano, those great highways, that numerous population, that commerce and industry, those strong Greek influences—imagine them all crowded into a deep valley, under an almost tropical heat, round a great lake, and you have the conditions in which Christianity arose and Christ Himself laboured.

We do not realise that the greater part of our Lord's ministry was accomplished at what may be truly called the bottom of a trench, 680 feet below the level of the sea.[2] As you go down into it by the road which our Lord Himself traversed between Nazareth and Capernaum, there come up to meet you some signals of its wonderful peculiarity. By two broad moors,[3] the grey limestone land falls from the ranges of Lower Galilee to a line of cliffs overlooking the Lake, and about 300 feet above it. These terraced moors are broken by dykes of basalt, and strewn with lava and pumice-stone. There are hardly any trees upon them; after rain the shadeless streams soon die, and the summer grass and bush crackle to tinder. The memories of these moors match their appearance; history and legend know them only as the

[1] For this chapter, see Map 2.
[2] Garrow Duncan on the Lake generally, *PEFQ*, 1926, 15, 65.
[3] Now the plateau of Sha'ara and the Sahel el-Aḥma.

scenes of flight and thirst and exhaustion. Across their southern end Sisera fled headlong and sought drink for his parched throat in the tent of Jael.[1] By the aspect of the northern end, the imagination of the early Church was moved to fix upon it as the *desert place* where, when the day was far spent and the exhausted multitudes were distant from their villages, our Lord brought forth a miracle to feed them.[2] And there, in Crusading times, the courage of Christendom was scorched to the heart, so as never to rally in all the East again. Where the heights of Ḥaṭṭin offer neither shade nor springs, the Crusaders, tempted, it is said, by treachery, came forth to meet Saladin. A hot July night without water was followed by a burning day,[3] to add to the horrors of which the enemy set fire to the scrub. The smoke swept the fevered Christians into a panic; knights choked in their hot armour; the blinded foot-soldiers, breaking their ranks and dropping their weapons, were ridden down in mobs by the Moslem cavalry; and though here and there groups of brave men fought sun and fire and sword far on into the afternoon, the defeat was utter. A militant and truculent Christianity, as false as the relics of the "True Cross" round which it was rallied, met its judicial end within view of the scenes where Christ proclaimed the Gospel of Peace, and went about doing good.

Through such memories, enforcing the effect of the arid landscape, you descend from the hills of Galilee to her Lake. You feel you are passing from the climate and scenery of Southern Europe to those of the barer tropics. The sea-winds, which freshen all Galilee and high Hauran beyond, blow over this basin, and the sun beats into it with unmitigated ardour.[4] The atmosphere, for the most part, hangs still and heavy, but the cold currents, as they pass from the west, are sucked down in vortices of air, or by the narrow

[1] See p. 256; cf. Ewing on "Meroz", Hastings' *DB*.

[2] Beyond the sterility nothing justifies this tradition.

[3] 5th July 1187. The battle is described from the Crusading side by Bernard the Treasurer; from the Saracen by Beha ed-Din (*Life of Saladin*, xxxv). Robinson, *BR*. iii. 245-249, gives a summary of these.

[4] For notes of temperature, winds, and storms: Robinson, *BR*, iii; Merrill, *East of Jordan*; Frei, *ZDPV*, ix. 100 f.; Tristram's writings; Macgregor, *Rob Roy on the Jordan*, etc. The first reliable statistics by Dr. Torrance in 1890 are given by Glaisher, *PEFQ*, 1896, p. 92: Mean monthly temp. from 51° January to 90° August; lowest 34.3° Jan.; highest 111° Sept.; mean daily range from 13.5° Dec. to 28.3° May. In England the highest difference in the barometer between 8 A.M. and 4 P.M. is in June 0.025 in., at Tiberias the mean for the year was 0.081, nearly four times as much. On 87 days between May 4 and Nov. 1, counting every day in August, temp. was over 100° Fahr. The mean of the high day temp. for the year 85°, at Jerusalem 72.6°; mean temp. 74, Jerus. 63.2°. Rainfall for 11 months 22.38 in., Jerus. 23.92. Also E. K. Bisht's data for Tiberias, *PEFQ*, 1909, etc.

gorges that break upon the Lake.[1] Hence sudden storms for which the region is notorious—

The wind, the tempest roaring high,
The tumult of a tropic sky.

In such conditions a large population and industry would have been as impossible as at the other end of the Jordan, but for two features—the Lake itself and the wealth of fountains and streams which feed it from Lebanon. In that torrid basin, approached through sterile surroundings, the Lake feeds every sense of the body with life. Sweet water,[2] full of fish,[3] a surface of sparkling blue, tempting breezes from above, bringing forth breezes of her own, the Lake of Galilee is at once food, drink, and air, a rest to the eye, coolness in the heat, an escape from the crowd,[4] and a facility of travel welcome in so exhausting a climate. Even those who share not her memories of Christ feel enthusiasm for her. The Rabbis said: "The Lord hath created seven seas, but the Sea of Gennesaret is His delight."

The Lake lies like a harp, with the bulge to the north-west. It is nearly thirteen miles long,[5] and its greatest breadth eight.[6] The wider north end is the more open. The Jordan escaping from a long gorge, enters through a delta of his own deposits. To the west of this is thorny, thistly moorland, sloping north to a height which leaves over it only Hermon visible, though the basin of Merom lies between. North-west this moorland steepens, rising to the bulk of the hills about Ṣafed, and then, as the coast of the Lake trends more rapidly southwards, it drops upon the level Ghuweir—or "little Ghor"—almost certainly the *land of Gennesaret*, four miles broad.

[1] Canon G. N. Livett writes me an interesting confirmation of this from his experience of such vortices in 1911.

[2] Some travellers have found in the water "a slight brackish taste" (so Robinson's companions, but not himself, *BR*, iii. 261). But this approaches unpleasantness only in shallow waters near saline springs. Elsewhere the words of Josephus, iii *Wars*, x. 7, are not exaggerated. γλυκειά τε ὅμως ἐστὶ καὶ ποτιμωτάτη.

[3] See p. 300. [4] Mark vi. 32, etc.

[5] Large Survey Map, from the influx of Jordan to Semakh.

[6] Greatest depth reported 250 metres at the north end, Lortet, *Dragages exécutées dans le Lac de Tibériade en Mai*, 1880; *Comptes Rendus Hebdom.* des séances de l'Académie des Sciences, Tome xci, Paris, 1880, pp. 500-502. But Barrois, *PEFQ*, 1892, 211 ff. after a history of previous attempts, records his own results, scarcely over 40 to 45 metres according to the season, the greatest depths on the axis of Jordan and almost on the Lake's meridian; the east side is steeper; "if Lortet's 250 metres is correct, it must be due to a fissure". Lortet's idea that the Lake was once connected with the Mediterranean, is disproved by Hull. See p. 302. On the peculiar fishes, see Tristram, and Merrill, *East of the Jordan*, p. 441.

[7] Gennesaret Γεννησαρέτ, the Land of G. Matt. xiv. 34; Mark vi. 53; Lake of G. Luke v. 1. The earliest use is in 1 Macc. xi. 67, Τὸ ὕδωρ Γεννησάρ (in this verse, for

South of the Ghuweir the hills close upon the Lake, with a valley breaking through from the plateau above. South of this valley they leave but a ribbon of coast, on which Tiberias lies, commanded by its black castle. In contrast to the green open slopes of the north, these dark, imprisoning cliffs, with their black *debris*, impose upon this part of the coast a sombre, sinister aspect, not unsuited for its association with the name of the gloomy tyrant, that, by a strange irony, has been stamped on a landscape from which the name of Jesus has vanished.[1] As the south end of the Lake approaches, the ribbon of coast widens, and the Jordan cuts through this, striking at first due west, and then south by the foot of the hills. Four miles broad, the Jordan Valley, the Ghor, leaves a wide prospect from the Lake southward, that is closed only by the cliffs of the gorge to which it narrows twenty miles away. From the east the Yarmuk Valley breaks in just below the Lake, distending the Ghor to the dimensions of a plain; and to the south of the Yarmuk rise the heights of Gadara, commanding this plain, and looking up the Lake to Tiberias and the north end. From the Yarmuk northwards up all the east side of the Lake runs a wall of hills, the edge of the plateau of Jaulan[2] or

---

Νασωρ read *Ἀσωρ* = Ḥaṣor, cf. Josephus, xiii *Antt.* v. 7). Josephus, *Γεννησάρ*, *Γ. λίμνη*, or *ὕδωρ* and *ἡ Γεννησαρῖτις*. Later Hebrew (Targums and Talmud) גניסר, גנוסר, and גינוסר. Targums identify the name with Chinnereth of the O.T. (כִּנֶּרֶת, Deut. iii. 17, Josh. xix. 35; כִּנְרוֹת, Josh, xi. 2; כָּל־כִּנֶּרֶת, 1 Kings xv. 20), applied both to the Lake and a town on the Lake, while in the last passage it perhaps covers all the north Jordan Valley. Some accept this identification (Dillmann, *PEF Map*, ed. 1891, etc.), but it is improbable. LXX transliterate כנרת by *χενέρεθ* and *χενέρωθ*. Even this can scarcely have been *Γεννησάρ*, גניסר, or גינוסר. The latter form points rather to a compound of גיא or גן. Chinnereth has been derived from כנור, "harp", as if through the shape of the Lake. *Talm. Bab. Meg.* 6*a*: "Chinnereth, *i.e.* Genesar, and wherefore is it called Chinnereth? Because its fruit is sweet like the artichoke, ככינרא' (not as Neub. *Géog. du Talm.* 215, "sweet as voice of a harp"). Wellhausen (*Gesch.* 220) derives the name from גיא and נסר by which Galilee is to be understood, the *form* Gennesaret being explicable as due to Chinnereth. Buhl (113, 229) prefers גן, the lake taking its name from the fertile district of Gennesaret. Schürer (*Theol. Lit. Zeit.* March 2, 1895) supports גן because of the Greek form and points out that the best reading in the only Mishna passage bearing the name, Maaseroth, iii. 7, is גניסר, pointed by *cod. de Rossi*, 138, גְּנֵיסַר. Masterman (*Bibl. World*) extends G. east towards Tell Ḥum.

[1] Lamartine (*Pilgrimage to the Holy Land*, Eng. ed. i, 269) speaks of "avalanches of black stones", "the black, naked hill", "the sombre and funereal character of the landscape about Tiberias".

[2] Hebrew גּוֹלָן, Golan, in classic Arabic Gaulan, but with natives of the district

Gaulanitis; a limestone plateau, but topped by a vast layer of basalt. You see the curious formation as you ascend the gorges which lead up from the Lake, for first you pass the dirty white lime strata, and then the hard black rocks of the volcanic deposit. Some of the gorges—like that of Fiķ, opposite Tiberias, where Hippos stood—are open and gradual enough to have been used as high-roads in all ages; but others farther north are wild and impassable.[1] The wall which the plateau presents to the Lake is higher and more constant than the hills down the west side, but does not come so close to the beach. Except at Kersa, the east coast is about half a mile broad, well watered and fertile.

The view which the whole basin presents has been likened to one of our Scottish lochs. This would be one of the least wooded. Few lochs in Scotland have surroundings so stripped of trees as those of the Lake of Galilee are to-day. Except for some palms lingering in Gennesaret, a scattering of thorn bush round the coast, brakes of oleander on the east shores, and small oaks up the gorges to the Jaulan plateau, trees are not to be seen. The mountain edges are bare, and so are the grey slopes to the north, lifted towards Hermon as a Scottish moor to a snowy Ben. Only one town is visible, Tiberias, a fevered place of over 8500 inhabitants; besides there are not more than three or four villages round the coast. There are no farmsteads,[2] nor crofts, such as break the solitude of our most desolate Highland lochs. The lights which come out at night on shore and hill are camp-fires of wandering Arabs. It is well known how seldom a sail is seen on the Lake.

How different it was in the days when Jesus came down from Nazareth to find His home and His disciples upon these shores! Where there are now no trees there were woods; where there are marshes, there were gardens; where there is but a boat or two, there were fleets of sails; where there is one town, there were nine or ten. We know this from Josephus, who describes the province he governed and fought over only thirty-four years after our Lord's ministry—too short a time for the country to have changed.

The Plain of Gennesaret had "soil so fruitful, that all sorts of trees would grow upon it, for the temper of the air is so well blended that it suits those many sorts, especially walnuts, which require the colder air" (relatively to the rest), "and flourish there in great plenty. There are palm trees, which grow best in hot air; fig trees also and olives near them, which require an air more temperate." This conjunction was due to the steep slope of the Galilean

---

shortened to the same first syllable as in Hebrew, with soft *g*—*gô*, or *jô*, Schumacher's *The Jaulân*.

[1] Like the Wady Jeramaya described in Schumacher's *The Jaulân*, 253.

[2] Except the German colony near 'Ain eṭ-Ṭabigha.

hills, which fall from as high as 4000 feet above the sea, north of Ṣafed, to 680 below at Gennesaret. In the days of the pride of the land, what a plunge through nature it must have been, when one came down from oaks, through olives, sycomores and walnuts, to palms with roots washed by the Lake. "One may call this place the ambition of Nature, where it forces plants naturally enemies to agree together: it is a happy contention of the seasons, as if each of them laid claim to this country, for it not only nourishes different sorts of autumnal fruits beyond men's expectation, but preserves them a great while. It supplies men with the principal fruits, grapes, and figs continually during ten months, and the rest of the fruits, as they ripen together through the whole year."[1] Even now one sees proof of that luxuriance in the rich patches of garden upon Gennesaret, in the wealth of flowers on the surrounding slopes, and in the maidenhair fern that springs up wherever a stream gives water and a ruin throws shade.[2] About Tiberias the land was probably as bare as now, but from the foot of the Lake to Beth-shan was cultivated for wheat, and the incoming valley from Tabor[3] holds oleanders deep enough to cover a regiment of horse. The east plateau, bare to-day, was well wooded even to a recent time, for the names imply the presence of forest and copse,[4] while some wadies by which you descend to the Lake, have oaks, terebinths, planes, and carobs, and others are full of bush and brake.[5]

There were nine cities round the Lake, each said to have had not less than 15,000 inhabitants, and some probably more. Of these the sites of Tiberias and Magdala on the western shore, and of Gadara and Hippos on the east hills are certain. Beth-saida and Capernaum were at the north end, though where exactly, who can tell? Taricheæ is a matter of controversy, and so is Chorazin. But this we know, that whatever be the sites to which these names were originally attached, their towns formed round the now bare Lake an almost unbroken ring of building.

Tiberias is said to occupy the site or neighbourhood of Rakkath, an ancient town of Naphtali,[6] and as Rakkath probably means *strip*, or *coast*, this may

[1] Josephus, iii *Wars*, x. 8.

[2] The gardens about Irbid, on the plateau above the Lake, are beautiful. On the Wady el-Ḥamam, which, true to its name, shelters numberless wild blue-grey doves, see Schumacher, *ZDPV*, xiii. 67.

[3] Wady Fejjas.

[4] Schumacher, *The Jaulân*, 15, 17, 22, 23.

[5] There were thick woods round the Lake, even in Arculf's time, A.D. 700.

[6] *Talm. Jer. Meg.* 2*b*. *Talm. Bab. Meg.* 6*a* gives other identifications. When the foundations were laid, human bones were discovered. The site cannot have coincided with an old town, but may have covered the cemetery adjoining. Neubauer (*Géog. du Talm.* 209) quotes from *Tal. Bab. Sanh.* 12 proof that in the 4th cent. Tiberias was called Rakkath.

be. The Herods did not raise their cities from virgin sites, but generally rebuilt some old town. Why Herod chose this site is clear. There would have been difficulty in adapting to his designs for a capital towns so full of commerce as Taricheæ and Capernaum; he would prefer a site dominated by a hill, where he could build a castle, yet be near the shore, and no doubt he found an advantage, perhaps pecuniary, to be near Baths famous throughout the Roman world.[1] In what year the building was begun or finished is uncertain, but at the earliest not more than five or six years before our Lord began His ministry on the Lake.[2] Herod's plans were large. Ruins indicate a wall three miles long.[3]

Besides the imposing citadel were a palace, a forum, and a synagogue.[4] But the buildings were the best of the town. No true Jew would set foot on a site defiled at once by the bones uncovered in digging the foundations, and by the heathen images staring from the castle walls. Failing to get respectable citizens, Herod swept into his city the scum of the land. *Non abfuerat omen*: he had called it after Tiberius.

That the city was new, artificial and unclean partly explains its absence from the records of Christ's ministry. Our Lord avoided the half-Greek cities, and among courtiers and officials would have been less at home than among the common people of the country. But the surroundings of Tiberias,

[1] Cf. Pliny, *H.N.* v. 15, "Tiberiade aquis calidis salubre".

[2] Or A.D. 20-22. Lewin, *Fasti Sacri*, n. 1163, and Schürer (*Hist.* II, vol. i. 144) fix on A.D. 26 on the ground that Josephus does not mention the building of Tiberias till after Pilate became Procurator of Judæa (xviii *Antt.* ii, cf. 3 with 2). This is too late, for (*a*) a coin of Tiberias under Claudius (De Saulcy, *Numis. de la Terre Sainte*, 334), is dated in the 33rd year of the city, and Claudius died in 54; if this coin be his, it drives us back to 21; (*b*) two coins of Tiberias under Trajan (*Ibid.* 335) bear 80 and 81 of the city: as he began to reign in 98 they forbid us going farther back than A.D. 18; (*c*) but on a third coin under Trajan (*Ibid.* 336, No. 4, Pl. xvii), of date 81 of the city, the emperor is called only *Germanicus*, and not also *Dacicus*, which title he won in A.D. 103. This gives A.D. 22 for an upper limit. The evidence of this coin is to be preferred to that of another (whether we read *ΓΕΡΜ* or *ΓΕΡ . Δ*) mentioned by Schürer, 145. These facts are stronger than the ambiguous evidence of Josephus, by which Schürer fixes the date as 26. The interest of the question lies in the fact that Tiberias is mentioned in no gospel but the Fourth.

[3] Schumacher, *PEFQ*, 1887, 85 ff. The walls included the citadel of Herod, but not the baths, as Furrer maintains, *ZDPV*, ii. 54. Josephus' expression that the baths were *ἐν Τιβεριάδι*, *Life*, 16, ii *Wars*, xxi. 6, must be interpreted "in the district of Tiberias" (Schürer). In xviii *Antt.* ii. 3, iv *Wars*, i. 3, the baths are outside the city, *'Εμμαοῦς* or *Ἀμμαοῦς* = חמתה.

[4] The palace on the Acropolis, Jos. *Life*, 12; Schumacher, *PEFQ*, 1887, 87 ff. Josephus destroyed it. The Forum was used during Josephus' occupation: *Ib.* 17, etc. The synagogue or *Προσευχή μέγιστον οἴκημα*, *Ib.* 54.

too, were repellent.[1] The city, a long strip like its predecessor, *the Ribbon*, was drawn out on the narrowest part of the coast. The hue of its volcanic environment was as of rusty mourning and the atmosphere more confined than on the north of the Lake. The fresh westerly breezes which blow through the summer strike the Lake well out on its surface, and leave the air inshore below the cliffs stagnant and close.[2] Tiberias is feverish. Capernaum and Beth-saida must have been more healthy, and through them besides ran the greatest of the Galilean thoroughfares, the Via Maris, pouring a stream of busy life. Life, physical and mental, was more in current in the cities of our Lord's choice than in that of Herod's. Yet while Bethsaida and Capernaum have passed, Tiberias endures; and the name of the morbid tyrant still stamps a region from which that of Jesus has vanished. The obvious reason is the black acropolis above Tiberias.[3] Capernaum, where Matthew sat at custom, depended on the great road, and faded when commerce took a new direction. But Tiberias, the only defensible site, at once on the Lake and on a hill, became the seat of the government of the province, which in time took from it its designation. That is why the name of the foreign emperor, first embalmed here in a sordid flattery, is still buried in this obscurity. But Christ went up those roads to rule the world.

The Baths of Tiberias lie a mile from the south end of the city wall. Amidst the wreckage of fortune and of name with which this coast is strewn, these springs, ministering to the changeless sorrows of humanity, have preserved their reputation and their name. Hammath they were in the Old Testament, Emmaus when the Greeks came, and to-day Ḥummam.[4] Patients come from all parts of Syria, chiefly in June and July, when the neighbourhood is crowded. Like other medicinal baths in the East, they heal also the feuds and quarrels of the population. The peninsula on which the baths of Gadara stand is, as we shall see, considered neutral ground by rival tribes around it. So was it here. When Josephus and John of Gischala divided

[1] Schürer is wrong: "the most beautiful spot in Galilee", *Hist.* I, ii. 19; "a beautiful and fertile district", *ib.* ii. 143.

[2] Dr. Ewing, late of Tiberias, informs me that this is correct. Many have noticed it: Robinson, Macgregor, etc. Tiberias lies in face of the hot south winds blowing up the Ghor, cf. Frei, *ZDPV*, ix. 100 f.

[3] When Saladin took Tiberias in 1187, the citadel did not yield to him till after the battle of Ḥaṭṭin.

[4] Ἀμμαθοῦς, not Ἀμμαοῦς, is the right reading in xviii *Antt.* ii. 3, iv *Wars*, i. 3 (Niese). There are four springs at about 144°: "The deposit consists chiefly of carbonate of lime with a very small proportion of muriatic salts", Robinson, *BR*, iii. 259, 260. Merrill, *East of Jordan*, mentions a cave filled with steam at 86°, on the hill on which the castle stands.

Galilee into rival camps, the latter, pretending sickness, requested from Josephus a safe-conduct that he might visit the baths at Emmaus, and it was granted.[1] Doubtless also the existence of these wells reconciled the Jews to Tiberias, and changed that banned and cursed site into one of the four sacred cities of the Jews, with thirteen synagogues. The baths were famed across the ancient world. Pliny speaks of Tiberias "calidis aquis salubris"[2]: and on a coin of Tiberias under Trajan is a figure of Hygeia, feeding the serpent of Aesculapius, and sitting on a rock from beneath which breaks a spring.[3] Our Lord paid no visit to this spring as He did to the pool of Bethesda, but the patients brought to it from all parts of Syria probably swelled the numbers who were laid at His feet. There are now in Tiberias, for His sake, a physician and a hospital, with the same opportunities.[4]

Of equal importance with Tiberias was Taricheæ, for according to Pliny,[5] in his day it gave its name to the whole Lake; it had a large population in 52 B.C., when we first hear of it[6]; it was a centre of industry and commerce, and in Josephus' time a greater stronghold of Jewish patriotism than almost any other in Galilee. But there is a mystery about Taricheæ. The name is neither in the Gospels nor upon the Lake to-day. Till definite proof be discovered, the site will continue a matter of debate, for the evidence we have is so balanced on either side that authorities have changed their opinions more than once.[7] We have one certain datum,[8] that Taricheæ was thirty

[1] ii *Wars*, xxi. 6. [2] *HN*, v. 15.

[3] De Saulcy, *Numis. de la Terre Sainte*, 335, Trajan, 1, 2: Plate xvii. 9.

[4] The Medical Mission of the Church of Scotland under Dr. Torrance.

[5] *HN*, v. 15.

[6] xiv *Antt.* vii. 3. Cassius visited it again in 43, writing to Cicero "ex castris Taricheis", Cic. *ad Familiares* xii. 11. The next mention of it is in Strabo, xvi. 2, 45. Nero gave it with Tiberias to Agrippa II (xx *Antt.* viii. 4; ii *Wars*, xiii. 2).

[7] The question was discussed by officers of the English Survey: *PEFQ*, 1877, 10 ff., Wilson, originally in favour of the south site at Kerak, here fixes on Mejdel; 121, Kitchener on Kh. el-Ḳuneiṭtriyeh, 2 m. N of Tiberias; 181, Conder quotes Pliny. In 1878, p. 79, H. K. K.; 190 ff., Conder argues for Kerak. Ebers, Guthe (*Pälastina*, i. 317 f., 501), and Socin (*Bädeker*, 1876) favour the north site, Mejdel. Discussion continues through *ZDPV*, viii. 95, Spiers (Mejdel); ix. 104 ff. Frei (do.); x. 120, Jakob; xi. 216 ff., van Kasteren seeks to remove objections to Kerak from Vespasian's advance on Tiberias, by taking the latter not along the coast, but by the plateau; xii. 145 ff., Furrer argues against Kerak and for a north site, both for Taricheæ and Emmaus of Vespasian's camp; 178, Dechent, against this second Emmaus; xiii. 140, Buhl answers objections to Kerak, and fixes Vespasian's camp at Ḥummam; 194, Furrer replies for Mejdel; 281, Guthe sums up for Kerak, changing from his former position. Schürer (*Hist.* I, i. 224) favours the south site. Albright, *Annual American Sch. Orient. Res. Jerus.* 1921-22, identifies it with Magdala.

[8] Josephus, *Life*, 32.

stadia, or three and three-quarter miles from Tiberias; was it north or south of Tiberias, was it at Kerak at the issue of the Jordan from the Lake, or at Mejdel on the Plain of Gennesaret? Pliny says south,[1] but his evidence as to other towns is not correct, and we cannot depend on him. The classic passage is the description by Josephus of Vespasian's advance from Scythopolis on Tiberias first and then on Taricheæ. It is argued that this proves Taricheæ to the north of Tiberias, for Vespasian could not have left it on his flank while attacking the latter, nor could the fugitives from Tiberias have fled, as described, to Kerak, for that would have been in the face of the Romans' advance up the coast. Mejdel has, therefore, been fixed upon, and as Josephus tells us that Vespasian's camp lay between Tiberias and Taricheæ at Emmaus, where were hot springs,[2] these have been recognised in wells two miles north of Tiberias, at the mouth of Wady 'Amwas or Abu el-'Amis.[3] The advocates of Kerak maintain that Emmaus can only be the baths south of Tiberias, that the mention of a plain between Tiberias and Taricheæ precludes Mejdel, while they seek to turn the objections to Kerak which rise from Vespasian's advance by understanding the latter to have taken place not along the coast past Kerak, but by the plateau. To this statement of the discussion three points are to be added. Kerak is not overhung with hills from which arrows could be shot into it, as Josephus describes Taricheæ to have been.[4] Josephus speaks of going to Arbela from Tiberias through Taricheæ,[5] which implies that the latter lay north of Tiberias. On the other hand, the only echo of the name of Taricheæ in later times is found on the south of the Lake.[6] The second point has been mentioned, but has not received its proper emphasis: the third has been overlooked. On opposite sides, they leave the question on the same delicate balance as the rest of the evidence. A more decisive discovery would be the presence of brine in considerable quantity at some point on the coast: failing that, the south end

[1] *HN*, xv. 3. [2] Josephus, iii *Wars*, x. 1: cf. iv *Wars*, i. 3.

[3] 'Amwas, Frei, *ZDPV*, ix. 104 ff.: Abu el-'Amis Eng. map.

[4] ὑπώρειος, iii *Wars*, x. 1. [5] *Life*, 59 and 60.

[6] In the Jichus ha-Ṣadiḳim (end of 16th cent.) which mentions next to the Baths of Tiberias a סראקה, that is like a corruption of Taricheæ. See p. 386 of Carmoly's *Itineraires de la Terre Sainte des xiii*[e]*-xvii*[e] *siècles*.—Conder's identification of Taricheæ with Takar or Takar-Aar of the Mohar's travels (*Handbook*, p. 279) cannot be thought of, for Taricheæ is Greek. Nor is Neubauer's identification of Taricheæ with the Talmudic בית ירח, which he supposes corrupted to תריח, likely; though בית ירח is placed near Sennabris, probably by the issue of the Jordan (*Géog. du Talmud*, p. 216, cf. with p. 31). Kerak he supposes a corruption of בית ירח = קיר ירח. This is equally unlikely. More probable is the hypothesis that Kerak is a reminiscence of Rakkath.

of the Lake as nearest to the Dead Sea, would be the most convenient position for such curing-yards as formed the staple industry of Tarichеæ.[1] Kerak, too, lies on a peninsula, just where the Jordan issues from the Lake, and is the only position on the coast which now suits Josephus' description of Tarichеæ as washed on more than one side by the sea.

Tarichеæ is a Greek word, and means "pickling places", and Strabo says that "at Tarichеæ the Lake supplied excellent pickling-places".[2] The pickled fish of Galilee were known through the Roman world: not only were large quantities taken up to Jerusalem at the season of the yearly feasts for the multitudes gathered there, but barrels were carried round the Mediterranean. Josephus describes Tarichеæ as full of materials for ship-building, and with many artisans.[3] The harbour could shelter a fleet of vessels. That so important a place, and moreover one not like Tiberias, official and foreign, but thoroughly Galilean, as Josephus testifies, and a centre of the disciples' own craft, should not be mentioned in the Gospels is remarkable.[4] The reason may be that, at this date, Tarichеæ was still Greek—the name implies that its industry at least was of foreign introduction. But if the town really lay at the south-west corner of the Lake, we must remember that this district seems never to have been visited by our Lord and His disciples. Perhaps it was out of the way of those main roads which they selected for their journeys, and yet not solitary enough to afford them a retreat. Not only Tarichеæ is omitted from the Gospels; nothing south of Gennesaret is mentioned, neither Tiberias nor the Baths, nor Sennabris, nor Tarichеæ, nor Homonœa, nor Scythopolis.[5]

[1] Seetzen (*Reisen*) reports the name Mellaḥa, "salt", as heard by him near Kerak. Robinson (*BR*, iii. 263) suspects a confusion with 'Ain Mellaḥa on Lake Ḥuleh; but Frei reports that, while he missed the name Sinn en-Nabra, Mellaḥa was given him as a place to be sought on the hill slopes, and van Kasteren heard the coast-level called Mellaḥa (for these see n. 7, p. 292), and Guérin reports Khurbet el-Mellaḥa. If this be so it would go far towards fixing the southern site.

[2] xvi. ch. ii, § 45. Pickled fish (*Ταρίχη*) were much known in the Roman and Greek world. Some places on the Egyptian coast had the name *Ταριχέαι*. The Galilean port is called *Ταριχέαι*, *Ταριχαῖαι*, and *Ταριχαία*.

[3] iii *Wars*, x. 6.

[4] Large draughts of fish, such as in the Gospels, must have been carried to Tarichеæ to be cured. They could not be otherwise used in that climate.

[5] How little is to be inferred from the silence of the Gospels about places mentioned in Josephus is to be seen from the converse silence of Josephus about Nazareth. He agitated and fought well over Galilee, he mentions villages as obscure as Nazareth, and yet is silent about it. Homonœa (Jos. *Life*, 54), *Ὁμονοία*, 30 stades from Tiberias, Arḍ el-Ḥamma (Furrer, *ZDPV*, ii. 52), or Umm Junia as on *PEF Map*, 1891. On the lost Philoteria, to the south of the Lake, Polybius v. 10, cf. Schürer, I, i. 196.

North of Tiberias lay Magdala, the present Mejdel on the Plain of Gennesaret,[1] and Capernaum, Beth-saida, and Chorazin upon sites which may always remain in dispute. Chorazin might be Kersa on the eastern shore, but is more probably the present ruins[2] of Kerazeh north of Tell-Ḥum. Capernaum has been assigned both to Tell-Ḥum, three miles SW of the issue of Jordan and to Khan Minyeh on the north edge of Gennesaret; but the evidence is on the whole in favour of the latter,[3] and one may fix the house of Jesus, as Mark calls it, the birthplace of the Gospel, at that north-east corner of fair Gennesaret, where the waves beat now on an abandoned shore, but once there was a quay and a busy town, and the great road from east to west poured its daily stream of life.

[1] Migdal-el, cf. Josephus. See Ewing "Magadan", Hastings' *DB*. Mark viii. 10 gives Dalmanutha. In the Talmud are various Magdalas or Migdals, one a Sabbath journey from Tiberias and so nearer this than Mejdel; Buhl thinks S of Tiberias, perhaps Mejdal Minya. There was, too, M. Sebo'ayya (Buhl, 225 f.).

[2] With which Willibald, 723-726, identifies it.

[3] Capernaum was Kephar-Nahum, the village of Nahum. A strong Christian tradition from the 6th cent. on fixed it at Tell Ḥum, and this site is preferred by Wilson, Furrer, Ritter, Guérin, Guthe, Buhl, Masterman, Socin (*Baed.* ed. 3) and Schürer (II, ii. p. 71). Christian tradition has erred in regard to other sites, *e.g.* Sychar. Tell Ḥum is an impossible contraction from Kephar-Nahum. There is no Tell at the place, and Guérin (*Galil.* i. 279) is right in deriving the name from Tanhum, a Rabbi buried here (cf. *Jichus ha-Abot* in Carmoly, *Itiner., etc., des xiii*[e]*-xvii*[e] *siècles*, 449, 478; *Jichus ha-Ṣadiḳim, ib.* 385, sets there the tombs of Nahum and Tanhum). Tell Ḥum is on the great road, and near the frontier, so it suits Capernaum as a customs city, but it is waterless, with no such fountain as Josephus describes in Capernaum, iii *Wars*, x. 8, nor near enough to Gennesaret to suit his data. For reasons for Tell Ḥum from the fine synagogue discovered there see Masterman's description and argument, *Studies in Galilee* (1909), 71 ff. But that was not necessarily the Capernaum synagogue emphasised in the Gospels (Mark i. 21, iii. 1, 5; Luke vii. 1-10, etc.); indeed, good authorities date it from the 2nd cent. A.D.

For Khan Minyeh tradition is nearly as old. Arculf (670) found Capernaum here, and in 1334 Isaac Chilo (*Les Chemins de Jérus.*, Carmoly 259), who arrived at Kefar-Nahum, says that here aforetime dwelt Minim, the Jews' name for Christian converts. The Talmud defines sinners, or Minim, as "sons of Kefar-Nahum". So Conder and others see Minim survive in Minyeh. Furrer (*ZDPV*, ii. 58 ff.) objects that a nickname would scarcely survive where the real name had died, and Gildemeister (*ib.* iv. 194 ff.) says Minyeh, which he spells from old authorities *el-munja*, is the Arabic word (in Egypt and Spain), from the Greek *μονή* and = mansio, villa, steading, small village. Here, in the 11th cent., lay a place Munjat Hischam (Kazwini's *Lexicon*). Hischam was dropped; in 1430 el-Munja is mentioned as a large village, after which even the Lake is called (el-Munja is the Spanish Almunia). Tristram, *Israel*, gives the form Miniyeh; so Delitzsch derives the name from Mineh, *harbour*. However this may be, Khan Minyeh suits the description of Josephus, iii *Wars*, x. 8; he might as easily be brought here when wounded on the Jordan (*Life*, 71-73) as to Tell-Ḥum. The references in the Gospels to Capernaum suit Khan Minyeh. There are ruins, Quaresmius,

With regard to Beth-saida, it has been supposed by most that the references in the Gospels imply two places of that name. Of one of these there can be no doubt, Bethsaida, Fisher-Home, was a village on the east bank of Jordan, and near the river's mouth, which the tetrarch Philip rebuilt and named Julias, in honour of the daughter of Augustus.[1] This is the Beth-saida to which Jesus withdrew on hearing of the Baptist's death,[2] and near which *was the desert place,*[3] described by John[4] as on *the other side of the Sea of Galilee*, where the five thousand, who had followed Him *on foot* by the fords over Jordan,[5] were miraculously fed. The level plain on the east of the Jordan, the Baṭaiḥa, so fertile that some have claimed it for Gennesaret, still helps us to understand how there was much *grass in the place.*[6] When the meal was over, Jesus, we are told, constrained His disciples to *go before to the other side towards Beth-saida.* Does this oblige us to admit another Beth-saida on the western coast? Some, however, unwillingly,[7] conclude that it does, and have found the second Beth-saida either as a suburb of Julias on the west bank of Jordan,[8] or farther along the coast at 'Ain eṭ-Ṭabigha.[9] But when Jesus urges His disciples *to go across* to Beth-saida, this does not imply a crossing to the west, for Josephus speaks of "sailing over from Tiberias to Taricheæ", though these towns lay on the same side of the Lake.[10] And in this case it would be natural for Jesus to wish to return from the scene of the miracle, which we may place some way down the eastern coast, to Beth-saida-Julias, for, according to Luke, He had just fled there from Herod's jurisdiction

ii. 568, both on the plain (Robinson and Merrill (*E. of Jordan*, 301 f.) who found a city wall) and on the hill, Schumacher (*ZDPV*, xiii. 70: place-names Tell el-'Oreime, Dahr es-sillam, Arḍ es-siḳi umm Je'ade[?]). Robinson, *LBR*, 348-358; Conder, *Handbook* and *TW*; Henderson, *Pal.* 158 f.; Keim's *Jesus*, Eng. ed. ii. 367 ff.; Stanley, *Sin. and Pal.* 384, etc. Also the well and stream of Ṭabigha is near enough to be Josephus' "fountain of Capernaum", and across the steep rock above Khan Minyeh is an excavated passage, now a path, which may well have been a duct for the copious water that Josephus says watered Gennesaret. On the whole after all those years of argument I still incline to my opinion of 1894 that Khan Minyeh represents Capernaum. Further see my article in *Enc. Bibl.* 1899; and on opposite sides of the question, Herbert Rix, *Tent and Testament*, 1907, App. D, and Masterman, *Studies in Galilee*, 1909, ch. iv. Recent private letters confirm my opinion.

[1] xviii *Antt.* ii. 1; ii *Wars*, ix. 1. On its position cf. xviii *Antt.* ii. 1, which fixes it on the Lake with *Life*, 72, near Jordan; cf. ii *Wars*, xiii. 2, across Jordan, though this may be the other Julias of Herod Antipas.

[2] Luke ix. 10. [3] Mark vi. 31; Matt. xiv. 13. [4] John vi. 10.

[5] One is now two miles from the mouth, *PEF Large Map*.

[6] John vi. 10; they sat on *green grass*, Mark vi. 39; *on grass*, Matt. xiv. 19.

[7] Reland (653-655), who feels himself very unwillingly shut up to two Bethsaidas. Henderson, *Pal.* 156, 157.

[8] Thomson, *Land and Book.* [9] Fürer v. Haimendorf, 1566. [10] *Life*, 59.

in the west. The Fourth Gospel speaks of *Beth-saida in Galilee*,[1] but this need not mean that it lay west of the Jordan, for, as we have seen, the province of Galilee ran right round the Lake, and included most of the level coastland on the east.[2] It is not, therefore, necessary to demand more than one Beth-saida.[3] Wherever these three—Capernaum, Beth-saida, and Chorazin—may have been, the well-nigh complete obliteration of all of them is remarkable in this, that they were the three towns which our Lord condemned to humiliation.

Down the east coast the city of Gergesa has been identified with the ruins known as Kersa, at the only portion of that coast on which the steep hills come down to the shore.[4] Farther south there is the gorge of Fiḳ or Aphek, up which the great road ran from Scythopolis to Damascus. On a long camel's-neck of hill, which fills the middle of this gorge, the Ḳula'at el-Ḥoṣn, Gamala has been placed,[5] but more probably it is Hippos, with Aphek, now Fiḳ, near, as described by Eusebius.[6] Hippos, however, is claimed for Susiyeh, above the same gorge. [7] Apheḳ lay a little higher up on

[1] xii. 21.

[2] As the Turkish Ḳad'at Tubariyeh (cf. ii *Wars*, xx. 4). Even Judas of Gamala is sometimes called Galilean, xviii *Antt.* i. 6. Ptolemæus, A.D. 140, reckons Julias to Galilee, but by that time it had been definitely attached to the latter (A.D. 84).

[3] So also Holtzmann, *Jahrb. für Prot. Theol.* 1878, No. 2, 283 f. Buhl reaches this conclusion on the same evidence, and pertinently adds that the native town Bethsaida need not have been the same as the half-heathen Julias which Jesus would hardly have entered, but was probably the latter's port. He quotes Schumacher, *ZDPV*, ix. 319, that Beth-saida may have been the present ruins, el-'Araj on the sea, and connected with et-Tell, the site of Julias, by a street. But see xviii. *Antt.* ii. 1. Descriptions and arguments by Rix and Masterman in works cited above should be consulted.

[4] Gergesa is not a sure reading and Gerasa is contested. Keim, *Jesus*, has argued for Gadara. Westcott and Hort prefer *Γαδαρηνῶν* in Matt. viii. 28, *Γερασηνῶν*, Mark v. 1, Luke viii. 26. If *Γέρασα* was the name of the town it may well be Kersa or Gersa (so first Thomson, *Land and Book*, ii. 35; Warren, Hastings' *DB*, "Gerasenes"; G. A. Smith, *American Journ. of Theol.* iv. 106). Origen knew of a city Gergesa. In 1283 Burchardus writes "Gerasa civitas in littore maris sita est sub monte Seyr contra Tiberiadem fere, sed modicum declinans ad aquilonem." Cf. Furrer, *ZDPV*, xxi (1899), 184 f.

[5] See, for the arguments between this and Gamli, Schürer, *Hist.* ii. 1; Furrer, *ZDPV*, ii. 149 f., and Van Kasteren, *ib.* xiii. 215 ff., place it in Jamli on the Rukkad, but against this Schumacher, *ib.* xv. 175, who suggests el-Eḥṣun (*N. Ajlun*, 116).

[6] Josephus places it on the E coast, 30 stadia from Tiberias (xiv *Antt.* iv. 4, xv. vii. 3, xvii. xi. 4; ii *Wars*, xviii. 1, 5; *Life*, 9, 65). Susiyeh is properly of the plain S of the gorge, Arḍ Susiyeh. Cf. Rabbinic Susitha.

[7] Clermont-Ganneau was the first to suggest that Susiyeh, the Arab equivalent of Hippos, might be found here, and the discovery was made by Schumacher, *PEFQ*, 1887, 36 ff.; *The Jaulân*, 244; Neubauer, *Géo. du Talm.* 238 f.

the plateau, the present village of Fiḳ. And Gadara looked up the Lake from the heights immediately south of the Yarmuk.[1] Below Gadara, in the Ghor, there must have been villages, some by the Lake like the present Semakh, and some at the foot of the hills, where ruins now lie.[2]

This catalogue of the towns on the Lake of Galilee, if it fail to fix for us the sites of many, cannot but help our imagination to realise the almost unbroken line of buildings by which the Lake was surrounded. Of this her coasts still bear the mark. As the Dead Sea is girdled by an almost constant hedge of driftwood, so is the Sea of Galilee by a scarcely less continuous belt of ruins—the drift of her ancient towns.[3] In the time of our Lord she must have mirrored within the outline of her guardian hills little else than city-walls, houses, synagogues, wharves, and factories.[4] Greek architecture hung its magnificence over her simple life: Herod's castle, temple, and theatres in Tiberias; the bath-houses at Hammath; a hippodrome at Taricheæ; and, farther back from the shore, the high-stacked houses of Hippos; the theatre in Gadara, looking up the Lake with the Acropolis above it, and the paved street with its triumphal archway; the Greek villas on the heights about Gadara; with a Roman camp or two, high enough up the slopes to catch the western breeze, and daily sending its troops to relieve guard in the cities. All this was what imposed itself upon that simple life on fields and roads and boats, which we see in the Gospels, sunny and free. Amid the sowing and reaping, the fishing and mending of nets, the journeying to and fro upon foot, simple habits of the native life, do we not catch some shadows of that other world, which had grown up around it, in the crowds that are said to grind on one another in the narrow lanes, like corn between millstones[5]; in the figures of the centurion, the publican, and the demoniac crying that his name was Legion; in the stories of the pulling down of barns and the building of greater, of opulent householders leaving their well-appointed villas for a time with every servant in his place, and the porter set to watch, of markets and *streets*, as well as *lanes*[6]; in the comparison of the towns on the Lake to great cities—Sodom and Gomorrah, Tyre, Sidon

[1] For Gadara see ch. xxix.

[2] Over the road down the Ghor, SW from Gadara, at the foot of the hill.

[3] "These accumulated fragments, the multitude of towns, and the magnificence of the constructions of which they were proofs, recalled to my mind the roads which lead along the foot of Vesuvius from Castellamare to Portici. As there, the borders of the Lake of Gennesareth seem to have borne cities instead of harvests and forests." —*Lamartine*.

[4] There were tanneries and potteries by the present 'Ain eṭ-Ṭabigha.

[5] Mark v. 24: *συνέθλιβον αὐτόν*; cf. Luke viii. 42; *συνέπνιγον αὐτόν*.

[6] *Go ye out into the streets and lanes.*

and Nineveh; in the mention of the sins of a city,[1] and of Mammon and *all the things after which the Gentiles seek*, and in the acknowledgment that Galilee was a place where a man might *gain the whole world.*[2]

Twice I have seemed to see the Lake as it lay in those thronged days. One of these occasions was among the tombs of Gadara. Some peasants had just dug up the gravestone of a Roman soldier, whose name was given —P . . . Aelius, and that he had lived forty years, and served nineteen; also that he was of a Legion, the Fourteenth.[3] As I read this last detail—and the word is still stamped on other stones in the neighbourhood—I realised how familiar that engine of foreign oppression had been to this region, so that the poor madman could find nothing fitter to describe the incubus upon his own life. *My name is Legion*, he said, *for we are many*. The second occasion was at Fiḳ, as I looked across the site of Gamala and down the gorge, on the Lake and the houses of Tiberias opposite—their squalor glorified in the mid-day sun. I saw nothing but water and houses, and the sound came over the hill of a bugle of a troop of Turkish horse. It was a glimpse and echo of that time when Greek cities and Roman camps environed the Lake. Yet only a glimpse; for Gamala should have been stacked with her high houses, and the Lake dotted with sails, and on the air there should have been the hum of tens of thousands of people crowded in a few square miles. The only sound I heard, save the bugle, was of bees. The scene differs from what it was as much as a wood in winter from a wood in summer, or a bay at ebb from a bay near full tide, when the waters are rushing and the boats are sailing to and fro.

The industries of the Lake of Galilee were agriculture and fruit-growing; dyeing and tanning, with every department of a carrying trade; but chiefly

[1] Luke vii. 37. [2] Luke ix. 25.

[3] The whole inscription read as follows:

DM
P . AEL . . .
BI . . . . . ZΛ
. . . . . . IOB
MILES LEG XIIII
G AÑO XL
STIP XIX ER
VDES INSTIT
VTI M GAI
VS ET RVFI .
US PROCV
RAVERVNT

Publius (?) Aelius . . . A soldier of the Fourteenth Legion, Gemina, in his fortieth year, and nineteenth of service; the heirs designate, Marcus Gaius and Rufinus (?), saw to everything.

fishing, boat-building, fish-curing. Of the last, which spread the Lake's fame over the Roman world before its fishermen and their habits became familiar through the Gospel, there is no trace in the Evangelists. The fisheries were pursued by thousands of families. They were no monopoly; but the fishing-grounds, best at the north end of the Lake, where the streams entered, were free to all. And the trade was profitable.[1]

In the ranks of those who pursued this free and hardy industry Christ looked for His disciples. Not wealthy, they were independent, with no servile tempers, and no private or trade wrongs disadjusting their consciences. This was one reason why our Lord chose them. In that age it would have been easy to gather, as David did into the Cave of Adullam, all in debt, or in distress or discontented, or run away from their masters. But such would not have been the men to preach a spiritual gospel, the coming, not of a national, but of a universal, kingdom. Men brought up, however justly, to feel the wrongs of their class or of their trade before anything else would have been of no use to Christ. Just as futile would those "innovators" have proved, whom Josephus describes to have largely composed the population of Galilee. Christ went to a trade with no private wrongs: and called men not from their dreams, but from work they were content to do from day to day till something higher should touch them. And so it has come to pass that not the jargon of the fanatics and brigands in the highlands of Galilee, but the speech of the fishermen of her Lake, and the instruments of their simple craft, have become the language and symbolism of the world's religion.

XXII. *THE JORDAN VALLEY*[2]

Among the rivers of the world the Jordan is unique by a twofold distinction of Nature and History. Hundreds of other streams are more large, useful, or beautiful; none has been more spoken about by mankind. Other rivers have awakened a richer poetry in the peoples through whom they pass—for the references to Jordan in the Bible are few, and, with two or three exceptions, prosaic—but of none has the music sounded so far or so pleasantly, across the world. There are holy waters which annually attract a greater

[1] See above on Taricheæ, pp. 292-294. Frei reports that, in one cast of the net from the shore, he saw a fisherman secure 28, and he infers an enormous wealth of fish in the Lake, *ZDPV*, ix. 102. On the kinds of fish, see Hasselquist's *Travels*; Tristram, *The Land of Israel*; Merrill, *East of Jordan*, i. 41. They are chiefly a kind of mullet.

[2] For this chapter, see Maps 2, 5, and 6.

number of pilgrims, but to none do pilgrims travel from such various and distant lands. In influence upon the imagination of man, the Nile is perhaps the Jordan's only competitor. He has drawn to his valley one after another of the greatest races of the world; his mystery and annual miracle have impressed the mind equally of ancient and of modern man. But the Nile has never been adopted by a universal religion. To the fathers of human civilisation that silent flood, which cut their land in two, across which their dead were ferried, and the Lord Sun himself passed daily to his death among the desert hills, was the symbolic border of the next world. But who now knows this, who feels it, save as a fact of ancient history? Whereas, still to half the world, the short, thin thread of the Jordan is the symbol of both frontiers of the spirit's life on earth—the baptism through which it passes into God's Church, and the waters of death which divide this pilgrim fellowship from the Promised Land.

The Nile and the Jordan, otherwise so different, are alike in this, that the historical singularity of each has behind it as remarkable a singularity of physical formation. Both valleys were laid open by the same geological disturbance,[1] and it left them equally monstrous and unique. Every one knows the incomparableness of the Nile, solitary and stupendous, which, unfed for a thousand miles by tributary or by rain, has sustained of his own resource the civilisation of a mighty empire, and still, by his annual flood, bestows on the desert a fertility not excelled in any country, which has the fountains of heaven and of the great deep in its fortune. In its own way the Jordan is as solitary and extreme an effect of natural forces. There may be something on the surface of another planet to match the Jordan Valley: there is nothing on this. No other part of our earth, uncovered by water, sinks to 500 feet below the level of the ocean.[2] But here we have a rift more than one hundred and sixty miles long,[3] and from two to fifteen broad, which falls from the sea-level to as deep as 1292 feet below it at the coast of the Dead

[1] Hull, *PEF Survey Memoirs, Geology*, 108; Dawson, *Mod. Science in Bible Lands*, 588; Gregory, *Proc. Brit. Assoc.* 1894. See below.

[2] Other parts of continents below ocean-level are: the level of the Caspian Sea more than 80 feet below that of the Black Sea; part of the Caspian coasts; a depression between Lake Elton and the Ural, in which a lake used to lie, but is now dry, 151 feet below the Black Sea. The Fayum, part of which is 5 to 20 feet under sea-level; and the Shott Melr'ir marshes and salt fields in the Sahara, from 95 to 279 feet below the Mediterranean. The Liukchin oasis in Central Asia; the lowest part, the salt lake Bojaite, is about 330 feet below Turfan, itself 160 feet below the sea (*Izvestiya* of the Russian Geogr. Soc. i. 1894, quoted *Scottish Geogr. Maga.* x. 542). Also part of SE Arabia as just (1931) found by Mr. Thomas.

[3] From just below Lake Ḥuleh, where the dip begins, to where on the Arabah S of the Dead Sea, the valley rises to sea-level.

Sea, while the bottom of the latter is 1300 feet deeper. In this trench there are the Jordan, nearly one hundred miles long; two great lakes, twelve and fifty-three miles in length; large tracts of arable country, especially about Gennesaret, Bethshan, and Jericho; regions once populous like the coasts of the Lake of Galilee; and the sites of some famous towns—Tiberias, Jericho, and the "Cities of the Plain". Is it not true that on earth there is nothing else like this deep, this colossal ditch?

Geologists[1] tells us that while these regions were still covered with water, from which the granite peaks of Sinai alone protruded, deposits of limestone were laid upon the ocean-bed. Under pressure from east and west the limestone rose above the water in folds, running north and south.[2] Two of these are now the ranges on either side of the Jordan Valley, but the Valley is due, not only to their elevation, but to a rupture of the strata between them. This "fault" is not confined to that portion of the Valley which is beneath sea-level: it extends from Northern Syria, between the Lebanons, down the Jordan and along Wady Arabah to the Gulf of 'Aḳaba, three hundred and fifty miles.[3] Had the two long folds risen in isolation from each other, the valley would have been an arm of the Red Sea stretching to the foot of Lebanon, and in that case how changed the history of Palestine must have been! But the two folds were not disconnected. As they rose from the waters there rose between them, near their south end, a diagonal ridge of limestone, still visible about forty-five miles to the north of the Gulf of 'Aḳaba on the water-shed between 'Aḳaba and the Dead Sea.[4] This not only shut out the Red Sea, but shut in part of the old ocean-bed with a large quantity of salt water.[5] There followed a period of great rains, with perpetual snow and glaciers on Lebanon, during which the valley was filled with fresh water for two hundred miles,[6] or one long lake from the Sea of Galilee to some fifty miles south of the present end of the Dead Sea. How the valley passed from that condition to its present is not clear. Some think the change

[1] Hull, *PEF Mem. Geol.* Pt. IV, ch. i. 108 ff.; Dawson, *Mod. Science in Bible Lands*, ch. viii and App. iv; Lartet, *La Mer Morte*; Conder, *TW*, 217 ff.; Blanckenhorn, *ZDPV*, 1896.

[2] "Early in the Miocene epoch, by tangential pressure of earth's surface due to contraction, by the secular cooling of the crust."—Hull, p. 108.

[3] Dawson, p. 442.

[4] "The water-parting crossing the valley has continued as such ever since the region emerged from the ocean."—Hull, *ib.* 20.

[5] Hull, 109 (also 120), accounts for the peculiar fauna and flora of the Lake of Galilee and Jordan by their original connection with the ocean, 109, 110. They suffered the change experienced elsewhere, *e.g.* on the Caspian Sea, of the passage from salt to fresh water.

[6] Hull, 15, 113, with sketch-map, 72, showing the lake; Dawson, 444.

of climate—great decrease of rain with the disappearance of the glaciers—enough to account for the gradual shrinking of the one large lake to two smaller ones.[1] There are, however, traces of various sea-beaches so distinct, and some so far apart, that it has been inferred that the confinement of the water successively within these must have been caused as much by sudden convulsions, for which the region has been notorious, as by gradual desiccation. This is supported by the fact that, within the observation of man, the Dead Sea has not become smaller, but rather increased.[2] Volcanic disturbances on a large scale took place in the Jordan Valley within comparatively recent times.[3]

In this rift from the Lebanons to the Red Sea are six distinct sections: the Beḳa‘ between the Lebanons; Upper Jordan, from its sources at the foot of Hermon through Lake Ḥuleh to the Lake of Galilee; this Lake; Lower Jordan to its mouth at Jericho; the Dead Sea; and, thence to the Gulf of ‘Aḳaba, the Wady Arabah. The first and last fall outside our area, and we have already visited the Lake of Galilee; there remain Upper Jordan, Lower Jordan, and the Dead Sea.

1. *The Upper Jordan*[4]

The great valley of Palestine, as it runs out from between the Lebanons, makes a slight turn east round the foot of Hermon, so that Hermon not only looks right down the rest of its course, but is able to discharge into this three-fourths of the waters which gather on his high and ample bulk. By these and streams, which break from the rest of the surrounding hills, the floor of the valley is soaked in moisture. Once, probably, it was all a lake. To-day this has shrunk to its lower end, the so-called Lake of Ḥuleh, and the rest is marsh and fat meadow, with a few mounds and terraces covered by trees. Four streams, which unite before entering the lake, contest the honour of being the source of the Jordan. The only one which does not spring upon the east watershed is the Nahr Bareighit, which comes down the Merj ‘Ayun from a source slightly separated from the valley of the Liṭany. It is the smallest. The next, Nahr Ḥaṣbany, springs half a mile to the north of Ḥaṣbeya, from a buttress of Hermon, and comes south between Hermon and the Jebel Dahar. This is the longest of the four, and most in the line of Jordan itself, but it has much less water than either of the other

[1] Hull, 115. [2] Conder, *TW*, 210, 220. [3] Nötling, *ZDPV*, 1885.

[4] On the name Jordan see Seybold, *MuNDPV*, 1896, 10, 26, and my note *Amer. Journal of Theol.* 107.

two—Nahr Leddan, the heaviest but the shortest, springing from Tell el-Ḳaḍi, in the bosom of the valley itself; and Nahr Banias, which has the most impressive origin of all four, in the roots of Hermon, and gathers the most tributaries. It is these two which have generally been regarded as the sources of Jordan.[1]

Travellers usually arrive first at the source of the Leddan, a mound, perhaps a hundred yards long, and rising some sixty feet above the plain before the plain rises to Hermon. Draped by trees and bush, it is plumed and crested by a grove of oaks. On the west side, through huge boulders, whose lower half its rush has worn bare, a stream, about twelve feet broad by three deep, breaks from the bowels of the earth; while another, more shallow and quiet, appears higher in a jungle of reeds and bushes. This opulent mound is called Tell el-Ḳaḍi, and Ḳaḍi means the same as Dan. It is, therefore, supposed to be the site of Laish or Leshem, which the Danites took for their city.[2] But this might also be fixed at Banias, and with more probability,[3] for Banias is a better site than Tell el-Ḳaḍi for the capital of the district, and we cannot conceive any tribe as able to hold Tell el-Ḳaḍi who did not also hold Banias.[4]

Paneas lies scarcely an hour north of Tell el-Ḳaḍi. From the latter you pass a well-watered meadow, covered by trees, and a broad terrace with oaks, like an English park, till you come to the edge of a gorge, through which roars a headlong stream, half stifled by bush. A Roman bridge takes you over, and through a tangle of trees, brushwood, and fern you break into sight of a high cliff of limestone, reddened by the water oozing over its face

[1] No ancient writer mentions any sources of Jordan but these two last at Dan and Banias. Josephus styles that springing from Dan "the so-called Little Jordan", iv *Wars*, i. 1, cf. viii *Antt.* viii. 4; again, "the Lesser Jordan", v *Antt.* iii. 1. The source at Banias he calls the reputed fountain of Jordan, i *Wars*, xxi. 3; iii *ib.* x. 7. In the latter passage he tells his story of Lake Phiala as the ultimate source, from which he says it had been proved, by throwing chaff into it, that the fountains at Banias were fed. Phiala, "120 stadia on the way to Trachonitis", is probably Birket er-Ram, Robinson, *BR*, iii. 614 ff. *Onomasticon*, sub *Λεῖσα* (Laisa), gives Paneas as the source. From Arculf (700) on through Willibald (722), and the series of narratives and chronicles in Crusading times (Saewulf, Fetellus, Benjamin of Tudela, De Joinville, etc.), and later Maundeville (1322), Felix Fabri (1480)—the story runs that Jordan springs from two sources, Jor and Dan, at the foot of Lebanon, near Banias. (But Daniel (1106) calls the two issues from the Lake of Galilee, Jor and Dan.) How the names arose is clear. Dan was known to have lain there, and they took the second syllable to be its name. Jor, it was easy to suppose, was the name of the other fountain. But the ancients and mediævals located Dan, not at Tell el-Ḳaḍi, but at Paneas.

[2] See p. 60. In Josephus' time, when it was called Daphne, there was "a temple of the golden calf", iv *Wars*, i. 1.

[3] *Onomasticon*, art. *Λεῖσα*.

[4] See pp. 308, 309.

from the iron soil above.[1] In the cliff is a cavern. Part of the upper rock has fallen, and from the *débris* of boulders and shingle below bursts and bubbles along thirty feet a full-born river. The place is a sanctuary of waters, and from time immemorial men have drawn near to worship. As you stand within the charm of it, a charm not uncommon in the Lebanons, you understand why the early Semites adored the Baalim of the underground waters even before they raised their gods to heaven, and thanked them for the rain.[2] This must have been one of the chief seats of the Baalim, perhaps Baal-gad of the Book of Joshua.[3] When the Greeks came they also felt the presence of deity, and dedicated the grotto, as an inscription testifies, to Pan and the Nymphs.[4] Hill, cavern, and fountain were called the Paneion,[5] and town and district Paneas.[6] In 20 B.C. Herod the Great received the district from Augustus,[7] and built him a temple of white marble, setting the bust of Cæsar hard by the shrine of Pan.[8] Philip, tetrarch of this region, embellished the town and called it Cæsarea,[9] known as his Cæsarea—Cæsarea Philippi—to distinguish it from his father's on the sea-coast.[10] The official designation was altered by Agrippa II[11] to Neronias, which was used along with the name Cæsarea even under Marcus Aurelius,[12] but then died out. Cæsarea lasted a little longer in conjunction with Paneas,[12] till Paneas survived alone, and has survived to the present, only that Arabs, with no *p* upon their lips, spell it Banias.[13]

The extraordinary mixture of religious and political interests which gathered upon this charming site during the first centuries of our era may be seen at a glance, in its rich confusion, upon the pageful of the town's coins

[1] "From a hundred to a hundred and fifty feet", Robinson, *LBR*, 106.

[2] W. R. Smith, *Religion of the Semites*, 97, etc.

[3] Josh. xi. 17, xii. 7, xiii. 5; also a Baal-Hermon. Jud. iii. 3.

[4] *Πανί τε καὶ Νύμφαις* on the rock of the grotto.

[5] Josephus calls the "place" *τὸ Πάνειον*, xv *Antt.* x. 3; i *Wars*, xxi. 3; iii *Wars*, x. 7, the name of the fountain; Eusebius, *HE*, vii. 17, of the hill. In Josephus' time the cave overhung an unfathomable pool.

[6] See Schürer's note, *Hist. of Jewish People*, II, i. 133. *Πανιάς* or *Πανεάς*, properly an adjective, designates both the *country* (xv *Antt.* x. 3, etc.; cf. Pliny, *HN*, v. 18) and the *town* (xviii *Antt.* ii. 1).

[7] On the death of Zenodorus, the previous lord of these parts, xv *Antt.* x. 3; i *Wars*, xxi. 3.

[8] xviii *Antt.* ii. 1.

[9] *Ibid.*; iii *Wars*, ix. 7.

[10] xx *Antt.* ix. 4.

[11] De Saulcy, *Numismatique de la Terre Sainte*, 315, 316: Plate xviii, cf. No. 7 with No. 8.

[12] *Ibid.*

[13] بانياس. The tradition of its Greek origin was strong among the Arabs, only they took its founder to have been Balnias, *i.e.* Pliny!

which De Saulcy has reproduced.[1] On one, we have the syrinx or pipe of Pan; on a second Pan leaning on a tree, playing a flute; on a third the mouth of the cavern, with a rail in front and Pan within, again leaning on a tree playing the flute; on others the laurelled head of Apollo, a pillared temple, and inside the figure of Poppæa, Nero's wife, whom he kicked to death and then raised to divine honours; various emperors with their title Divus, and the town's title, "Cæsarea—August, Sacred and With Rights of Sanctuary—under Paneion."[2] This proves that the two systems of religion were carried on together, and that Pan was worshipped in the grotto, whose niches still bear his name, while divine honours were paid to Cæsar in the white temple that stood perhaps on the cliff above,[3] the site of the present Mohammedan shrine of Sheikh Khaḍr, or St. George.[4]

While both these sanctuaries were open, and men thus worshipped side by side the forces of nature and the incarnation of political power, Jesus came with His disciples to the coasts of Cæsarea Philippi. Never did the place better earn its title of Asylos, or shelter nobler fugitives. The journey of our Lord and His disciples was, in the first instance, a retreat from Jewish hostility to the neutrality of Gentile ground. But it became also the occasion of His resolution to return to meet the Jews, and the death which lay ready for Him in their hate. From this farthest corner of the land Jesus set His face steadfastly to Jerusalem. The scenery had already been consecrated by the crisis and turning of a soul, by the hope which another exile had seen break through his drenching sorrow, like as the sun breaks through the mists and saturated woods of the hills around.

"... From the land of Jordan,
And the Hermons, from the hill Mizar,
Deep unto deep is calling at the noise of thy waterfalls:
All thy breakers amd billows are gone over me.
With a breaking in my bones mine enemies reproach me,
While they say to me all the day, Where is thy God?

Why art thou cast down, O my soul?
And why art thou disquieted upon me?

[1] *Op. cit.* Plate xviii.

[2] *Op. cit.* Plate xviii, No. 8. *ΚΑΙC . CEB . IEP . ΚΑΙ . AC . ΥΠ . ΠΑΝΙΩ . AC.* is for ἄσυλος, with rights of asylum or sanctuary.

[3] The exact position of Herod's temple is unknown. Hewn stones are scattered all over the place.

[4] See p. 123.

> *Hope thou in God: for I shall yet praise Him,*
> *Health of my countenance, and my God.*"[1]

This Psalm, amidst its sympathetic scenery, may well have come into the hearts of these fugitives, and accomplished its due ministry to Him, Who at such crises in His life, summoned no other angel to His aid than some such winged word of Scripture. Yet even these high matters cannot have absorbed the disciples' attention, where so many pagan sanctuaries broke the beauty of the scene with their challenge to all that was best in the Jewish heart. That a mere man, however exalted, should have a temple built to him and especially by a Jewish prince, had filled Jewry with indignation. The little company of wayfarers must have talked of this obtrusive sanctuary. It is, therefore, striking that there and then they emphasised their own Master's claims upon the faith of mankind, and that the first clear confession of Christ's divine Sonship was made near the shrine in which men already worshipped a fellow-man as God. These were the two religions which were soon to contest the world—the marble temple covering the bust of an Emperor, the group of exiles round the leader whom His own people had rejected. They appeared to have this in common, that they were centred in individuals, that they both responded to the longing of the age for some embodiment of authority, that each paid divine homage to a man. Yet, even on that single point of resemblance, there was this distinction between them. He in the temple was only an official, the temporary symbol of a great power,

[1] Psalm xlii-xliii. *The Land of Jordan* usually means in O.T. land across Jordan. *Hermons* (not Hermonites) must refer to the triple peaks of Hermon. If these two identifications hold, the standpoint of the Psalmist is fixed in the corner between Hermon and Jordan, where Banias stands. To the two localities the Hill Mizar, מִצְעָר, is placed in apposition. It may mean, as it stands, Hill of Littleness. But it may also be a proper name; and it is remarkable that in the neighbourhood there should be two or three names with the same or kindred radicals: (1) Za'ura زعورا; צ often weakens to ז (Wright's *Comp. Grammar*, 58, 61); (2) Wady Za'arah, زعارة, above Banias; (3) Khurbet Mezara, مزارا. I suggest these may be reminiscent of a hill in this district, called Mizar; none other would have been put by the Psalmist in apposition to the Hermons. Cheyne: "To me this appendage to 'Hermonim' seems a poetic loss. Unless the little mountain has a symbolic meaning I could wish it away." I cannot see this; symbolic meanings for Hermonim and Mizar are forced, and even if we got a natural one, it would be out of place after the literal *Land of Jordan*. To employ all as proper names is suitable to a lyric. Baethgen's interpretation (following Smend) of the Hill of Littleness as equal to Mt. Zion in contrast to Hermon, and of the three factors, Jordan, Hermon, Zion, as equivalent to the Holy Land; and his translation, *I remember those far from the land of Jordan, and the Hermons, far from the little hill*, are forced and improbable.

to-day's dispenser of its largess, to-morrow to be succeeded by another. But the little band of fugitives outside clung to their Leader for His own eternal sake. He was the Kingdom, He was the Religion, everything lay for ever in His character and His love. Herod built the temple to Augustus for the same reason for which he had paid homage to Cæsar and Antony, or for which his children ascribed divine honours on this same spot to Claudius and Nero—because each of these for the moment had all things in his gift. But it was because they counted all things but loss for His sake that the disciples turned there and then to Christ, with a love and allegiance which could never be transferred to another, any more than God Himself might be imagined to yield to a successor in the faith of His creatures. And again, while the emperor compelled allegiance by his rank, his splendour, his power, Christ turned that day from the symbol of all this to seek His kingdom by the way of sacrifice and death. *Ye know that the rulers of the Gentiles lord it over them, and the great impose their authority upon them. . . . The Son of Man came not to be ministered unto, but to minister, and to give His life a ransom for many.* This was a contrast on which Christ often dwelt: nowhere can we better value the alternative which it presented to that generation, than here at Cæsarea by the sources of Jordan, where we see the apotheosis of the Gentile spirit in the temple raised to an Augustus by the flattery of a Herod, and Christ with His few disciples turning from it to His Cross and Sacrifice.

Before we leave this end of the Jordan Valley, we must notice one function which it has performed throughout history. Running up into the Lebanons, this long hollow is the gate from the north into Palestine, and Banias, which was a fortress as well as a sanctuary, is the key of the gate. It is true that *the entering in of Hamath*, the other end of the pass through the Lebanons, is spoken of as if it were the northern entrance into Palestine, but it is only the approach. Here in Dan lay the limit of the land of Israel. Beyond were rugged indefensible mountain ranges. If we may compare the region with one more extensive, the Lebanons were to Israel, for military purposes, what the mountains of Afghanistan are to India, and the fortress at Banias below Hermon, on the roads to Damascus and up the Beḳa', has a position not unlike that of Peshawur, near the entrance to the Khyber—though by the Syrian fortress there flows no river like the Indus. Did an invader come south between the Lebanons? He had to fight here: the battle by which Antiochus the Great won Palestine from the Ptolemies took place near Paneas.[1] Nor could the masters of Palestine hold the Upper Jordan except at the same time they held Banias. During the Latin Kingdom of Jerusalem the fortress

[1] 198 B.C. Polybius, xvi. 18; xxvii. 1.

was contested by Frank and Saracen. Did the Franks take it, then the rich valley was theirs. Did the Saracens win it back, then the Franks[1] in their castle of Hunin, on the opposite hills of Naphtali, were obliged to arrange with them for a division of the pastures and fields between. And in the Ninth Crusade, when an expedition of Louis of France conquered all the Jordan Valley, they were obliged to retire from it, because they failed to capture also the castle of Banias.[2]

It is these illustrations, taken from all parts of history, of the impossibility of holding the meadows and springs of Upper Jordan, without also holding Banias and its castle, which make it seem probable that Leshem or Dan was the present Banias, and not (in spite of the name) Tell el-Ḳaḍi. If there be in this latter name, which is doubtful, some reminiscence of the synonymous Dan,[3] then it is possible to suppose that we have here what we have in many places, the transference of a name a few miles from its original site. On all other appearances than the shadowy name, Banias, and not Tell el-Ḳaḍi, is the ancient capital of the Danites, the northern limit of the land of Israel.[4]

Curiously enough the two are now politically separate, Tell el-Ḳaḍi in Palestine under the British Mandate but Banias in the Province of Syria under France, the frontier[5] since 1922 running between them.

The rest of this plain is of little historical interest. Lake Ḥuleh is Lake Semechonitis of Josephus[6] but hardly the Waters of Merom of the Book of Joshua.[7] The open water girt by swamps and jungles of the papyrus reed is

[1] "The lands in the plain belong half to the Franks and half to the Moslem, and here is the boundary, called 'The Boundary of Dividing'." Ibn Jubair (A.D. 1185) in Le Strange, *Pal. under Moslems*, 418.

[2] A.D. 1253, De Joinville, *Memoirs of Louis IX*, Pt. ii. One of the most stirring accounts in all the Chronicles of the Crusades.

[3] Ḳaḍi = Dan = Judge.

[4] Buhl thinks my argument insufficient and holds to the old opinion. Tell el-Ḳaḍi = Dan. But the military difficulties remain, and Deut. xxxiii. 22, *Dan leaps from Bashan* suits Banias not Tell el-Ḳaḍi.

[5] This starts from Ras en-Nakura on the Levant, runs E to Yarun, thence NE to Ḳades, NNE to Metulleh, across Jordan to Tell el-Ḳaḍi and Banias, thence SSW to the Bridge-of-the-Daughters-of-Jacob and S on the river to the Lake, along its E shore to opposite Tiberias, thence SSE to el-Hamme station on the railroad.

[6] v *Antt.* v. 1; iii *Wars*, x. 7; iv *Wars*, i. 1; upon it Seleucia.

[7] xi. 5 f. The name *The Height* suits a lake so far above that of Galilee, and the neighbourhood is possible for chariots; but *waters* suggest springs not lake, and we have no means of fixing the scene of Joshua's victory. *Onomasticon* puts water of Merran near Dothan, 12 m. from Sebaste. The origin of the name *Ḥuleh* is unknown; the same as Ulatha (see ch. xxiv) and ימא דחולתא of the Talmud (Neubauer, 24, 27 ff.). Winckler (*Gesch. Israels*, ii, *Völker etc. d. alten Orients*, 3) reading Gen. xiv

now not more than five miles by five[1] and might easily be drained to the purifying of the insect-infested air; but probably it once covered the surrounding plain especially to the north.[2] From the lower end of the Lake the Jordan enters the Great Rift below sea-level. It descends a narrow gorge in almost continuous cascade, falling 680 feet in less than nine miles, and then through a delta of its own deposits glides quietly into the Lake of Galilee. Six miles above this Lake it was spanned by the Bridge-of-the-Daughters-of-Jacob on the high-road between Damascus and Galilee.[3] Here (when the retreating Turks had blown up one of its arches) the British cavalry, after their conquest of Esdraelon and Lower Galilee, crossed the river on 27th September 1918, upon their advance by Ḳuneiṭra to Damascus.

2. *The Lower Jordan: the Ghor*[4]

From the Lake of Galilee to the Dead Sea the Jordan Valley is sixty-five miles long. Down the west are the mountains of Galilee and Samaria, with the break between them of the Vale of Jezreel. They stand from 800 to 1500 feet above the valley floor, with higher ranges behind. On the other side run the hills of Gilead, their long level edge some 2000 feet above Jordan, and broken only by the incoming valleys of the Yarmuk and Jabbok. Between these two ranges the valley varies in breadth from two to fourteen miles. For thirteen miles south of the Lake the breadth is hardly more than four, then expands to six or seven in the Plain of Beth-shan, which rises by terraces towards the level of Esdraelon. Ten miles south of Beth-shan the Samarian hills press eastward, and for the next thirteen the river runs closely by their feet, and the valley is two miles wide. Again the Samarian hills withdraw, and the valley widens first to eight miles and then to fourteen, which is the breadth at Jericho. What we have, therefore, between Galilee and the Dead Sea is a long narrow vale twice expanding—at Beth-shan and Jericho—to the

---

as a Palestine ed. of a Babylonian legend takes the original to have described a Hebrew defeat at Kedesh-Naphtali; *Salt Sea* might be Ḥuleh for Will. of Tyre calls it Meleha, which Winckler takes as Mellaḥa still attached to a wady with brook on the W bank. But all this depends on a precarious analysis of Gen. xiv, and one cannot think of Ḥuleh being *salt*. How does Hazazon-tamar come in? See Buhl, 113, and Ewing's "Meroz" in Hastings' *DB*.—Semechonitis is compared with Samkhuna of the Amarna Letters (Flinders Petrie, *Hist. of Egypt*, ii. 278, 317).

[1] The best account is in Macgregor's *Rob Roy on the Jordan*.

[2] Cf. Quaresmius, *Elucid. Terrae Sanctae*, Vol. II, vii, ch. xii, fol. 872.

[3] See pp. 277 f. For the country between the Lakes, Schumacher, *ZDPV*, xiii.

[4] See *PEF Mem. Jerus.*, Append. 473 ff.

dimensions of a plain. The Old Testament bestows on it both of the Hebrew names for valley—Deep and Opening.[1] Greek writers call it the Aulōn or Hollow,[2] and Arabs el-Ghor, or the Rift.[3] But Josephus twice gives it the name of the "Great Plain", which he also applies to Esdraelon.[4]

A large part of this valley is of exuberant fertility, and, as we shall see, the whole might be cultivated. The Jordan runs in too deep a channel to be easily useful for irrigation, but a number of affluents from both sides offer abundant moisture during the greater part of the year.[5] Some of these springs and brooks, rising far below the level of the ocean, and in soil impregnated with chlorides and sodium, are bitter and warm. In many parts are mounds and ridges of grey marl, salt and greasy, with stretches of gravel, sand, clay, and other *débris* of an old sea-bottom, that assume the weirdest shapes, and give a desolate aspect to the Vale. But notwithstanding this poison, vegetation is rank, especially in spring. The heat is of a forcing-house. Wherever water comes, the flowers rise to the knee, and herbage often to the shoulder.[6] The drier stretches are covered by broom, thistle, or intricate thorn-bush; by the streams are brakes of cane and oleander.[7] The streams dash down to the Jordan, tearing up the surface of the country by their spring floods and heaping across flowers and grass the loosened marl and ruin of cane-brake. Swamps abound, and there is malaria. Towards Jericho the vegetation grows less and less rank[8]—a plain of thorn-groves with a swamp or two, and then the ground breaks away, discoloured or crusted with salt, and bearing only a few succulent plants, to the shingly beach and blue waters of the Dead Sea. Although there is so much fertility, the stretches of sour soil, unhealthy

[1] עמק of the south end, Josh. xiii. 27; בקעה of the north under Hermon, Josh. xi. 17 (LXX *Πεδία*); Josh. xii. 7 (LXX *Πεδίον*), and of the south end, Deut. xxxiv. 3. See above pp. 249 ff.

[2] *Αὐλών*. So, *e.g.* Diod. Sic. ii. 48. 9; xix. 98. 4; Theophrastus, *Hist. Plant.* ii. 6. 8; ix. 6. 1; Dioscorides, i. 18.

[3] الغور.

[4] Once in its extent, iv *Wars*, viii. 2: *τὸ μέγα πεδίον καλεῖται ἀπὸ κώμης Γινναβρὶν* (at the S end of the Lake of Galilee) *διῆκον μέχρι τῆς Ἀσφαλτίτιδος λίμνης*; once at Jericho, iv *Antt.* vi. 1, *ἐπὶ τὸν Ἰορδάνην κατὰ τὸ μέγα πεδίον Ἱεριχοῦντος ἀντικρύ*. Probably to the Jordan Valley the same name refers in 1 Macc. v. 52, though the beginning of Esdraelon may be meant. In such an ambiguity perhaps the name was transferred from Esdraelon, which it suits, to the Jordan Valley, that is not so truly described by it. In 1 Macc. xvi. 11, *τὸ πεδίον Ἱεριχώ*.

[5] There is now a power-house on Jordan nearly opposite Beisan, a stage in the electrification of the land, a head-race canal bringing water from the Yarmuk reservoir (*Times*, 7th Jan. 1931). See below, p. 314.

[6] Conder, *TW*, 225 ff.

[7] On the flora and fauna see Warren, "Jordan", Hastings' *DB*.

[8] The wheat fields of the ‘Adwan E of Jordan are due to irrigation.

jungle, obtrusive marl, and parched hillsides out of reach of the streams, justify the Hebrew name of Arabah or Desert.[1] In the New Testament also the Valley is called a Wilderness.[2]

Down this broad valley there curves and twists a deeper, narrower bed —perhaps 150 feet deeper,[3] and from 200 yards to a mile broad.[4] Its banks are mostly of white marl,[5] and within these it is packed with tamarisks and other semi-tropical trees and tangled bush. To those who look down from the hills along any stretch of the Valley, this Zor, as it is called, trails and winds like an enormous green serpent, more forbidding in its rankness than open water could be, however foul or broken. This jungle marks the Jordan's wider bed, the breadth to which the river rises in flood. In the Old Testament it is the *Pride of Jordan*, and a symbol of trouble and danger. *Though in a land of peace thou be secure, how wilt thou do in the Pride of Jordan? He shall come up like a lion from the Pride of Jordan.*[6] It was long supposed that this referred to the spring floods of the river, and it is given in the English version as *swelling*, but the word means *pride*, and as one text speaks of the *pride of Jordan being spoiled*,[7] the phrase refers to the jungle, whose green ribbon looks so rich from the hills above. In that case we ought to translate it the *luxuriance* or *rankness* of Jordan. Though lions have ceased from the land, this jungle is still a covert for wild beasts, and Jeremiah's contrast of it with a *land of peace* is even more suitable to a haunted jungle than to an inundation. But it is floods which have made the rankness, they fill this wider bed of Jordan every year[8]; and the floor of the jungle is covered with deposits of mud and gravel, dead weed, driftwood and the exposed roots of trees.

Penetrating this unhealthy hollow you come soon to the Jordan itself. Remember that it is but a groove in the bottom of an old sea-bed, a ditch as deep below the level of the ocean as some of our coal-mines, and you will be prepared for the uncouthness of the scene. There is no yellow marl by the river itself.[9] Those heaps and ridges, which in higher parts of the Valley

[1] ערבה also in the plural in connection with certain districts. The Araboth of Moab and of Jericho.

[2] Mark i, cf. 4 and 5.

[3] Conder reckons 150 feet deeper at Beisan, *TW*, 215; and 200 feet at Jericho, *ib.* 216. Warren: 20 ft. at N end of the Ghor.

[4] Conder says ¼ m. to 2 m., but the latter must be close to the Dead Sea.

[5] Covered in spring with flowers (Conder).

[6] Jer. xii. 5, xlix. 19. l. 44.

[7] Zech. xi. 3.

[8] *Jordan overfloweth his banks all the time of harvest, i.e.* in April, Josh. iii. 15. "Abound as Jordan in the time of harvest", Ecclesiasticus xxiv. 26. For a flood see *MuNDPV*, 1897, 30.

[9] Yet the oscillating river sometimes touches the marl cliffs bounding the Zor.

look like nothing but the refuse of a chemical factory, have there been washed away. But there are hardly less ugly mudbanks, from two to twenty-five feet high, with an occasional bed of shingle, that is not clean and sparkling as in our rivers, but foul with ooze and slime. Dead driftwood is everywhere in sight. Large trees lie about, overthrown: and the exposed roots and lower trunks of the trees still standing are smeared with mud, save where they have been torn by passing wreckage. There are, however, open spaces, where the river flashes to the hills above and an easy path is possible to its edge. But in the lower reaches this is mostly where the earth is too salt to sustain vegetation; and so it may be said that Jordan sweeps to the Dead Sea through unhealthy jungle relieved only by poisonous soil.

The river itself is from 90 to 100 feet broad,[1] a rapid, muddy water with a zigzag current. The depth varies from 3 feet at some fords[2] to as much as 10 or 12. In the sixty-five miles[3] the descent is 610 feet, or an average of 9 feet a mile—not a great fall, for the Spey, and the Dee from Balmoral to Aberdeen both average about 14 feet a mile. But near the Lake of Galilee the fall is over 40 feet a mile,[4] and this impetus given to a large volume of water, down a channel in which it cannot sprawl and few rocks retard, induces a great rapidity. This has given the river its name: Jordan means the Down-comer. The swiftness is rendered more dangerous by the muddy bed and curious zigzag current which will easily sweep a man from the side into the centre of the stream. In April the waters rise to the wider bed, but for the most of the year they keep to the channel of 90 feet. Here, with infrequent interruptions of shingle, mostly silent and black in spite of its speed, but now and then breaking into praise and whitening into foam, Jordan scours along, muddy between banks of mud, careless of beauty, careless of life, intent upon its own work, which for ages by decree of the Almighty has been that of separation.

Most rivers, in valleys so wide and well watered, mean the presence of cities, or of much cultivation. But the valley of the Jordan never seems to have been populous.[5] Some towns were built in it, and gardens were numerous. Jericho, we have seen,[6] was a flourishing region, especially in the hands

[1] Lynch, *Narrative of U.S. Exped.*, makes the average 70 to 80. *MuNDPV*, 1899, 35, puts it at Damieh 40 metres.

[2] Le Strange crossed after rain near Beisan, where the water "scarcely reached the horses' bellies" (*Ride through Ajlun, etc.* in Schumacher's *Across Jordan*). For an Arab tribe's crossing near Jericho see Seetzen, *Reisen*, ii. 275 ff.

[3] Lynch, 265, says its course, zigzagging so much, must be 200 m.; if so the real fall is only 3 ft. a mile (Warren).

[4] Conder, *TW*, 215.

[5] Cf. Pliny, *HN*, v. 15: "accolis invitum se praebet".

[6] Ch. xiii, pp. 181 ff.

of the Romans, who knew how to irrigate. There seems to have been a forest of palms hence to Phaselis.[1] Farther up at Ḳurawa are fertile fields, and the richness of the country round Beth-shan is evident.[2] The whole of this side of the valley was famed through the ancient world for its corn, dates, balsam,[3] flax, and other products.[4] The early Christian pilgrims also lavish praise: the Arab geographers of the eighth to the twelfth centuries imply that there was still fertility in the Ghọr. They speak of the sugar of Beth-shan and Ḳurawa; and the Crusaders found sugar growing in Jericho.[5] On the eastern side of the valley was the large town of Livias or Julias, opposite Jericho,[6] immediately north of that some smaller towns, with the city of Adam perhaps at the present Tell Damieh and Succoth at Tell Deir 'Alla, but after these, till the Yarmuk is reached, nothing except some nameless villages, —unless Pella, which lay on the first terraces above the Valley, be reckoned to the Valley. The number of mounds, some of which have been found to consist of sun-dried bricks,[7] are probably remains not of cities but of brick-fields. The clay of the Valley was good for moulding, and Solomon placed in it his brass foundries for the building of the Temple.[8] But, from this absence of cities on the east of the Jordan, it must not be supposed that the land is not cultivable. Between the Yarmuk and Pella, sufficient streams break from Gilead to irrigate the whole region, the remains of ancient

[1] See p. 233. [2] Josephus. [3] Cf. Le Strange, *op. cit.* 270.

[4] Polybius, v. 70, says that the district between Beth-shan and the Lake could support an army, and there Vespasian settled his Legions. On the balsam, Diodorus Siculus, ii. 48. 9, xix. 98. 4, Dioscorides, i. 18; the dates and fertility of Jericho, Archelais and Phaselis, Pliny, *HN*, v. 15 (14), Strabo, xvi. ii. 41; the linen of Beth-shan, etc., *Totius Orbis Descriptio, Geogr. Gr. Minores*, Ed. Müller, ii. 513 ff.

[5] Cf. Le Strange's *Pal. under Moslems*, 53; Rey, *Les Colon. Franques*, p. 386. The name "sugar-mills" still attaches to some ruins at Jericho.

[6] On the site of Beth-haram or -haran (Josh. xiii. 27; Num. xxxii. 36) the *βηθαράμφθᾶ* of Josephus (ii *Wars*, iv. 2) where Herod had a palace; *βηθράμφθά*, according to Euseb., but Jerome Betharam (*Onomasticon*). He says it was called Livias by Herod, *i.e.* Antipas, in honour of the wife of Augustus, but Josephus names it Julias (xviii *Antt.* ii. 1; ii *Wars*, ix. 1). Livias was the older, as the Emperor's wife was received into gens Julia only by his testament (Schürer, *Hist.* II, i. 142). Placidus, a lieutenant of Vespasian, held it in 68f. (iv *Wars*, vii. 6; viii. 2). Theodosius, A.D. 530, *De Situ Terræ Sanctæ*, 65 (PPT, p. 14) describes it as 12m. from Jericho, near warm springs. He calls it Livias. It is now Tell er-Rameh.

[7] By Warren; see Conder, *TW*, 220, 221. But this is not certain, for all over the Valley are artificial mounds, 50 to 100 ft. high, where are passages for traffic.

[8] W of Jordan at Zarethan, 1 Kings vii. 46. צרתן probably the Zarethan of Josh. iii. 16, beside the city of Adam. On Adam, Zarethan, etc., see *PEFQ*, 1895, papers by Watson (253) on stoppage of Jordan, A.D. 1267, Dalton and Stevenson (334); *PEFQ*, 1896, Clermont-Ganneau and Stevenson (79 ff.). Also *MuNDPV*, 1899, 34 ff.

aqueducts are visible, and even, without elaborate irrigation, the few small villages have reaped good harvests of grain.[1] All up the east of the river we came across patches of cultivation, the property of various Bedawee tribes on the highlands to the east.[2] The dews are as heavy as in other parts of the land: the heat is tropical. The Arabah, then, in spite of its name, was once largely cultivated, and by simple methods of irrigation, drawn from the affluents of the Jordan, might again become a rich and fruitful land.[3] The opening of railways may begin another era, like that in which the fame of the fruits of the Jordan went out over the world.[4] Under a good Government dates, rice, sugar, flax, cotton and many more commodities might be grown in abundance.

Why, then, have towns always been few in the Valley? and why has it deserved the name of wilderness? The reasons are three. From early spring to late autumn the heat is intolerable, and parches all vegetation not constantly watered. At Pella and opposite Jericho we found the temperature in July at 104°; it has been known to rise in August to 118°.[5] The Arabs of the Ghor, the Ghawarineh, are sickly and degenerate. It is not to be wondered at that the Israelites who possessed the hills on either side should prefer to build their cities there, descending to the valley only for sowing and reaping their harvests. This is what many Samarian villages now do, as well as the Arabs of Moab[6] and the peasants of Gilead.

In ancient times the valley was infested with wild beasts. To extirpate them was one of the serious difficulties in Israel's conquest of the country.[7] But their covert and stronghold was the jungle of the Jordan; driven from the rest of the land they were secure here, and bred so fast that, as soon as a neighbouring province was deprived of its population, they overran it.[8] Lions are the most often mentioned in the Old Testament.[9] There are no

[1] We passed over this district in 1891, and were surprised at the many signs of cultivation, the great piles of corn in the few villages, and the old aqueducts: cf. *Pella*, 18, 19.

[2] For the north end, Schumacher, *Jaulân*, 148. The 'Adwan cultivate, or have cultivated for them, some of the south Valley. When we visited their main camp near Heshbon, 'Ali Di'ab, their chief, with a number of the men were absent securing their grain in the Valley.

[3] Cf. Le Strange, *op. cit.* 270.

[4] The Sultan of Turkey bought, for his private estate, a large part of the valley. We met his servants in several parts of it in 1891.

[5] Conder, *TW*. Yet in winter it can be chilly (Warren) and at nights cold. But see Blanckenhorn, *ZDPV*, xxxii. 38-109, "Studien über das Klima des Jordantals".

[6] Cf. Robinson, *LBR*. So we found with the 'Adwan Bedouin.

[7] Deut. vii. 22; xxxii. 24; Lev. xxvi. 6, 22; cf. Gen. xxxi. 39, *that which was torn of beasts*; Exod. xxii. 31; Lev. vii. 24; xvii. 15; xxii. 8; Amos v. 19; Hosea ii. 18; xiii. 7 f.; Isa. xi. 6 f., etc.

[8] 2 Kings xvii. 25.

[9] *Ibid.*; Jer. xlix. 19; etc.

lions to-day—the last was reported five hundred years ago[1]—but wild boars abound, and there are leopards and a kind of wolf.[2]

A more serious hindrance to settlement in the Jordan Valley was the frequency with which it was over-run by the Arabs. There were no towns on the level of Esdraelon. Except for the prehistoric town recently excavated on the Teleilat (little mounds of) Ghassul, five kilometres north of the Dead Sea, which was burned before the early Bronze Age[3] and never rebuilt, and Jericho itself, there were none in the Arabah[4]; for no site existed in either of these channels capable of resisting the desert swarms which poured through them. No walls have yet been found round the ancient city just mentioned; the Herods did not attempt to fortify Archelais or Phaselis, which were only villages; and neither Jericho nor Beth-shan successfully sustained a siege.

We must, therefore, seek for the *rôle* of this Valley in history in another direction than that along which its possible fertility points us. We find it in two functions:

(1) The Jordan was a border and barrier. We have seen how the river itself tells us this by the depth of its valley, its unuseful, unlovely course, its muddy banks and their rank jungle. And so we find it appreciated in literature. With few exceptions the references to Jordan in the Old Testament are geographical and prosaic; the Psalmist hears in it no music; the prophet speaks of its rankness and danger; it excites the ridicule of those who know its sister Syrian rivers[5]; the exiles by Babel's streams think not upon Jordan's rush of water but upon the arid Jerusalem; and when a symbol is needed of the water of life the Psalmist ignores his country's only river, and floods for his purpose the dry bed of the Kidron.[6] Jordan was only a boundary, a line to traverse, and, in nearly all texts in which the name occurs, this is governed by a preposition, *unto*, *over*, *across*.[7]

It is difficult to estimate the military value of such a frontier. Like other border rivers the Jordan has been often and easily crossed, but, unlike them,

[1] Many early pilgrims speak of them; the last were Abbot Daniel, 1100, and Poloner, 1421 (*PPT*).

[2] Conder saw a wolf, *TW*.

[3] A. Mallon, *Biblica*, xi. 1930, *PEFQ*, 1930, 172: "one of the oldest cities in Palestine" with proofs of "a developed and even luxurious culture". Father Mallon and M. R. Neuville have (1931) uncovered 35 acres of city ruins, "destroyed by fire and not by flood" on the Teleilat Ghassul, 5 km. *north* of the Dead Sea; "the uncovered city was four times larger than Jericho".

[4] But see next chapter on the Cities of the Plain.

[5] 2 Kings v. 12.

[6] *There is a river whose streams do glad the city of our God*, Ps. xlvi.

[7] Jordan as a border, Gen. xxxii. 10; Deut. iii. 20; xxvii. 4; Josh. i. 2; Num. xxxiv. 10-12. It is Ezekiel's border, xlvii. 18.

there do not appear to have been—below the Lake of Galilee at least—serious attempts to defend it until the late War. In the time of the Judges the fords were watched to prevent the escape of fugitives,[1] and once the Maccabees had a battle on the river.[2] But, in the greatest invasion of all, Israel crossed unopposed, and in her turn offered no opposition on Jordan either to Syrians, who came over just below the Lake, or to Arabs or Moabites farther south. David did not seek to check Absalom's crossing, nor the Byzantines that of the Arabs, nor the Crusaders that of Saladin, nor Napoleon that of the Turks.[3] Nor was the Arab drift into Western Palestine ever checked by the river, but only by a settled government to the east of it. In short, at no period has the eastern defence of the land been laid along Jordan; nor has the river been always a boundary between different states. North Israel lay on both sides, and in later days Peræa was counted with Judæa. Is then the frontier influence of Jordan entirely a reflection of the spiritual symbolism to which subsequent events exalted the river? This can hardly be said in face of the following facts. Moses dreaded the separation that Jordan would cause between the tribes left to the east of it and those who crossed.[4] To early Israel the crossing of Jordan was as great a crisis as the crossing of the Red Sea.[5] When David was made King in Hebron, it was Eastern Palestine which Abner chose for the rallying of Israel round Saul's house,[6] and David himself fled there when Absalom raised Judah against him.[7] There are many other passages taken from the everyday speech of the people, which prove how separating an influence they felt in that deep gulf with its super-heated airs, its jungle and rapid river.[8] We have but to compare the Jordan with another river flowing in line with itself, the Orontes, to see that, from whatever reason, the former was an effective frontier between the nomad and the husbandman, between east and west, to a degree never reached by the latter. Perhaps this effectiveness did not consist so much in shutting out invaders from the east as in giving to those who drifted over the river a visible and impressive reason why they should not return. All down Israel's history it is

[1] Judges vii. 24, Ephraim against Midian; xii. 5, Gilead against Ephraim.

[2] *Circa* 160; 1 Macc. ix. 32-49. The tactics are not clear. The fight seems to have been on the west bank, and the only use of the river was that made by the Jewish troops in swimming it so as to escape from the Syrians.

[3] Below the Lake of Galilee. On the N, where the Turks crossed by the Jisr Benat-Ya'kob and besieged Ṣafed, Murat drove them across the river again, and on the S all the fighting was W of Jordan, at the heights of Lubieh and on Esdraelon. The Turkish army was cut off from Damascus after it crossed Jordan, and found a base at Nablus.

[4] Num. xxxii. 6 ff. [5] Ps. cxiv. 3, etc. [6] 2 Sam. ii. 8 ff. [7] *Id.* xv-xvii.

[8] The frequency of the phrase *across Jordan*, and such names as the Mountains of the Abarim, *i.e. Those on the over-side.*

clear that the people knew themselves cut off from the east, that their land felt under them no more a part of Arabia, and that they trod it with the consciousness of another and a higher destiny than that of the Arab tribes from whom they finally broke when they *passed over Jordan*. In this moral effect upon the national consciousness the Jordan and its Valley exerted an influence, than which any strength it had as a military border was of less historical significance, until the late War. Then from March till May 1918, its lower fords and the bridges by them from Jisr ed-Damiyeh down to the Dead Sea were bitterly contested by the British and Turkish forces with success oscillating repeatedly between them. The river was then in flood, difficult and dangerous to swimmers, boats, and rafts alike, until bridges were thrown across it.

(2) Jordan has not only been associated with the figures of two of Israel's greatest prophets—Elijah and John the Baptist—but with the bestowal, at their hands, of the Spirit upon their successors.

We are not surprised that as his end approached Elijah should feel driven towards that border, across which he had first burst mysteriously upon Israel,[1] and to which he had withdrawn while waiting for his word to fulfil itself.[2] Stage by stage he came down from the high centre of the land to its lowest, lonely shelves.[3] *Tarry here, I pray thee, for the Lord hath sent me to Beth-el . . . to Jericho . . . to Jordan.* But at each stage Elisha said, *As the Lord liveth, and as thy soul liveth, I will not leave thee*; and when the little communities of prophets came out and said, *Knowest thou that the Lord will take away thy master from thy head to-day?* he answered, *I also know it, hold ye your peace.* So these two, leaving the sons of the prophets, passed down the falling land as the planets pass to their setting through groups of lesser stars. The mountains of The-Over-Side filled the view ahead of them, and in these mountains lay the sepulchre of Moses. He, who in his helplessness had fled for inspiration to Horeb, could not fail to wonder whether God was to lay him to rest beside his forerunner on Nebo. In front was no

[1] He was from Tishbe, in Gilead. In 1 Kings xvii. 1 read with LXX and Heb. text, *Elijah the Tishbite from Tishbē* (θεσβων) *of Gilead.* See Buhl, p. 257, van Kasteren, *ZDPV*, xiii. 207 ff., perhaps Istib in W Yabis. Klosterman suggests *the Jabeshite from Jabesh* (?).

[2] 1 Kings xvii. 3, *Turn thee east and hide thee by the brook Cherith, which is on the face of Jordan.* This phrase, which in Hebrew orientation means *east of Jordan*, excludes Wady Ḳelt behind Jericho; Cherith must be sought in Gilead, where the name has not been discovered.

[3] 2 Kings ii. The Gilgal is not that beside Jericho, but was either near the high-road between Bethel and Shechem, the present Jiljilia, 2441 ft. above the sea and over 3700 above Jordan, or Juleijil on the plain of Mukhna under Gerizim, see Schlatter, *Zur Topogr. u. Gesch. Pal.* 246 ff.; Buhl, *Geog.* 202 f., *Enc. Bibl.* "Gilgal".

promised land visible—nothing but that high sky-line eastward under the empty heaven. Behind was no nation waiting to press into the future—nothing but that single follower who persisted to the end. And so the end came. The river that had drawn back at a nation's feet, parted at the stroke of one man, and as he suddenly passed away to the God from whom he had suddenly come, it was one man whom he acknowledged as his heir, and to whom he left his spirit. Realise these two lonely figures in that unpeopled wilderness, the State invisible, the Church left behind in impotent gaze and wonder, and nothing passing between the two men save from the one the tribute to personal worth, and from the other the influence of personal spirit and force—realise all this on the lonely bank of Jordan, and you understand the beginnings of prophecy, the new dispensation in which the instrument of the Most High was to be not the State and its laws, not the army and its victories, not even the Church and her fellowship, but the spirit of the individual man. Not in vain the story tells us that it was with his mantle, symbol of the Prophet, that Elijah smote the waters, and Elisha smote them the second time on his return to his ministry. Jordan, that had owned the People of God, owns now the Prophet.

Elisha is represented as the first in Israel to employ the river for sacramental purposes. He said unto Naaman the leper, *Go and wash in Jordan seven times, and thy flesh shall come again to thee, and thou shalt be clean.* We do not again read of Jordan being thus used.

(3) These two events may have determined John the Baptist's choice of the theatre of his ministry. He found here both of his requisites, solitude and much water. He found also those vivid figures of his preaching—the slimy shingle, of which he said, *God is able to raise up of these stones children to Abraham*; the trees with *the axe laid to their roots*, for the Jordan jungle was a haunt of wood cutters[1]; and, on the higher stretches of the Valley, the fires among the dry scrub chasing before them the scorpions and vipers.[2] But chiefly must it have been the memories of Elijah and Elisha which came upon John and the crowds that listened to him. Israel's only river had by these prophets been consecrated to the two acts most symbolic of religion—the washing by water and the gift of the Spirit. And now where Elisha bade Naaman bathe his leprosy away, John called on Israel to wash and be clean: where Elijah bequeathed his spirit, John was to meet and own his successor. But it was no Elisha who came to take his sign from this second Elijah. *There cometh He that is mightier than I after me, the latchet of whose shoes I am not worthy to stoop down and unloose. I indeed have baptized you with water, but He shall baptize you with the Holy Ghost.... And Jesus was*

[1] Cf. 2 Kings vi. 1 ff.

[2] Cf. Stanley, *Sin. and Pal.*

baptized of John in Jordan, and straightway coming up out of the water he saw the heavens rending, and the Spirit, like a dove, descending upon Him; and there came a voice from heaven, Thou art My beloved Son, in whom I am well pleased.[1]

So what was never a great Jewish river has become a very great Christian one.

XXIII. *THE DEAD SEA*[2]

Surely there is no region of earth where Nature and History have more cruelly conspired, where so tragic a drama has obtained so awful a theatre. The effect of some historical catastrophes has been heightened by their occurrence amid scenes of beauty and peace. It is otherwise here. Nature, when she has not herself been, by some convulsion, the executioner of judgement, has added every aggravation of horror to the cruelty of the human avenger or the exhaustion of the doomed. The history of the Dead Sea opens with Sodom and Gomorrah, and may be said to close with the Massacre of Masada.

Last chapter described the formation of the Jordan Valley, by the enclosure of a bit of the ocean-bed, between two folds of the earth's surface, and by a subsequent depression to the present depth below the level of the sea. Of this extraordinary Rift or Sink, as it might be called, the Dead Sea occupies the forty-eight deepest miles, with an average breadth of nine to ten. The surface is 1290 feet below the Mediterranean, but the bottom is

[1] The place of our Saviour's baptism is uncertain. The traditional site is at the Makhaḍet Hajle. The Bethabara, where the Baptist is said by some MSS. of John i. 28 to be baptising when Jesus came to him, is placed by Conder at the ford 'Abarah, just N of Beisan (*TW*, 230). But a name like that, *ferry*, *crossing*, or *ford* (see p. 224, n. 6), probably occurred more than once down the river. The other more authentic reading is Bethany. The argument which the author of *Supernatural Religion* bases on the word Bethany against the Evangelist's knowledge of Palestine reveals his own ignorance both of the possibilities of the country in which several Bethanys may have lain, and of the rest of the Gospel, the writer of which expressly states that he knew the other Bethany near Jerusalem (xi. 18). On the possibility that the true reading is *βηθαναβρά* (cf. *βαιυθαναβρά* in LXX-B of Josh. xiii. 27) see Grove and Wilson, Smith's *DB*, 2nd ed. "Bethnimrah" and Rix, *Tent and Testament*, 175 ff.

[2] This name, first used by Pausanias and Galen, *Θάλασσα νεκρά*, is not in O.T., which gives *Salt Sea* and *Sea of the Arabah*; Arab. baḥr or Buḥeirat Luṭ, Sea of Lot; el-Baḥr el-Mayet by the Terâbin, Baḥr el-Fli by the Ẓullam, Buḥeirat el-Melḥ, by the Ṣḥûr (Musil). For this chapter, see Maps 9 and 10.

as deep again, soundings having been taken to 1300 feet. This is at the north-east corner under the hills of Moab, and not far from the entrance of the Jordan; thence the bed shelves upwards, till the whole of the south end of the sea is only from 8 to 14 feet deep.[1] These figures, however, vary from year to year, and after a very rainy season the sea will be as much as 15 feet deeper, and at the south end more than a mile longer.[2]

The Dead Sea receives, besides the Jordan, four or five smaller streams, but has no issue for its waters except through evaporation. This is raised to enormous proportions by the heat which prevails during the greater part of the year. The extracted moisture usually forms a haze impenetrable to the eye for more than a few miles, but sometimes columns of mist rear themselves from the sea, heavy clouds are formed, and thunderstorms rage the more violently for their narrow confines, as the torn coasts testify, with lightning and floods of rain. To the everlasting evaporation is due the bitterness of the sea. All rivers contain some salts, and all lakes without issue to the ocean become more or less briny. But the streams which feed the Dead Sea are unusually saline; they flow through nitrous soil, and are fed by sulphurous springs. Chemicals have been found in the water of the sea which are not traceable in its tributaries, and probably are introduced by hot springs in the sea bottom.[3] Along the shores are deposits of sulphur and petroleum springs. The surrounding strata are rich in bituminous matter, and after earthquakes lumps of bitumen are found floating on the water so as to justify its ancient name of Asphaltitis.[4] At the south-east end a ridge

[1] The west side is, as a rule, much shallower than the eastern. Some years ago the south end was fordable as far north as the Lisan (Burckhardt, *Travels*; Robinson, *BR*, ii). This and the submergence of a jetty at the north end prove that for long the volume of the sea has been increasing. (See p. 303.) On the sea generally and its fluctuations see E. Huntington, *Pal. and its Transformation*, chs. ix, xiv; E. W. G. Masterman, *PEFQ*, 1913, 192-197; 1917, 185.

[2] Robinson, *BR*, ii. 672, says that after heavy rain the marshes at the south end of the Dead Sea are covered by water to the extent of two or three miles.

[3] Bromine, chlorides of sodium, magnesium and calcium. Burckhardt was told that at the former ford the bottom waters felt warm to the feet.

[4] Bitumen is petroleum hardened by evaporation and oxidation, Dawson, *Mod. Science in Bible Lands*, 487 f. The bituminous limestone, which burns like bright coal (Burckhardt, *Syria*, 394), is the so-called Dead Sea stone from which articles are made for sale in Jerusalem and Bethlehem. The floating lumps probably are from petroleum springs in the sea-bed. These springs were more common in ancient times. Gen. xiv. 10 says the Vale of Siddim was *wells, wells, i.e.* full of wells, *of bitumen*, בֶּאֱרוֹת בֶּאֱרוֹת חֵמָר. Arabs call bitumen ḥommar, حمر. Burckhardt, *Syria*, 394; Strabo, xvi. ii. 42; Diod. Sic., ii. 48; xix. 98; Josephus (iv *Wars*, viii. 4), and Pliny (*HN*, v. 16) describes the sea as ejecting bitumen or asphalt. See Burckhardt, *Syria*,

of rock-salt, 300 feet high, runs for five miles, elsewhere there are deep saline deposits, and the bed of the sea appears to be covered with salt crystals.[1] To all these solid ingredients, precipitated and concentrated by the constant evaporation, the Dead Sea owes its bitterness and buoyancy. While ocean water contains from 4 to 6 per cent. of solids in solution, the Dead Sea holds from 24 to 26 per cent., or five times as much.[2] The water is nauseous to the taste and oily to the touch, leaving on the skin, when it dries, a crust of salt. But it is brilliant. Seen from far no lake on earth looks more blue and beautiful. Swim out upon it, and at a depth of 20 feet you can count the pebbles through the water. The buoyancy of the Dead Sea is known; it is difficult to sink the limbs deep enough for swimming; if you throw a stick on the surface, it seems to rest as on a mirror, so little actually penetrates the water. The surface is not always smooth, the heavy water rises easily; and in storm the waves are powerful. Lieutenant Lynch describes them beating on the bow of his boat like the blows of a sledge-hammer.[3] No fish can exist in the waters, but some lower forms of life are reported.[4]

These bitter and imprisoned waters, that are yet so blue and brilliant, chafe a low beach of gravel, varied by marl or salted marsh. Twice on the west side the cliffs come down to the water's edge, and on the east coast there is a curious peninsula, called el-Lisan, The Tongue, though the shape

---

394; Robinson, *BR*, ii. 228-230. (In the earthquakes of 1834 and 1837 masses of bitumen were cast ashore); Lynch, *Narrative*, 303; Blanckenhorn, *ZDPV*, xix. (1896), 1-59, xxi. (1898), 63 ff.; Gautier, "Dead Sea", *Enc. Bibl.* (1899); A. Musil, *Moab*.

[1] The ridge is Jebel, or Ḥashm, Usdum, Robinson, *BR*, ii. 206 ff., 481. Arabs take salt from this and the Lisan. Dredging brings up crystals of salts. For the S end of the Sea see Libbey and Hoskins, *The Jordan Valley and Petra*, vol. ii, ch. xii (1905).

[2] Hull (as below) gives for the Atlantic 6 lbs. of salt in 100 of water, for the Dead Sea, 24.57. Cf. the analyses in Robinson, *BR*, ii. 224, by Dr. Marcet, Gay-Lussac, etc., and by Hull, *PEF Mem. Geol.* p. 121.

[3] On the water of the Dead Sea, *PEF Geolog. Mem.*, Hull, pt. v, ch. i; Dawson, *Mod. Science in Bibl. Lands*, 472 ff.; Lartet, *La Mer Morte*; Lynch, *Narrative*. On its buoyancy, Jos. iv *Wars*, viii. 4.

[4] On my first visit I found on the north shore fish swimming in a pool separated from the sea by a bar of gravel two feet wide, and indistinguishable in taste. Yet when they were put in the sea they gasped and turned over dead. See Aristotle, *Meteorics*, ii; Galen, *de Simpl. Med.* iv, c. 19 (quoted by Reland): *φαίνεται ἐν ἐκείνῳ τῷ ὕδατι μήτε ζῶον ἐγγιγνόμενόν τι, μήτε φυτόν*. That birds cannot fly over the sea ("neque pisces aut suetas aquis volucres patitur", Tacitus, *Hist.* v. 6) is legendary. Robinson remarks that the absence of water-fowl is due to that of fish, *BR*, ii. 226. The multitude of shells are not land-shells, and cannot be explained as having come down Jordan and other streams. Perhaps they date from the time the sea was a fresh-water lake. Lortet, *PEFQ*, 1892, 48 ff., reports tetanus microbes and other pathogenic forms in the mud.

is more that of a spurred boot. This is formed of steep banks of marl, from forty to sixty feet high,[1] that shine over the blue waters like the walls of an iceberg. Elsewhere is gravel, clean and fair as the waters which lave it. But the gravel is crowned with an almost constant hedge of driftwood, every particle of which is stripped of bark and bleached, while much glitters with salt. You could not imagine a more proper crown for Death. With this the brilliant illusion of the Dead Sea fades, and everywhere beyond, to the heights of the surrounding hills, reign violence and desolation. If the coast is flat you have salt-pans, or a briny swamp; if terraced, there is a yellow, scurfy stretch of soil, with few thorn-bushes and succulent weeds. Ancient beaches are visible round it, steep banks from five to fifty feet of stained and greasy marl, very friable, with heaps of rubbish at their feet, and crowned by nothing but their own bare, crumbling brows. Some hold that these gave the region its name, the Vale of Siddim[2]; and in truth they chiefly haunt one's memory of the Dead Sea. Last crumbling shelves of the upper world, there are not in nature more weird symbols of forsakenness and desolation.

Behind these terraces of marl the mountains rise precipitous and barren on either coast. To the east the long range of Moab, at a height of 2500 to 3000 feet above the shore, seems broken only by the valley of the Arnon. The tawny limestone cliffs, capped with softer chalk, and streaked with marl, but blotted by outcrops of basalt or black limestone, stand near enough to the coast to be reflected in the still water, and at sunset, losing their blots, glow one uniform amethyst above the blue. In all Judæa there is no view like this, as you see it across the wilderness from the Mount of Olives. On the west coast the hills touch the water at two points, but elsewhere leave between them and the sea the shore already described, sometimes a hundred yards broad, sometimes a mile and a half. From behind the highest terrace of marl the hills rise precipitously in cliffs from 2000 to 2500 feet. No such valley cuts them as Arnon cuts the opposite range, but every three or four

[1] Lynch, *Narrative*, p. 297: "A bold, broad promontory, from 40 to 60 feet high, . . . a broad margin of sand at its foot, incrusted with salt and bitumen, the perpendicular face extending all round, and presenting the coarse and chalky appearance of recent carbonate of lime." With an ancient port Mayumas in its north bay.

[2] Conder, *TW*, 208, says the local name for these terraces is "sidd". From its root שׂדד = to level, שְׂדִּים is taken in the sense of level fields (Aq. Onk. etc.). LXX owns ignorance, translating *φάραγξ ἡ ἁλυκή*. Arabic in several forms means to level, also to obstruct. A derived noun, "sudd", pl. "sidadât", is a "hollow containing rocks, stones, and stagnant rain-water" (Freytag), and Gesenius takes the Hebrew as equivalent. On the surroundings of the Sea cf. Felix Fabri, *PPT*, ii. 164.

miles they are pierced by a narrow gorge, which continues in a broad gully through the marl terraces to the sea. These gorges are barren, save in their rocky beds, the only passages up them, where a few trees live on the water that trickles out of sight beneath the grey shingle. Otherwise, except at En-gedi, the west range is bare, unbroken, menacing; and there are few places in the world where the sun beats with so fierce a heat.[1] Beyond this rocky barrier stretches Jeshimon, or *Devastation*, the wilderness of Judæa, which we have already traversed.[2]

In this awful hollow, this bit of the infernal regions come to the surface, this hell with the sun shining into it, primitive man laid the scene of the most terrible judgement on human sin. The glare of Sodom and Gomorrah is flung down the whole length of Scripture history. It is the popular and standard judgement of sin. The story is told in Genesis; it is applied in Deuteronomy, by Amos, by Isaiah, by Jeremiah, by Ezekiel and Zephaniah, and in Lamentations.[3] Our Lord employs it more than once as the figure of the judgement He threatens upon cities where the word is preached in vain, and we feel the flame scorch our own cheeks.[4] Paul, Peter, Jude make mention of it.[5] In the Apocalypse the city of sin is *spiritually called Sodom.*[6]

The cities were five: Sodom, Gomorrah, Admah, Zeboim, and Bela or Zoar.[7] They lay on the floor of the Valley after which they were called *Cities of the Kikkar, or Circle.*[8] But exactly where, we cannot tell. Though the glare of this catastrophe burns still, the ruins it left have disappeared, and there remains almost no authentic trace of the names it has scattered to infamy across the world. A much-debated but insoluble question is whether the narratives in Genesis intend to place the cities north or south of the Dead

[1] For En-gedi, see pp. 183 ff.

[2] See chs. xiii–xv.

[3] Gen. xix; Deut. xxix. 23, cf. xxxii. 32; Amos iv. 11; Isa. i. 9 f., iii. 6, cf. xiii. 19; Jer. xxiii. 14, xlix. 18, l. 40; Zeph. ii. 9; Lam. iv. 6; Ezek. xvi. 46, 49, 53, 55.

[4] Matt. x. 15, xi. 24; Luke x. 12, xvii. 29.

[5] Rom. ix. 29; Isa. i. 9; 2 Peter ii. 6; Jude 7.

[6] Rev. xi. 8.

[7] Gen. xiv. 2. Sodom = סְדֹם, LXX *Σόδομα*, in the Arab tradition سدوم. Gomorrah = עֲמֹרָה, *Γόμοῤῥα*, غمورا. Admah = אַדְמָה, *Ἀδαμά*, ادموتا. Zeboim = צְבִים, or צביים, or צבאים, *Σεβωείμ*, صبوايم, or, صابورا. Zoar = צֹעַר or צוֹעַר, *Σηγώρ*, *Σόγορ*, صاعورا.

[8] A.V. Cities of the Plain, but כִּכָּר = circle. הַכִּכָּר used alone in Gen. xiii. 12, xix. 17, 29; Deut. xxxiv; 2 Sam. xviii. 23; but כִּכַּר הַיַּרְדֵּן, Circle of Jordan, Gen. xiii. 10; 1 Kings vii. 46, cf. Matt. iii. 5.

Sea. For the north are these points—that Abraham and Lot looked upon the cities from near Bethel,[1] that *Circle of Jordan* is not applicable to the south of the Dead Sea, that the presence of five cities there is impossible,[2] that the expedition of the Four Kings, as it swept north from Kadesh-Barnea, attacked Hazazon-tamar, probably En-gedi, *before* it reached the Vale of Siddim and encountered the King of Sodom and his allies[3]; that the name Gomorrah perhaps exists in Ṭubḳ 'Amriyeh, near 'Ain el-Feskhah[4]; and that the name Zoar has been recovered in Tell Saghur.[5]

But, on the other hand, at the south end of the Dead Sea there lay through Roman and Mediæval times a city called Zoara by the Greeks and Ṣughar by the Arabs, which all identified with the Zoar of Lot.[6] Jebel Usdum is the "uncontested representative of Sodom".[7] Hazazon-tamar may be not En-

[1] Gen. x. cf. v. 3 with v. 10.
[2] Conder, *PEFQ*, 1886, 139.
[3] De Saulcy and Conder.
[4] Gen. xiv. 7, 8. But see below.
[5] ساغور, pointed out by W. F. Birch, adopted by Conder, *Heth and Moab*, 154. Merrill, *East of Jordan*, 235, prefers Ektanu. His argument that Zoar of the Arab geographers lay N of the Sea is met by Le Strange, *Pal. under Moslems*, 286. In 1895 Birch wrote me his reasons for a north site, mainly as stated above; adding that a Zoar on the SE edge of the Sea would not be visible from Pisgah (Deut. xxxiv. 3) and that "in Isaiah xv. 4-6 and Jer. xlviii. 34 Zoar (near Sodom) is connected rather with places towards the N of Moab than with places towards the S."—Excavations at Tell Ghassul, 4 m. NE of the Sea on W el-Jorfeh disclosed stone foundations of houses with other remains reckoned to reach back to 3000 B.C. but destroyed about 2000 and claimed as the site of Sodom; report to the Pontificio Istituto Biblico, quoted in *Times*, July 23, 1930.
[6] *Ζωαρά* and *Ζοώρ* in Jos. iv *Wars*, viii. 4: "The Sea of Asphalt reaches to Zoar in Arabia"; cf. i *Antt*. xi. 4, xiv *Antt*. i. 4. *Ζωαρά* in *Onomasticon*, art. *βαλά*: "Still inhabited, lying on the Dead Sea, and holding a garrison of soldiers; balsam and palm grow by it, proofs of its ancient fertility." Zughar, also Sughar and Sukar, is mentioned by Arab geographers, Le Strange, *Pal. under Moslems*, 286 ff., as a station on the trade-route between 'Aḳaba and Jericho, one degree south of Jericho, "a city of heat near the desert", "on the shore of the overwhelming lake. . . . The mountains overhang the town." "Near Al-Karak, three days' march from Jerusalem, on the Higgâs border." "The lake is called after it"; "neighbouring people call the town Sakar, *i.e.* Hell; its water is execrable; no place equal to it in evil climate; its people are black-skinned and thick-set; its waters hot, as though the place stood over hell-fire. Its commercial prosperity is, like Bûzrah, on a small scale, and trade very lucrative"; "much arable land there"; "the trade is considerable, and markets greatly frequented." Arab writers identify it with Lot's Zoar. Crusaders knew the place as Segor, but called it Palmer (Will. of Tyre, xxii. 30). Clermont-Ganneau, *PEFQ*, 1886, 20, thinks the site may be not far from the Tawahin es-Soukhar, on the Ghor eṣ-Ṣafieh; here Kitchener (*PEFQ*, 1884, 216, with plan) found remains of antiquity, but none like temples, with the name Khurbet Labrush. Buhl, *Geog*. 271, favours identifying Zoar of Gen. and Deut. with Zo'ar of the Moslems, and notes that as in Ezek. xvi. 46, Sodom lay S of Judah.
[7] Clermont-Ganneau, *PEFQ*, 1886, 20. Usdum, اسدم, from Sodom as Arsuf

gedi, but the Tamar of Ezekiel, south-west of the Dead Sea.[1] The name Kikkar may have extended to the south of the Dead Sea, just as to-day the Ghor is continued for a few miles south of Jebel Usdum[2]; Jewish and Arab traditions fix on the south; and, finally, natural conditions are more suitable there than on the north to the descriptions of the region both before and after the catastrophe, for there is still enough water and verdure on the east side of the Ghor to suggest *a garden of the Lord*,[3] while the shallow bay and long marshes may, better than the ground on the north of the sea, hide the secret of the overwhelmed cities.[4]

Such is the evidence for the rival sites. We can only wonder at the confidence with which writers dogmatically decide in favour of one or the other.

And Yahweh rained upon Sodom and upon Gomorrah sulphur and fire—from Yahweh, from the heavens—and He overturned those cities, and all the Circle, and all the inhabitants of the cities, and that which grew upon the ground. And Lot's wife looked back as they fled to Zoar and became a pillar of salt. And Abraham looked down upon Sodom and Gomorrah, upon all the land of the Circle, and saw, and, behold, the smoke of the land went up like the smoke of a

---

from Resef, etc. De Saulcy reports ruins named Khurbet Usdum. We have other proofs that the name Sodom was here in comparatively recent times. Galen, Bk. iv, *De simplicium medicamentorum facultatibus*, mentions "salts of Sodom" from "the mountains surrounding the lake, which are called Sodom (*Σόδομα*)." At the Council of Nicæa was a Bishop Severus Sodomorum (*Acta Conc. Nic.*); if this reading be correct we must suppose that the district south of the Sea then held the name which was there in Galen's time, and is still found. So we can dispense with the explanation by Reland, p. 1020.

[1] Knobel, on Gen. xiv. 7; cf. Ezek. xlvii. 19, xlviii. 28.

[2] Robinson, *BR*, ii. 490; the division between el-Ghor and el-'Arabah is a line of white cliffs crossing the valley obliquely beyond the flat marshland S of the Sea. Thence to 'Aḳaba is the Arabah; north to the Lake of Galilee, the Ghor.

[3] Gen. xiii. 10; especially about the Lisan and W Kerak cultivated by the Ghawarineh.

[4] Robinson, *BR*, ii. 489, describes the Ghor at the S end of the Sea as "wholly unsusceptible of cultivation", except on the E side, "covered with shrubs and verdure, like the Plain of Jericho". The bay is very shallow, and was fordable some years ago (Robinson, *BR*, ii. p. 234 f.; Lynch, *Narrative*, p. 304 n.). Musil (172) was told by one Ḥanna el-Ḳalanze: "In the year of my birth (about 1830) an earthquake took place. Then vanished the way from el-Lisân to 'Ain Jedi through the Dead Sea. This way called el-Mḳêṭa, was 2-4 steps broad and in places 2-5 fingers under the water, so that it had to be delimited by poles. In the Ghazu expeditions the victors returned home with their booty very gladly across el-Mḳêṭa, because their way could not be cut off." Nothing prevents the theory that this end of the Sea was formed later than the Sea itself, Robinson, *BR*, ii. 604.

furnace.[1] Some have taken these words to describe such an eruption as that of Vesuvius upon Pompeii.[2] But there is no need to invoke the volcano, and those are more in harmony with the narrative, who judge that in this bituminous soil took place one of those terrible explosions and conflagrations, which have broken out in the similar geology of the oil districts of North America.[3] In such soil reservoirs of oil and gas are formed, and suddenly discharged by their own pressure or by earthquake. The gas explodes, carrying high into the air masses of oil which fall back in fiery rain, and are so inextinguishable that they float afire on water. Sometimes brine and saline mud are ejected, and over the site of the reservoirs are tremors and subsidences. Such a phenomenon accounts for the statements of the narrative.

The reality of the narrative, however, has been questioned by many. They argue that it is simply one of the many legends of overturned or burned cities, with the addition of the local phenomena of the Dead Sea, and of a grander moral than has been attached to any tale of the kind. But statements of this argument have three faults. They are based upon facts irrelevant, they omit some that are relevant, and they suppose that critics who maintain the truth of the narrative have some subjective or dogmatic reason for doing so. They appeal to the ease with which legends spring up everywhere of cities sunk beneath lakes or the ocean. But this is not relevant to our narrative, for it is striking that, though the presence of the Dead Sea offers every temptation for the adoption of such a legend, it is nowhere in the Bible even suggested that the doomed cities are at the bottom of the sea, but we hear of this first from Josephus.[4] That is a proof of the sobriety of the Biblical tradition. Again, the arguments against the latter fail to deal with the fact

[1] Gen. xix. 24-28.

[2] Fritz Nötling, *Das Todte Meer u. der Untergang von Sodom u. Gomorra, Deutsches Montagsblatt*, x. Jahrg. 27, 31, 33 (quoted *ZDPV*, xi. 126), seeks for the cities in Wady Zerḳa Ma'in in Moab, and accounts for their overthrow by a volcano. He points to the comparatively recent date of the lava streams east of Jordan. But towns in Wady Zerḳa Ma'in could not be called cities of the Kikkar, and the phenomena do not agree with a volcanic eruption.

[3] Robinson (*BR*, ii. 606 ff., Letter to Leopold von Buch) suggested the coincidence of volcanic and earthquake action, the stuff from the volcano setting on fire the bitumen released by the earthquake. Dawson, *Mod. Science in Bible Lands*, 488 ff., gives the theory described above.

[4] The one verse through which this notion of submergence might be forced on Scripture, though wrongly, is Gen. xiv. 3, *the Vale of Siddim, which is the Salt Sea.* These words do not necessarily mark the Vale and the Sea as coincident; and the verse only gives the Vale as the battle-field, not as the site of the cities. Nowhere else is the slightest suggestion of submergence. On the contrary, the site of Sodom is regarded not as sea-covered, but as salt and infertile soil. It is interesting that neither Strabo (xvi) nor Tacitus (*Hist.* v. 7) speaks of submergence. The more surprising is

that the phenomena it describes have all happened elsewhere in similar geological formations, and yet are so singular that it is not probable they were invented. And, thirdly, so far from its being a dogmatic interest which alone holds some to a belief in the narrative, the facts of the existence of the cities and of their overthrow in the manner described are accepted both by authorities in natural science and by critics of the Old Testament, who have no such interests to serve. The effort to prove the story wholly legend may be said to have failed.[1]

It is in accordance with the grace of God, making that first which was last and that last which was first, that this awful vale of judgement, to which its inhabitants sometimes gave the name of Hell, should be the scene of one of the most vivid and stupendous hopes of prophecy. To the north of Jerusalem begins the torrent-bed of the Kidron. It sweeps past the Temple Mount, past what were afterwards Calvary and Gethsemane. It leaves the Mount of Olives and Bethany to the left, Bethlehem far to the right. It plunges down among the bare terraces, precipices, and crags of the wilderness of Judæa—the wilderness of the Scape-goat. So barren and blistered, so furnace-like does it become as it drops below the level of the sea, that it takes the name of Wady en-Nar, or the Fire Wady. At last its dreary course brings it to

---

it that scholars like Siegried and Stade should twice have stated that the cities are sunk in the Dead Sea, *Handwörterbuch*, artt. סדם and עמרה.

[1] In the above paragraph I had in view an article by Cheyne in the *New World*, i, 1892, 236-245, which seems to have the three faults I have instanced. It dwells on the parallel afforded by stories of cities sunk beneath the ocean, which, as I have shown, are relevant only for pointing out how free the Bible story is from such an exaggeration, even though the Dead Sea must have suggested it. Cheyne also does not mention the scientific evidence. He ascribes belief in the described facts to an uncritical orthodoxy and doctrinal interests. This may be disproved by citing among scientists, Nötling, who both gives a site for the towns and a reason for their overthrow, and, among critics who cannot be charged with a dogmatic bias, Knobel who, on Gen. xix. 28, says: "Dem Bericht liegt ohne Zweifel eine Thatsache zu Grund". It is a pity for criticism that rejection of a narrative should be made without exhaustive review of the evidence, or that those who hold to the fact in it should be described as doing so for subjective reasons, when there is much evidence for it as fact. I do not feel that it matters anything to faith, whether the story be historical or not. But there is much evidence for it. Cheyne developed his views in "Sodom and Gomorrah", *Enc. Bibl.*, in which he notices some of the scientific evidence. See further, Skinner's *Genesis* (Intern. Crit. Comm.), 310 ff., and Driver's *Genesis* (Westm. Comm.), 202. The various narratives belong as follows: ch. xiii, Lot's settlement in Sodom, is from J, except vv. 6, 11 and 12, which are probably from P, ch. xiv, the defeat of the five kings, is from an unknown source outside the chief documents, and by some held to be contemporary with its events; ch. xix. 1-28 is from J, but v. 29 from P. The ghastly story, 30-38, is probably from another source.

the precipices above the Dead Sea, into which it shoots its scanty winter waters; but all summer it is dry. The imagination of a prophet who haunted the austere and weird, Ezekiel, filled the Wady of Fire with water from under the threshold of the temple, water that came up to the ankles, to the knees, to the loins, and then became *waters of swimming, a torrent that could not be crossed.* And the bare banks, that the sun blisters, had *very many trees on the one side and on the other.* And these waters *went down to the Arabah, and went into the* sour *waters and the waters were to be healed.* The Dead Sea was to swarm with fish, and it *shall come to pass, the fishers shall stand upon it from En-gedi to En-eglaim.* But in the midst of the vision there is a curious reservation of a utilitarian kind, *the fens and the marshes thereof shall not be healed, they shall be given for salt*—salt which under the Old Covenant the Dead Sea ever supplied for house or temple, meat or sacrifice, and still sends to Jerusalem by the camel trains you see traversing the coast from Usdum to En-gedi. But the vision opens out again. *And by the torrent upon the bank thereof, on this side and on that side, shall come up all trees for food, whose leaf shall not fade, neither shall the fruit thereof be consumed; it shall bring forth new fruit according to his months, because their waters issued out of the Sanctuary, and the fruit thereof shall be for food, and the leaf thereof for healing.*[1] So there is nothing—nothing too sunken, too useless, too doomed—but by the grace of God it may be redeemed, lifted, and made rich with life.

Passing over several of Herod's cruelties and his own awful end, which happened at Jericho within the Dead Sea regions, we come to the last historic scene on these bitter coasts—the Massacre of Masada.[2]

Masada, or es-Sebbeh as it is called to-day, lies on the coast, five hours south of En-gedi. Seen from the north it is an immense rock, half a mile long by an eighth broad, hewn out of the range that runs down the coast, and twisted round so as to point boldly north-east across the sea. It is isolated, precipitous on every side and inaccessible except in two places, where winding paths, half goat-tracks half ladders, may be followed by men in single file.[3] On the west this stronghold falls only some 400 feet upon a promontory that connects it with the range behind. Everywhere else it shows at least 1300 feet of cliff, but seaward as much as 1700. The fortresses are few that match this one in natural strength. But it is only when you

[1] Ezek. xlvii. 1-12.

[2] Tuch, "Masada die Herodianische Felsenfeste nach Josephus u. neueren Beobachtern" (*Reformationsfest*, 1863).

[3] Josephus notices these two approaches. One of them he calls the Snake. De Saulcy says he has flattered it. "C'est une escalade sans interruption."—*Voyage autour de la Mer Morte.*

come to it, as those who would attack it had to come, through the waterless wilderness of Judæa, that you feel its awful remoteness, its savage height, its power to turn armies of besiegers into stony despair. Masada is the Gorgon's head magnified to a mountain. After six hours' ride through the falling chaos of Jeshimon,[1] we found faint traces of a military road,—our Arabs called this Karossa el-Khufeiriyeh,—only to lose them on the edge of a cliff. Leading our horses down this cliff by a path, each turn of which was visible only when we came to it, we struck the bed of the Wady Ṣafṣaf, and followed it towards the bulk of rock which shut out the Dead Sea from our view, and soon towered above us. This was Masada, bare, brown, inaccessible, except for a narrow bank reared against it at a steep angle, and in its white colour distinct from the rock itself. The bank rose from the neck of land which connects the rock with the wady behind. We climbed it on foot. Half-way up we struck to the right along the almost precipitous rock, and then turned left by another sloping shelf, which brought us to a gateway with a pointed arch. A few more steps placed us on the summit. This is a plateau almost 700 yards long, and in breadth varying from 180 yards on the north to 250 on the south. The view is magnificent, and at first dazzled our eyes to the interesting ruins at our feet. We saw the Dead Sea in its whole length. En-gedi was clear to the north, Jebel Usdum clear to the south. The peninsula, el-Lisan, lay brilliant white on the brilliant blue of the water. Behind it ran the long wall of Moab, and over the top of this we discerned the position of Kerak. Only westward was the view confined, and yet it had its own fascination, for here rise the jagged cliffs of Jeshimon, with the uncouth valley running up through them. Immediately below is the neck of land coming out to Masada from this valley, the dizzy depths of the gorges on either side, and eastward the broad flat beach of the sea.

The ruins on Masada are the gateway already noticed, the *débris* of a wall running round the edge of the plateau, and on the latter cisterns and tombs, remains of a castle and palace, a chapel with the apse standing, and curious mosaics on the walls. The pointed arch of the gateway and the chapel are Byzantine or later. The rest of the ruins are Herodian. With them the real history of Masada is bound up.

Jonathan Maccabæus was the first to build a fortress on the rock.[2] Herod fled to it with his bride Mariamne in 42 B.C., when the Parthians took Jerusalem; and eight years later he elaborately built upon it. He enclosed the plateau by a wall seven furlongs in circumference with towers. He built a richly-furnished palace on the west, and floored it with stones of several colours—the mosaic still found. The top of the hill, which was of fat soil,

[1] See p. 211. [2] Hence the name מצדה = fortress.

he reserved for cultivation; he hewed many reservoirs for rain, and laid up in caverns immense quantities of wine, oil, pulse, and dates. It is said that these stores were still in good condition a century later, when Masada, along with Machærus and Hyrcaneum, fell into the hands of the Sicarii—the most fanatic of the Jewish patriots in the war of Independence. In A.D. 70 when Jerusalem fell, a band of them, being the last survivors of the garrison, fled with Eleazar to Masada.[1] They might well have thought themselves secure in a fortress so remote, and standing so furnished in the midst of so waterless a country. But they had Rome to deal with. Palestine is stamped all over with proofs of the power of the Romans, yet nowhere are you so forced into admiration of their genius as when you stand on that Dead Sea coast below Masada, between their two camps, or mark the wall they built around the rock, or the white ramp they raised against it. They laid a road across a waterless desert, brought their siege engines down cliffs, and fought for months, miles away from water and forage. The General was Flavius Silva, a lieutenant of Titus. On the earthen bank on the promontory he raised another bank of stones, and on that a tower plated with iron. This brought the battering-ram on a level with the edge of the plateau, and it breached Herod's wall. The defenders built an inner wall, that was but a trough of wood packed with earth, and the blows of the ram only made this more compact. Silva set it on fire. At first the flames were blown on the besiegers, but, the wind changing, the fire coursed through the whole wall. The Romans let it burn, and retired to their camps for the night. Next morning they planted their ladders and prepared the assault. But no one met them, and on the plateau nothing moved except the still smouldering fire. The first of the storming party stood still on the tops of their ladders and sent across the silence a great shout. Then two women with some children came out of a cave, and told that when the inner wall took fire, Eleazar gathered his men and urged them, rather than fall into Roman hands, or let their wives and children so fall, to kill the latter, and then to slay each other. Moved by his words into a fury, not one drew back or scrupled, but, kissing them with tears, each slew those who were dearest to him. Then by lot ten of the men were chosen to fall upon the others, who received their death-blows lying stretched upon their families. And of those ten one was chosen who slew the other nine, and, setting fire to all their property that had been gathered together for burning, he fell upon his own sword. The two women who now met the Romans had hidden themselves with five children, and these were the only survivors of a garrison of nearly one thousand.

[1] Josephus, vii *Wars*, viii f.

BOOK THREE

EASTERN PALESTINE

XXIV. *OVER JORDAN: THE GENERAL FEATURES*[1]

"Who," says Dean Stanley, "that has ever travelled in Palestine has not longed to cross the Jordan Valley to those mysterious hills which close every eastward view with their long horizontal outline, their overshadowing heights, their deep purple shade?" He justly calls them "the most novel feature of the Holy Land", "the elevating and solemn background of all that is poor and mean in the scenery of Western Palestine". Only part of their impressiveness is due to their height, enhanced by the depression of the Jordan Valley below them; they derive the most of their fascination from their sustained line of elevation. As you see this from afar, you feel the promise of a spacious country behind—high, healthy areas of life, an open and richly furnished stage for history.

This promise is amply fulfilled when you cross Jordan and climb the range of Eastern Palestine. The country is about 150 miles long from Hermon to the south end of the Dead Sea; its breadth, from the edge of the Jordan Valley to the edge of the desert, varies from thirty to eighty. Yet throughout this extent the average elevation is nearly 2000 feet above the level of the sea, or 2800 above the average level of Jordan. The consequence is a temperate climate lifted above the almost tropic heats which surround it to west and south. In winter the snow lies for days at a time[2]; even in November and March there are frosts[3]; and the temperature falls low enough to explain the Arab saying that the cold has one of its homes in the Belḳa.[4] Through summer there seems to be more rain, mist, and cloud than upon the other side of Jordan,[5] and the days are swept by breezes from the west with the freshness of the sea upon them. Jaulan and Hauran were called by the Romans Palestina Salutaris[6]; and Oliphant says that "cool-blowing" is an epithet Arab poets are fond of applying to the Nuḳra, or southern end of

[1] For this chapter, see Maps 2, 5, 6, and on pages 56-7.

[2] Seetzen (*Reisen*, vol. i) had during February very deep snow.

[3] Burckhardt (*Travels in Syria*, 92) reports strong hoar frosts in November in Hauran. Merrill (*East of Jordan*, 358) found ice in the heart of Gilead on March 18th with a temperature in the air of 38°.

[4] The portion of the Eastern range from Arnon to Jabbok.

[5] Burckhardt, *passim*, Buckingham, *Travels*, chs. xviii. ff.; Post, *PEFQ*, 1888, 191, 203 ff.

[6] *ZDPV*, xxii. 131 f., xxiii. 112.

Hauran.[1] We traversed Eastern Palestine during twenty-two days of mid-summer,[2] and were able to test the climate. We had thrice dense mists,[3] and several very cold evenings. Every morning about ten a breeze sprang up from the west, and lasted till sun-down, so that although the noon temperature in the Jordan Valley, as often as we entered it, was at least 103°, on the table-land above we seldom had it over 90°.[4] Whether upon the shadeless plain of Hauran, where the ripe corn swayed like the sea before the wind,[5] or upon the ridges of Gilead, where the oak branches rustled and their shadows swung to and fro over the cool paths,[6] most of the twelve hours were almost as bracing as the dawn, and night fell, not, as in other parts of Palestine, to repair, but to confirm, the influences of the day. Eastern Palestine is a land of health. This was our first impression, as we rose to Hauran by the steppes south of Pharpar, the wind blowing over from Hermon, and this our last impression, when we regretfully struck our tents on the pastures of Moab, where the dry herbage makes the breezes as fragrant as the heather the winds of our own Highlands. Victory and Good Fortune were the favourite deities of the later Pagans of this region, but their temples might more fitly have been dedicated to the goddess Hygeia.[7]

But Eastern Palestine does more than fulfil its promise of fresh air. Broad and breezy as it looks from afar, it also looks barren, and when you come upon it surprises you by its fertility. Next to its air, its waters are its most charming feature. West of the Jordan no rivers run, and only a few perennial streams, but here are at least four rivers—Yarmuk, 'Arab, Jabbok and Arnon, of which the Yarmuk, with its great falls, is as large as Jordan.[8] These rivers drain the country and the desert behind. They run in deep gorges, below the average level of the plateau, but are fed by numerous springs and streams, which, with the winter snow and rains, sufficiently water the higher lands.[9] Luxuriant vegetation is almost universal, and agriculture prosperous. In the most northerly of the three divisions of the country, from Hermon to the Yarmuk, a large part of the surface, a rich volcanic soil, is tilled for wheat, the rest covered by a thick herbage.[10] This is Hauran, the granary of Syria, and the hilly district to the west of it was once thickly wooded. The middle region, Gilead, between the Yarmuk and the Jabbok, has its ridges covered by forests, under which you may march for the day in breezy and fragrant

[1] *Land of Gilead*, 102. [2] June 16-July 7, 1891.

[3] At Ghabaghib, Irbid (see p. 63, n. 9), and Wady Yabis.

[4] But in the gorges that cut the plateau it was stifling; cf. Burckhardt in the Arnon, July 14, p. 273.

[5] See ch. xxx. [6] Post, *PEFQ*, 1888, 200: "cool air of the uplands".

[7] Ewing, *PEFQ*, Jan. 1895, No. 124. [8] Before it receives Yarmuk.

[9] Except on the Belḳa. [10] See ch. xxix.

shade[1]; the valleys hold orchards of pomegranate, apricot, and olive, there are many vineyards, on the open plains are fields of wheat and maize,[2] and the few moors are rich in fragrant herbs.[3] Gilead bore perfume and medicine for the whole Eastern world. They who first break from her into history are *a company of Ishmaelites with their camels bearing spicery and balm and myrrh, going to carry it down to Egypt.*[4] It became a proverb, *Is there no balm in Gilead, is there no physician there!* and again, *Go up into Gilead and take balm!*[5] In the third division, south of the Jabbok, the forests gradually cease, and Ammon and Moab are mostly high, bare moors with few jungles of bush. They are occasionally cultivated for wheat and once bore the vine.

More famous than the tilth of Eastern Palestine is her pasture. We passed through at the height of the shepherd's year. From the Arabian deserts the Bedouin were swarming to the fresh summer herbage of these uplands. We should never have believed the amount of their flocks had we not seen, and tried to count them. One afternoon which we spent at Edrei, the 'Aneezeh tribe,[6] that roams from Euphrates to Jordan, drove their camels upon the plain to the north of the town, till we counted nearly a thousand feeding, and there was a multitude more behind. Next day we passed their foes, the Beni-Ṣaḥr, one of whose camel-herds numbered four hundred, and another two hundred. We looked south-east from the hills above 'Amman, and there were hundreds more of the Sherarat Arabs from Ma'an. *Profusion of camels shall cover thee, camels of Midian and Ephah, all of them from Sheba shall come.*[7] The Arabs had also many sheep and goats. The herds of the settled inhabitants were still more numerous. In Moab the dust of the roads bore almost no marks but those of the feet of sheep. The scenes which throng our memory of Eastern Palestine, are (besides the threshing-floors of Hauran) the streams of Gilead in the heat of the day with the cattle standing in them, or the evenings when we sat at the door of our tent near the village well, and would hear the shepherd's pipe far away, and the sheep and goats and cows with the heavy bells would break over the edge of the hill and come down the slope to wait their turn at the troughs. Over Jordan we were never

[1] Burckhardt, *Travels*, 348. "Grateful shade of fine oak and pistachios, with a scenery more like that of Europe than any I had yet seen in Syria"; Post, *PEFQ*, 1888, 200. Oliphant (*Land of Gilead*, 160) quotes 2 Sam. xviii. 8: *the wood devoured more people that day than the sword*; of the valley in which 'Ajlun lies he says it was "a view such as one would expect to find in the Black Forest". On the fertility of Gilead, 129 f.

[2] Like the Buḳei'a and the plateau above, near es-Salṭ.

[3] On the botany, Post, *PEFQ*, 1888.

[4] Gen. xxxvii. 25.

[5] Jer. viii. 22, xlvi. 11; known as Balsamum Gileadense.

[6] Or a branch of it—the Oulad-'Ali.

[7] Isa. lx. 6.

long out of the sound of the lowing of cattle or of the shepherd's pipe.

And thus one understands why so much of the annals of this country is taken up with the multiplying of cattle, tribute in sheep and wool,[1] and the getting of spoil by tens of thousands of camels, and hundreds of thousands of sheep.[2] Bulls of Bashan and fat kine of Bashan are proverbial throughout the Old Testament. "Thou canst not," runs an Arab saying, "find a country like the Belḳa" for cattle and sheep.[3] When Moses overcame Midian the spoil was reckoned at more than half a million of sheep, 72,000 beeves, and 61,000 asses.[4] *When the children of Reuben and of Gad, who had a very great multitude of cattle, saw the land of Jazer and Gilead,* they asked it for themselves, *for the place was a place for cattle.*[5] When Reuben lingered in his own country and would not cross Jordan to the help of the Lord against the mighty, Deborah taunted him:

By the water-courses of Reuben great were the resolves!
Why didst thou abide among the sheep-hurdles?
To listen to the bleating of the flocks?
By the water-courses of Reuben were great resolves of heart![6]

The king of Moab was *a sheepmaster*, and his tribute to Israel 100,000 lambs, and 100,000 rams with the wool.[7] Flocks and pastures have ever been the wealth, the charm, the temptation of Eastern Palestine.

The third general feature of Eastern Palestine is its openness to the desert. Bashan, Gilead, and Moab all roll off, with little barrier, upon the Arabian plateau. Consequently they have been exposed in all ages to the invasion of the hungry nomads, some of whom swarm upon them every year for pasture, while others have settled down into more permanent occupation[8]: living in movable camps, but cultivating the soil. These are the Ishmaelites and Midianites of the Old Testament; *children of the East*, who made Gilead their base of operation against Western Palestine. It was sons of Ishmael whom Balak called to help him against Israel. Their sheikhs went with the elders of Moab to bring Balaam from the farther east to curse the people of Yahweh,[9] and the last war Moses undertook was to avenge Yahweh upon Midian.[10] In the days of the Judges they swarmed across Jordan, and every spring, pitching their black tents in Jezreel, swept off the harvests from the valleys of Ephraim. But Gideon beat them back over the river, and finally

[1] 2 Chron. v. 9; 2 Kings iii. 4. [2] 2 Chron. v. 21. [3] Burckhardt, 369.
[4] One cannot vouch for these. [5] Num. xxxii. 1. [6] Judges v. 16. [7] Kings iii. 4.
[8] The Arab tribes of E Palestine are distinguishable into: (1) Bedouin, whose range lies within E Palestine, like the 'Adwan, Beni-Ṣaḥr, etc.; (2) who come in every year from Arabia like the 'Aneezeh, or a branch of them, Ruwala, the Sherarat, the Wuld 'Ali, *ZDPV*, xx. 104.
[9] Num. xxii. 6. [10] Num. xxxi.

broke them upon Moab. *He took the two kings of Midian, Zebah and Zalmunna, and discomfited all the host.*[1] The *Day of Midian* was very decisive.[2] But though, for many centuries to come, Israel had nothing to fear on this frontier from Arabia, the tides rose again in the close of her history,[3] and even till now they have flowed and ebbed unceasing. You stand to-day on one of the Moab hills, and looking east you see a tossed and weary land, as destitute of signs of life as mid-ocean. Yet as irresistibly and almost as regularly as ocean is drawn by the moon, so have these trackless wastes been swept by tides of men, drawn on by hunger and the hope of spoil. Successive civilisations—Semitic, Greek, Roman, and Turkish—have kept them back for a time, but as these decayed, they have swept in again with the regularity and remorselessness of the sea. Scattered across Hauran and Gilead were Greek cities, the military walls and roads of the Roman Empire, castles and towers of the Turks. But to-day those are all in ruin, and the names of many forgotten. Whereas the Bedawee pitches his camps about them, herds his sheep in their courts, and calls himself by the very names which his ancestors bore there in the days of Gideon. Recently a Zeeb still led a Midianite tribe in Moab.[4] The Beni-Mesaid pitched their summer camp where an inscription of A.D. 214 records the presence of a nomad tribe of the same name.[5] They have extorted the same blackmail; if this was withheld, they have swept off harvests in the same ruthless fashion.[6] We found Arab tents pitched near the flourishing town of Irbid, and in the tents a Bedawee chieftainess, to whom the Irbid people, in spite of having a Turkish lieutenant-governor and a troop of soldiers in their midst, paid annual tribute for the security of their crops. The tax was called by a euphemism Brotherhood, and the town which yielded it known as the Sister of the tribe that made the demand. It was so established a custom that Government allowed it, and even took a percentage of their spoil from the nomads.[7] But it was among the ruins of an ancient city that we felt most the force of these desert tides upon Eastern Palestine. At Pella, overlooking the Jordan, there was once a town, with a castle, colonnades, mausoleums, pagan temples, and a Christian cathedral. You can now distinguish these only by their basement lines and a few pillars. Scarcely one stone stands upon another. But close beside them, when we were there, stood the tents of a Bedawee tribe. Frail houses of hair, they were here five thousand years ago, ere civilisation spread

[1] Judges viii. 12. [2] Isa. ix. 4 (Eng. Vers.). [3] Josephus, xiii *Antt.* xiii. 3.

[4] 'Ali Di'ab = Zeeb = wolf, the chief of the 'Adwan.

[5] Waddington, 2287: *φυλὴ Μοζαιεδήνων.*

[6] Or burned them, Burckhardt, *Travels*, etc.

[7] "Brotherhood", Khuwwah; "Sister", Ukht. Burckhardt describes the system in Hauran, *Travels*, 300 ff.; Schumacher, *ZDPV*, xxii. 180.

from the Nile and the Euphrates, and they flowed in again upon the decay of one of its most powerful bulwarks. For the Arabs have been like the ocean, barred for a time, yet prevailing at last over the patience and virtue of great empires.

We have now discovered the secrets of the confusing history of Eastern Palestine. Here is a land blessed more than most with health and fertility, but its health has been paralysed by its danger, its fertility checked and blasted by the floods of barbarism to which it lies exposed. And hence the mingled brilliance and ineffectiveness of the history of this province—the civilisation which sprang so quickly and richly from its soil, the ruins which cover it to-day. No land possesses greater power of recuperation, but except for the first five centuries of our era its enemies have never given its wounds time to heal. Israel planted east of Jordan tribes as valiant and righteous[1] as those she brought to the west, and on a richer soil. Yet they had no part in the greatness of the nation, and the Kingdom and Church of God were built upon Western Palestine. Ammon and Moab were wealthier than Judah and Ephraim, yet they never reached even the political achievements of the latter. We read of cities in Eastern Palestine in early times, but which of them became famous? We know the sites of only a few. The land of Uz has been identified with various parts of Eastern Palestine; and indeed one could not get a better summary of the history of the region than the story of the substance of Job and the disasters which swept it away. But two other proofs may be given of the same insecurity of so fertile a province.

One is the existence of subterranean fortresses and towns, and of towns which are of the next degree to subterranean, being built in the heart of these intricate mazes of lava which have spread and cracked open in the north-east of the region.[2]

[1] Num. xxxii, Deut. iii. 12 ff.

[2] The most famous is Edrei, on which see pp. 386 f. In an inscription in Ḳanawat (Wadd. 2329) Agrippa I blames the inhabitants for dwelling in caves and bids them build houses, Joseph. xiv *Antt.* xv. 5; xv *Antt.* x. 1; xvi *Antt.* ix. 1. Strabo (xvi. ii. 20) mentions caves in the Trachons (wrongly in mountains beyond the Trachons), one of which could hold 4000 robbers; cf. Wetzstein, *Reisebericht über Hauran u. die Trachonen*, 36 ff.; also on the caves in Zumle and Eṣ-Ṣuweit, 46 f.; named by William of Tyre (xxii. 21), "Cavea Roob". In Gilead caves are only less numerous. Oliphant (*Land of G.* 147, 161 f.) was told by his guides and the officials of an underground village in Gilead, Belvola, but did not find it. He thinks it near Jebel Kafkafa. He heard of subterranean dwellings at Rehab, east of the Ḳula'at ez-Zerḳa (p. 218). On the caverns at 'Araḳ-el-Emir, see Conder's *Heth and Moab*, pp. 169 ff., *PEF Mem. E. Pal.*, and my *Jerusalem*, ii. 425, 462; for cities in the lava mazes, Wetzstein, *op. cit.*, Porter, *Five Years in Damascus*, ii. The Leja is covered with ruins. The remains of

The careful, elaborate architecture of these refuges testifies at once to the high culture of the inhabitants and the frequency of the barbaric invasions against which they took such precautions. History corroborates; from Strabo to Wetzstein we read again and again of how the population was run to earth,[1] and travellers tell us that cityfuls of men, in order to avoid some new line of Arab invasion, have migrated in a night to some other city which had lain empty for years from a similar cause.[2] This sudden transference of numbers of the inhabitants is extraordinary; no two travellers, between whose visits ten years have elapsed, give the same account of the cultivation or populousness of the same district.

But this combination of opulence and insecurity, which is the chief feature of Eastern Palestine, is perhaps most clearly illustrated by the fortunes upon her of Greek civilisation. These healthy and fertile plateaus were early discovered and occupied by the Greeks. Veterans of Alexander the Great founded cities; the Seleucids and Ptolemies in turn attempted to organise the region. Yet in spite of this no permanent civilisation was here achieved till the coming of the Romans. Across Jordan Greek remains of the Seleucid age are the merest fragments[3]; nor does history record there any real progress. It required the genius of Rome, the power of the Legions, the organisation of the Empire, to build a bulwark between Syria and the desert; and even those powers took nearly two centuries to their task. We shall follow the details later. Here it is only necessary to state that Pompey brought the first Legions to Eastern Palestine in 64 B.C.; that from that year the Greek cities date their civic eras, as if previously they had no history; that Greek coins and inscriptions begin to multiply; that the underground cities are abandoned, and that Greek art and letters abundantly flourish. About A.D. 106 Trajan creates another province between Syria and the east borders of the Empire, thus removing her even from touch with the desert.[4] Then follows the rule of the Antonines. Eastern Palestine is covered with roads; her fields cultivated for some centuries in peace, and her cities permitted to multiply to such an extent that to-day the astonished traveller, as he passes across her

---

one town, Mismieh, are three miles in circumference, and so situated that "it was necessary to cut a road through the lava bed in order to reach the city, which no doubt enjoyed immunity from attack, since the rock fields about it are almost impassable".—Merrill, *East of Jordan*, 16.

[1] Wetzstein, *Reisebericht*, etc. 46. On the cave-fort of Crusading times Röhricht, *Gesch. Königreichs Jerus.* 249, 347, Will. of Tyre, xxii, ch. 15.

[2] Burckhardt, Post, *op. cit.*

[3] One or two inscriptions may date from the Seleucids; see Burckhardt.

[4] Brünnow and v. Domaszewski, *Die Provincia Arabia*, 3 vols. 1904.

once more Arab-swept surface, can stand almost nowhere but the sites of two or three of them are in his view.

That till now no power but Rome has ever held Eastern Palestine secure against the desert, is the crowning feature of the strange history of this land.[1]

Under the new government of the land, Arab subject to British supervision and French, excavations and other explorations have already been in progress, and should throw much further light on the ancient history of Transjordan.

XXV. *THE DIVISIONS AND NAMES OF EASTERN PALESTINE*

Eastern Palestine may be said to stretch from Hermon to the south end of the Dead Sea. To form a clear idea of its provinces we must note the three large rivers which cut it at right angles to the Jordan—the Arnon, Jabbok, and Yarmuk. Of these the Arnon has nearly always formed the political boundary to the south.[2] The other two, the Jabbok and Yarmuk, divide Eastern Palestine into three provinces. The southern face of Hermon continued east by the Jebel el-'Aswad is properly the northern boundary; but round on the east of Hermon is room for the territory of Damascus. Separated by Anti-Lebanon from the west and the north, Damascus is thrown upon Eastern Palestine. But its slope to the desert, while the rest of the country drains to the Jordan, as well as the low line of hills to the south of it, distinguish the territory of Damascus from the three provinces which form Eastern Palestine proper. These we now take from north to south. Physically they are distinct.

1. *The Three Natural Divisions*

Across the northmost division, from Hermon to the Yarmuk, the limestone basis of the country is covered by volcanic deposits. The stone is basalt, the soil rich, red loam resting on beds of ash, and there are vast "ḥarras" or eruptions of lava, suddenly cooled and split open into tortuous shapes. Down the edge of the Jordan Valley and the border of the desert run rows of extinct volcanoes. The centre of this province is a plain, about fifty miles

[1] On some success by the Turk, *ZDPV*, xx. 96 f.

[2] Israel's territory never went south of Arnon.

long by twenty broad, scarcely broken by a hill, and almost treeless. This is Hauran proper. To the west of this, above the Jordan, is the hilly and once wooded district of Jaulan; to the east the "ḥarras" and extinct volcanoes; and in the south-east the range of Jebel Hauran or Jebel ed-Druz. All beyond is desert draining to the Euphrates.

South of the Yarmuk the volcanic elements almost disappear and the limestone comes to the surface. We had proof of the suddenness of the change. In every village of Hauran we had seen ancient inscriptions, still legible in the hard basalt; but when we crossed the Yarmuk we found almost none and little carving—limestone is not a material to have preserved them.[1] Between the Yarmuk and Jabbok the country is mainly disposed in high ridges, fully forested; eastward are plains.

South of Jabbok the ridges and forests alike diminish, till by the north end of the Dead Sea the country is a treeless plateau, in winter bleak, in summer breezy and fragrant. This plateau is broken only by deep, wide, warm valleys like the Arnon, across which it rolls south beyond our present survey. Eastward it is separated from the desert by low rolling hills.

These three sections, then, are physically distinct from each other, from the territory of Damascus to the north and from Edom to the south. It is unfortunate that through ancient history we do not find the same definiteness of political division and nomenclature. In Eastern Palestine names are everywhere adrift. We are best able to fix those of to-day and from them work into the past.

2. *The Political Names and Divisions of To-day*

In 1915 the British Government promised King Husein of the Hejaz to recognise the independence of the Arabs, and by the later Sykes-Picot agreement territory was assigned them from Aleppo to Damascus and all Transjordan southwards. But after the war this was prevented by political complications, especially strife between the French and the Arabs. The Emir Feisal, who with Colonel Lawrence had led the Arab forces in invading Eastern Palestine and in their part in capturing Damascus, held rule in that city after the Armistice, but in 1920 was ejected by the French,[2] who incorporated it in their Province of Syria. Transjordan, which had been

[1] S of Yarmuk the inscriptions we found were nearly all in basalt. So in Gadara, on the edge of the volcanic area; in Gerasa both on limestone and basalt; between Yarmuk and Jabbok one or two extinct craters and outcrops of basalt.

[2] Feisal became King of Iraḳ (Mesopotamia).

divided into its three natural parts, 'Ajlun, the Belḳa, and Kerak (south to 'Aḳaba), "was left politically derelict", till in 1921 Emir 'Abdullah, second son of Husein, brought its three districts again under one government, with a governor for each and sub-governors, and was provisionally recognised as Administrator of Transjordan by the Mandatory Government in Jerusalem. This was confirmed by the Colonial Office in London in 1922, and in 1923 Sir Herbert Samuel announced at 'Amman that "His Majesty's Government will recognise the existence of an independent Government in Transjordan, provided that such a Government is constitutional, and places His Majesty's Government in a position to fulfil its international obligations in respect of the territory." The Emir rules through a small Council at 'Amman, the capital, where also a British representative resides, directed by the High Commissioner in Jerusalem. An annex of September 1922 to the Palestine Mandate provides that the Articles on the Jewish National Home in Western Palestine do not apply to Transjordan.[1]

3. *The Names and Divisions of Yesterday*

Under the Turks the chief line of political division was the Jabbok.[2] By this all Eastern Palestine, except Damascus, was divided into two Mutasserafliks or Provinces, to which in 1893 a third was added south of the Arnon, with a Kaimakam and small garrison at Kerak and a police garrison at Ma'an. South of the Jabbok, and comprising the ridges and table-land to the Arnon, was the natural division, the Belḳa. The Belḳa was administered from Nablus but had its own local capital at es-Salṭ.[3]

North of the Jabbok, and as far as the territory of Damascus, extended the Mutasseraflik of Hauran,[4] with its capital at el-Merkez,[5] and divided thus: Between the Jabbok and the Yarmuk the wooded district of 'Ajlun was administered from Irbid. North of the Yarmuk, along the Jordan Valley to the slopes of Hermon ran Jaulan[6]; divisible into a southern and more arable,

[1] For the above see the High Commissioner's Reports, 1924-25, etc.

[2] Strictly, the south border was the Arnon, but practically the Belḳa extended farther south.

[3] *MuNDPV*, 1896, 45.

[4] *Sic*, and not "The Hauran".

[5] Early Arab geographers called all the country from Damascus to the Belḳa, Saouad of Damascus (Rey, *Col. Franques*, p. 434). Those quoted by Le Strange (*Pal. under Moslems*, p. 34) extend the territory of Damascus to the borders of the Belḳa, and name as districts Jaidur, Jaulan, Hauran with capital Buṣra, el-Bathanieyyah with Edrei, or Adhra'ah. On boundaries, *ZDPV*, xx. 68.

[6] Surveyed and described by Schumacher, *The Jaulân*, 1888, from *ZDPV*, 1886;

and a northern and more rocky half; the whole administered from el-Ḳuneiṭrah. The east border was the 'Allan, a tributary of the Yarmuk, and Wady Ruḳḳad. But still east of this lies the town Sahem el-Jaulan, and in Porter's day Jaulan extended to the Hajj Road. Other divisions of the Mutasseraflik of Hauran, each under a Kaimakam, were Jebel ed-Druz, administered from es-Suweda, Der'at, and Buṣr el-Ḥariri.[1]

The great plain east of Jaulan is called Hauran in the narrow but popular sense of the name.[2] It stretches from the territory of Damascus to the district of 'Ajlun, from the Jebel 'Aswad to the Wady Shelaleh or Upper Yarmuk. The south end is called en-Nuḳra, "the hollow hearth" of the Bedouin, for it lies low between the hilly Jaulan on the west, the Leja and more distant Jebel Hauran on the east, and the ridge of Zumleh behind Edrei on the south. The name Hauran extends vaguely towards the desert, but the features are so varied as to be separately designated. To the east of the plain there is the Leja—the long, low flood of lava, "the tempest in stone" —twenty-four miles by ten to twenty.[3] East of this is another plain, Wady Liwa or Nimreh, the upper part of which is called Arḍ el-Betheniyeh[4]; while to the south of this is Jebel Hauran or Druz, on which Druze Sheikhs held themselves half independent of the Government.

From Damascus the Hajj Road crosses Hauran to Muzeirib, on the sources of the Yarmuk, and the desert east of 'Ajlun and the Belḳa.[5] It is an ancient line of traffic to the Gulf of 'Aḳaba, but in Arab history a more frequented route to Arabia held east through Bozrah, and in those days Bozrah, or Eski-Shem, disputed with Damascus the front rank among cities in this region.

With these divisions of to-day and yesterday we go back to the disposition of the land in the Greek period and at the time of Christ, and in Old Testament history.[5]

Steuernagel, *Der 'Adschlun*, after Schumacher, 1925. The area is about 560 square miles.

[1] Hartmann (*ZDPV*, xiii. 61) put es-Salṭ also under Hauran.

[2] See p. 356 for a proposed derivation of Hauran.

[3] Length from Burak to Tell Dubbeh; breadth in the south at Shuhbah twenty miles, but tapering gradually to a round headland on the north.

[4] So in Stubel's chart, and Fischer and Guthe's map.

[5] The arrangement of Eastern Palestine at the time of the Crusades would disturb our study of its ancient divisions, so I put as much as we know here. The Crusaders called Eastern Palestine Oultre Jourdain. To the south the Seigneurie of Krak and Montreal extended from the Arnon to Mount Sinai (Rey, *Colonies Franques*, p. 393, cf. 19). The territory of Suete, or Suhete, was Jaulan, under the Principality of Galilee (*Ibid.* 434). The name is either the same as Suwade of Arab geographers or modern Eṣ-Ṣuweit = الصويت, Wetzstein, *Reisebericht*, 46. Did the Crusaders firmly

4. *Divisions and Names in the Greek Period: the Time of Christ*

In the Greek period the general name for Eastern Palestine was Cœle-Syria.[1] This had at first been bestowed upon the hollow between the Lebanons,[2] and was thence loosely stretched over all Southern of Syria except Phœnicia.[3] But before the Romans came it seems to have been restricted again to the east of Jordan, and by officially separating it from Phœnicia and Judæa, the Romans confirmed this restriction.[4] To Josephus, Cœle-Syria is all Eastern Palestine,[5] and the only town west of the Jordan which belonged to it was the capital of the Decapolis, Beth-shan.[6]

Thus restricted to Eastern Palestine, Cœle-Syria consisted, south of the Yarmuk, of Peræa and the interlaced region of Decapolis, and, north of the Yarmuk, of the various provinces which in the time of Christ made up the tetrarchy of Philip,—Gaulanitis, Auranitis, Batanæa, Trachonitis, and Ituræan land. That is to say, while with the Turks the Jabbok was the principal line of division, and the Yarmuk subsidiary, in Greek days the Yarmuk was the chief frontier with the Jabbok subsidiary.

Peræa was properly identical with the modern Belḳa, or the region between Jabbok and Arnon. In one passage Josephus says that it stretched from Pella, or from south of the Jabbok, to Machærus just north of the Arnon, and from the Jordan to Philadelphia.[7] But the name, which simply means

---

hold Gilead? Some of its castles probably date in part from them, and their marks are on ruins about Heshbon. Baldwin I took tribute about Es-Salṭ in 1118 (Rey, p. 435). Two expeditions reached Bozrah in 1113 and 1119. In 1125 and 1129 they did not advance beyond Suete. See further, ch. xxviii.

[1] *Κοίλη Συρία*; cf. Nöldeke, *Hermes*, x. 167, n. i.

[2] To which it is perhaps still confined in 1 Esdras iv. 48.

[3] "Cœle-Syria and Phœnicia", 1 Esdras ii. 17, 24, 27; vi. 29; vii. 1; viii. 67; 1 Macc. x. 69; 2 Macc. iii. 5, 8, where Jerusalem is one of its towns; 2 Macc. iv. 4; viii. 8; x. 11. Polybius, v. 80, and Diodorus Siculus, xix. 59, include the Philistine coast. Even Josephus once uses it in this sense, xiv *Antt.* iv. 5: "Cœle-Syria as far as the river Euphrates and Egypt"; Felix Fabri, *PPT*, i. 198, seems to take it equal to Syria N of Galilee.

[4] In 47 B.C. they gave the military charge of it to Herod, xiv *Antt.* ix. 5. *στρατηγὸς τῆς Κοίλης Σύριας*, i *Wars*, x. 8. In this passage Cœle-Syria is distinct from Samaria (8), Galilee (5), and, of course, Judæa; cf. Pliny, *HN*, v. 9.

[5] xiii *Antt.* xiii. 3, including Moab and Ammon; cf. i *Antt.* xi. 5, but in a narrow sense xv *Antt.* iii. 8.

[6] xiii *Antt.* xiii. 2. Further Pseudo-Aristeas in Swete, *Introd. to O.T. in Greek*, 520; Strabo, xvi. ii. 21.

[7] iii *Wars*, iii. 3.

the *land across*, must have been used also in a wider sense, for elsewhere Josephus calls Gadara, on the banks of the Yarmuk, the capital of Peræa.[1] North of the Yarmuk Peræa did not stretch. By Herod's will, confirmed by Augustus, Peræa was assigned with Galilee to Antipas. Geographically this was an awkward conjunction, for Galilee is the district with which Peræa has the slightest natural connection, while it was thus cut off from the regions immediately opposite, across the Yarmuk and the Jordan. There were, however, reasons, racial and religious, for the arrangement. North of Yarmuk the inhabitants were mainly Greek, and across Jordan Samaria was Samaritan; but in Peræa, as in Galilee, Jews formed the bulk of the population[2]; and, narrow as the strip must have been which connected the two provinces, it formed an easy and convenient passage. The Jews regarded Peræa, Galilee, and Judæa as the three Jewish provinces[3]; and when Galilean pilgrims came up to Jerusalem by Peræa, they felt they had travelled all the way on Jewish soil. When Mark says, *Christ cometh into the borders of Judæa and over Jordan*, he means Peræa by the latter.[4] Here Christ met Jewish doctors, who tempted Him, a Jewish ruler who knew the law, and Jewish mothers who brought their children to Him, that He might lay His hands upon them.

North of Jabbok Peræa intermingled with "the region of Decapolis".[5] Only vaguely can Decapolis be called a geographical quantity. It was really the part of Eastern Palestine in which lay the cities of that famous league, their suburbs and the territories over which they had influence and rights of property. These cities lay mostly south of Yarmuk, but at least four were north of that river. As we are to discuss them separately, more need not be said here.

When we come north of Yarmuk, the definition of boundaries and names in the Greek period is more difficult. Our starting-point is Philip's legacy under the will of Herod, confirmed by Augustus in 4 B.C. This gives Philip's tetrarchy as Gaulanitis, Batanæa, Trachonitis, Auranitis, and "part of the house of Zenodorus" about Paneas, or practically all from Hermon to the Yarmuk and the frontier of Nabatæa, which ran south of Kanatha and Hebran, but north of Bozrah and Salkhat.[6] The same is defined by Luke as

[1] iv *Wars*, vii. 3. Schlatter (*Zur Topographie u. Geschichte Palästinas*, 48 ff.) insists that another Gadara or Gadora, "probably es-Salṭ", is meant.

[2] Josephus, xx *Antt.* i. 1; iv *Wars*, vii. 4-6.

[3] So frequently in the Mishna-Neubauer, *Géog. du Talmud.*

[4] Mark x. 1, Westcott-Hort: τὰ ὅρια τῆς Ἰουδαίας καὶ πέραν τοῦ Ἰορδάνου.

[5] Pliny, *HN*, v. 16: *Decapolitana Regio*, "has urbes intercursant".

[6] xvii *Antt.* viii. 1, Gaulanitis, Trachonitis, Paneas; xi. 4, Batanæa, Trachonitis, Auranitis, and a certain part of the house of Zenodorus; xviii *Antt.* iv. 6, Trachonitis, Gaulanitis, the nation of the Batanæans; ii *Wars*, vi. 3, Batanæa, Trachonitis, Auranitis,

Ituræa and the region of Trachonitis, or, as some render it, the *region Ituræan and of Trachonitis*.[1]

There is no doubt about Gaulanitis. That province must have been practically the same as the present Jaulan, or the country along the Jordan Valley between the Yarmuk and Hermon, with an uncertain east border along perhaps the 'Allan. Like Jaulan, Gaulanitis was divided into an Upper and a Lower Department,[2] and, as by the Turks, the east coast of the Lake of Galilee was cut off from it, and administered from Tiberias.[3] The north end of Gaulanitis seems also to have been known by the names of Ulatha[4] and Paneas.

Nor is there difficulty about Auranitis. The name is the same as Hauran. We have no definition of its limits, but probably, like Hauran, it was the plain east of Jaulan,[5] with the same loose extension south to the Nabatæan border,[6] and south-east to Jebel Ḥauran, the Mons Alsadamus or Asalmanos of Ptolemy.[7]

Our difficulties begin with Batanæa. Batanæa was the Greek form for Bashan,[8] and originally applied, like the latter, to all the country north of the Yarmuk. But in a special sense Batanæa was distinguished from Trachonitis and Auranitis as only a part of Philip's tetrarchy.[9] It bordered on Trachon-

---

and parts of Zeno's house about Jamnia, for which read Paneas. In iii *Wars*, iii. 5: The region of Gamala, and Gaulanitis, and Batanæa, and Trachonitis are parts of the kingdom of Agrippa. "This country begins at Mt. Libanus", *i.e.* Anti-Lebanon, "and the fountains of Jordan, and reaches breadthway to the Lake of Tiberias", *i.e.* the south end, "and in length extends from a village called Arpha", unknown, "as far as Julias", *i.e.* Beth-saida on Jordan. "Its inhabitants are Jews and Syrians mixed." Jos. seems to take Gaulanitis for all N of Yarmuk, describing Og as King of Galaaditis (iv *Antt.* v. 3). If Solyma (*Life*, 37) be Salem of to-day this carries the name E to Jebel Druz. But again he distinguishes Gaulanitis from Hippene and Gamalitis (iii *Wars*, iii. 1, 5). For the frontier between Philip's tetrarchy and Nabatæa, see pp. 411, 413, 415.

[1] Luke iii. 1: τῆς Ἰτουραίας καὶ Τραχωνίτιδος χώρας.

[2] Josephus, iv *Wars*, i. 1.

[3] See p. 271, n. 4.

[4] Perhaps the same name as the modern Lake Ḥuleh. Josephus, xv *Antt.* x. 3. See pp. 309 f.

[5] See p. 345.

[6] Probable from this that Zenodorus wished to sell Auranitis to the Nabatæans, xvii *Antt.* x. 2.

[7] Wetzstein, 90, Ασελδαμός, Ασαλμανός.

[8] So iv *Antt.* vii. 4; ix *Antt.* viii. 1; and *Onomasticon*, art. Βασάν: αὕτη Βασανῖτις ἡ νῦν καλουμένη Βαταναία.

[9] xv *Antt.* x. 1; i *Wars*, xx. 4. In *Life*, 11, Josephus talks of "the Trachonites in Batanæa". Ecbatana should be read Βαθυρά, see p. 412.

itis,[1] the territory round the Leja; the road by which Jewish pilgrims came from Babylon to Jerusalem passed across it,[2] and it seems to have been near the territory of Gamala in Gaulanitis.[3] Probably, therefore, Batanæa lay between the Leja and Gilead, in En-Nuḳra.[4] The name was still here in the fourth century[5] and in the tenth,[6] but has drifted to the east of the Leja.[7] Doubtful is the suggestion that we should recognise Batanæa in the *Bethany beyond Jordan, where John was baptizing*.[8]

Trachonitis was the territory containing the Trachon or Trachons. These are described by Strabo as "the two so-called Trachones behind Damascus".[9] The name, the only Greek one among those we are discussing, corresponds to the two stretches of lava, "tempests in stone", which lie south-east of Damascus—the Leja and Ṣafa.[10] Each is called by Arabs a Wa‘ar, meaning rough, stony tract, and equivalent to Trachon. The latter, beyond the reach of civilisation, was little regarded, and the Leja became the Trachon *par excellence*, as is proved by two inscriptions at either end of it—in Musmi‘eh, ancient Phæna, and at Bereke, each of which is called a chief town of the Trachon.[11] Trachonitis was obviously the Trachon, *plus* some territory round it.[12] In the north it extended west from the Leja to the districts of Ulatha and Paneas in north Jaulan[13]; and in the south it bordered with Batanæa,[14] but also touched Mons Alsadamus, Jebel Ḥauran.[15] Philo uses Trachonitis for the whole tetrarchy of Philip.[16]

[1] xvii *Antt.* ii. 1: "the toparchy called Batanæa, which country is bounded by Trachonitis".

[2] *Ibid.* 2.

[3] This is to be inferred from Josephus, *Life*, 11.

[4] See p. 345.

[5] Eusebius, *Onomasticon*, places Ashtaroth and Edrei or Adraa in Batanæa.

[6] Idrisi (Wetzstein, *Reisebericht*, 87) places Edrei in Betheniyeh.

[7] See p. 345.

[8] John's Gospel, i. 28, Westcott and Hort. The suggestion is Conder's. Bethany is the name of a town, defined *across Jordan*, to distinguish it from the other Bethany. Batanæa did not need this.

[9] Strabo, xvi. ii. 20. *Τραχών* = a rough, stony place.

[10] Wetzstein, *Reisebericht*, 36 ff.

[11] That in Musmi‘eh is given by Burckhardt, p. 117, and Wadd., 2524; date about A.D. 225; that in Bereke by Wadd., 2396. The word is *μητροκωμία* which, used twice, can scarcely be metropolis (Merrill, *East of Jordan*, 20), but is chief town of a group of villages.

[12] Josephus gives *Τράχων* in xv *Antt.* x. 1 (cf. xvi *Antt.* iv. 6), but in the parallel passage, i *Wars*, xx. 4, *Τραχωνίτις*.

[13] xv *Antt.* x. 3. The Leja itself could scarcely be described as bordering with Ulatha.

[14] Josephus, xvii *Antt.* ii. 1, 2.

[15] Ptolemy (v. 15, 4) has *Τραχωνίται Ἄραβες* under Mons Alsadamus.

[16] *Legat. ad Cajum*, 41. In the fourth century Eusebius places Trachonitis north-east of Bozrah, south of Damascus, and in the desert.

The portion of Philip's tetrarchy most difficult to define is the Ituræan. Did this cover or overlap Trachonitis, or was it a separate province? Luke's reference[1] is ambiguous, and we have no echo of the name to guide us.[2] In ancient times much is said of the Ituræi, a vigorous, emphatic breed of men, famous as archers. They are sung by Virgil and Lucan[3]; fight with Cæsar in Africa;[4] rattle with their arrows through the Forum, a defiant bodyguard for Mark Antony, till Cicero cries out against the insult to the Senate.[5] They were wild bordermen between Syria and Arabia, to both of which they were reckoned by ancient writers. They were of an Ishmaelite stock,[6] like the Nabatæans, and Strabo speaks of them as mixed with Arabs, and inhabiting the same inaccessible highlands.[7] It is probably because of their semi-nomadic character that for long there was no region definitely called Ituræa; except once by Tacitus, the name is not used as a noun before the fourth century and doubtfully even then.[8] But the tribe had a more or less distinct territory, on which, like many other nomads of the Syrian border, they settled for a time, as a kingdom with a capital. Schürer has proved this to have been in the main Anti-Lebanon, capital Chalcis in the Beḳa'; for a time the sway of their ruler extended over Lebanon also.[9] In 105 B.C. their territory

---

[1] Luke iii. 1. See p. 348.

[2] Jedur, جيدور, the name of the plain to the north of Hauran, has been quoted by many as equivalent to Ituræa (Robinson, Conder, etc.), but on what grounds it is impossible to see. The words are utterly different.

[3] *Georg.* ii. 448; *Pharsalia*, vii. 230, 514. Vibius Sequester, *de Gentibus*: "Ithyrei usu sagittae periti."

[4] *Bell. Afric.* 20.

[5] "They"—'the barbarians', as he calls them—"filled these very benches." *Philippics*, ii. 19, 112; xiii. 18.

[6] They are no doubt the same as the יְטוּר, Jetur, of Gen. xxv. 15, mentioned with other Ishmaelite tribes of Arabs. Cf. 1 Chron. i. 31, v. 19.

[7] xvi. ii. 18: τὰ μὲν οὖν ὀρεινὰ ἔχουσι πάντα Ἰτουραῖοί τε καὶ Ἄραβες. 20: ἔπειτα πρὸς τὰ Ἀράβων μέρη καὶ τῶν Ἰτουραίων ἀναμὶξ ὄρη δύσβατα.

[8] W. M. Ramsay, *Expositor*, Jan., Feb., April 1894. The only Greek passage in which Ituræa appears before the 4th cent. is Josephus, xii *Antt.* xi. 3, in older editions: Πολεμήσας Ἰτουραίαν. But this should be as in Niese, Ἰτουραίους, given in some codices, and more suitable to the grammar. See *Expositor*, March 1894, p. 236. This reading removes the last Greek precedent for τῆς Ἰτουραίας in Luke iii. 1 as a noun. Schürer still speaks of Ituræa as a noun, reading in xiii *Antt.* xi. 3 Ἰτουραίαν.

[9] Schürer, *Hist. of Jewish People*, Eng., div. 1, vol. ii, Append. i: "History of Chalcis, Ituræa, and Abilene." His evidence for Anti-Lebanon is fourfold. (1) Jos. xiii *Antt.* xi. 3, places the Ituræan country in the north of Galilee, in 105 B.C. (2) On an inscription of about A.D. 6 (Ramsay, p. 147) Q. Æmilius Secundus relates that sent by Quirinius "adversus Ituræos in Libano monte castellum eorem cepi" (*Ephemeris Epigraphica*, 1881, 537-542). (3) Dion Cassius (xlix. 32) calls Lysanias king of the

bordered with Galilee,[1] and Schürer thinks their name covered also part of Galilee; this is improbable. If the name thus spread down the slopes of Anti-Lebanon west to Galilee, it may also have extended down the same hill south-east upon the districts of Paneas, and east towards Trachonitis. The Ituræans were Arabs, and Strabo's statement that they inhabited inaccessible highlands along with Arabs must refer to districts east of Anti-Lebanon. We gather, then, that the Ituræans extended farther east than Schürer seems willing to admit. At the same time Strabo distinguishes the two Trachons from the parts occupied by Ituræans and Arabs together. We may therefore conclude that the Ituræans, though scattered towards Trachonitis, occupied a distinct territory. About 25 B.C., however, part of the Ituræan domains south of Hermon was under the same ruler as Trachonitis, Zenodorus by name.[2] Again, in 20 B.C., that same part of Ituræan territory and Trachonitis were both under Herod; and from 4 B.C. to A.D. 34 under Philip.[3] Now, it is not impossible that the names of territories bordering each other and under the same ruler overlapped. As a fact, we have seen that Philo called all Philip's tetrarchy Trachonitis. Conversely, did "Ituræan" spread across Trachonitis? We have no evidence that it did during the first century. But this is possible. Within the last few years the Druzes emigrating from Lebanon have bestowed their name on Jebel Hauran, which is as often called Jebel Druz. The Ituræans might have effected a similar transference of their name to Trachonitis, especially in A.D. 6, when the Romans captured their seats in Anti-Lebanon.[4] At the same time Strabo, writing after this event, still keeps Ituræan territory and Trachonitis distinct. The questions, therefore, whether Luke meant by his words two distinct portions of Philip's tetrarchy, or two equivalent or overlapping names for it; and whether, on either of these interpretations of his words, he was correct—are questions to which the geographical data of the first century supply us with no certain

---

Ituræans, and the same writer (lix. 12) and Tacitus (*Ann.* xii. 23) calls Soemus governor of the same; but Lysanias ruled the Lebanon from the sea to Damascus, with his capital at Chalcis, and Soemus was tetrarch at Lebanon (Jos. *Vita*, xi). (4) Above all, Strabo puts the Ituræans in Anti-Lebanon (xvi. ii. 18): *τὴν Ἰτουραίων ὀρείνην;* 18: *τίνα καὶ ὀρεινὰ ἐν οἷς ἡ Χαλκὶς ὥσπερ ἀκρόπολις τοῦ Μασσύου* (*i.e.* the Beḳa').

[1] xiii *Antt.* xi. 3. See p. 270.

[2] xv *Antt.* x. 1; i *Wars*, xx. 4. "Zenodorus, who had leased the house of Lysanias, king of the Ituræans" (Dion Cassius, xlix. 32), which included Ulatha and Paneas and the country round about.

[3] In whose tetrarchy "a certain part of the house of Zenodorus" represents the Ituræan region S and SE of Hermon.

[4] See previous page.

answer. It is true that Eusebius in the fourth century makes Ituræa and Trachonitis equivalent; but the name Ituræa was dead by his day, and his evidence cannot rank with that of the first century.[1]

Behind Ituræa, on the Upper Abana or Barada, lay Abilene, which Luke gives as the tetrarchy of Lysanias,[2] and in the Beḳa' Chalcis, but these are beyond our limits.

In New Testament times the whole region east and south of Eastern Palestine was known as Arabia. The population were an Arab tribe or tribes known as the Nabatæans,[3] who at the beginning of the third century had settled down to agriculture and commerce. About 100 B.C. they became a powerful kingdom. Their capital was Petra,[4] but their influence extended round Syria, from Damascus, which fell to them in 87 B.C., when they defeated the Syrians,[5] to Gaza,[6] and to the centre of Arabia.[7] Their inscriptions are scattered over Eastern Palestine, where they had many settlements,

[1] From my article, *Expositor*, March 1894. To that Professor Ramsay replied, April, 288, n. 1, 298 ff., and to this my answers are: (1) I am his ally in so far as I brought evidence for the *possibility* of the overlapping of Trachonitis and the Ituræan name. (2) I repeat that, leaving aside Luke iii. 1, there is no evidence in the 1st cent. of such overlapping. (3) My objection to Eusebius is not so much to his errors as a geographer for his own day, as that his date in the 4th cent. makes his testimony about the 1st inferior to that of a 1st cent. writer Strabo, who distinguishes the Trachons from "the parts of the Ituræans". (4) Ramsay seems led to extend the Ituræans as far as over the Trachon by his theory (which on p. 300 he wrongly imputes to me) that "the Ituræans were the one warlike tribe of the whole region"; they were not; to the E were Arabs distinct from, but partly mixed with, them (Strabo, xvi. ii. 18, 20), and Nabatæans (if these be distinct, which is doubtful, from Strabo's Arabs) holding Damascus when Rome was not, and allies of Arabs of the Trachon (see below); when Ramsay says, "the true home of such a race (*i.e.* as the Ituræans) is *not* the long settled and well-governed land between Lebanon and Anti-Lebanon" he ignores (*a*) how often such land in Syria was seized and governed by such a tribe, and (*b*) that Ituræans did settle on Anti-Lebanon and in the Beḳa' with Chalcis as their capital. On this Schürer seems to me correct (above, p. 350). Bedouins and Turcomans long warred in the Beḳa'; in 1898 part of the 'Aneezeh tribe paid the fellahin for the right of grazing on their stubble (Von Oppenheim, *Vom Mittelmeer z. Pers. Golf*, i. 26 n.).

[2] Luke iii. 1. The capital of Abilene was Abila, the ruins of which are still to be found at Suḳ on the Barada.

[3] Identified by some with the Nebaioth of the Old Testament.

[4] Jos. xiv *Antt*. i. 4; xvii *Antt*. iii. 2, etc. etc.; i *Wars*, vi. 2, etc. Strabo, xvi. ii. 34; iv. 2. 18, especially 21 ff.; Pliny, *HN*, vi. 28.

[5] Jos. xiii *Antt*. xv. 2; i *Wars*, iv. 7.

[6] xiii *Antt*. xiii. 3.

[7] At Hejra, or Meda'in eṣ-Ṣaliḥ, on the Hajj route to Mecca, there are great numbers of Nabatæan tombs and inscriptions; Doughty, *Arabia Deserta*, vol. i; *Corpus Inscript. Semiticarum*, Pars II, tom. i. 183 ff.

and in Arabia, but have even been found in Italy, proving the extent of their trade.[1] Their relations with Rome we follow later on.[2]

5. *In Old Testament Times*

When we pass back into the Old Testament we again find Eastern Palestine, now known as Over-Jordan or Abarim,[3] divided into three. But the lines of division are not now Yarmuk and Jabbok, but Yarmuk and that line twenty-five miles south of Jabbok, which divides the table-land of Moab from the ridges north of it.[4] All south of this to the Arnon is Mishor or Table-land; all north of it, as far as the Yarmuk, is Gilead; and all north of Yarmuk is Bashan.[5]

The Mishor,[6] or Table-land, covered the south half of the Belḳa; sometimes called Mishor of Medeba,[7] which town is conspicuous across it, it was also the Sharon[8] of Eastern Palestine.

The rest of the Belḳa, from Heshbon to the Jabbok, formed the south half of Gilead[9]; the other half lay between Jabbok and Yarmuk,[10] equivalent to the modern district of ʻAjlun.[11] The whole region was called Gilead, Land of Gilead, and Mount Gilead,[12] the last of which survives on the ridge south of the Jabbok, Jebel Jelaʻad.[13] Once Gilead is used for Gad.[14] But with that

[1] *CIS*, as in previous note; also for the Greek ones, Waddington.

[2] Chapters xxvi and xxx.

[3] עבר ירדן, sometimes with מזרחה, eastward. עברים = men or regions *on the other side*.

[4] Coincident with Wady Ḥesban.

[5] For these three see Deut. iii. 10; iv. 43; cf. Josh. xx. 8; xiii. 9 ff.

[6] המישור, Auth. Eng. Ver., *plain country*, or plain; Rev. Ver., *plain*; margin, *table-land*.

[7] Josh. xiii. 9, 16.

[8] From same root as מישור, 1 Chron. v. 16. Neubauer, *Géog.* 47 ff.

[9] Deut. iii. 12: *half Mt. Gilead;* Josh. xii. 2: *half Gilead even to Jabbok.*

[10] Deut. iii. 13: *the rest of Gilead.* Josh. xii. 5, cf. 1 Kings iv. 19.

[11] P. 537. The Yarmuk was the north border, for (1) the country of Gad, practically Gilead, ran to the Sea of Galilee (Deut. iii. 16); (2) Gilead marched with Geshur and Maacah (Josh. xiii. 11). These two in Jaulan.

[12] In the Hexateuch JE uses all three. *Gilead*, Num. xxxii. 26 (J); *Land of G.*, Num. xxxii. 1 (JE), Josh. xvii. 5, 6 (JE); *Mt. G.*, Gen. xxxi. 21 (E), 25 (J). D *Gilead* (Deut. ii. 36, iii. 15, 16, xxxiv. 1 (D or R?); Josh. xii. 2, 5, xiii. 11), except once, *Mt. G.* (Deut. iii. 12). P *Gilead* (Josh. xiii. 25, 31) and *Land of G.* (Num. xxxii. 29; Josh. xxii. 9, 13, 15, 32).

[13] Burckhardt, *Syria*, 348.

[14] Jud. v. 17, cf. 1 Sam. xiii. 7.

elasticity which characterises names across Jordan, Gilead is at least twice used of all Eastern Palestine to Dan.[1] This seems to be the sense of the word in the Maccabees[2]; Josephus uses it with both the narrower and the wider application.[3]

Bashan, or The Bashan,[4] had its east border on Salecah, now Salkhat, the nearest town of importance to the Arabian desert,[5] and included Edrei,[6] Ashtaroth,[7] now Tell ‘Ashtara, and Golan.[8] That is, Bashan proper covered the land known in Greek times as Batanæa, the south end of the plain of Hauran.[9] In this narrower application the name does not appear to have come west to Jordan, for between it and that river lay Geshur and Maacah.[10] But in a wider sense Bashan extended to Hermon, and covered all north of Gilead.[11] The long edge of mountain east of the Lake of Galilee is the Bashan which the prophets so often couple with Carmel. *Dan*, says a poet, *is a lion's whelp; he leaps from Bashan.*[12] This carries the name to the foot of Hermon. Whether Hermon itself was known as *mount* or *mountains of Bashan*, or whether the latter designates all that eastern range, is uncertain. The poet says, *mountains of bold heights*[13] *are the Mount of Bashan.* This epithet, not applicable to the level edge of the table-land, might refer either to the triple summits of Hermon,[14] or to the broken cones that are scattered across Bashan, and in their volcanic form differ from the softer, less imposing heights of Western Palestine.[15]

[1] Deut. xxxiv. 1; Josh. xxii. 9, 13, 15, 32.

[2] *Γαλαὰδ*, 1 Macc. v. 1, 17, etc., *Γαλααδῖτις*, v. 20; excludes Ammon and Jazer to the S but includes part of Hauran, xiii. 22; Judith i. 8, xv. 5.

[3] i *Antt.* xix. 10, the hill Galadēn, the country *Γαλαδηνή*; iv *Antt.* v. 3; vi *Antt.* v. 1; ix *Antt.* viii. 1: *Γαλααδῖτις*, so also LXX; xii *Antt.* viii. 2, 3; in 3 for "Galilee" read "Gilead"; xiii *Antt.* xiii. 4.

[4] The article in all historical statements of the kingdom of Og, always king of *the* Bashan (Num. xxi. 33; Deut. i. 4, etc.; even Psalms cxxxv. 11, cxxxvi. 20), or the territories of Manasseh (Josh. xvii. 1, xxi. 6, etc.) except 1 Chron. v. 23; sometimes in poetry (Deut. xxxiii. 22), and prophecy (Isa. ii. 13; Jer. xxii. 20; l. 19; Amos iv. 1). But in these more often omitted: Psalm xxii. 13 (Eng. 12); lxviii. 17, 23 (Eng. 16, 22); Isa. xxxiii. 9; Ezek. xxvii. 6, xxxix. 18; Micah vii. 14; Nahum i. 4; Zech. xi. 2.

[5] Deut. iii. 10; Josh. xii. 4, xiii. 11; 1 Chron. v. 11. [6] Deut. iii. 10; Josh. ix. 10.

[7] Deut. i. 4; Josh. ix. 10, xii. 4, xiii. 12, 31. [8] Deut. iv. 43; Josh. xx. 8, xxi. 27.

[9] 1 Chron. v. 23 seems to limit Bashan to the south of this plain.

[10] Josh. xii. 4 f., xiii. 11, 13 imply Geshur and Maacah as W of Bashan, probably occupying Jaulan. Cf. Guthe, *ZDPV*, xii. 232.

[11] Deut. iv. 43; 2 Kings x. 33. [12] Deut. xxxiii. 22.

[13] Psalm lxviii. 15. גַּבְנֻנִּים, *protuberances, bulgings, humps*; גִּבֵּן, hump-backed, Lev. xxi. 20. In the Targums גיבנא is a hill-top, גְּבִינֵי, eyebrows.

[14] So Olshausen, and Baethgen; cf. p. 307.

[15] So Delitzsch. Wetzstein compares גבנון with Syriac gabnun and Arabic gabulun,

Within Bashan lay Argob, probably equivalent to our "Glebe".[1] It bordered on Geshur and Maacah,[2] and contained threescore fortified cities. Sometimes Argob seems equivalent to the kingdom of Og in Bashan, and sometimes to all Bashan. But the name always given it of the Measured Lot[3] of Argob, implies that it was some well-defined district within Bashan.[4] For the same reason many[5] have thought it to be the Leja, which lies so well marked off from the surrounding country, but for this there is no further evidence. Nor was the Argob identical with the Havvoth-Jair, or *Tent-villages of Jair*.[6] Of these we have two different accounts: one that they were *camps* taken by Jair, the son of Manasseh, in the days of Moses[7]; the other that they were thirty cities belonging to the thirty sons of Jair, a Gileadite, one of the minor Judges.[8] The first account has been mixed with that of the conquest of Argob in a verse in Deuteronomy, which bears proof of having been altered to effect this.[9] Argob and Havvoth-jair were not the same: Argob a region full of walled and gated cities, the Havvoth-jair a collection of Bedouin camps. But the absolute proof of their difference is that a passage

---

"a roof with a gable end". He is wrong when (with Cheyne) he confines the general term *mount* = range, or *mountains of Bashan*, to Jebel Ḥauran, even though it were true that the Hill of Salmon, in the previous verse, be the same as Ptolemy's Mons Asalmanos (v. 15). Cf. Guthe, *ZDPV*, xii. 231.

[1] ארגוב or הארגוב, probably from רגב, a clod. [2] Deut. iii. 14. [3] הבל

[4] Always in Bashan, Deut. iii. 4, 13 f.; 1 Kings iv. 13.

[5] So Porter, Conder, Henderson, *PEF Map*.

[6] חות יאיר. חוה is probably the same as the Arabic حواء, hiwâ, pl. احوية, Ahwîyât. the Bedawee goat hair-tent, applied also to a collection of houses. Freytag, *sub voce*. Hence Hivites, חִוִּי.

[7] Num. xxxii. 41. From perhaps E. [8] Judges x. 3-5.

[9] Deut. iii. 14. I do not think we can say with Dillmann that this is an insertion, for an insertion would not bear marks of being altered from something else. It tells us that *Jair took the Hebel* or *lot of Argob*, singular, *and called them*, plural. This means that a plural noun originally stood in place of *the Hebel of Argob* (*them* cannot be *the coasts* of the intervening clause). This can only have been *tent-villages of Gilead*, or some such expression. How clumsily the change has been made is seen from this that Bashan אֶת־הַבָּשָׁן, is not in place, which is earlier in the sentence, but now stands where it is ungrammatical. But if either the above explanation or any other of the origin of this verse be wrong, the text is so confused that we could not prefer it to the evidence of verse 4, which says the towns of Argob were not Havvoth, tent-villages, but walled and gated cities; nor to 1 Kings iv. 13, which separates Argob from Havvoth-Jair, reckoning the former to Bashan, the latter to Gilead. But if we put aside Deut. iii. 14, we must also strike out at least the last clause of Josh. xiii. 30, P, which calls the tent-villages of Jair cities, and, against 2 Kings iv. 13, puts them in Bashan.

in First Kings expressly separates them, placing the camps of Jair in Gilead and Argob and its cities in Bashan.[1]

The only other Old Testament name which it is necessary to mention is Hauran or Havran of Ezekiel, which he gives with Damascus and Gilead, as comprising Eastern Palestine.[2] There is little doubt that this is the same as Auranitis and Hauran, which also, like the Hebrew, is a proper name, without the definite article. It is at least worth noting that a district lying so hollow between mountains, and to part of which Arabs give the name of their hollow hearth, en-Nuḳra, should have a title capable of being split into *Havr* or *Hawr*, *a hole*, and *-an*, a common termination of place-names.

These, then, are the greater divisions of Eastern Palestine, with their names respectively to-day, and under the Turks, at the Crusades, in New Testament, and in Old Testament, times. We sum them up in the following comparative table on next page.

In the next chapters we take these divisions successively from the south northwards.

XXVI. *THE LAND OF EDOM*[3]

I add this new chapter for two reasons: the ancient kinship and close neighbourhood of Israel and Edom, and because now under the British Mandate for Palestine the province or emirate of Transjordan reaches south to 'Aḳaba, the ancient Elath, as once upon a time did the government and the commerce of Jewish kings.

In the Old Testament Edom is properly the name of the people[4] and like Moab is by itself doubtfully applied to their land, and certainly not till

[1] 1 Kings iv. 13. Here, however, it is right to say that some regard the *villages of Jair, the son of Manasseh in Gilead*, as an insertion. Still we know from other passages that the Havvoth-Jair were in Gilead, but Argob is always placed in Bashan. Buhl, 118 f., equally rejects the identification as due to confusion. For Argob he suggests Suwet, where Wetzstein says are the ruins of 300 towns. Ṣuweit is E of Gilead, but geologically connected with Bashan. Cf. Driver, *Deuteronomy*, 48 f.

[2] Ezek. xlvii. 16, 18, חַוְרָן. Hauran appears in an inscription of Shalmaneser II; cf. Winckler, *Keilinschrift. Handbuch z. A.T.* 10 f. In the Mishna Hauran is a mountain, Neubauer, *Géog. du Talmud*, 426.

[3] For this chapter, see Map on pages 56-7.

[4] Num. xx. 18 f., JE, 1 Sam. xiv. 47, etc., etc.; when of the land it is feminine, Jer. xlix. 17, Ezek. xxv. 13 f., and so even of the people, Mal. i. 4. How readily it

Names To-day	Under the Turks	At the Crusades	In New Test. Times	In Old Test. Times
		WHOLE TERRITORY		
TRANSJORDAN	—	Oultre-Jourdain	Cœle-Syria	Over-Jordan. Abarim.
		(a) DAMASCUS		
Damascus	el-Ghuṭa (geogr.) Liwa of Damascus (administrative)	— —	Damascus	Aram of Damascus.
		(b) NORTH OF THE YARMUK		
HAURAN	HAURAN (Mutasseraflik of)	—	TETRARCHY OF PHILIP (+Decapolis, etc.)	ALL BASHAN. (+Half-Gilead).
	(1) Jaulan	Suwete or Suhete	Gaulanitis	Geshur (?). Maacah (?). The town Golan.
	(2) Hauran proper		Auranitis	Hauran (Ezekiel).
	(3) Leja	—	Trachon(itis)	(?)
	(4) Arḍ el-Betheniyeh	—	Batanæa (?)	Bashan, in narrower sense.
	(5) En-Nuḳra	—	—	Argob (?).
	(6) Jebel Ḥauran or Drûz	—	Mount Ἀσαλμανός	Mount Bashan (?).
		(c) BETWEEN YARMUK AND JABBOK		
Ajlun	(7) ‘Ajlun	—	Region of Decapolis, with part of Peræa	Half-Gilead.
		(d) BETWEEN JABBOK AND ARNON		
The Belḳa	The BELḲA	—	Part of Peræa	Half-Gilead. The Mishor.
		(e) SOUTH OF ARNON		
Kerak to ‘Aḳaba	Kaimakamate of Kerak and S	Seigneurie of Krak and Montreal	Moabitis. Nabatæan territory	Moab and Edom.

later writers, the regular names for that being *land* and *field* or *territory* of Edom.[1] Parallels are *land of Seir*,[2] *Mount Seir*,[3] and *Seir* alone[4]; the people being *sons of Seir*,[5] but also *Esau* or *sons of Esau*[6] and their land *Mount of Esau*.[7] The names of some Arab tribes come from ancestors, or localities, or sacred animals, or from political relations as "confederates", "clients",[8] or from livelihood as "cattlemen", or from character or noble descent.[9] So with some tribal names in the Old Testament, but which are true of Edom, Esau, and Seir is not certain. Edom is variously taken, as the name of a god,[10] as a variant of Adam, *man*,[11] or as a reflection of the *red* rocks east of the Arabah, or of the Hebrew tradition that Rebekah's elder twin *came forth red like an hairy garment*, but this continues *they called his name Esau* not Edom.[12] In Assyrian the root means "make", "produce", and hence perhaps Hebrew adamah, *soil* or *ground*.[13] Other place-names have the same radicals.[14] Assyrian for the people is U-du-mu,[15] but the Hebrew form is supported by the Greek Edom and Idumæa.[16] Seir seems *hairy*, and for a land may imply a shrubby or wooded aspect.[17] Something can be said for the similar explanation of Esau.[18]

In Hebrew tradition Jacob or Israel and Esau or Edom were the twin-sons

---

passed from people to land we see, *e.g.* in 2 Kings iii. 20; sometimes it may be either, *e.g.* Num. xxxiv. 3, Josh. xv. 1.

[1] אֶרֶץ אֱדוֹם, Gen. xxxvi. 16 f., 1 Kings ix. 26, etc., and שְׂדֵה, Gen. xxxii. 4, SE, Jud. v. 4, whether *wild country* or *territory*; also *a wilderness of Edom*.

[2] Gen. xxxii. 4 (A.V. 3). [3] Gen. xiv. 6, P, Josh. xxiv. 3, JE. [4] Deut. ii. 4, etc.

[5] 2 Chron. xxv. 11, 14, but Gen. xxxvi. 20 f. *Horites*.

[6] Deut. ii. 4 f., Mal. i. 2, etc. [7] Obad. 8 f., 19, 21.

[8] Sabaean, "subjects" or "clients".

[9] See Doughty's *Arabia Deserta* and lists in Von Oppenheim, *Vom Mittelmeer z. Pers. Golf*, ii. 67 ff.

[10] Obed-edom, *worshipper of Edom*, Stade, *Gesch.* i. 21, W. R. Smith, *Rel. of Semites*, 43; cf. W. M. Müller, *As. u. Eur.*, 315 f.

[11] Baethgen, *Beiträge*. [12] Sayce and others. [13] Friedrich Delitzsch.

[14] Josh. iii. 16, xix. 36, Gen. x. 19, Hos. xi. 8, etc.

[15] Delitzsch, *Paradies*, 295; due as in other names to vowel-assimilation (my *Jerusalem*, i. 257).

[16] The rare Ἀβδοδόμ, LXX, 1 Chron. xv. 24, א, xvi. 38, hardly proves Odom the older form, W. M. Müller, *As. u. Eur.*, 316.

[17] Also in Judah and Ephraim, Josh. xv. 10, Jud. iii. 26; in *Amarna Letters* matât Shi-iri, Winckler's ed. 181, line 26; cf. *KAT*³ 201, Zimmern, *Zeitschrift für Assyriologie*, vi. 251; Ramses III says he defeated the Sa-a-ira of the Bedawee tribes (Papyrus Harris, W. M. Müller, 135 ff., Nöldeke, *Enc. Bibl.* 1182).

[18] Gen. xxv. 25: Arabic ʿIṣu; ʿatha or ʿathia is compared but doubtfully. Targ.

of Isaac and Rebekah, tent-dwellers in the Negeb,[1] half-nomads, taking to agriculture[2] like some tribes to-day. From this stage the two diverged. Esau is *a cunning hunter*, *a man of the field*, *field* in its sense of *wild*. South of the Negeb, land now roamed by wild 'Azazimeh, where the only livelihood was hunting, robbery, or war, Esau was to live by the sword, serve his brother for a time and then break his yoke.[3] Jacob is *a quiet man*,[4] so far civilised but still in tents. Another tradition describes him later migrating into Canaan, a cattle-breeder with flocks and slaves, already beyond the nomadic stage, when he is met by Esau with four hundred men.[5] His fear of his brother, the gift he offers him, his timid doubts of its sufficiency, Esau's offer of protection and Jacob's refusal of this, reflect the relations usual between Arabs from the desert and lately settled fellâhin, as the latter increase in substance, and in fear of the Arabs pay them blackmail. Esau returns to Seir, Jacob goes on to Succoth and *builds him an house*—the verb implies stone or brick—with booths for cattle; though sometimes still in tents yet buying ground from the settled habitants, practising commerce, and offered intermarriage with the dwellers in towns.[6]

Israel coming out of Egypt finds the sons of Esau settled under a king in a land of vines from which they had driven the Horites or cave-dwellers, and this land it is clear from Israel's journeys was the range east of the Arabah, from the south of the Dead Sea to the Gulf of 'Aḳaba.[7] But though the Arabah, a deep valley ten or twelve miles broad, seems a decisive border it did not confine Esau to the east of it. The geographic and historic unity of the ranges on both sides of it must be emphasised.[8] They largely

---

Jonathan derives Esau from 'asah, *make*, as if ready-made, with hair, teeth, etc., which recalls the Assyr. root of Adam given above. Phœnician Usoos, a mythical hunter, has been compared, Philo Byblius in Eus. *Præp. Evang.* i. 10. 10, W. R. Smith, *Rel. of Sem.* 448. Müller, 316 f. finds the feminine in 'A-si-ti, a desert wild-rider.

[1] Gen. xxiv. 67, xxv. 27; on the Negeb see above, pp. 189 ff.

[2] By the well Lahai-roi, Gen. xxv. 11; *sojourners* (settled immigrants) *in the land*, xxvi. 3; as far as Philistine Gerar, 6; sowing seed and reaping harvests, 12; camping in the Vale of Gerar, digging wells 17 f.; thence to another well and to Beersheba, 22 f.

[3] Gen. xxvii. 26 ff., 39 f.

[4] Gen. xxv. 27; תָּם here not perfect, but *finished*, *orderly*, *refined*, Sc. douce (Skinner) New Hebr. *harmless*; A.V. *plain*, and LXX, ἄπλαστος, mislead.

[5] Gen. xxxii. f., JE.

[6] Gen. xxxiv. 8 ff., 12 ff., 20 ff., P.

[7] Num. xx. 14 ff., JE, Deut. ii: others take Horites as "white race", Maspero (340) compares, *e.g.* Khar for S Palestine.

[8] See Trumbull, *Kadesh-barnea*, 83 ff., Buhl, *Gesch. der Edomiter*, 22 ff.

share the same drainage. From both the most water is carried off by Wady el-Jeib, the main channel of the Arabah, while the south part of each drains towards the Gulf of ʻAḳaba; and though the west range sends a few streams to the Mediterranean, and the east some into the Arabian desert, these are but a small proportion of the whole. Nor has the Arabah ever proved a social or political frontier. Across it Edom's territory stretched into the wild land south of the Negeb.

In Kadesh Israel were on or near the border of Edom,[1] and the border later assigned to themselves west of the Arabah and towards the desert of Zin was *along by the side of Edom*.[2] The name Seir appears west as well as east of the Arabah,[3] and the conflicts of Jewish kings with Edom for the routes between Palestine and the Red Sea imply the claims of Edom to the region south of the Negeb.[4] Later the Nabatæans commanded both sides of the Arabah; Rome's Palestina Tertia included Areopolis, Rabbath-moab and Petra to the east and Beorsaba (Beersheba) and Elusa to the west[5]; and ninety years ago Petra was under the Turkish governor of Gaza[6]; while the same Arab tribes, in whole or in part, have ever roamed over both sides of the Arabah.[7]

The two mountain ranges with the great valley between form a square of about 125 miles either way, from the Arabian desert westward and from the latitude of Beersheba to that of the head of the Gulf of ʻAḳaba. Few territories of this size cover such a range of soils. In parts well-watered, in others with a precarious agriculture, the most is unproductive. Minerals are unknown, save salt and some phosphates and copper. But a historical importance far beyond the degree of its own resources is given to the territory by its position. It is a land of passage which not only bears lines of traffic between Egypt and Syria and between the Red Sea or Arabia (including the Sabæan country, with its frankincense)[8] and the Levant,[9] but by its very wildness

[1] Num. xx. 16, *the uttermost of the border* of Edom.

[2] Num. xxxiv. 3 JE, Josh. xv. 1, P; xi. 16 f. (deut,) sets the S limit of Joshua's conquests at Mt. Halak, *the bare mount, that goeth up to Seir*, probably Jebel Ḥalaḳ, beginning a range which divides the sandy desert on its west from pastoral ground on its east, Musil, *Edom*, ii. 8 f.

[3] Deut. i. 44. [4] 2 Sam. viii. 14, 1 Kings ix. 26, xxii. 47 f., 2 Kings viii. 20 ff., etc.

[5] Reland, *Palæstina*, I, ch. xxxiv. [6] Robinson, *BR*, ii. 547.

[7] *E.g.* Haweytat, Dhullam, Kaʻabineh (Rob. ii. 55. 3 ff.), and others.

[8] Data in Minæan inscriptions and Gk. and Lat. geographers; Pliny, *HN*, xii. 33, gives 65 daily marches for camels from Thomna (Thomola vi. 32) in the incense land to Gaza.

[9] From ʻAḳaba (Elath) to Maʻan and Petra, or to the latter more direct by the Arabah; to ʻAin el-Weibeh 80 m. from ʻAḳaba and so to Gaza 8 days or to Hebron. See Robinson, *BR*, ii. 580 ff., and for a summary of all the routes in this region my

grants its tribes the control, and some of the profit, of that traffic. To this we may add its military importance as a difficult frontier, or rather a No-Man's-Land, between Egypt and the powers of south-western Asia, and as having borne for centuries the *limes* of the Roman Empire. Then, too, the traditions which fixed on Sinai as The Mount of The Giving of the Law in the peninsula between the Gulfs of Suez and 'Aḳaba,[1] with the institution of Holy Places there in sympathy with those of Jerusalem, and the rise of Mecca as the centre of Islam, have drawn across this land the pilgrimages of three religions.[2] Yet of late traders and pilgrims alike have been much diverted from Edom and Seir by the Suez Canal[3] and the Hajj and other railroads.[4]

Of the Inner Syrian Range from Hermon to the Red Sea, Eastern Edom or Mount Esau is the southmost section, some 112 miles long by 25 to 30 broad.[5] It stands distinct from the rest of the Range by features of its own, and entrenched from the Plateau, or Mishor, of Moab by the greatest of the cañons which cut the Range, the Wady el-Ḥeṣa-Ḳeraḥi. The Mount is not so cleft by deep cañons as Moab and Gilead are, draining wholly to the Jordan or Dead Sea, but throws off its waters both on to the Arabian desert

---

art. "Trade and Commerce", *Enc. Bibl.* From Ma'an it is 10 journeys to Damascus.

[1] But *Blackwood's Magazine*, Feb. 1931, gives strong reasons for tracing the Exodus up the coast of the Levant by the Serbonian Bog and fixing Sinai on the hills to the east. *Yesterday and To-day in Sinai*, 1931, by Major C. S. Jarvis, Governor of Sinai.

[2] For pilgrim routes in Middle Ages see Robinson, *BR*, i. 561 ff.

[3] Musil, *Edom*, i. 38.

[4] I have drawn the above data from: A. Notices and lists on monuments of the Ancient Empires; the O.T. with the few in Josephus and fewer in Talmud; defective information in Gk. and Lat. geographers; Bk. xix Diodorus Siculus on Antigonus' campaign; the Antonine Itinerary, Peutinger Tables, Onomasticon, Notitia Dignitatum and the Madaba Mosaic Map (below, p. 375, n. 6); Nabatæan inscriptions, Roman milestones, Christian texts, a few coins. B. Meagre itineraries of pilgrims, cents. 6-19; Arab geographers and historians; records of the Latin Kingdom of Jerusalem, of expeditions of Baldwin I and III to Wady Musa and 'Aḳaba and of Crusaders (who did not hold Gaza) at Kerak, Shobek, and Petra, etc. (cf. *Les Colonies Franques dans les xii et xiii siècles*, ch. 9, Röhricht, *Gesch. Königreich Jerusalem*, 394). C. Modern travels, from 1806 on, data of which to 1840 are given by Ritter, *The Geog. of Pal. and Sinaitic Peninsula* (Eng. by Gage, 1846), the first scientific treatment of the region; later travels to 1893 used by Buhl, *Gesch. der Edomiter*; Hull, *PEF Mem.*; *Geology of Arabia Petræa*, etc., especially in the Arabah, 1888; the more recent journeys of Houston, Gray Hill, Wilson (all in *PEFQ*), F. E. Hoskins, Libbey and Hoskins, Dalman and Kennedy; Brünnow and Domaszewski, *Die Provincia Arabia*, 1904-6; Musil's *Edom*; see too Woolley and Lawrence, *The Wilderness of Zin* (Ṣin), *PEF Annual*, 1914.

[5] As reckoned from Musil's map; Buhl about 160 kilom. long.

and into the Arabah. Again, Mount Esau attains a general elevation of 4000 to 5000 feet above sea-level, far higher than that of Hauran,[1] Gilead, or Moab, which gives it in parts a different climate and aspect. On the plateau that forms the back of the Mount the temperatures are lower and snow lies deeper and for longer at a time[2]; while summer travellers are more often conscious of resemblances to the landscapes of Europe.[3] Again, the main crest or comb of the range does not run immediately above the great depression on its west, but considerably further east, leaving room for lower ranges and shelves of plateau. Most distinctive is the obtrusion of the underlying rocks. Of these great stretches are laid bare by the eastward recession of the upper limestones. Whereas looking east on Moab you see an almost unbroken wall of mountain all limestone save for its lowest courses of purple sandstone flashing upon the Dead Sea, the western aspect of Mount Esau is more graded in form and varied in colour. From the lacustrine marls and undulating sands of the Arabah, below or at or even 500 feet above sea-level, rise, sometimes to 2000 feet, rugged masses of red granite and porphyry, and above these rich red, yellow and white sandstones on successive levels with steep escarpments between them, varied not only by dykes of the lower rock bursting up, and by a frequent conglomerate of these and itself, but also by limestone strata, which the violent "fault" has dragged down from above. The depth of this sandstone is reckoned at from 1500 to 2000 feet. Over and behind it lie the long white and yellow terraces of limestone, which form the crest of the range and the plateau at its back. The volcanic features, basalt blocks and ridges on the plateau and in some valleys, are apparently secondary as on the rest of the Syrian Range, but not so numerous. The

[1] Except, of course, the Jebel Ḥauran.

[2] Burckhardt, p. 402, climate extremely agreeable, though heat very great in summer, yet never suffocating, because of a prevailing breeze; winter very cold, deep snow, and frosts sometimes till middle of March. Irby and Mangles, on May 26 excessive cold in lat. S of Delta of Egypt, W wind. Palmer, April 6-10 on uplands above W Musa, snow and hail, 6 inches on ground and several feet drifting into tents. Wilson (*PEFQ*, 1899, 309), climate colder than Palestine's, snow common in winter and spring, summer hot but nights cool on plateau. Musil (*Edom.* i, 269), in winter 1898 on E slope of Jebel esh-Shera (11 m. SW of Ma'an) at 4200 ft. (1280 m.) snow lay 4 days in such mass Arabs could not leave their tents.

[3] Doughty. i. 39: "the limestone moorland of so great altitude resembles Europe, there are hollow, park-like grounds with ever-green oak"; Wilson, *PEFQ*, '99, 307; "general aspect of limestone plateau not unlike those of Sussex downs or Yorkshire wolds"; Musil, *Edom*, i. 37: "Wir ritten über hohes Durrgras an vielen starken Buṭm-Bäumen und dichtem Gebüsche vorbei, und es kam mir vor, als wäre ich plötzlich in einen Europäischen Wald versetzt."

mineral resources are meagre, in one place copper and in several gorges salt.[1]

The variety of Mount Esau is thus greater than that of the Range to the north. Besides the cool stony plateaus, which it has like the latter but lifts higher, its west flank is a series of ridges, shelves, and strips of valley, mazes of peaks, cliffs, and chasms that form some of the wildest rock scenery in the world. In the sandstone above the Arabah are the Shîḳs (shafts), clefts or corridors between perpendicular rocks. Springs emerge between the porous upper strata of limestone and at the contact of the latter with the sandstone. On the limestone plateau devoid of springs cisterns preserve some of the winter rain, and at various periods dams and reservoirs have caught the surface waters in both the shallow and the deep wadies. These and the terraces distribute the annual moisture and nourish a varied vegetation. Almost treeless on its slopes to the desert[2] the mount bears on its back and west flanks plentiful timber,[3] groves of the evergreen oak and the buṭm or terebinth,[4] and stretches of juniper,[5] a conifer with a trunk often a foot in diameter, which fetches a good price in Kerak and Ma'an. The egriot or cherry is, or was, in demand at Damascus and Gaza for pipe-stems.[6] Poplar and willow are frequent along Wady Ḥesa and found elsewhere on the limestone.[7] Below 3000 feet flourish laurels, oleanders and tamarisks, ṭarfa. The sycomore, never growing above 1000, is infrequent. Nubk or thorn, and retem or broom abound and, in wadies running into the Arabah and Wady Ḥesa, thick bush and reeds. Honeysuckle, caper, and other trailers are also found, and a flowering aloe in Wady Musa.[8] The range of levels is hospitable to fruit-trees. On the limestone the olive, fig, and vine flourish as in Palestine, with the less frequent pomegranate, carob, and mulberry. Most are found too on the west sandstones but less fertile.[9] Even of Ma'an Doughty says, "the boughs of her fruit-trees hang over the clay orchard

[1] On the geology, besides works mentioned above, see Larter, *Exploration Géol. . . . de l'Idumée*, 1878.

[2] There are poplars and fruit-trees on the waters at Ma'an.

[3] Besides references below see Chichester Hart, *Some Account of the Fauna and Flora of Sinai, Petra and W 'Arabah* (*PEF*, 1891).

[4] Some woods take 1½ hr. to ride through (Musil, *Edom*, i. 299).

[5] Junip. Phœnicea, Arab. 'ar'ar (Hart, 38, etc.), luzzab = hard, "an almost black cypress" (Musil, i. 37), but see Brünnow, *ZDPV*, xxxii. 168.

[6] Ar. keraz (Musil, i. 38).

[7] Doughty.

[8] Irby and Mangles, on May 24; without flower, Dalman, 25.

[9] I heard Arabs judge the olives not comparable to Judæa's. Dalman on the poorness of the olives (*Petra*, 1) means those on sandstone. Idrisi, 5, says esh-Shera and el-Jebal very fertile, in olives, almonds, etc. Strabo (xvi, iv. 26), "the Nabatæan

walls into the inhuman desert".[1] Acorn and terebinth berries are eaten and the juniper fruit is made into sweetmeats.[2]

On the high plateau and elsewhere winter rains bring out a long, thick grass still green in May, but by July or August dry and hard.[3] Pasture abounds—"the greatest sheep flocks which I have seen of the Arabs were in the rocky coomb-land between Shobek and Petra",[4]—and even on the hardest slopes of the mountain and out on the desert is fodder for camels. Where soil lies barley and wheat may be sown. The stony back of the range is arable, "in the best sheltered plains are corn-plots, arḍ-ba'al, nourished only by rain".[5] But the richest fields are the higher shallow wadies, the wider part of others, and basins watered by rivulets or artificial channels from springs. At one time or another rock-cut conduits have rendered fertile unpromising shelves on the west slope. The same make possible gardens of lentils, onions, garlic, and other vegetables. Hewn terraces look like old vineyards.

This agriculture was variously exposed to the wilder countries about it. Except when the land was held by a firm government in Petra or other centre, with influence over the desert roads, or when the Roman frontier ran down the east border, the plateau and its slopes to the desert lay open to the nomad swarms of Arabia, and the peasants could pursue their cultivation, as many did till recently, only under blackmail. To this testify numerous ruins of watch-towers, especially by cisterns on the plateau, and travellers notice how springs have been guarded by forts or block-houses. The whole range is crossed annually by Bedawee tribes between their winter resorts in the Arabah and spring or early summer pastures east of the Hajj road.[6] Under good government the fellâhin would welcome these nomads for the trade they stirred, and for what they paid or exchanged for stubble and water, but in times of disorder they rendered cultivation unprofitable.[7] Yet the narrowness of the defiles, and the enclosure of many basins by easily defended ridges, secured in some places the persistence of a settled population and of agriculture through all political conditions: *dweller in the clefts of the rock, the height is his habitation, that saith in his heart, Who shall bring me down to earth?*[8]

---

land produces everything except olive-oil, oil of sesamum is used" may refer not to Edom but to Arabia Felix.

[1] *Arabia Deserta*, i. 33. [2] Musil, *Edom*, i. 37 f. [3] Doughty, i. 37; Musil, *passim*.

[4] Doughty, i. 39.

[5] *Ibid.*; Musil, ii. 239, contrasts the fertile main range with its barren east spurs.

[6] Musil, *Edom*, ii. 15. [7] Cf. Num. xx. 19.

[8] Obad. 3, Jer. xlix. 16, *the rock*, ha-sela', 2 Kings xiv. 7.

Mount Esau was thus productive enough to provide its people with material for trade with Arabia, Egypt, and Syria, especially timber, oil, copper, and cattle, aromatic and medicinal herbs, and vegetable alkali.[1] But the *treasures of Esau*, and the wealth attributed to the Nabatæans were perhaps rather due to their command of the transit trade from Arabia and the Red Sea to the Levant as described. Amos and Obadiah imply that they were slave-traders.[2] The sources of the bitumen which the Nabatæans exported to the Greek world lay outside the land of Edom proper.[3]

Though, unlike the rest of the Syrian Range, Mount Esau is not cut across by wadies draining it right through from the desert to the Arabah, it is yet divided by definite lines into districts with distinctive names. About 30 miles (48 kilos.) south of Wady Ḥesa, the Range, which has risen to a table-land of about 4900 feet (1500 m.) and even to a summit of 5280[4] feet is cleft south-east from the Arabah to the watershed by the broad, profound W el-Ghuweir; and a little south from the top of this but across the watershed (somewhat lower here) starts the long Wady Abu-l-Ḥamam that runs to the desert. This diagonal line, near the middle of which stands Shobek,[5] is the boundary between two districts, el-Jebal north, and esh-Shera south.[6] El-Jebal[7] is no recent name. It occurs in Hebrew, Gebal[8] with other general terms, Edom, Moab, Ammon. In Samaritan[9] and late Hebrew[10] it renders the Hebrew Seir, and in the Talmud stands for both a district and a town.[11] Josephus gives Gobolitis as part of Idumæa,[12] and Gebalitai[13] with Edomites and Amalekites as the objects of Amaziah's expedition; Eusebius and Jerome

[1] Isa. lx. 7, *rams of Nebaioth*; Eupolemus, *Fragm. Histor. Graec.* iii. 26 on the importation to Judah of cattle from Arabia, which may be Edom; Strabo, xvi, iv. 18, "Nabatæa abounding in cattle"; 26, "sheep with white fleeces, oxen large, but no horses, only camels"; Pliny, *HN*, xii. 46 (21), the best Myrobalanum, an oily fruit, is in Petra, 54 (25), from Petra hypericon to adulterate balsam, xiv. 9 (7), Petritan wine, but this may be from another Petra, xxi. 72, "the most esteemed scented rush is that in Nabatæa named teuchites" with medicinal properties; if the Lemon-grass Andropogon schoenanthus, it is found in Arabia, cf. Jer. vi. 20, *incense from Sheba and sweet-cane from a far country*, Isa. xliii. 24, Exod. xxx. 23. Burckhardt, p. 411: Arabs gather kali in esh-Shera and sell the soap-ashes in Gaza.

[2] Amos i. 9, Obad. 14. [3] See next chapter. [4] Musil's figures.

[5] Wilson, *PEFQ*, 1899, 320, "The Shōbek gap".

[6] Musil gives the border as W el-Ḥammam, Dalman as the shallow sidd Daḥdil which runs into the top of W el-Ghuweir, and separated the Turkish ḳada, or district of eṭ-Ṭafileh, chief town of el-Jebal, from that of Ma'an, chief of esh-Shera (*ZDPV*, xxxi. 265 f.).

[7] Sometimes given for its chief town eṭ-Ṭafileh. [8] Psalm lxxxiii. 8.

[9] Deut. xxxiii. 2. [10] Targum, Gen. xxxii. 4. [11] Neubauer, *Géog. du Talmud*, 67.

[12] ii *Antt.* i. 2, iii *Antt.* ii. 1, with Petra. [13] ix *Antt.* ix. 1.

take Gebalene as equivalent to Idumæa.[1] Jebal, Arabic for "mountains", does not appear in Hebrew till after the Exile of Israel, when Edom had been driven from Mount Esau by their Arab supplanters. Nor is the name distinctive of the section when this is seen from the west, for the *whole* of Mount Esau here appears broken up into "mountains". But to Arabia the southern section, esh-Shera, presents a continuous declivity, while el-Jebal is a ridge dominated by high black summits and running into other ridges.[2] The fitness of the Arab name on the Arab side is obvious.

The name of the next division, esh-Shera, has nothing to do with Seir, and may be akin to Arabic shara, "exposed and dry". Dalman finds it in the name of the Nabatæan god Du-Shara, "He of Shara", patron of Petra.[3] Arab geographers combine it sometimes with that of el-Jebal as of one province, at others stretch esh-Shera alone over all Mount Esau even to Zughar or Zoar as its capital. But more correctly they also confine it to the south part of the Mount with Odhruḥ as its capital.[4] From the beginning of esh-Shera, Jebel el-Hisheh, the range rises south, mainly on two parallel ridges, one to 5412 feet (1650 m.) and then declines till in Jebel el-Ḥafir (or Kafir), it sinks to the plain Ḳedriyyat. Here esh-Shera and the upper limestones of the range together cease, all beyond is sandstone, and the hills run no longer north and south, but east and west,[5] forming the next division, el-Ḥesma, that stretches into Arabia, a high plateau with truncated cones and on its west "a forest of mountains", which rise to 2000 feet above the plain, the heads nearly 6000 above sea-level[6]; southwards it falls on the granite round the Gulf of 'Aḳaba. Other divisions are Iram, "a black basalt mountain landscape",[7] south-east of the Ḥesma plateau, and el-Jafar, a swampy district east of esh-Shera, on which its eastern waters die out.

Historic sites on Mount Esau or Edom from the Gulf northwards are 'Aḳaba, Elath, Ezion-geber, thence up the Arabah to Petra, and thence to Ma'an and up the east of the range to Odhruḥ, Shobek, Bozrah, Ṭafileh.

El-'Aḳaba, the Ascent or Pass,[8] frequent in compound names,[9] well

[1] *Onomasticon sub Γέθεα*, also Gebalitica. [2] Musil, i. 2, ii. 14.

[3] *Petra*, 49. [4] Le Strange, *Pal. under Moslems*, 24, 32, etc.

[5] Burckhardt, 435 ff., Doughty, i. 45, etc., Musil, i. 2, 265, 270, etc. Brünnow's highest figure is 1615 m., Blanckenhorn's 1709 m. (*Hedschaz-Bahn*, 57).

[6] Doughty, i. 46, Burckhardt, 729: "higher than any of Shera".

[7] Musil, i. 4, see, too, Yakut, i. 212, Le Strange, 457.

[8] The root is that of *Jacob*. One form of it is to "strike with the heel", a plural means "the turns of camels being watered", "exchange", "a road over a mountain, up or down" (Lane). To-day in Egypt "uḳb is end or hinge of a door" (Spiro).

[9] Sometimes 'A. el-Muṣriyeh, the Egyptian, to distinguish it from 'A. esh-Shemiyah, the Northern or Syrian, the descent of the Hajj Road from the limestone esh-Shera on to the sandstones of Arabia (Doughty, i. 51).

deserves to stand alone here as The Pass *par excellence*. From time immemorial it has served as both ingress and egress between sea and land, between Arabia and the highlands of Sinai and Palestine, "The Gateway of Arabia". On the east, and some two miles from the head, of the Gulf, it has stood from an unknown date, a strong Turkish castle, now partly ruined, holding till the Great War a small garrison, with some peasants' mud-built hovels about it and a line of palms.[1] On its gravel beach above the almost tideless waters no harbour is possible, but across the Gulf, here barely two miles wide, is the Jeziret Fara'un, Pharaoh's Isle, with ruined fortifications and a narrow channel between it and the west coast, said to be the best harbour in the Gulf north of Daḥab.[2] 'Aḳaba is not so named in the Bible but has two other names which belong to this end of the Gulf, Elath and Ezion-geber. Elath (or Eloth, perhaps Date-Palms) was *on the shore of the Red Sea in the land of Edom*,[3] once Judah's and restored to her and rebuilt by Uzziah, but again taken by Edom.[4] For a time called Berenike[5] the name Elath survived for many centuries as Aila, Ailath or Ailam, with trade to India,[6] and the Gulf itself was called The Aelanitic. Aila was the seat of a bishop. Twice was it held by the Crusaders, first till Saladin retook it in 1170, and again in 1182-83, when it was occupied by Renaud de Chatillon, Lord of Karak and Montreal, who had galleys carried in pieces on camels across the desert from Ashkelon, and having rebuilt them blockaded the Island then called Graye, which was still held by the Moslem, but for a brief time the Frankish ships dominated the Gulf and part of the Red Sea.[7] An Arab geographer calls Aila "Waila the harbour of Palestine, emporium of the Hejaz, rich in palms and fishes".[8] A considerable centre till the fifteenth century, its remains may be some mounds a little north of the Castle of 'Aḳaba.[9]

With Elath Hebrew records join Ezion-geber,[10] where Solomon *made a navy of ships beside Eloth*,[11] and Jehoshaphat *made ships of Tarshish to go to Ophir for gold, but they went not for the ships were broken at Ezion-geber*.[12]

[1] Robinson, *BR*, i. 241; F. E. Hoskins, *From the Nile to Nebo*, 313, etc.

[2] Ritter, i. 73, Robinson, i. 237, F. E. Hoskins, 295 ff. (the fullest), T. E. Lawrence, *PEF Annual*, 1914-15, 130 ff., plate iii; opposite on the W coast the Well of Ṭaba', SE end of frontier between Egypt and Palestine.

[3] 1 Kings ix. 26, cf. Deut. ii. 8.

[4] 2 Kings xiv. 22, xvi. 6 (for *Aram* read Edom).

[5] Jos. viii *Antt.* vi. 4.

[6] *Onom.*; Theodoret, *Quaest. in Jer.*, 100. 49; Procopius, *Bell. Pers.* i. 19.

[7] *Chron. d'Ernoul et de Bernard le Trésorier and others.* Rey, 21 f., 155 ff.

[8] Muḳaddasi (10th cent.), Le Strange, 549.

[9] Robinson, i. 241, but Hoskins at W Ṭaba'.

[10] Deut. ii. 8, LXX, γασιὼν γάβερ.

[11] 1 Kings ix. 26-28.

[12] 1 Kings xxii. 48, 2 Chron. xx. 36 f.

This harbour is variously located: as the channel between Pharaoh's Isle and the west coast, with "enormous ruins" on this near the head of the Gulf[1]; and, because of the similar consonants in Ezion and Ghadian (Ṛadian),[2] at the well of this name, twelve miles up the Arabah,[3] to which the Gulf may once have extended.[4] Ezion or Ghadian may mean "where the Ghada (Ṛada) tree abounds".

On Elath-'Aḳaba converge many ancient routes: those from Suez over the Sinai Peninsula, that which continues them into Arabia, and two northwards. Of these one, entering the south end of Mount Edom by Wady Ithm (or Yetem), continues along the east border of the Mount with Roman milestones (one of Trajan) and "a bit of Roman wall", to Ma'an for Moab and Damascus; and tradition assigns it to Israel coming from Kadesh-barnea *by the way of the Red Sea to compass the land of Edom . . . from Elath and Ezion-geber.*[5] The other goes straight up the Arabah for Gaza (to which a caravan track strikes north-west from 'Ain el-Weibeh, the best oasis in the Arabah, over the Neḳb Merzeba),[6] and for Beersheba, Hebron, and Jerusalem. Up this road, past the watershed of the Arabah, some 50 miles from the Gulf, rises "a gigantic, majestic" mountain[7] in coloured strata, a shining landmark for all the country round, Jebel Neby Harun, Mount of the Prophet Aaron, which from Josephus[8] onward has been accepted by Jews, Christians, and Moslems[9] as *Hor—The Mountain*, where the priestly writers place the death and burial of Aaron, the brother of Moses.[10] This they describe as *on the edge of the land of Edom*,[11] but we have seen that Edom's land stretched west as well as east of the Arabah, and Mount Hor is more naturally placed near Kadesh-barnea, where Jebel Madara, north-west of 'Ain Ḳadeis, has been suggested for it.[12]

[1] Hoskins, 297.

[2] Lagarde, *Übersicht . . . der Nomina*, 157.

[3] Robinson, i. 250 f., Driver, *Deut.* 35, f.

[4] Musil, i. 254, ii. 183 ff., 187, 199, describes the oasis Ma-Ghadian with remains of fortification and gardens on what is now desert; his guide told of a town there with many ships but violent rain brought down from the wadies such masses of stone that the sea was pushed back to 'Aḳaba; the likeness of LXX, *'Εμαεσειών* to Ma-Ghadian is striking.

[5] Num. xx. 22 f., xxi. 4, Deut. ii. 1, 8.

[6] Musil, ii. 204.

[7] Musil, i. 284, pl. 84 ff.

[8] iv *Antt.* iv. 7.

[9] Jerome, *De Situ, etc.*, "juxta Petram"; Mas'udi (A.D. 943), i. 94; Yakut (13th cent.), iii. 559—both in Le Strange, 73, 74.

[10] Num. xx. 22 f., xxi. 4, xxxiii. 37 ff., Deut. xxxii. 50.

[11] Num. xxiii. 37. Doughty and Hoskins favour Jebel Harun.

[12] Trumbull, *Kadesh-barnea*, 127 ff.; but G. B. Gray on Num. xx. 22 says while "the site satisfies the conditions of the text, it is philologically most hazardous"; see too Woolley and Lawrence, *PEF Annual*, 1914-15, 69-71.

Round the south-east of Jebel Neby Harun and on its north side narrow defiles lead up from the Arabah to the edge of the most singular and most famous site on Mount Edom, the Wady Musa,[1] in which lies the city of Petra. It is beyond the capacity of these pages to compass the features of this incomparable and fascinating basin, only some 1250 yards by from 250 to 500, in which nature and human art have worked together as nowhere else in the world; and the reader is referred to the descriptions of its wonders by modern travellers from Seetzen onwards.[2] By her position and its security, and by her later importance, Petra must have been at a very early period a centre of commerce between Arabia and all to the west and north of her.[3] But it is very doubtful whether the Old Testament ever refers to Petra; the name usually taken for her, Ha-Selaʻ, The Rock,[4] being too general for a single town. Josephus says, "the capital of all Arabia, formerly Arkē, Arkem or Rekemē, is now called Petra by the Greeks".[5] Towards the end of the fourth century B.C. the place was twice attacked by the forces of Antigonus, one of the Greek rivals for the Seleucid sovereignty; but these assaults, not till after they gained much spoil, were repulsed by "the Arabs",[6] doubtless the supplanters of the Edomites, the Nabatæans, who in the second century had their capital in Petra. In 55 B.C. Gabinius, a general of Pompey, brought the town and district under the Romans, who called the region Arabia Petræa after it; and in 105 the Nabatæan kingdom was added to the Roman province of Arabia. The buildings and carvings of Petra are of Nabatæan art, strongly influenced by Greek forms. Christianity soon came to the district, and Bishops of Petra sat in the early Councils of the Church. But before the fifth century the prosperity of Petra had vanished, and except in connection with a Crusading expedition to the alleged Val de Moise,[7] the name Petra disappears.

[1] "Of Moses", because a tradition of Jewish or Christian origin, adopted by Islam placed here the striking by him of water from the rock: Jerome, *De Situ, etc.*, 144; Yakut (13th cent.) in Le Strange, 548.

[2] Especially Irby and Mangles; Wilson, *Lands of the Bible*, x; Robinson *BR*, i; Stanley, *Sinai and Palestine*, 87 ff.; Musil, Brünnow and Domaszewski, and Dalman, who gives the fullest account of the rock-cut shrines and tombs with their carvings, and the castle of masonry.

[3] Minæan (S Arabia) inscriptions of the 8th and 7th cents. B.C. name a Maʻan el-Muṣeriyeh about here, a junction of trade-routes, which may well be Petra, as in Maʻan very ancient remains have still to be found.

[4] Jud. i. 36, Isa. xvi. 1, Obad. 3; in 2 Kings xiv. 7, where it is probably a town, taken by Amaziah and thereafter called Joktheel, this place never appears again, and so seems too unimportant to be Petra.

[5] iv *Antt.* iv. 7, vii. 1, according to various codd.

[6] Diodorus Siculus, Bk. xix.

[7] Rey, *Les Colonies Franques*, 396 f.

One of the intricate shîḳs or corridors through the deep rock of Wady Musa, called *The* Shîḳ, leads up from Petra by the village of Eljy on a five hours' march south-east to Ma'an, a small double-town, due with its gardens and orchards to several springs in an otherwise inhospitable area.[1] It is the last Syrian merkez or rest-station on the Hajj Road, and has a market and on the railway a station. Thence to Jauf, the nearest oasis in Arabia, is ten camel-marches. Ma'an is said to have been a Roman military post, and has been suggested as the Ahamant of the Crusaders.[2] Under the Turks it was the seat of a kaimakam, with a garrison and a camp; to-day it is the headquarters of the Liwa or administrative district of Ma'an. Besides the Hajj Road and the rail by Ḳaṭrane to 'Amman, another road with ancient remains runs north 21 miles to Shobek, on whose height Baldwin I built the castle of Mons Regalis, Montreal, commanding the route from Damascus to Egypt. It was taken by the Saracens in 1188, and later rebuilt by the Mamelukes. The capital of esh-Shera under the Turks, it is now the centre of a subdivision of the district of Ma'an. South of Shobek is Odhruḥ[3] with a well, a brook, and considerable ruins; and northwards are Buṣeira, the *Bozrah in the land of Edom*, threatened by the prophets[4]—"no more winefats at Bozrah but her fields even now are fruitful vineyards"[5]; and eṭ-Ṭafileh,[6] capital of the Turkish district el-Jebal, with a kaimakam and garrison and (it is said) 9000 Arab inhabitants, now the centre of the Kerak Liwa of Transjordan.

We now follow the operations of the Arab forces of the Emir Feisal, under Ja'far Pasha, an expert soldier who had left the Turkish army, and Captain Lawrence.[7] They captured 'Aḳaba on 6th July 1917, just before General Allenby arrived in Palestine, and henceforth were to act in co-ordination with him. Aided by an Air Force they harassed and threatened Ma'an from August onwards, but were unable to take it. Early in October, however, they occupied Shobek, and in December eṭ-Ṭafileh. The railway stations south and north of Ma'an were taken by them, and the rails torn up to prevent the Turkish forces still in the Hejaz from coming north; while two raids by the allied natives of the region reached, and for a time held, part of the railway between Ḳaṭrane and 'Amman as well as el-Mezra' on the east

[1] See Doughty, i. 33 f., Musil i. 272, "no ancient remains".
[2] Rey, *Les Colonies Franques*, 22, 398.
[3] Doughty; Utherah, "a principal ruined site".
[4] Amos i. 12, Isa. xxxiv. 6, lxiii. 1; Buṣeira = Little Bozrah.
[5] Doughty, i. 38
[6] Plan in *Mil. Operations Eg. and Pal.* 399.
[7] What follows is based on ch. xvii, "The Arab Campaign", of *Military Operations, Egypt and Palestine, June 1917 to the End of the War*, by Captain Cyril Falls, 1930.

shore of the Dead Sea. On 6th March 1918, Feisal's forces had to retire from eṭ-Ṭafileh to Shobek before a superior German-Turkish force from Kerak, but they re-occupied it on 18th March. Further advance was stayed by the failure of the two British expeditions across Jordan, 21st March–2nd April, and 1st May, to take 'Amman and hold es-Salṭ,[1] and summer passed before General Chaytor's force from the Jordan Valley occupied 'Amman on 25th September. Thence a detachment was sent south, to which the disheartened garrison of Ma'an fleeing north surrendered at Ziza on the 29th, the while a column of Feisal's host actually took Der'a and reached Sheikh Sa'd; and effected union with British forces for the final advance on Damascus.

XXVII. *THE LAND OF MOAB AND THE COMING OF ISRAEL*

In contrast to the Land of Edom, a broken mountain-range with lofty peaks, the Land of Moab[2] is a more or less sustained plateau, Hebrew Ha-Mishôr,[3] mainly of limestone, resting upon sandstone with outcrops of basalt, and cut across from the desert, *The Wilderness east of Moab*,[4] to the Dead Sea by several valleys, shallow at their upper ends, deepening westward and with considerable plains, but less passable towards their issue upon the sea. The border between the two Lands is the Wady Ḥesa-Ḳeraḥi.[5] From this the Land of Moab stretches north, divided by the valleys into four parts, which with their names are as follows[6]:

1. *Arḍ el-Kerak*, the southmost of the four, is also the largest, extending

[1] See below, p. 397.

[2] Except in Jer. xl. 11 and (doubtfully) Num. xxi. 11 the O.T. takes *Moab* as the people not the land (D, deut. passages, and P); *field* or *territory of M.* Num. xxi. 20 E?, Gen. xxxvi. 35 P, Ruth i. 1 f. etc.; Moab not necessarily land even in Jud. iii. 29, Amos ii. 1 f., Zeph. ii. 8 f. Eusebius-Jerome *Μωάβ* and *Μωαβῖτις*; Latin inscription at Ḳuṣr el-Bsheir Mobenium. *MuNDPV*, 1897, 38.

[3] See p. 353.

[4] Num. xxi. 11, Deut. ii. 8.

[5] Sometimes pronounced Ḥesi and Aḥsa; Yakut ii. 266 el-Ḥasa.

[6] Besides older works see *PEF Mem. E. Palestine*, 1889; Doughty, *Arabia Des.* i, 1888; Brünnow and Domaszewski, *Die Provincia Arabia*, vols. i-iii, 1904-9; Libby and Hoskins, *Jordan Valley and Petra*, i, 1905; Musil, *Arabia Petræa* i, *Moab* 1907; G. A. Smith, "Moab", §§ 1-9, *Enc. Bibl.* 1902; *PEFQ*, 1904, 1905, and *Atlas of the Hist. Geog. of the Holy Land*, Maps 29 f., 1914.

from Wady Ḥesa north to Wady Mojib or Arnon. On the whole well-watered it is drained by wadies within itself as well as by the Arnon affluent, Wady es-Sulṭani or Mkheres, which may be taken as its natural boundary on the east. All travellers affirm the fertility, and signs of a large ancient population, both of which somewhat revived after the Turkish Government was established in Kerak. The most important ancient sites are Kerak and Rabba, Rabbath-Moab,[1] Areopolis of the Greeks, which Musil takes to be Ar Moab, a name sometimes applied to the whole district: *To the children of Lot I have given Ar for a heritage*[2]; a little south is Marma el-'Eir, possibly 'Ir or Ar Moab. Among others he describes Beit-el-Karm, sometimes called Ḳaṣr Rabba, and Dimneh, ancient Dimon,[3] Seil el-'Arabi the Nahal ha-'Arabim,[4] Khurbet ed-Dunn Dennaba, and finds in el-Jelimeh the Aigaleim of Eusebius, but another el-Jelimeh south-east of Kerak is more probable. El-Kerak itself, Kerakka of the Targums, Ptolemy's Charakmoba,[5] Mōbou Charax of Uranius,[6] Krak or Crac of the Crusaders, stands on one of the finest positions offered by nature to the military engineer. The town was entered by zigzag tunnels under its walls, through which I found in 1904 recent breaches, and was told that the chapel I sought in the Frankish citadel had ceased to exist. Probably el-Kerak is Kir-hareseth or Kir of Moab of the time of Hebrew kings and prophets. The name Harasha applies to a lower stretch of Wady Kerak.[7] Musil suggests or approves other identifications.[8] The Transjordan Liwa or administrative district of Kerak extends into Edom with a secondary centre at eṭ-Ṭafileh.

2. *El-Kura*, from the Mojib or Arnon to the Wady el-Waleh, which I found less fertile than the Kerak district, has fewer place-names, though some ruins, including Roman, are on prominent sites. On the Roman Road is Dhiban, that I heard pronounced Ziban, the extensive remains of Dibon

[1] Not in O.T., first in Josephus, xiv *Antt.* i. 14, *Ῥαβαθά*.
[2] Deut. ii. 9, 29.
[3] Isa. xv. 2, Jer. xlviii. 2.
[4] Isa. xv. 7.
[5] Steph. Byz. quoting Ptolemy, but MSS. of Ptol. v. 17 read *Χαρακωμα* and the map has it S of Petra. Coins of Caracalla spell the name as Ptolemy does (*Rev. Numism.* 1899, 274).
[6] *Fragmenta Hist. Græc.* iv. 526.
[7] Brünnow, *MuNDPV*, 1895.
[8] Seil en-Numera with Nimrim, Isa. xv. 6; Fas with Luhith, el-'Araḳ with Horonaim, Isa. xv. 5 f., Jer. xlviii. 5, 34, they mean the same; el-Kerye (in Seil el-Ḳeraḥi) with Zoar, for the slogan of its folk is "Be heroes, O dwellers in Zoghar"; Khanzireh and Habel with the Crusaders' casalia Cansir and Hable, "in the land of Crac"; other sites are Moteh, near the Roman Road, where Moslems first encountered Byzantines and were defeated; Ftiyan above W el-Mkheres, commanding communications S and N; close to it the Roman el-Lejjun; Dat-ras commanding the road and plain; Mḥayy "greatest fortress I have seen in SE Moab".

in which was found the famous inscription of Mesha, King of Moab in Omri's time; a double city with a citadel in the south half, and south again a fortified knoll, all three surrounded by walls, some of the remains being older than the Byzantine which prevail. Besides the main road four or five others converge upon it. North-west are a group of sites once of importance to judge from their ruins.[1] South-east, where the Roman Road drops into the Arnon valley, are ruins with the name 'Aḳraba, "scorpion", often applied to such zigzag descents; and a mile and a half farther east, also on the edge of the plateau with another descending road, traces of a tower, wall, and gate. 'Ara'er, the ancient *Aroer on the lip of the wady*,[2] which also Eusebius sets above Arnon "on the eyebrow of the hill". The south limit of Sihon's kingdom, it was that of David's and of North Israel's east of Jordan.[3] East and south-east along the edge of the Wady Mojib other remains including towers, and on a promontory over its upper stretch, Wady Sa'ideh, the formidable ruins of Medeyyne, Jerome's Madian "juxta Arnonem et Areopolin"; which Musil suggests may be *the City of Moab*, *'Ir-Moab*, *at the end of the border of Arnon*,[4] and *the city*, *ha-'Ir*, *in the midst of the wady*.[5] We may even identify it with Ar or Ar Moab, for in texts in which this seems a city and not a district,[6] it is probably the same as 'Ir-Moab,[7] being described as *the border of Moab*, to which the cliff of the *valleys of Arnon stretches*, and *it leans on the border of Moab*.[8]

3. *El-Jebal* from Wady Waleh north to Wady Zerḳa Ma'in, is the narrowest division but with important sites. The wadies east of the main road which flow south into Seil Heydan or el-Ḥammam were named to me differently[9] from what Musil records, though we agree on ez-Zerdab in which some of them unite. El-Ḳreyat, Kiriathaim,[10] would repay excavation; when I saw it in 1904 it was still free from the re-settlement that destroys so many ancient remains in Moab. Mkaur is Machaerus, and its castle Ḳaṣr el-Meshnekeh (the name given me), Herod's castle, the prison of John the Baptist, with a view over to the Mount of Olives and a part of Jerusalem. The plan drawn by my companion and my own notes[11] correspond with Josephus' account in all details save one, the position of the "lower city"

[1] Esh-shḳeḳ, "the Fissure", Barza, Dhafra, edh-Dheheybeh, "place of gold", a frequent place-name, not the Di-zahab of Deut. i. 1.

[2] Deut. ii. 36, etc., Josh. xii. 2.

[3] Deut. ii. 36, iv. 48, 2 Sam. xxiv. 5, 2 Kings x. 33.

[4] Num. xxii. 36.

[5] Josh. xiii. 9, cf. Deut. ii. 36.

[6] See G. B. Gray on Num. xxi. 14 f., and G. A. Smith, "Ar", *Enc. Bibl.*

[7] Deut. ii. 18.

[8] Num. xxi. 15.

[9] *PEFQ*, 1905, 46.

[10] Jer. xlviii. 1, 23.

[11] *PEFQ*, 1905, 226 f.

relative to the castle.[1] For the ruins called Mkaur are not close to the castle as Josephus implies, but nearly a mile east across a valley. They are, however, as far as I could judge, Byzantine, and the town they represent may not have been built till long after the destruction of Herod's castle by Lucilius Bassus in A.D. 71 or 72. In neither the Hasmonæan nor the Herodian period is Machærus described except as a stronghold, an outlying fortress of the Jews towards the Nabatæans. Any town of the same name would be immediately under it, say on the south whither the causeway runs from the castle. After A.D. 72 (so far as I know) we do not find Machærus described as a fortress; probably the folk of "the lower city" deprived of protection there moved to the ridge where are the Byzantine ruins now called Mkaur. This ridge, named to Musil ed-Deyr, but to me eṭ-Ṭeyr, bears for some distance north stone circles and platforms, more frequent than I saw elsewhere in Moab, as far as Khurbet 'Aṭṭarus, Ataroth; but as I saw no domestic ruins except at their two ends their long straggling line indicates an important religious centre. North-east of the Khurbet by an ancient track I came to a conspicuous elevation crowned by a mound of stone ruins for which the name Rujm, Cairn, of 'Aṭṭarus was given me. It lies on the brink of the deep Wady Zerḳa Ma'in, and as you look up to it from the bed of the latter it forms the summit of what Musil calls Jebel 'Aṭṭarus. The stones represent not a cairn so much as a ruined platform, round which seemed to me remains of a wall. That within two miles are two sites of the name is remarkable. But the Old Testament gives both Ataroth and Atroth-shophan,[2] the Samaritan for which, Shephim, suggests *heights*, suitably to Rujm or Jebel 'Aṭṭarus. Both Khurbet and Rujm were fenced cities. There are hot springs below Machærus, eṣ-Ṣara or ez-Zara, Zereth. The ancient road I followed from Mkaur by 'Aṭṭarus to Libb Musil also gives, and shows how it continues east to the upper waters of Wady el-Waleh, there Wady eth-Thamad, and the desert. Near its crossing of the two trunk roads north and south is ed-Dlelet-el-Gharbiyyeh, once a strong town on the south limit of "the fruitful plain of Madeba, with a lofty castle commanding the three roads" (Almon) Diblathaim.[3] Other sites are Libb, Lemba, or Libba of Josephus,[4] Umm el-Walid, which Musil suggests as Jahaz,[5] and Ziza which reminds him of the Zuzim.[6]

4. *El-Belḳa*,[7] from Wady Zerḳa Ma'in north to the sources of the Zerḳa and the borders of Ammon, the best-known division of Moab, is covered by

[1] vii *Wars*, vi. 1 ff. [2] Num. xxxii. 3, 34 f.
[3] Num. xxxiii. 46, LXX, Γελμών Διβλαθάιμ. [4] xiii *Antt.* xv. 4, xiv *id.* i. 4.
[5] Num. xxi. 23, *towards the desert.* [6] Gen. xiv. 5.
[7] "Pied Land", Doughty, i; not the same as the present Liwa of the name.

Conder's survey, supplemented by Musil's, and the most easily visited by travellers. It falls into two parts. One is the main plateau with shallow wadies, fertile beds below stony ridges, rich opportunities of pasture and husbandry, with remains of the ancient culture of the olive and the vine, which it were easy to restore. As it is, much grain is produced; in 1904 I saw corn dealers from Jerusalem buying up the harvests before they were reaped. There are few springs, the dams and reservoirs of the Greek period are in ruin, and when the winter rains failed as in 1900-1 famine ensued. The other part of this northmost division of Moab consists of the rugged wadies breaking from the plateau into the Ghor. In these, below the softer strata of limestone, springs appear, and even a waterfall at the 'Uyun Musa, on which Musil's photographs of July 1901 show more water than I found in July 1891. The numerous ruins in this division are mainly of Byzantine cities. The most interesting are those of Medeba,[1] the town which gave its name to the whole plateau, *unto Dibon.*[2] Assigned to Reuben, it was not Israel's in David's reign,[3] was recovered from Moab by Omri, was speedily Moab's again; a fortress in the Maccabæan age,[4] mentioned by Ptolemy and in the *Onomasticon*, an episcopal city in the province of Arabia,[5] and now Madaba. The ruins are of the town's walls, streets, reservoirs, ten churches, the famous mosaic map,[6] and other mosaic floors found (says Musil) "in every private house, for we have to do here with a native branch of art highly important in art-history."

With Medeba in importance was Heshbon, the city of Sihon, too often mentioned in the Old Testament,[7] and by Josephus,[8] for a full enumeration of the instances. In modern Ḥesban, on the edge of a wady of the same name, 600 feet above 'Ain-Ḥesban, upon two hills over 2900 above sea-level, are remains of a castle, temple, great reservoir, and other buildings, mainly Roman, but with marks of the Crusaders. With Heshbon was always joined Elealeh, now el-'Al, two miles or so to the north. Other admitted identifica-

[1] מֵידְבָא, Num. xxi. 30 (Syriac reads *midbar*, desert); 1 Chron. xix. 7; Isa. xv. 2; on the Moabite stone מהדבא; in 1 Macc. ix. 36, *Μηδαβά*.

[2] Josh. xiii. 9, 16.

[3] 1 Chron. xix. 7.

[4] Jos. xiii *Antt.* i. 4, ix. 1, etc.

[5] Reland, p. 217.

[6] A. Schulten, *Die Mosaikkarte von Madaba* (1900); W. Kubitschek, *Mitth. d. Geogr. Gesellsch.* of Vienna, 1900, Heft. 11 f.; *MuNDPV*, 1897, 1902.

[7] חֶשְׁבּוֹן, Num. xxi. 25-28, 30, etc., etc.; Isa. xv. 4, xvi. 8 f.; Jer. xlviii. 2, etc.; Song of Sol. vii. 4.

[8] '*Ησεβών* or '*Εσεβών* and its district '*Εσεβωνῖτις*, xii *Antt.* iv. 11, ii *Wars*, xviii. 1, etc.

tions are those of Mount Nebo and Pisgah,[1] and Mephaath with Nefa'.[2] Others suggested are Bamoth-baal or Bamoth[3]; or identified are—on the south slopes of Mount Neba the town of Nebo with Khurbet el-Mkhayyet, Beth-peor with Sheikh Gazel, the valley, Ha-Gai, with that of the Wells of Moses, Ashdoth-pisgah with W en-Na'am, Abel-shittim with W es-Seyale, and Beth-jeshimoth with Khurbet es-Sweyimeh. Callirrhoë, to which Herod was brought in his last illness, was most probably the hot springs of Wady Zerḳa Ma'in.[4] Others find Callirrhoë farther north at eṣ-Ṣara (or ez-Zara).[5] The Survey Map marks a fragment of an ancient road from Jericho towards the Zerḳa Ma'in hot springs but fails to continue it up to them. Nor could I find one in 1904, and my guides denied there was any. In 1906 others[6] found basalt pavement above the hot springs, and traces of a road "in well-arranged gradients and boundary walls" at the top with more remnants farther on, and Musil tells how from Barrakat below Mount Nebo, south-west he saw the white line of "the ancient road from Jericho to the springs of Zara or Zerḳa Ma'in" traversing Abu-l-Ḥasan, one of the broad stages by which the Land of Moab rises from the Dead Sea. I still think Josephus means by Kallirrhoë, "down on" which he says the springs were situated, the main stream of the Zerḳa Ma'in. If the aged and sick king had to be brought by the road which passes them what was the use of carrying him farther?[7]

In this division of the Land of Moab the dolmens and cromlechs are very numerous, especially at el-Ḳweiḳiye, or as the Bedu pronounce it, el-Ḳweiziye.

The passage of the Arnon brings Israel into light upon Eastern Palestine.

[1] See pp. 380 ff. [2] Clermont-Ganneau, *PEFQ*, 1902, 260 f.

[3] Num. xxi. 19, xxii. 41, Isa. xv. 2: A.V. *high places.*

[4] Probably also Nahali-el, *Wady of God*, Num. xxi. 19. Jos. xvii *Antt.* vi. 5, i *Wars*, xxxiii. 5, Pliny, *HN*, v. 16, 72, describe the wells of Callirrhoë as flowing into the Dead Sea though their immediate issue is into the W Zerḳa Ma'in, but that implies that all the valley was identified with the wells and supports Conder's identification of it with Nahali-el. In vii *Wars*, vi. 3 the valley is described as N of Machærus, and part of it is called Baaras, with wells hot and cold, fresh salt and sulphur. Jerome (*Onom.*) gives Baaru "in Arabia (the Roman Province) ubi aquas calidas sponte humus effert", and Bare near Cariathaim; Eusebius defines *Βεελμεών* as "a very large village near the Mount of the Hot waters". Jerome, *Quæst. in Lib. Gen.*, says Callirrhoë was Lasha, Gen. x. 19.

[5] Seetzen, Dechent (*ZDPV*, vii. 196 ff.), Musil and others.

[6] Drs. Cropper and Bacon, *PEFQ*, 1906, 297.

[7] See my article, *PEFQ*, 1905, 223 f.

We have a list of the stations of their journey before this, but the sites of these are not now discernible,[1] and even the Brook Zered,[2] given as the limit of the wilderness, did not mark the beginning of the Promised Land. The Arnon is afterwards drawn as the south frontier of Israel east of Jordan. Aroer, on its banks, was the Beersheba of the East. We see Israel as soon as they cross it entering upon war for their heritage.

That Israel had to do battle after passing the Arnon was due to a recent change in the political disposition of Eastern Palestine. The country from the Jabbok to the Arnon properly belonged northwards to Ammon, and south to Moab. But shortly before Israel's arrival, Sihon, an Amorite king from Western Palestine, had crossed the Jordan, and driving Moab south over Arnon, and Ammon east to the sources of the Jabbok, had founded a kingdom for himself between these two rivers. Israel had come up the eastern border of Moab, but, in order to reach Jordan, had to strike west across Sihon's territory. Moses asked for rights of passage. Sihon refused, and Israel prepared for battle. They were now upon some branch of the Arnon, but high up it. Their route had perhaps followed the present Hajj Road.[3]

The Arnon, the present Wady el-Mojib, is an enormous trench across the plateau of Moab. It is about 1700 feet deep, and two miles broad from edge to edge of the cliffs which bound it, but the floor of the valley down which the stream winds is only forty yards wide.[4] About fifteen miles up from the Dead Sea the trench divides into branches, one running north-east, the other south-south-east, and each again dividing into two. The plateau up

[1] Num. xxi. 10, 11*a*, E. Oboth unknown, but on the plateau E of Edom, Arḍ Suwan, Flint-Ground (Arabia Petræa (?), Doughty, *Ar. Des.* i. 28 f.); Iye-Abarim, *heaps of the dwellers*, or *regions, on the Other-side* (to distinguish it from Iim of Judah, Josh. xv. 29) *on the border of Moab in the wilderness which is before Moab towards the sunrising* (Num. xxi. 11). Israel kept thus far E to avoid not only the settled parts of Moab, but like the Hajj, the deeper stretches of the cañon between Edom and Moab, Wady el-Ḥesa. Once over the shallower stretches of this, where the Hajj Road crosses, they were in *the wilderness of Moab*. To show the way across the wady are cairns which tempt one to emend the name to 'Iye ha-'Oberîm, *heaps of the passengers*. For the region see Doughty, *Ar. Des.* i, and Musil, *Moab*.

[2] Deut. ii. 13, LXX, *Ζάρετ*, not again in O.T. nor in Josephus; Madaba map *(Δ)APEZ*, a wady to the sea S of Kerak. North of Wady el-Ḥesa the Hajj Road crosses W es-Sulṭani, a south affluent of Arnon and a landmark on this route where water can be had by digging, a suitable camping-place (Musil, *Moab*, 316, 319, n. 15). This Israel crossed, like the Hajj from SW to NE not as Musil implies from E to W; Dillmann gives either W Feranj or Seil Sa'ideh a branch of Arnon.

[3] Num. xxi. 21, where the embassy to Sihon is related *after* the list of the stations on the journey.

[4] Burckhardt, *Syria*, 372.

to the desert is thus cut not only across but up and down, by deep ravines, and a difficult frontier is formed. You see why the political boundary of Eastern Palestine has generally lain here, and not farther south. The southern branch, the present Seil Sa'ideh, called also Safiah, is the principal,[1] but all the branches probably carried the name Arnon right to the desert. Not *the valley* but *the valleys* of Arnon are named in the fragments of song upon Israel's passage:

Waheb in Suphah (we passed) *and the valleys of Arnon,*
And the cliff of the valleys, which stretches to Ar's seat,
And leans on the border of Moab.[2]

The first words are obscure. Suphah may survive in Safiah.[3] The *cliffs* or *declivities* of these Moab valleys are impressive, and every traveller speaks of them.[4] Ar is not Rabbath Moab, which lies south of the Arnon, but Ar, or 'Ir, of Moab, which stood on Moab's border, and, as we saw, may be Medeyyne.[5] On the north bank, just before the valley divides, stand the ruins of 'Ara'er, *the Aroer on the lip of the valley of Arnon,* which we have already called the Beersheba of Eastern Palestine.[6]

From the Upper Arnon, then,—Deuteronomy calls the place *Wilderness of Kedemoth,*[7]—Israel sent to Sihon for leave to cross his territory, and Sihon refusing came out to battle at Jahaz, a strong place near Kedemoth,[8] in the south-east corner of Sihon's territory. The result was the defeat of Sihon, and the occupation of his land by Israel. *Wherefore they that sing taunt-songs say,*—the "mashal" opens with the challenge of Israel to the Amorites to return and rebuild their city (ver. 27), then (vv. 28, 29) describes how the Amorites had come there, by taking the country from Moab, and returns (ver. 30) to the keynote of Israel's victory—

27 *Come ye to Heshbon!*
Let the city of Sihon be built and set up again!

[1] *Ibid.* p. 373. It carries the name Mojib up to the desert.
[2] Num. xxi. 14, 15. For Waheb (accusative) LXX read *Ζωόβ*.
[3] صفيه
[4] Especially Burckhardt, 400 f. *Cliff,* אשד not elsewhere, but plural אשדות frequent for *slopes.*
[5] Above, p. 373.
[6] Above, p. 377.
[7] Deut. ii. 26 f.
[8] Jahaz, יהץ, Num. xxi. 23; Deut. ii. 32; Isa. xv. 4; Jer. xlviii. 34; but Jahzah, יהצה, Josh. xiii. 18, xxi. 36: Judges xi. 20; Jer. xlviii. 21; and 1 Chron. vi. 78—is twice with Kedemoth, Josh. xiii. 18, xxi. 36 f., which must have lain east; twice seems a limit of Moab, distant from Heshbon, Isa. xv. 4; Jer. xlviii. 34; and once placed on the plateau of Moab, *Ib.* 21. On the Moabite Stone, 19, 20, spelt like the shorter Hebrew, and given as a fortress, near Dibon. The following lines are Num. xxi. 27-30.

28 *For fire had*[1] *gone forth from Heshbon,*
Flame from the fortress of Sihon,
Had devoured Ar of Moab,
And consumed[2] *the high places of Arnon.*

29 *Woe unto thee, Moab!*
Thou art undone, people of Chemosh!
He hath given his sons to be runaways,
His daughters to captivity,
To the king of the Amorites, Sihon!

30 *But we shot at them, Heshbon was undone—unto Dibon,*[3]
And we laid waste unto Nobah (?) which lies on the desert.[4]

The war against Sihon is declared to be unhistorical by some who refer the song to a conquest of Moab by Israel in the ninth century. Their reasons are that the war is given in but one of the documents of the Pentateuch, that the song traces an invasion from north to south, not from south to north, and that if *king of the Amorites, Sihon*,[5] be omitted, the whole reads of an invasion by Israel of Moab, beginning at Heshbon and extending to the Arnon. But the document which tells the story is the oldest of the documents; its date, at the latest in the eighth century, forbids that its authors could have confused a war in the ninth century with one in the fourteenth; and it is not contradicted by other documents. Such an invasion of Eastern Palestine by Amorites from the west was possible; while we cannot understand, if the facts were not as stated, any motive for inventing the tale.[6]

Sihon defeated and Heshbon overthrown, the country was clear for the advance of Israel from the Arnon. Their goal was the Jordan, and their

[1] The verb, from its position, must be rendered pluperfect.
[2] So LXX, *κατέπιεν*, as if בלעה. Hebrew, בעלי: *Baals of the high places of Arnon.*
[3] *Dibon, the City of King Mesha*, D. Mackenzie, *PEFQ*, 1913, 57.
[4] The text is uncertain. The above is that of Dillmann, based on the Peshitto. Daibon is the proper spelling, as we see from דיבן of the Moabite Stone. Nophah is unknown (there is a Naifeh south-east of Ma'an), but a Nobah lay NE of Heshbon near Jogbehah (Jud. viii. 11). This would be inconsistent with the words, אשר עד מידבא, for Medeba lies south of Heshbon. But Peshitto reads אשר על מדבר, *which is on the desert.* For Niram, *we shot at them*, LXX read ninam, *their offspring*, and the last line *γυναῖκες ἔτι προσεξέκαυσαν πῦρ ἐπὶ Μωάβ.* So v. 30 may run thus: *Their offspring is perished fr. Heshbon to Dibon, their women childless from the slopes to the desert.* See G. A. Smith, *Early Poetry of Israel*, 66.
[5] Num. xxi. 29.
[6] See Appendix on "The Wars with Sihon and Og".

nearest way over the treeless Plateau, which stretches north from Arnon, and then down one of the glens which break from the west of Heshbon into the Arabah. The Plateau is without springs, and Israel's stations would be fixed by three water-courses which cut it between the Arnon and Heshbon. One itinerary gives four stations: Beer, where Israel had to dig for water, and sang the Song of the Well, some spot near the Upper Arnon[1]; Mattanah[2]; Nahali-el, or the Valley of God, not an unfit name for Wady Zerḳa Maʿin with healing springs[3]; Bamoth,[4] High Places, which may be represented by the ancient cromlechs and altars about Wady Jideid.[5]

Here Israel were to exchange the desert, their horizon during forty years, for the first full sight of the Promised Land. The next station is *the glen in the field of Moab, by the headland of Pisgah, which looks out over Jeshimon.*[6]

During their journey over the table-land, Israel had no outlook westward across the Dead Sea. For westward the Plateau rises a little and shuts out all view, but on the other side of the rise it breaks into promontories slightly lower than itself, which run out over the Arabah and Dead Sea Valley, and afford a view of Western Palestine. Seen from below, or from across Jordan, these headlands, rising three or four thousand feet by slope and precipice from the valley, stand out like separate mountains. But eastward they do not rise from the Moab Plateau—they are simply projections or capes of the latter, and you ride from it on to them without feeling a difference of level, save for a decline of a few feet. Israel, passing Bamoth, had arrived at the inland end of one of these headlands—almost certainly that which breaks from the Plateau half-way between Heshbon and Medeba, and runs out, under the name of Neba, nearly opposite the north end of the Dead Sea. The ridge is about two miles long, and its level top perhaps half a mile broad. It is flinty limestone, mostly barren, yet where it breaks from the Plateau, fertile, and, on the July day we crossed, this end was covered with yellow corn and reapers. Before you descend from the rising ground, which

[1] Num. xxi. 16-18. In 18*b* read (with LXX) *from Beer* for *from the wilderness*. Beer is not Dibon, Conder, *PEFQ*, 1882, 86; Israel would not need to dig water there, and seems to have passed to the east.

[2] The only names to-day even remotely echoing this name are Umm Denieh and Butmah, the name of the upper course of the Wady Waleh.

[3] Conder, *Ib.* See p. 376.

[4] Not *Bamoth in the valley*, as the *PEF Red. Map* calls it (also Conder, *PEFQ*, 1882 86), following the mistaken English of Num. xxi. 20. Read *from Bamoth* to *the glen* or *ravine*.

[5] Conder, *PEFQ*, 1886, 85 ff.; *Heth and Moab*, 145 ff.

[6] Num. xxi. 20, E, *the glen that is in the territory of Moab*, but D the *glen* or *gorge*, גיא, *opposite Beth-peor* (Deut. iii. 29, iv. 46, xxxiv. 6). In P Beth-peor is by itself (Josh. xiii. 20).

alone divides it from the Plateau, you instinctively seek the nearest high mound for a last view backwards. There is the Plain of Moab, southward broken only by the eminence of Medeba and the hollow of Arnon, but in front it rolls unbroken, unvaried save by the shadows of a few clouds on the featureless hillocks into the infinite east. You turn west, descending through the corn-fields, and traverse the flinty ridge to the limestone knoll upon it, which bears the name of Ras, or Head, of Neba.[1] You have lost the eastern view, but Western Palestine is in sight; only the hither side of the Jordan Valley is still invisible, and north and south the view is hampered by the near hills. Follow the ridge to its second summit, Ras Siaghah, and you are on a headland, which, though lower than Ras Neba, stands free of the rest of the range. The whole of the Jordan Valley is now open from En-gedi, beyond which the mists become impenetrable, to where, on the north, the hills of Gilead seem to meet those of Ephraim. The Jordan flows below: Jericho is visible beyond. Over Gilead Hermon can be seen in clear weather, but the heat hid it from us. The view is almost that described as the last on which the eyes of Moses rested, the higher hills of Western Palestine shutting out possibility of a sight of the sea. It is certainly the position described: *the head of the Pisgah, which looketh down* or *over upon*, *the face of Jeshimon*, whether this be the wilderness of Judæa across the Dead Sea, or the stretch of waste-land east of Jordan, just below our point of view.[2]

It was probably the well-watered glen north of the Neba-Siaghah ridge, the Wady 'Ayun Musa, which Israel descended and camped in. It would depend on the season, whether the host stayed about its plentiful waters, now called the "Wells of Moses", or at once went down to the warm plains

[1] Neba in Bedawee dialect is "mountain back", Dalman *MuNDPV*, 1900, 23.

[2] *Looketh down* or *over upon* = נִקְשְׁפָה, of God from heaven, Ps. cii. 20 (19); and of men out of, and down from, a window, 2 Sam. xxiv. 20; Gen. xxvi. 8; Song vi. 10. The chief idea seems to be not *forth*, but *down*, and, if so, this Jeshimon will not be the wilderness of Judæa, but the tract of barren land E of Jordan, N of the Sea, in which בית ישמות lay, Josh. xii. 3, xiii. 20; Ezek. xxv. 9. Cf. Dillmann *ad locum*.

Pisgah is used with the article, either ראש הפסגה, *summit of the Pisgah* (Num. xxi. 20, xxiii. 14 (JE); Deut. iii. 27, xxxiv. 1), or אשדות הפסגה or אשדת, *slopes of the Pisgah* (Deut. iii. 17, iv. 49; Josh. xii. 3, D; and Josh. xiii. 20, probably P). The ראש is described as *looking down on Jeshimon, over against Jericho, and commanding a view of Shittim*. Siaghah, now attached to the foreland, has no connection with Pisgah, the letters of which, or their equivalents, are found in Ras Feshkhah, a headland on the other side of the Sea. The name Mount Nebo, הר נבו, is only in two passages, both probably P: Deut. xxxii. 49, where it is one of the Abarim range, over against Jericho, and Deut. xxxiv. 1, where it is the same as Pisgah, LXX, *Ναβαύ*. The town Nebo is in Num. xxxii. 3, 38, xxxiii. 47; Isa. xv. 2; Jer. xlviii. 1, 22; 1 Chron. v. 8, generally next to Baal-meon. On Nebo, F. E. Hoskins, *Nile to Nebo*, 355 ff.

of Shittim beside the Jordan. One thing is certain; this journey, though in the Book of Numbers it is described before the war with Sihon, must have come after the latter. No host so large and cumbered could have ventured down any of the glens from the Plateau to the Jordan before their warriors had occupied Heshbon, for Heshbon commands these glens.

To Nebo again the sacred story brings Moses to close his life—again to that long platform where the host he had guided for forty years first lost their desert horizon, and saw the Promised Land open. And somewhere below the platform the Lord buried Moses—*in a valley in the land of Moab, over against Beth-peor, but no man knoweth of his sepulchre to this day*. Between the streams, that in these valleys spring full-born from the rocks, and the merry corn-fields on the Plateau above, are some thousand feet of slopes and gullies, where no foot comes, the rock is crumbling, and silence reigns, save for the west wind moaning through the thistles. Here Moses was laid. Who would wish to know the exact spot? The whole region is a sepulchre.

Nebo and the neighbouring hills were also the stations and altars of Balaam. Balak brought him from the Arnon, and they took their first position at Bamoth-baal, which must have lain back from the edge of the hills, for Balaam could see from it only the farther edge of Israel's camp on the plain below.[1] The seer's second station was in the field of Zophim, or *the Gazers*, which is given as on *the head of Pisgah*,[2] where seven altars were built. The third station was *the head of Peor that looketh down on Jeshimon*—the same index as for Nebo itself, yet probably a point still nearer the plain of Shittim.[3] The places at which Balaam took his stand and looked for omens were probably sanctuaries. The range is covered with the names of deity—Baal, Nebo, Peor. Nor could there be more suitable platforms for altars, nor more open posts for observing the stars or the passage of clouds, or the flight of birds across the hollow of the Arabah.[4] *The field of Gazers* was rightly named. To-day the hills have many ancient altars and circles of stones upon them.[5]

[1] Num. xxii. 41. Bamoth-baal was perhaps Bamoth, the station of Israel, xxi. 19, On Balaam's altars see Conder, *PEFQ*, 1882; and *Heth and Moab*. On his oracles, G. A. Smith, *Early Poetry of Israel*, 67 ff., and the references there.

[2] Num. xxiii. 14.

[3] פעור, a mountain of this name is not elsewhere found. בית פעור, Josh. xiii. 20, is given with Ashdoth-pisgah and Beth-jeshimoth, which means that it lay down towards the plain. *Onomasticon*, ὄρος Φογώρ, by the ascent from Livias (Tell Rame) and Βεθφογώρ, 6 Rom. m. E of Livias.

[4] Cf. Num. xxiii. 23, where *enchantment* and *divination* should be *omens*, as of birds and clouds (cf. xxiv. 1, *he went not, as at other times, to seek for omens*), and *soothsaying* by watching arrows, or looking into entrails.

[5] Conder, *op. cit.*

Besides the distant campaign against Og, king of Bashan,[1] Israel waged war—impossible to avoid in those desert-bordering regions—with the Midianites.[2] No geographical data are given.

The rest of the geography of Moab carries us into the period of the kings and prophets.

The territory of Sihon between the Arnon and the Jabbok, and as far east as Jazer, the border of the children of Ammon, was divided between the tribes of Reuben and Gad. These high, fresh moors, the dust of whose paths still bear no foot-marks save of sheep and cattle, had attracted the two tribes, which, not crossing the Jordan, failed to rise like the others from the pastoral to the agricultural stage of life. They asked Moses for the land, and he divided it between them. The division is hard to define: we have two accounts. In one[3] the cities of Reuben cluster about Heshbon, while Gad's are both south on the Arnon and north of all Reuben's. In the other,[4] from a different document, Reuben has all to the south of Heshbon, Gad all to the north, the Wady Ḥesban being the probable boundary. Neither account is early, and the former may represent the distribution of the two tribes when Reuben was dwindling.[5] All we know is that both must have had constant warfare with Moab, who would not be kept south of Arnon, and that, in course of this warfare, Reuben disappeared. The Moabite inscription of the middle of the ninth century mentions the men of Gad, and places them immediately north of Arnon, but does not know of Reuben.[6] Towards the beginning of the ninth century Moab was as far north as Medeba,[7] but Omri drove him back across Arnon, and he was tributary to Israel all Omri's days and Ahab's.[8] Then he revolted, and sweeping north, took and rebuilt towns we already know between the Arnon and Nebo.[9]

[1] See pp. 386 f. [2] Num. xxxi.

[3] Num. xxxii. 34 ff. (E). Gad had Dibon, Ataroth (modern 'Aṭṭarus), Aroer, Atroth-shophan unknown, Jazer and Jogbehah north near Jabbok, Beth-nimrah unknown, and Beth-haran, see p. 314. Reuben had Heshbon, Elealeh, now el-'Al, N of Heshbon, Kiriathaim, now Ḳureiyat, S of Wady Zerḳa Ma'in, Nebo, Baal-meon, and the unknown Sibmah.

[4] Josh. xiii. 15 ff. (P?).

[5] Stade, *Gesch.*, 148; he seems wrong when he maintains that, at the crossing of Jordan, Reuben had no territory about Heshbon, and only came there later. No trace of this, and Stade owns not to be able to discover Reuben's seat before it was Heshbon.

[6] l. 10: "men of Gad had dwelt in the land of Ataroth from of old".

[7] Or Mĕhēdaba, Moabite Stone, ll. 7 f.; *MuNDPV*, 1897, 49 ff.

[8] 2 Kings i. 1, iii. 5. Mesha puts his revolt in the middle of Ahab's reign, l. 8. We might correct the narrative by this contemporary document: but the death of a king was the usual moment for a revolt like Mesha's.

[9] Aroer, Dibon, Jahaz, Kiriathaim, Beth-bamoth, Baal-meon, Mĕhēdeba, Beth-diblathaim; he destroyed Ataroth and Nebo.

He does not profess to have taken Heshbon. The kings of Judah, Israel, and Edom contrived to defeat Moab,[1] but without result. Mesha or his successors must have pushed their conquests farther north, for in the time of the prophets we find Moab, except for a short interval, in possession of all their ancient territory even north of the Wady Ḥesban.[2] From Moab the land passed to Arabs and Nabatæans.[3]

The Hasmonæans won back for Israel these seats of Reuben. That curious personage, the Jewish priest Hyrcanus, driven by his brothers across Jordan, had built the wonderful castle and caves of Tyrus, now 'Araḳ el-Emir, and established a kind of kingdom. But he killed himself in 176 B.C.[4] John Hyrcanus took Medeba,[5] and Alexander Jannæus made the Moabites tributary.[6] He built, as the Jewish bulwark to the south, the fortress of Mekawar,[7] in Greek Machærus, to-day Mkaur. It was given up to the Romans, and destroyed by Gabinius, but Herod rebuilt it, making another Masada.[8] Pliny calls Machærus the second citadel of Judæa.[9] It lay on the border of Peræa, or the tetrarchy of Herod Antipas; to the south were the domains of Aretas, Herod's father-in-law, king of the Nabatæans.[10] When, for Herodias, Herod intrigued to divorce the daughter of Aretas, she begged to be sent to Machærus, and Herod having let her, she escaped from it to one of her

[1] 2 Kings iii.

[2] Amos (vi. 14) sets the boundary of the kingdom of Jeroboam II at the brook of the Arabah. If this means some water-course S of the Dead Sea, he had again reduced Moab, which is probable. Isa. xv, xvi speaks of Heshbon, Elealeh, and Jazar as Moabite; Jer. xlviii. 45, Heshbon stands outside Moab; Ezek. xxv. 9, Medeba is Moab's.

[3] 1 Macc. ix. 35 ff.: τοὺς Ναυαταίους; the υἱοὶ 'Ιαμβρὶ ἐκ Μηδαβά may be compared with the name Ia'meru, יעמרו, in the Nabatæan inscription from Umm er-Reṣaṣ, *CIS*, ii. 195, and Ἀμαραίου παῖδες, Jos. xiii *Antt.* i. 2; Clermont-Ganneau, *Journal Asiatique*, 1891, p. 542.

[4] Josephus, xii *Antt.* iv. 11. For 'Araḳ el-Emir see Merrill's *East of Jordan*, 106 ff.; Tristram, *Land of Israel*, 520; Conder, *Heth and Moab*, 168 ff.; De Vogüé, *Le Temple de Jerus.* 37 ff., pl. xxxiv. f.; De Saulcy, *Voyage*, etc., i. 211 f.; Duc de Luynes, *Voyage . . . à la Mer Morte*, 30 ff.; *PEF Mem. E. Pal.* i. 65 ff.; Gautier, *Au delà du Jordain*, 50 ff.; G. A. Smith, *Jerus.* ii. 404, 425, *Callirrhoë and Machærus, Un. F.C. Maga.* Feb. 1895.

[5] xiii *Antt.* ix. 1. About 127 B.C. *ZDPV*, xxxiv. 110, Hyrcanium.

[6] *Ibid.* xiii. 5. Before 90 B.C.

[7] מכור or מכוור. Some readings in the Talmud and Targums insert a *v* or *b* (Lightfoot, *Opera*, Ed. Leusden, ii. 582; Levy, *Neuhebräisches Wörterbuch*, *sub voce* מכוור). Josephus gives Μαχαιροῦς; Pliny, Machærus. For its building by Alexander Jannæus see Josephus, vii *Wars*, vi. 2.

[8] Josephus, xiv *Antt.* v. 2; vi. 1; vii *Wars*, vi. 2; i *Wars*, vii. 2.

[9] *HN*, v. 16.

[10] Josephus, xviii *Antt.* v. 1.

father's camps on the Arnon.[1] We have two inscriptions from about this date of the *strategi* or commanders of these camps.[2] Aretas, like Herod, was a vassal of Rome, but instead of appealing to his suzerain to right the wrong done to his daughter, he prepared to go to war against Herod. Herod moved south to Machærus to meet him, bringing his new wife, Herodias, and her daughter Salome. Aretas lingered, and Herod turned to deal with another foe, whom his scandalous conduct had roused within his own domains.[3] John the Baptist, preaching in Peræa, had denounced the marriage of Herodias, and Herod arrested and cast him into the dungeons, which Machærus held beneath its palace. Here the revelry of the king's birthday took place, and, in the same moments within the same walls, the murder of the prophet.[4] Machærus overlooks the Dead Sea—it was another of those tragedies, for which nature has furnished so sympathetic a theatre.[5] But it was not the last. Like Masada Machærus formed a refuge for the Jewish zealots, who escaped from the overthrow of Jerusalem. Though unable to take it by storm, the Romans compelled its surrender through sheer menace, slaughtered a large part of the garrison and razed the walls.[6]

Thus Moses and John, the first and the last of the prophets, thirteen centuries between them, closed their lives almost on the same spot. Within sight is the scene of the translation of Elijah.

[1] *Ibid.* Josephus cannot have meant to say what some of his words imply, that Machærus belonged at this time to Aretas. There had been no reason of peace or war for Herod's surrender of this fortress; the rest of this passage implies that Herod let his wife go to a fortress still his own, and it is only *after* she reaches Machærus that Josephus talks of her coming "into Arabia", and under charge of her father's generals. The clause assigning Machærus to Aretas must be corrupt.

[2] One at Umm er-Reṣaṣ, the other at Medeba. *Corpus Inscrip. Semit.*, Pars. ii, tom. ii, Nos. 195, 196; the former A.D. 39, the latter 37. The latter does not prove the possession of Medeba by Nabatæans for it is not *in situ*, and may have been brought from a distance. In any case, the position of the Jews and Nabatæans in Moab in 37 tells us nothing upon the question of the previous note.

[3] Matt. xiv. 3 ff.

[4] Josephus (xviii *Antt.* v. 2) is our only authority for the murder of the Baptist in Machærus. Matthew (xiv. 3 ff.) and Mark (vi. 17 ff.) mention no place. Keim's observation (*Jesus of Nazara*, iv. 217) that Mark vi. 21 implies Tiberias is gratuitous, and an answer is supplied by himself (*Ib.* 218, note 1), when he points out that Galilee, as in Mark's account, is used by Josephus of the whole tetrarchy of Antipas. Wieseler's theory, that the banquet was in Livias, the execution in Machærus, is impossible.

[5] See p. 320.

[6] Josephus, vii *Wars*, vi. 2 f. On the present site see Burckhardt, Tristram, Conder, G. A. Smith, *Callirrhoë and Machærus.*

XXVIII. *ISRAEL AND OTHERS IN GILEAD AND BASHAN*[1]

We proceed to what, through so many centuries, was Israel's only proper territory east of Jordan, the Land of Gilead. Gilead, let us remember, extends from the edge of the plateau of Moab to the Yarmuk, and is halved by the Jabbok. Israel's defeat of Sihon gave them the southern half, and brought them to this river. But the Sacred Narrative carries Israel in the days of Moses across the north half[2] of Gilead up to Bashan. To the story of Sihon it adds that of Og.

We are not offered the same evidence in this case as in the previous. No song is preserved to illustrate the war against Og, and the story is confined to the Deuteronomic documents. So even critics, who believe in the reality of Sihon and his overthrow by Israel, doubt whether Og existed or Israel made so early an advance so far as Bashan.

I give elsewhere[3] answers to these doubts, and here need only emphasise the geographical probability of Israel's advance towards Bashan before they crossed Jordan. Israel, it is certain, were settled for a time in Moab, the country to the north was attractive, no obstacle like Jordan shut it off, and a chief such as Og is described would not be quiescent before so strong an invader on his own side of the river. No other invader of Syria from the south-east has crossed Jordan without conquering Eastern Palestine, sometimes even as far as Damascus.[4] Og is represented as governing the country to the Jabbok. But there is no record of Israel's advance from the Jabbok to the Yarmuk. Og met them at Edrei, east of the source of the latter. Edrei, the present Adhra'a,[5] is a strong position on the south of the gorge that forms the southern boundary of the plain of Hauran. The gorge winds, and with a tributary ravine, isolates the present city on all but the south side, by which it can be approached on the level. But the citadel is cut off upon a hill which stands forward on the gorge, and probably with the caves below held the ancient town. These caves are one of the wonders of Eastern

[1] For this chapter, see Map, pages 56-7. [2] On this, el-Kefarat, *ZDPV*, xx. 112 ff.

[3] Appendix on "The Wars against Sihon and Og".

[4] One thinks of how Nabatæans pushed up to Damascus, in face of Greek powers, and how Mohammedans took Damascus before Jerusalem.

[5] אדרעי, Modern Arabic, Dara'at, but Bedouin preserve the ancient pronunciation Azra'at; Greek *Ἄδράα*. *ZDPV*, xx. 118.

Palestine. They form a subterranean city, a labyrinth of streets with shops and houses on either side, and a market-place.[1] How old the whole is we cannot say. The Bible makes no mention of so great a marvel, which is probably to be dated from later times. Bashan was full of cities[2] besides Edrei, but almost none of the present ruins go back beyond the Christian era.

Less clear than Israel's conquest of Og is their occupation of his land, for the accounts differ, and many hold that the interpretation of them is, that Manasseh's settlement in Half Gilead (north of the Jabbok) and in Bashan took place not before Israel's passage of the Jordan, but from Western Palestine, and after the settlement of the tribe north of Ephraim. There are reasons against this, and in favour of the earlier settlement: on our present evidence, the matter remains uncertain.[3] But at whatever period Hebrew tribes first settled in Gilead, Gilead continued to be the peculiar domain of Israel east of Jordan. The reasons for this, with the consequent movements

[1] Wetzstein, *Reisebericht*, 47 f.; Porter, *Five Years in Damascus*. From the entrance in the gorge we penetrated for fifty yards, and were stopped by a recent fall of rock. Our guides said the passage was blown up by the Kaimakam to close the labyrinth to fugitives from military service and justice.

[2] Deut. iii.

[3] Num. xxxii. 1, JE states only Reuben and Gad asked for land E of Jordan. Other sources add to their settlement there that of the half-tribe of Manasseh (Deut. and Num. xxxii. 33, assigned to the redactor). Deborah's song speaks of Machir as if a western clan (Jud. v. 14). The story how Machir, son of Manasseh, took Gilead, and Jair, son of Manasseh, took its camp-villages, and called them Havvoth-jair, is attached by an earlier document (J) to that of the settlement of E Palestine under Moses (Num. xxxii. 39 ff.). But Judges x assigns Havvoth-jair to Jair a Gileadite under the Judges (see p. 355). Wellhausen says (*Hist.*[2] 33) this makes "probable" the invasion of Gilead by Manasseh after the conquest of W Palestine. Stade (*Gesch.* 163) thinks it happened when Reuben and Gad, whom he supposes to have first settled in Gilead, pushed S to Moab. But, as we saw, p. 383, Reuben and Gad were in Moab from the first, and Stade gives no proof for the movement he imputes to them. Budde (*Richt u. Sam.* pp. 32 ff.) points out that the sons of Joseph could not (Josh. xvii. 14-18) have complained that they had only one lot, if besides their western territory they had already from Moses land E of Jordan, and by inserting "Gilead" in ver. 18, makes this the new lot which Joshua granted. But there is no sign of "Gilead" having fallen out of the text, or being meant by Joshua. Nor could it have helped the House of Joseph against the Canaanites of W Palestine (ver. 18) to possess Gilead. As Stade observes (*Gesch.* 163), it is not clear that Joshua granted them a second lot. Arguments for the invasion of N Gilead from W Palestine are thus inconclusive. Note, on the other side, Gilead is said to be father of Abiezer and Shechem (Num. xxvi. 29 f. P; Josh. xvii. 2, JE), and therefore older in Manasseh's history than these western towns of the tribe, and while Judges xii. 4 (probably from the period of the early Kings) speaks of some Gileadites as late immigrants into their land, it assumes that Manasseh had previously occupied this. Cf. Driver, "Manasseh", Hastings' *DB*.

of history in Gilead, are as clear as the questions of her various localities and sites are obscure. Gilead is only a half-explored country.

Why Gilead constituted the eastern domain of Israel may be understood from her formation. Gilead is the only part of Eastern Palestine which corresponds to the territories of Israel in the West. Gilead is mountain or hill-country between the plateaus of Moab and Hauran. Hauran was swept by the Aramæans or Syrians, a people with chariots; north of the Yarmuk Israel seldom got footing. Moab and the level country east of Gilead were swept by Arabs and Ammonites. But neither Aram from the north, nor Ammon from the south, though they sometimes carried fire and sword across Gilead, was able to drive the Hebrews from those wooded ridges between Moab and the Yarmuk, which formed almost as integral a portion of Israel as the hill-country of Judah, or that of Ephraim. Gilead was also in close communication with Western Palestine, as neither Bashan nor Moab could be.

Thus we find in Gilead, from the earliest times to the Assyrian captivity, Hebrew communities, centres and rallying-places for Hebrew dynasties, Hebrew character and heroism, with prophecy, the distinctive glory of Hebrew life. Deborah's song substitutes Gilead for Gad as the name of a tribe in Israel.[1] In pursuit of the Midianites Gideon finds in Gilead two communities, Succoth and Penuel, from which he expects the same devotion to Israel as he would from towns in Ephraim.[2] Two of the Judges are Gileadite. One, Jair, lives on the east of the province, the border of the desert, where men inhabit not cities but camps.[3] The other is the imposing figure of Jephthah, Israel's champion against Ammon who occupied the land on the Upper Jabbok. The story of Jephthah throbs with the sense of common interest between Gilead and Ephraim.[4] Mizpah in Gilead was the gathering-place of all Israel against Benjamin.[5] When the Ammonites threatened the helpless Jabesh-gilead, Saul proved his title as king of All-Israel by succouring this Eastern city,[6] a service which its citizens remembered when they rescued his body from insult at Beth-shan, and gave it burial with themselves.[7] With some thought of all this Abner vainly tried in Gilead to restore Saul's dynasty.[8]

By victories over Ammon and Aram of Damascus and Zobah, David was the first to bring all Eastern Palestine under Israel.[9] So completely had

[1] Jud. v. 17. [2] Jud. viii.

[3] Jud. x. 3-5. See p. 551. Nobah went still farther east to Kanatha in the Jebel Ḥauran, Kenath, Num. xxxii. 42.

[4] Jud. x. ff. [5] Jud. xx. 1. [6] 1 Sam. xi. [7] 1 Sam. xxxi. 11-13. [8] 2 Sam. ii.

[9] 2 Sam. viii and x. The exact degree of the subjection of Aram to David is left in doubt. Zobah lay to the north of Damascus.

David won the hearts of Eastern Israel that when Absalom's rebellion broke out he sought refuge in Gilead, and made his headquarters Mahanaim, where Abner had crowned Ishbosheth. The woods of Gilead live before us in the story of the subsequent battle, when the rough *woodland multiplied to devour more people than the sword*, and Absalom was hanged by his long hair in the oak.[1] Solomon did not retain all the Eastern conquests of his father, and in his day Damascus grew to that power which made her, for the next three centuries, a formidable foe to Israel.[2] After the Disruption Gilead remained with the northern kingdom, opposite which it lay, and with which it had communication by the fords of Jordan.[3] Jeroboam fortified Penuel, and, for a time, may have made it his capital.[4] Soon afterwards Gilead gave Israel a great personality. *Elijah the Tishbite* breaks across Jordan from *Tishbe in Gilead*[5] with the same suddenness as in the end he disappears across the same river. In Gilead we must also seek for the Brook Cherith, the scene of his retreat.[6] In the reign of Ahab Damascus and Israel fought as allies against Assyria,[7] but from this event onward they were foes. They met on Israelite territory and Aram was beaten, met again at Aphek, on Aramæan territory above the Lake of Galilee, where the great road still comes along from Damascus to the Jordan,[8] and Aram was beaten once more. Later, the Aramæans took Ramoth in Gilead, and Ahab fell in the effort to regain it.[9] After some years, in which Aram kept up war against Western Palestine[10] and besieged Samaria,[11] Joram, grandson of Ahab, won back Ramoth-gilead, but it was still contested by Aram,[12] and Jehu was serving in the garrison when anointed to destroy the House of Omri. In Jehu's reign, and perhaps because of the internal troubles following his

[1] 2 Sam. xviii. 8, 10; on the name Ephraim (ver. 6), E of Jordan, see p. 223.

[2] The idea that Solomon built Tadmor or Palmyra must be abandoned. For Tadmor in 1 Kings ix. 18 read Tamar, a town in Judah. See p. 184.

[3] On the connection of Ephraim with Eastern Palestine see pp. 223-224.

[4] So it seems from the close connection between his abandonment of Shechem and building of Penuel, 1 Kings xii. 25.

[5] 1 Kings xvii. 1, LXX. Khurbet Istib S of W Yabis with a ruined chapel, Mar Elyas; cf. Van Kasteren, *ZDPV*, xiii. 207; *MuNDPV*, 1898, p. 20, for frequency of Elijah's name about the Jabbok.

[6] Described as *before*, *i.e.* east of, *Jordan*, 1 Kings xvii. 3, 5; see Schulten, *Die Mosaikkarte von Madaba*, 11, for traditional evidence for this. Cf. Eusebius, *Onom.*, *sub χορρά*; Irby and Mangles' *Travels*.

[7] At Ḳarḳar in 854 B.C.

[8] The present Fiḳ. Wellhausen and W. R. Smith are wrong in identifying this with Aphek where the Philistines mustered. See p. 260. The narrative of the war between Israel and Aram, 1 Kings xx.

[9] 1 Kings xxii. [10] 2 Kings v. 2, vi. 8. [11] *Id.* vi. 24 ff.; vii. [12] *Id.* ix. 1, 4, 14.

usurpation of the throne, Hazael of Damascus, sweeping to the Arnon, was able to conquer all Israel's possessions east of Jordan.[1] Probably to the barbarities of this campaign, in which Aram was joined by Ammon and Moab, Amos refers: *For three transgressions of Damascus, yea for four, I will not turn it away; for they have threshed Gilead with threshing-sledges of iron. For three transgressions of the children of Ammon, yea for four, I will not turn it away; for they have ripped up the mothers of Gilead—to enlarge their border!*[2] Moabite bands *used to invade* Western Palestine *at the coming in of the year*, and Hazael and Ben-Hadad, kings of Aram, *oppressed Israel all their days.*[3]

During these evil times the prophet Elisha, borderman as he was (from Abel-meholah on Jordan),[4] expert in camp-life, ambush and scouting,[5] and with political foresight,[6] had also been the moral stay and inspiration of his broken people—altogether,[7] through those three distracting reigns, *the chariot of Israel and the horsemen thereof.*[8] His bequest to Israel was hope: dying, he prophesied that the young Joash should thrice smite the Syrians at Aphek.[9] And so it came to pass. Joash recovered from Aram what Jehoahaz had lost,[10] and under the next, the long reign of Jeroboam II, Israel enjoyed supremacy up to her ideal borders, Hamath and the Dead Sea, and probably occupied part of the territory of Damascus.[11] This lasted fifty years. Hosea treats Gilead as if it were as integral a part of the kingdom as Ephraim.[12] But then came the flood which was to devastate both Western and Eastern Palestine. In 734 *Tiglath-pileser, king of Assyria, came and took Ijon, Abel beth-maacah, Janoah, Kedesh, and Hazor, and Gilead, and Galilee, all the lands of Naphtali, and carried them captive to Assyria.*[13] The eastern territories of Israel were left to the Ishmaelites. Isaiah does not mention Gilead. Micah has only a prayer that God's flock may *pasture again in Bashan and Gilead, as in days of old.*[14] To Jeremiah Gilead is only a figure and a proverb, whose pathos is deepened by her abandonment by Israel; *Is there no balm in*

[1] 2 Kings x. 32. [2] Amos i. 3, 13. [3] 2 Kings xiii. 3, 20.

[4] 1 Kings xix. 16, somewhere on Jordan, probably S of plain of Bethshan; Judges vii. 22; 1 Kings iv. 12. Eusebius and Jerome (*Onom.*, Ἀβελμαελαί) place it in the Ghor, 10 m. S of Bethshan, at a spot called Βηθμαιελά Conder, 'Ain Helweh, 9½ m. S of Bethshan, but Hölscher, *ZDPV*, xxxiii. 16 ff., Tell el-Ḥammi, 13 kiloms. S of Bethshan; cf. Thomsen, *ZDPV*, xxxvii. 187.

[5] These qualities, different from those of Elijah, are obvious: 2 Kings iv. 38 ff., vi. 1-23, especially, 12: *Elisha, the prophet, telleth the king of Israel the words thou speakest in thy bedchamber.*

[6] 2 Kings viii. 7 ff.; ix. 3. [7] *Id.* vi. 13-17. [8] *Id.* xiii. 14. [9] *Id.* xiii. 17.

[10] *Id.* xiii. 25. [11] 2 Kings xiv. 28, not Damascus itself.

[12] Hosea vi. 8, xii. 11. Cf. Obad. 19. [13] 2 Kings xv. 29. [14] Micah vii. 14.

Gilead, no physician there?[1] But in the days of the captivity Zechariah names Gilead as a promise: *I will bring them again out of the land of Egypt, and gather them out of Assyria; and I will bring them down into the land of Gilead and Lebanon.*[2] The returned people shall be so many that Gilead shall be needed, and even Lebanon, for the overflow of them.

Such then is the ancient history of Gilead, a history of constant war, the tangled lines of which become intelligible when you recognise the position of this territory—high forest ridges between Jordan and the desert, between the plateaus of Moab and Hauran. But when you come to details, and seek to fasten names, and trace the scenery of separate events, you are baffled. In all Syria sites are nowhere less fixed than in Gilead. Only one identification is certain; perhaps two more are probable.

The certainty is the Jabbok or Yabboḳ.[3] One has seen this Jabbok from childhood—the midnight passage of a ford, the section of a river gleaming under torches, splashed and ploughed by struggling animals, cries of women and children above the noise; and then, left alone with the night, the man and the river—for the narrative betokens sympathy between the two tortuous courses[4]: the wrestle with God beside the struggling stream, and dawn breaking down the valley on a changed life. To-day there is no river which you associate more with the height of noon: groups of cattle standing to the knees in water, brakes of oleanders soaked in sunshine, and a fair array of fields on either side, scattered over with reapers and men guiding water by ancient channels to orchards and gardens. From first to last, the valley of the Jabbok is of great fertility. The head-waters of the river rise on the edge of Moab, only some eighteen miles from the Jordan, yet to the east of the water-parting. Thus the river flows at first desertwards, under the name of ʻAmman, past Rabbath-ammon[5] to the Hajj road. There it turns north, fetches a compass north-west, cuts in two the range of Gilead, and by a winding bed flows west-south-west to the Jordan. The whole course, not counting the windings, is over sixty miles. The water is shallow, always fordable, except where it breaks between steep rocks, mostly brawling over a stony bed, muddy, and, at a distance, of a grey-blue colour, which gives it

[1] Jer. viii. 22. [2] Zech. x. 10.

[3] Breadth at mouth 8-10 metres, *MuNDPV*, 1899, 35; cf. *Bibl. Sacr.* 1877, 742; 1878, 411 ff.

[4] יַבֹּק Yabboḳ, and יֵאָבֵק, Ye'abheḳ = *he wrestles.* The narrative connects the wrestling both with the river and with the place called Penuel.

[5] See the next chapter, on the Decapolis.

the name Zerḳa. The best fields are upon the upper reaches, where wheat is grown, but almost nowhere on the banks are you out of sight of sheep, or cattle, or tillage. A road from Jordan follows the valley to the desert, another runs from the desert by ʻAmman to the west.[1] The river has always been a frontier and a line of traffic. Some day the valley will be populous and busy. Yet the highest fame of Jabbok will ever be its earliest, and not all the sunshine, ripening harvests along its live length, can be so bright as that first gleaming and splashing of its waters at midnight, or the grey dawn breaking on the crippled Israel. The history of Gilead is a history of war and struggle, civilisation enduring only by perpetual strife. But upon the Jabbok its first hero was taught how man has to reckon in life with God also, and that his noblest struggles are in the darkness, with the Unseen.

The two sites on Gilead, whose identification is probable, are both named in Gideon's pursuit of the Midianites. Succoth may be Tell Deir ʻAlla, a high mound in the Jordan Valley, about a mile north of the Jabbok.[2] Jogbehah is echoed in Jubeihah, or Ajbeihat, on the road from Salṭ to ʻAmman.[3] *Gideon went up by the way of them that dwell in tents east of Nobah*, unknown, *and Jogbehah*. This may mean the road up the Jabbok itself. In any case, Gideon, going east, came from Succoth to Penuel, as Jacob, going west, came from Penuel to Succoth. Penuel was probably a prominent ridge near the Jabbok, not necessarily south of this, and above Succoth.[4] We are equally ignorant of Mahanaim. It lay presumably north of the Jabbok, and of the great gorge of Jordan, on the border of Gad, and not far from Jordan —an important city, fit for a capital.[5] The other famous names cannot be

[1] Merrill, *East of the Jordan*, ch. xxx: "Exploration of the Jabbok".

[2] The identification is Merrill's (*E. of Jordan*, pp. 385-388; cf. Conder, *Heth and Moab*, p. 183), through words of the Talmud (Shebiith ix. 2, Gemara) that the later name of Succoth was דרעלה, Dar'ala. This leaves the matter only probable. Psalm lx. 6: the Vale of Succoth, between Shechem and Gilead; cf. *MuNDPV*, 1899, p. 21.

[3] Jud. viii. 11, cf. Num. xxxii. 35, 42. This is Van de Velde's suggestion. We visited the ruins in 1891, finding nothing but some Greek carvings. The name Ajbeihat in my diary, was given me by Arabs. Jubeihah is on the *PEF Map*.

[4] That Penuel was prominent is likely from the Phœnician headland known as θεοῦ πρόσωπον (Strabo, xvi. ii. 15 f.). Gen. xxxii.2 5-33 implies it was near Jabbok; Jud. viii. 8-11, above Succoth. If Jacob came from the N, Penuel was S of Jabbok; if from the E, Penuel may have been on either bank, for the east road down Jabbok valley crosses the river more than once. Merrill suggests Tulul edh-Dhahab, round and between which the Jabbok forces its way into the Jordan (pp. 390-392). Conder puts Penuel on Jebel Oshaʻ, Schumacher on Medwar-nol (*MuNDPV*, 1901, p. 2).

[5] Gen. xxxii. 1-10 (vv. 4-14*a* belong to J, vv. 1-3, 14*b* ff. to E) seems to put Mahanaim near Jordan, which would make Jacob approach Jabbok from the N. Abner,

certainly fixed—mizpah, Ramath-mizpah, Ramoth-gilead, and the Land of Tob. Mizpah, the scene of Laban's covenant with Jacob, has been placed by Conder at Suf, a place of dolmens and stone-circles between 'Ajlun and Jerash.[1] This may be, but in the diversity of other accounts of a mizpeh in Gilead, one of which, Jephthah's story, places it on the border of Ammon,[2] another implies that it lay more to the west,[3] another puts Ramath-mizpeh on the north border of Gad,[4] while another speaks of a Maspha or Mizpeh in the far north-east[5]—what certainty can we have that these are the same? or, if they are, what site will suit them all? Ramoth-gilead, assigned to at least five different places, probably lay north of them all, near the Yarmuk, for it was on debatable ground between Aram and Israel.[6] The name of Land of Tob, north of Mizpah,[7] may survive in the Wady and village of Ṭaiyibeh, east of Pella.[8]

But while these ancient sites are uncertain, it must be remembered that no province has at the present day sites which, by nature and the part they have played in modern history, are more definitely stamped as likely to have

---

crossing Jordan, came through the Bithron or Gorge (2 Sam. ii. 29), a name which suits the central portion of the Jordan Valley, to Mahanaim. The Kikkar, across which Ahimaaz ran to Mahanaim (*id.* xviii. 23) is probably Kikkar of Jordan (see pp. 223, 324). Conder (*Heth and Moab*, 185 ff.) places Mahanaim near the Buḳei'a E of Salṭ, a region, though "well-watered" and with "important ruins", not likely for a chief town, and hardly on the border of Gad, where Mahanaim is placed by Josh. xiii. 26. Merrill (p. 437) suggests Khurbet Suleikhat, 300 ft. above the Ghor, in W 'Ajlun, which wady Buhl, 121, suggests for Bithron, a Roman road running up it from 'Ajlun towards Mahanaim; he would not seek Cherith here; cf. v. Kasteren, *ZDPV*, xiii. 205, on Kh.-Mahne or Mahnā or Mahnī (*MuNPDV*, 1897, p. 2; 1898, p. 20). Visited by Seetzen, *Reisen*, i. 385.

[1] Gen. xxxi. 49. Conder, *Heth and Moab*, 181 f.; Oliphant, *Land of Gilead*, 209-216.

[2] Jud. x. 17, xi. 11, 29, 34. Nothing in this, thinks Hölscher, hinders us from putting Mizpah far north; fixing Ramoth at er-Ramta he finds Mizpah at Beit-Ras (*ZDPV*, xxix. 139 f., cf. *MuNDPV*, 1897, 66, 1899, 19); Budde (*Richter*, 86), not S of the Jabbok.

[3] Or Israel would hardly gather here against Benjamin, Jud. xx. f.

[4] Josh. xiii. 26.

[5] Taken by Judas Maccabæus, 1 Macc. v. 35.

[6] 1 Kings xxii. 2 Kings ix. See too the order of the cities of refuge from N to S in Josh. xxi. 38.

[7] And not, as Conder says, the district in which Mizpah lay; Jephthah came from it to Mizpah, which the story places near the land of Ammon.

[8] The *n* in Syriac of 1 Macc. v. 13, and the Greek of 2 Macc. xii. 17, is not a radical, but a termination, *Τώβιον* or *Τούβιον, Τουβιηνοί*. Hence *PEF. Red. Map* is wrong in suggesting Tibneh, S of Ṭaiyibeh. Hölscher (*ZDPV*, xxix. 142) says the village sheikh gave him its older name as 'Efre, and takes it as the Ephron of 1 Macc: and *Γεφροῦν* of Polybius, v. 70. 12, See below, p. 395.

been among the famous sites of old. It is impossible to believe that es-Salṭ[1] with its Jebel Osha', 'Ajlun with its famous view-point and fortress in the Ḳula'at er-Rubaḍ, Pella, Gadara, Irbid, Remtheh, were not famous in the history of Israel in Gilead. Surely they were used. It may be the meagreness of detail in the Old Testament which prevents us from identifying Mizpah with far-seeing Ḳula'at er-Rubaḍ, Mahanaim, with so worthy a capital for Gilead as 'Ajlun, or so historical a site as Pella; or from placing Ramoth-gilead at Reimun,[2] or at es-Salṭ, or at the Ḳula'at er-Rubaḍ, though I feel it necessary, from what the Old Testament says of the frequency with which Ramoth-gilead was contested by Aram and Israel, to put it farther north on or near the Yarmuk.[3] Irbid[4] and Remtheh, on the north-east, are strong sites; the former was the capital of the Turkish district 'Ajlun, the latter a station on the Hajj road, immemorial line of traffic. Both must have been prominent in ancient times.

But all that can be done to-day is to state the topographical problems of Israel in Gilead, and leave their solution till the discovery of fresh evidence.

After returning from exile Jews spread across Eastern Palestine, and came in conflict, as we have seen them in the Shephelah, with the race of Greek settlers who flowed in the wake of Alexander the Great. Hellenism came to terms with the native paganism: the two amalgamated. But the Jews, few and weak, kept to themselves, and when the religious war broke out in the

[1] Schlatter (*Zur Topogr.* 44 ff.) proposes es-Salṭ with its well Jador for the Gadara given as the capital of Peræa (Jos. iv *Wars*, vii. 3), distinct from Gadara on the Yarmuk, which he takes as that captured by Antiochus 218 and 198 and by Alex. Jannæus (Polyb. v. 271, Jos. xii *Antt.* iii. 3, xiii *Antt.* xiii. 3, 1 *Wars*, iv. 2). This is improbable. He takes S Gadara as the Gadora of Ptolemy and Gedôr of the Talmud (Neubauer); Buhl approves (255 n.).

[2] So Conder. Buhl (262) prefers the ruins el-Jala'ad, not 3 m. S of Jabbok, which suits the data of Eusebius, that Ramoth was 15 Rom. m. W of Philadelphia on Jabbok; he identifies it with the town of Gilead, Hos. vi. 8, cf. Jud. xii. 7, LXX, Cod. Alex. and Lag.

[3] G. A. Cooke, who visited es-Salṭ in 1894, points out that O.T. references to Ramoth show it as of strategic and administrative importance for Bashan on the one hand (1 Kings iv. 13) and Aram and N Israel on the other, accessible from Samaria town and Jezreel by road (1 Kings xxii. 37, 2 Kings viii. 28 f., ix. 16), therefore considerably N of the Jabbok, and suitable for chariots (1 Kings xxii. 31 ff.) while es-Salṭ is not so. This evidence of a N site for Ramoth, which I suggested, is welcome; see Addenda, ed. 2, Driver's *Deut.* p. xx.

[4] Raboisson (*Rev. de la Terre Sainte*, 1894), equates it with Laribda of Assurbanipal's campaign.

second century they were sorely pressed in their various cities.[1] Judas Maccabæus, who had conquered the Ammonites under a Greek leader,[2] achieved a second victorious campaign,[3] the course of which is hard to trace, but it brought him as far east as Bozrah. He took that town, and next, Dathema, or, by another reading, Rametha, in which we may trace an echo of Ramoth of Gilead,[4] and next, Maspha,[5] Casphon,[6] Maged, Bosor,[7] and other cities of the country of Galaad. The heathen mustered at Raphon,[8] probably Raphana of the Decapolis on the Yarmuk, but Judas defeated them and took Karnain,[9] with its temple to Atargatis. Then, gathering all Jews who would come back with him, he returned by "a great and well-fortified" city called Ephron,[10] which he was forced to take before he could pass, and crossed the Jordan at Beth-shan.

Alexander Jannæus[11] again brought Gilead within the territories of Israel. First he took Gadara, but seems to have been repulsed from Amathus, a strong fortress just north of the Jabbok, now Amatha.[12] On a second campaign, after overcoming "the Moabites and Gileadites", he destroyed Amathus and its Greek defenders, but was defeated on the Yarmuk by Obodas, the Arabian. "He was thrown by means of a multitude of camels into a deep valley"—a fate singularly like that which the Arabs inflicted on the Byzantine army in A.D. 634, forcing them by sheer weight of numbers into a defile in the same neighbourhood.[13] But Alexander, though a dissolute man, was a determined captain. He returned to Eastern Palestine, and though it cost him a three years' campaign, 84-81, he reduced the country. In Gilead

[1] 1 Macc. v. 9.

[2] 1 Macc. v. 6-8.

[3] 1 Macc. v. 24 ff.; the wilderness into which he went three days' journey must be east of Ammon and Gilead, whence he turned on Bozrah.

[4] 1 Macc. v. 9: Greek *Δάθεμα*; Syriac, Rametha. This would confirm the northern position of Ramoth. See above, p. 394.

[5] Not necessarily Mizpah of Gilead; Syriac Alim, Josephus Malle.

[6] *Χασφώρ* (v. 26), *Χασφών*, *Χασφώθ* (v. 36).

[7] *Μακέδ* and *Βοσόρ*.

[8] V. 37, *Ραφὼν ἐκπέραν τοῦ Χειμάῤῥου*. See next chapter.

[9] V. 43 f., *Καρναΐν*.

[10] Vv. 46 ff. *'Εφρὼν*; Syriac, Ophrah.

[11] 104-78 B.C..

[12] Josephus (xiii *Antt.* xiii. 3; i *Wars*, iv. 2) says that Amathus was taken by Alexander, but mentions his repulse and departure to other fields immediately. The *Onomasticon* places Amathus 21 m. S of Pella.

[13] Josephus, xiii *Antt.* xiii. 4, places the rout of Alexander's army near Gadara, but in i *Wars*, iv. 4, near Gaulana, *i.e.* Golan. We must not suppose the two were the same place—though Gadara, not mentioned in the O.T., nor identified with any O.T. name, is not an impossible site for Golan, standing as it does on the border of Gaulanitis. More probably Golan lay N of Yarmuk, and the above passages prove it near the latter and Gadara. Sahem el-Jaulan (see p. 345) is 17 m. NE of Gadara and 3 from the Yarmuk.

he took Pella, Dion, and Gerasa; in Bashan Golan, Seleucia, and Gamala.[1]

Thus all Gilead and Bashan with Moab were again Israel's, and this terrible debauchee repeated the triumphs of a David and a Jeroboam II. Another Semitic power, the Nabatæan, held all to the East, and Damascus. The Greek cities were Judaised. Hellenism lay prostrate.

So matters continued till the arrival of Pompey and the Roman Legions in 64 B.C. These closed the dominion of Israel in Bashan and Gilead, and opened a new period in the history of Eastern Palestine, which we shall follow in the next two chapters. But here we may take in the operations over Jordan of the Crusaders and of the British Army in 1918.

We have followed the operations of the Crusaders through their Seigneurie of Kerak and Montreal, extending from the Gulf of ʻAḳaba to the latitude of Medeba. To the north of this, in Gilead and Bashan, their hold, curiously enough, was more intermittent and less secure. Their principal expeditions across Jordan were in 1113, 1118-19, when they took Edrei and Bozrah, and even penetrated the Leja, and in 1125 and 1129 when they confirmed for a time their possession of Suete or Suhete, which Arab writers of that century call Souad or Saouad, and apply to all the region between Damascus and the Belḳa, but which has been more particularly identified with Jaulan, east of the Lake of Galilee and the Upper Jordan. Suete was a fief of the principality of Galilee. In Gilead itself, to which their name, La Terre d'Oultre-Jourdain, more properly applied, their power was mainly confined to annual tributes first levied by Baldwin I on the fertile districts of Arx Aijlun, as the Latins called Ḳulaʻat er-Rubaḍ, above ʻAjlun, which citadel Saladin afterwards re-fortified, and of Szalt, as es-Salṭ was then spelt. Baldwin II reached Jerash, and destroyed its fortress as too far east from Christian territory. In 1157 troops of the Franks had to recapture a castle "en la terre de Galaad", probably er-Rubaḍ; and, among other expeditions, one in 1183 reached Elealeh, north of Heshbon. In 1229 Frederick II was granted by the Sultan Kerak, es-Salṭ, the Ghôr and other places; and in 1259 Beibars rebuilt his line of defence from Damascus to Bozrah, ʻAjlun and Es-Salṭ.[2]

[1] Josephus, xiii *Antt.* xv. 3, 4; i *Wars*, iv. 8. For Pella, Dion, Gerasa see next chapter. Pella was destroyed, for the inhabitants would not accept Judaism. On Golan see previous note and p. 354. Seleucia, Σελευκεία (distinct from Seleucia on the Tigris, xiii *Antt.* vii. 1; xviii *Antt.* ix. 8, and other cities of the name founded by Seleucus Nicator), lay east of Lake Ḥuleh (iv *Wars*, i. 1) on an unknown site. Josephus fortified it (ii *Wars*, xx. 6; *Life*, 37), a centre of revolt against the Romans (iv *Wars*, i. 1). For Gamala, see p. 297.

[2] The above details are mostly from William of Tyre's chronicle and Beha ed Din; see, too, Rey.

In the spring of 1918 came the British attempts upon north Moab, 'Amman, a centre of the German-Turkish Army of the East, and south Gilead. Crossing, and with difficulty bridging, the Jordan on March 22-23, at the ford of Ghoraniyeh, the starting-point of a high-road to es-Salṭ, and thence by Ṣuweiliḥ to 'Amman, and at the ford of Hijlah, from which tracks run through the foothills direct to the Plateau and 'Amman, our troops cleared the enemy out of the Ghor, east of the river. With difficulty because of the weather and the ground, but against little military opposition, one force took es-Salṭ on the 25th, and others, by the mountain-tracks direct on 'Amman, reached Na'ur and 'Ain es-Sir on the edge of the Plateau, till by the 28th a British line confronted, and partly surrounded, 'Amman behind its protecting gorges and fortifications. On the 30th they attacked but were repulsed, and the same night all British arms were withdrawn, even across Jordan, leaving only an outpost at Ghoraniyeh—"the Army's first failure since the second battle of Gaza a year before". Though not inferior in number to the foe, weather and ground had been too much for them. Through April Turkish attacks on the Jordan bridge-heads were repulsed, and on April 30 the British advanced once more upon Debari and other points in the foothills, and even got near es-Salṭ, but on May 4 had again to yield, and all troops were withdrawn west of Jordan save at the bridge-heads.[1]

To-day 'Ajlun is a Liwa of Transjordan, with headquarters at Irbid and subordinate centres at 'Ajlun and Jerash.

XXIX. *GREECE OVER JORDAN: THE DECAPOLIS*[2]

Greek immigration flowed into Palestine in the wake of Alexander the Great.[3] Numbers of his veterans settled in Northern and Eastern Syria, while the dynasties, founded by his generals at Antioch and in Egypt, welcomed the arrival of multitudes more of their race. The settlements of these immigrants assumed the Greek form of civic communities, democratic in constitution, and aiming at independence, but often subject to the great powers of the East, or to local tyrants.[4] On the coast the Greeks absorbed the Philistine and Phœnician cities; east of the Jordan they more frequently occupied positions not formerly historical.

[1] Falls, *Military Operations, Egypt and Palestine*, 1917-18, chs. xv-xvii.

[2] For this chapter, see Map on pages 56-7 and Map 2.

[3] But see Hölscher, *Pal. in Pers. u. Hellen. Zeit.* 68.

[4] See pp. 394-396.

The oldest Greek settlements in Eastern Palestine were Pella and Dion, which, as their Macedonian names suggest, were probably founded by Alexander's own soldiers.[1] Nearly as old were Philadelphia on the site of Rabbath-ammon, Gadara, and Abila, all of them important fortresses by 218 B.C.[2] Bozrah was a strong Greek centre in the time of the Maccabees.[3] Gerasa and Hippos are not mentioned till later.[4] Of none of these cities have inscriptions or coins been found of a date earlier than the arrival of the Romans.[5]

The freedom of the Greek cities of Palestine was taken from them by the Jewish princes; Pompey "restored them to their citizens",[6] and they date their civic eras from the year of his Syrian campaign, 64-63 B.C. The measure of their independence must have varied between the time of Pompey and that of Trajan. They had communal freedom, their own councils,[7] the rights of coinage, of asylum, of property and administration in the surrounding districts, and of association with each other for defensive and commercial purposes. But from the first they were "put under the Province of Syria".[8] Their administration of politics and law was subject to revision by the Governor, they were taxed for imperial purposes, their coins bore *the image of Cæsar*, they were liable to military service,[9] and while they appear to have had no Roman garrison,[10] Roman generals used them for the quartering of the legions.[11] The position at this time of the Greek cities in Syria must not be compared to that of Greek cities in Europe. In Europe and in Asia the

[1] The Macedonian Pella was the birthplace of Alexander, and a second Asiatic Pella was in North Syria. The suggestion of Tuch (*Quæstiones de Fl. Josephi libris historicis*, p. 18) that Pella is Greek for פחלא, equivalent to the modern Faḥil is not so improbable as Schürer supposes (*Hist.* ii. 1, 114), for it is difficult to understand how Faḥil could have risen from Pella. In the Talmud Paḥil or Paḥel. Dion was a town of Macedonia, and Stephanus Byzantinus attributes the Syrian Dion to Alexander himself.

[2] Polybius, v. 71, xvi. 39; Jos. xii *Antt.* iii. 3; Stark, *Gaza*, 381. [3] See p. 395.

[4] Gerasa, when taken by Jannæus; Hippos, when freed by Pompey.

[5] With the doubtful exception of a coin of Dion of 89-88 B.C., De Saulcy, 378 ff. The next earliest seems one of Gadara of 56 B.C. *Ibid.* 294.

[6] Jos. (xiv *Antt.* iv. 4; i *Wars*, vii. 7) mentions Gadara, Hippos, Pella, and Dion, as freed by Pompey, but Abila, Kanata, Kanatha, and Philadelphia also dated coins from 64-63 B.C., the Pompeian era. The era of Gerasa is uncertain, yet an inscription points to 62 B.C. (Crowfoot, in work cited below, p. 400, n. 1). Only some coins of Scythopolis date from Pompey. The coins of Gadara and Pella show that these towns assumed the name "Pompeian" (De Saulcy, 293, 398 f.).

[7] See p. 406.

[8] Josephus as in note 6. [9] Jos. ii *Wars*, xviii. 19.

[10] Save at request of the citizens, iv *Wars*, vii. 3 f.

[11] As Vespasian wintered Legions v and x in Scythopolis, iii *Wars*, ix. 1.

relations of Greece and Rome were very different. In Europe Rome was the conqueror, and might be regarded as the oppressor, of Greece; in Asia the Roman power was the indispensable ally and safeguard of the Greeks, and their interests could never be opposed. Therefore, even when the authority of the Empire over these cities was enforced by instances so extreme as the gift by Augustus of some of them to Herod,[1] the inhabitants at first made no resistance, and, indeed, in Herod they found an overlord of Hellenic sympathy.[2]

Confederacies of Greek cities were common under both the Republic and the Empire,[3] and formed for commerce and the cultivation of the Hellenic spirit against alien races. Their most famous Oriental instance was the Decapolis. The origin of this League is nowhere mentioned, but to those familiar with the history of the period its reason is obvious. Between 64 B.C., when Pompey constituted the Province of Syria, and A.D. 106, when Trajan succeeded in making the Roman government effective up to the desert, Eastern Palestine remained exposed and unsettled. The Romans left the government to their Semitic vassals, Zenodorus, Herod, and the Nabatæan princes,[4] but these made little of the work. Bands of Arab robbers scoured Eastern Palestine, and even in A.D. 40 the settlers in Hauran were driven underground.[5] It is this period of unsettlement, when the forces both of order and disorder were Semitic, which is covered by the history of the Decapolis. We may therefore venture to recognise in the latter a League of Greek cities against the Semitic influences east and west of Jordan, from which Rome had freed them, but could not yet give them full protection.[6] As at least two of the cities, Hippos and Gadara, were given by Augustus to Herod, it is possible that the League did not arise till after Herod's death in 4 B.C., when these cities regained their independence; but it is more probable that it had existed since the enfranchisement of many of the towns by Pompey, and the necessity even then for Greeks to support each other against the Semites. This does not imply that the population of the cities was exclusively Greek. Their commerce would bring to them, perhaps in considerable numbers, Arabs and Jews, in whose languages, as well as in

[1] E of Jordan, Hippos, Gadara; W, Gaza, Ashdod, Joppa, Straton's Tower were given to Herod in 30 B.C.; xv *Antt.* vii. 3; i *Wars*, xx. 3.

[2] Gadara alone appears to have difficulties with Herod, xv *Antt.* x. 2 f.

[3] For Greece, cf. Mommsen, *Prov. Rom. Empire*, Eng. i. 264 f.

[4] See especially Josephus, xv *Antt.* x. i.

[5] An inscription of that year describes the population as living in caves and underground cities, Waddington, 2329.

[6] The name Decapolis does not occur before Pliny, Josephus, and the Gospels of Matthew and Mark.

Greek, inscriptions have been found. The religion of the Decapolis, as we shall see, was, in contrast to that of other towns in Eastern Palestine, predominantly Hellenic; but the remains of a Jewish synagogue have been discovered in Gerasa,[1] the Nabatæan Du-Sara was worshipped in Edrei, and in several of the Decapolis Ashtoreth, though under the Hellenised form of Astarte.

The Decapolis, according to its name, consisted at first of ten cities. Look at the sites of these, trace the roads which connect them, and you recognise the military and commercial policy of their confederation.[2]

The Plain of Esdraelon gives passage from the coast to Jordan. At the inland end of this the Ten Cities begin, and scatter fanwise along the main routes of traffic across Jordan to the desert. Scythopolis was the only member of the League west of Jordan,[3] indispensable to her eastern fellows by her command of their communications with the sea and with the Greek cities of the coast.[4] From Scythopolis three roads cross Jordan and traverse Eastern Palestine. The other original members of the Decapolis lay either on these roads or on the road they ran to join—the line of commerce between Damascus and Arabia along the border of the desert. Immediately across Jordan and at the beginning of the three roads lay Pella, Gadara, Hippos. The positions of these are undisputed—Pella on the southern, Gadara on the central, Hippos on the northern or Damascus road.[5] They stood just above the Jordan Valley; they were not twenty-five miles apart, their territories touched, and thus together they commanded the edge of the eastern table-land. Across this we now follow the three roads, to which they held the entrance. The road from Pella struck south-east over the hills of Gilead, and may be traced both by the directions of Eusebius and by some monuments, to which we were able to add by the fortunate discovery of a milestone.[6] On this road lay three other members of the Decapolis—Dion, on

[1] J. W. Crowfoot, *Churches at Jerash* (Supplementary Papers, 3, of the *BSAJ*, 1931), a preliminary report of the Yale-British expeditions to Jerash, 1928-30, a most valuable contribution to the history and art of the Decapolis, with 13 plates and a plan.

[2] Ammianus Marcellinus (4th cent.); "Arabia . . . opima varietate commerciorum, castrisque oppleta validis et castellis . . . hæc quoque civitates habet inter oppida quædam ingentes, Bostram, Gerasam atque Filadelfiam, murorum firmitate cautissimas" (Bk. xiv. 8, 13).

[3] But Marquardt, *Röm. Staatsverwaltung*, i. 392 ff., makes a strong case for Samaria's inclusion. See my *Jerusalem*, ii. 374, 378, 388.

[4] On Scythopolis (Bethshan), see pp. 235 ff.

[5] Hippos had coins with horse, Pegasus, woman holding him: De Saulcy.

[6] This road, of which Eusebius tells us in the *Onomasticon*, artt. *Ἀρισώθ* and *'Ιαβεῖς Γαλάαδ*, was traced by Merrill past Miryamin, Kefr Abil, Maklub, and Wady Mahneh to 'Ain Jenneh (*East of Jordan*, 357; Le Strange, *Across Jordan*, 277). In Kefr Abil

an undiscovered site[1] near Pella, and Gerasa[2] (Jerash), and Philadelphia ('Amman), the farthest south. The central road, which travelled past Gadara, led towards Raphana, an original partner of the League, whose site is uncertain,[3] and, after passing some cities that joined the League later, reached Kanatha, the most easterly of the Decapolis at the foot of Jebel Ḥauran.[4]

---

we confirmed this by finding a Roman milestone, used as a pillar in the mosque, the inscription on which stands as on the left of these two columns, and may be restored as on the right. Others in *MuNDPV*, 1899, 90 f.

MP	Imperator Cæsar
I..IVS	M(arcus)Aurelius Ant
VSAVG	oninus Augustus
I A	[Parthicus Maximus?]
I II ET	Trib(unicia) Pot(estate)? Co(n)s(ul) II. et
	Imperator Cæsar
I VERVS	L(ucius) Aurelius Verus
IICOSIb	Trib(unicia) Pot(estate) II.? Co(n)s(ul) II.
IFILI	Divi Antonini Filii
POTES	Divi Hadriani Nepotes
PARTHICI	Divi Trajani Parthici Pro-
IVI	-nepotes Divi Nervæ Ab-
EPOTES	-nepotes

1 Dion must have lain a little SE of Pella. Ptolemy, v. 15, gives the longitude and latitude: Scythopolis, 67° 20′, 31° 55′; Pella, 67° 40′, 31° 40′; Dion 67° 30′, 31° 45′; Gerasa, 68° 15′, 31° 45′. The position in Mommsen's map is, therefore, wrong. Josephus mentions it with Gerasa (xiii *Antt.* xv. 3, for Essa read Gerasa) and with Pella (xiv *Antt.* iv. 4). It is not given by Polybius in the campaign of Antiochus, 218 B.C. (Pol. v. 70). Steph. Byzan. is ambiguous: *Δῖον . . . κτίσμα Ἀλεξάνδρου ἢ καὶ Πέλλα ἧς τὸ ὕδωρ νοσερόν; ἢ καὶ Πέλλα* is not certain, or it would prove the identity of Pella and Dion. It is singular that the *Excerpta ex Græca Notitia Patriarchatuum*, Reland, 215, should give, under Palestina Secunda, Pella in the plural, *Πέλλαι*, and no Dion, but another list, p. 217, has no Pella, and reckons Dion with Gerasa in Arabia. Eusebius, too has Pella in the plural, *Onomasticon*, art. *Αἰμάθ*. Reland quotes an epigram on the bad water mentioned by Steph. Byzan.: "Sweet is the water of Dion to drink, but drink it and thou losest thy thirst, and straightway thy life." De Saulcy says there is a well near Kefr Abil, called by the Arabs 'Ain el-Jarim, or "The Fatal Well". Merrill (*East of Jordan*, 298) suggests Eidun for Dion, but that is too much NE. Dion will probably be found about Ba'un or 'Ajlun. Further, Schumacher's *Pella* (*PEF*, 1888).

2 On Gerasa see *ZDPV*, xviii. 126; Schumacher, "Dscherasch", *ZDPV*, xxv. 100 ff.; cf. *MuNDPV*, 1898, 57 ff., 1900, 18; and Crowfoot, *op. cit.*

3 Raphana was probably the Raphōn of 1 Macc. v. 37-43 (see p. 395) and xii *Antt.* viii. 4, near Ashtaroth-karnaim, and on a wady—perhaps Nahr el-Awared, a tributary of the Yarmuk. Buhl suggests Tell esh-Shehab in a wady of that name where are remains of fortifications, and I found the stele of Sety I. He also suggests that Kapitolias was Raphon. Wetzstein had equated them.

4 Kanatha is the Kenath of the O.T. (Num. xxxii. 42; 1 Chron. ii. 23; see p. 388,

Some have hesitated to place one of the earliest Greek cities so far east, but many Greeks were in the neighbouring Bozrah even in the time of Judas Maccabæus[1]; Kanatha had always been a place of importance, and now, with Philadelphia and Gerasa, it represented the Decapolis on the margin of the desert, and on the route from Damascus to Arabia which ran along this. Damascus itself appears to have been an honorary member of the league. These, then—Scythopolis; Pella, Dion, Gerasa, and Philadelphia; Gadara, Raphana, and Kanatha; Hippos and Damascus—were the original ten, from which the Decapolis received its name.[2]

But to these others were added. Ptolemy gives eighteen names, leaving out Raphana and adding nine others, which it is interesting to note lay mostly towards Damascus, and away from the Decapolitan region proper in North Gilead.[3] The most important of the additions were three. Abila lay about twelve miles east of Gadara, on a branch of the Yarmuk.[4] Kanata is distinguished from Kanatha by the different spelling of its name on coins and inscriptions, as well as by the fact that an aqueduct which one inscription describes as running to Kanata started too low to carry water to Kanatha. From another inscription Wetzstein has placed Kanata at el-Kerak, in the Nuḳra, but the neighbouring el-Ḳuniyeh seems rather to echo the name.[5] Kapitolias, which from its Latin name appears to have been added to the

---

n. 3), now called Ḳanawat, but according to Wetzstein (*Reisebericht*, p. 78) by the Bedouin always Ḳanawa. But see Moore on Jud. viii. 11 and Socin, *Baedeker*² 313. We were turned back by the authorities on our visit to Ḳanawat and Bozrah. Full accounts of the ruins in Burckhardt, *Syria*, 83; Buckingham, *Travels among Arab Tribes*, 242 ff.; Porter, *Five Years in Damascus*, ch. xi; Merrill, *East of the Jordan*, 36-42. Inscriptions in Wadd. 2329-2363; Wetzstein, *Ausg. Inschr.* (see p. 15, n. 1), 188-193. For coins, De Saulcy (*Numis. de la T.S.* 400 f.). Porter gives an adequate argument for identifying Kanatha with Ḳanawat. In the Peutinger Tables it is 37 R. m. from Aena (Phæna), which is 24 from Damascus. *Κάνωθα* and *Κέναθα* were other forms.

[1] See p. 395.

[2] They form the earliest list, Pliny, *HN*, v. 16 (18). Damascus must have been unknown to Josephus as a member of the League, for he calls Scythopolis the greatest of the Decapolis.

[3] See next page.

[4] On a Palmyrene inscription (Reland, pp. 525 ff.), *Ἄβίλη τῆς Δεκαπόλεος* (distinct from Abila on the Abana NW of Damascus, after which Abilene, Luke iii. 1, was named). First discovered by Seetzen (*Reisen*, i. 371 f.), 1806, the site and ruins described by Schumacher, *Abila of the Decapolis*; cf. *Onomasticon*, art. 'Αβέλ; De Saulcy, *Numis. de la T.S.* 308-312.

[5] See Wadd. 2296 (about the aqueduct), 2329, 2412*a*-9. Wetzstein, *Ausgewählte Inschr.* 183-186. De Saulcy, *Numis. de la T.S.* 399 ff., plate xxiii, where on 8 is *KANATHNΩN*, a coin of Kanata, but on 10 *KANAΘ-NΩN*, a coin of Kanatha.

Decapolis after Trajan extended the Empire to the desert,[1] either was Beit-er-Ras, House of the Headland, a few knolls with remains of Greek carving near Irbid, or lay farther north.[2] Other towns of this wider Decapolis were such as Edrei, Bozrah, already in the Amarna Letters,[3] and some of their neighbours.

Each of these cities not only had its suburbs but commanded besides a large territory, with villages.[4] Round Hippos was Hippene,[5] round Gadara a country of the Gadarenes.[6] Gadara had a sea-board on the Lake of Galilee. Some of her coins bear a trireme. We did not, however, realise how far the property and influence of the Greek cities extended till we followed the aqueduct which brought water to Gadara from as far east as Edrei.[7] Such long works prove that the cities of the Decapolis possessed rights and authority at distances even greater than those separating them from each other. The Decapolitan region, as Pliny calls it,[8] *the borders of the Decapolis*, as styled in the Gospels,[9] was, therefore, no mere name, but a sphere of property and effective influence. The territories of Scythopolis, Pella, Gadara, and Hippos, which adjoined each other, alone represented a solid belt of country along the Jordan.[10] East and north-east from this ran the aqueduct of Gadara for more than thirty miles; all Gilead itself was at one time called the region of Gerasa.[11] If, then, we omit Damascus, we may determine the "region of the Decapolis" to have been most of the country south-east of the Lake of Galilee across Gilead to the desert, but Pliny's words that it was penetrated by the tetrarchies, forbid us to assume it as absolutely solid.[12]

From this investigation we turn to a description of these Greek cities, their sites, buildings, and the life which thronged them.

When the Greeks occupied new sites their choice was mainly determined

[1] It dated its era from 97 or 98, the accession of Trajan, De Saulcy, p. 305.

[2] Beit-Ras suits the position of Kapitolias in the Peutinger Tables; but not, as Schürer points out (*Hist.* II, i. p. 106, n. 205), the data of the Itinerarium Antonini, which require a site farther north. We found no inscriptions, but beautiful Greek carving at Beit-Ras, which lies on the road from Edrei to Gadara. Schumacher, *N. Ajlun*, 154 ff., says the name before the building of the present village was Kef er-Ras; cf. *ZDPV*, xx. 173; P. Thomsen, *id.* xxxiii, reports new discoveries.

[3] Flinders Petrie, *Hist. of Egypt*, ii. 303, 313.

[4] Jos. *Life*, 65.

[5] Jos. iii *Wars*, iii. 1.

[6] Mark v. 1, according to one reading.

[7] Schumacher (*ZDPV*, xx. 184) shows it probable that this aqueduct started from el-Chrebi W of Wady Shellale, on which no arches have been found, and that the Ḳanāṭir Fira'ūn by Edrei belonged to an aqueduct which, after achieving its main end in Edrei, went S into the Zumal hills.

[8] v. 15, "Decapolita regio".

[9] Mark vii. 31.

[10] Did it wholly cut off Peræa from Galilee?

[11] Jerome in the fourth century.

[12] Pliny, *HN*, v. 16. See above, p. 347.

by questions of commerce and defence. Thus Hippos has no water, but lies on an eminence just above the Lake of Galilee, where the road breaks north-east to Damascus. Thus Gadara[1] stood on a headland above the Jordan Valley—a broad, fresh stage for city life, which steep, deep slopes on three sides constituted a fortress. In spite of its feeble spring, this is so incomparable a site, that even if it was not historical before the Greeks—which is so unlikely that one is inclined to fix here Ramoth-gilead—the Greeks could not have neglected it. But the favourite Greek site was different: a mound or ridge by a shallow stream—one of the characteristic Peræan brooks, ten to twelve feet wide, and a foot deep, with a smaller mound, perhaps, on the other side, and meadow and arable land adjoining. These are the features common to Scythopolis, Pella, Gerasa,[2] Philadelphia, Abila, and Kanatha, most of which have besides a far and splendid view. The architectural features were also similar. There were the usual buildings of a Greek city of the Roman period, the colonnaded street, arch, forum, temple, theatre, bath, and mausoleum, in florid Doric and Corinthian, with the later Christian basilica among them, and perhaps a martyrion, or martyrs' monument. Approach any of these sites of the Decapolis, and this is the order in which you meet with their remains. Almost at the moment at which your eye catches a cluster of columns, or the edge of an amphitheatre against the sky, your horses' hoofs clatter upon pavement. You cannot ride any more. You must walk up this causeway, which the city laid out from its gates. You must feel the clean tight slabs of basalt, so well laid that most lie square still. You must draw your hand along ruts worn deep by the chariot wheels of fifteen, eighteen centuries ago. If the road runs between banks there will be tombs in the limestone, with basalt lintels, and a Roman name in Greek letters, perhaps a basalt or limestone sarcophagus flung out on the road by an Arab hunter for treasure. If it is a waterless site like Gadara you find an aqueduct running with the road, the pipes hewn of solid basalt, with a diameter like our drain-pipes, and fitting to each other with flanges. But if it be the more characteristic site by a stream, you come to one of those narrow parapetless Roman bridges which were the first to span the Syrian rivers, and had till recently so few successors. You reach the arch, or heap of ruins, that marks the old gateway. Within is an open space, probably the forum, and from this through the city you can trace the line of the long colonnaded street. Generally nothing remains but the bases of the columns, as *in the street called Straight* of Damascus, or as at Gadara; but at Philadelphia ten or twelve columns still stand to their full height, and

[1] Guthe on two Gadaras, *MuNDPV*, 1895, p. 5.

[2] For inscriptions in Gerasa see *MuNDPV*, 1895-1902.

in the street of Gerasa nearly two hundred. This last was lined by public and private buildings, with rich façades. At Gadara you see a by-street with plain vaulted buildings, probably stores or bazaars.

The best preserved buildings are the amphitheatres, the most beautiful are the temples.

Some cities of the Decapolis had each two amphitheatres. Those ample, solid basins, with their high tiers of benches for spectators, were either built above vaulted chambers used for the actors, the victims, and the wild beasts of the shows; or else, as at Philadelphia, Kanatha, and one of the Gadara theatres, they rested on the hollow side of a hill. They faced in all directions, north and west—the Philadelphian, the Gerasan two, and one of Gadara looked due north, but the second Gadarene west, and those of Kanatha and Scythopolis west or north-west. The largest was the Philadelphian, holding about seven thousand spectators; the rest varied from two to four thousand. Over against the benches, in some theatres, the post-scenium still rises, a high wall ornate with pillars, brackets, and niches. Several cities contained another place of Greek amusement. Where the stream, after passing through the town, issues from the wall, you also see, as at Gerasa, the banks of a Naumachia, with remains of tiers of benches behind them. For even on the borders of the desert the wave-born Greeks built their mimic seas, and fought their sham sea-fights. With all these public stages, most of the cities had their annual *Παγκράτια*, or games in which every kind of athletic exercise was exhibited.

Some of the temples were beautiful, as we may see from the ruins at Kanatha and Gerasa. Oblong in shape, their central hall was from fifty to seventy feet by thirty to fifty. They were peripteral, with a double row of columns in the front. They did not stand on the highest part of the town, but on platforms approached by stately steps. The religion of the Decapolis was predominantly Greek. In other towns of Eastern Palestine we find the shrines of many of the Nabatæan gods, either with their own names, or thinly disguised under those of their Greek counterparts. But in the Decapolis the gods of Hellas were supreme. Almost alone of Semitic deities was Astarte worshipped, the tower-crowned Astarte, but she was practically Hellenic. Each city worshipped her, but had in addition its own *Τύχη* or Civic Fortune, sometimes unnamed. In Scythopolis the people were chiefly devoted to Dionysus[1] and Astarte, in Pella to Pallas, in Gadara to Zeus, "the most high Zeus", Pallas, Herakles and Astarte, in Kapitolias to Astarte and Zeus, in Abila to Herakles and Astarte, in Kanatha to Zeus and Pallas, in Gerasa to Artemis—"Artemis of the Gerasenes", like "Diana of the

[1] See p. 239.

Ephesians"—in Philadelphia to Pallas, but especially to Herakles, "the Good Fortune of the Philadelphians".[1]

Like the rest of Palestine the cities of the Decapolis yielded to the progress and triumph of the Cross, and for the next centuries, sometimes on the lower courses of the Pagan temples or with even fuller use of their architecture, numerous churches, basilicas, and cathedrals arose, whose ruins impress the traveller still with their size and richness; for example at Bozrah, but especially at Gerasa, now Jerash, where extensive discoveries have been made by the co-operation of British and American archæologists. Jewish synagogues have also been traced in the Decapolis, the remains of one in Gerasa showing fine architecture and beautiful mosaics, but about A.D. 530 it was converted into a Christian church. By the eighth century nearly all the Christian buildings fell into ruin, perhaps less through the iconoclasm of Islam than by the numerous earthquakes with which Eastern Palestine has been afflicted.[2]

You also find the ruins of the Ten Cities strewn with relics of their political constitution. The ambiguous character of their freedom—municipal independence[3] subject to the revision and patronage of the imperial authorities—could not be better illustrated than by two fragments which I turned up in a street in Gerasa. One was the half of a tombstone of a member of the City Council with his title still legible—

ΒΟΥΛΕΥΤΗΣ

The other was two feet of basalt with enormous letters, from an inscription of honour to an emperor—

αυ ΤΟΚΡΑΤ *ωρ*

Fragments like these may be found in almost every ruin of the Decapolis, and bear as decisive testimony as any political treatise to the double character of the Decapolitan constitution. Tombs of Bouleutai are found everywhere.[4] I append one we routed out of the modern cemetery at Edrei, where it did duty, upside down, as the headstone of a sheikh recently deceased. It dates from "the fourth year of the Cæsars Marcus and Lucius" (Marcus Aurelius

[1] See the coins of these cities in De Saulcy, *Numis. de la T.S.* Edrei alone of the Decapolis has a Semitic deity, Du-Sara, on whom see next chapter: De Saulcy, p. 375.

[2] On the churches and synagogue of Jerash, their history and art, see Crowfoot, *op. cit.*

[3] See above, p. 398.

[4] Josephus gives the βουλή of Tiberias at 600 members, ii *Wars*, xxi. 9; and that of Gaza at 500, xiii *Antt.* xiii. 3. Those of Scythopolis, Gadara, and Gerasa, can hardly have been less.

and Lucius Verus), A.D. 165.[1] The Decapolis never forgot Pompey; Gadara and Pella call themselves Pompeian. Nearly all the emperors appear on their coins. Gadara has a full list from Augustus and Tiberius onward, but it was with the Antonines, 130-180, that the Ten Cities were most flourishing. The Antonines made the roads, and under them Gerasa put on her splendour.

On some ruins of the Decapolis there are still visible carven epigrams, reflections on death, and longer pieces of Greek verse. These faintly witness to the literary activity of the Ten Cities at the beginning of our era. We have seen what famous centres of Hellenism were the coast cities in those days. But the Decapolis had also its personages in Greek literature. Gadara produced Philodemus the Epicuræan, a contemporary of Cicero, Meleager the epigrammatist, Menippus the satirist, Theodorus the rhetorician, the tutor of Tiberius,[2] and others.[3] Gerasa also was a mother of great teachers.[4]

We may now touch again a subject we touched before—the influence of this Greek life on Galilee, and the beginnings of Christianity. The Decapolis flourished in the time of Christ's ministry. Gadara, with her temples and amphitheatres, her art, games, and literature, overhung the Lake of Galilee, and the voyages of its fishermen. A leading Epicuræan of the previous generation, the founder of the Greek anthology, some famous wits of the day, the reigning emperor's tutor had been bred within sight of the homes of the writers of the New Testament. Philodemus, Meleager, Menippus, Theodorus were names of which one end of the Lake of Galilee was proud, when Matthew, Peter, James, and John were working at the other end. The temples of Zeus, Pallas, and Astarte crowned a height opposite to that which gave its name to the Sermon on the Mount. Bacchus, under his Greek name, ruled the territory down the Jordan Valley to Scythopolis. Another temple to Zeus stood on the other side of Galilee, at Ptolemais, almost in sight of Nazareth. We cannot believe that the two worlds, which this landscape embraced, did not break into each other. The roads which crossed Galilee from the Decapolis to the coast, the inscriptions upon them, the constant

[1] Copied at Edrei, June 21, 1891, from a small slab of basalt:—

ΓΑΙΟCΛΟVΚΙΟC
ΒΑCCΟCΒΟVΛΕV
τΗCΕΠΟΗCΕΝο
ΕΚΤωΝΙΔΙωΝΤΟ
ΜΝΗΜΑΕΤΔΚΑΙCΑΡ
ΝΜΑΡΚΟΥΚΑΙΛοΥΚΙΟV.

[2] Strabo, xvi. ii. 29; cf. Schürer, *Hist.* II, i. 29.

[3] Reland, p. 775; Schürer, p. 104.

[4] Stephanus Byzantinus, under *Γέρασα*, mentions three, Ariston, Kerykos and Plato. Cf. Schürer, *op. cit.* pp. 29, 121.

trade between the fishermen and the Greek exporters of their fish, the very coins—everywhere thrust Greek upon the Jews of Galilee. The Aramaic dialect had begun to fill with Greek words. It is hard to believe that our Lord and His disciples did not know Greek. But, at least, in that characteristic Greek city overhanging the Lake of Galilee, in the scholars it sent to Greece and Rome, we have proof that the Kingdom of God came forth in no obscure corner, but in face of the kingdoms of this world.

XXX. *HAURAN AND ITS CITIES*[1]

We pass from the Decapolis to other cities of Eastern Palestine, very different in origin and character.

In the Decapolis the life was Greek. Rome gave the shelter, and the authority of the Empire was supreme, but the arts, letters, manners, and religion were of Greece. On those noble stages of life the seeds of Hellenism had been planted for three hundred years; as soon as Pompey fenced them, there sprang up the characteristic forms of Greek civilisation. With the cities of Hauran and the Trachon it was different. Their civilisation mostly dates from a century later than that of the Decapolis, and was not pure Greek, but a mixture of Greek and Semitic, still cast, however, in the moulds of the Empire. In the Decapolis Rome sheltered Greeks; in those other cities she disciplined half-Greek Syrians and wild Arabs.

To understand this we must survey Hauran and the story of its slow civilisation first by Roman vassals and then by the emperors themselves.

Ḥaurān, or "Hollow",[2] is the name given to the great plain which stretches south from Hermon, between Jaulan and the Leja, and thence, between the mountains of Gilead and the Jebel Ḥauran, runs out upon the Desert. In a wider application the name covers also the Leja and all fertile ground to the east.

To this great Plain you rise from Pharpar[3] and the lands of Damascus by a series of terraces, each three to four miles broad. When you have shaken off some hills to the east you are out upon Hauran proper, 2000 feet high, and the ground stretching level to the horizon. Hermon shuts off a quarter of heaven in the north-west, but round the rest of the circle you feel the openness, the light, the equal sweep of prairie air. Is it night—over the free distance the bells of the camel-caravans reach your ears an hour before the camels pass. Is it morning—the mists as they lift have nothing higher than

[1] For this chapter, see Map on pages 56-7. [2] See p. 356.
[3] The present Nahr el 'Awaj is probably Pharpar.

a tower to tear themselves from, and the Hajj road unrolls to the horizon. Is it noon—the heat does not swelter above the shadeless soil, but the wind sweeps fresh as at sea, with the swing of fifty open miles upon it. The surface of the plain is broken only by a mound or two, a few shallow watercourses, some short outcrops of basalt, and villages of the same stone, the level black line of their roofs cut by a tower or the jagged gable of an old temple. All else is a rolling prairie of rich red soil, under wheat, or lying for the year fallow in pasture. It is a land of harvests, and if you traverse it in summer it fills you with the wonder of its wealth. Through the early day the camels, piled high with sheaves, five or seven swaying corn-stacks on a string, draw in from the fields to the threshing-floors. These lie along the village walls, each some fifty square yards of the plain, trodden hard and fenced by a low, dry dyke. The sheaves are strewn to the depth of two or three feet, and the threshing-sledges, curved slabs of wood, studded with basalt teeth, are dragged up and down by horses, driven by boys who stand on the sledges and sing as they plunge over the billows of straw. Poor men have their smaller crops trodden out by donkeys driven in a narrow circle three abreast, exactly in the fashion depicted on the old Egyptian monuments. When the whole mass is cut and bruised enough, it is tossed with forks against the afternoon wind, the chopped straw is stored for fodder in some vault that has kept the rain out since the days of Agrippa or the Antonines; but the winnowed grain is packed in bags and carried on camels to the markets of Damascus and Acre. The long lines of these "grain-boats" sail down the summer roads; one evening at Ghabaghib, our first station out of Damascus, we counted 187 pass our tent, and at the Bridge-of-the-Daughters-of-Jacob, *over Jordan the Way of the Sea*, the train of them has been known not to break all night through. Hauran wheat is famous round the Levant. The failure of the camel carriage to export an average crop—some years part has to be left to rot unreaped—reconciles one to the invasion of Hauran by the Haifa-Damascus railway.

The fertility of this Plain is not more striking than its want of trees. Except the groves lately planted round the governor's seat at El-Merkez, we saw practically no trees in Hauran.[1] The people, therefore, used marvellously little timber. The threshing-sledges, the yokes and ploughs, the long axles on which the giant millstones were trundled from the Leja[2] to

[1] Though on the Jebel Ḥauran there are many oaks.

[2] In the 1st ed. I spelt Lejjah as if from Ar. *lujj*, "mass of water", "great depth of sea", and by comparison "rough place on a mountain" (Kamus), see page 411. Conder gives lejja as N Syrian for "basalt" (*Crit. Rev.* iv. 289). But the pronunciation seems to be with one *j*—Lejah, accent on the last syllable. So Burckhardt, Ledjah; Wetzstein, Lega; Burton and Merrill, Lejah; Fischer and Guthe, el-Ledschah; and

Damascus, in every village a few doors, stools, and boxes—that was all. The rafters, the ceilings, most of the doors, the lattices and window-bars were of stone. The originality to which this want of wood stimulated in the ancient architects of Hauran will be noticed farther on, but here we may linger for a little on the singular appearance which the unrelieved use of the sombre basalt gave to towns built fifteen hundred years ago, and in many cases still standing as the builder left them. One remembers the weirdness of wandering as a child through the Black Cities of the *Arabian Nights*; one felt this weirdness again in the cities of Hauran. Under the strong sun, the basalt takes a sullen sheen like polished ebony; the low and level architecture is unrelieved even by threads of mortar, for the blocks were cut so fine, and lie so heavy on each other, that no cement was needed; there was, besides, an absence of trees, bush, ivy and all green. This weirdness was naturally greatest where the cities, emptied of their inhabitants more than a thousand years ago, still stood tenantless. An awful silence filled the sable ruins; there was never a face, nor a flower, nor the flutter of a robe in the bare, black streets. But the fascination was shared even by the towns into which this generation had crept back, and patched their ruins with bricks of the last winter's mud. In these, I have seen the yellow sheaves piled high against the black walls, and the dust of the threshing-floors rising thick in the sunbeams, but the sunshine showed so pallid and ineffectual above the sullen stone, that what I looked on seemed to be, not the flesh and blood and labour of to-day, but the phantasm of some ancient summer afternoon flung magically back upon its desolate and irresponsive stage. From such dreams one was wakened by the fresh Hauran wind, the breath and quickening of the Plain.

This rich and healthy Plain is dominated by Hermon. On Hauran you are never out of sight of Hermon. Eighty miles away he is still visible, and even on the slopes of Jebel Ḥauran the amphitheatres were so arranged that over the stage the spectators might have a view of the great hill. It is a singular companionship of a noble mountain and a noble plain.

"There is right at the west end of Itaille,
Down at the root of Vesulus the cold,
A lusty plain abundant of vitaille,
Where many a tower and town thou mayest behold
That founded were in time of fathers old,

Ewing (in a letter to me), el-Lejá. This may be the same as Ar. laja', "refuge" or "asylum" (Kam.). And the N Syrian noun for "basalt" would be derived from the region from which N Syria chiefly procures basalt mill-stones. See p. 410.

And many another delectable sight;
And Saluces this noble country hight."

On the east the Plain is framed by a long low line of blue. As you approach, the blue darkens, and stands out an irregular bank of shiny black rock, from thirty to forty feet high, split by narrow crevasses as the edge of a mud-heap is split on a frosty day. Climb it and you stand on the margin of a vast mass of congealed lava, three hundred and fifty square miles in extent, which flowed out upon the Plain from some of the now extinct craters in the centre of it, and cooling, broke up into innumerable cracks and fissures. Sometimes it looks like an ebony glacier with irregular crevasses. Elsewhere it "has the appearance of the sea, when in motion beneath a dark, cloudy sky, and when the waves are of good size, but without any white crests of foam".[1] Here and there the eddies of liquid lava have been caught in the very swirl of them; or, as it broke in large bubbles and curved over in sluggish waves, the viscous mass has been fixed for ever to the forms of sharp-edged hollows and caverns. This "petrified ocean" is without neither soil nor fresh water. Springs abound, there are a few small lakes, and many fields. The ruins of villages are numerous, and a number of the crevasses have been widened to admit the passage of roads.

This Leja, this Trachon, not high but wild and intricate, almost bridges the plain between Hermon and Jebel Ḥauran, and has at most periods enabled the inhabitants of these two ranges to combine and tyrannise over the populations of Hauran proper and Damascus.

In the beginning of the first century before Christ Hermon was held by the half-settled Ituræans; Western Hauran was under the Jew, Alexander Jannæus, while the Nabatæans occupied everything else to the east, including Damascus, the rest of Hauran, and the Leja.[2] When the Romans came in 64 B.C.,[3] besides freeing the Greek cities of Gaulanitis and Gilead from the Jews, they drove the Nabatæans to the southern edge of Hauran, where their northernmost cities continued to be Bozrah and Salkhat.[4] But the Romans did not then occupy Hauran itself.[5] For the next forty years the reports are

[1] Merrill, *East of Jordan*, p. 11.

[2] See end of last chapter.

[3] Pompey sent Scaurus with the first legions to Damascus in 65 B.C. and himself followed in 64; when he went to Europe next year he left Scaurus behind, who subdued the Nabatæans.

[4] There is a Nabatæan inscription in Bozrah of the eleventh year of Malchus II (not Malchus I, as Schürer, *Hist.* div. I, vol. ii. 335, for there was an earlier Malchus, known from a coin, whom Schürer omits from his lists), *i.e.* about 40 B.C., *CIS*, II, i. No. 174. Schürer (*Theol. Lit. Zeitung*, March 2, 1895) holds this doubtful.

[5] There was a Roman governor in Damascus at least from 44 to 42 B.C. (xiv *Antt.* xi. 7, xii. 1; i *Wars*, xii. 1, 2). About 36 Mark Antony gave Cleopatra "Cœle-Syria"

meagre. In 25, Trachonitis and Hauran were under the nominal rule of one Zenodorus, who had also leased part of the Ituræan domains on the slopes of Hermon.[1] He did not protect the peaceful inhabitants from the robbers of the Leja, and they appealed to Varro, Governor of Syria. Augustus ordered Varro to replace Zenodorus by Herod, who had already conducted war in this region, and to whom Gadara and Hippos,[2] on its western borders, for the time belonged.[3] Herod had difficulty with the Arab robbers of the Leja,[4] and their allies the Nabatæans.[5] It was only after he had put a garrison of 3000 Idumæans in Trachonitis, and called a Jew named Zamaris from Babylonia, and built for him in Batanæa fortresses and a village called Bathyra,[6] that he was successful. Zamaris kept down the robbers of the Leja,[7] "protected Jews coming up on pilgrimage from Babylon", and, when Herod declared freedom from taxes, "the land became full of people".[8] A few public buildings were erected. A temple near Kanatha was built, in the bulk of it, by Herod,[9] and the ruins contain an inscription recording the erection of a statue to him. This is the earliest Greek inscription discovered

---

(see p. 346) and parts of the Judæan and Arab territories (Jos. xv *Antt.* iii. 8, iv. 1, 2; i *Wars*, xviii. 5).

[1] xv *Antt.* x. 1; i *Wars*, xx. 4. That Zenodorus was ruler of Trachonitis is expressly said; that he also ruled Auranitis is obvious from his attempt to sell it to the Nabatæans (xv *Antt.* x. 2).

[2] In 32 B.C. Herod had been defeated by Nabatæans at Kanatha (i *Wars*, xix. 2; at Kana, xv *Antt.* v. 1), but had afterwards subdued them.

[3] Since 30 B.C.: xv *Antt.* vii. 3; i *Wars*, xx. 3.

[4] Varro himself had previously punished them, i *Wars*, xx. 4.

[5] First he routed the Trachonites, "procuring peace and quietness for the neighbouring peoples" (xv *Antt.* x. 1; i *Wars*, xx. 4). But they, "obliged to live quietly, which they did not like, and when they took pains with the ground it bare but little", took advantage of his absence in Rome to revolt (xvi *Antt.* ix. 1). His troops subdued them, forty of their chiefs escaping to Nabatæa. On his return he slew some who remained in Trachon, whereupon the forty fugitives had a blood-feud against him, and, in alliance with the Nabatæans, harassed his borders. Herod put a garrison of 3000 Idumæans into Trachonitis. But, in taking the punishment of the Nabatæans into his own hands, he displeased Augustus. The Nabatæans, on this, "refused to pay for their pastures", *i.e.* overran Hauran, as usual every year, with their own flocks. Then he called Zamaris as above (xvii *Antt.* ii. 1-3).

[6] xvii *Antt.* ii. 1, 2. Does the name Bathyra survive in Buṣr (el-Ḥariri) on the south margin of the Leja?

[7] It is not asserted that he conquered the Leja itself.

[8] xvii *Antt.* ii. 1, 2.

[9] At Seia, now Sei‘, half an hour from Kanawat, De Vogüé, *Syrie Centrale: Archit, Civile et Religieuse*, i, pl. 1. It had been Nabatæan. The inscription in Wadd. 2364 the erector Obaisatos.

in these regions.[1] Herod was evidently the pioneer of civilisation in Hauran.

At Herod's death in 4 B.C., Philip, his son, received for a tetrarchy Gaulanitis, Batanæa, Trachonitis, Auranitis, and a "certain part of the domain of Zenodorus", or all the country from Hermon to the Yarmuk.[2] He was greatly helped by Jakim, son of Zamaris, who supplied him with cavalry.[3] His just and gentle reign has no annals; the only account of his kingdom is that of Strabo, who, writing of the Trachons about A.D. 25, when Christ was beginning to preach in Galilee, says "the barbarians used to rob the merchants most generally on the side of Arabia Felix, but this happens less frequently since the destruction of robber bands under Zenodorus, by the good government of the Romans, and as a result of the security afforded by the soldiers stationed in Syria".[4] Thus though Arab raids still happened, they were less frequent. In the records of Christ's ministry we hear no rumour of Arabs, but we see bits of the bulwark which, Strabo says, was keeping them away—the Centurion, the Legion, the superscription of Cæsar. Something of the difficulties of communication, and the insecurity which prevailed in spite of the Romans, may be felt in such parables as that of the binding of the strong man and spoiling of his goods, or that of the husbandmen who slew their master's heir.

At Philip's death in 34 his tetrarchy was taken back into the Province of Syria, but allowed to administer its own revenues.[5] In 37 Caligula bestowed it upon Herod Agrippa,[6] who afterwards received the rest of his grandfather's domains. Agrippa's territory extended as far east as the farther slopes of the Jebel Ḥauran, where an inscription of his has been discovered.[7] But the Nabatæans, under King Aretas, still held Bozrah and Salkhat, and for the time Damascus had been yielded to them by the Romans. Paul tells us that when he came back to Damascus from Arabia, three years after his conversion, *an ethnarch under Aretas the king*[8] *held the city of the Damascenes*[9]; and while we have imperial coins of Damascus under Augustus and Tiberius down to A.D. 33, we have none under Caligula or Claudius, or till the ninth year of Nero in 63. How Damascus had come from the Romans into the hands of Aretas we do not know[10]; and we are equally ignorant of the reasons that led

[1] The date of another monument and inscription at Suweida (Soada) of Odairatos, the son of Annelus, is uncertain. It belongs to the first century either before or after Christ. Wadd. 2320; De Vogüé, as above, pl. 1.

[2] See pp. 346 ff. [3] xvii *Antt.* ii. 1-2. [4] Strabo, xvi. ii. 20. [5] xviii *Antt.* iv. 6.

[6] xviii *Antt.* vi. 6-10; ii *Wars*, ix. 5. [7] At el-Mushennef, Wadd. 2211.

[8] Aretas iv, 9 B.C. A.D. 40. [9] 2 Cor. xi. 32, cf. Acts ix. 23 ff.

[10] Some think he took it by war on the withdrawal of the troops of Vitellius, at the death of Tiberius (xviii *Antt.* v. 3). So Neander, *Planting, etc., of the Christian Church,*

the Nabatæan ethnarch to take the side of the Damascus Jews, and seek, on their request, to arrest Paul.[1] Three years earlier the synagogues of Damascus had presumably sufficient independence and authority to give up to Paul and his commission from the high priest such Jews as had gone over to Christianity. On that occasion Paul's journey to Damascus from Jerusalem took him across some part of Hauran. The Arabia into which he went after his conversion was not Hauran, as some imagine,[2] but either the lonely Ḥarras to the east of the Leja or Nabatæa proper,—Bozrah, Salkhat, Petra, and farther south, perhaps, to Sinai.[3] Agrippa found Hauran not yet perfectly civilised. In a proclamation of date A.D. 41 he appears to exhort the inhabitants to leave off their beast-like manner of life in caves, and build themselves houses.[4] This proclamation breathes the confidence of ability to protect the Hauranites, and has even been called "the point of departure for the architectural history of the country".[5] Certain it is that whereas from before this date we possess only two Greek inscriptions[6] from Hauran among many in the Nabatæan language, Greek inscriptions now rapidly multiply, and we have numerous records in stone of the building of public edifices.

Agrippa died in 44, in the fashion described in the Book of Acts,[7] and as his son Agrippa was just seventeen, the Romans resumed the administration

---

Eng. iii. 2; Porter, *Five Years in Damascus*, i. 103. But that Romans should let Damascus go by war seems incredible; so Conybeare and Howson, *Life and Epistles of St. Paul*, and Schürer favour the theory that Caligula gave Damascus to Aretas (*Hist.* I, ii. 357 f.). Perhaps when Herod Agrippa got Philip's tetrarchy, it was felt by Caligula that the foe of the Herodian house should also get territory. Aretas had defeated his sworn foe Herod Antipas a few years before (xviii *Antt.* v. 3).

[1] The Jews of Damascus were numerous and powerful (ii *Wars*, xx. 2; vii *Wars*, viii. 7), but perhaps there had been under Caligula's rearrangement of Syria a new agreement of Aretas with Agrippa and the Jews.

[2] *E.g.* Woldemar Schmidt, in Herzog's *Real-Encyclopädie* (ed. 2) xi. 364.

[3] Gal. i. 16, 17, cf. *On Mount Sinai*, iv. 25. Whether Paul preached in Arabia is very doubtful. It does not necessarily follow, as Porter thinks, from a comparison of ver. 16 with ver. 17 in Gal. i.

[4] Wadd. 2392*a*, an inscription in Kanatha. But the inscription is fragmentary, and the interpretation doubtful. The proclamation cannot have been meant for Kanatha, a free city, with coins since Pompey's time.

[5] De Vogüé, *Architecture Civile et Religieuse de la Syrie Centrale*.

[6] One about the statue to Herod, see p. 412; another on a monument at Suweida, ancient Soada, S of Kanawat, also in Nabatæan. Wadd. 2320; De Vogüé, *op. cit.* pl. 1; *CIS*, Pars II, tom. i. No. 162, where it is ascribed because of the form of the Nabatæan letters, to 1st cent. B.C.

[7] xii. 20 ff., cf. Josephus, xix *Antt.* viii. 2; ii *Wars*, xi. 6.

of all Palestine by a Procurator under the Governor of Syria.[1] The only inscription from this period is in Nabatæan, at Ḥebran south of Kanatha, of the seventh year of Claudius Cæsar.[2] From this we learn that the boundary between the Roman province (or kingdom of Agrippa) and the Nabatæan kingdom ran south of Ḥebran, but north of Bozrah and Salkhat for these were cities of the Nabatæan kings.[3]

In 50, Agrippa II received from Claudius the kingdom of Chalcis in the Lebanon,[4] and in 53 the old tetrarchies of Philip and Lysanias,[5] so that once more Hauran came under a Jewish prince. He was the worst of his line. This enthusiast for Nero, this trifler with Paul, this pander to his sister's shame, this purveyor of Roman rejoicings at his people's overthrow, this royal camp-follower, this ape whom Titus led about, caused himself to be styled in his Hauran inscriptions the Great King, Lover of Cæsar, Pious, Lover of Rome.[6] He called his first capital after Nero,[7] through sore humiliation he held to all the Flavian emperors, and it is perhaps a sign of the same subserviency that the only inscription which has been discovered recognising the three months' reign of Otho is one upon Agrippa's domains in Hauran.[8] There are still extant several buildings from the second Agrippa's reign, and numerous inscriptions: the latest portions of the temple at Sei',[9] a temple at

[1] xix *Antt.* ix. 1, 2; ii *Wars*, xi. 6.

[2] שנת שבע לקלדיסקיסר; in *CIS*, Pars II, tom. i. No. 170. It records the erection of a portal by Maliku, a priest of the goddess Allât.

[3] For Bozrah see above, p. 411. In Salkhat are two inscriptions: one of the 17th year of Malchus III (not Malchus II, Schürer, see p. 411, n. 4), about A.D. 65; the other of the 25th year of Rab'el, A.D. 95 or 96.

[4] The kingdom of his uncle Herod; xx *Antt.* v. 2; ii *Wars*, xii. 1.

[5] The latter included Abila and the Lebanon domains of Varus, which stretched far north (xx *Antt.* vii. 1, a curious order; ii *Wars*, xii. 8); parts of Galilee and Peræa were added (xx. *Antt.* viii. 4; ii *Wars*, xiii. 2).

[6] *βασιλεὺς μέγας, φιλοκαίσαρ, εὐσεβὴς καὶ φιλορώμαιος*; at Si'a, Wadd. 2365.

[7] See p. 305.

[8] Found by us on the top of a straw-store at Ṭuffas, two hours NW of el-Muzeirib, on 19th June 1891 (*Critical Review*, ii. 59). On the death of Nero in 68, Agrippa II, and Titus, the latter sent by Vespasian, set out from Syria to Rome to salute Galba, but heard on the way of his death. Agrippa went on to salute Otho, but Titus returned to his father with the news, and Vespasian's legions, then east of the Lake of Galilee, within a few hours of Ṭuffas, took the oath to Otho. Here is the inscription in curious oblong letters; the *Ω* shaped like the Hebrew letter shin:

L ΔΡΥΠΕΡΤΗƐΑΥΤΟΚΡΑΙ....
CΤΟΥΜΑΡΚΟΥΟΘΩΝΟƐƐΩΤΗΙ ....
ΛΟΦ ΙΗƐΔΙΟΓΕΝΟΥƐΠΑΤΗΡΠ..
ƐΤΟ ΝƐΥΝ ΑΙƐΔΥƐΙΨΑΛΙƐΙΟΙΚ..
ΓΚ ΕΙΑƐΧΑΡΙΝΤ . .

[9] See p. 412, n. 9.

eṣ-Ṣunamein, on the Hajj road south of Damascus, inscriptions there and elsewhere.[1] Agrippa died in 100, and his territories seem again to have fallen within the Province of Syria.

During this period the Nabatæans continued to surround Agrippa's territories on the south, where they still occupied Bozrah and Salkhat[2]; and on the east, where they held a post as far north as Admedera,[3] the first station between Damascus and Palmyra—Damascus had been taken back from them by the Romans under Nero[4]—but in 106 A.D., Trajan, by Cornelius Palma, Governor of Syria, brought the whole Nabatæan kingdom into the Empire, and created from it the new Province of Arabia with Bozrah as the Capital.[5]

This was the most decisive step in the history of Hauran. The fertile plain was no longer the ragged edge of civilisation, but an inner province of the Empire. Between the wilderness and herself there was organised another Roman province, and the Roman frontier. Therefore with A.D. 106 the often checked civilisation of Hauran may be said to have got fairly under way. The Romans immediately instituted public works. The aqueduct already mentioned from el-Afine to Kanata was built by Cornelius Palma,[6] and other aqueducts and reservoirs are to be assigned to about the same date.

[1] We found the slab with the inscription at eṣ-Ṣunamein, serving as the end of the sheikh's dust-box. I reproduced it in the *Critical Review*, ii. (1892), p. 56; it was previously given in *ZDPV*, vii. (1884), 121 f. It records the dedication of a portal, with little victories, images, and lions, to "Zeus the Lord". The double date, "the 37th year, which is also the 32nd of King Agrippa", I explained by the difference between Agrippa's right to succeed his father in A.D. 44-45 and actual accession to a kingdom in 49-50. Schürer (*Hist.* div. 1, vol. ii. 194 f.) refers the smaller number to an era of Agrippa II beginning in 61, and the greater to a supposed era beginning five years earlier in 56. For this latter there is no evidence. De Saulcy is right in interpreting the former as an era, not of Agrippa but of Cæsarea-Philippi. I hold to the interpretation I gave.

[2] Two Nabatæan inscriptions at Salkhat: one of the 17th year of Malchus III (not Malchus II) about A.D. 65; one of the 25th year of Rab'el, A.D. 95 or 96; a third of uncertain date; *CIS*, Pars II, tom. i. Nos. 182-184. The name Nabatæan survived for some years the fall of the kingdom: "Annalus the Nabatæan" on an inscription of 140, Wadd. 2437, Ewing, 94.

[3] The present Ḍmer or Maḳṣurah, *CIS*, Pars II, tom. i. No. 161. This inscription also belongs to the reign of Rab'el, 71-106 A.D.: cf. Wadd. 2562 g.

[4] A.D. 53-68.

[5] Dio Cassius, lxviii. 14: *Πάλμας τῆς Συρίας ἄρχων τὴν Ἀραβίαν τὴν πρὸς τῇ Πέτρᾳ ἐχειρώσατο, καὶ Ῥωμαίων ὑπήκοον ἐποιήσατο.* Cf. Reland; Mommsen, *Prov. of the Roman Empire*, II; A. G. Wright, *PEFQ*, 1895, with boundaries, list of places, etc.; Robinson Lees, *Geogr. Journal*, 1895, v. 19; in Umm el-Jemal 16 m. SSW of Bozrah, a Roman frontier inscription, Wadd. 2057*a*, *b*, *MuNDPV*, 1896, 49 f.

[6] Wadd. 2296-97; cf. 2301, 2308.

During the second and third centuries, basilicas, temples, theatres,[1] multiplied in the old cities: but a still more evident sign of prosperity was the rise of many villages to the rank of cities. Those ruins, so numerous that as you travel across Hauran you are never out of sight of some of them, so strongly built of basalt that from many it seems as though their inhabitants had fled but yesterday—those are the shells of the Roman peace. In some primeval tranquillity of man, "giant cities of Bashan" may have risen, as is alleged,[2] on this margin of the desert; but if so, these are not their ruins. With the exception of a stray inscription to a Hebrew Herod or Agrippa, to a Nabatæan Malchus or Rab'el, themselves but Roman vassals, there is in Hauran no written record of a life earlier than the beginning of the Empire by Trajan. Thereafter inscriptions abound. The letters are Greek, the religion of which they speak may be Syrian, but the civil power they acknowledge is Rome. The Legions have left their stamp everywhere. In Bashan there is scarcely a single ruin but bears upon it the name of at least one of the Emperors. As in Decapolis, so in Hauran, you stumble on bits of basalt with some of the syllables of Autokrator upon them: the letters are Greek, but they only translate Imperator. The gods of the temples bear Semitic names, or have received their Greek equivalents, Zeus, Herakles, Athene, Tyché, and so forth, but it is a Valens, a Caius, a Publius, a Lucilius, an Ulpius, who are inscribed as benefactors of the temples. It is Flavii, Bassi, and Cornelii who are buried around them. Where two generations are named the name of the father is nearly always Semitic, that of the son is frequently Latin, and never Greek—a curious proof of the Latinising of the natives. "Farewell, O Rufus, son of Ath! veteran, aged 65"[3]; "of Valens, son of Azis"[4]; "Bassos, son of Zabd"[5]; "Hadrian, son of Malekh."[6] Seldom is this reversed, but we found a tombstone, near Sheikh Miskin on the Hajj road, with the name "Authos, son of Priscus".[7] Sometimes it is a native of Germany or of Gaul, drafted here for service on the Arabian border, whose epitaph tells us how he died thinking of his fatherland: ". . . . born(?) and

[1] Like the one in Bozrah.

[2] Porter, *Giant Cities of Bashan*. Cf. Wetzstein, *Reisebericht*, pp. 81 f.

[3] *θάρσ(ε) Ῥοῦφέ Ἄθου οὐετρανός ἐτ(ῶν)οέ*, Wadd. 2039.

[4] *Οὐαλεντος Ἄζιζου*, Wadd. 2046.

[5] *βάσσος Ζαβδοῦ*, Wadd. 2070 i.

[6] At Khurbet el-Araje, Wadd. 2196. *Ἀδριανοῦ τοῦ καὶ Σοαίδου Μαλέχου ἐθνάρχου, στρατηγοῦ νομάδων τὸ μνημίον ἐτῶν λβ'. Ἄδδος ἀδελφὸς ἐτῶν κή.* Contemporary with the Emperor Hadrian. Cf. 1982, 2070, 2079, 2174.

[7] *Αὖθος Πρεισκου ἔτη?*, *Critical Review*, ii. (1892). On the road to el-Merkez, a little way out of Sheikh Miskin, is a cairn which the slab with this inscriptions surmounts. The shepherds affirmed it to be the tomb of Sheikh Mohammad el-'Ajamy; cf. Schumacher, *Across Jordan*, p. 118, for a Sheikh el-'Ajamy, whose tomb is shown at el-'Ajamy on the Upper Yarmuk.

a lover of his country, having come from Germany and died in the Agrippian troop, was taken back to his own."[1]

It is, however, in her roads, and the records of her frontier, that fullest proof of Rome's power survives. The Roman roads diverged from Damascus—one skirting Hermon to Cæsarea-Philippi; two crossing Gaulanitis to the Jordan bridges above and below the Lake of Galilee, one striking south through the Leja to Bozrah, and perhaps one down the east of the Leja to Kanatha. At right angles to these ran others, especially the Great Eastern road from Gadara to Edrei, Bozrah, Salecah, and thence boldly into the desert in the direction of the Persian Gulf.[2] "The Raṣif, or Roman road in these lands, is twelve paces broad, and is divided by five rows of upright stones into three divisions of equal breadth, the two outer rows are bordered by a ditch more or less deep, according to the level."[3] When we pass on to the borders of the desert, we see how marvellous was the line of the Roman defence. In the border villages, or by the roads as they plunge into the waste towards Palmyra or the Euphrates, marked by rows of black stones, on some hillock with no view but the desert, we read the official marks of the Legions, and the rough *graffiti* which the soldiers scribbled through the tedium of their desert watch.[4] Even more conspicuous is the skill by which Rome won the nomads to her service and fastened them down in defence of the border they had otherwise fretted and broken. On chiefs of tribes were bestowed the titles Phylarch, Ethnarch, and Strategus of the Nomads.[5]

Behind this Roman bulwark there grew up a unique civilisation talking Greek, imitating Rome, but at heart Semitic. We have seen how overrun with Arabs Hauran was before Rome came, how her earliest civilisers were themselves Semites—a Herod, a Philip, an Agrippa, "three thousand Idumæans", a colony of "Babylonian Jews"; and how an Arab civilisation, the Nabatæan, grew up south of Hauran. Nor did the Semitic influences upon Hauran cease when Rome made her frontiers secure to the east of it. The

[1] *. . . νετος καὶ φιλόπατρις ἀπὸ Γερμανίας ἀνέλθων καὶ ἐν εἴλῃ Ἀγριππιανῇ ἀποθανῶ(ν) εἰς τὰ ἴδια μεθηνέχθη*, Wadd. 2121.

[2] Impossible to ascertain the exact dates. The roads through the Leja may be as old as its conquest by Varro, 23 B.C. See p. 412. Most milestones are of the Antonines.

[3] Wetzstein, *Reisebericht*, 73.

[4] At Namara, for instance, a day's journey from the frontier villages of Hauran into the desert. Among the *graffiti Θαῖμος Σίδμου* and *Γάδδυς δρομεδάρι(ο)ς*, Wadd. 2267 (on the dromedary troops, cf. Wadd. 1946, 2424), the names of the Second and Third Legions. *Id.* 2279, 2281.

[5] "Phylarch", Wadd. 2404, etc.; for "Ethnarch", "Strategus of the Nomads", see inscription on p. 417, n. 6; also Wadd. 2112, at el-Hit, where Waddington thinks he found evidence of the presence of an Augustan band, Acts xxvii. 1; the fragment is *σπείρης Αυ. . . .* Cf. Ewing, 70: *Θεῷ Αὔμου*; Wadd. 2441; Ewing, 88.

nomads continued to immigrate in even greater numbers than before, yet not to rob but to settle, and add their own weight to the resistance which Rome offered to the tides of the desert. Of these immigrations the most distinguished was that of the Beni-Jafn, who left Yemen in A.D. 104, and towards the close of the century settled within the borders of the Empire.[1] But there were many who came with and after the Beni-Jafn, and the border garrisons seem to have been largely composed of Arab soldiers. The Greek and Latin elements of the population, as in other Oriental provinces, did not endure. Hauran must have remained essentially Semitic. The Greek of the inscriptions is Greek written by Semites: containing blunders and barbarisms, and betraying the influence of the Semitic phonology.[2] We saw that in the families which rose to the position of having an ornate tomb, or of being able to dedicate a temple, the name of the father was nearly always Semitic—a contrast to the monuments of the Decapolis, in which Semitic names are infrequent. Again, in the temples of Hauran, the names of the gods are not altogether Greek,[3] as in the Decapolis, but we meet with Baalsamîn, Du-Sara, ʻAthi, Aziz, Aumos, Allât, Vagrah, Adad from Khabab,[4] Ogenes at ʻAry,[5] and the curious Theandrites. Herod's temple at Seiʻ is dedicated to Baalsamîn, Baal of the Heavens,[6] probably the Zeus Megistos Keraunios of the Greek inscriptions. Du-Sara was a Sun-God, giver of fertility and joy, whom the Greeks identified with Dionysus.[7] His symbols, the vine and the wine-cup, still ornament lintels in many villages of Hauran; the chief centres of his worship were Petra and el-Ḥejr in Central Arabia, but it is a proof of the distance to which Nabatæan commerce extended that we find two tablets dedicated to him at Rome and Puteoli. Allât was "the mother of the gods, the goddess of Salkhat", which city was sacred to her.[8]

[1] See pp. 30 f.; cf. Wadd. 2110, 2413 n.

[2] Wadd. 2081, *σεννοτου* שנת: 2090, *πόντων πάντων*: cf. 1916, 2049-53, 2457, Ewing, 74.

[3] But Heracles at Nejran, Wadd. 2428, Ewing, 114.

[4] Ewing, 51.

[5] Wadd. 2440, Ewing, 99.

[6] בעשמין contracted from בעלשמין, *CIS*, Pars II, No. 163.

[7] Nabatæan, דושרא, *CIS*, Pars II, tom. i. No. 157 at Puteoli; 160 at Rome; 190 Umm el-Jemal, south of Bozrah, frequently in the monuments of el-Ḥejr, 197 ff. Greek *Δουσαρης*, Wadd. 2023; 2312 with *ἀνίκητος*, also applied to *Ἥλιος*, 2392. Cf. *Δουσαριος*, 1916. Epiphanius (*Haeres.*) describes the feast at Petra on the winter solstice in honour of Du-Sara and his virgin mother. See also Tertullian, *Apolog*. 24. In *ZDMG*, xiv. 465, the name is derived from Sheraa, a chain of mountains in Arabia, as if "Lord of Shera". Cf. Baethgen, *Beiträge zur Semitischen Religionsgeschichte*, 94-97. See above, p. 366.

[8] *CIS*, Pars II, tom. i. Nos. 170, 171, 182, 183, 185; 182 runs: "this is the house which Ruḥu, son of Malkhu, son of Akhlibu, son of Ruḥu, built to Allât, their goddess."

Aziz, the Mighty, 'Athi and Aumos were of lower rank.[1] The Greek name
Theandrios or Theandrites is as puzzling as interesting: the Semitic original
is unknown.[2]

In the architecture of Hauran native elements are no less conspicuous.
We have no more the imitations of the Greek orders which we found in the
Decapolis; but the lines and the ornaments are determined both by the
habits of Oriental art and by the nature of the material with which Hauran
architects had to work. The oldest building, the temple of Sei',[3] was erected
by Herod, a prince already under Hellenic influence; but its Greek lines are
modified by Eastern ideas.[4] De Vogüé thinks that in its ruins we see reflections of the Temple at Jerusalem, which was not only contemporary but
likewise the work of Herod. It was, however, the peculiarity of their material
which chiefly influenced the architects of Hauran. Their country was
practically treeless; they had to construct entirely of stone, and the basalt
at their disposal not only served for masonry, but allowed itself to be cut
into beams, slabs, lattice-work, and other shapes for which wood was usually
employed. Consequently the building of Hauran developed a style of its
own. This took the form of a series of parallel arches, across which were laid
long rafters of basalt,[5] and on these the slabs of the ceiling. Some of the
roofs are still solid; above the rafters of others are scattered a number of big
stones, so that you have a trellis roof through which the sunshine is fretted
on the floor. But frequently[6] the roof took the form of the cupola, and in this
you see the "first essays towards the Byzantine style of architecture, and
especially towards putting the cupola on a square by means of spherical
pendentives".[7] The parallel arches, straining outwards, required exterior

---

(אלהתחם, against Renan's theory that "goddess" was impossible in Semitic). In
185 Allât is with Vagrah. Cf. Baethgen, *Beiträge*, etc. 98, 99.

[1] Aziz, Wadd. 2314 (Suweida), identified on an inscription in Dacia with Apollo;
'Athi on an inscription at Egla (el-'Ageilat) Batanæa, Wadd. 2209. Θεῷ αὐτῶν Ἐθάῳ
worshipped at Palmyra under the name עתי. To Αὖμος at Deir el-Leben, Wadd.
2392, 2394, on a large temple of A.D. 320, on which he seems identified with the Sun.
Cf. 2463 and 2464 (Hauran in Trachonitis); on the latter the name Aumos belongs to
a Christian.

[2] Θεάνδριος, Wadd. 1905; Θεανδρίτης, 2046, 2481, Ewing, 44.   [3] See p. 412.

[4] On the principles of the architecture of Hauran the authority is De Vogüé, *Syrie
Centrale. Architecture Civile et Religieuse*; for the basis of the above paragraphs, see
the *Avant Propos* of this work.

[5] De Vogüé describes the slabs as laid directly on the arches, but in the specimens
I examined the long basalt beams intervene.

[6] As in the Menzil at eş-Şunamein and elsewhere.

[7] De Vogüé. The oldest specimen of cupola is at Umm ez-Zeitun, dating from
A.D. 282.

bulwarks; and, consequently, along many of the public buildings are solid buttresses running the length of the walls, and built in the form of steps and stairs. We found them the favourite benches of the village school, when the sun was not too fierce; the bright children, scattered over these ancient buttresses, composed a charming picture. The elevation of the buildings is generally low, but never mean; the decorations few and simple. The basalt allowed less carving than the limestone of Gilead, but has preserved the inscriptions. It is a wonder to see the carved stone lattices of the windows, and the stone doors turning on stone hinges.

Most of the public buildings appear to have risen under the Antonines and Septimius Severus: Temples, Basilicas, Theatres, and the round towers, which all civilisations have found indispensable in war with the Arabs.[1]

But there had entered Hauran a new force, which was gradually to change both the religion and the art of the land.

The early course of Christianity across Jordan is obscure. In Western and Northern Syria, in Mesopotamia and Persia, we have comparatively full accounts of the organisation of the Church, but in Eastern Syria and Arabia her early history is almost a blank. We know of our Lord's ministry in Decapolis and Peræa,[2] of Paul's conversion and the band of disciples at Damascus,[3] and of Paul's possible ministry in Arabia.[4] The Christians of Jerusalem fled from the siege to Pella,[5] where it is said the Ebionite heresy first developed,[6] and the Christianity of Eastern Palestine is described as of this Judaistic kind—enforcing the Mosaic law, affirming the human birth of Christ, abjuring Paul as a heretic, and looking for the return of Christ to found an earthly kingdom.[7] But of this there are no remains, not even at Pella, and the earliest record we have of an active Christianity in Hauran is of the establishment of a monastery in A.D. 180 by 'Amr I, a Ghassanide prince. About A.D. 218 Origen paid two visits east of Jordan; the first on the call of the Governor of Arabia to explain to him his doctrine,[8] and the

[1] Cf. Uzziah's use of towers, 2 Chron. xxvi. 9, 10; and that of the Turks along the Hajj road. Doughty, *Arabia Deserta*, i. *passim.*

[2] Mark v. 1 and x. 1.

[3] Acts ix; 2 Cor. xi.

[4] Gal. i. 15-17: *But when it was the good pleasure of God . . . to reveal His Son in me, that I might preach Him among the Gentiles . . . I went away into Arabia, and again I returned unto Damascus.*

[5] Eusebius, *HE*, iii. 5.

[6] Epiphanius, *adv. Hæres.* xxx. 2.

[7] E of the Dead Sea gathered the Elkesaites, another heretical sect, taking their name from חיל כסי, their title for the Holy Ghost, also given to their sacred book. They practised many Mosaic and Essene rites, and worshipped Christ as the Son of God; Epiphanius, *Hæres.* xix, xxx, liii; Eusebius, *HE*, vi. 38; Theodoret, *Fabularum Hæreticarum*, vii.

[8] Eusebius, *HE*, vi. 19.

second to an Arabian Synod, at which he overthrew the heresy of Beryllus, Bishop of Bozrah, and propounded the eternal generation of the Son.[1] From Shuhba in Trachonitis came the first Christian emperor. Philip the Arabian was the son of a Bedawee chief, was at least a nominal Christian, and occupied the Imperial throne from 244 to 249.[2] The Christians of these regions must have suffered, like those of the rest of Syria, in the persecutions under Decius and Diocletian,[3] and, perhaps, owing to the latter's order for the destruction of Christian buildings we have few Christian remains earlier than his day. Traces of these persecutions are still eloquent in Hauran—one cryptogram for Christ, *ΙΧΘΥΣ* of the catacombs[4]; another *ΧΜΓ*, found only here, and probably meaning "Christ born of Mary"[5]; a possible allusion to Mary masked in heathen terms, *Πότνια Νύμφη*[6]; above all, many bits of basalt with the words, or syllables of the words, Martyr and Martyrs' Monument.[7] These latter meet you in almost every village, rendering its dust dear to your Christian heart. Even the nomads raised monuments to the Martyrs.[8] One longer inscription: "For the Repose of the Martyrs who have fallen asleep"[9] reminds us of Stephen. The erection of such memorials proves a day in which Christianity was able to show itself in public, and others record its gradual triumph over paganism. Amid the names of Zeus, Athene, Du-Sara, Allât, which stamp the ruins, you read that of our Lord carven with equal boldness in face of the sun, as

ΙΗΣ + ΟΥΣ

or a proclamation of the "One God"[10]; or the triumphant words,[11]

+ ΧΡΙΣ + ΤΟΣ ΝΙΚΑ +

On these follow longer inscriptions: prayers, dedications, quotations from Scripture, epitaphs. At Umm el-Jemal: "Prayer of Numerianus (and) John

[1] *Ibid.* vi. 20, 33, 37.
[2] *Ibid.* vi. 34; cf. Uhlhorn, Herzog, *Real-Encyc.* xi. pp. 613 ff.; cf. Wadd. 2071 ff.
[3] Decius, A.D. 249-251; Diocletian began persecution in 303.
[4] Wadd. 2362. Wadd. 2465; Ewing, 82, has the monogram P.
[5] *Χρίστος ἐκ Μάριας γεννηθεῖς*, Wadd. 1936, 2145. De Rossi, *Χρίστος, Μιχαήλ, Γαβριήλ.*
[6] Wadd. 2145.
[7] *Μαρτύριον.* As these "martyries" were used as chapels, and many churches contained them, *ἐκκλησία* and *μαρτύριον* are sometimes used by early writers as equivalent.
[8] *E.g.* Wadd. 2464, where the *Μαρτύριον* was raised by a Phylarch.
[9] *Ὑπὲρ τῆς ἀναπαυσέως τῶν κεκοιμένων Μαρτύρων*, Wadd. 1920.
[10] *Εἷς Θ* . . . Wadd. 2057, cf. 2066.
[11] Wadd. 2253.

—From the womb of (our) mother our God art thou; forsake us not."[1] At Salkhat, in wretched Greek, scribbled in an obscure chamber, "Aouos, Moses, for the forgiveness of sins".[2] In several places, "Help, O Christ". On the lintel of a house at Ṭuffas: "Jesus Christ be the shelter and defence of all the family of the house, and bless their incoming, and their outgoing."[3] Sometimes the intercession of the saints is sought, as at Sahwet el-Khiḍr, in the Chapel of St. George: "Holy George, receive: also Scholasticius the offerer do thou guard by thy prayers, and for Comes his brother ask repose."[4] It is remarkable that the quotations from Scripture are from the Old Testament in the LXX version, but sometimes, as in the prayer quoted, adapted for application to Christ. "This is the gate of the Lord, the righteous shall come in by it."[5] "If the Lord watch not the city, in vain doth the watchman keep awake."[6] On the portal of the Church of St. John, now the Great Mosque in Damascus: "Thy kingdom, O Christ, is an everlasting kingdom, and Thy dominion endureth from generation to generation."[7]

Pagan and Christian inscriptions contrast in two respects. Pagans parade the names of the donors, offerers, and dedicators. With a modesty, too strange to the givings of the modern Church, the Christian inscriptions nearly always omit the names, as thus: "Remember, Lord, the founder, of whom Thou knowest the name."[8] Another, but less clear, contrast is found among the tombs. Heathen epitaphs, in Decapolis or Hauran, are mostly without hope. Romans, in lawyer-like form, record only the name, rank, and age of the dead, and how the tomb was built.[9] Greeks indulge in sentiment and reflection; their hope is ambiguous. "After all things a tomb" is on the lintel of a tomb at Irbid.[10] *Καὶ Σύ*, Even thou, is a common *memento*

[1] Ps. xxii. 10, 11; Wadd. 2068. [2] Wadd. 2010.

[3] As I copied it, the inscription reads a little differently (*Critical Review*, ii. p. 60) from Schumacher's copy, *Across the Jordan*, p. 21. The quotations are from the Psalms: cxxi, etc. Cf. Wadd. 2068, 2537.

[4] Wadd. 1981, cf. 2126. [5] Ps. cxviii. 20; Wadd. 1961.

[6] Ps. cxxvii. 1; Wadd. 2390, cf. 2501.

[7] The portal above roof of the silversmiths' bazaar: Ps. cxlv. 13.

[8] Wadd. 2087, etc. Cf. the inscription on the font at Bethlehem. But see 2249 for an instance of the name being given.

[9] See the inscription we discovered at Gadara, p. 299 of this volume.

[10] Merrill (*East of Jordan*, 293), reads *Μετὰ Πάντα Τ(οῦτο)*; Clermont-Ganneau (*Recueil*, etc. 17) *Τ(άφος)*. The latter is correct; my copy shows *a* as the second letter of the word. I have modified the contrast I drew between Pagan and Christian epitaphs. I took οὐδεὶς ἀθάνατος = nobody is immortal, and as only on Pagan tombs. But W. M. Ramsay (*Exp*. Jan. 1895, 58 f.) thinks the phrase = nobody is free from death, and holds most of its instances as Christian (Wadd. 1897, 1986, 2459, and perhaps 2032, 2050, and Ewing, 163). W. E. Crum (*Academy*, Jan. 19, 1895) cites four

mori. The Greek heart breaks on the stone; the farewell seems final. "Thou hast finished" is a common epitaph. "Titus, son of Malchus, farewell, thou hast finished untimely, (thy) years twelve, farewell!"[1] Or the dead are told that theirs is the inevitable fate, nobody is deathless. "Be of cheer, Helen, dear child, no one is deathless. I have laid thee beside thy mother, Gavaia. . . ."[2] This οὐδεὶς ἀθάνατος is very common. Its most striking appearance is on the Mount of Olives, over against the Church of the Resurrection.[3] Its occurrence on Christian tombs is not accompanied by exultation or vision of another life. Yet a quiet confidence reigns. The dead are "they that sleep"; the living pray for their repose, or offer a prayer for themselves, as: "May the soul of Gerontius be saved."[4]

Other expressions of faith and feeling are: "O Christ, our God"; "The Peace of Christ to all"; "Peace to all men + the Holy Catholic Church of the Lord."[5]

The Church of Eastern Palestine was organised in the second and third centuries, for in the beginning of the fourth its bishops and metropolitans were many, as witnessed by the Acts of the Councils of Nicæa and Chalcedon. At the former Damascus had a metropolitan with seven suffragans. Bozrah was the ecclesiastical, as well as the civil, metropolis of Hauran. The diocese had its own theology, as we have seen, in Origen's time, and its synods. The town was a centre of trade, only second to Damascus—a tradition preserved in its present name of Old Damascus. It was full of monks.

The earliest Christian buildings were destroyed under Diocletian. They were probably the martyries, little chapels built over a martyr's grave. After the victory over paganism the first churches were the basilicas of the An-

Coptic tombs with "not any deathless". Both think Christians took the phrase from Pagans. Revillout had called it "essentiellement matérialiste et syrienne"; Clermont-Ganneau (*Arch. Res.* i, 367 ff.), giving Christian instances, traces it to Semitic sentiment. Christians probably put new meaning into the words. Further, Ramsay takes καὶ σύ as the dead's reply to the greeting, and τελευτάω as probably only *to die*. On the analogy of ὁ βίος ταῦτα (very common) he reads on the Irbid tomb μετὰ πάντα ταῦτα after all—this.

[1] On a pillar now in a stable in Gadara, *Critical Review*, ii. 61; cf Clermont-Ganneau, *Recueil*, p. 21.

[2] Wadd. 2032, cf. 1986; ἐπαύσετο Αὖθος. But 2247 (ἅμα θεοῖς) and 2322 express hope. Cf. also 2432, Ewing, 112.

[3] Wadd. 1897, cf. 2429. There is a beautiful epitaph given by Wadd. 2322:

Ὕπνος ἔχει σε, μάκαρ, πολυήρατε, δῖε Σαβῖνε
καὶ ζῇς ὡς ἥρως καὶ νέκυς οὐκ ἐγένου.
εὕδεις δ' ὡς ἔτι ζῶν ὑπὸ δένδρεσι σοῖς ἐν τύμ(βοις)
ψυχαὶ γὰρ ζῶσιν τῶν ἄγαν εὐσεβαίων.

[4] Wadd. 2492.

[5] Wadd. 2500, 2061, 2519.

tonines and other emperors, and then imitations of these. But during the fourth and fifth centuries there developed the style known as Byzantine—the dome above the square chamber. The two finest churches were that of St. George at Zorava, of date 514,[1] and the cathedral at Bozrah of 512. St. George's consists of two concentric octagons in a square crowned by drum and cupola; against the eastern face of the exterior octagon is built the choir, terminating in an apse; each angle of the square outside the octagons holds a smaller apse; on the west are three portals; on the north and south one each. This church bears the inscription beginning, "The assembly of demons has become the house of the Lord." The cathedral of Bozrah was four-square and crowned by a dome, with a longish apse. An inscription in Bozrah[2] gives a form of the Greek original for church, *κυριακόν*, "The Lord's house", *κυρικόν*, which is as nearly as possible the same as the forms at the other end of Christendom, *kerk* and *kirk*.

The latest Christian buildings in Hauran are of the middle of the seventh century. In the beginning of that the camel-driver, Mohammed, used, on his journeys from Arabia, to visit Bozrah, and, it is said, learned there, from the monk Hariri, all he ever knew of Christianity.[3] Mohammed died in 632. By 634 the hosts whom his doctrines inspired overran Hauran, defeated on the Yarmuk the Christian army, and by 635 took Damascus. Subsequently we have only two Christian buildings in Hauran, the monastery Deir Eyoub, with date 641,[4] and a church of St. George at el-Kafr, 652.[5] The Christianity and the Hellenism of the province dwindled to fragments of their former selves.[6] The vitality of Hauran was blasted. We have no worthy buildings from the Mohammedan period; the structures of former days were mutilated and abused, the theatre at Bozrah made a castle, cathedrals and churches turned to mosques. Other barbarians have understood, interpreted, developed the civilisations which they conquered, and so did the Arabs in other parts of the world. But in the desert-bordering Hauran, on which ruder and ruder swarms beat up as the centuries went on, were only abuse, neglect, decay; and the sole conservative elements, which ensured that at least we should have some ruins of ancient days, have been the hardness and weight of Hauran basalt, and the superstitious reverence of the Arabs for inscriptions, which they have treasured and employed—generally

[1] On site of a temple to Theandrites, Wadd. 2569? The relics of St. George seem taken to Zorava early in the 6th cent., Wadd. 2498.

[2] Wadd. 1920. [3] *Yakut*, i. 64; the *Marâsid*, i. 425, 441. [4] Wadd. 2413.

[5] Ewing, 153, 665 A.D. in Wadd. 1997.

[6] Ewing, 150, seems to describe the building of a church at el-Kafr in 720.

on end, or wrong-side up—as tombstones or as charms over the doors of their houses. Hauran has continued fertile and full of villages to the present day, but the villages have known no security, sheltered no stable populations; and the land has been scoured by nomads.[1] The great towns became shells in which little clans huddled for shelter. In Bozrah were, in 1891, not more than forty families.

The Crusaders made two expeditions to Bozrah, and besieged Damascus. But none of these adventures effected anything, and though their coins have been found in Hauran they got no settlement there.[2]

The advance of the Allied Forces in September 1918, across Hauran upon Damascus, was by lines converging from east and west upon their common goal. We have seen that the 4th British Cavalry Division with batteries of Artillery marched from Beisan on Irbid, Arbela, and er-Ramta, which they found cleared of the enemy by the 27th. Next day they reached Dera' at Station on the rail-road, and were in touch with Lieut-Col. Lawrence, and a column of Feisal's Arabs, mostly enforced by "wild camel-men" from the immediate east, glad to turn against their Turkish oppressors. In concert with them on their flank they moved on to el-Muzeirib and up the Hajj road to Sheikh Miskin on the 29th, and leaving the retreating Turks to be harassed by the Arabs, by Zeraḳiyeh reached Kisweh, within ten miles of Damascus. Meanwhile the Australian Mounted and 5th Cavalry Divisions, having crossed the Jordan below the Bridge-of-the-Daughters-of-Jacob, passed Ḳuneiṭra, and after being held up for a little by the enemy reached Sa'ara on September 30th. From this across the Nahr el-'Awaj, by some identified with the River Pharpar, rises Jebel 'Aswad, separating Hauran from the fields south of Damascus. Sa'ara is eighteen miles from Damascus. A Brigade of the Division pushing north occupied both Ḳaṭana on the old Roman road and Kaukab (Cochaba) ten miles from the city. Thus on September 30th the Desert Mounted Corps were at the gates of Damascus, the Australian Mounted Division at el-Mezzeh, two miles to the west, and some Brigades in command of the Baradeh Gorge; the 5th Cavalry Division at Kaukab with a Brigade on the hills east of 'Ashrafîyeh, and the 4th mainly at Zeraḳiyeh on the Hajj road, but a Brigade at Khan Dennun seven miles nearer the city. The Arab forces had reached the north-east of the city. On October 1st Damascus was taken.[3]

Damascus has seen many races approach her in the course of her long history, but surely never before 1918 such a variety as together accomplished

[1] See pp. 339, 340. [2] On the Crusaders over Jordan, see p. 345.

[3] For the above see Lawrence, *Revolt in the Desert*; C. Falls, *Military Operations, Egypt and Palestine from June 1917, etc.*, ch. xxvi.

her capture. For the Allied Armies contained besides British Yeomanry and Artillery, Indian Regiments from the Deccan and Poona, Australian Horse, French Spahîs and Chasseurs d'Afrique, Feisal's regular Arabs from the Hejaz, and Arab irregulars from the desert immediately east of Hauran.

XXXI. *DAMASCUS*

Damascus[1]—never claimed for Israel and never under a Hebrew prince[2]—lies beyond the limits of the Holy Land, and of our present survey. But she has ever been the goal of the roads of the lands we have traversed, the dream and envy of their peoples. We have met her fame everywhere. She has seen the rise, felt the effect, and survived the passage, of the forces which have strewn Syria with ruins. Not a fallen city have we visited but Damascus was old when it was built, and still exists long after many have perished. Amid the growth and decay of the races, civilisations and religions, which have thronged Syria for four thousand years, Damascus remains the one perennially great Syrian city. Before we cease our survey she demands our homage, with such appreciation as we may attempt of the secret of her eternal youth. Beyond appreciation we need not go: we have recorded the main facts of her history.[3]

Damascus lies about seventy miles from the sea-board, upon the east of Anti-Lebanon, and close in to the foot of the hills. You reach her from Beyrout by the carriage-road or the rail-road which first climb over Lebanon into "Hollow Syria", and then by the easy passes of Anti-Lebanon cross into the valley of the Abana, with which they issue upon a plain 2300 feet above the sea, and in extent thirty miles by ten. This plain is bounded west by Hermon, north by an eastern offshoot of that hill, east by a row of extinct volcanoes, south by the river 'Awaj, probably the Pharpar, and by a low range that shuts off Hauran.

Like the slopes of Anti-Lebanon behind it, this plain would be as desert as the rest of the country to the Euphrates were it not for the river Abana.

[1] Probably Hittite Damashunas, Garstang, Index of Hittite Names, *Suppl. Papers, BSAJ*, 1923.

[2] For an apparent exception see p. 390.

[3] For her roads to the sea, her place between the Mediterranean and the far East, see ch. xx; for her connection with Israel, ch. xxviii; for her relations to Eastern Palestine, ch. xxv; for her place in the Decapolis, ch. xxix; for her history under Rome and the Nabatæans, ch. xxx.

The Abana bursts from the heart of Anti-Lebanon, runs a course of ten miles in a narrow gorge, and from the mouth of this flings itself abroad in seven streams. After watering the greater part of the plain, it dies away in a large marsh. Over the green of this marsh you see from Damascus at sunset low purple hills twenty-five miles off. They are the edge of the Eastern desert: beyond them is nothing but a rolling waste, and the long ways to Palmyra and Baghdad.

It is an astonishing site for what is said to be the oldest, and is certainly the most enduring, city of the world. For it is incapable of defence and remote from the sea and the main lines of commerce. From the coast of Syria it is doubly barred by those ranges of snow-capped mountains whose populations enjoy more tempting prospects to the north and west. But look east and you understand Damascus. You would as soon think of questioning the site of New York or Sydney or San Francisco. Damascus is a harbour of refuge upon the earliest sea man learned to navigate. Because there is nothing but desert beyond, or immediately behind this site; because this river, the Abana, instead of wasting her waters on a slight extension of the fringe of fertile Syria, saves them in her narrow gorge till she can fling them out upon the desert, and there, instead of slowly expending them on the doubtful possibilities of a province, lavishes her life at once in the creation of a single city, and straightway dies in face of the desert—because of all this Damascus, remote and defenceless, has endured throughout history, and must endure. Nineveh, Babylon, and Memphis easily conquered her. She probably preceded and has outlived them. She was twice supplanted—by Antioch, and has seen Antioch decay, by Baghdad, and Baghdad had to yield. She has been often sacked, and twice at least the effective classes of her people were swept into captivity, but that did not break the chain of her history. She was once capital of the world from the Atlantic to the Bay of Bengal,[1] but the vast empire went from her and the city continued to flourish. Standing on the edge of fertility, on the shore of the much-voyaged desert, Damascus is indispensable alike to civilisation and to the nomads. Moreover, she is the city of the Mediterranean world, which lies nearest the far East, and Islam has made her the western port for Mecca.

The plain on which Damascus lies is called the Ghuṭa. Too high to be marshy, the Ghuṭa is shot all over by the cold, rapid waters of the Abana, which serve equally in bringing life and in carrying off corruption. Verdure springs profusely. As you look down from one of the bare heights to the north you see some hundred and fifty square miles of green—thronging and billowy as the sea, with the white compact city rising from it like an island.

[1] Under the Omaiyade Khalifs in the end of the seventh century.

There is apparently the lavishness of a virgin forest, but when you get among it you find neither rankness nor jungle. The cultivated ground is extensive, most of it in orchards and plantations, but there are also flower gardens, parks, and corn-fields of considerable size—none, however, so spread as to disturb the distant impression of close forest.

It is best to enter Damascus in summer, because then everything predisposes you for her charms. You come down off the most barren flanks of Anti-Lebanon. You cross the plateau of Ṣaḥra ed-Dimas, six shadeless miles that stretch, with the elasticity of all Syrian plains in haze, till you almost fancy you are upon enchanted ground rolling out with you as you travel. But at last the road begins to sink, and you come with it into a deep rut, into which all the heat and glare of the broad miles behind seems compressed. The air is still, the rocks blistered, the road deep in dust, when suddenly a bank of foliage bursts into view, with a white verandah above it. The road turns a corner; you are in shadow, on a bridge, in a breeze. Another turn and you have streams on both sides, a burn gurgling through bushes on the left, on the right not one stream but one banked over the other, and the wind in the poplars above. You break into the richer valley of the Abana itself. You pass between orchards of figs and of apricots. For hedges there are the briar rose, and for a canopy the walnut. Pomegranate blossoms glow through the shade; vine-boughs trail across the briar; a little waterfall breaks on the edge of the road. To the left the river, thirty feet of dark green water with white curls, shoots down a steep, smooth bed. And all this water and leafage are so lavish that the broken mud-walls and slovenly houses have no power to vex the eye, exulting in the contrast of the valley with the bare brown hills that shut it in. For two miles more you ride between trees, through a village, over a bridge, between high banks of gardens, road and river together, flecked with light. You come between two streams, one washing the roots of aged fig-trees, past a quarry where the desert sinks in cliff upon the road, beside an old aqueduct whose Roman masonry trails with brambles. The gorge narrows, there is room only for the aqueduct and river, with the road between, but just as the cliff comes near enough to overhang the road the hills turn sharply off, and the relieved river slackens and sprawls between islands. You are out on the plain; there are gardens and meadows; men and boys, horses, asses, and geese loaf upon the grass and the shingle; great orchards, with busy people gathering apricots, stretch on either side. Still no city is visible. A mile more of orchards, then through the walnuts a crescent gleams, and the minaret it crowns. You come upon a grassy level, cut by the river into two parks. There is a five-arched bridge, and over the bridge minarets and low white domes. You pass some public gardens, cross the river, ride between it and another garden with lofty trees, and halt in a square, with the serai, courts of justice, prison, and barracks of what was the principal garrison of Syria. The river has disappeared under the square by three tunnels, from which it passes in lesser conduits and pipes to every house and court in the city. By the north walls a branch breaks again into the open; here the chief gardens spread beneath walnuts and poplars, and the water rushes by them swift and cold from its confinement. So at least it was in 1891 and 1901.

With the long gardens of Damascus, the paradise of the Arab world, you must take the Bazaars of Damascus, in which many other worlds meet the Arab. Travellers are often disappointed with both gardens and bazaars. It is not to be expected that Westerns should feel the charm of the waters of Damascus as the desert Bedawee does. But if any one confesses the bazaars dull, he has neither eye for colour nor wit to read the city's history in the faces she gathers to them from Nubia to the Caucasus. It is a perpetual banquet of colour. There were blots when I was there—foreign prints and cheap clocks, second-hand carriages from Beyrout, the dusty streets themselves, where they break into the open glare. But in the long dusk tunnels, shot by solid shafts of light, all else is beautiful—old walnut-wood, brown tobacco bales, carpets, spotted brown scones in the bakers' shops, tawny sweet-meats, golden Hauran wheat, piles of green melons, tables of snow from Hermon, armour and rich saddle-bags, human dresses, but especially human flesh—the pallid townsman, the brown fellâh, the Druze with mountain blood in his cheek, the grey Jew, the black and blue-black negroes. Besides Turk and Hebrew, the great racial types are three: Bedawee Arab, Greek, and Kurd. They are the token of how Damascus lies between the Levant, the Desert, and that other region of the world to which we are apt to forget that Syria has any avenue—the highlands of Armenia. Saladin, her greatest Sultan, was a Kurd: the Kurd sheep-masters used every year to send their flocks for sale to the Lebanons, the Kurdish cavalry always formed the most vigorous part of the Turkish garrison.

Even the Bazaars of Damascus fail to exhaust the significance of the city. To gather more of this you must come out upon the three great roads which go forth from her—west, south, and east. The west, or south-west, road travels by Galilee to the Levant and the Nile. The south, leaving the city by the "Gates of God",[1] takes the pilgrims to Mecca. The east is the road to Baghdad. Egypt, Arabia, Persia—this city of the Khalifs lies in the midst of the three, and the Mediterranean is behind her.

As for her relations to Syria, Damascus never had in these but one rival,

[1] Bauwâbat-Allah, Turkish Mişr Kapusi, Egyptian Gate.

and this only so long as a European power ruled in the East. Antioch was the creation of the Greeks (330 B.C.), the capital of the Seleucid dynasty, the residence of the Roman Legate in Syria, and the centre of Eastern Christianity. During the thousand years of European supremacy Damascus fell second to Antioch, and her history is obscure. But so soon as the Moslem came (they took Damascus in 634, Antioch in 635), the city on the Desert rose again to the first rank, the city on the Levant began to decline. For one hundred years, 650 to 750, Damascus had the Khalifate under the Omaiyades; and once for all she was bound to Mecca by the Hajj. Under Arab rule Damascus has even absorbed the Christian fame of Antioch, for though the Patriarch takes his title from Antioch, he resides in Damascus. The fortunes of the two cities during the Crusades reflect the same relations. The European forces made Antioch their centre, but never took Damascus.

In the history of religion, Damascus was the stage of two great crises. She was the scene of the conversion of the first Apostle of Christianity to the Gentiles; she was the earliest Christian city to be taken by Islam. It was fitting that Paul's conversion, with his first sense of a mission to the Gentiles, should not take place till his journey brought him to Gentile soil. The Cathedral, which rose on the ruins of the heathen temple, was dedicated not to Paul but to John the Baptist. When the Arabs took Damascus in 634 this Church was divided between Mohammedans and Christians. Seventy years later it was absorbed by the conquerors and rebuilt to become one of the greatest, if not of the richest, of the mosques of Islam. The rebuilding destroyed all the Christian features, except that which, above the south portal, preserves this prayer and prophecy: *Thy kingdom, O Christ, is an everlasting kingdom, and Thy dominion endureth for all generations.*[1]

[1] See J. E. Hanauer, "Damascus: Notes on Changes Made in the City During the Great War", *PEFQ*, 1924, 68 ff.

APPENDICES

APPENDIX I

SOME GEOGRAPHICAL PASSAGES AND TERMS IN THE OLD TESTAMENT

Reference is made on pp. 55, etc. to passages in the O.T. which give the chief physical features of Palestine.

(*a*) The earliest seems to be Jud. i. 9. Looking W from the hills above Jericho the writer describes Judah as *going down to fight the Canaanites who dwelt on the Mount, the Negeb, and the Shephelah.* Budde (*Richter u. Samuel*) argues that this verse is not of the original Jahwist narrative on the ground that it contradicts ver. 19, *Judah possessed the Mount, but could not drive out the inhabitants of the Valley, because they had chariots of iron.* But ver. 9 only says that Judah went down to attack the Canaanites in the Mount, the Negeb, and the Shephelah, while ver. 19 deals with the result, that it was successful only so far as the mountain. Again Budde seems to take Shephelah and 'Emeḳ or Valley as the same. But Shephelah is low hills between Philistia and the Judæan range, including hill and vale. 'Emeḳ is valley or plain-land. I see no reason, therefore, for separating ver. 9. Note, too, that Judah *went down* to the Mount, etc., which can only mean that to the writer this tribe did not depart on a separate path of conquest from the rest of Israel till after Israel reached the crest of the Central Range.

The rest of the passages form a group in one style, the Deuteronomic.

(*b*) In Deut. i. 7 Israel are ordered to journey to the *Mount of the Amorite*, the Central Range, representative of the whole land, *and to all his neighbours.* Then the main features of the country are given from E to W—*the Arabah*, or Jordan Valley, *the Mount*, or Central Range, *the Shephelah, the Negeb, the Coast of the Sea, the land of the Canaanite. Lebanon* is added, and all north to the *great river, the Euphrates*, the ideal border of the Promised Land.

(*c*) In Josh. x. 40 *all the Land*, as far as conquered by Joshua, and therefore exclusive of the Maritime Plain, is *The Mount, the Negeb, the Shephelah, and Slopes* (A.V. *springs*).

(*d*) Josh. xi. 16 gives this as the *Mount, all the Negeb, and all the Land of Goshen*—an unknown extent from Gibeon (Josh. x. 41; cf. xv. 51) south across Judah, and out upon the Negeb, not that Goshen where Israel settled in Egypt—*the Shephelah, the Arabah, the Mount of Israel*—the Central

Range within the north kingdom of Israel—*and its Shephelah*, the lower and more open hills between the hills of Samaria and Carmel, with resemblances to *the* Shephelah opposite Judah. No other interpretation seems feasible; but, if correct, the date of the passage is after the kingdom of Israel was separated from Judah.

(*e*) In Josh. xii. 8 we find *The Mountain, the Shephelah, the Arabah, the Slopes, the Desert*—on the skirts of the land—*and the Negeb*. The Mountain or Central Range was named in its portions: *The Mountain—hill country—of Judah* or *Judæa*,[1] *the Mountain of Ephraim*,[2] or *of Israel*, or plural, *Mountains of Samaria*, for the range scatters; and in Galilee, *the Mountain of Naphtali*.

All these refer to Western Palestine. Divisions and names of E Palestine are in chap. xxv. As in the west, *mount* is applied to the hills of Moab; *mountains of Abarim*, to Gilead and to Bashan. There is, besides, Ha-Mishôr, the plateau of Moab.

Some words are necessary on the O.T. geographical terms. For HILLS or HEIGHTS Hebrew has: הר har, applied either to a range, or hill-country (also in plural), or to a great hill like Hor (Num. xx. 22), or to smaller hills like the citadel of Jerusalem (Isa. xxii. 5), or Samaria; LXX mostly ὄρος and ὀρεινή; גבעה gibe'ah, *hill*, as distinguished from *mountain* הר, but also interchangeable with the latter, Isa. xl. 4; Job xv. 7; Prov. viii. 25. Like הר of Zion, Isa. x. 32; Ezek. xxxiv. 26, but never like הר used of a range or hill-country; as in Canticles iv. 6, a high place; LXX generally βουνός.

בָּמָה bamah in the singular only of artificial high places; but once or twice in the plural natural heights (Micah i. 3; Jer. xxvi. 18; Ezek. xxxvi. 2; cf. 2 Sam. i. 19, 25).

עֹפֶל 'ophel=swell, bank, mound; as a common noun only for tumours (cf. *tumulus*, from *tumeo*); as a name with the article (except Isa. xxxii. 14; Micah iv. 8) it was the rising ground of the Temple, cf. 2 Chron. xxvii. 3; Neh. iii. 26, etc.; also a part of Samaria, 2 Kings v. 24; a part of Dibon, Moabite Stone, 22.

אֲשֵׁדוֹת 'ashedoth, slopes; so with כְּסָלוֹת as in כ״ תבר, Josh. xix. 12; cf. Josh. xix. 18, Modern Iksal. צַד ṣadh=side, 1 Sam. xxiii. 26; 2 Sam. xiii. 34; יַרְכָּה yarcah=thigh, Jud. xix. 1, 18, etc.; צֵלָע ṣela'=rib, 2 Sam. xvi. 13; שְׁכֶם shechem=back, Gen. xlviii. 22; כָּתֵף katheph=shoulder, Josh. xv. 8, 10; xviii. 10, of hills, also the coast of Philistia rising from the sea,

[1] Luke i. 39, etc. [2] Authorised Version, *Mount Ephraim*.

Isa. xi. 14; ראש rôsh, Arabic râs=headland, foreland, summit; even אַזְנוֹת 'aznoth=ears; אזנות תבור Josh. xix. 34, though impossible to say to what exactly this refers. קֶרֶן ḳeren=horn.

שְׁפִי shephî, a bare hill; נָפָה naphah elevation, raised land, only in Naphath-Dor, the rise of Carmel behind Dor; תֵּל tel (in composition Tell=Arabic Tell) the mound of rubbish on which a village stands, Josh. xi. 13; Jer. xxx. 18; also the heap caused by the ruin of a city, Deut. xiii. 16, etc. As a place-name, it does not seem to have occurred in ancient Palestine. The instances of it in the O.T. refer to Babylonia, Ezek. iii. 15; Ezra ii. 59; Neh. vii. 61. Other words for height (geographical) are מָרוֹם marôm (cf. רוּמָה Rumah, a place, 2 Kings xxiii. 36, and רָמָה Ramah); מִשְׂגָּב misgab, Ps. xviii. 2 (3). A summit is ראש or אָמִיר 'amîr Isa. xvii. 6.

מַעֲלֶה ma'aleh=ascent, used with names, *e.g.* Aḳrabbim, or "the scorpions", Num. xxxiv. 4; Josh. xv. 3; Jud. i. 36; Adummim, Josh. xv. 7, see p. 181; Gur, 2 Kings ix. 27, see p. 268 n.; Ziz, 2 Chron. xx. 16, see p. 185 n. 8; Luhith in Moab, Isa. xv. 5; Jer. xlviii.5; Beth-horon, Josh. x. 10; cf. 1 Macc. ii. 16; Jud. viii. 13. מוֹרָד morad is the opposite, the descent from Ai to Jericho, Josh. vii. 5; of the Beth-horon, Josh. x. 10; 1 Macc. iii. 24; of Horonaim, Jer. xlviii. 5=ascent of Luhith. Other words for "pass" were מַעְבָּרָה, מַעְבָּר (see p. 224) and נֶקֶב neḳeb, common in Arabic, which in the O.T. is only used as a proper name, Josh. xix. 33; אֲדָמִי הַנֶּקֶב LXX Ἀρμὲ, καὶ Ναβὸκ or Νακὲβ.

For Valley are these: On עֵמֶק 'emeḳ=*deepening*, and בִּקְעָה biḳ'ah =opening, see pp. 249 f.; for 'emeḳ LXX gives mostly *κοῖλας*, also *φάραγξ*, *πεδίον*, *αὐλών*. Elah (1 Sam. xvii. 2, 19), Hebron (Gen. xxxvii. 14), Aijalon (Josh. x. 12; cf. Isa. xxviii. 21), Jezreel (Josh. xvii. 16; Judges vi. 33; vii. 1; Hosea i. 5) are the only places called 'emeḳ identified past doubt. There were also the Vales of Siddim (Gen. xiv. 3, 8); of Rephaim (Josh. xv. 8), probably SE of Jerusalem; Achor (Josh. vii. 24), probably a pass from Jordan into Benjamin; Shaveh (Gen. xiv. 17); Keziz (Josh. xviii. 21); Beth-rehob (Judges xviii. 28), probably the N end of the Jordan Vale; Berachah (2 Chron. xx. 26); Baca (Ps. lxxxiv. 6); Succoth (Ps. lx. 6; cviii. 7), part of the Jordan Valley; Jehoshaphat (Joel iii. 2, 12; cf. v. 14). Like בקעה, עמק is applied to all parts of the Jordan Valley (Josh. xiii. 27; perhaps xviii. 28;

Ps. lx. 6); but unlike בקעה never extended to any plain so wide as that of the Euphrates, or like the central triangle of Esdraelon (see p. 250). Like בקעה it is used generically for valley-land, either *ager*, that can be ploughed (Job xxxix. 10; Ps. lxv. 14, Heb.) or *campus*, fit for military manœuvres (Job xxxix. 21; Josh. xvii. 16). Hence its extension was natural to the Philistine plain (Jer. xlvii. 5). On בקעה see p. 250. It is applied to plains like Esdraelon, or that of Jordan under Hermon (Josh. xi. 17; xii. 7), or at Jericho (Deut. xxxiv. 3), even to the valley of the Euphrates (Ezek. iii. 22; xxxviii. 1; Gen. xi. 2), and the Maritime Plain. LXX renders it by πεδίον. The Arabic equivalent is the vale between the Lebanons, the Beḳ'a, البقعة and other level tracts surrounded by hills, *e.g.* Buḳei'a, البقيعة, on the Belḳa, E of Salṭ, which we crossed in 1891 from the Jabbok, a high secluded vale, about 4 miles by 3, with mountains all round. Also the Buḳei'a, E of Shechem, and the Buḳei'a in Judah, above the N end of the Dead Sea. A surrounding of hills seems necessary to the name Biḳ'ah as if land *laid open*.

גַּיְא or גַּי gai (גֵּיא Isa. xl. 4; גֵּיא Zech. xiv. 4) is nearer our *glen* than *valley*, generally used for narrower openings than בקעה or עמק. Sites to which it was applied are: one of the gorges descending from the Moab plateau (Num. xxi. 20, Deut. iii. 20, etc.); the valleys of Hinnom, Josh. xv. 8, etc., etc., and Jiphthah-el, Josh. xix. 14, 27, perhaps Wady el-Ḳurn in Galilee. In Ps. xxiii. 4, evidently a ravine, in Zech. xiv. 14 a rent or cleft through a hill; in 1 Sam. xvii. 3 perhaps the ditch of the stream through the 'emeḳ (see p. 161). LXX φάραγξ (usually) αὐλών, κοῖλας, νάπη, or transliterated γῆ.

שָׁוֶה shaveh=level, Eng. *dale*, Gen. xiv. 5, in Moab a proper name; xiv. 7—מְצוּלָה, מְצוֹלָה meṣulah, meṣolah=a deep, but only once a valley bottom, מְצֻלָּה meṣullah, Zech. i. 8. פַּחַת, ravine, abyss (2 Sam. xviii. 17; cf. Ezra ii. 6, etc.; Neh. vii. 11). נַחַל both a stream and its valley.

For Plains, besides עמק and בקעה, is מישור mîshôr=level, generally of table-land, especially Moab (Deut. iii. 10; Josh. xiii. 9, 16; Jer. xlviii. 21, see p. 353), but also Bashan (1 Kings xx. 23-35). In 2 Chron. xxvi. 19 some (*e.g.* Siegfried-Stade, *Handwörterbuch*) refer it to the Jordan Plain, but it may be Moab. In Zech. iv. 7, opposed to הַר. From the same root is שָׁרוֹן shārôn, always as a proper name, and except in 1 Chron. v. 16, where it refers to a region E of Jordan (cf. Neub. *Géog. du Talmud*, 47) always of the Maritime Plain from Carmel to Joppa (see pp. 114 ff.); LXX δρύμος (Isa. lxv. 10, etc.) and πεδίον (Song ii. 1; 1 Chron. xxvii. 29). On שְׁפֵלָה not *plain*, but *low hills*, see fully, pp. 143 ff. אָבֵל 'Abel, a meadow always in composition, Abel-beth-maacah (1 Kings xv. 20, etc.) or Abel-maim, 2 Chron. xvi. 4, perhaps Abil el-Ḳamh (Rob. *LBR*); Abel-shittim of the acacias, Num. xxxiii. 49) opposite Jericho; Abel-meholah (of the dance or the whirls (?), see p. 390 n. 4); Abel-keramim (of vineyards, Jud. xi. 33); Abel-mizraim (of Egypt, Gen. l. 11). In 1 Sam. vi. 18 read אבן for אבל. For שָׂדֶה field, see pp. 72 f. כַּר *a watered field*, Isa. xxx. 23. כִּכָּר, p. 324. גָּלִיל, p. 269.

On מדבר (German *Trift* from *treiben*) from דבר to drive (*i.e.* herds to pasture), Jer. xxv. 24=*land not sown*. Our version renders *wilderness*, or *desert*. It is properly land roamed by nomads in opposition to land occupied by tillers of the soil. ערבה arabah=desert-steppe, used generally as parallel to Midbar (Isa. xxxvi. 6, etc.; Zech. xiv. 10, etc.), from the same root as Arabia and Arab; but with the definite article generally confined to the Jordan Valley, Deut. ii. 8, etc., etc. (see p. 312). יְשִׁמוֹן yeshimon, *devastation*, a stronger word, see p. 211, as applied to Judah; in a general sense Deut. xxxii. 10; Isa. xliii. 19, 20; Ps. lxviii. 7, etc.

For River, the most comprehensive is נהר *stream*, Ger. *Fluss*, for a river, Gen. ii. 10; Job xl. 23, but also for smaller streams and even artificial ones, canals (Ex. viii. 1; Ezek. xxxi. 4; Ps. cxxxvii. 1). The River, הנהר=the Euphrates, Gen. xxxi. 21, etc., etc., but in Isa. xix. 5 singular, 6 plural, the Nile. The Naharaim of Aram-naharaim are probably the Euphrates and Khabur (*ZAT*, iii. 307 f., Budde, *Urgeschichte*, 445 f.). נהר is also used of the sea, and in plural of its currents or tides (?), Ps. lxvi. 6, xxiv. 2 (but here probably of the deep under the earth).

נחל naḥal=Arabic wady, Greek χειμάῤῥοος, Ital. *fiumára*, a winter-torrent and its valley, 1 Kings xvii. 3, *hide in Naḥal Kerîth*, and 4, *drink of the Naḥal*. Valleys of this kind to which it is applied in the O.T. are Kidron, 2 Sam. xv. 23; el-'Arish, the *river of Egypt*, Num. xxxiv. 5; Josh. xv. 4, etc.; Eshcol, Num. xiii. 23, etc.; Kanah, W Kaneh, Josh. xvi. 8; Sorek, W es-Surar, Jud. xvi. 4; Gerar, Gen. xxvi. 17, cf. 1 Sam. xv. 5. But נחל is also used for large perennial streams like Arnon (Num. xxi. 14; Deut. ii. 24, iii. 8), Jabbok (Gen. xxxii. 23; Deut. ii. 37). Other נְחָלִים not identified are Zered (see p. 377). Besor N of Judah (1 Sam. xxx. 9, 10, 21); Gaash in Mt. Ephraim (Josh. xxiv. 30; Jud. ii. 9, etc.; 2 Sam. xxiii. 30; 1 Chron. xi. 32); Cherith (p. 389); Gad (2 Sam. xxiv. 5); Shittim (Joel iii. 18). A perennial stream is נחל איתן, LXX generally χειμάῤῥοος, even of Arnon and Jabbok; but also *φάραγξ* of Kishon (Josh. xix. 11); Arnon (Deut. ii. 24); Eshcol (Num. xiii. 23); and *ποταμός* of el-'Arish, 1 Kings viii. 65; *νάπαι*, Num. xxvi. 6.

יְאוֹר ye'or=the Nile, Gen. xli. 1-3, etc.; plural Nile-canals, Ex. viii. 1; Isa. vii. 18; Nahum iii. 8; canals in general, Isa. xxxiii. 21; river in general, Dan. xii. 5-7. LXX *πόταμος*, save Isa. xxxiii. 21, *διώρυγες*, xxxvii. 25 (*συναγωγὴν ὕδατος*). שִׁיחוֹר or שְׁחוֹר or שִׁחֹר is parallel to יְאוֹר the Nile, Isa. xxiii. 3; cf. Jer. ii. 18. In Josh. xiii. 3 either the Pelusiac branch of the Nile, or W el-'Arish.

פֶּלֶג peleg, Arabic fâleîj (cf. *πέλαγος*, *fluctus*)=stream, Jud. v. 15, 16; Ps. i. 3; xlvi. 4; lxv. 9, etc. אוּבַל=river, Dan. viii. 2, 3, 6; so יוּבַל, Jer. xvii. 8. (מיכל 2 Sam. xvii. 20 is corrupt.) Canal or conduit is תְּעָלָה te'alah=bringing up (of Elijah's trench, 1 Kings xviii. 32, etc.; of Jerusalem conduits, 2 Kings xviii. 17; xx. 20; Isa. vii. 3), or שֶׁלַח shelaḥ=(water) shoot, Neh. iii. 15. אָפִיק is river-bed, Ps. xviii. 16; stream, Ps. cxxvi. 4; Wady, Ezek. vi. 3. יַד *hand*=river-side, as we say Dee-side, Deut. ii. 37. שָׂפָה=lip, is bank or brink, Josh. xi. 4, etc.; קָצֶה=end, is either mouth of a river, Josh. xv. 5; xviii. 19, or edge of its waters, Josh. iii. 8, 15; גְּדוֹת= banks, Josh. iii. 15, etc. Spates or floods are קדמים (probably, see p. 256 n. 1); שֶׁטֶף (Ps. xxxii. 6, etc.); שִׁבֹּלֶת (Isa. xxvii. 12; cf. Jud. xii); and perhaps זֶרֶם, though this is rather the burst of rain that makes the flood. מִשְׁבָּר =breaker, originally billow, 2 Sam. xxii. 5; Jonah ii. 3; but in Ps. xlii. may be cataract. גל parallel to it Jonah ii. 4=heap or mass of water. הַמַּבּוּל= The Deluge.

On Wells and Springs see p. 71. Besides עַיִן and בְּאֵר are מַעְיָן, a collective of עַיִן, Josh. xv. 9, etc.; מוֹצָא מַיִם fountain-head (Ps. cvii. 33, 35, etc., of Ras el-'Ain, p. 71). מָקוֹר poetical for a dug spring, Jer. li. 36, etc.; מַבּוּעַ probably=gushing, Isa. xxxv. 7; xlix. 10; גֻּלֹּת bubbling springs, Josh. xv. 19; Jud. i. 15. באר or בּוֹר a dry בְּאֵר, Gen. xxxvii. 20; but also for water, Jer. vi. 7, etc.

Cisterns, Lakes, Pools, and Ponds.—For Gennesaret and Dead Sea the word is ים=sea; a bay of this is לָשׁוֹן=tongue or מִפְרָץ (or harbour, see p. 105); its bed קַרְקַע Amos ix. 3; בְּרֵכָה pool or tank, 2 Sam. ii. 13, etc.; מִקְוֶה a reservoir, Isa. xxii. 11; אֲגַם pond of standing water, Ps. cvii. 35, etc.; גֵּב ditch, 2 Kings iii. 16; Isa. xxx. 14.

APPENDIX II

STADE'S THEORY OF ISRAEL'S INVASION OF WESTERN PALESTINE

(See p. 187)

Stade's Theory of Israel's Invasion of Western Palestine, vol. i. pp. 123, 141 of *Geschichte des Volkes Israel*. It may bewilder the reader that it should be necessary to seek a theory so very different from the biblical account, but Stade has evidently felt compelled to this by unwillingness to attribute to Israel any save physical impulses in crossing Jordan, and by his belief that Israel could never have overcome the Canaanites. We shall see how far justified are these presuppositions. After the death of Moses (this is the theory) Israel continued to reside E of Jordan for a very long time, during which they passed from the nomadic to the agricultural stage, and increased in numbers. E Palestine became too small for them, and separate clans were forced to seek new homes across Jordan. About their passage into W Palestine Stade asserts: *First*, that they did not cross at once as a united body, but gradually, clan by clan. Joshua is legendary, an Eponymous of Ephraim, one of the clans. *Second*, they crossed peacefully, and won land W of Jordan by purchase or treaty. *Third*, they crossed not at Jericho, for opposite Jericho then lay Moabite, not Israelite, territory, but at Jabbok, where the Israelite population E of Jordan was most dense. Such is Stade's theory. Its presupposition—that Israel had no impulse to cross Jordan except a physical one, no memory of her forefathers' possession of the land, no consciousness yet of national unity, no impetus derived from the leadership of Moses, no desire for a national territory on surer ground than the E of Jordan afforded, nothing but the spilling over of her increasing numbers—that is simply impossible to prove, even if it were not opposed to the entire body of Israelite tradition, and inconsistent with Israel's subsequent history. Is it possible that so ancient (it is found in the earliest poems), so widespread (it occurs in every source) a tradition, as that Israel was conscious of her unity and her leadership by Yahweh in crossing Jordan, can be wrong? Is it possible that Israel, which became what she did, had not already (after all Moses did and taught) some sense of national destiny, and was not left to the drift of an increasing population? But to go on from this presupposition which I think groundless, to the three points deduced from it. *First*, that the passage of Jordan was gradual, clans by clans, and that Joshua was no real person. Stade bases his assertion that Joshua is the personification of the clan Ephraim on his notion that he is known to only one of the documents, the Ephraimite E. But Kuenen (*Onderzoek*, sec. ed. §13), Dillmann and Budde (*ZATW*, vii. 133; *Ri. u. Sam.*) have shown that Joshua was known also to the Judæan source J—of which Kittel rightly says, that "it can hardly be doubted" (*Gesch.* i. 248). But if Joshua was real, we have a personal centre for the whole people crossing Jordan and settling upon W Palestine, only less strong than that round which they had previously been kept united, *viz.* Moses. *Second*, Stade supposes that Israel's occupation of the land was peaceful. In W Palestine there was much forest-land unoccupied on the hills. Part of this the Canaanites, who had the towns and the valley-land, sold or gave to Israelite clans, in order to prevent Israel's military seizure of land (the possibility of which, observe, Stade admits). His arguments are (*a*) that the Canaanites were too strong for Israel to acquire land by force; (*b*) that the Israelite occupation was only partial and for long outside the chief houses; (*c*) that for long Israel lived in peaceful relations, intermarriage, etc., with Canaan. But (*a*) is not true. It is probable (from extra-biblical evidence) that W Palestine was then inhabited by tribes disunited and weakened by wars. This was not the only time in Syria's history that Arab tribes in the flush of their strength and hope defeated degenerate, though better equipped, settled populations. Stade admits both that the Canaanites submitted to a peaceful occupation only under fear of a military one, and that certain tribes of Israel (Dan, Simeon, and Levi) did win their land by the sword. Again (*b*) is admitted in the narrative, and is as compatible with a warlike as with a peaceful invasion. A partial occupation by war is in harmony with all we know of Semitic warfare—the fierce rush at a territory, and if success does not follow, exhaustion, acquiescence with what has been gained. Nor is (*c*) incompatible with a military invasion of this kind. But turning from these reasons to the assertion itself—if Stade be right that Israel won parts of W Palestine by treaty and purchase, why is there no trace in the narratives of such transactions? Why is the tradition of a military conquest so solid?

With this, and with Stade's *Third* position, Geography comes in. He holds that Israel could not have crossed at Jericho, for E Palestine opposite Jericho was at this time not Israelite but Moabite territory. Yet this is by no means correct. What we do know is that in later times E Palestine opposite Jericho was in Moab's hands; but this is a reason *against* supposing that the tradition of Israel's crossing there was a late tradition. Stade says that tradition merely fixed on the Jordan at Jericho as a likely place; but would this have seemed a likely place when the E bank was in Moab's hands? The rise of a tradition of the passage of the Jordan just here became more and more improbable as the centuries went on. Turning to W Palestine, we find strong geographical reasons for the passage at Jericho which I have already given on pp. 187 f. In W Palestine Israel was divided at first into two parts: the Joseph tribes settled in Mt. Ephraim, and Judah on the plateau S of Jerusalem, but in between were Canaanite settlements.[1] Now, what point of entrance better corresponds than Jericho to this disposition of the tribes? Had Israel crossed at the Jabbok, it is not easy to see how some tribes got into Judah as well as some into Mt. Ephraim, unless you suppose (so Oort's *Atlas*) that the tribe Judah never crossed Jordan, but came to its settlements through the Negeb: a supposition for which there is no real evidence. But take the statement of the Book of Joshua (to which more than one document contributes) that Israel as a whole crossed by Jericho. Then how natural is the subsequent disposition of the tribe—for roads lead up from Jericho equally into Mt. Ephraim, the plateau of Benjamin, and the centre and south of Judah. Again, the easy capture of Jericho is a fact which the subsequent history of the town renders probable. Jericho never once stood a siege. Finally, the existence of Israel's central camp at Gilgal for a considerable period, while the hill-country was being subdued (Josh. x. 43), receives an interesting proof in support of its possibility from the analogous case of the Canaanites who ruled the hill-country from Gilgal as a centre (Deut. xi. 30).

Further see H. P. Smith, *O.T. Hist.* (1903), who admits as certain only Israel's settlement in E Palestine before the invasion of Canaan proper; W. Phythian-Adams. *PEFQ*, 1927, 34-47, using the results of the German excavations; J. Garstang, *id.* 96-100, pointing out the uncertainties but concluding that the "red" city of Jericho was destroyed between 1400 and 1700 B.C. with liability to error of 50 years on either side; on recent excavations, *id.* 1930, 123-134; also his *Josh. Jud.* (1931) throughout.

[1] Although the tribe of Benjamin had occupied its territory, as Kittel shows (*Gesch.* p. i. 265 f.), there is no reason for supposing that this tribe was not formed till after the settlement of Ephraim. It was there from the first, on the territory which the Book of Joshua assigns to it.

APPENDIX III

THE WARS AGAINST SIHON AND OG

(See pp. 377 ff. and 386 ff.)

The War against Sihon the King of the Amorites.—The unreality of this and the reference of the song (Num. xxi. 27-30) to an invasion of Moab by Israel in the 9th century, have been urged by Meyer (*ZATW*, 1881, 118 ff.); Stade (*Gesch.* i. 117 ff.); and Addis (*Documents of the Hexateuch*, i. p. 174). But Dillmann (in *Numbers*[2], 128 ff.), Kuenen (*Onderzoek*, i. 13, 13), Wellhausen (*Hist.*), support the fact of the war. The arguments may be summed up: Reasons against the reality of the war against Sihon: (1) Mentioned only in E (Num. xxi) and D (ii. 24 ff.: Jud. xii. 13 is, according to Budde, an insertion from E, *Richter u. Sam.* 125); (2) Neither P nor J says anything of it; but (3) on the contrary both represent Sihon's land as still in possession of Moab, or at least with the name of Moab; *e.g.* P Num. xxii. 1, Israel camped *in 'Arboth-Moab, opposite Jericho*, and JE (Num. xxii. 41; xxiii. 14, 28) Balak of Moab brings Balaam to Bamoth as if his own territory.

To these it may be replied, (1) E is the oldest document; (2) though neither P nor J mentions war with Sihon, they give no story nor detail inconsistent with such a war. They do not say that Israel took the land between Arnon and Jabbok from Moab or Ammon, and the only trace of war between Moab and Israel is a fragment of E's own in Josh. 24, 9; (3) though Moab had been driven by Sihon from her territory, her name would remain attached to it. Dillmann points out that Sihon's conquest of Heshbon need not imply that all the Moabites were banished. Again D, which gives the war with Sihon for the land between Jabbok and Arnon, yet calls the latter the land of Moab (i. 5; xxviii. 69 (Heb.); xxxiv. 5).

There can be no objection to the story itself; nothing is incredible in it. If later all Israel under David, and N Israel under Omri, crossed Jordan and occupied the territory of Moab, Amorites may have done the same. And nothing was to be gained by inventing the story.

We come to the song (Num. xxi. 27 f.). Those who believe it does not refer to a war on the Amorites, at Israel's entrance to the land, but to an invasion of Moabite territory from W of Jordan, in the 9th cent., allege that the course of conquest it marks is from N to S, the line of the latter invasion, but they have to omit *the king of the Amorites Sihon* in ver. 29, and take Sihon as king of Moab. But against ver. 29*d* there is no objection, apart from this theory. Leave it, and take the first line of conquest traced in vv. 28, 29 as that of Sihon over Moab, and you do not violate the geography.

To sum up: the theory that the war with Sihon is unhistorical, and that the poem refers to a conquest by Israel of Moab in the 9th cent., can only be held by sacrificing vv. 26 and 29*d*, against neither of which is any objection apart from this theory; while the story of the war against Sihon as told by E is neither improbable nor inconsistent with the data in J and P, nor likely to have been invented.

See further Cornill, *Hist.* 45, Bennett, "Moab", Hastings, *DB*.

2. THE WAR WITH OG, KING OF BASHAN.—This war has not the same evidence in its support. In Num. xxi the account of it is an insertion (vv. 33 ff.) from the hand of a Deuteronomic writer. Characteristic phrases of D occur in it. Nor, save perhaps in three cases, is there mention of this war in the Hexateuch, outside the Deuteronomic passages, Num. xxi. 33 ff.; Deut. i. 4; iii; iv. 47; xxix. 7; Josh. xii. 4. The doubtful passages are Num. xxxii. 33, assigned by Kautzsch to a late edition; Josh. ix. 10, which he assigns to JE, but Dillmann regards as inserted, and Josh. xiii. 30, probably from P. 1 Kings iv. 19 is Deuteronomic. The story, therefore, we owe to the Deuteronomist, and we have no reminiscence of it as of the war with Sihon in the song. On this account, many who admit Sihon as historical, decline to receive Og. It is a case where proof is impossible; and we have not as much evidence as in Sihon's case. At the same time Og was bound with Sihon in the memory and tradition of the people, and it is difficult to see how he can have been invented. There is no geographical obstacle to a campaign N of Jabbok. Edrei would be as likely a place for Israel to fight with a king of Bashan as any other, while the fact that no battles are mentioned farther N towards Damascus, or E of the Lake of Galilee, where it would have been even easier for the popular memory to have invented victories for Moses, is proof that the tradition was restrained by historical facts. Critics, who assign to Israel a long residence E of Jordan, should be ready to admit an extension of their conquest northward by the easiest route to places so attractive as those of Bashan, before the crossing of Jordan was attempted.

APPENDIX IV

BIBLIOGRAPHY OF EASTERN PALESTINE

Authorities on the East of Jordan are as follows (I mark those I have not seen by an asterisk): Volney, *Voyage en Syrie*, etc., 1783-1785, II. (Eng. 1812); Seetzen's *Reisen durch Syrien*, 1806; Burckhardt, *Travels in Syria and the Holy Land in* 1810-1812 (1822); Buckingham, *Travels in Palestine, through the Countries of Bashan and Gilead in* 1816 (London, 1821); *Travels among the Arab Tribes east of Syria*, etc. (London, 1825); Irby and Mangles' *Travels in Egypt, Syria*, etc., 1817, 1818 (London, 1822); *Schubert (and Roth), *Reise in's Morgenland*, 1837 (first to discover the depth of the Dead Sea below the Mediterranean); Robinson, *Bib. Res.* (1838), especially vol. ii; Molyneux's "Expedition to Dead Sea, 1847", in *Journ. of Royal Geogr. Society*, xviii. 126 ff.; Lynch's *Narrative of U.S. Expedition in* 1848; in 1852 Robinson visited Pella and W Yabis (*Later Bib. Res.* sec. viii.); Porter, *Five Years in Damascus, with Travels, etc., in Palmyra, Lebanon, and the Hauran* (London, 1855); *Roth in Petermann's *Mittheilungen*, 1857-1858, about Kerak S to 'Aḳaba; G. Rey, *Voyage dans le Haouran et aux bords de la Mer Morte in* 1858; Wetzstein, *Reisebericht uber Hauran u. die Trachonen* (1858), (Berlin, 1860); *Wetzstein's and Dörgen's expedition farther south in 1800; Petermann's *Mittheil.* 1866; De Saulcy in 1863 visited Ammon, Ḥesban, etc., *Voy. en Terre Sainte*, i. 1865; *Duc de Luynes, *Voy. d'exploration à la Mer Morte, à Petra, et sur la rive gauche du Jourdain* en 1864 (pub. 1874), vol. ii, with Mavor's and Sanvaire's expedition to Kerak, Shobek, etc.; Wilson and Anderson, 1866, in *PEFQ*, vol. i; Warren, *Reconnaissance of Jordan Valley*, 1867; and *PEFQ*, i, ii; Palmer and Drake, *Desert of Tih and Country of Moab, PEFQ*, 1871; the Kieperts travelled from 'Amman by Gadara to Muzeirib in 1870, **Zeitschrift des Ges. für Erdkunde* (Berlin, v); Northey's *Expedition E. of Jordan in* 1871 (*PEFQ*, 1872); Tristram's *Land of Moab*, 1874; Porter's journey of 1874, *PEFQ*, 1881; Kersten's to Dead Sea and Moab, 1874, *ZDPV*, ii; Expedition of American Society, 1876, in Merrill's *East of the Jordan* (London, 1881); Schick's journey to Moab, 1877, is given with map in *ZDPV*, ii; Langer's short journey, 1881, in **Mitth. d. Geogr. Ges. in Wien*, 1882; Burton and Drake, *Unexplored Syria*; Laurence Oliphant's *Land of Gilead*, 1880. In 1881 Conder and Mantell began that survey of E Palestine, which the Turks brought to a conclusion; see *PEFQ*,

1881-1882, *PEF Mem.* on E Palestine, Conder, *Heth and Moab*, 1885. In 1884 Hull and Kitchener surveyed the S end of Dead Sea and regions round, *PEFQ*, 1884, and Geolog. vol. in *PEF Mem.* In 1884 Guy Le Strange visited Pella, Ajlun, and the Belḳa, *PEFQ*, 1885, also in Schumacher's *Across Jordan*, which gives Oliphant's *Trip to NE of Lake Tiberias.* Schumacher's surveys and travels, 1885 onward, in *Across the Jordan, Exploration and Survey of part of Hauran and Jaulan* (London, 1886); *The Jaulân*, surveyed for the *DPV* (Eng. 1888); *Pella; Ajlun; Abila of the Decapolis* as supplement to *PEFQ*, 1889. Scharling, *Hauran: Reisebilder aus Palästina* (Bremen, 1890). In *ZDPV* among others: Stubel, *Reise nach den Diret et Tulul*, etc., with map, XII; Van Kasteren, *Journey in Gilead*, XIII, *PEFQ*, 1888. *Narrative of a Scientific Expedition in the Trans-Jordanic Region*, 1886.

In 1895 these: Rob. Lees, *Geogr. Journ.*, *PEFQ*; F. J. Bliss, "Exped. to Moab and Gilead" and "Inscriptions Coll. in Moab", 371 ff.; W. Ewing, "Journey in Hauran"; cf. "Gk. and other Inscriptions", ed. by A. G. Wright and A. Souter; also Wright, "The Rom. Prov. of Syria, and Arabia". *ZDPV*, Schumacher, Es-Salṭ, 65 ff., Medeba, 113 ff., Dscherash, 126 ff., cf. 141. *MuNDPV*, R. Brünnow, "Reisebericht", 65 ff., 81 (cf. 1896 with photos); Kiepert, 24 ff., *Der Bote aus Zion*, 33 ff.; L. Gautier, *Au delà du Jourdain.* In 1896: *PEFQ*, Gray Hill, "Journ. E. of Jordan, etc.", *MuNDPV*, "*Ein Fusstour, etc.*" (from *Die Warte des Tempels*, 1895). During the last thirty-five years, articles and notices in *PEFQ*, *Bibl. World*, *JBL*, *ZDPV*, *MuNDPV*, and other periodicals, as well as various handbooks for travellers are too numerous to mention. But these volumes must be noted: Von Oppenheim, *Vom Mittelmeer z. Pers. Golf*, i. 1899; L. Gautier, *Autour de la Mer Morte*, 1901; A. Musil, *Arabia Petræa*, i *Moab*, ii f. *Edom*, 1907; R. E. Brünnow and A. von Domaszewski, *Die Provincia Arabia*, 3 vols., 1904-1909; W. Libbey and F. E. Hoskins, *The Jordan Valley and Petra*, 2 vols., 1905; Gertrude L. Bell, *The Desert and The Sown*; J. Kelman, *From Damascus to Palmyra*, 1908; G. A. Smith and J. G. Bartholomew, *Atlas of Hist. Geog. of the Holy Land*, the relevant maps, 1915.

The volumes and articles on the inscriptions of Eastern Palestine will be found given on p. 34, n. 7.

APPENDIX V

ROADS AND WHEELED VEHICLES IN SYRIA

(See p. 220)

Judah's progress in chariots is interesting. Joshua houghed horses and burnt chariots taken in war (Josh. xi. 6, 9). David houghed most horses, but kept a hundred (2 Sam. viii. 4). Solomon had 1400 chariots, in chariot cities, and with the king at Jerusalem (1 Kings x. 26). There would be few there for the ground was unsuitable, and the depôts were in the Arabah or Shephelah where they would be of more use. A Beth-marcaboth was in the Negeb. The only instances of chariots driving into Jerusalem are given on p. 220. See, too, 2 Sam, xvi, where Absalom is said to have chariots, whether in Jerusalem is uncertain; and Isa. xxiii, where Assyrian chariots fill the valley of Jehoshaphat.

Wheeled vehicles drawn by oxen were used in agriculture from early times, 1 Sam. vi. 10; 2 Sam. vi. 3 (in Amos ii. 13 perhaps threshing-rollers). As a nomadic race, settled in a hilly country, Israel would not soon take to wheels; and the earliest carts or waggons in the Bible came from Philistia or Egypt (1 Sam. vi. 10; Gen. xlv. 19, etc.). Chariots were introduced from Mesopotamia, and later from Egypt (which had the chariot and horse from Asia). Syrians, with their flat country S of Damascus, were strong in chariots, and Samaria lay on the main road between Egypt and Damascus, which crossed her NW corner, and was used by chariots (*Travels of an Egyptian*, see p. 115).

Roads, in our sense, were not necessary for waggons and chariots. In 1891, E of Jordan, we met Circassians driving bullock-carts from Damascus to Jerash and Rabboth-ammon. But artificial roads of some kind appear to have existed in Palestine from the earliest times. The מסלה, A.V. *highway*, is *heaped up*, often only for temporary purposes, such as the visit of royalty, cf. Isa. xlv, lxii, 10 (I saw the like on the visit of Khedive Tewfik to Siout in Upper Egypt in 1880); but also for permanent use, Num. xx. 19; Jud. xx. 31; 1 Sam. vi. 12; 1 Chron. xxvi. 16; Jer. xxxi. 21. Roads were enjoined to the cities of refuge (Deut. xix. 3).

In the N.T., outside Revelation, horses and chariots, except once, do not exist, a contrast to the O.T., and proof of the pacific plebeian kingdom of

Him who came *riding upon an ass*. The exception is the chariot of the treasurer of Queen Candace (Acts viii. 28 ff.).

The Romans were the first to make great roads in Palestine, and this not till Hadrian and the Antonines. The milestones are chiefly of Antoninus Pius and Marcus Aurelius, but the oldest is of Hadrian.[1]

After the Moslem invasion the first Khalifs kept up the Roman roads in Syria, with a service of stage-coaches and posts. The Latin *mile* was adopted, الميل el-Mîl. One Arab milestone was found between Jerusalem and Jericho, at Khan el-Ḥathroura, inscribed as by "the servant of God, Abd-el-Melik, prince of believers. The mercy of God be to him. From Damascus to this milestone is 109 miles." This was Khalif Abd-el-Melek ibn-Merwan, 65-86 of the Hejra, builder of the mosque of Omar. Clermont-Ganneau, *Recueil d'Archéologie Orientale*, 201 ff.: "Une Pierre Milliaire Arabe de Palestine du Ière siècle de l'hégire."[2]

In the times of the Crusades, "the royal roads, which replaced the Roman ways, still appear to have been used by wheeled vehicles. As for others, there is every cause to think that they were only mule-paths."[3]

The decay of these roads, and the disappearance of wheeled vehicles from the land—till recently—was due to the conquest of Syria by nomad and desert tribes whose locomotion was on animals. The few roads and carriages now in existence are of Frank, Jewish, or Circassian origin. By 1894 were the Alpine road from Beyrout to Damascus, with branches, and roads from Jaffa to Jerusalem, Jerusalem to Jericho and Hebron, Jaffa to Nablus, and Haifa to Nazareth; also one partly made from Damascus along the Hajj route. But especially since the War roads have been multiplied. There are said to be "now 400 m. of metalled main roads and 440 of secondary serving 177 villages. Many hundreds of tracks connecting scattered villages and settlements are used by motors and other wheeled traffic in the dry weather" (*Enc. Brit.*, 14th ed. "Palestine").

In 1892 the Beyrout-Damascus railway was opened, in 1892 that from Jaffa to Jerusalem, 1895 that from Haifa by El-Muzeirib to Damascus, 1901-1904 Damascus to Ma'an, extended by 1908 to Medina. In 1906-1908 a broad-gauge line was laid from Aleppo to Riyak on the Beyrout-Damascus

[1] Cl.-Ganneau, "Une Inscription Romaine de Bettir". *Comptes Rendus de l'Académie des Inscriptions, etc.* 1894.

[2] Another of the same Khalif near Bab el-Wad on the Roman road to Jerusalem, De Vogüé and Cl.-Ganneau, as in previous note, 27 ff., 259 f. Lagrange, *Rev. Biblique*, iii, 1894, 136 ff., argues (inconclusively) for the Arab mile = 2500 metres. On this paragraph see Arculf, A.D. 700 in Bohn's *Early Travels*, 7.

[3] Rev, *Colonies Franques*, 254.

line, with a branch to Tripoli in 1911, taken up in 1917. The Great War brought about a large increase. The Turks laid down a line from N of Tullkarm to Lydda on the Jaffa-Jerusalem line and from the Junction-Station on this ran two branches to Beersheba and to near Gaza. The British by March 1917 had completed their railway from Ḳantarah on the Suez Canal almost to Gaza, and by January 1919 brought it on to Haifa. See the Railway Map 1914-1919, accompanying *Military Operations, Egypt and Palestine, June 1917 to the End of the War*, compiled by Captain Cyril Falls, maps by Major A. F. Becke, 1930.

APPENDIX VI

THE JEWISH COLONIES IN PALESTINE

This list has been compiled from *The Handbook of Palestine and Trans-Jordan*, by Luke and Keith-Roach, and from some official documents and other sources. The Colonies vary much in size and the number of colonists. By far the largest are Petaḥ-Tiḳweh with some 6500 inhabitants, Rishon-le-Ziyon with over 2000, Reḥoboth and Ziḳron-Ya'aḳub over 1000, down to smaller settlements of several hundreds or only a few scores. There are Agricultural Experiment Stations at Reḥoboth, Tell-Abhibh (Aviv), and Gebhath (Gevath).

Judæa—south of Jaffa: Miḳweh-Israel, Naḥlat-Yehuda, Rishon-le-Ziyon, Be'er Ya'aḳub, Nes Ziyona, Kfar Aharon, Reḥoboth, 'Ekron, Gedera, Be'er Tubhia, Ruḥama, Ben-Shemen, Ḥulda, Kfar Uria, 'Artuf.

Judæa—north of Jaffa: Naḥlat Gannim, Naḥlat Yiṣḥak, Shekhunat Borochov, Ramat Gan, Bnei Beraḳ, Petaḥ-Tiḳweh, Ra'anana, Ramatayim, Ḳiryath Sha'ul, 'Ir Shalom, Herzlia, Magdiel, Kfar Saba, Kfar Mala.

About Jerusalem: Ḳiryath 'Anabhim, Moza, 'Emeḳ Arazim, 'Aṭaroth, Nebhe Ya'aḳub.

Samaria: Gan Shmuel, Kerkur, Gedera, Benyamina, Zaramia, Caesarea, Shfeia, Bat Shlomo, Ziḳron-Ya'aḳub, 'Athlit, Gibh'ath 'Ada, Tirah.

Esdraelon: Naḥlat Ya'aḳub, Ḥarthiya, Yazur, Nesher, Kfar Yehoshu'a, Ziḳron Abhram, Sheikh Abreḳ, Kfar Baruch, Manor, Jedda, Yugoslavian group, Sharona, Hashron, Pinsk, Gwata, Abu Shusha, Nahalal, Afuleh, Merhabhia, Balfouria, Kfar Yeladim, Tel 'Adashim, Kfar Gide'on, Zerifin, Kneifes, Ginegar (Jinjar), Kfar Yeḥezkiel, 'Ain Harod, Tel Yoseph, Ḥephṣibah, Beth Alfa, Gebha'.

Lower Galilee: Kfar Tabor, Segera, Miṣpah, Kfar Ḥittim, Migdal, Kinnereth, Degania A and B, Markenhof, Gesher Neḥalim, Menaḥamiya, Betania, Yabhniel, Beit Gan.

Upper Galilee: Rosh Pinna, Maḥanayim, Ayeleth Hashaḥar, Mishmar Hayarden, Yesod Hama'ala, Tel Hai and Kfar Gil'adi, Gibh'ath Haḥoṣbhim, Metulleh, 'Ain Zeitun.

MAPS

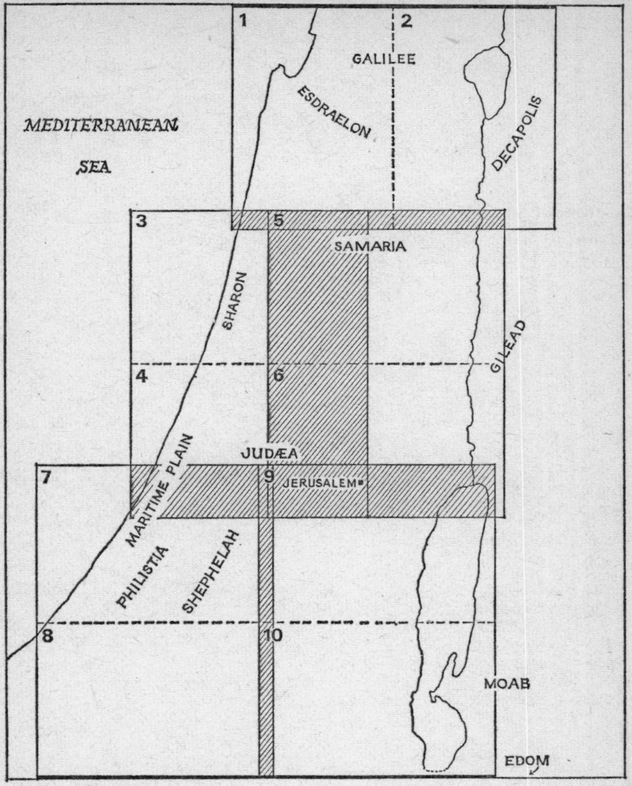

These maps are simplified from George Adam Smith's original coloured maps by the omission of modern settlements, roads and railways; but all the author's placings of Biblical localities are included unchanged.

In all the maps names run due east-west.

Scale of Maps

0 1 2 3 4 6 8

or approximately 5 ½ miles to 1 inch

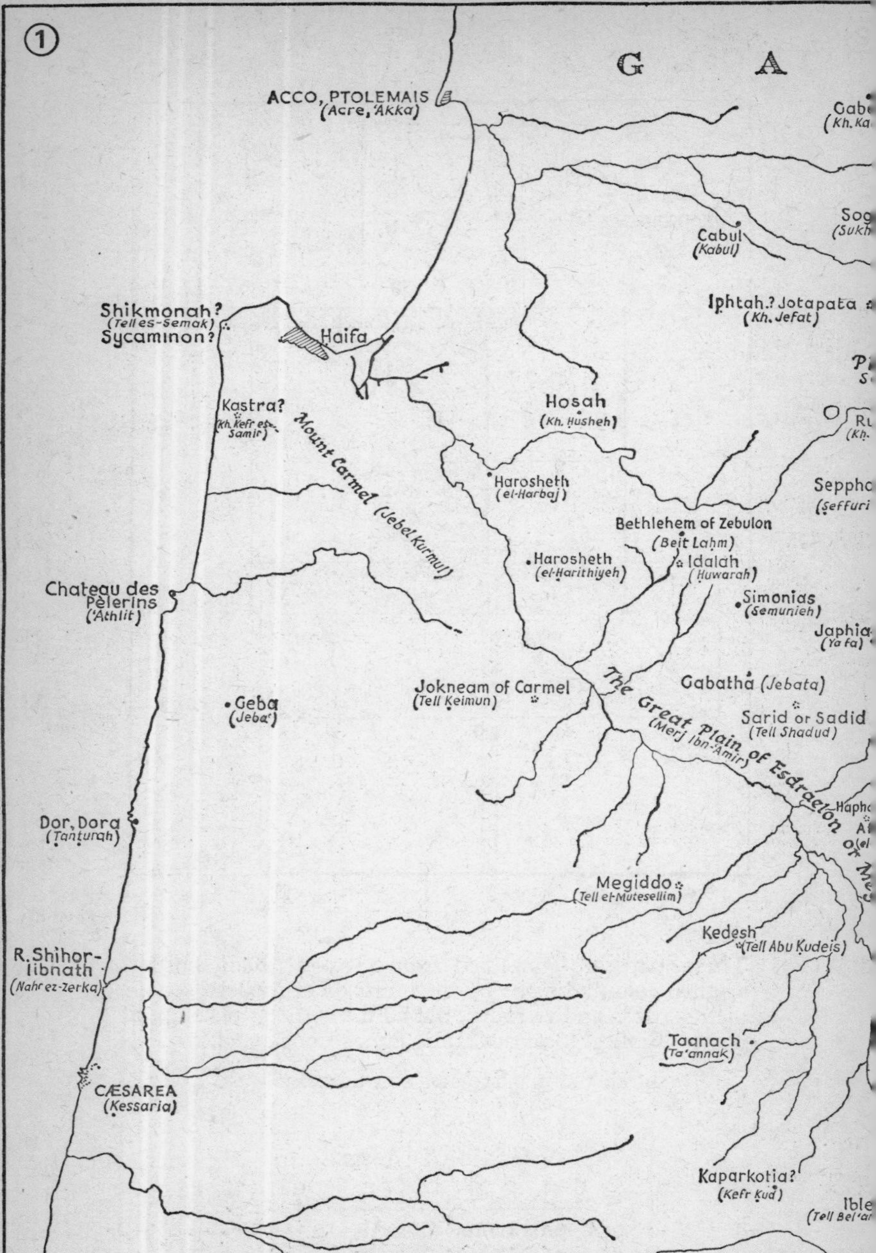
1
G A
ACCO, PTOLEMAIS
(Acre, 'Akka)
Cabul
(Kabul)
Iphtah.? Jotapata
(Kh. Jefat)
Shikmonah?
(Tell es-Semak)
Sycaminon?
Haifa
Kastra?
(Kh. Kefr es-Samir)
Mount Carmel (Jebel Kurmul)
Hosah
(Kh. Husheh)
Harosheth
(el-Harbaj)
Bethlehem of Zebulon
(Beit Lahm)
Harosheth
(el-Harithiyeh)
Idalah
(Huwarah)
Simonias
(Semunieh)
Chateau des Pèlerins
('Athlit)
Japhia
(Ya fa)
The Great Plain of Esdraelon
(Merj Ibn-'Amir)
Jokneam of Carmel
(Tell Keimun)
Gabatha (Jebata)
Geba
(Jeba')
Sarid or Sadid
(Tell Shadud)
Dor, Dora
(Tanturah)
Megiddo
(Tell el-Mutesellim)
Kedesh
(Tell Abu Kudeis)
R. Shihor-libnath
(Nahr ez-Zerka)
Taanach
(Ta'annak)
CÆSAREA
(Kessaria)
Kaparkotia?
(Kefr Kud)
Aphek? (el-Mejdel)
Aphek? (Baka)
Dothan (Tell Dothan)

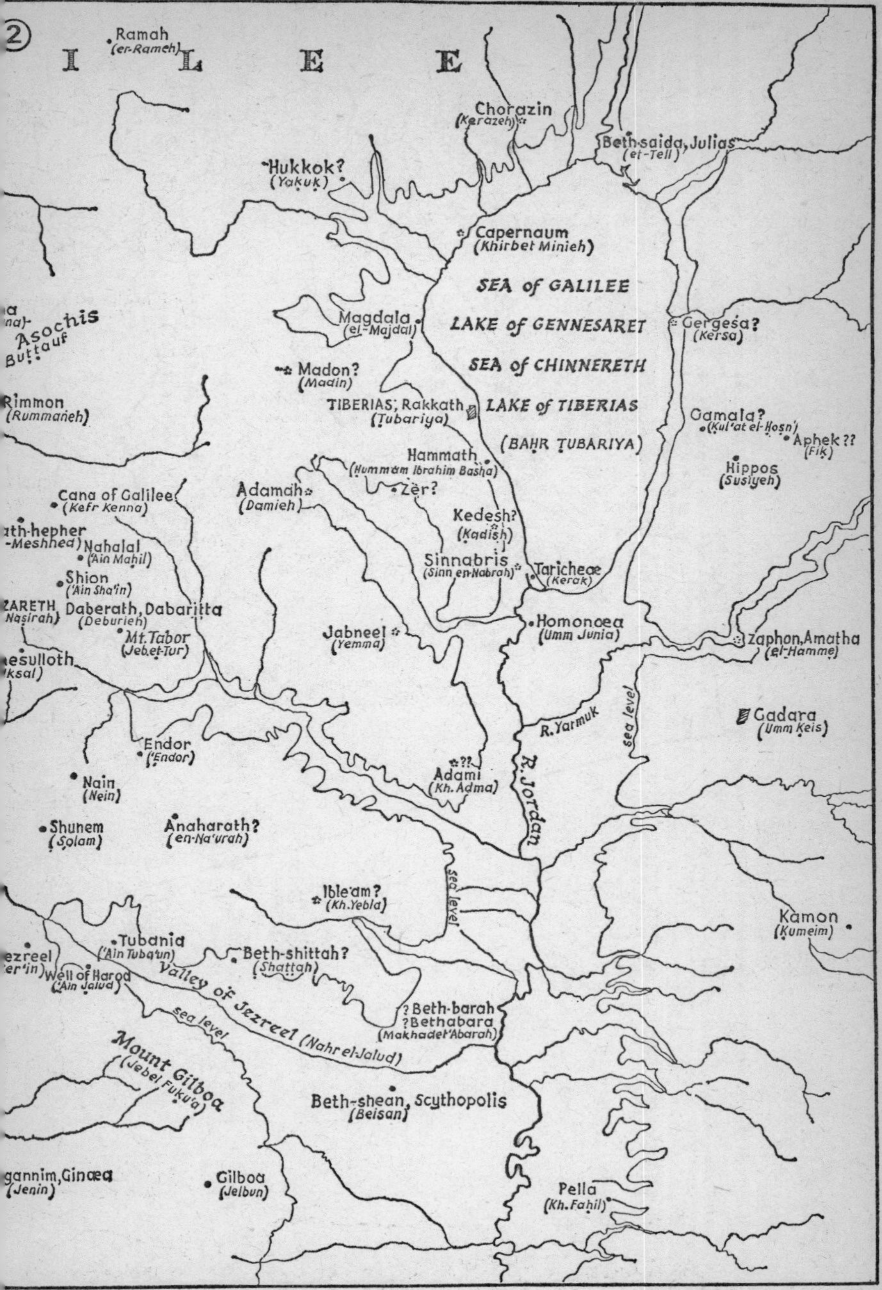

2
Ramah
(er-Rameh)
I L E E
Chorazin
(Kerazeh)
Beth-saida, Julias
(et-Tell)
Hukkok?
(Yakuk)
Capernaum
(Khirbet Minieh)
SEA of GALILEE
LAKE of GENNESARET
SEA of CHINNERETH
LAKE of TIBERIAS
(BAHR TUBARIYA)
Magdala
(el-Majdal)
Asochis
Buttauf
Madon?
(Madin)
Gergesa?
(Kersa)
Rimmon
(Rummaneh)
TIBERIAS, Rakkath
(Tubariya)
Gamala?
(Kul'at el-Hosn')
Aphek ??
(Fik)
Hammath
(Humm'am Ibrahim Basha)
Hippos
(Susiyeh)
Zer?
Cana of Galilee
(Kefr Kenna)
Adamah
(Damieh)
Kedesh?
(Kadish)
Nahalal
('Ain Mahil)
Sinnabris
(Sinn en-Nabrah)
Taricheae
(Kerak)
Shion
('Ain Sha'in)
Daberath, Dabaritta
(Deburieh)
Homonoea
(Umm Junia)
Mt. Tabor
(Jebel-et-Tur)
Jabneel
(Yemma)
Zaphon, Amatha
(el-Hamme)
R. Yarmuk
sea level
Gadara
(Umm Keis)
Endor
('Endor)
R. Jordan
Adami
(Kh. Adma)
Nain
(Nein)
Shunem
(Solam)
Anaharath?
(en-Na'urah)
sea level
Ible'am?
(Kh. Yebla)
Kamon
(Kumeim)
Tubania
('Ain Tuba'un)
Beth-shittah?
(Shattah)
Well of Harod
('Ain Jalud)
Valley of Jezreel (Nahr el-Jalud)
sea level
? Beth-barah
? Bethabara
(Makhadet 'Abarah)
Mount Gilboa
(Jebel Fuku'a)
Beth-shean, Scythopolis
(Beisan)
gannim, Ginaea
(Jenin)
Gilboa
(Jelbun)
Pella
(Kh. Fahil)

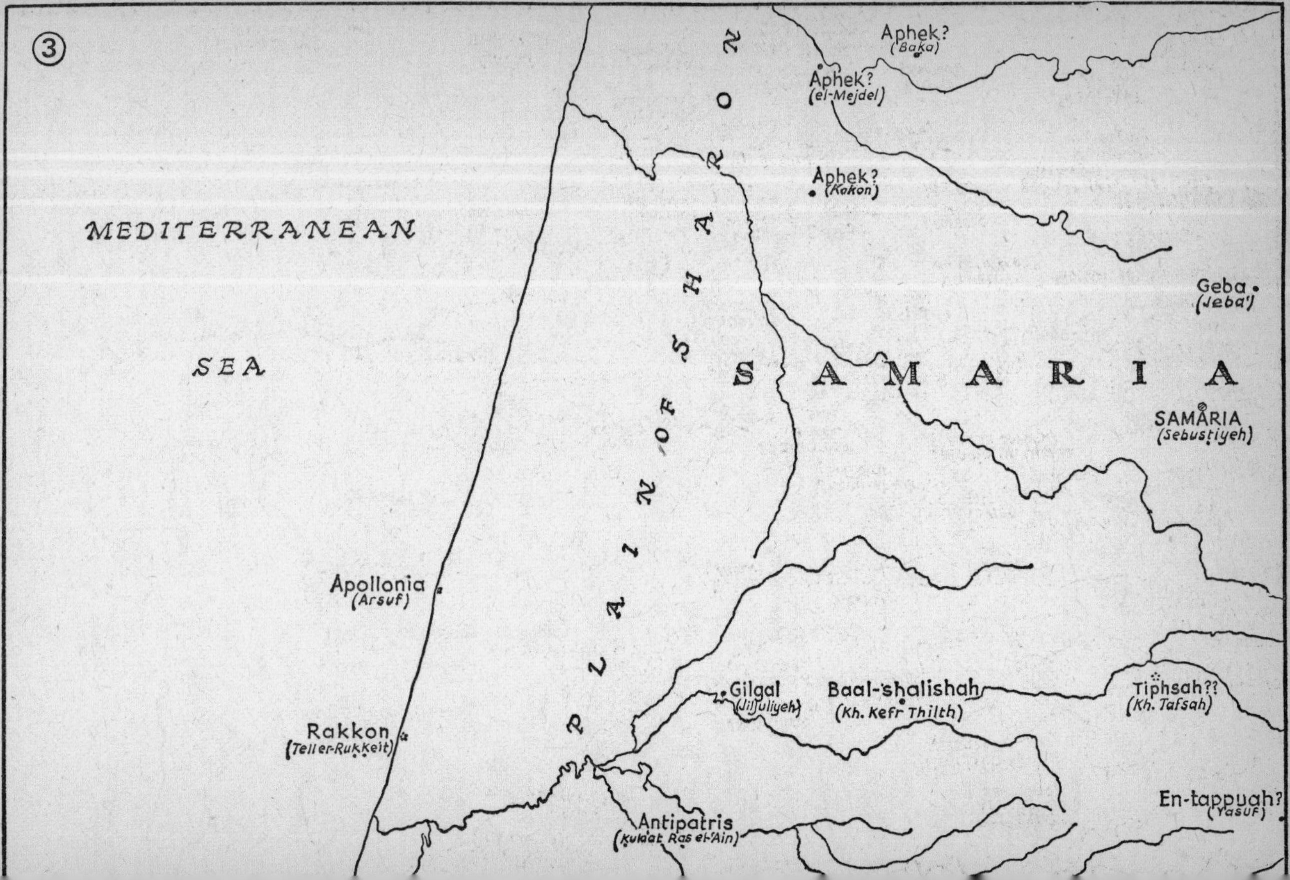
3
MEDITERRANEAN
SEA
PLAIN OF SHARON
SAMARIA
Aphek?
(Baka)
Aphek?
(el-Mejdel)
Aphek?
(Kakon)
Geba
(Jeba')
SAMARIA
(Sebustiyeh)
Apollonia
(Arsuf)
Rakkon
(Tell er-Rukkeit)
Gilgal
(Jiljuliyeh)
Baal-shalishah
(Kh. Kefr Thilth)
Tiphsah??
(Kh. Tafsah)
En-tappuah?
(Yasuf)
Antipatris
(Kulaat Ras el-Ain)

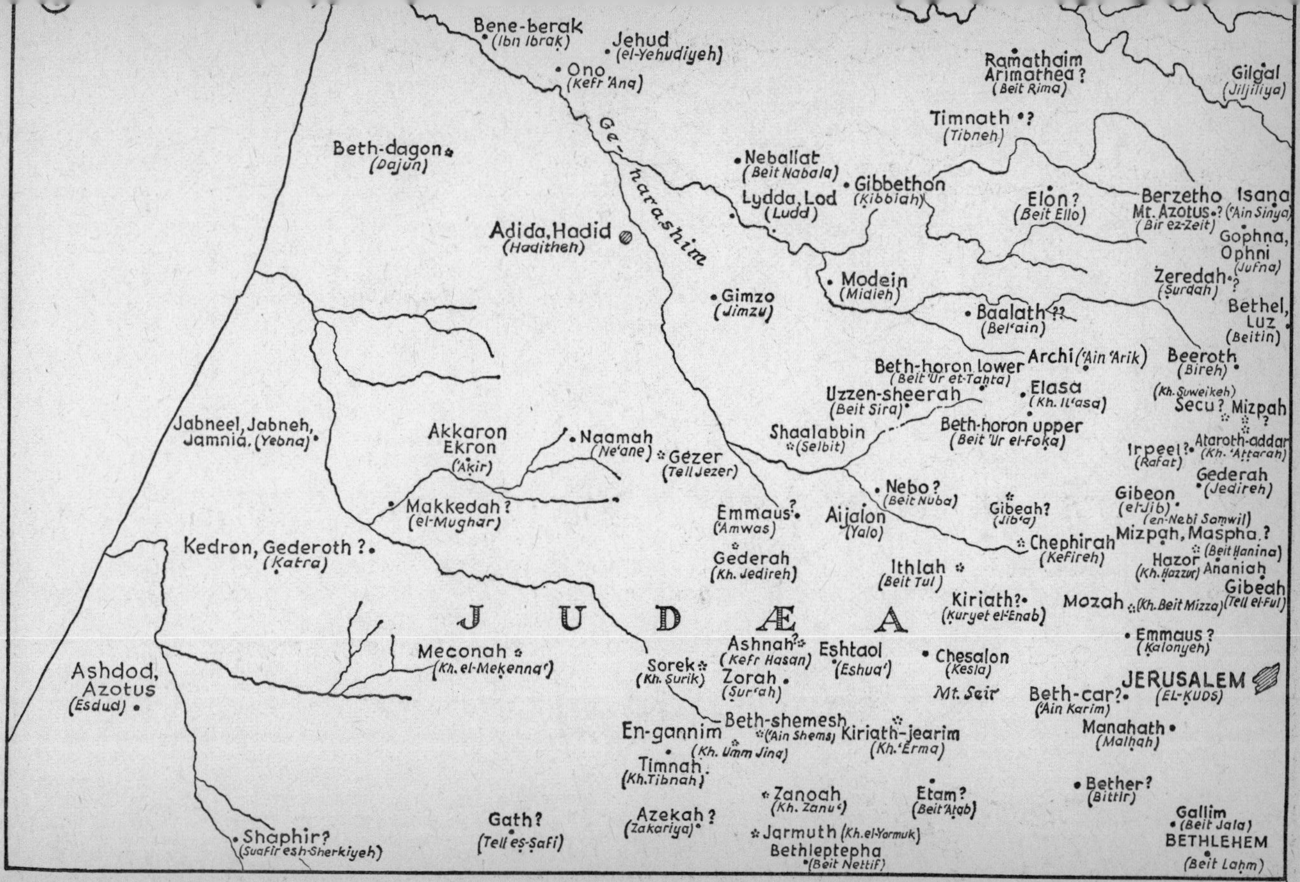
Bene-berak (Ibn Ibrak)
Jehud (el-Yehudiyeh)
Ono (Kefr 'Ana)
Ramathaim Arimathea? (Beit Rima)
Gilgal (Jiljiliya)
Timnath? (Tibneh)
Beth-dagon (Dajun)
Ge-harashim
Neballat (Beit Nabala)
Gibbethon (Kibbiah)
Lydda, Lod (Ludd)
Elon? (Beit Ello)
Berzetho
Isana ('Ain Sinya)
Mt. Azotus? (Bir ez-Zeit)
Gophna, Ophni (Jufna)
Adida, Hadid (Haditheh)
Zeredah? (Surdah)
Modein (Midieh)
Gimzo (Jimzu)
Baalath?? (Bel'ain)
Bethel, Luz (Beitin)
Archi ('Ain 'Arik)
Beeroth (Bireh)
Beth-horon lower (Beit 'Ur et-Tahta)
Elasa (Kh. Il'asa)
(Kh. Suweikeh)
Secu?
Mizpah?
Uzzen-sheerah (Beit Sira)
Beth-horon upper (Beit 'Ur el-Foka)
Shaalabbin (Selbit)
Ataroth-addar (Kh. 'Attarah)
Irpeel? (Rafat)
Jabneel, Jabneh, Jamnia (Yebna)
Akkaron Ekron ('Akir)
Naamah (Ne'ane)
Gezer (Tell Jezer)
Gederah (Jedireh)
Nebo? (Beit Nuba)
Gibeon (el-Jib)
(en-Nebi Samwil)
Makkedah? (el-Mughar)
Emmaus? ('Amwas)
Aijalon (Yalo)
Gibeah? (Jib'a)
Chephirah (Kefireh)
Mizpah, Maspha? (Beit Hanina)
Hazor (Kh. Hazzur)
Ananiah
Kedron, Gederoth? (Katra)
Gederah (Kh. Jedireh)
Ithlah (Beit Tul)
Gibeah (Tell el-Ful)
Kiriath? (Kuryet el-'Enab)
Mozah (Kh. Beit Mizza)
JUDÆA
Emmaus? (Kalonyeh)
Meconah (Kh. el-Mekenna')
Ashnah? (Kefr Hasan)
Eshtaol (Eshua')
Chesalon (Kesla)
Ashdod, Azotus (Esdud)
Sorek (Kh. Surik)
Zorah (Sur'ah)
JERUSALEM (EL-KUDS)
Mt. Seir
Beth-car? ('Ain Karim)
Beth-shemesh ('Ain Shems)
En-gannim (Kh. Umm Jina)
Kiriath-jearim (Kh. 'Erma)
Manahath (Malhah)
Timnah (Kh. Tibnah)
Zanoah (Kh. Zanu')
Etam? (Beit 'Atab)
Bether? (Bittir)
Gath? (Tell es-Safi)
Azekah? (Zakariya)
Jarmuth (Kh. el-Yarmuk)
Bethleptepha (Beit Nettif)
Gallim (Beit Jala)
BETHLEHEM (Beit Lahm)
Shaphir? (Suafir esh-Sherkiyeh)

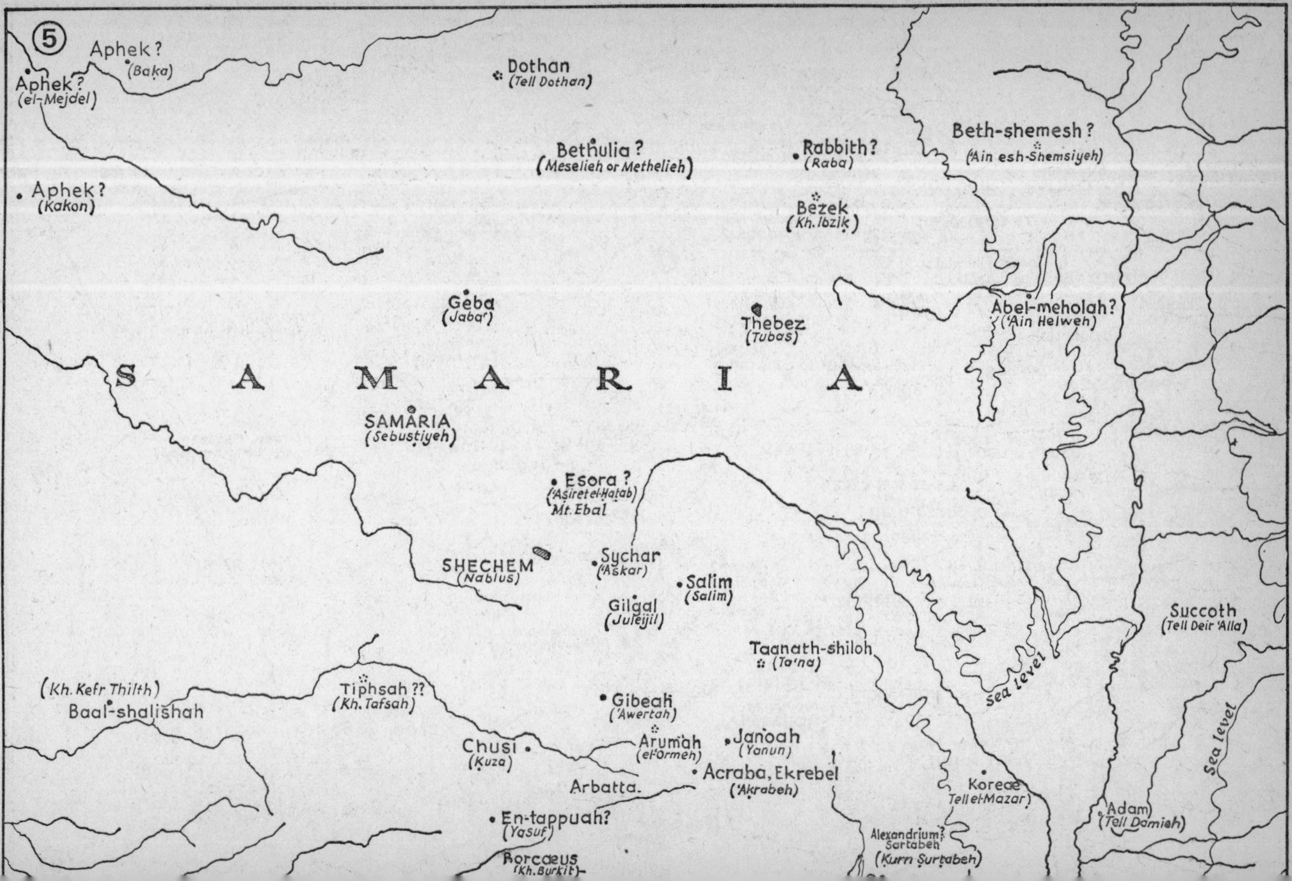
5
Aphek?
(Baka)
Aphek?
(el-Mejdel)
Aphek?
(Kakon)
Dothan
(Tell Dothan)
Bethulia?
(Meselieh or Methelieh)
Rabbith?
(Raba)
Bezek
(Kh. Ibzik)
Beth-shemesh?
('Ain esh-Shemsiyeh)
Geba
(Jaba')
Thebez
(Tubas)
Abel-meholah?
('Ain Helweh)
S A M A R I A
SAMARIA
(Sebustiyeh)
Esora?
('Asiret el-Hatab)
Mt. Ebal
SHECHEM
(Nablus)
Sychar
('Askar)
Salim
(Salim)
Gilgal
(Juleijil)
Taanath-shiloh
(Ta'na)
Succoth
(Tell Deir 'Alla)
Sea level
Sea level
(Kh. Kefr Thilth)
Baal-shalishah
Tiphsah??
(Kh. Tafsah)
Gibeah
('Awertah)
Arumah
(el-'Ormeh)
Janoah
(Yanun)
Chusi
(Kuza)
Acraba, Ekrebel
('Akrabeh)
Arbatta.
Korece
Tell el-Mazar)
Adam
(Tell Damieh)
En-tappuah?
(Yasuf)
Alexandrium?
Sartabeh
(Kurn Surtabeh)
Borcaeus
(Kh. Burkit)

6
Shiloh (Seilun)
Thormasia (Turmus 'Aya)
Phaselis (Kh. Faṣa'il)
River Jordan
Ramathaim Arimathea ? (Beit Rima)
Gilgal (Jiljiliya)
Timnath ? (Tibneh)
Gibbethon (Kibbiah)
Elon ? (Beit Ello)
Berzetho
? Mt. Azotus (Bir ez-Zeit)
Isana ('Ain Sinya)
Baal-hazor (Tell el-'Aṣur)
Chephar-ammoni (Kefr 'Ana)
Gophna, Ophni (Jufna)
Aphairema, Ophrah? Ephraim (Et Taiyibeh)
Modein (Midieh)
Zeredah (Ṣurdah) ?
Naarah? (Kh. el-'Aujah et-Taḥta)
Baalath ?? (Bel'ain)
Bethel, Luz (Beitin)
Rock Rimmon (Rumman)
Sea level
Zemaraim (Kh. es-Sumrah)
Archi ('Ain 'Arik)
Beeroth (Bireh)
Ai, Aiath ?? (Kh. Ḥayyan)
Beth-horon lower (Beit 'Ur et-Taḥta)
Elasa (Kh. Il'asa)
Uzzen-sheerah (Beit Sira)
(Kh. Suweikeh) Secu
Dok ('Ain ed-Duk)
Rock Oreb ? ('Ushsh el-Ghurab)
Mizpah? (Tell en-Naṣbeh)
Beth-horon upper (Beit 'Ur el-Foka)
Ataroth-addar (Kh. 'Aṭṭarah)
Michmash (Mukhmas)
Irpeel (Rafat)
Gederah (Jedireh)
Nebo ? (Beit Nuba)
Gibeon (el-Jib)
Geba, Gibeah (Jeba')
Jericho (er-Riḥa)
Gilgal (B. Jiljulieh)
Aijalon (Yalo)
Gibeah (Jib'a)
(en-Nebi Samwil) Mizpah, Maspha
Gorge of Pheretai
Parah (Kh. Fara)
Chephirah (Kefireh)
Azmaveth (Hizmeh)
Ithlah (Beit Tul)
Hazor (Kh. Ḥazzur)
Ananiah (Beit Hanina)
? Alemeth, Almon (Kh. 'Almit)
Beth-hoglah ('Ain Ḥajlah)
Kiriath? (Kuryet el-'Enab)
Mozah (Kh. Beit Mizza)
Gibeah (Tell el-Ful)
Anathoth ('Anata)
Adummim (Tal'at ed-Damm)
Debir (Thoghret ed-Debr)
JUDÆA
Emmaus? (Kalonyeh)
Eshtaol (Eshua')
Chesalon (Kesla)
Mt. Seir
Bethphage (Kefr et-Tor)
JERUSALEM (EL-KUDS)
En-shemesh ('Ain Haud)
Beth-car ('Ain Karim)
Bethany ('Azariyeh)
Beth-jeshimoth (Suweimeh)
Kiriath-jearim (Kh. 'Erma)
Manahath (Malhah)
Bether ? (Bittir)
Etam ? (Beit 'Aṭab)
Gallim (Beit Jala)
BETHLEHEM (Beit Laḥm)
EL GHOR

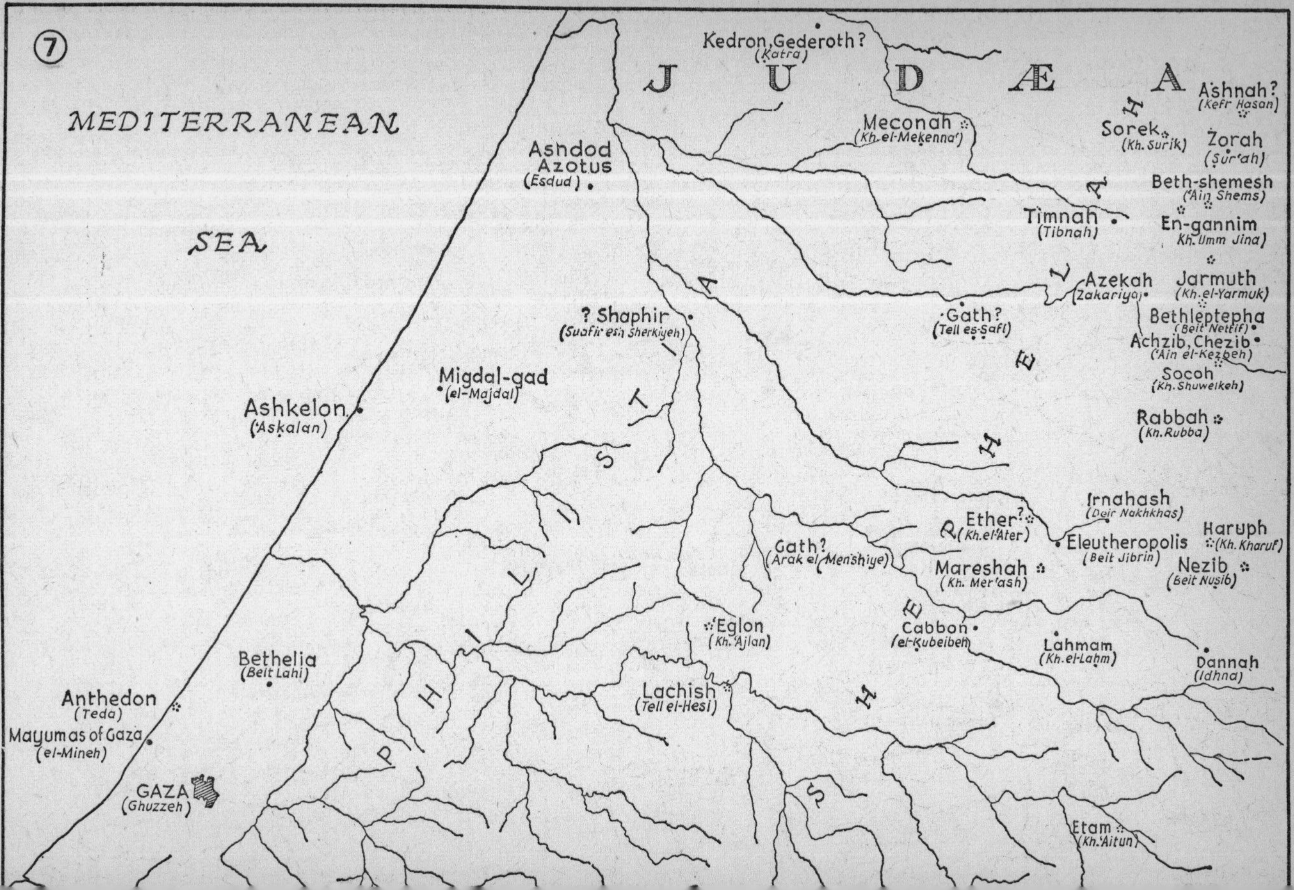
7
MEDITERRANEAN
SEA
JUDÆA
SHEPHELAH
PHILISTIA
SHEPHELAH
Kedron,Gederoth? (Katra)
Meconah (Kh. el-Mekenna')
Ashdod Azotus (Esdud)
Ashnah? (Kefr Hasan)
Sorek (Kh. Surik)
Zorah (Sur'ah)
Beth-shemesh ('Ain Shems)
Timnah (Tibnah)
En-gannim Kh. Umm Jina)
Azekah (Zakariya)
Jarmuth (Kh. el-Yarmuk)
Bethleptepha (Beit Nettif)
Achzib, Chezib ('Ain el-Kezbeh)
Socoh (Kh. Shuweikeh)
? Shaphir (Suafir esh Sherkiyeh)
Gath? (Tell es-Safi)
Rabbah (Kh. Rubba)
Migdal-gad (el-Majdal)
Ashkelon ('Askalan)
Irnahash (Deir Nakhkhas)
Ether? (Kh. el-'Ater)
Haruph (Kh. Kharuf)
Eleutheropolis (Beit Jibrin)
Gath? (Arak el Menshiye)
Mareshah (Kh. Mer'ash)
Nezib (Beit Nusib)
Eglon (Kh. 'Ajlan)
Cabbon (el-Kubeibeh)
Lahmam (Kh. el-Lahm)
Dannah (Idhna)
Bethelia (Beit Lahi)
Anthedon (Teda)
Lachish (Tell el-Hesi)
Mayumas of Gaza (el-Mineh)
GAZA (Ghuzzeh)
Etam (Kh. 'Aitun)

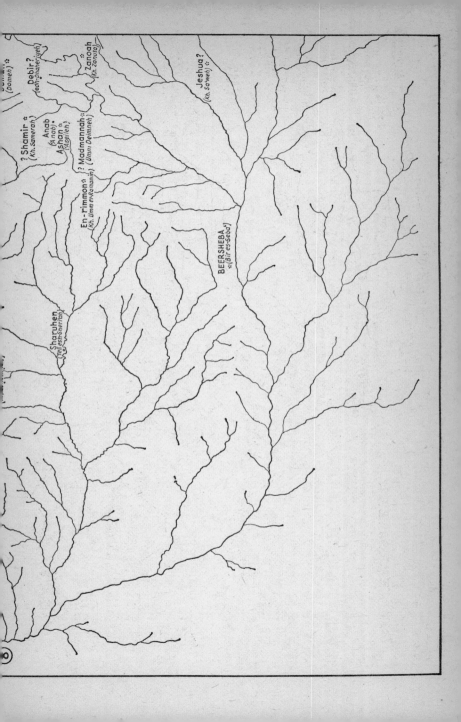

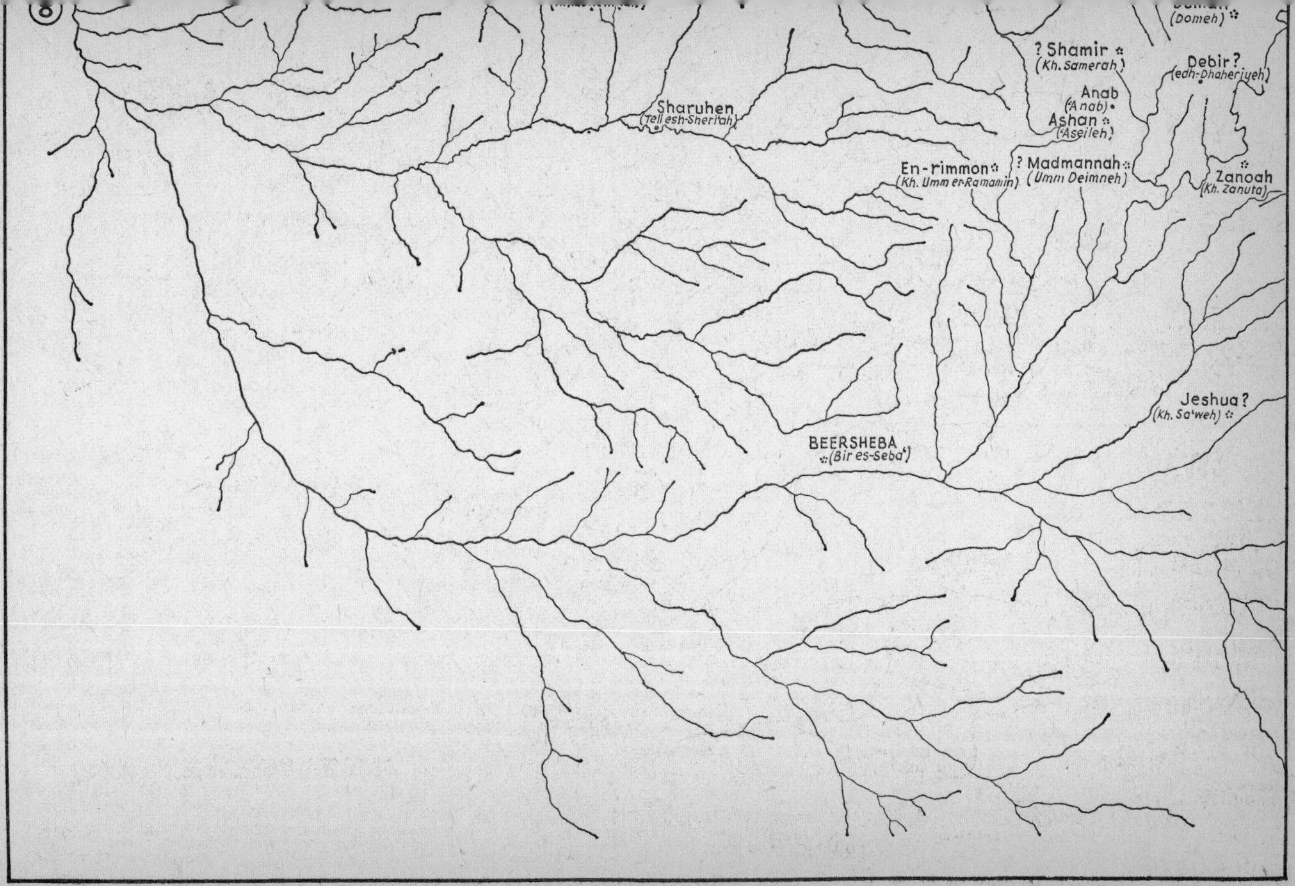

8
(Domeh)
? Shamir
(Kh. Samerah)
Debir?
(edh-Dhaheriyeh)
Anab
('Anab)
Ashan
('Aseileh)
Sharuhen
(Tell esh-Sheri'ah)
En-rimmon
(Kh. Umm er-Ramamin)
? Madmannah
(Umm Deimneh)
Zanoah
(Kh. Zanuta)
Jeshua?
(Kh. Sa'weh)
BEERSHEBA
(Bir es-Seba')

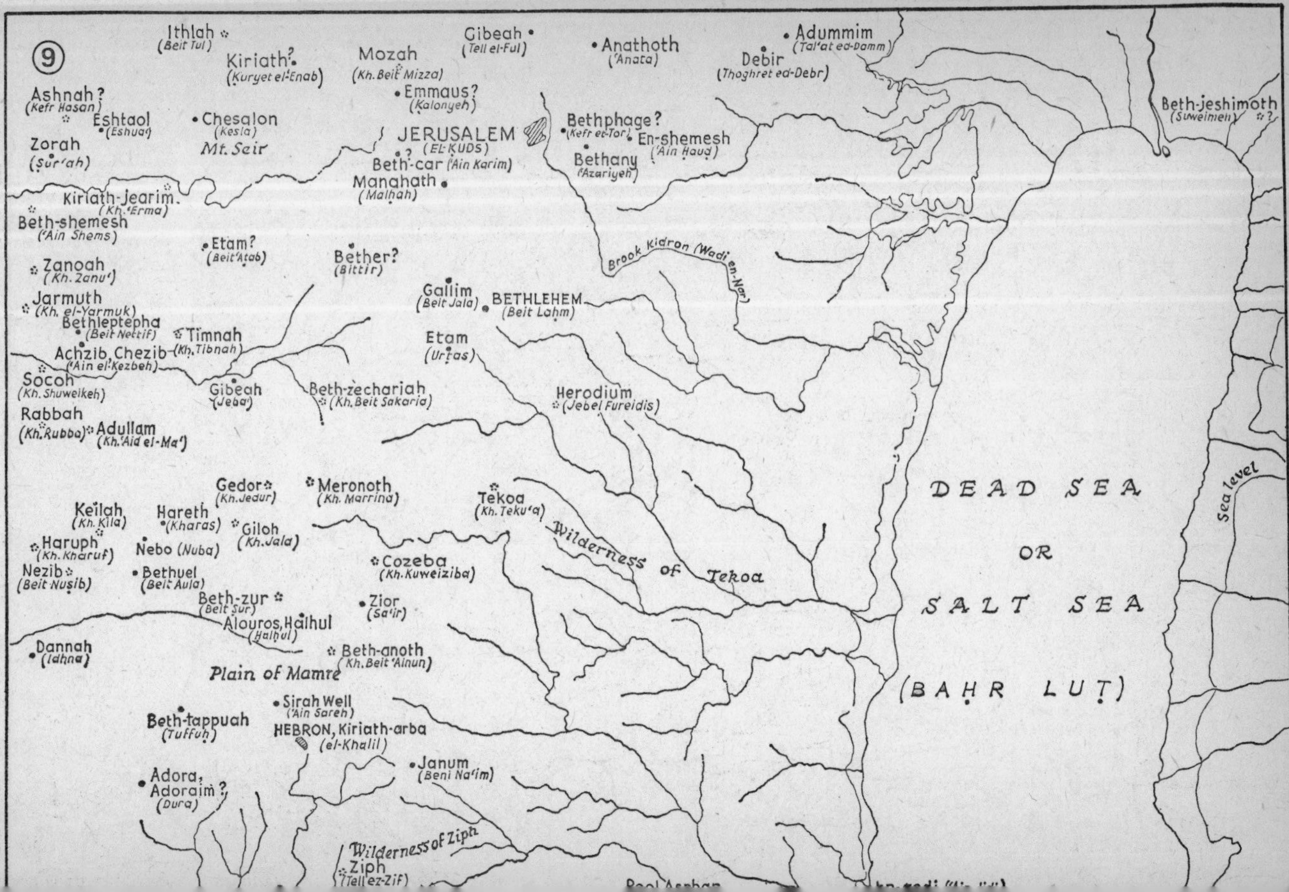
9
Ashnah? (Kefr Hasan)
Eshtaol (Eshua')
Zorah (Ṣur'ah)
Ithlah (Beit Tul)
Kiriath? (Kuryet el-Enab)
Chesalon (Kesla)
Mt. Seir
Mozah (Kh. Beit Mizza)
Emmaus? (Kalonyeh)
Gibeah (Tell el-Ful)
JERUSALEM (EL-KUDS)
Beth-car ('Ain Karim)
Manahath (Malhah)
Anathoth ('Anata)
Debir (Thoghret ed-Debr)
Adummim (Tal'at ed-Damm)
Bethphage? (Kefr et-Tor)
En-shemesh ('Ain Haud)
Bethany ('Azariyeh)
Beth-jeshimoth (Suweimeh) ?
Kiriath-jearim (Kh. 'Erma)
Beth-shemesh ('Ain Shems)
Etam? (Beit 'Atab)
Bether? (Bittir)
Brook Kidron (Wadi en-Nar)
Zanoah (Kh. Zanu')
Jarmuth (Kh. el-Yarmuk)
Bethleptepha (Beit Nettif)
Timnah (Kh. Tibnah)
Achzib, Chezib ('Ain el-Kezbeh)
Gallim (Beit Jala)
BETHLEHEM (Beit Lahm)
Etam (Urṭas)
Socoh (Kh. Shuweikeh)
Gibeah (Jeba')
Beth-zechariah (Kh. Beit Sakaria)
Herodium (Jebel Fureidis)
Rabbah (Kh. Rubba)
Adullam (Kh. 'Aid el-Ma')
Gedor (Kh. Jedur)
Meronoth (Kh. Marrina)
Tekoa (Kh. Teku'a)
Keilah (Kh. Kila)
Hareth (Kharas)
Giloh (Kh. Jala)
Haruph (Kh. Kharuf)
Nebo (Nuba)
Wilderness of Tekoa
Cozeba (Kh. Kuweiziba)
Nezib (Beit Nuṣib)
Bethuel (Beit Aula)
Beth-zur (Beit Ṣur)
Zior (Sa'ir)
Alouros, Halhul (Halhul)
Dannah (Idhna)
Beth-anoth (Kh. Beit 'Ainun)
Plain of Mamre
Sirah Well ('Ain Sareh)
Beth-tappuah (Tuffuh)
HEBRON, Kiriath-arba (el-Khalil)
Janum (Beni Na'im)
Adora, Adoraim? (Dura)
Wilderness of Ziph
Ziph (Tell ez-Zif)
DEAD SEA OR SALT SEA (BAHR LUT)
Sea level

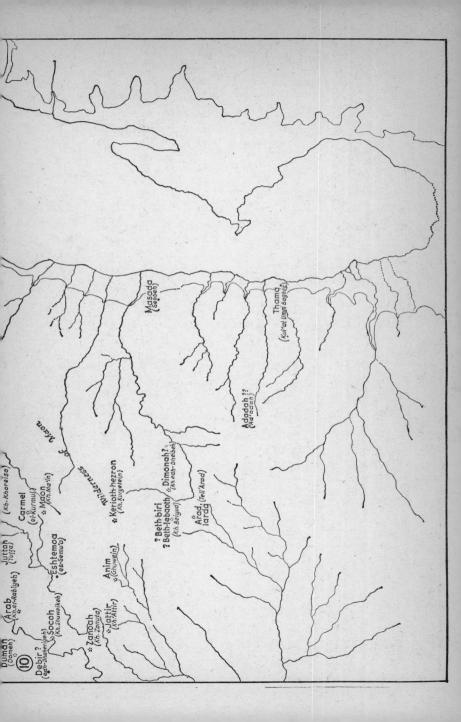

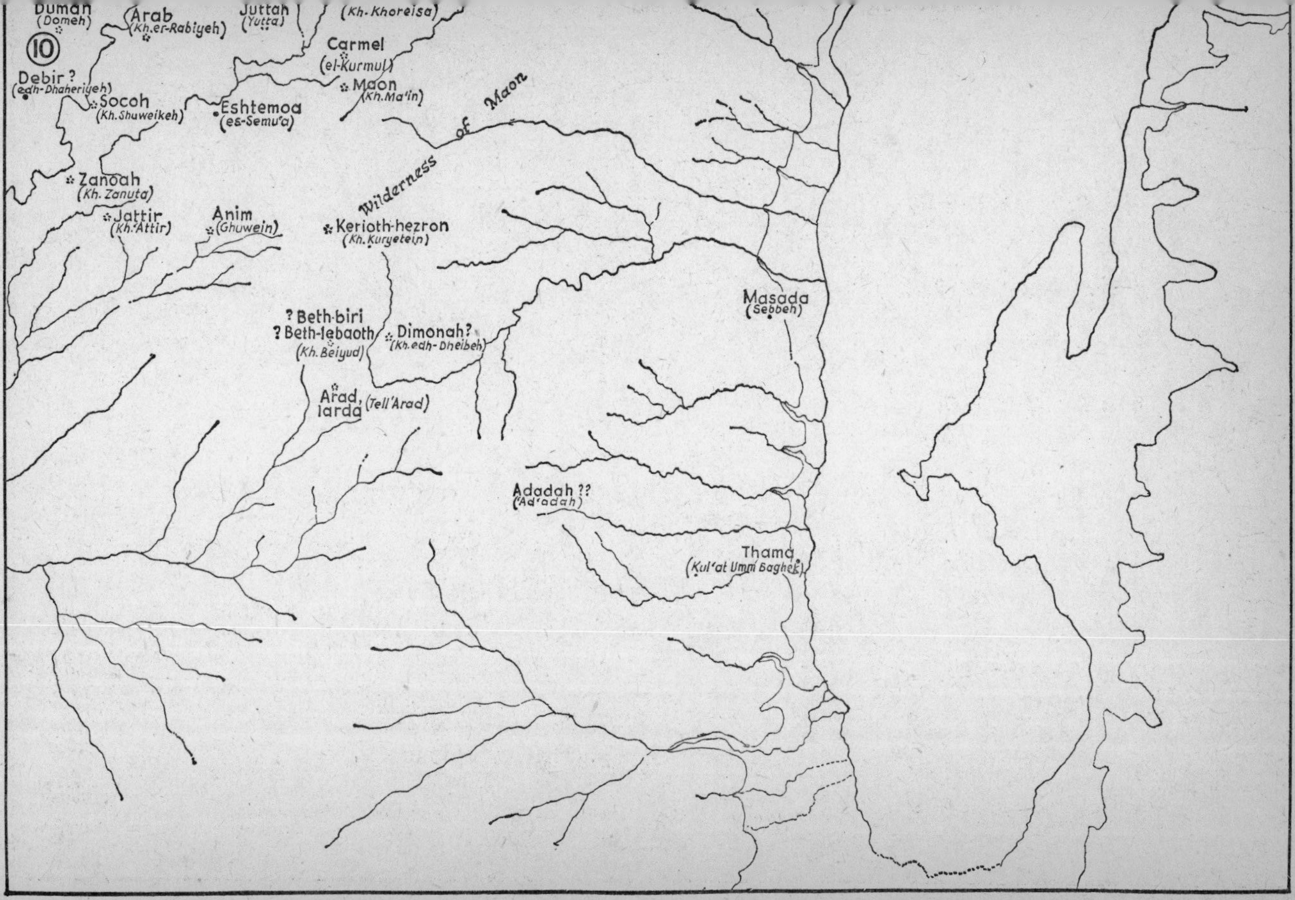

10
Duman
(Domeh)
Arab
(Kh. er-Rabiyeh)
Juttah
(Yutta)
(Kh. Khoreisa)
Carmel
(el-Kurmul)
Maon
(Kh. Ma'in)
Debir?
(edh-Dhaheriyeh)
Socoh
(Kh. Shuweikeh)
Eshtemoa
(es-Semu'a)
Wilderness of Maon
Zanoah
(Kh. Zanuta)
Jattir
(Kh. 'Attir)
Anim
(Ghuwein)
Kerioth-hezron
(Kh. Kuryetein)
Masada
(Sebbeh)
? Beth-biri
? Beth-lebaoth
(Kh. Beiyud)
Dimonah?
(Kh. edh-Dheibeh)
Arad, Iarda
(Tell 'Arad)
Adadah ??
('Ad'adah)
Thama
(Kul'at Umm Baghek)

INDEXES

INDEX

This index has been planned to conform, as far as possible, with that of the Twenty-fifth Edition, and to extend its scope

INDEX OF AUTHORITIES

(For Abbreviations of Titles, see pages 14 and 15)
See also Appendix IV (Bibliography of Eastern Palestine) on pp. 446-7.

INDEX TO MAPS

1. Biblical Names

2. Arabic Names